Strategic Alliances

The Globalization of the World Economy

Series Editor: Mark Casson
Professor of Economics
University of Reading, UK

Wherever possible, the articles in these volumes have been reproduced as originally published using facsimile reproduction, inclusive of footnotes and pagination to facilitate ease of reference.

For a list of all Edward Elgar published titles visit our site on the World Wide Web at
http://www.e-elgar.co.uk

Strategic Alliances

Edited by

Paul W. Beamish

Professor of International Business
Ivey Business School, University of Western Ontario
Canada

THE GLOBALIZATION OF THE WORLD ECONOMY 2

An Elgar Reference Collection
Cheltenham, UK • Northampton, MA, USA

Published by
Edward Elgar Publishing Limited
8 Lansdown Place
Cheltenham
Glos GL50 2HU
UK

Edward Elgar Publishing, Inc.
6 Market Street
Northampton
Massachusetts 01060
USA

A catalogue record for this book is available from the British Library.

Library of Congress Cataloguing in Publication Data
Strategic alliances / edited by Paul W. Beamish
    (The Globalization of the world economy : 2)
    Includes bibliographical references and index.
    1. Strategic alliances .   I. Beamish, Paul W., 1953-   .
II. Series.
HD69.S8S773   1998
338.8--dc21
                                        98-21066
                                          CIP

3 2280 00681 4388

ISBN 1 85898 694 X
Printed and bound in Great Britain by MPG Books Ltd, Bodmin, Cornwall

Contents

Acknowledgements

The editor and publishers wish to thank the authors and the following publishers who have kindly given permission for the use of copyright material.

Academy of Management for articles: Bryan Borys and David B. Jemison (1989), 'Hybrid Arrangements as Strategic Alliances: Theoretical Issues in Organizational Combinations', *Academy of Management Review*, **14** (2), 234–49; Arvind Parkhe (1993), '"Messy" Research, Methodological Predispositions, and Theory Development in International Joint Ventures', *Academy of Management Review*, **18** (2), April, 227–68; Aimin Yan and Barbara Gray (1994), 'Bargaining Power, Management Control, and Performance in United States–China Joint Ventures: A Comparative Case Study', *Academy of Management Journal*, **37** (6), December, 1478–517; Andrew C. Inkpen and Paul W. Beamish (1997), 'Knowledge, Bargaining Power, and the Instability of International Joint Ventures', *Academy of Management Review*, **22** (1), January, 177–202.

Braybrooke Press for article: Jean-Louis Schaan (1988), 'How to Control a Joint Venture Even as a Minority Partner', *Journal of General Management*, **14** (1), Autumn, 4–16.

Harvard Business Review for articles: J. Peter Killing (1982), 'How to Make a Global Joint Venture Work', *Harvard Business Review*, **3**, May–June, 120–27; Gary Hamel, Yves L. Doz and C.K. Prahalad (1989), 'Collaborate with Your Competitors – and Win', *Harvard Business Review*, **89** (1), January–February, 133–9.

Institute for Operations Research and the Management Sciences for article: Arvind Parkhe (1993), 'Partner Nationality and the Structure–Performance Relationship in Strategic Alliances', *Organization Science*, **4** (2), May, 301–24.

Journal of International Business Studies for articles: Donald J. Lecraw (1984), 'Bargaining Power, Ownership, and Profitability of Transnational Corporations in Developing Countries', *Journal of International Business Studies*, **XV** (1), Spring/Summer, 27–43; Erin Anderson and Hubert Gatignon (1986), 'Modes of Foreign Entry: A Transaction Cost Analysis and Propositions', *Journal of International Business Studies*, **17** (3), Fall, 1–26; Paul W. Beamish and John C. Banks (1987), 'Equity Joint Ventures and the Theory of the Multinational Enterprise', *Journal of International Business Studies*, **19** (2), Summer, 1–16; Bruce Kogut and Harbir Singh (1988), 'The Effect of National Culture on the Choice of Entry Mode', *Journal of International Business Studies*, **19** (3), 411–32; J. Michael Geringer and Louis Hebert (1989), 'Control and Performance of International Joint Ventures', *Journal of International Business Studies*, **XX** (2), Summer, 235–54; Benjamin Gomes-Casseres (1990), 'Firm Ownership Preferences and Host Government Restrictions: An Integrated Approach', *Journal of International Business Studies*, **21** (1), 1–22; Oded Shenkar and Yoram Zeira

(1992), 'Role Conflict and Role Ambiguity of Chief Executive Officers in International Joint Ventures', *Journal of International Business Studies*, **23** (1), 55–75; Stephen B. Tallman and Oded Shenkar (1994), 'A Managerial Decision Model of International Cooperative Venture Formation', *Journal of International Business Studies*, **25** (1), 91–113; C. Patrick Woodcock, Paul W. Beamish and Shige Makino (1994), 'Ownership-Based Entry Mode Strategies and International Performance', *Journal of International Business Studies*, **25** (2), 253–73; John H. Dunning (1995), 'Reappraising the Eclectic Paradigm in an Age of Alliance Capitalism', *Journal of International Business Studies*, **26** (3), 461–91; Peter J. Buckley and Mark Casson (1996), 'An Economic Model of International Joint Venture Strategy', *Journal of International Business Studies*, **27** (5), Special Issue, 849–76.

Management International Review for articles: F.J. Contractor and P. Lorange (1988), 'Competition vs. Cooperation: A Benefit/Cost Framework for Choosing Between Fully-Owned Investments and Cooperative Relationships', *Management International Review*, Special Issue, 5–18; P.J. Buckley and M. Casson (1988), 'A Theory of Co-Operation in International Business', *Management International Review*, Special Issue, 19–38; M.A. Lyles (1988), 'Learning Among Joint Venture Sophisticated Firms', *Management International Review*, Special Issue, 85–97.

Michigan State University Press for article: Paul W. Beamish (1993), 'The Characteristics of Joint Ventures in the People's Republic of China', *Journal of International Marketing*, **1** (2), 29–48.

Sloan Management Review Association for article: Erin Anderson (1990), 'Two Firms, One Frontier: On Assessing Joint Venture Performance', *Sloan Management Review*, **31** (2), Winter, 19–30.

John Wiley & Sons Ltd for articles: Jean-François Hennart (1988), 'A Transaction Costs Theory of Equity Joint Ventures', *Strategic Management Journal*, **9** (4), July–August, 361–74; Bruce Kogut (1988), 'Joint Ventures: Theoretical and Empirical Perspectives', *Strategic Management Journal*, **9** (4), July–August, 319–32; Gary Hamel (1991), 'Competition for Competence and Inter-Partner Learning Within International Strategic Alliances', *Strategic Management Journal*, **12**, Special Issue, Summer, 83–103.

Every effort has been made to trace all the copyright holders but if any have been inadvertently overlooked the publishers will be pleased to make the necessary arrangement at the first opportunity.

In addition the publishers wish to thank the Library of the London School of Economics and Political Science and the Marshall Library of Economics, Cambridge University for their assistance in obtaining these articles.

Introduction

Paul W. Beamish

The study of strategic alliances and joint ventures has been one of *the* major areas of business research in the 1980s and 1990s. In this 'age of alliance capitalism', this is no surprise. Much of the top research on strategic alliances has taken place from an international perspective. This is a consequence of the practitioner need to devise organization forms that allow them to better compete in the complex global environment.

The 27 papers which were carefully selected for this volume consider the key theoretical and empirical contributions of leading scholars. These contributions variously consider strategic alliances using different theoretical lenses, as one of many alternative organization forms, and from design, on-going management, and performance-improving perspectives.

In this Introduction the papers in this volume are organized into six sections. The six sections focus on The Joint Venture as a Mode of Foreign Entry; Performance; Control; Learning Within Alliances; Bargaining Power; and Theory. The comments which follow on each paper sometimes draw directly from the abstracts. As will be immediately evident, an overlap exists between the sections.

The Joint Venture as a Mode of Foreign Entry

One of the dominant issues within the entire area of strategic alliances deals with the question of choosing the appropriate mode of entry for foreign markets. The first paper we consider is by Anderson and Gatignon (1986; Chapter 1, this volume). They were recipients of the 1996 JIBS Decade Award for the most influential paper from the 1986 volume of *Journal of International Business Studies* (JIBS). This paper offers a transaction cost perspective for investigating the entry mode decision. The authors illustrate the feasibility of clustering 17 entry modes into the degree of control the mode provides the entrant. Further, they propose that the most efficient entry mode is a function of the trade-off between control and the cost of resource commitment. Finally they advance a series of testable propositions delimiting the circumstances under which each mode maximizes long-term efficiency.

At about the same time that Anderson and Gatignon were examining the entry mode decision, other scholars were also considering a mode choice decision. Two articles originally presented at a 1986 conference at Rutgers' University appeared in a special issue in 1988 of *Management International Review*. The first of these by Contractor and Lorange (Chapter 8) provided a cost–benefit framework for choosing between fully-owned (or wholly-owned investments) and forms of cooperative relationship. The authors noted that both direct and indirect incremental costs and benefits must be examined. They felt that the cooperative mode is preferred over the go it alone alternative when the incremental net benefit of the former over the latter is greater than the other partners' share of the profits.

Buckley and Casson (Chapter 6) provided a theory of cooperation in international business in their 1988 paper. They noted how cooperation could be analysed from both an economic and an organizational perspective. Of particular note in their paper was how some joint venture types provide a suitable context in which the partners can demonstrate what they called mutual forbearance and thereby build up trust.

A decade after the presentation of their original work on their theory of cooperation, Buckley and Casson provided a more detailed and comprehensive economic model of international joint venture strategy. In their 1996 paper (Chapter 7) the strategic choice between joint ventures, licence agreements and mergers was analysed using eight factors suggested by internalization theory. The model explained the increasing role of joint ventures in the 1980s in terms of the accelerating pace of technological innovation and the globalization of markets. It offered a range of predictions about the formation of joint ventures within and across industries, across locations and over time. It also laid out a powerful modelling technique that has numerous applications elsewhere in international business strategy. Although this paper has only recently been published, it is destined to be a cornerstone of future economics-oriented research dealing with international joint ventures.

The next three papers within the entry mode area are all important empirical contributions. The first of these by Beamish and Banks (Chapter 4) examines equity joint ventures and the theory of the multinational enterprise. This paper was the winner of the 1997 JIBS Decade Award for the most influential article published in the 1987 volume of *Journal of International Business Studies*. The paper extends the internalization approach to the theory of the multinational enterprise to include an expanded role for equity joint ventures. Using the transaction cost paradigm of Williamson, the paper explains why joint ventures may sometimes be preferred over wholly-owned subsidiaries. In support, empirical work on joint venture performance in developing countries is presented which demonstrates that under certain conditions, joint ventures can be the optimal, not the second best, mode of foreign direct investment.

A more recent contribution by Woodcock, Beamish and Makino (1994; Chapter 26) examines ownership-based entry mode strategies and international performance. The ownership entry modes examined are the wholly-owned modes of acquisition and new venture entry and the nonwholly-owned mode of joint venture. The theoretical relationship is developed for international entry modes that is based on the contingency characteristics of resource requirements and organizational control factors. This paper suggests that different entry modes have different performance outcomes based on their resource and organizational control demands. A theoretical model, although developed using the eclectic theoretical approach, is based largely on concepts and relationships previously delineated in contingency theory. The hypotheses suggest that new ventures should outperform joint ventures and joint ventures should outperform acquisitions. An empirical test using a sample of 321 Japanese firms entering the North American market provides supporting evidence.

The final paper in this section looks at the effect of national culture on the choice of entry mode. Kogut and Singh (1988; Chapter 18) note that the characteristics of national cultures have frequently been claimed to influence the selection of entry mode. Their article investigates this claim by developing a theoretical argument for why culture should influence the choice of entry. Two hypotheses are derived which relate culture to entry mode choice. One hypothesis focuses on the cultural distance between countries, the other on attitudes towards uncertainty avoidance. Their hypotheses are tested by analysing data on 228 entries into the US market by acquisition, wholly-owned greenfield and joint venture. Empirical support for the effect of national culture on entry choice was observed.

Performance

Not surprisingly, performance related issues have been the single greatest area of investigation on research dealing with strategic alliances. The first paper by Anderson (1990; Chapter 2) considers the ways in which joint venture performance is examined. Her article, written for more of a practitioner audience, argues that performance evaluation becomes particularly difficult because joint ventures are undertaken for varying purposes in highly uncertain and risky settings. She argues that conventional performance measures are therefore misleading under such circumstances. She proposes a way to evaluate the effectiveness of joint ventures by classifying them into four categories and then for each, suggesting which factors should be considered in evaluation.

The second paper, by Beamish (1993; Chapter 3), was based on a meta-analysis of many studies on joint ventures and was derived in part from an earlier article on a related subject entitled, 'The Characteristics of Joint Ventures in Developing Countries' which was published in *Columbia Journal of World Business*. It looks at joint venture performance and eleven other characteristics of equity joint ventures across three regions: developed country market economies, developing country market economies and developing country planned economies (in particular, China). The eleven other characteristics examined include the reason for creating a joint venture, the frequency of association with government partners, the overall use of joint ventures versus other modes of foreign involvement, the origin of the foreign partner, the proportion of intended joint ventures actually implemented, the use of joint ventures with a predetermined duration, the most common level of ownership for the multinational enterprise forming a joint venture, the number of autonomously managed ventures, the ownership-control relationship, the control-performance relationship in successful joint ventures, the instability rate and a managerial assessment of dissatisfaction with performance.

Hamel, Doz and Prahalad (1989; Chapter 12), following an examination of 15 strategic alliances, suggest that success or failure in strategic alliances should be judged by the shifts in competitive strength on both sides. Their conclusions are that firms benefiting most from competitive collaboration see collaboration as competition in a different form, harmony as the most important measure of success, cooperation as limited, and learning from partners as paramount. They suggest that mutual gain is possible for companies if both have converging strategic goals and diverging competitive goals, if they have modest size and market power compared with industry leaders, and if both believe that they can learn from the other and limit access to proprietary skills. They suggest that whether collaboration results in competitive surrender or revitalization depends foremost on what employees think the purpose of the alliance is to be.

The final paper in this section examines partner nationality in the structure–performance relationship in strategic alliances. Parkhe (1993; Chapter 22) notes how alliances are complex to manage successfully because of the opportunity and incentive to cheat and profit at the partner's expense. As a consequence, alliances are frequently subject to high instability, poor performance and premature dissolution. His study addresses the question of whether it is possible to promote more stable cooperation and higher alliance performance through a realignment of companies' incentives. This question is addressed empirically using work in game theory. The study's data strongly supports the hypothesis that alliance performance is linked to alliance structure.

Control

A major area of investigation within the joint venture literature relates to the question of control, that is 'Who is in charge in the joint venture?' Killing (1982; Chapter 16) provides us with a basic typology about ways of managing a joint venture. He introduces the idea of shared management versus dominant parent management control within joint ventures using a sample of 37 joint ventures involving mostly North American and western European companies. Killing suggests that the most effective form of control is the situation where one partner dominates decision making control within the venture. There has been a large volume of subsequent empirical research which has looked at the question of whether or not control should be dominated or shared (or perhaps split) within joint ventures. The results are mixed with respect to whether there is one best form of control.

In many parts of the world it has historically not been easy for the foreign investor to take a majority equity position with its investments, or alternately there are sometimes significant incentives for the foreign investor to take a minority equity position. This leaves unanswered the question, 'How do you exercise control or influence in a joint venture even as a minority partner?' This is the issue which Schaan (1988; Chapter 23) explored in his study of joint ventures operating primarily in Mexico. He noted that to ensure joint venture success, managers must seek to maintain a subtle balance between the desire and need to control the venture and the need to have harmonious relations with the partners. He noted that a number of mechanisms can be employed to enable all interested parties to monitor developments and shape decisions that affect the joint venture. These include: board meetings, the provision of parent company services, key personnel appointments, organizational and structural context, informal mechanisms and integrating with the parent organizations. Even in a minority equity situation, a series of measures are recommended to enhance the likelihood of successful control. These include: policies governing parental intervention; diplomacy; governance of the joint venture manager; formal assessments and arrangements for resolving disagreements.

Geringer and Hebert (1989; Chapter 10) review and synthesize prior studies addressing the conceptualization and operationalization of control within international joint ventures as well as the international joint venture control-performance relationship. Their paper presents a conceptualization of control as well as a conceptual framework for studying control within joint ventures.

Yan and Gray (1994; Chapter 27) examine the relationship between bargaining power, management control and performance in joint ventures. The results of their comparative case study of four ventures between partners from the US and The People's Republic of China are discussed. They provide evidence that the relative levels of joint venture partners' bargaining power has a significant impact on the pattern of parent control in the joint venture's management.

Learning/Knowledge Accumulation

During the past decade a small group of scholars have investigated whether or not joint ventures are appropriate vehicles for organizational learning or knowledge accumulation. Among the earliest papers was Lyles's (1988) article dealing with 'Learning Among Joint Venture Sophisticated Firms' (Chapter 20). She examined the role of organizational learning in four firms and developed a learning framework that had several levels of learning. Lower level learning was based on repetition and routines and involved association building. Higher level learning involved an adjustment of overall missions, beliefs and norms.

Arguably the major contribution to date within the learning stream has been Hamel's (1991) article (Chapter 13). This paper was based on detailed analysis of nine international alliances which yielded a fine grained understanding of the determinants of inter-partner learning. The study suggested that not all partners are equally adept at learning and that asymmetries in learning alter the relative bargaining power of partners. It also suggested that stability and longevity may be inappropriate metrics of partnership success, that partners may have competitive as well as collaborative aims in relation to each other, and that process may be more important than structure in determining learning outcomes.

The third and final example within the learning stream which we consider is by Kogut (1988; Chapter 17). He compares the perspectives of transaction costs and strategic behaviour to explain the motivation to joint venture. The transaction cost approach is derived from Williamson. Its arguments are driven by cost minimizing solutions and joint ventures are analysed as an efficient solution to the hazards of economic transactions. The strategic behaviour perspective in contrast stems from theories concerning its influence on a firm's competitive positioning. It places joint ventures in the context of competitive rivalry and collusive agreements to enhance market power. Kogut proposes a theory of joint ventures as an instrument of organizational learning. The view here is joint venture as a means by which firms can learn or seek to retain their capabilities. The perspectives provide distinct, occasionally overlapping, explanations for joint venture behaviour. The theories probably will apply differently according to contextual factors and the type of research questions being considered.

Bargaining Power

A bargaining perspective can be applied both in relation to bargaining power between a multi-national enterprise and a host country as well as between two different firms. The first two of the three papers in this section consider the bargaining power relationship between the firm and the country in which the firm is investing.

Lecraw (1984; Chapter 19) observed that as the bargaining power of the multinational enterprise in his sample increased relative to the bargaining power of the host country, and as the desire of the multinational for a high level of equity ownership increased, the percentage equity ownership of the multinationals in their subsidiaries also increased. The relationship between percentage equity ownership and subsidiary success from the multinational viewpoint however was J-shaped. High and low levels of equity ownership were associated with high levels of success. Control of critical operational variables by the multinational was directly related to success.

Gomes-Casseres (1990; Chapter 11) suggests that two approaches may explain how multinational enterprises select ownership structures for subsidiaries. The first argues that firms prefer structures that minimize the transaction costs of doing business abroad. The second argues that ownership structures are determined by negotiations with host governments whose outcomes depend on the bargaining power of the firm. His paper presents a framework integrating these two approaches. He provides empirical support to the view that attractive domestic markets increase the relative bargaining power of host governments. He finds no support for other hypotheses of this school, such as those predicting that firms in marketing and R&D intensive industries have more bargaining power than others. These latter factors were apparently more important in determining firm ownership preferences. Further, the paper measures when government ownership restrictions deter firm entry, concluding that relatively large firms and those with high intra-system sales are deterred more than others.

More recently, Inkpen and Beamish (1997; Chapter 15) have examined the relationship between knowledge, bargaining power and the instability of international joint ventures. They argue that, although the high rate of instability of international joint ventures has been well documented, the underlying reasons for the instability require clarification. Their paper develops a theoretical framework for instability of international joint ventures which is grounded in a bargaining power and dependence perspective. Instability is defined as a major change in partner-relationship status that is unplanned and premature from one or both partners' perspectives. The core argument is that the instability of international joint ventures is associated with shifts in partner bargaining power. Shifts in the balance of bargaining power occur when partners acquire sufficient knowledge and skills to eliminate a partner dependency and make the international joint venture bargain obsolete. The primary focus is on the acquisition of local knowledge by the foreign partner (as opposed to merely accessing this local knowledge) and the impact that this acquisition of knowledge has on the stability of the venture.

Theory

Numerous theoretical lenses have been employed in the consideration of strategic alliances. In this section we consider a variety of theoretical perspectives.

Dunning (1995; Chapter 9) in the third instalment of his eclectic paradigm which has been published in *Journal of International Business Studies* (see Dunning 1980, 1988) discusses the implication of the advent of alliance capitalism for the theorizing about the determinants of multinational enterprise (MNE) activity. He argues that due to the increased porosity of the boundaries of firms, countries and markets, the eclectic (or Ownership Location Internationalization) paradigm of international production needs to consider more explicitly the competitive advantages arising from the way firms organize their inter-firm transactions, the growing interdependencies of many intermediate product markets, and the widening of the portfolio of the assets of districts, regions and countries to embrace the external economies of interdependent activities.

The same year in which the second instalment of Dunning's eclectic paradigm was published (1988) Hennart provided a transaction cost theory of equity joint ventures (Chapter 14). In his paper the insights of transaction cost theorists are used to develop a static theory of equity joint ventures. Equity joint ventures may be either scale joint ventures or link joint ventures. Scale joint ventures arise when parent firms attempt to internalize a failing market but indivisibilities caused by scale or scope economies make full ownership of relevant assets inefficient. Link joint ventures result from the simultaneous failing of the markets for the services of two or more assets whenever these assets are firm-specific public goods and significant management costs would be entailed in acquisition of the firm holding them. All joint ventures can be explained as a means to bypass inefficient markets for intermediate inputs. If assets can be shared at low marginal cost (public goods), replication is more expensive than acquisition. A joint venture will be chosen over a takeover if the assets each party need are a subset of those held by its partner.

More recently, Tallman and Shenkar (1994; Chapter 25) argue that while cooperative venture formation is typically explained in terms of the market imperfections concepts of industrial organization economics models or the transaction costs economics approach of internalization models, such models do not provide a sufficient explanation of the original decision by MNE managers to establish an international cooperative venture. They develop a model of international cooperative venture formation that is centered on the decision making process of MNE executives. Central issues for managerial decisions are developed from the organizational studies literature. A framework delineating the sequence and criteria used in the decision to form international cooperative ventures is developed from these defined areas and from existing models. Propositions pertaining to the venture decision process are outlined.

A more specialized contribution to theory within the international alliances literature is provided by Shenkar and Zeira (1992; Chapter 24) in their consideration of role theory. Their study examines the organizational and personal correlates of role conflict and role ambiguity of chief executive officers (CEO) heading international joint ventures. Role conflict was found to be lower when the number of parent firms was higher and when the CEO had spent more years with the organization. Role ambiguity was found to be lower when the CEO had more years of education, when the power distance and masculinity/femininity gap between parents were lower and when the individualism/collectivism and uncertainty avoidance gaps were higher. The implications of these findings for role theory and international management are discussed.

The final two papers consider a variety of theoretical issues requiring resolution within the strategic alliances area. In the first of these by Borys and Jemison (1989; Chapter 5) a series of theoretical issues within organizational combinations are considered. These authors suggest that within hybrid organizational arrangements, two or more sovereign organizations continue to pursue common interests. They suggest that different operations, production philosophies and administrative systems can be coordinated through (1) pooled inter-dependence (drawing from a common resource) (2) sequential interdependence (ensuring a fit between points of contact) and (3) reciprocal interdependence (partners exchanging output). A network of institutionalized expectations provides a stable reference point from which organizational members may coordinate their actions.

In the final paper, Parkhe (1993; Chapter 21) notes that while several theoretical dimensions have been emphasized in the literature, researchers have not addressed certain crucial questions at the heart of the international joint venture (IJV) relationship. Consequently, individually useful IJV studies have not coalesced into a collectively coherent body of work with an underlying theoretical structure. This weakness in theory development may stem from the convergence of hard methodological approaches with soft behavioural variables. In proposing and justifying a research programme toward deeper understanding of voluntary interfirm cooperation, a theoretical framework for IJVs is presented. A typology of theory development approaches is also developed. The framework and typology are applied to demonstrate how a near term shift in foci can accelerate rigourous IJV theory development.

Acknowledgement

The assistance of Andrew Delios, Charles Dhanaraj and Andrew Inkpen in developing and compiling the list of papers considered within this volume is gratefully acknowledged.

References

Beamish, P.W. (1985), 'The characteristics of joint ventures in developed and developing countries', *Columbia Journal of World Business*, Fall, **XX**, 13–19.

Dunning, J.H. (1980), 'Toward an eclectic theory of international production: some empirical tests', *Journal of International Business Studies*, **11** (2), 9–13.

Dunning, J.H. (1988), 'The Eclectic Paradigm of International Production: A Restatement and Possible Extension', *Journal of International Business Studies*, **19** (1), 1–31.

[1]

MODES OF FOREIGN ENTRY:
A TRANSACTION COST ANALYSIS AND PROPOSITIONS

Erin Anderson* and Hubert Gatignon**
The Wharton School
University of Pennsylvania

Abstract. A "frontier issue" in international marketing is the appropriate choice of entry mode in foreign markets. The objective of this paper is to offer a transaction cost framework for investigating the entry mode decision. This framework provides 1) a theoretical basis for systematically interrelating the literature into propositions, 2) propositions about interactions which resolve the apparently contradictory arguments advanced to date. Specifically, the paper:

- illustrates the feasibility of clustering 17 entry modes into the *degree of control* the mode provides the entrant;

- proposes that the most appropriate (i.e., most efficient) entry-mode is a function of the tradeoff between control and the cost of resource commitment

- advances testable propositions delimiting the circumstances under which each mode maximizes long-term efficiency.

The entry mode literature is reviewed in the context of these propositions, and guidelines are derived for choosing the appropriate mode of entry, given certain characteristics of the firm, the product, and the environment.

*Erin Anderson is Assistant Professor of Marketing at the Wharton School, University of Pennsylvania, which she joined in 1981. She received the Ph.D. from the UCLA Graduate School of Management. She has published in the *Rand Journal of Economics, Marketing Science,* and the *Sloan Management Review.*

**Hubert A. Gatignon has been an Assistant Professor of Marketing at the Wharton School, University of Pennsylvania since 1981. He obtained an MBA from UCLA in 1975 and a Ph.D. in Management from UCLA in 1981. Professor Gatignon has published in *Marketing Science,* the *Journal of Marketing Research,* the *Journal of Consumer Research,* and the *Journal of Marketing.*

The authors gratefully acknowledge the financial support of the Wharton Center for International Management Studies. The comments of Yoram Wind, Jean-Francois Hennart, and three anonymous reviewers, as well as Charles Goodman and Leonard Lodish, are greatly appreciated, as is the assistance of Shari Powell.

Received: August 1985; Revised: November 1985 & March 1986; Accepted: March 1986.

2   JOURNAL OF INTERNATIONAL BUSINESS STUDIES, FALL 1986

A firm seeking to perform a business function (e.g., production management, distribution) outside its domestic market must choose the best "mode of entry" (institutional arrangement) for the foreign market. The would-be entrant faces a large array of choices, including: a wholly-owned subsidiary, a joint venture (in which the entrant could be majority, equal, or minority partner), or a nonequity arrangement such as licensing or a contractual joint venture.

The impact of entry modes on the success of foreign operations is great, leading Wind and Perlmutter (1977) to identify entry modes as a "frontier issue" in international marketing. Entry modes differ greatly in their mix of advantages and drawbacks. The tradeoffs involved are difficult to evaluate and little understood. Several surveys of how firms actually make the entry mode decision (reviewed in Robinson 1978) indicate that few companies make a conscious, deliberate cost/benefit analysis of the options.

What is the best mode of entry for a given function in a given situation? Despite the existence of relevant evidence, the literature does not suggest how the manager should weigh tradeoffs to arrive at a choice that maximizes risk-adjusted return on investment. Instead, much of the literature contains many seemingly unrelated considerations, with no identification of key constructs. Often, a consideration is mentioned as part of a case study, with little indication of how the factor should affect other situations. Further, relevant work is scattered across books and journals in several disciplines, obscured by varying terminology, and separated by differences in problem setup, theory, and method.[1]

The objective of this paper is to develop a theory, expressed in testable propositions, for integrating the literature on entry into a unified framework. The theory, which comes from industrial organization, is explicitly concerned with weighing tradeoffs and with maximizing an economic criterion: long-term efficiency. In particular, the theory includes interactions between determinants of entry modes, interactions that help resolve contradictory arguments in the literature.

This review develops testable propositions concerning the following question: Under what circumstances is an entry mode the most efficient choice in the long run? Efficiency in general terms is the ratio of output to input. In the international context we mean the entrant's long-run return on its investment in an entry mode, adjusted for risk. Hence, we address the impact of a mode on both the numerator (returns) and denominator (investment) over the long-time horizon.[2]

Section one of this paper categorizes modes of entry into varying degrees of control by the entrant. Section two presents a transaction cost theory of entry modes, which generates a set of propositions. Entry mode research is reviewed in the context of these propositions. The paper concludes with suggestions for empirical research.

MODES OF ENTRY AND CONTROL

The classical approaches to long-term strategic decisions, such as entry mode choice, emphasize choosing the option offering the highest risk-adjusted return on investment in the feasible set. Yet, the literature on the entry mode choice makes little direct mention of risk or return. Instead, the issue is structured in terms of the degree of control each mode affords the entrant (Daniels, Ogram, and Radebaugh 1982, Robinson 1978, Robock, Simmonds, and Zwick 1977, Vernon and Wells 1976). But why such emphasis on control?

The Preeminent Role of Control

Control (the ability to influence systems, methods, and decisions) has a critical impact on the future of a foreign enterprise. Without control, a firm finds it more difficult to coordinate actions, carry out strategies, revise strategies, and resolve the disputes that invariably arise when two parties to a contract pursue their own interests (Davidson 1982). Further, the entrant can use its control to obtain a larger share of the foreign enterprise's profits. In short, control is a way to obtain a higher return.

Yet control, while obviously desirable, carries a high price (Vernon 1983). To take control, the entrant must assume responsibility for decision-making, responsibility a firm may be unwilling or unable to carry out in an uncertain foreign environment. Control also entails commitment of resources, including high overhead. This in turn creates switching costs, reducing the firm's ability to change its institutional arrangement should its choice turn out to be suboptimal. Resource commitment also increases the firm's exposure, i.e., the possibility of losses due to currency changes (Davidson 1982). Thus, to assume control is also to assume some forms of risk.

Control, then, is the focus of the entry mode literature because it is the single most important determinant of both risk and return. High-control modes can increase return and risk. Low-control modes (e.g., licenses and other contractual agreements) minimize resource commitment (hence risk) but often at the expense of returns. Firms trade various levels of control for reduction of resource commitment in the hope of reducing some forms of risk while increasing their returns. Hence, focusing on control is consistent with the classical risk-adjusted return perspective.

The viewpoint adopted in this paper is that international entry mode choices are most usefully and tractably viewed as a tradeoff between control and the cost of resource commitments, often under conditions of considerable risk and uncertainty. Preserving flexibility should be a major consideration of most firms in making the tradeoff. Flexibility, the ability to change systems and methods quickly and at a low cost, is always an important consideration, particularly in lesser-known foreign markets (where the entrant is likely to change systems and methods as it learns the new environment). This view is consistent with Holton (1971), who argues that control, risk, and flexibility are principal considerations (Mascarenhas 1982).

Classifying Modes of Entry

The objective of this review is to suggest major factors that determine what degree of control maximizes long-run efficiency. The theory of the efficiency of modes of entry treated in section two relies on the existence of a mapping to a control dimension but not on any particular mapping. For purposes of illustration, we suggest, in this section, a mapping from entry modes to the degree of control they afford the entrant.

As a caveat, there are many ways to gain control and many variations within any one form of entry mode (Kindleberger 1984, Hayashi 1978). For example, a minority partner might exercise influence out of proportion to ownership, due to such factors as a special contractual arrangement, expertise, or status as a government body. Hence our discussion is very general, and exceptions to our mapping can be found. Consequently, this discussion is intended to demonstrate the feasibility of a mapping, empirical tests of which are independent from the theory proposed in section two. Indeed, a valuable research contribution would be the development of a detailed theory of the relationship between control and governance structure.

A Suggested Clustering of Entry Modes

Although there is no tested, accepted theory as to how much control each entry mode affords, both the "management" (Root 1983) and the "economic" (Calvet 1981, Caves 1982) streams of research offer information as to the clustering of entry modes. Figure 1 illustrates how 17 entry modes can be grouped in terms of the amount of control (high, medium, low) an entrant gains over the activities of a foreign business entity.

As shown in Figure 1, dominant equity interests (wholly-owned subsidiary or majority shareholder) are expected to offer the highest degree of control to the entrant (Root 1983, Davidson, 1982, Bivens and Lovell 1966, Friedman and Beguin 1971, Killing 1982).

Balanced interests (plurality shareholder, equal partnership and balanced contracts) are shown as medium-control modes based on the notion of a "credible commitment" (Williamson 1983) or "hostage." Firms forming a venture with a high likelihood of trouble (such as equal partnerships) will have difficulty locating a suitable partner. To attract a partner, the entrant may need to put up something to lose, a sort of good-faith collateral, known as credible commitment. For example, in a slightly unbalanced venture, the over 50%-partner may concede favorable contract clauses (such as veto power). These clauses can be so favorable that a firm may have more control with a 49% share than a 51% share (Friedman and Beguin 1971). Or the commitment may be the most critical positions in the

Figure 1
Entry Mode Classified by the Entrant's Level of Control

High-Control Modes: Dominant Equity Interests

Wholly-owned subsidiary
Dominant shareholder (many partners)
Dominant shareholder (few partners)
Dominant shareholder (one partner)

Medium-Control Modes: Balanced Interests

Plurality shareholder (many partners)
Plurality shareholder (few partners)
Equal partner (50/50)
Contractual joint venture
Contract management
Restrictive exclusive contract
   (e.g., distribution agreement, license)
Franchise
Nonexclusive restrictive contract
Exclusive nonrestrictive contract

Low-Control Modes: Diffused Interests

Nonexclusive, nonrestrictive contracts
   (e.g., intensive distribution, some licenses)
Small shareholder (many partners)
Small shareholder (few partners)
Small shareholder (one partner)

foreign entity: the exposed partner can demand to fill them with its own personnel, a method preferred by Japanese multinationals (Hayashi 1978).

In a 50-50 relationship, the hostage is a peculiar one — the venture itself. Friedman and Beguin (1971) point out that equality in equity capital can "lend a special feeling of partnership to the two partners" (p. 372), adding "the risk of deadlock itself acts as a powerful incentive to the partners, encouraging them to find solutions to disagreements by discussion and compromise" (p. 377).

In certain nonequity modes, moderate control comes from daily involvement in the operation and from expertise. These modes include:

— *Contract management* (an ongoing relationship) in which the entrant performs specified functions and in which the entrant has representation on the management committee that oversees the venture's activities,

— *Contractual joint ventures*,

— *Restrictive exclusive contracts*,

— *Franchising* (a form of licensing in which the use of a business system is granted).[3] Franchising offers medium control because the typical agreement includes incentives to adhere to the system's rules and allows a high degree of monitoring of the franchisee's activities.

— Contracts that are *exclusive but nonrestrictive* or *nonexclusive but restrictive*. Either restrictiveness or exclusivity give the entrant moderate control, though by different means. Restrictive contracts circumscribe the other party's freedom of action, while exclusive contracts (simultaneously a reward and a protection against competition) motivate the other party to cooperate (Stern and El-Ansary 1982).

Low-control modes are ones in which the entrant has diffused interests. These include nonexclusive, nonrestrictive contracts (multiple unrestricted licenses and intensive distribution) and minority equity positions.

We reiterate here that there are many ways to gain control. Our list is not exhaustive: In particular, we note that entrants may build stable relationships or networks with other parties in which the long-term interests of both parties allow the development of norms. Although this area has received relatively little research attention, developments have been made by Hakansson (1984) and Williamson (1985).

We now turn to propositions concerning the degree of control that is most efficient for a variety of conditions. Given a ranking of entry models on control, it is then possible to recommend an entry mode for a given entry situation.

A TRANSACTION COST ANALYSIS OF FOREIGN MODES OF ENTRY

What is the best entry mode for a given setting? Obviously, a large number of factors bear on the answer. The intent of this review is to propose constructs and mechanisms derived from a unified theoretical framework. This framework is similar to the general approach of several new theories of foreign investment (Kindleberger 1984, Caves 1971, 1982, Hennart 1982, Rugman 1982), which concern why multinational firms exist. In this paper, we develop these theories for one specific issue: choice of mode of entry. Our analysis builds on the existing literature by proposing detailed relationships between constructs corresponding to the ideas presented in the more general theories. As we develop these empirically testable propositions, we contrast them with predictions from other, frequently more well-known frameworks to suggest how they differ and to spur empirical research designed to sort out competing predictions. We also review findings that bear on each proposition.

Our mapping from governance structure to control (Figure 1) looks something like a progression from less integrated to more integrated. Williamson (1979) suggests that degree of integration proceeds from complete non-integration (classical marketing contracting between two parties) to complete integration (one entity "contracts" internally to perform a function), passing through intermediate points. Underlying this progression is the transference of authority from paper (a contract) to entities (arbitrators, parties to a transaction), culminating in the consolidation of authority by one party. This progression of authority is a growing degree of control.

Control and integration are closely related, since integration gives a firm legitimate authority to direct operations. Hence, we employ a theory of vertical integration to generate propositions about the desirability of various modes of entry offering various degrees of control. The theory, transaction cost analysis, combines elements of industrial organization, organization theory, and contract law to weigh the tradeoffs to be made in vertical integration (and by extension, degree of control) decisions.

We begin with the assumption that the market being entered has at least enough potential that the firm can recoup the overhead of a high-control entry mode. If this is not the case, high-control modes are not worth considering (Williamson 1979). However, for markets large enough to break even on the fixed cost of a high-control mode, the entrant has a choice to make. In these circumstances, the efficiency of an entry mode depends on four constructs that determine the optimal degree of control, following a transaction cost analysis. These constructs are:

1. *transaction-specific assets*: investments (physical and human) that are specialized to one or a few users or uses;

2. *external uncertainty*: the unpredictability of the entrant's external environment;

3. *internal uncertainty*: the entrant's inability to determine its agents' performance by observing output measures;

4. *free-riding potential*: agents' ability to receive benefits without bearing the associated costs.

Figure 2
A Transaction Cost Framework For Analyzing the Efficiency
of Entry Modes

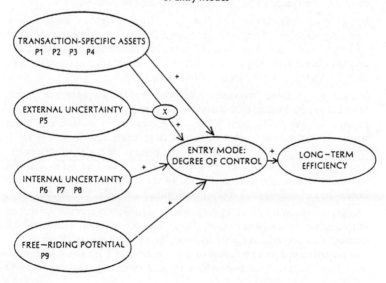

Figure 2 is an overview of the framework, which shows that these four factors should be positively associated with the entrant's degree of control. The four factors, their rationale, and their corresponding propositions about entry modes are discussed one by one in this section.

Figure 3 restates the propositions in a more accessible form and lists the conditions under which the modes in the high-control cluster are most appropriate.

TRANSACTION-SPECIFIC ASSETS

Transaction cost analysis approaches the entry mode question with the following promise: a low level of ownership is preferable until proven otherwise. We label this premise the "default" hypothesis.

The default hypothesis accords with an assumption fundamental to economics, that is, that market outcomes tend to be efficient when competition is strong. Competitive pressures drive parties to perform effectively at low cost and to deal with each other in fairness, honesty, and good faith lest they be replaced. Hayashi (1978) gives the example of foreign sales agents competing to carry out distribution for a Japanese entrant. Hayashi finds that where competition among agents is active, the resulting business relationship is highly cooperative. In general, where suppliers of a good or service are readily available, a firm may take advantage of their expertise and economies of scope and scale in performing their specialized function by writing a contract with one supplier, confident that a new supplier may be found if the relationship is unsatisfactory (Williamson 1981b). Accordingly, firms are advised to avoid integration whenever the supplier market is competitive. In this way, the firm can have both a high return and low risk.

By not integrating (or investing directly), a firm avoids the drawbacks of a company division. Overhead is minimized, as is company politics, communication distortion, and the possibility that an inside division will become obsolete or inefficient because it is shielded from the pressures of daily competition for contracts (Williamson 1975).

Integration (or direct investment) is, however, justified when the market mechanism no longer encourages performance, i.e., when competitive pressure is low. Williamson (1979) argues that most transactions begin when competition is intense but some degenerate into lock in ("small numbers bargaining") when the contract partner becomes irreplaceable. Then the partner may extract new contract terms, become inflexible, and otherwise violate the letter and spirit of the agreement ("opportunistic" behavior, i.e., self-interest seeking with guile) with relative impunity.

Degeneration into lock in occurs when "transaction-specific assets" of considerable value accumulate. These are investments (physical and human) that are valuable only in a narrow range of transactions, that is, specialized to one or a few users or uses (Williamson 1981b). An example of a physical transaction-specific asset is a stamping machine to make

Figure 3
When A Mode of Entry is Most Efficient

When Dominant Entry Interests Are	Based on	When Balanced Interests Are	Based on	When Diffused Interests Are	Based on
Conditions		Conditions		Conditions	
Transaction-Specific Assets		**Transaction-Specific Assets**		**Transaction-Specific Assets**	
Products or processes highly proprietary	P1	Products or processes moderately proprietary	P1	Products or processes not proprietary (open knowledge)	P1
Products or processes unstructured, ill understood	P2	Products or processes semi-structured, moderately well understood	P2	Products or processes well structured, routinely understood	P2
Products highly customized to each user	P3	Products adaptable to user groups	P3	Products complete standardized	P3
Introductory and growth stages of product life cycle	P4	Later growth and early maturity strages of product life cycle	P4	Mature stage of product life cycle	P4
Interaction: Transaction-Specific Assets/External Uncertainty		*Interaction: Asset Specificity /External Uncertainty*		*Interaction: Transaction-Specific Assets/External Uncertainty*	
Products or processes highly *proprietary and political or economic instability acute*	P5	Products or processes somewhat *proprietary and political or economic instability moderate*	P5	Products or processes not *proprietary and political or economic instability acute*	P5
Products or processes unstructured, *ill understood, and political or economic instability acute*	P5	Products or processes semi-structured, *moderately well understood, and political or economic instability moderate*	P5	Products or processes well structured, *routinely understood, and political or economic instability acute*	P5
Products highly customized to each *user and political or economic instability acute*	P5	Products adaptable to user groups *and political or economic instability moderate*	P5	Products completely standardized *and political or economic instability acute*	P5
Introductory and growth stages of product life cycle and political or economic instability acute	P5	*Later growth or early maturity stages of product life cycle and political or economic instability moderate*	P5	Mature stage of product life cycle *and political or economic instability acute*	P5
Internal Uncertainty		**Internal Uncertainty**		**Internal Uncertainty**	
Firm has considerable international experience	P6	Firm has moderate degree of international experience	P6	Firm has little international experience	P6
Sociocultural distance is great	P7b	Sociocultural distance is moderate	P7a, P7b	Sociocultural distance is great	P7a
Benefits of doing business the entrant's way are large	P7c	Modest benefits to doing business the extrant's way	P7c	Small (if any) benefits to doing business the entrant's way	P7c
Foreign business community is very small	P8	Foreign business community is of substantial size	P8	Foreign business community is very large	P8
Free-Riding Potential		**Free-Riding Potential**		**Free-Riding Potential**	
Brand name is extremely valuable	P9	Brand name carries some value	P9	Brand name not valued	P9

parts to the specifications of one manufacturer (Klein, Crawford, and Alchian 1972). Human transaction-specific assets include working relationships and knowledge of the idiosyncrasies of a firm and its activities. Transaction-specific assets usually develop over time, coming to assume a larger role the longer the transaction has continued. Frequently these experience-based assets are not very valuable. But where they significantly contribute to performance, the partner who acquires them becomes hard to replace.

When transaction-specific assets are likely to become valuable, transaction cost analysis suggests that firms are better off either integrating the function (exerting maximum control) or redesigning tasks so that general purpose assets will suffice. If the firm integrates, it will still become locked in, but to employees rather than outsiders. Opportunism can be combatted by exercising legitimate authority, monitoring behavior, and offering more varied incentives than can be used with outsiders. If instead the firm redesigns the task, it loses the value generated by specialized assets. However, both small numbers bargaining and overhead can be avoided, which sometimes offsets the loss of specialization benefits.

The preceding discussion has focused on ownership as a means of exerting control. More recent developments in transaction cost analysis (see Williamson 1985 for a summary) have begun to stress other ways to gain control, ways that fall in the large zone between classical market contracting and vertical integration. Many of the arrangements found in international operations fall into this zone (relational contracting). Research that explores the development of relational contracts promises to make a valuable contribution to our understanding of modes of entry (see Hakansson 1984).

We now turn to four propositions applying the notion of transaction-specific assets to the entry mode decision. The appropriate entry mode is a function of a number of variables taken simultaneously. For clearer exposition, our propositions deal with one factor at a time.

Transaction-Specific Assets: Proposition 1

The concept of transaction-specific assets suggests the following proposition:

> P1:   Modes of entry offering greater control are more efficient for highly proprietary products or processes.

Proprietary knowledge is an important type of specialized asset. On the surface, proprietary products and processes would seem appropriate for a low level of control, licensing, because there is something of value to license (Root 1983). Indeed, firms with high R&D expenditures (which generate proprietary knowledge), do more licensing *per se* (Caves 1981). However, Calvet (1981) points out that proprietary knowledge is subject to hazards of transmission and valuation. Such knowledge is often ill codified and difficult to transmit across organizational boundaries. Furthermore, the classic problem of valuation of information arises: the buyer cannot know what the knowledge is worth (what bid to make) unless the knowledge is disclosed, at which point the acquirer need not pay for it. This obliges information-holders to exploit it themselves, resulting in high levels of ownership, and hence control, of a foreign business entity. Ownership has the added advantage of encouraging teamwork and keeping the (employee) team together (Williamson 1981b).

If a particular practice is efficient and an industry is competitive, we may expect to see firms that have survived in that industry following the efficient practice (Lilien 1979). Hence, systematic practices that firms follow constitute information about what mode is efficient. In the entry mode literature, it appears that firms do exert more control as proprietary content increases. Research and development expenditures (which generate proprietary knowledge) increase the extent of licensing (Telesio 1979) but increase the extent of direct investment even more (Davidson and McFetridge 1984, Caves 1982, Davidson 1982). Stopford and Wells find a negative relationship between research and development expenditures and the proportion of subsidiaries organized as joint venture rather than wholly-owned subsidiaries. This implies that firms tend to reserve proprietary knowledge for entry vehicles they control completely. In a similar vein, Coughlan and Flaherty (1983) study the use of wholly-owned distribution (high control) vs. independent distribution (low control) by U.S. semiconductor manufacturers operating in foreign markets. They find that high control is more often employed for technically sophisticated products, which tend to have higher proprietary content than unsophis- ticated products. This corresponds to a finding in the literature on intra- firm trading, which considers the extent to which a multinational firm manufactures its own inputs and markets its own outputs. Intra-firm trade indicates that a firm not only is integrated (common ownership) but acts integrated (is self-sufficient). Hence, the forces that drive integration (high control) should also drive intra-firm trading (Lall 1978). Lall (1978) and Helleiner and Lavergne (1979) find that intra-firm trading is strongly related to R&D spending, an oft-used proxy for proprietary content and technological sophistication.

Transaction-Specific Assets: Proposition 2

Another implication of the concept of asset specificity is:

> P2: Entry modes offering higher degrees of control are more efficient for unstructured, poorly-understood products and processes.

It is particularly difficult to use low-control entry modes for more ill- structured, poorly-understood activities and knowledge. Teece (1976) refers to a "common code" of understanding of what the problem and its parameters are. The common code of understanding is a transaction- specific asset that is critical for amorphous functions (Johanson and Vahlne 1977). Teece (1976), in a path-breaking empirical study of technology transfer costs, strongly supports this idea. He finds that the costs of the entrant's first transfer across national boundaries are much higher than the costs of subsequent transfers. This occurs because the first transfer is ill understood. Thus, development personnel must interact heavily with production personnel to solve the inevitable unforeseen problems. Fortunately, the firm moves down the learning curve by developing and codifying solutions, which are applied to subsequent transfers of this technology. For such ill-structured, poorly understood activities as first transfers of technology, high-control entry modes are preferable to preserve and extend the common code of understanding.

Teece (1983) suggests complexity is a proxy for the degree to which products and processes are ill-structured and poorly understood. In accordance with proposition 2, Wilson (1980) finds licensing (low control) is more common for simpler products, while direct investment (higher control) is more common for complex products. Davidson and McFetridge (1984) find that radical new products are more likely to be transferred to a virtually wholly-owned affiliate (at least 95% equity) than to an independent firm (less than 5% equity).

Transaction-Specific Assets: Proposition 3

P3:   Entry modes offering higher degrees of control are more efficient for products customized to the user.

Customized products demand considerable local knowledge. On the surface, this presents no difficulties, since the entrant can contract with a local independent entity that has that knowledge. But by the nature of customization, the entrant must work actively with the local entity to tailor the product to the user. Accordingly, working relationships must be developed between personnel from each company (contractor and contractee). Those relationships will include a knowledge of what to expect from individuals and of how to communicate. These working relationships constitute an asset specific to the contractor-contractee transaction. Holton (1971), Keegan (1974), and Kobrin et. al. (1980) note the strong reliance of decision-makers on such relationships when assessing other foreign opportunities, which underscores their importance. Since these relationships exist only with the current contractee, the entrant is locked in. Team effects have been created, and control is needed to preserve them (Williamson 1981b).

Johanson and Vahlne (1977) suggest that people-intensive tasks are particularly ill-structured. If so, we would expect such customized businesses as management consulting, banking, and advertising to be dominated by high-control entry modes. Caves (1981) surveys anecdotal evidence that service firms such as these are more likely than other firms to go abroad, often at the urging of domestic clients making their own international entries. Presumably, this occurs because clients want to preserve and extend the intimate knowledge and working relationship already built up with service firms. Weinstein (1974), in his survey of U.S. advertising agencies expanding abroad, finds over 60% of foreign affiliates are at least majority-owned by the parent agency. In distribution, Coughlan and Flaherty (1983) find high-control distribution methods used more often for products with high service requirements, a characteristic of customized products.

Transaction-Specific Assets: Proposition 4

P4:   The more mature the product class, the less control firms should demand of a foreign business entity.

Immature product classes have a high proprietary content (Chandler 1977), raising the transmission and valuation problems mentioned earlier. Further, technological and market knowledge of a new product class is not yet common. Hence, only the innovator's personnel know the product and its markets. To avoid becoming locked in to outsiders who acquire that knowledge, control is required. Thus, newer technology is likely to be handled by wholly-owned subsidiaries (high control) (Williamson 1979).

Specialized knowledge comes into the open market as the innovation diffuses. Over time transaction-specific assets associated with an innovation become general purpose assets associated with a well-established product. Chandler (1977) documents this diffusion for products and processes that were an innovation in the U.S. in the nineteenth century. As this diffusion occurs, we should expect to see less integration, as less administrative control is needed. Hence, older technology is likely to be licensed or handled by a joint venture (lower control) (Williamson 1979).[4]

In the international entry mode literature, Weinstein (1974) finds that U.S. advertising agencies entered foreign markets beginning in 1915, when large-scale advertising was a novel way of doing business. Consistent with P4, Weinstein finds that the first advertising agencies going abroad were highly likely to start subsidiaries from scratch and to own them 100%. In later years, when advertising became common, U.S. entrants became more likely to acquire existing firms and to take less equity, often minority positions.

Teece (1976) finds that technology transfer costs (absorbed by transferor and transferee) decline sharply in mature product classes (measured by the age of the technology and the number of competitors using similar or competing technology). Because the requisite knowledge is well codified and widely available for hire, the entrant does not need to supplement the control offered by the market mechanism.

This product class effect has been suggested for various reasons in the entry mode literature. One reason advanced is that the likely gains are lower with mature products, so that management will prefer investing resources in more promising sectors (Bivens and Lovell 1966). Another explanation is that firms with immature products are in a better bargaining position with local authorities. Because their product is difficult to duplicate, they can force host governments and local partners to grant them more ownership and control and do not need the expertise of partners (Bivens and Lovell 1966, Davidson 1982). As the product matures, the advantage erodes, creating pressure to give up control. Vernon (1977) calls this the "obsolescing bargain."

We now turn to propositions about the impact of external uncertainty, the second of the four transaction cost constructs, on the viability of entry modes.

EXTERNAL UNCERTAINTY

External uncertainty is the volatility (unpredictability) of the firm's environment. Williamson (1979) hypothesizes that firms should react to volatility by avoiding ownership, since it commits them to one operation that may not be appropriate when the next environmental shift occurs. Rather, firms should retain flexibility and shift risk to outsiders. This suggests that in the absence of transaction-specific assets, the default option, market contracting, is unchanged by volatility. We should not expect higher-control entry modes to be more efficient than lower-control modes in volatile settings.

But what if transaction-specific assets accumulate such that the entrant becomes locked in to a partner in a shifting environment? Then flexibility, the major reason not to integrate in the face of uncertainty, is lost anyway. Further, frequent shifts mean frequent negotiation of new arrangements, presenting the agent with many occasions to behave opportunistically and inflexibly. In short, uncertain environments aggravate the normal difficulty of working with irreplaceable agents, making the combination of uncertainty and specificity a potent double bind. This suggests that given some degree of asset specificity, control becomes more desirable as uncertainty increases.

This idea is represented in Figure 3. The horizontal line (no transaction-specific assets) indicates that without specificity (TSA), uncertainty should be unrelated to the degree of control sought. But given specificity, marked by an X, uncertainty increases the need for control. The strength of this relationship increases as specificity increases.

External Uncertainty: Proposition 5

In international operations, external uncertainty (unpredictability) is an important factor. External uncertainty is typically labeled "country risk," which can take many forms, e.g., political instability, economic fluctuations, currency changes (Herring 1983).[5] Some writers argue that firms react to unpredictability by exerting control to manage their volatile affairs and resolve disputes (Killing 1982, Bivens and Lovell 1966). Unfortunately, this commits the entrant to an operation that may turn out to be inappropriate as unforeseen circumstances develop (Root 1983). Further, in volatile environments, a product or technology may be obsolete by the time a high-control administrative mechanism is in place. Hence, firms may license in fast-changing industries simply to get their returns before they disappear (Caves 1981).

Transaction cost analysis suggests that in volatile environments, entrants are better off accepting low-control entry modes (the "default option"). This not only avoids resource commitment but frees entrants to change partners or renegotiate contract terms and working arrangements relatively easily as circumstances develop and change.[6] Low control maintains flexibility — unless flexibility has already been lost through the accumulation of transaction-specific assets.

Hence:

P5: The greater the *combination* of country risk (e.g., political instability, economic fluctuations) and transaction-specificity of assets (proprietary content, poorly understood products, customization, product class immaturity), the higher the appropriate degree of control.

This proposition is an interaction,[7] expressed as an X in Figure 2, and occurs in addition to the effect of asset specificity alone (propositions 1 through 4). An interaction implies that each source of unpredictability should interact to magnify (add to) the separate impact of each source of transaction-specific assets: the proprietary nature of products and processes (P1), ill-understood products and processes (P2), customizing products to the user (P3), and the immaturity of a product class (P4). An entrant in these circumstances is likely to find the problems of managing irreplaceable agents magnified, since the risky, changing environment presents numerous occasions for agents to shirk and to renegotiate to their advantage.

In a nutshell, proposition 5 suggests that environmental unpredictability plays a major role when asset specificity is high, magnifying the need for control that specificity creates. When specificity is low, unpredictability does not change the default option, low control, for the firm can deal with unpredictability by changing agents. Instead of exerting control (and assuming the corresponding risk), the entrant can retain flexibility and let the competitive market mechanism operate to generate returns (Mascarenhas 1982).

INTERNAL UNCERTAINTY

The third factor in the transaction cost framework is internal uncertainty. Internal uncertainty exists when the firm cannot accurately assess its agents' performance by objective, readily available output measures. This may occur when good measures of output are not available, or when the relationship between inputs and outputs is ill-understood (Ouchi 1977), making it difficult to specify what performance level to expect. Uncertainty internal to the firm makes control more desirable regardless of the level of asset specificity involved (Williamson 1981a). When performance cannot be specified or measured easily, firms can monitor inputs rather than evaluate outputs. Further, firms can use a variety of subtle incentives to develop goal congruence and loyalty. Thus, employees may act in the firm's best interest even if a firm cannot precisely specify what to do.

When internal uncertainty is high, control is needed to impose subjective judgement and to monitor inputs (behavior). This presupposes that management knows how people should behave and how to judge hard-to-quantify results. In the domestic environment, this is likely to be the case, as management has learned to manage over time. But the international setting is another matter. Entrants new to the international setting are unlikely to know how to overcome internal uncertainty. Further, firms that operate in competitive industries and try to exert control before they know how to use it will make serious errors that should depress efficiency (Teece 1976, p. 46).

Internal Uncertainty: Proposition 6

Accordingly,

> P6:   The entrant's degree of control of a foreign business entity should be positively related to the firm's cumulative international experience.

Proposition 6 has been extensively discussed in the literature that describes what managers do (which may or may not be efficient). There is some indication that firms do behave according to this proposition. A popular conception in the international management literature is that of a firm as a humanlike entity, "maturing" (Stopford and Wells 1972) as it acquires experience in international markets. The international neophyte fears the unknown, consequently overstating risks and understating returns of international markets (Davidson 1980). Overly conservative, the firm avoids setting up a foreign business entity and merely exports (Bilkey 1978). With the limited experience of exporting, the firm gains confidence and becomes more aggressive in nondomestic markets, moving toward more direct investment rather than export (Bilkey 1978, Weston and Sorge 1972) or licensing (Telesio 1979).

Still hesitant, the firm selects nearby, culturally similar countries (Engwall 1984, Davidson 1980, Bilkey 1978). With experience comes enhanced understanding, competence, and confidence, as well as more accurate perception of foreign risks and returns. The firm enters more distant, different countries (Davidson 1980) and with new adventuresomeness acquires a taste for control, for active management of the entity (Root 1983). Unlike the neophyte firm, content to let someone else run the international side of the business, the more experienced firm is confident, assertive, desirous of control, and willing to take risks to get it. Further, the firm has probably set up a headquarters staff for international operations and is eager to get the most form this overhead (Davidson 1980, 1982). Accordingly, experience should lead to more control, which proposition 6 suggests is the most efficient outcome.

Proposition 6 is not without controversy in the descriptive literature. Conceivably, the relationship between international experience and the *observed* degree of ownership is negative, i.e., that inexperienced firms demand higher ownership levels than do more experienced firms. This argument is based on the ethnocentric orientation of many international neophytes. Ethnocentrism leads inexperienced firms to demand to have their own nationals in key positions, which is easier to achieve via ownership than negotiation (Weichmann and Pringle 1979). Over time, firms become comfortable with local differences, develop working relationships with local people, and become confident that they can use local expertise to their advantage. At this point, firms are more willing to delegate control (Shetty 1979), which is reflected in lower degrees of ownership.

This counter-argument is a market power proposal: it assumes that firms have the latitude to follow their preferences even if the result is inefficient. In contrast, transaction cost analysis assumes inefficient practices are extinguished by market pressures. This implies that in noncompetitive industries, we may observe that the entrant's degree of control is negatively related to the firm's international experience. In other words, an inefficient practice may be observed where managers have the slack to implement their preferences at the sacrifice of long-term results.

Internal Uncertainty: Proposition 7

A particularly potent form of internal uncertainty is created by sociocultural distance. The difference between home and host cultures, although difficult to measure, has intrigued researchers in the international area. It is often argued that the greater the sociocultural difference between home and host countries, the lower the degree of control an entrant should and does demand. This is explained by the higher uncertainty executives perceive in cultures that are truly "foreign" to them. Not knowing, being comfortable with, or even agreeing with the values and operating methods of the host country, executives may shy away from the involvement that accompanies ownership (Root 1983, Davidson 1980, 1982, Richman and Copen 1972). Uncertainty due to sociocultural distance may also cause executives to undervalue foreign investments (Root 1983). Further, transferring home management techniques and values is difficult where the operating environment is very dissimilar to that of the home country (Richman and Copen 1972, Alpander 1976). Finally, sociocultural distance also creates high information costs, which firms may avoid by turning management over to partners or licensees (Root 1983).

Goodnow and Hansz (1972) support this viewpoint in an empirical study of how much control large U.S. firms exert when going overseas. Via cluster analysis, they sort 100 countries into three groups that roughly correspond to increasing sociocultural distance from the United States. Goodnow and Hansz also group entry modes into three types: strong control/high investment, moderate control/modest investment, and weak control/low investment. They find firms reduce their control and investment as they move away from socioculturally similar countries.

Not all writers agree. The Conference Board (Bivens and Lovell 1966) suggests that some firms react to sociocultural distance by demanding

18   JOURNAL OF INTERNATIONAL BUSINESS STUDIES, FALL 1986

rather than avoiding ownership so that they may impose their operating methods. Such firms do not trust local management or non-local partners and prefer the control to "do it their way." Richman and Copen (1972) point out that being foreign gives a firm latitude to be different, to break the rules of the local culture to a point, because foreigners are expected to do things differently. Hymer (1976) contends that local firms, because they do not have the disadvantage of operating in a foreign culture at a distance, will always outperform foreign firms unless the entrants have a distinctive advantage. On occasion operating methods that do not fit local culture will constitute the necessary advantage that enables foreigners to compete with locals on their home ground.

In short, the entry mode literature conflicts concerning the impact of sociocultural distance. Transaction cost analysis suggests both views are correct for the following reason. Sociocultural distance makes internal uncertainty very high, since the environment is unknown. Furthermore, an entrant transferring its operating procedures and methods to a very different setting will have to train its agents heavily. Once they learn the entrant's ways, agents will have acquired valuable knowledge and relationships that are of little use to other firms in that country, making these assets transaction-specific (see Richman and Copen for examples). Given that the management problems created by sociocultural distance are now aggravated by specificity, an entrant is better off to demand control.

Alternatively, the entrant may decide to give up the benefits of employing its own methods, design an operation that uses local (general purpose) methods, and have little control. This is the design reaction to the prospect of specific assets. With specificity designed out, the problems of sociocultural distance can be managed by transferring risk to external agents, thereby reducing flexibility. If the foregone specialization benefits are not too large, designing out specificity is the efficient solution.

Which is the more efficient reaction to sociocultural distance: creating specificity and using a high-control mode or designing out specificity ("going native") and using a low-control mode? The answer depends on the gains from doing business in unconventional foreign ways for a given culture. Transaction cost analysis suggests the effect of cultural differences is as follows:

P7:   When sociocultural distance is great:

         a: Low-control levels are more efficient than intermediate levels;

         b: High-control levels are more efficient than intermediate levels;

         c: High-control levels are more efficient only when there is a substantial advantage to doing business in the entrant's way.

Proposition 7c suggests that when operating in a very different environment, "our way" is not automatically the best way. Put differently, the default option, low control, should not be given up without a reason. Proposition 7b reflects the control reaction to sociocultural distance: a firm running an operation in a very different culture is bound to manage "our way," thereby creating specificity. The control that created lock in is now needed to manage it, but the firm benefits from its freedom to operate unconventionally. In contrast, proposition 7a reflects the design reaction to sociocultural distance: lacking control, a firm manages "as it's done here," losing specialization benefits but avoiding lock in. Intermediate levels of control are undesirable because they offer the worst of both possibilities — neither freedom to be unconventional nor low commitment to be flexible.

As a corollary, entrants are unlikely to write contracts with outsiders that impose the entrant's style on the contractee. By so doing, the entrant would enter small numbers bargaining without gaining much control over the partner. A testable implication is that franchising, which by nature imposes a management style on an independent, should decline as sociocultural distance increases.

Internal Uncertainty: Proposition 8

Richman and Copen (1972) point out that the problems of sociocultural distance can diminish over time even if the culture is stable. This occurs because as more foreign firms enter the country, the pool of local personnel trained in these methods grows. Not only do firms train managers, but their presence arouses awareness, which in turn causes host-country nationals to obtain a business education abroad. The process is slow but has a cumulative effect (which Richman and Copen detail in the case of India). Eventually, the pool is large enough that an entrant finds enough local contractees available to constitute an open market in management skills. In short, these skills have diffused to become general purpose and readily available rather than narrowly available and specific to the few companies using them. This suggests:

> P8: The larger the foreign business community in the
> host country, the lower the level of control an
> entrant should demand.

Proposition 8 occurs because over time the entrant will find multinational management skills widely available, in spite of sociocultural distance (Seidler 1972 details this process for the transfer of American-style accounting methods to less developed countries). This diffusion of skills removes a major barrier to licensing (a low-control mode), which is the unavailability of "suitable" local firms (Caves 1981). Hence, management of the foreign entity can be contracted out to a pool of knowledgeable personnel, not necessarily employees, who can be controlled by the threat of replacement. In this vein, Contractor (1984) finds evidence that licensing becomes more lucrative relative to direct investment as a country's indigenous technical capability increases.

FREE-RIDING POTENTIAL

A potential control problem arises whenever one party can "free ride" on the efforts of others, receiving benefits without bearing costs. For example, McDonald's has charged its French franchisee with riding on the company's international goodwill and recognition to attract customers without maintaining the cleanliness standards that support the company name (*Time* 1981). Transaction cost analysis suggests that ceteris paribus, where the potential for free-riding ("demand externalities") is high, entry modes offering higher control are more efficient.

Free-Riding Potential: Proposition 9

This suggests:

> P9:   Entry modes offering higher degrees of control are more
>   efficient the higher the value of a brand name.

When a brand name is valuable, short-term gains can be had at the expense of the long term. Firms will take control to protect their brand name from degradation by free-riders (Davidson 1982) or to prevent the local operation from using the name in an inconsistent manner, thus diluting or confusing the international positioning of the brand (Holton 1971). Caves (1981) highlights the danger of local partners, who have less to lose from degrading a brand than does the entrant. Caves reviews both anecdotal and survey evidence that firms demand higher ownership levels when standardization of the product's design, style, quality, and name is part of the entrant's strategy. Since the strategy depends on assurance of all the name connotes (a "goodwill asset" or "reputation effect"), quality control is critical and free-riding is especially damaging.

These findings suggest high control is appropriate for heavily advertised brands. However, there is some contradiction in the empirical literature. Lall (1978) and Helleiner and Lavergne (1979) find that high advertising levels are associated with low intra-firm trading (low integration, low control), suggesting that valuable brand names can be efficiently marketed via low-control entry modes. Their explanation is that heavily advertised products tend to be unsophisticated consumer goods, which many agents are capable of handling, making low control appropriate. This explanation is consistent with propositions 1 through 4 concerning transaction-specific assets.

Yet heavy advertising does make free-riding more likely and control more desirable. This situation illustrates the value of the default option (low control) in transaction cost analysis. Beginning from low-control modes, a firm is advised to exert more control for valuable brand names (e.g., more heavily advertised brands). Hence, a firm is better off franchising its heavily advertised brands rather than merely licensing them in non-restrictive, nonexclusive fashion. However, the firm may not need to go so far as a joint venture or majority-owned affiliate. Proposition 9 proposes that more restraints be added (higher-control entry modes) as brand value increases, rather than proposing that high control is always appropriate. Hence proposition 9 fits the empirical literature and illustrates the control-flexibility tradeoff.

STRATEGIES FOR EMPIRICAL TESTS

The measurement strategy used by researchers to date has largely consisted of using single-item measures that are themselves proxy variables (e.g., R&D spending to indicate the construct "extent of proprietary information"). This approach, which is practical in light of the difficulty of obtaining international data, has yielded promising results. Clearly, hypothesis testing would be even stronger if psychometric methods were used to develop composite measures of each construct, thereby reducing reliance on single-item measures of complex constructs.[8] One advantage of this method is that the interpretability of findings using proxy variables would be greatly enhanced if they were embedded in a composite measure. Further, the proxy variable approach would be a stronger test if researchers were able to rule out alternative explanations by controlling for the impact of a greater range of covariates than is typical in entry mode studies.

These suggestions are particularly useful for researchers designing their own data collection instruments, which allows them greater degrees of freedom in their approach and provides a closer correspondence between theory and data (Williamson 1985). Outside the entry mode field, some research involving primary data collection has resulted in multi-item measures of transaction cost constructs. These measures are described in Walker and Weber (1984), Anderson (1985), and Anderson and Coughlan (1985).

An empirical test of transaction cost propositions is incomplete without the inclusion of two classes of predictor variables. One class concerns government restrictions, which narrow the feasible set of entry modes (Teece 1984). The other class concerns "production cost" factors, e.g., taxes, labor costs, and transportation costs. Ultimately, an efficient entry mode is based on the sum of production and transaction (governance) costs, given the feasible set. Production cost factors correlated with transaction cost factors will bias estimates of effects unless included as covariates. Further, a more complete picture of entry modes emerges when production factors are considered (Williamson 1985).[9]

A direct test of the long-term efficiency of an entry mode would be difficult to make. Efficiency data are highly proprietary and, even if obtainable, reflect potentially large short-run effects. We suggest that an appropriate and more tractable empirical research approach is to study prevailing practice (usage of entry modes) in competitive industries, which tend to extinguish inefficient choices (Lilien 1979). An example would be to predict the impact of explanatory variables on the odds of choosing a higher-control mode over a lower-control mode at a given point in time.

An approach that is even closer to the long-term nature of the propositions is to study what practices survive over time (e.g., using a hazard rates model). Although the time dimension introduces new variables, it does approximate the working out of inappropriate choices.

CONCLUSION

The transaction cost propositions advanced here are not suggested as an all-inclusive answer. Other factors will of course enter and may be very powerful in some settings. As indicated earlier, the framework applies to an entry decision where the choice is real. For a firm already operating in a foreign market with an existing mode of operation, the concepts discussed in this paper are certainly relevant. However, additional factors related to switching costs must be considered. The proposed framework also has limited value in situations where governmental, competitive, or information restrictions eliminate a large number of options. Nonetheless, the transaction cost approach is a useful way to structure the issues. This is particularly helpful when dealing with poorly understood issues and a long list of potentially relevant variables whose direction of effect is difficult to predict.

Simplification is a critical first step when dealing with complex problems. Our analysis ignores or downplays considerations that play a major role in some settings. In particular, we assume that an entrant, having decided to operate in a given market, has a choice of entry modes. This ignores possible government restrictions and assumes the entrant is contemplating a volume of business sufficient to carry the overhead of a high-control entry mode, at least over the long run (Williamson 1979). Further, we do not consider possible interactions between decision to enter and choice of entry mode.

Finally, we assume the entrant wants to operate a profitable business venture in the host country. To the extent that a foreign operation's objectives may be subordinate to the strategy needs of a parent multi-national, other objectives may take precedence. In turn, the multinational's need to trade off subsidiary profits for system profits obliges the MNC to exert more control than the transaction cost default option suggests (Caves 1982). In general, higher degrees of control are more appropriate for entrants that closely coordinate global strategies.

Given these limitations, what can be gained from the framework proposed here? Much of the literature on modes of entry does not suggest hypotheses but considerations. The pros and cons of, say, licensing, are weighed against an alternative that is usually unspecified. Hence, predictions are difficult to make. In contrast, the framework presented here yields testable propositions based on the control-resource commitment tradeoff. A notable advantage of transaction cost analysis in this regard is the "default" hypothesis: low-resource commitment is preferable until proven otherwise. The presence of a default hypothesis is especially helpful for theory testing because it provides a testable prediction.

Transaction cost analysis has been extended in recent years to cover a range of control rather than the extremes of integrate or contract out (Williamson 1985). In this form, transaction cost analysis brings to the entry mode problem an emphasis on the growth of ties that bind, on uncertainty, on the balancing of risks (credible commitments)and on the scale of operations. These constructs have been used to bring together many of the diverse ideas (such as the effect of sociocultural distance) expressed in the managerial and economic literatures and order them into testable propositions under a consistent rationale. Some of these propositions are new (e.g., the effect of the foreign business community), while others serve to clarify debates in the literature (e.g., the effect of sociocultural distance). The propositions also emphasize the interactions derived from the transaction cost analytical framework. Other interactions could be observed in empirical work in the sense that the joint effect of two variables could be greater than the sum of their independent effects. However, the rationale for these interactions goes beyond a transaction cost analytical framework. While the approach is incomplete, it is a useful starting point in examining tradeoffs among modes of entry.

In this paper we have developed a systematic approach to the entry mode issue. The propositions summarized in Figures 2 and 3 are testable. It is hoped, these propositions will encourage empirical research into an important area, as well as provide guidelines to management about how to match entry modes with their situations.

NOTES

1. Caves (1982) and Hennart (1982) undertake ambitious surveys of both the economic and international business research on multinational enterprise, including the entry mode issue. This paper builds on their works. We develop testable propositions (involving tradeoffs and interactions) as to when each mode of entry is likely to be effective. This is made possible by adopting an explicit criterion of long-term efficiency and employing a transaction cost perspective.

2. The purpose of developing the theory presented here is to help managers choose which form of entry to employ in a foreign market. Therefore, the theory concerns only situations where there is a set of options from which to choose. Further, the long-term orientation confines us to durable entry modes. We do not address short-term contracting (e.g., nonrenewable one-year licenses). The long-term efficiency criterion does not apply to a short-term arrangement. Consequently, this analysis does not offer insight about the length of contract. Nonetheless, the long-term perspective is necessary when the firm makes a long-term commitment to a market. See Kindleberger (1984) for a discussion of long vs. short-term contracts.

3. Franchising arrangements are frequently exclusive as well.

4. A product class may have reached the mature stage in the entrant's home country but not the host country. Hence, indigenous capability is not yet widely available, and the entrant who contracts with and trains a local independent entity is creating transaction-specific assets. The relevant level of product maturity, therefore, is in the host country.

5. For practical purposes, risk and uncertainty are synonymous (Herring 1983).

6. Many firms choose to retain low resource commitment but trade off the renegotiation aspect of flexibility by writing long-term licenses.

7. Interactions are typically operationalized as a multiplication of two terms (here, specificity and uncertainty). The multiplicative term is high when both factors are high (combined presence) and low when either factor is low (lack of combined presence). Of course, both terms must be positive for the interaction to meanfully express the combined presence of two factors.

24   JOURNAL OF INTERNATIONAL BUSINESS STUDIES, FALL 1986

8. Nunnally (1978) is perhaps the most cited reference on psychometric methods and offers concrete suggestions for overcoming the data limitations that are bound to arise in conducting field research.

9. Accounting for production costs is particularly important when considering introducing a new product line into a foreign market where the firm has an ongoing operation. While product addition is an entry, it is an incremental decision. Hence, it is the incremental costs that are relevant. For example, Davidson and McFetridge (1984) find that if firms have an affiliate in place, they are more likely to add product to the affiliate's line than to seek other arrangements. This is because the fixed costs of the affiliate have already been incurred; the additional operation generates only marginal costs.

SELECTED REFERENCES

Alpander, Guvenc G. (1976), Use of Quantitative Methods in International Operations by U.S. Overseas Executives, *Management International Review*, 10 (1), 71-77.

Anderson, Erin (1985), The Salesperson as Outside Agent or Employee: A Transaction Cost Analysis, *Marketing Science* 4 (Summer), 234-254.

_____ and Anne T. Coughlan (1985), Distribution of Industrial Products Introduced to Foreign Markets: Independent Versus Integrated Channels, Working Paper 85-033, Department of Marketing, The Wharton School.

Bilkey, Warren J. (1978), An Attempted Integration of the Literature on the Export Behavior of Firms, *Journal of International Business Studies*, 9 (Spring-Summer), 33-46.

Bivens, Daren Kraus and Enid Baird Lovell (1966), *Joint Ventures with Foreign Partners*, New York: the National Industrial Conference Board.

Calvet, A.L. (1981), A Synthesis of Foreign Direct Investment Theories and Theories of the Multinational Firm, *Journal of International Business Studies*, 12 (Spring-Summer), 43-59.

Caves, Richard E. (1982), *Multinational Enterprise and Economic Analysis*, Cambridge: Cambridge University Press.

_____ (1971), International Corporations: The Industrial Economics of Foreign Investment, *Economica*, 38, 1-27.

Chandler, Alfred D. (1977), *The Visible Hand: The Managerial Revolution in American Business*, Cambridge, Mass.: The Belknap Press.

Contractor, Farok J. (1984), Choosing Between Direct Investment and Licensing: Theoretical Considerations and Empirical Tests, *Journal of International Business Studies*, 15 (Winter),167-188.

Coughlan, Anne T. and M. Therese Flaherty (1983), Measuring the International Marketing Productivity of U.S. Semiconductor Companies. In David Gautschi, ed., *Productivity and Efficiency in Distribution Systems*, 123-149, Amsterdam: Elsevier Science Publishing Co., Inc.

Daniels, John D., Ernest W. Ogram, Jr., and Lee H. Radebaugh (1982), *International Business: Environments and Operations*, 3d edition, Reading, Mass.: Addison Wesley.

Davidson, William H. (1982), *Global Strategic Management*, New York: John Wiley and Sons.

_____ (1980), The Location of Foreign Direct Investment Activity: Country Characteristics and Experience Effects, *Journal of International Business Studies*, 11 (Fall), 9-22.

Davidson, William H. and Donald G. McFetridge (1984), International Technology Transactions and the Theory of the Firm, *The Journal of Industrial Economics*, 32 (March), 253-264.

Eiteman, David K. and Arthur I. Stonehill (1973), *Multinational Business Finance*, Reading, Mass.: Addison-Wesley

Engwall, Lars (1984), ed., *Uppsala Contributions to Business Research*, Uppsala, Sweden: Acta Universitatis Upsaliensis.

Evan, William M. (1965), Toward A Theory of Inter-Organizational Relationships, *Management Science*, 11 (August), B-217-B-230.

Friedmann, Wolfgang G. (1972), The Contractual Joint Venture,*Columbia Journal of World Business*, 7 (January-February),57-63.

Friedmann, Wolfgang G. and Jean-Pierre Beguin (1971), *Joint International Business Ventures in Developing Countries*, New York: Columbia University Press.

Goodnow, James D. and James E. Hanz (1972), Environmental Determinants of Overseas Market Entry Strategies, *Journal of International Business Studies*, 3 (Spring), 33-50.

Hackey, D. (1976), The International Expansion of U.S. Franchise Systems: Status and Strategies, *Journal of International Business Studies*, 7 (June), 65-75.

Hakansson, Hakan (1984), ed., *International Marketing and Purchasing of Industrial Goods*, New York: John Wiley and Sons.

Hayashi, Kichiro (1978), Japanese Management of Multinational Operations: Sources and Means of Joint Venture Control, *Management International Review*, 18 (4), 47-57.

Helleiner, G.K. and Real Lavergne (1979), Intra-Firm Trade and Industrial Exports to the United States, *Oxford Bulletin of Economics and Statistics*, 41 (November), 297-311.

Hennart, Jean-Francois (1982), *A Theory of Multinational Enterprise*, Ann Arbor: The University of Michigan Press.

Herring, Richard J., ed. (1983), *Managing International Risk*, Cambridge: Cambridge University Press.

Holton, Richard (1971), Marketing Policies in Multinational Corporations, *California Management Review*, 13 (4), 57-67.

Hymer, Stephen (1976), *The International Operations of National Firms*, Cambridge: MIT Press.

Johanson, Jan and Jan-Erik Vahlne (1977), The Internationalization Process of the Firm — A Model of Knowledge Development and Increasing Foreign Market Commitment, *Journal of International Business Studies*, 8 (Spring-Summer), 23-32.

Keegan, Warren J. (1974), Multinational Scanning: A Study of the Information Sources Utilized by Headquarters Executives in Multinational Companies, *Administrative Science Quarterly*, 19 (September), 411-421.

Killing, J. Peter (1982), How to Make A Global Joint Venture Work, *Harvard Business Review*, 60 (May-June), 120-127.

Kindleberger, Charles P. (1984), *Multinational Excursions*, Cambridge: The MIT Press.

Klein, Benjamin, Robert G. Crawford, and Armen A. Alchian (1972), Vertical Integration, Appropriable Quasi-Rents, and the Competitive Contracting Process, *Journal of Law and Economics*, 21 (October), 297-325.

Kobrin, Stephen J. (1976), The Environmental Determinants of Foreign Direct Manufacturing Investment: An Ex Post Empirical Analysis, *Journal of International Business Studies*, 7 (Fall-Winter), 29-42.

Kobrin, Stephen J., John Basek, Stephen Blank, and Joseph La Palombara (1980), The Assessment and Evaluation of Noneconomic Environments by American Firms: A Preliminary Report, *Journal of International Business Studies*, 11 (Spring-Summer), 32-46.

Lall, Sanjaya (1978), The Pattern of Intra-Firm Exports by U.S. Multinationals, *Oxford Bulletin of Economics and Statistics*, 40 (August), 209-222.

Lee, Woo-Young and John J. Brasch (1978), The Adoption of Export as an Innovative Strategy, *Journal of International Business Studies*, 9 (Spring-Summer), 85-93.

Lilien, Gary L. (1979), ADVISOR 2: Modeling the Marketing Mix Decision for Industrial Products, *Management Science*, 25 (February), 191-204.

Mascarenhas, Briance (1982), Coping With Uncertainty in International Business, *Journal of International Business Studies*, 13 (Fall), 87,98.

Newbould, Gerald D., Peter J. Buckley, and Jane C. Thurwell (1978), *Going International: The Experience of Smaller Companies Overseas*, New York: John Wiley and Sons, Inc.

Nunnally, Jum C. (1978), *Psychometric Theory*, Second Edition, New York: McGraw-Hill.

Puxty, Anthony G. (1979), Some Evidence Concerning Cultural Differentials in Ownership Policies of Overseas Subsidiaries, *Management International Review*, 19 (2), 39-52.

Richman, Barry M. and Melvyn Copen (1972), *International Management and Economic Development*, New York: McGraw-Hill.

Robinson, Richard C. (1978), *International Business Management: A Guide to Decision Making*, 2nd edition, Hinsdale, Ill.: The Dryden Press

Robock, Stefan H., Kenneth Simmonds, and Jack Zwick (1977), *International Business and Multinational Enterprises*, Howmewood, Ill.: Richard D. Irwin.

Root, Franklin J. (1983), *Foreign Market Entry Strategies*, New York: AMACON.

Rugman, Alan M. (1982), *New Theories of the Multinational Enterprise*, New York: St. Martin's Press.

Rummel, R.J. and David A. Heenan (1978), How Multinationals Analyze Political Risk, *Harvard Business Review*, 56 (January-February), 67-76.

Seidler, Lee J. (1972), Nationalism and the International Transfer of Accounting Skills. In A. Kapoor and Phillip D. Grubb, eds., *The Multinational Enterprise in Transition*, 233-242, Princeton: The Darwin Press.

Shetty, Y.K. (1979), Managing the MNC: European and American Styles, *Management International Review*, 19 (3), 39-48.

Stern, Louis W. and Adel El-Ansary (1982), *Marketing Channels*, Englewood Cliffs, N.J.: Prentice Hall.

Stopford, John M. and Louis T. Wells, Jr. (1972), *Managing the Multinational Enterprise*, New York: Basic Books.

Teece, David J. (1983), Technological and Organizational Factors in the Theory of the Multinational Enterprise. In Mark Casson, ed., *The Growth of International Business*, 51-62, New York: George Allen and Irwin.

_____ (1976), *The Multinational Corporation and the Resource Cost of International Technology Transfer*, Cambridge: Ballinger Publishing.

Telesio, P. (1979), *Technology Licensing and Multinational Enterprises*, New York: Praeger.

Time (1981), Big Mac Attack, (September 14), 56.

Vernon, Raymond (1983), Organizational and Institutional Responses to International Risk. In Richard J. Herring, ed., *Managing International Risk*, 191-216, Cambridge:Cambridge University Press.

_____ (1977), *Storm Over the Multinationals*, Cambridge: Harvard University Press.

_____ (1966), International Trade and International Investment in the Product Life Cycle, *Quarterly Journal of Economics*, (May), 190-207.

_____ and Louis T. Wells (1976), *Manager in the International Economy*, Englewood Cliffs, N.J.: Prentice Hall.

Walker, Gordon and David Weber (1984), A Transaction Cost Approach to Make-or-Buy Decisions, *Administrative Science Quarterly*, 29 (September), 373-391.

Weichmann, Ulrich and L. Pringle (1979), Problems that Plague Multinational Marketers, *Harvard Business Review*, 57 (4), 118-124.

Weinstein, Arnold K. (1974), The International Expansion of U.S. Multinational Advertising Agencies, *MSU Business Topics*, 10 (Summer), 29-35.

Weston, J. Fred and Bart W. Sorge (1972), *International Managerial Finance*, Homewood, Ill.: Richard D. Irwin.

Williamson, Oliver E. (1985), *The Economic Institutions of Capitalism*, New York: Free Press.

_____ (1983), Credible Commitments: Using Hostages to Support Exchange, *American Economic Review*, 83 (September), 519-540.

_____ (1981a), The Economics of Organization: The Transaction Cost Approach, *American Journal of Sociology*, 87 (3), 548-577.

_____ (1981b), The Modern Corporation: Origins, Evolution, Attributes, *Journal of Economic Literature*, 19 (December), 1537-1568.

_____ (1979), Transaction Cost Economics: The Governance of Contractual Relations, *Journal of Law and Economics*, 22 (October), 233-62.

_____ (1975), *Markets and Hierarchies: Analysis and Antitrust Implications*, New York: The Free Press.

Wilson, Brent D. (1980), The Propensity of Multinational Firms to Expand Through Acquisitions, *Journal Of International Business Studies*, 11 (Spring-Summer), 59-65.

Wind, Yoram and Howard Perlmutter (1977), On the Identification of Frontier Issues in International Marketing, *Columbia Journal of World Business*, 12 (Winter), 131-139.

Wind, Yoram, Susan P. Douglas, and Howard V. Perlmutter (1973), Guidelines for Developing International Marketing Strategies, *Journal of Marketing*, 37 (April), 14-23.

[2]

Two Firms, One Frontier: On Assessing Joint Venture Performance

Erin Anderson　　　　　　　　　　*The Wharton School*

THE INCREASING POPULARITY OF JOINT VENTURES, particularly for international operations, has underscored the importance of a difficult question: how should the performance of a joint venture be assessed? Performance evaluation, never an easy task, becomes exceptionally difficult because joint ventures are often undertaken for amorphous purposes (such as opening a window on a technology) and in highly uncertain, risky settings. Conventional performance appraisals tend to be misleading under such circumstances. This article examines how appraisals are usually conducted and proposes an alternative model.

Sloan
Management
Review

19

Winter 1990

ALTHOUGH JOINT VENTURES have been used for decades as a way to organize a business, in recent years they have been used much more widely. They have enjoyed such a surge of popularity, in fact, that more joint ventures and cooperative arrangements have been announced since 1981 than in all previous years. Even U.S. multinationals, long noted for their penchant to own subsidiaries outright rather than to share ownership, have recently been willing to consider joint ventures when entering a new business. Some observers predict that joint ventures are the wave of the future for reasons such as heightened global competition, increased risk, ever-larger projects, and the fast pace of technological change.

Whatever the reasons, a joint venture (that is, at least two companies pooling resources to create a new, separate organization) is now an accepted way to organize a business. This acceptance raises a difficult question: how is the performance of a joint venture to be evaluated? At first glance, the answer seems clear: evaluate them just like a division of the parent. But which parent? And what if a joint venture "does well," but at the expense of a parent's interests? To further complicate the picture, joint ventures are especially likely to be used in risky, uncertain settings. In such an environment, any business is difficult to evaluate because profit is a long-term proposition and because there are no performance baselines for comparison. Finally,

many joint ventures are not intended to fill standard business objectives (such as making profits). Instead, they are created to learn a technology, open a market, "keep a window" on an opportunity, or block a competitor.[1] It is not easy to assess how well a venture (or, for that matter, a corporate division) meets qualitative objectives such as these.

This article asks two questions. One, how do businesses currently evaluate the performance of their joint ventures? And two, how could they do it better? To answer the first question, I surveyed reports in the business press and found that firms typically fall back on the same methods they use to evaluate internal divisions with unambiguous goals that are operating in stable, low-risk settings. Even though they realize that this approach is not appropriate for most joint ventures, firms often use such standard methods for lack of an operationally feasible alternative.

How could they do it better? This article proposes a sensible way to evaluate the effectiveness of joint ventures. I classify joint ventures into four categories. Then, for each category, I suggest which factors should be considered (and which should be ignored) in evaluation. The objective is to help managers do a better job of:
• determining how to compensate the individuals involved in the venture,
• determining levels of resource commitment,
• determining if and when the parent should in-

tervene, and
* forecasting a partner's reaction to the joint venture.

How Do Businesses Evaluate Their Joint Ventures?

To answer my first question, I searched in two business press databases for information on joint ventures. The search uncovered more than 3,000 articles and books that appeared within the last two decades. Yet, even though joint ventures are the object of intense interest, remarkably few of these publications address performance assessment. Most of them address reasons for establishing a joint venture, descriptions of the creation of specific ventures, or guidelines for selecting a partner. In short, the *possibilities* of joint ventures seem to generate more attention than their *results*. There is startlingly little information on how (and even if) firms monitor and weigh their joint ventures' performance. This omission may reflect business practice: there is some evidence that companies often give only passing attention to deciding how and when to monitor joint venture performance.

The most comprehensive data comes from a Conference Board survey of 168 large firms engaged in at least one international joint venture. These firms tend to evaluate the venture much as they do one of their own divisions. Imposing a formidable amount of paperwork on the venture, these parents typically evaluate performance using financial reports, supplemented by whatever can be gleaned from informal visits by parent executives.

That firms treat their ventures as they do their own divisions is understandable—it is a familiar path of least resistance, one likely to be viewed as legitimate by parent personnel. But here I will argue that ventures usually *are* different. Reverting to the familiar, routine assessment of financial performance may be comfortable, but it is unlikely to produce accurate assessments of joint venture performance.

Why Are Joint Ventures Different?

Most joint ventures should not be evaluated using the standard operating procedures that corporate headquarters applies to wholly owned divisions with conventional business objectives. One important reason is that the interests of the joint venture and the parents are often in conflict. For example,

a venture may enjoy excellent market acceptance and provide high return on investment, which is good performance from one parent's viewpoint. Yet another of the parents may be unhappy because the venture refuses to use one of its divisions as a supplier. From one parent's perspective, then, the joint venture is performing poorly. Indeed, the same venture may be rated very differently depending on the viewpoint adopted. Parents that evaluate performance strictly in accord with their own interests, as they do with subsidiaries, risk alienating their partners. Performance evaluation requires incorporating multiple viewpoints, if only to forecast the partners' reactions and future behavior.

Joint ventures are different from wholly owned divisions in another important way: their organizational politics are much more complicated. Because joint ventures have multiple parents, they may be viewed as "outsiders" by parent personnel, who question their commitment to the corporation. Thus, joint ventures are more likely to become scapegoats and "political footballs," especially when the parent itself has performance problems. Divisions of the parent may find it easy to blame the joint venture for their own shortcomings. Headquarters personnel may become suspicious and hypercritical of the venture, particularly if an explanation for corporate shortcomings is needed. And joint ventures are particularly easy to criticize with impunity because venture managers simply cannot be as visible to a parent as most subsidiary managers are. Hence, joint ventures are especially vulnerable players in the game of corporate politics.[2] Too often, the result is a politically expedient performance assessment that is premature and overly harsh. This scenario is especially likely if performance evaluation draws no distinction between subsidiaries and joint ventures.

Why Not Stick to Profitability Measures?

Aside from the partners' interests, the difficulty of evaluating joint venture performace may seem overblown. Why not simply use profitability indicators? For many businesses, profitability is an excellent index of performance. What makes joint ventures so different?

The answer lies in the joint venture's setting. While they may be used for many purposes, joint ventures are especially popular in risky, uncertain situations, for it is there that firms are most likely to concede some control if that will spread risk

Joint
Ventures

20

Anderson

Erin Anderson is Associate Professor in the Marketing Department, The Wharton School, University of Pennsylvania. Dr. Anderson holds the B.S. degree from the University of the Pacific and the Ph.D. degree from the Graduate School of Management, UCLA. Her research centers on interorganizational issues, particularly the effect of control on the performance of marketing functions.

and expand expertise. But when risk and uncertainty are high, profitability by itself is a poor measure of the joint venture's value (or, for that matter, any business's value). For start-up, high-risk businesses, profits, if any, are in the future, and high costs are in the present.

The standard way to allow for this when evaluating performance is to use discounted cash flow analysis (DCF). But DCF is seriously flawed in risky, uncertain settings. There are four major problems.[3] The first is that while subjective estimates of operating results (such as revenue) may be feasible, converting these estimates into cash flows is extremely difficult, especially for later years in the projection. Second, period-by-period long-run forecasts are so difficult that they often end up being mechanical extrapolations of short-term trends. These estimates have the specificity needed for DCF analysis, but they overlook strategic concerns, such as technological changes. Third, uncertainties are very difficult to incorporate. A standard response is to raise the discount rate, but this penalizes uncertain projects exponentially into the future, thereby biasing against significant risk taking.

Fourth, and most important, many joint ventures are really options. They allow a parent to maintain a doorway into a market or a technology. If the opportunity eventually looks promising, the parent can exercise its option to enter. Otherwise, the firm can walk away. Unfortunately, DCF analysis does not adequately account for the value of an option—nor, for that matter, does any other analytical technique.

In more general terms, many, if not most, joint ventures operate in settings where current financial results are bound to suggest poor performance. Yet the venture may be making satisfactory progress toward longer-term goals, or meeting current goals that are not financial in nature. Standard operating procedure, then, will misstate the venture's performance. When are financial criteria appropriate? And what other criteria should be used? To answer this question, let us turn to a more general one: how can we evaluate the performance of *any* organization?

Measures of Performance and the Input-Output Continuum

A large literature addresses the issue of performance assessment, without offering much resolution.[4] "Organizational performance" is a controversial term.

Researchers have been unable to resolve these issues theoretically, and little research has addressed organizational effectiveness empirically. Indeed, some writers have suggested abandoning the effort: why, they argue, do we need to "keep score" anyway? Clearly, this is an impractical suggestion. An organization's performance *must* be compared and evaluated before decisions can be made. Without explicit ranking and rating, firms (particularly large ones) cannot decide where to invest and whom to reward. So performance assessment cannot be evaded or finessed away.

A major reason for the controversy is a lack of clarity about what an *indicator* of performance is (we might call it an "output" of an organization's functioning) and what a *determinant* of performance is (an "input"). Both researchers and managers tend to mix performance indicators and determinants (inputs and outputs) according to their own theories of what works. For example, employee satisfaction is often used as an indicator of a high-performing organization (an output), but others classify satisfaction as a cause of performance (an input), and still others ignore satisfaction altogether on the grounds that it is neither indicator nor determinant.

Another thorny issue concerns accounting for circumstances. Many a division manager has tried to convince "corporate" that effectiveness measures should be unique to each organization and its current life cycle stage. Different results should be expected depending on an organization's history, resources, and environment; what is good performance for a small, struggling firm in a hostile environment constitutes failure for a larger, established firm in a munificent environment. Yet determining the appropriate baseline is no trivial affair.

Given these problems, it is almost surprising to find that there *is* some consensus about what "performance" means. In one study experts rated the similarity of seventeen indicators/determinants of performance.[5] Multidimensional scaling, used to summarize the experts' judgments, revealed that they view organizational performance in three dimensions, named by their end points. These are as follows: stability versus flexibility; well-being of individuals (e.g., morale) versus well-being of the organization (e.g., profit); process (e.g., planning) versus outcome (e.g., productivity). This study highlights a dilemma encountered in practice: it is often difficult to judge the short-term results (outputs) without considering how these results are

Sloan
Management
Review

21

Winter 1990

being achieved (inputs). The study's inability to separate determinants and indicators of performance reflects the reality that these two facets are usually intertwined.

How do businesspeople think of performance? One answer comes from a periodic survey of America's "most admired companies" by *Fortune* magazine. Firms that executives rate as "most admired" are characterized by a combination of growth, profit, high (but not the highest) return on stockholders' equity, consistent avoidance of losses, consistently positive earnings, occasional improvements in operating results, good bond ratings, and stable management.[6] It is interesting that while most of these factors are financial and clearly results oriented, others (such as stable management) are nonfinancial and related to long-term performance. In short, executives seem to rank organizational performance by considering a "package" of inputs and outputs, weighed over time.

A number of writers argue that the "package" approach is the correct way to evaluate a business,

even though it is cumbersome, difficult, and subjective. Empirical support is provided by a recent study which finds that traditional accounting figures, including profitability measures, are statistically not enough to distinguish excellent from ordinary firms.[7] Excellent firms are also distinguished by their operating characteristics and methods (inputs), suggesting the need to view performance as a combination of many factors. In support of this position, a Conference Board survey of top executives finds strong sentiment that financial measures assess only one facet of performance and that a number of other factors, many of them qualitative, must be weighed.

But this is easier said than done. Managers, like most people, often simplify complex tasks (such as performance assessment) by ignoring or downgrading a great deal of information and adopting simple heuristics. Corporate managers, while they profess to weigh many factors in assessing performance, often simplify the job by giving a very high weight to one factor; from habit, sheer profitability is likely to be that factor. And firms used to receiving and processing "the financials" will simplify the job by using that information — and little else. As noted earlier, the result is a significant misstatement of a joint venture's performance.

In sum, the generic problem of how to rate a business unit's performance is especially knotty. Theory and practice seem to converge on a "package" approach, in which inputs and outputs are weighed to arrive at a composite index of effectiveness, which is then used to allocate resources. But considering diverse indicators and then comparing an organization's "score" to some baseline means that evaluation must be done with a strong element of subjectivity. This, in turn, creates substantial differences of opinion about performance. Management cannot and should not ignore them by resorting to simple comparisons on one or two readily available measures (such as profitability).

The Input-Output Continuum

In developing criteria it may be useful to classify performance measures along a continuum ranging from input to output measures (see Figure 1). At the output extreme are the "results" measures that most people use to assess current performance: these are financial measures, of which profitability is the most commonly used.[8] At the input extreme are indicators of states (e.g., high morale,

Figure 1	The Input-Output Continuum for a Joint Venture

Input

The State of the Venture Organization
Harmony among partners
Morale
Productivity
Financial resource indicators
Adaptiveness
Innovativeness

Learning
Unfamiliar market
Unfamiliar technology

Marketing Intermediate Variables
Relative product quality
Relative price

Marketing Measures of Performance
Market share
Customer satisfaction

Financial Measures of Performance
Profit rate
Cash flow

Output
"Performance"
or "Payoff"

Longer-
Term
Orientation

Shorter-
Term
Orientation

coordinated action).

The input extreme represents variables that should determine (create) measurable results. Inputs represent what the organization is doing (e.g., using resources) and how it is struggling to achieve eventual results (outputs). It is important to note that inputs are *not* themselves measures of the results most commercial organizations set as goals. Yet inputs are included in most discussions of performance because they are thought to be indicators of the organization's health and viability. An organization can score well on output measures (e.g., be currently profitable), yet score poorly on input measures (e.g., have alienated employees, have too much money tied up in accounts receivable). Eventually, poor inputs will show up in poor outputs; therefore, input measures should be considered to assess longer-term effectiveness. As Figure 1 shows, then, the input-output continuum also corresponds to a longer-shorter term orientation.

Note, however, that many theories about inputs leading to outputs are not well supported empirically. In other words, many theories are wrong or seriously incomplete, suggesting that more often than not it is unclear what the "right" levels of inputs are. Assessing inputs is a risky, subjective affair that requires developing a theory of what the "right" inputs are. We will return to this problem in a later section; it has profound implications for the assessment of joint venture performance.

Figure 1 shows the input-output progression for a joint venture. Below each category of indicators are examples (suggestive but not exhaustive) of what the category includes. The "state of the joint venture organization" is an important class of inputs. These factors reflect the functioning of the joint venture organization and include such factors as morale, productivity, turnover, safety rates, planning, flexibility, and ability to obtain resources. One indicator unique to joint ventures is harmony among the partners. Harmony is manifested in, among other things, coordinated efforts and good interpersonal relations. Harmonious partners do not guarantee a high-performing joint venture, but it is difficult to imagine a venture that enjoys lasting success if partners are suspicious and conflicting.

While these factors are not themselves effectiveness measures, they should portend future effectiveness. Also grouped under the state of the organization are some of the indicators that controllers track, such as accounts receivable and inventory levels. These variables show how the business uses resources and reflect the strategy the organization pursues (e.g., maintain high inventory to provide quick delivery). Although these financial figures are often confused with output measures, they actually reflect use of *resources*.

The next category, learning, is an output. Many joint ventures are created for the purpose of learning something, often an unfamiliar market, technology, or management technique. If the learning occurs, the joint venture has achieved something that should contribute to current and future performance.

Once a product is marketed, the joint venture can be assessed on marketing intermediate variables (such as selling quality products at target price levels). While marketing an inexpensive, high-quality product does not constitute performance per se, it leads to the eventual achievement of marketing performance objectives such as high market share and high customer satisfaction. Meeting marketing objectives should contribute to financial results, which are the "bottom line" of Figure 1 (literally), and which are unambiguous measures of outputs.

Evaluating the Joint Venture

The most basic issue in joint venture performance evaluation is the question of whose performance to assess. Parents have their own objectives in creating joint ventures, and obviously a venture's performance against these objectives is relevant. But it is not the only—indeed, not even the most important—basis for measuring results. I argue that joint ventures should be evaluated *primarily as stand-alone entities* seeking to maximize their own performance, not the parents'. This perspective frees the venture from parent politics and parochial viewpoints. Further, encouraging the joint venture to find its own way promotes harmony among parents (since sacrificing the venture's stand-alone performance to suit one parent is not likely to suit the others). Most joint ventures face a steep climb to begin with, as their high rates of dissolution show. Giving them the freedom to find their own best way increases their relatively slim chances of survival and prosperity. Further, giving the venture autonomy facilitates learning and innovation, which are primary reasons to enter a venture.

Further, where the interests of parent and joint venture diverge, one should be dubious of the parent's motives. For example, a joint venture may refuse to use a parent division as a supplier, thereby

Sloan
Management
Review

23

Winter 1990

increasing venture performance at the expense of parent performance. Here, a reasonable suspicion is that the division makes a nonviable product (if not, why must the venture be forced to be a customer?). Obliging the joint venture to subsidize the parent division merely postpones that division's day of reckoning—and drags the joint venture down with it.

Principles for Setting Performance Weights

Regardless of the performance viewpoint adopted, a critical issue in assessing joint venture performance is how heavily each element of the input-output continuum should be weighted. For example, how important is learning—versus, say, marketing performance—for a given joint venture?

William Ouchi offers a very useful approach; he sets up the performance assessment problem in two dimensions, as shown in Figure 2.[9] Dimension number one is how extensively managers understand the "transformation process" (how inputs become outputs). This is akin to asking if the evaluator knows *in detail* what management should do

(the task definition). Evaluators who understand the transformation process quite well know what works and can tell if management is making the right moves. In contrast, managers who understand the transformation process poorly are not in a good position to tell management to change its approach: their recommendation may well be wrong.

Dimension number two reflects how thoroughly the firm is able to assess, measure, and judge results. It comes as a rude shock to students to discover how often management lacks good information or cannot use what information it has. Experienced managers know that their indicators are often wrong or hopelessly out of date. Further, they also know that "the numbers" may be accurate but difficult to interpret, putting the evaluator in a poor position to say whether performance is good or bad.

Crossing these two dimensions (knowing what to do and having good indicators of results) yields four cells, numbered I, II, III, and IV in Figure 2. These cells represent various levels and sources of ignorance about organizational performance.

One of the most common scenarios is Cell III, in which the firm doesn't understand the transformation process well. This makes it difficult to tell the joint venture what it should do. Should it spend more on R&D? Reorganize? Change market focus? Change product features? It is not clear to the evaluator whether the joint venture is making the wrong moves; reasonable people disagree about the proper strategy. Indeed, the strategic management literature suggests that this is very frequently the case: the "correct" strategy is by no means clear for many businesses, nor is it clear which strategies are "wrong" (although strong opinions abound at later stages, when it becomes clear from the outputs whether the company succeeded or failed).

Fortunately, in Cell III, the evaluator does not need to worry, for corporate management *can* assess outputs. Not only does it have good information about outputs, but the firm has baselines. It knows what level of output is good (should be expected) and what level indicates problems. Hence, in Cell III, the evaluator can ignore inputs (or give them little consideration) and can base his or her assessment on outputs. In short, Cell III evaluators can demand performance without being obliged to tell the joint venture how to get it. Transformation can be left to the venture's discretion, and its management can be held accountable for results.

Cell II presents the opposite scenario. The evalu-

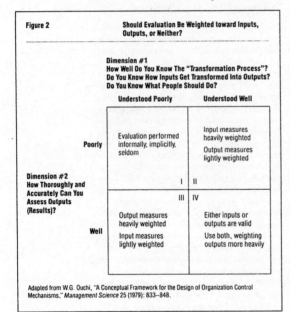

Figure 2   **Should Evaluation Be Weighted toward Inputs, Outputs, or Neither?**

Dimension #1
How Well Do You Know The "Transformation Process"?
Do You Know How Inputs Get Transformed Into Outputs?
Do You Know What People Should Do?

		Understood Poorly	Understood Well
	Poorly	Evaluation performed informally, implicitly, seldom	Input measures heavily weighted Output measures lightly weighted
		I	II
Dimension #2 How Thoroughly and Accurately Can You Assess Outputs (Results)?		III	IV
	Well	Output measures heavily weighted Input measures lightly weighted	Either inputs or outputs are valid Use both, weighting outputs more heavily

Adapted from W.G. Ouchi, "A Conceptual Framework for the Design of Organization Control Mechanisms," *Management Science* 25 (1979): 833–848.

ator may have poor knowledge of outputs. Perhaps sales figures are imprecise, margins are unstable, or market share is anybody's guess. Alternatively, the evaluator may be able to measure these figures but does not have a baseline, which makes it impossible to tell whether, say, ten firm orders in the first year in this market is good or bad. Obviously, unavailable or uninterpretable output information makes outputs difficult to assess.

Fortunately, the evaluating firm understands the transformation process: it knows what the joint venture *should* be doing, even if the results are difficult to judge. Input measures should be weighted heavily and the (faulty) output measures weighted lightly. The resulting evaluation will be imprecise and subjective. Some managers, more comfortable with the apparent objectivity of number-based assessment, question the value of evaluating inputs in Cell II conditions. Yet subjective evaluation is often a reasonable approximation. It meets the parent's need to decide whether to intervene or to reallocate, the parent's need to forecast its partners' satisfaction with the joint venture, and venture management's need for feedback. This last issue is crucial, as sustained ambiguity eventually hurts management's morale and motivation.

Cell IV is a utopian scenario: the firm knows what to do and can assess the results. Either outputs or inputs can be valid, so the evaluator may use either; Ouchi does not specify which is preferable. Some writers suggest that firms use whichever information is cheaper to collect, which will often be inputs. On the other hand, corporate management has a tendency to overcontrol, that is, to dictate behavior even when local managers are in a better position to judge the situation and react accordingly. So management may wish to concentrate on output measures because this approach gives managers the freedom to pursue innovative strategies — as long as they can produce results.

There is much to be said for using *both* input and output measures in Cell IV, putting somewhat more emphasis on output measures. Using input measures builds in a longer-term focus, while using output measures preserves local managers' autonomy as long as they can achieve outputs.

If Cell IV is utopian, Cell I is nightmarish. Neither inputs nor outputs are good indicators of performance; attempts to weigh and use them are arbitrary. Indeed, any performance evaluation is arbitrary, making it an especially frustrating exer-

cise. Ouchi suggests that under these conditions, performance evaluation is such a poor approximation that it is of limited value. Instead, he recommends that managers be guided not by their performance evaluations but by a strong corporate culture that generates organizational commitment. Commitment, in turn, motivates employees to discern and carry out those actions that are in the firm's best interest, even though the firm's ignorance keeps it from prescribing appropriate inputs or assessing levels of output. Ouchi recommends that evaluations be kept informal and implicit in Cell I and that they not be done often.

Figure 3 suggests how Ouchi's principles of selection can be applied to joint ventures. I begin by categorizing ventures into those where the parent can assess output measures only poorly.

Assessing a Joint Venture's Outputs

Firms that cannot assess outputs because they cannot measure them operate in information-poor environments. Such joint ventures:
• operate in new or experimental product classes (R&D ventures);
• exist primarily to learn ("knowledge acquisition" ventures);
• exist primarily to demonstrate feasibility (e.g., experimental manufacturing ventures); or
• exist primarily to thwart a competitor.

For these joint ventures, the standard output measures are irrelevant or will be measurable in the distant future, if at all. These ventures are often relatively young.

More often, firms *can* measure outputs with some confidence — but do not know how to interpret the numbers. They cannot tell what a "good" result is because they lack a baseline (a reasonable performance expectation). Joint ventures falling into this category:
• operate in little-known markets;
• operate in the introductory or early growth stage of the product life cycle; or
• face poorly defined competition (especially if entry barriers are low, allowing the competitive set to change rapidly).
Again, these ventures are often recently formed.

In contrast, parents tend to be able to measure and judge outputs for joint ventures that operate in mature product classes, sell to familiar markets, face defined competition (often stabilized by bar-

Sloan
Management
Review

25

Winter 1990

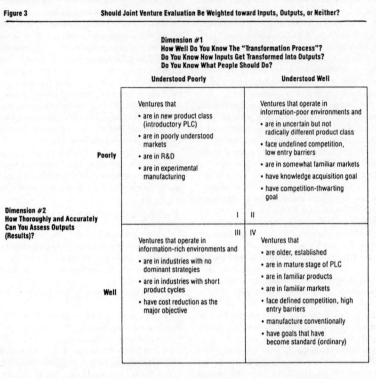

Figure 3   Should Joint Venture Evaluation Be Weighted toward Inputs, Outputs, or Neither?

**Dimension #1
How Well Do You Know The "Transformation Process"?
Do You Know How Inputs Get Transformed Into Outputs?
Do You Know What People Should Do?**

	Understood Poorly	Understood Well
Poorly	Ventures that • are in new product class (introductory PLC) • are in poorly understood markets • are in R&D • are in experimental manufacturing	Ventures that operate in information-poor environments and • are in uncertain but not radically different product class • face undefined competition, low entry barriers • are in somewhat familiar markets • have knowledge acquisition goal • have competition-thwarting goal
	I	II
	III	IV
Well	Ventures that operate in information-rich environments and • are in industries with no dominant strategies • are in industries with short product cycles • have cost reduction as the major objective	Ventures that • are older, established • are in mature stage of PLC • are in familiar products • are in familiar markets • face defined competition, high entry barriers • manufacture conventionally • have goals that have become standard (ordinary)

**Dimension #2
How Thoroughly and Accurately
Can You Assess Outputs
(Results)?**

riers to entry), and have standard profit-making goals. These joint ventures, which are often older, operate in information-rich environments that enable a firm not only to acquire but also to interpret indicators of outputs.

The Joint Venture's Transformation Process

When does the parent understand the transformation process well enough to know which inputs to reward and which to discourage? Joint ventures that operate in known markets or use well understood technologies are likely to have this understanding. So are joint ventures that produce mature products and those whose major purpose is nonexperimental manufacturing. If the objective is thwarting competition or acquiring knowledge, it is relatively clear what steps the venture should be taking (though it is not always clear if the objective has been achieved).

In contrast, the parent will be less sure which are the right inputs in ventures whose purpose is to experiment or develop, since it may take years to know if efforts in these directions are misguided. Ventures operating in lesser-known technologies or markets or in immature product classes also present a puzzle: the appropriate actions are often debatable. This is also true when an industry has no dominant strategy (many strategies appear equally viable) and when product cycles are short (there is little time to experiment).

When to Give a Venture a Long Leash

Using these ideas, Figure 3 classifies joint ventures into Ouchi's four cells. The model suggests that the traditional formal evaluation, heavily based on output measures and frequently updated, is appropriate for Cell IV joint ventures. These ventures, which tend to be older, may manufacture or sell mature products for familiar markets and tend to have standard (profit-making) goals. Frequently these businesses are cash cows. They may perform conventional manufacturing or face defined competition, stabilized by entry barriers. In such settings, the parent has a thorough understanding of what inputs to reward *and* can measure and judge outputs precisely.

Strikingly, such businesses are less likely to be joint ventures. Even if they started as joint ventures, they tend to convert into wholly owned subsidiaries by the time they mature.[10]

Some joint ventures fall into Cell III: the firm is unsure of the best way to produce results but can ascertain whether they have been achieved because these are information-rich settings. Often these are more mature industries in which there is no dominant strategy—because many approaches work—or in which product cycles are short, leaving little time to find the best approach. Sometimes the major objective of these ventures is cost reduction: where cost measures are good, the parent can tell if this goal has been achieved even if it is unsure which costs to cut and how.

A disproportionate number of joint ventures fall into Cell I, where the parent's ignorance is extensive. ("Ignorant" firms—i.e., firms moving into an unfamiliar field—are most likely to seek help in the form of a partner.) Here, where implicit, informal, and rare performance evaluations are called for, we find joint ventures entering new product classes or new markets, as well as R&D ventures and experimental manufacturing ventures. These are the riskiest, most uncertain joint ventures, and they should be given a long leash. Ouchi's taxonomy suggests that formal and frequent performance evaluation is of little use in reducing the parent's risk and uncertainty. Indeed, carrying out a formal evaluation may be counterproductive; it may steer joint venture managers in the wrong direction (emphasizing the wrong inputs), or prematurely shut a joint venture down (overreacting to low early levels of outputs). It is ironic that for-mal, frequent performance evaluation, a procedure intended to improve a joint venture's functioning by detecting problems, may actually reduce the joint venture's chances of succeeding.

Somewhere between the more mature joint venture (Cells III and IV) and the joint ventures in amorphous environments (Cell I) lies the joint venture that the parent can understand well enough to direct (Cell II). These ventures' outputs are difficult to measure or judge, as they operate in information-poor environments. But management understands what the ventures *should* be doing. Performance can be formally and frequently assessed on inputs, giving little weight to outputs. These ventures exist for definable, if nonstandard reasons (such as acquiring knowledge or thwarting competition), which means that certain activities (inputs) can be prescribed. They may be in the early growth stage of the product life cycle, sell or manufacture an uncertain but not radically different product class, operate in somewhat familiar markets, or face an undefined or unstable set of competitors. For such joint ventures, outputs are unsatisfactory measures because information is sparse or difficult to interpret. But some inputs can be recognized as desirable (or undesirable) and used as a basis of assessment.

Of course, input assessment is more subjective than output assessment. So Cell II joint ventures cannot be evaluated with the same level of objectivity as Cell III and IV ventures. The parents should not dismiss performance evaluation, but they should carry it out differently than they would at more mature joint ventures.

Probably most joint ventures start out in Cell I, where formal evaluation is of little value. Eventually, they become well enough understood to move to Cell II, where input evaluation is appropriate. Or they may move to Cells III and IV, where they can be evaluated by the formal, frequent, output-oriented methods standard for many company divisions. The sidebar (on Du Pont Corporation) details how one company learned to adjust its evaluation methods as its ventures changed cells.

The progression from input to output orientation is by no means unique to joint ventures. Most new organizations focus initially on inputs (acquiring resources, getting set up), while paying relatively little attention to outputs. However, as organizations mature, their focus shifts away from inputs and toward end results.[11] Furthermore, the

Sloan
Management
Review

27

Winter 1990

Joint
Ventures

28

Anderson

Du Pont: Joint Venture Pioneer

Du Pont first engaged in joint ventures near the turn of the century and has pursued more than forty joint ventures since 1950, in a broad array of businesses. Widely regarded as a company with a cohesive corporate culture, Du Pont is supported by a program of internal management development, promotion from within, and rewards for being a "team player" (versus "turf protector"). Today, Du Pont profits from that cohesion in the thorough yet flexible way it evaluates joint ventures. However, this was not always the case.

Before 1970, Du Pont joint ventured primarily in response to government pressures in such countries as Mexico and Japan, exercising 100 percent ownership wherever possible. Ventures were evaluated in a formal, stylized manner using financial criteria for the most part. Although it still preferred 100 percent ownership, after 1970 Du Pont began to undertake joint ventures for a variety of reasons. And as Du Pont's motivations for venturing became broader, more complex, and more strategic, so too did its criteria for evaluating venture performance.

Today Du Pont is organized into worldwide business centers, which may be centered on either a product or a market. Annually, the venture head and a representative from the most closely related worldwide business center set profit goals and evaluate performance. In addition to financial measures, mostly relating to return per resource committed, other criteria are used. These include:

- how safely and ethically the venture operates;
- environmental impact of the venture;
- the venture's innovativeness;
- degree to which the venture satisfies the other partners (this is to forestall discontent);
- degree to which the venture fills the need of its host country (this is to forestall government interference);
- degree of learning about industries, technologies, management techniques, the partner's skills, or countries;
- how smoothly the venture runs (personnel and coordination issues);
- ability to repatriate profits; and
- how well the venture meets goals based on the reasons it was created. Some of these reasons are utilizing capacity, affecting competition, gaining market share, generating other opportunities, and helping spur the sale of other Du Pont products.

Performance criteria vary by venture and strongly reflect the reasons the venture was created. Du Pont considers that flexibility is necessary because each venture is unique; the performance criteria must also be unique. One constant exists: safety, health, and environmental dimensions (what Du Pont personnel call "the SHE issues") are always a must. The company refuses to venture with partners who do not meet its SHE standards. Should a venture violate these standards, Du Pont will buy out the partner, fix the problem at its own expense, or, if all else fails, leave the venture.

As ventures mature and markets change, criteria change. In particular, once a project is authorized, it has a "proof period." After year three (proof year for established products) or year five (proof year for ventures involving new product categories), much greater emphasis is placed on financial measures, reflecting the maturing of the venture and the parent's correspondingly appropriate shift from input to output measures.

Potential conflicts with partners are explicitly focused upon when the venture is created. At that time, Du Pont presses for agreement about goals. Afterwards, the venture is evaluated as to how well it meets the partner's goals as well as Du Pont's. This is based on Du Pont's experience-based belief that the venture must be a win-win situation if it is to be healthy and survive. Hence, ventures are not forced to suboptimize their own performance to benefit Du Pont.

A striking feature of Du Pont's procedure is its relatively low level of procedural formality. This appears to be a conscious strategy whose purpose is to reduce bureaucracy, focus on action, encourage initiative, retain flexibility, and stimulate broad-ranging evaluation. As mentioned earlier, while performance criteria are well defined, neither weights nor scores are formalized, although they are used. Because of the strategic goals of many ventures, subjective information is used freely to judge whether the broad objectives of the venture are being met. Du Pont can also be adaptable in the timing of evaluations.

In short, Du Pont appears to focus on subjective strategic performance as well as formal performance criteria—and to recognize that a strong emphasis on outputs is inappropriate for young ventures, though appropriate for mature ones.

■

idea of evaluating a business entity close to the input extreme earlier on and closer to the output extreme as it matures can be applied to business *arrangements* as well as to business entities.

But a corporation's joint ventures are more complex and vulnerable than its internal ventures. Joint ventures are more complex because multiple interests must be balanced, and because the operating environment is often more risky and uncertain than those the parent would be willing to enter alone. And joint ventures are more vulnerable because they fall victim to corporate politics more easily than do internal divisions. The risks—premature intervention, overcontrol, excessive pessimism, and reduced commitment—can be avoided more readily if the corporation recognizes that most joint ventures should be evaluated more subjectively and with a longer time horizon than is typically used.

I have argued that most joint ventures must be given considerable time before they are ready to be judged on traditional output measures. The need for patience is underscored by a study of Fortune 500 firms that started new (wholly owned) businesses with the intent of diversifying.[12] The median startup took seven to eight *years* to show a positive return on investment or positive cash flow, and *no* ventures had positive cash flow in their first two years. Strikingly, many of the startups that turned positive early (in ROI terms) failed to retain their profitability. Many of the executives involved found these results astonishing, yet, upon reflection, concluded that these numbers were indeed realistic. Considering that joint ventures are often used in the riskiest of circumstances, the need for patience should be even greater. While waiting, the parent should rely on input measures, gradually shifting its emphasis to the output measures as the venture matures.

Paralleling the increased use of joint ventures is the new popularity of "strategic alliances" such as long-term supply contracts and joint research and development. These arrangements, while they do not create a separate business entity, have much in common with joint ventures. They can and should be evaluated in the same manner.

Conclusion

Evaluating a joint venture is one of the most difficult challenges a partner (parent) faces. Evidence suggests that most parents treat the joint venture as though it were a subsidiary, perhaps ignoring conflicts of interest among parents. Many parent firms evaluate immature ventures too formally, with too much emphasis on financial criteria and not enough emphasis on input measures. The results are likely to be premature termination or a cutback in commitment before a venture has had time to realize its potential. In particular, young joint ventures need a long leash. All too often, corporate parents recognize this at the time of creation. But at the time of evaluation, they revert to their familiar performance assessment procedures: formal, frequent, and financial. Joint ventures require a more balanced, often more subjective approach if their promise is to be realized. ∎

Sloan
Management
Review

29

Winter 1990

References

The author gratefully acknowledges the financial assistance of the Reginald Jones Center for Management Policy, Strategy, and Organization, via a grant from AT&T. Helpful comments were provided by Bruce Kogut, Edward Bowman, William Ross, David Larcker, and David Reibstein (of the Wharton School), Edward Zajac (of the Kellogg Graduate School of Management, Northwestern University), the Marketing Strategies Steering Group (of the Marketing Science Institute), Steven Sherman and Joseph Zycherman (of AT&T), Edward J. Zinser, Steven L. Griffith, Paul H. Hirzig, and T. Bruce Weaver (all of Du Pont), and an anonymous reviewer. This article is excerpted from a working paper on joint venture evaluation available as Working Paper #88-14 from the Jones Center, The Wharton School, 2000 Steinberg-Dietrich Hall, Philadelphia, PA 19104.

1
For a discussion of motives for forming joint ventures, see:
J. Hennart, "A Transaction Costs Theory of Equity Joint Ventures," *Strategic Management Journal* 9 (1988): 361–374; and
B. Kogut, "Joint Ventures: Theoretical and Empirical Perspectives," *Strategic Management Journal* 9 (1988): 319–332.

2
K. Harrigan, "Why Joint Ventures Fail," *Euro-Asia Business Review*, July 1987, pp. 20–26.

3
S. Myers, "Finance Theory and Financial Strategy," *Interfaces*, January–February 1984, pp. 126–137.

4
For a good overview of this literature, see:
P. Goodman and J. Pennings, "Critical Issues in Assessing Organizational Effectiveness," in E. Lawler, D. Nadler, and C. Cammann, eds., *Organizational Assessment*, (New York: Wiley-Interscience, 1980, pp. 185–215); and
A. Lewin and J. Minton, "Determining Organizational Effectiveness: Another Look and an Agenda for Research," *Management Science* 32 (1986): 514–538.

Joint
Ventures

30

Anderson

5
See R. Quinn and J. Rohrbaugh, "A Spatial Model of Effectiveness Criteria: Towards a Competing Values Approach to Organizational Analysis," *Management Science* 29 (1983): 363–377.

6
Cameron (1986) argues that effective companies avoid extreme levels of any one criterion of effectiveness. Instead, they seek to do well on a variety of criteria and to satisfy multiple constituencies (shareholders, employees, customers, and so forth). Cameron's description is similar to *Fortune*'s most admired firms: although they avoid the highest levels of ROE (as well as negative earnings), they manage to do well on multiple criteria. See:
K.S. Cameron, "Effectiveness as Paradox: Consensus and Conflict in Conceptions of Organizational Effectiveness," *Management Science* 32 (1986): 539–553.

7
B. Chakravarthy, "Measuring Strategic Performance," *Strategic Management Journal* 7 (1986): 437–458.

8
G. Foster, *Financial Statement Analysis*, 2nd Edition (Englewood Cliffs, NJ: Prentice-Hall, 1986).

9
W.G. Ouchi, "A Conceptual Framework for the Design of Organization Control Mechanisms," *Management Science* 25 (1979): 833–848.

10
B. Kogut, "A Study of the Life Cycle of Joint Ventures," in F. Contractor and P. Lorange, eds., *Co-operative Strategies in International Business* (Lexington, MA: Lexington Books, 1988, pp. 169–186).

11
K. Cameron and D. Whetten, "Perceptions of Organizational Effectiveness over Organizational Life Cycles," *Administrative Science Quarterly* 26 (1981): 525–544.

12
R. Biggadike, "The Risky Business of Diversification," *Harvard Business Review*, May–June 1979, pp. 103–111.

[3]

The Characteristics of Joint Ventures in the People's Republic of China

ABSTRACT

This paper compares the characteristics of international equity joint ventures in the People's Republic of China (PRC) with joint ventures in developing country market economies. The characteristics of Sino-foreign joint ventures were derived from twelve studies published since 1986, including the author's new sample. Twelve joint venture characteristics are reviewed along dimensions of design, management and performance.

Joint ventures in PRC are frequently used, created due to government pressure and with government partners, and often formed with partners from ethnically related countries. Further, many intended joint ventures are never implemented, and those that are implemented have often been set up for a predetermined duration. The foreign partner most commonly has a minority equity position, and those who have used split control have seen stronger performance. Overall joint venture stability has been high, but is expected to decline, and foreign partner satisfaction with performance is low.

During the past decade, no country saw the formation of more equity joint ventures with foreign firms than did the People's Republic of China (PRC). Agreements for more than 12,000 equity joint ventures with foreign partners were signed in addition to the more than 8,000 contractual joint ventures. The total contract value of these ventures exceeded US$30 billion (Table 1).

For the managers of many multinational enterprises (MNEs), a PRC joint venture was their first experience with joint ventures in a planned-economy developing country. As many managers discovered, their assumptions underlying the formation and subsequent management of these ventures were not the same as those underlying joint ventures in developed countries or in market-economy developing countries. Fundamental differences exist in the various environments in which these ventures are found (Austin 1990).

Earlier research (Beamish 1985) summarized the differences between joint ventures (JVs) in developed versus developing countries according to eight characteristics: reason for creating the joint venture; frequency of association with government partners; ownership level; ownership-control relationship; control-performance relationship; number of autonomously managed ventures; instability; and performance. The developing-country data for the 1985 study were from JVs in countries with market economies. Data about foreign-local JVs in LDC-based planned economies were not included for two reasons: (1) there were few countries that operated with primarily planned economies, and

Paul W. Beamish

Submitted June 1992
Revised August 1992
October 1992

© *Journal of International Marketing*
Vol. 1, No. 2, 1993, pp. 29-48

(2) their usage of foreign joint ventures was limited. With the escalating use of joint ventures in the PRC, and the opening of the Eastern Bloc to foreign involvement, by the early 1990s the phenomenon of foreign-local joint ventures in planned economies was well entrenched. Many foreign firms and general managers were already aware of some of the design, management, and performance issues with joint ventures in other parts of the world. The opening of the planned economy markets to the possibility of joint venturing brought with it both excitement and a desire to learn more about what to expect if they did invest.

The primary purpose of this paper is to compare 12 characteristics of joint ventures in the world's dominant developing country planned economy—the PRC—with joint ventures in developing country market economies. The four additional characteristics not examined in the 1985 study are: origin of investment; announced joint ventures actually enacted; use of JVs versus other modes of involvement; and use of JVs with a predetermined duration. The selection of these additional characteristics was based on recommendations from joint venture managers concerning their relevance, data availability, and fit with theory.[1]

A secondary objective is to update selected material in terms of key new or overlooked literature. Although the complete earlier discussion in Beamish (1985) of the eight characteristics in the initial two environments will not be repeated, data on the four new joint venture characteristics in developed countries will be provided.

Table 1. Foreign Investment in China 1979-1990

	Number of contracts signed	Contracted amount (US$ billion)	Utilized amount (US$ billion)
Direct investment (1979-89) of which:	21,734	33.80	14.91
Joint ventures	12,191	12.55	6.85
Cooperative enterprises	8,018	18.08	7.40
Wholly foreign-owned enterprises	1525	3.17	0.66
Direct Investment (1988)	5,945	5.30	3.19
Direct Investment (1989)	5,779	5.60	3.39
Direct Investment (1990-6 mos)	2,784	2.40	1.20
Total Direct Investment (1979 - mid-1990)	24,518	36.20	16.11

Sources: *Canada China Trade Council Newsletters* April 1989, September 1990.

Paul W. Beamish

The findings on the characteristics of joint ventures in the PRC were derived from twelve studies published during the past five years (see Table 2 for details on authors, year of publication, sample size, year data collected until, and foreign partner nationality), including the author's new 22 firm sample of equity joint ventures in the PRC. This latter data were collected through 46 personal semi-structured interviews conducted in the PRC between 1988-90. These interviews averaged two hours in length. Where possible, interviews were held with, and questionnaires administered to, both the Chinese and foreign partners and the joint venture general manager. More than one perspective on each joint venture was obtained to increase our confidence in the findings.

The basic interview guide had been developed and tested in samples of joint ventures in market-economy developing countries. For details see Beamish (1985) and Lee (1990). Interviews were conducted in joint ventures located in and around the cities of Beijing, Tianjin, Xian, Guangzhou, and Urumqui. Chinese co-researchers assisted with the interviews conducted in Chinese. Unlike the other eleven studies, this latter sample includes joint venture observations subsequent to the June 1989 events at Tiananmen Square. A broad-based convenience sample was used, and included equity joint ventures in both manufacturing (i.e. Babcock and Wilcox boilers) and service (i.e. Kentucky Fried Chicken restaurants). It involved low technology (i.e. Tang Dynasty Dinner Theatre) and high technology (i.e. Hybrid-Skylake animal breeding).

Each of the 12 studies did not look at all 12 characteristics. The number of authors who examined particular characteristics varied: their observations will be reported in the relevant section. Where possible, the findings of the other authors were coded according to the same criteria used in the new sample. The focus of these other authors was on JVs in the PRC. Generally, they did not attempt to compare their results with those of JVs in market-economy developing countries. The meta-analysis of JVs in the current study is compared to the meta-analysis of JVs in market-economy developing countries contained in Beamish (1985), which did not include JVs in the PRC.

In all instances data are reported on the basis of frequency of response. While this methodology did not permit the use of "hard" statistical analysis (beyond frequencies), the combination of meta-analysis, use of multiple respondents, and personal interviews, increases the perceived validity of the ratings used, and findings observed. Inter-informant reliability was very high.

The equity joint venture is the oldest form of foreign investment in post-Mao PRC, the law dating to 1979. In an equity joint venture the distribution of dividends is fixed according

RESEARCH METHODOLOGY

to each shareholder's capital contribution, and the venture is a limited liability corporation. According to the original but since relaxed joint venture law, the Chinese side was required to hold at least a 50 percent equity interest.

Table 2. Studies on Joint
Ventures in China

Author	Publication Date	Sample Size	Data Up To	Partner Nationality
Daniels, Krug & Nigh	1986	11	1983	U.S.
Chen	1986	931	1985	Various
Davidson	1987	47	1985	U.S.
National Council	1987	155 + 39	1986	U.S.
Campbell	1987	38*	1985	Various
Paloheimo & Lee	1988	33	1988	Singapore
Beamish & Wang	1989	840	1986	Various
Gao	1989	56	1988	Various
Teagarden & Von Glinow	1990	67	1989	Primarily U.S.
Shenkar	1990	20	1989	U.S., HK, UK
Boisot and Child	1990	30	1989	Various
Beamish	1993	22	1990	Various

*One-third of a sample of 115 were involved with liaison work in equity joint ventures.

In a cooperative, or contract, joint venture, there is greater flexibility. The distribution of dividends is not necessarily fixed according to each partner's capital contribution, and there is no minimum 25 percent participation by the foreign party. This structure avoids the issue of valuation of foreign technology and equipment.

Unfortunately, it is not always clear in some of the studies cited whether equity and contractual joint ventures are mixed within the samples. The data in the new sample and most of the previous studies refer to equity joint ventures. Teagarden (1990) notes that the distinction between equity and contractual joint ventures may not be significant. She found that the form affected strategic issues such as level of investment and choice of technology to be transferred. However, ongoing operations were not significantly influenced by form.

The next section reviews the characteristics of equity joint ventures in the PRC. These characteristics are contrasted with those in market-economy developing countries in order to determine which are common to both and which may be region/economic-type specific. Managerial relevance (already noted) and theoretical significance (discussed in section following) both warrant an examination of these characteristics. The underlying hypothesis is that each of the twelve characteristics of joint ventures in market-economy developing countries will be similar to the characteristics of joint ventures in planned economy developing countries. Previous research (Austin 1990, Beamish 1985) has demonstrated that variability exists in the characteristics of joint ventures *between* developed and developing countries. While the explanation of the differences has been couched in terms of economic development level, we realistically expect that there are other variables—such as culture and political system—which explain part of this variability. In order to probe the impact of other variables, it is necessary to control for certain dimensions *within* either developed or developing countries. Our objective in this study is to control as much as possible for the economic development level of the country, which will hopefully allow us to better understand the impact of other variables such as type of economic system.

Nonetheless, because *all* of the joint ventures compared here are from developing countries—heretofore aggregated together—we start with the common underlying hypothesis of similarity of JV characteristic due to economic level.

The twelve characteristics to be considered have been divided into three broad sections: Designing the Joint Venture; Managing the Joint Venture; and Joint Venture Performance. These categories broadly correspond to the Strategy-Structure-Performance paradigm within the Strategic Management field.

• **Venture Creation Rationales**

The major reasons for using the equity joint venture organization form are:

(a) government requirement or pressure (suasion) as a condition of market entry; (b) a need for the other partner's skills—be they technological, managerial, or the knowledge to work within the local market; and/or (c) a need for the attributes or assets of the other partner. Assets include such things as cash, patents, and raw material sources while attributes might include the use or manufacture of certain products or services.

Both Teagarden (1990) and the new study (19 of 22 cases) found that during the past decade, the major reason given by foreign partners for using the joint venture form in the PRC was government pressure. A similar pattern has been observed in developing countries with market economies, where indigenization pressures also exist.

Venture creation rationales and all of the other characteristics are summarized in Table 3. Column 3 of this table contains the characteristics as they apply to the PRC.

THE CHARACTERISTICS OF EQUITY JOINT VENTURES
Designing the Joint Venture

The Characteristics of Joint Ventures in the People's Republic of China **33**

Table 3. Summary of
Differences of Joint-Venture
Characteristics

Characteristics	Developed Country Market Economy	Developing Country Market Economy	Developing Country Planned Economy (China)
Major reason for creating venture*	Skill required	Government pressure	Government pressure**
Frequency of association with government partners*	Low	Moderate	Very High
Overall use of JVs versus other modes of foreign involvement	Significant	High (but contingent on country, industry, and technology level)	Very high** (regardless of country, industry or technology level)
Origin of foreign partner	Other developed countries	Developed countries	Ethnic Related Countries (i.e. Hong Kong)
Proportion of intended JVs actually implemented	High	Relatively high	Low (under 50%)
Use of JVs with a pre-determined duration	Low (except in certain industries)	Low	High
Most common level of ownership for MNE*	Equal	Minority	Minority**
Number of autonomously managed ventures*	Small	Negligible	Negligible**
Ownership-control relationship*	Direct (dominant control with majority ownership; shared control with equal ownership)	Difficult to discern because most MNEs have a minority ownership position	Indirect**
Control-performance relationship in successful JVs*	Inconclusive	Shared or split	Split control**
Instability rate*	30%	45%	Low
MNE managerial assessment of dissatisfaction with performance*	37%	61%	High**

* Characteristics for developed and market economy developing countries indicated with an
   asterisk were previously summarized in Paul W. Beamish, "The Characteristics of Joint
   Ventures in Developed and Developing Countries," *Columbia Journal of World Business*,
   Fall 1985, p.12-19.

** Indicates support for the hypothesis that this characteristic of joint ventures in China is
   similar to joint ventures in market economy developing countries.

Despite the government pressures to use the joint venture
organization form, solid theoretical reasons also exist.
Hennart (1988), and Beamish and Banks (1987), among others, have provided the general argument for the existence of
joint ventures. The latter study suggested that when multinational enterprises from developed countries are faced with
higher adaptation and information requirements than they
are accustomed to, particularly in culturally dissimilar countries, the joint venture form may be indicated. Certainly most
foreign investors in the PRC confront such requirements.

Paul W. Beamish

• **Frequency of Association with Government Partners**

While every country sees some level of public sector/private sector joint venturing, the frequency of association with government partners tends to be higher in developing countries. Nowhere is the frequency higher than in the PRC.

A cornerstone of the PRC's economy since 1949 has been the near total level of public rather than private ownership. Even with the commencement of the open-door policy in 1976, government ownership of major businesses has remained constant.

During the past decade, a small private sector was allowed to emerge, and various "free market" bazaars sprang up. However, the government has not encouraged the private sector to form JVs with foreign firms. None of the 22 ventures in the new sample were with Chinese private sector firms. Without a radical policy shift, the very high frequency of association with government partners will likely continue.

• **Use of JVs Versus Other Modes of Foreign Investment**

The United States has long been, and remains, the largest national foreign investor in the world according to the number of investments. While current data is difficult to obtain, as the summary below indicates, roughly 25,000 foreign investments were in place as of 1981. The 15,000 non-fully owned subsidiaries—60 percent of total investments—were made up of an unspecified mix of equity joint ventures (which involved the creation of a new business) and stakeholdings in existing businesses.

Foreign Investment by U.S.-Based Companies

Minority or Equal Owned	Majority Owned	Fully Owned
(10 - 50%)	(51 - 99%)	(100%)
12,000	3,000	10,000

Source: Contractor and Lorange (1988), estimates as of 1981.

Although the bulk of U.S. foreign investment involves some form of cooperation, (see also Pisano and Teece 1989; Baughn and Osborne 1990) and the use of joint ventures is significant, the single most frequently used mode is the wholly owned subsidiary. Comparable data on the use of JVs versus other modes from firms in other developed countries were not compiled.

Within market economy developing countries, the use of joint ventures as a form of foreign direct investment is also significant. Using the Harvard MNE data base, Austin (1990) noted that as of 1975, 45 percent of the U.S. MNE subsidiaries in developing countries were joint ventures. Using

The Characteristics of Joint Ventures in the People's Republic of China   **35**

more recent data, Kogut (1988) found that 38 percent were joint ventures, although wide variability was observed among industries, countries, and over time. In the majority of market economy developing countries, the requirement to use the joint venture form is more closely linked to particular sectors of the economy. For example, the desire to acquire experience with a new technology can serve as an impetus to a government to require joint ventures in that sector. When the source of foreign investment is from one market economy developing country to another, the frequency of joint venture usage jumps (Vernon-Wortzel and Wortzel 1988), often to more than 80 percent (Wells Jr. 1983; and Wells 1988).

As Table 1 indicates, the overall use of equity joint ventures in the PRC has been very high, particularly in relation to wholly owned subsidiaries. During the early 1990s, foreign firms in the PRC are confronting a different government attitude toward the use of the joint venture form of organization. The past decade has seen an evolution in the thinking of the Chinese government from Requiring JVs → Permitting Wholly Owned Subsidiaries → Encouraging Wholly Owned Subsidiaries. The implication of this new freedom of mode choice for foreign firms is that they will be better able to align their equity share with their objectives for entering the Chinese market. Shenkar (1990) and Teagarden (1990) have noted that there are a wide variety of objectives of foreign (and Chinese) firms for establishing operations. In Campbell's (1986) study, only one-third of the firms felt that an equity joint venture was the only secure long-term strategy for the PRC.

•Origin of Foreign Partner

Both trade and worldwide investment flows have long shown that the bulk of foreign investment from developed countries is to other developed countries; the origin of the foreign partner in joint ventures in developed countries is typically another developed country (Killing 1983; Hergert and Morris 1988).

Most foreign investment in market-economy developing countries using joint ventures is believed to originate from developed countries. Certainly this has been the case in the Caribbean (Beamish 1985) and Korea (Park 1990). This pattern of developed to developing country trade is notwithstanding the substantial trade that takes place among multinationals where each is from a developing country (Wells Jr. 1983).

With respect to the PRC, official government statistics and all of the samples point to Hong Kong as the primary source of joint venture investment. In early 1991, Taiwanese investment had begun to replace that from Hong Kong for the lead position. This would not be surprising given the much larger size of Taiwan and the cultural and language ties. This shift to a 'Greater PRC' economy (including PRC, Hong Kong, and Taiwan) suggests that the origin of the foreign partner for most PRC joint ventures is one that is not particularly foreign.

•Announced JVs Actually Enacted

In the vast majority of cases, if a public announcement is made of the plans to establish an international joint venture, the joint venture will in fact be established. This enactment level holds true in both developed and developing market economies, particularly if the announcement is made in an established western publication such as Mergers and Acquisitions. The enactment rate, based on studies that have reported such data, is over 90 percent (see, for example, Beamish 1988). Announced-but-not-implemented joint ventures are in fact so unusual that it is often only during methodological descriptions in doctoral dissertations that evidence is reported about these types of non-qualifying ventures in the sample.

The situation with respect to Chinese equity joint ventures appears to be dramatically different. As Table 1 noted, less than half the contracted investment had been disbursed. More significantly, many of the signed contracts will never be implemented; yet the PRC remains unwilling to provide an accurate restatement.

The gap between signed and implemented agreements is the result of many factors. First, due in part to the Chinese bureaucracy, there is an inevitable time-lag between signing and start-up. Teagarden (1990), for example, found a three-year lag. Second, some of the Chinese partners have encountered difficulties in obtaining even small levels of foreign exchange. In a survey of firms interested in the PRC, foreign exchange control was the most important issue identified by North American managers (Punnett and Yu 1990). Third, because the persons who sign an agreement are often different from those who have to implement it, there is enormous scope for delay or cancellation. Fourth, many of the proposed joint ventures were very small, and thus more vulnerable to economic fluctuations. Many were so small in fact, that they would not even be included in typical market-economy sample sets. For example, the Mergers and Acquisitions Rosters exclude transactions valued at less than US$1 million. Such incomplete reporting regarding small joint ventures in some market economies suggests that it may be incorrect to assume such a high implementation rate.

•Use of JVs With A Predetermined Duration

Within market-economy developed countries it is not common practice to have an equity joint venture agreement with a predetermined duration in place. While many executives do not expect their joint ventures (or wholly owned subsidiaries) to last indefinitely, neither do they normally set them up with an expiration date. A similar situation was observed by Beamish (1988) in market economy developing countries.

Some joint venture researchers have argued that there are conditions under which joint ventures with a predetermined duration will occur. According to Harrigan (1988), so-called fade out joint ventures between horizontal competitors in a U.S. domestic setting will be used as a gradual means of divesting, and will occur under conditions of slow, stagnant or declining demand coupled with low-demand uncertainty.

For much of the past decade, the PRC, unlike other countries, enforced a fade-out provision for Sino-foreign equity joint venture investments. Over half of the equity joint ventures formed in the PRC until 1985 (Beamish and Wang 1989) contained a provision whereby the entire business would became wholly Chinese owned at the end of ten years. Although the number of equity joint ventures in the PRC with predetermined durations remains high, recently, some of these earlier contracts have been extended after implementation. Over the past few years, the standard duration has increased to 15-30 years (Engholm 1989) and recently the laws have been changed allowing up to 50 years for equity joint ventures. There is no predetermined duration for cooperative ventures.

The fact that some Chinese enterprise managers have demonstrated a willingness to renegotiate the length of the joint venture agreement—even after the joint venture has gone into operation—provides solid evidence for Williamson's (1975) point that opportunistic behavior is not necessarily an inevitable aspect of interfirm behavior. Such evidence is significant because it provides theoretical support for the general use of joint ventures in the PRC.

• Ownership Level of Foreign Firm

Beamish and Wang (1989) found that the foreign firm had a minority equity position in most of the 805 equity joint ventures formed in the PRC until 1986. Sixty percent of the foreign firms had a minority equity position, 31 percent had equal equity and only 9 percent had a majority equity holding. Similar results were observed by Engholm (1990) and Boisot and Child (1990).

It is possible that more foreign firms will take a larger equity position now that the Chinese government has begun to encourage the use of wholly foreign owned businesses in the PRC. However, if the experience of foreign firms in market economy developing countries is any guide (see Franko 1989), most will continue to take a minority equity position since this often affords political advantages in the host country and tax advantages in both the home and host country. Tax advantages in the home country result from the minority-owned JV being treated as an investment whereas majority-owned JVs are considered wholly owned subsidiaries. In the host country, overall corporate tax rates are often lower if a local firm has a majority equity position.

•Number of Autonomously Managed Ventures

On occasion, joint ventures in developed countries are managed with little direction or control from either parent (Killing 1983) or—at the extreme—by a management team which did not originate from either partner. Such an approach is unusual in market-economy developing countries.

None of the studies of Sino-foreign JVs in the PRC indicated any autonomously managed joint ventures. The existence of joint venture autonomy would be extremely surprising in the PRC given that one of the reasons for the preponderance of joint ventures is a desire by the Chinese to learn about the operating methods of foreign firms.

•Ownership-Control Relationship

Although there is no necessary correlation between level of foreign ownership and amount of foreign control in joint ventures, certainly one often exists. In developed countries the most common relationships between foreign ownership and foreign control are minority equity with subordinate control, equal equity with shared/split control, and majority equity with dominant control. The potential for such a correlation breaks down, however, when there is local government legislation or pressure limiting foreign company ownership—common in developing countries—or when there are three or more partners.

In developing countries, including the PRC, foreign firms are typically able to exercise somewhat greater control than their equity levels would suggest. It is unclear whether this is due to the nature of their contribution, or to a more sophisticated knowledge of the control mechanisms available (Schaan 1983). Both the new sample (17 of 22 cases) and Boisot and Child (1990) indicated that shared/split control is the most common of the three types in the PRC. As noted earlier, most foreign firms have a minority equity position although equal ownership is quite common.

The perceived foreign ownership ceiling has recently been lifted in the PRC. The number of majority foreign owned JVs will increase somewhat, likely with a corresponding increase in the amount of dominant foreign control.

•Control-Performance Relationship

The measure of control used here was derived from Killing (1983). He measured control by administering a questionnaire in which managers were asked to assess the jointness

Managing the Joint Venture

Joint Venture Performance

of decision making regarding nine decisions (product pricing, product design, production scheduling, production process, quality standards, replacing a functional manager, budget sales targets, budget cost targets, and budget capital expenditures). To assess the jointness of decision making, six categories of decisions were considered (made by JV General Manager alone, made by JVGM with input from local parent, made by JVGM with input from foreign parent, made by local parent alone, made by foreign parent alone, and made jointly by parents). Then, depending on the response, ventures were classified as dominant, shared, split, or independently controlled.

Killing (1983) observed a correlation between dominant control by one partner in developed country joint ventures and superior joint venture performance. Since then, however, inconclusive and contradictory results have been reported. For example, Awadzi (1987) and Kogut (1988) observed no relationship in their developed country studies on the Control-Performance Relationship; Blodgett (1987), however, found a positive relationship between shared control and high performance.

In market-economy developing countries, a correlation between shared/split control and joint venture success was previously observed and has been reinforced by Austin (1990). Similarly in the PRC, Shenkar (1990), Teagarden (1990) and the new sample found it effective to divide up control along functional lines. To have one partner making nearly all the decisions—as would be the situation with a wholly owned subsidiary or dominant control joint venture—increases the probability of poor performance in the PRC. The local economy, politics, and culture in the PRC are so far removed from the experience of most Western firms and managers as to make dominant foreign control extremely risky. Similarly, the lack of technology and managerial skills by the Chinese makes dominant control by them equally risky. As a result, shared or split control is the principal means by which success may be achieved. Cory (1982) provides earlier support for this view in his study of joint ventures in Yugoslavia.

• Instability Rate

A frequently used—but imperfect—measure of joint venture performance is stability. A joint venture is considered unstable (Franko 1971) when: (a) the holdings of the foreign firm cross the 50 percent ownership line (since control may have shifted with the equity change); (b) when the holdings of the foreign firm cross the 95 percent ownership line (since the business is now essentially wholly owned); (c) the MNE sells out; (d) the JV is liquidated; or (e) there is a major reorganization (Killing 1983). If any of these conditions were observed in the new sample, the JV was considered unstable.

Both the National Council (1987) and the new sample (16 of 22 cases) observed relatively stable joint ventures in the PRC. The low instability rate is explained by five factors:

(A) for those JVs that serve the Chinese market *and* have raw material quota allocated to them, there is a greater assuredness of the future of the JV and, hence, fewer market pressures on the MNE to consider reorganization.

(B) because it takes longer to negotiate JVs in the PRC than in other countries, there is more time to ascertain the "appropriate" ownership level.

(C) because MNE partners generally perceive it as difficult to change the contract (due to a Chinese bureaucracy that they do not comprehend), they are less likely to seek adjustments in the ownership levels.

(D) because many JVs originally had what MNEs considered to be a short-duration fade-out provision (ten years), some MNEs did not deem it worthwhile to renegotiate.

(E) most JVs have been in operation less than ten years. In other countries, the start dates stretch back further; so by definition we would expect higher instability rates elsewhere.

Joint ventures in the PRC are likely to be less stable in the future. The longer a JV has been in operation, the greater will be the number of reorganizations/liquidations, as performance problems arise. In addition, with the relaxing of government pressures to use the joint venture organization form, and despite the performance implications, some managers will consider converting their minority equity ventures to majority or wholly owned businesses.

•**Performance**

International joint venture performance has been measured in numerous ways. Beamish (1988) observed a strong correlation between objective financial measures (i.e. 15 percent ROE) and subjective measures (i.e. managerial assessment) in market economy LDCs, while Geringer and Hebert (1991) report similar results in developed countries. The current study used a managerial assessment to measure performance.

The performance of Sino-foreign joint ventures has been measured in a variety of ways also. No matter what the measure used, however, a similar pattern is evident. With the exception of Campbell (1986), most studies where the data were collected prior to 1989 tended to view performance as satisfactory/acceptable. Since then however, as Teagarden and Von Glinow (1990), Shenkar (1990), and the new sample have found, performance problems have accelerated. Over half (14 of 22) of the MNE partners have indicated a dissatisfaction with performance and this is unlikely to change. Many firms have lost patience with the PRC and are unwilling to continue to wait for hard-currency profits to materialize. This loss of patience is first a result of the lapse of time. In the early years, many MNEs judged their PRC ventures by different criteria than those used with their other foreign affiliates. Such an approach was never defensible in the long term. Escalating inflation rates, as well, have made many MNEs realize that there will not be *steady* growth in the PRC—that in fact the attractiveness of the market will ebb and flow.

Second, the opening of Eastern European markets provides new, unexpected alternatives to doing business in the PRC and ones where physical, cultural, and economic gaps are not as wide for some investors. If the PRC and the Eastern European markets had opened up at the same time rather than ten years apart, we might never have seen the same MNE rush to the PRC. Even without these latter two reasons, a high level of performance difficulties can be expected with Sino-foreign joint ventures in the PRC, due to both their structural complexity and environmental diversity (see Shenkar, 1990; Von Glinow and Teagarden 1988).

Other reasons for the loss of patience include chagrin about the deaths, imprisonments, and refugee exodus resulting from the June 1989 events of Tiananmen Square. For example, numerous high-potential students who were in the west for training—including managerial training—at the time of the crackdown, exercised the option of applying for the refugee status that many governments offered.

IMPLICATIONS FOR MANAGEMENT AND RESEARCH

The present study has documented twelve characteristics of equity joint ventures in the PRC relative to joint ventures in market economy developing countries. In only seven of 12 cases was there support for the hypothesis that the characteristics of joint ventures in market economy developing countries would be similar to the characteristics of joint ventures in planned economy developing countries.

The primary implication for managers is to suggest the value in adopting a contingency approach to their involvement with joint ventures. Just as previous research noted the importance of not treating JVs in developed countries the same as those in developing countries, the study points out the importance of not assuming that JVs *within* developing countries have similar characteristics. While many characteristics are common, others are quite different. To adopt a common approach to the establishment and management of joint ventures—irrespective of whether it is located in a planned or market-economy developing country—may result in the organization taking on an unnecessary risk. For example, even for the manager experienced with joint ventures in

Paul W. Beamish

market-economy developing countries, there are five characteristics unique to China. We will look at the possible impact of each in turn.

The first characteristic that sets China apart is the fact that the frequency of association with government partners is far higher in the PRC than in other developing countries. The high probability of having to have a government partner in China means that the foreign partner cannot make the same assumptions about the partner's profit motivations, speed of decision making, desire for employment efficiency, and so forth that would more likely characterize JVs between two private sector organizations in developing countries. These are fundamental assumptions in most market-economy ventures. When they are called into question, the incentive to invest in China is reduced.

Second, the fact that most of the JV investment in China has come from ethnically related countries (especially newly industrialized Hong Kong and Taiwan) provides ample support for the impact of "psychic distance" on investment decisions. Because China was self-sufficient in many areas and closed to the Western world for so long, Western culture has made fewer inroads there than in many other developing countries. As a consequence, the foreign investor to China may encounter even more adjustment problems than they would in other developing countries.

A third unique characteristic is that less than half of the intended JVs in China have actually been implemented. In other developing countries, a signed JV agreement means that an implemented JV will very likely result (that is, a deal is a deal). In China, a signed agreement may or may not result in an implemented joint venture. For foreign companies that sign JV agreements in China, this uncertainty of result must be factored in to the company's entire foreign investment plans.

Fourth, the use in China of JVs with a predetermined duration—even if the provision is now being relaxed—still provides an additional pressure on foreign investors to China, which is not present in other developing countries. We need look no further than the 1997 return of Hong Kong to China to see how the impact of a fade-out provision is felt on managerial decision making well before the legislation actually takes effect.

The final characteristic that sets China apart, relative to other developing countries, is stability. Of particular relevance to managers is that, unlike other developing countries, there is currently not a correlation in China between stability and performance. While the current instability rate is low in China, managers need to guard against complacency, because this does not mean most JVs are, or will be, performing satisfactorily. For firms contemplating first-time entry into the Chinese market via the joint venture form, a basic understanding of some of these unique characteristics of joint ventures in the PRC can assist in making a better investment decision.

Future research is required along a number of dimensions:

(1) The Developed Country category should be split out at a minimum to examine the practices of Japanese firms. Gerlach (1987) has noted that fundamental differences appear to exist between the Japanese approach to alliances and the approaches found elsewhere. Campbell (1986) observed significant differences between Japanese and American firms in their assessments of the desirability of having daily management control by the Chinese partner in equity joint ventures.

(2) A comparison of the characteristics of other types of alliances with equity joint ventures is needed.

(3) While the present study examined 12 characteristics, investigation of additional characteristics and, more importantly, greater examination of the reasons for the particular characteristics, would be appropriate. For example, Ganitsky and Watzke (1990) have suggested the need to synchronize the time reckoning systems of joint venture partners. As well, more emphasis is needed on characteristics associated with the actual management of joint ventures.

(4) All economies evolve, and the characteristics present at one point in time cannot be expected to remain static. The rapidly changing economies of the Newly Industrialized economies, the PRC, and Eastern Europe—and the role of joint ventures within and between them—warrants attention.

(5) Methodologically, the meta-analysis which was used to explain certain of the characteristics is subject to the usual limitations of this type of approach.

THE AUTHOR

Paul W. Beamish *is the Davis Professor of International Business at The Western Business School, The University of Western Ontario, where he teaches international strategy. He is the senior author of* International Management: Text and Cases, *published by Irwin in 1991, and editor of the* Journal of International Business Studies. *In 1987-88 he was a consultant to The World Bank on Technology Transfer to China. He is the director of Western's China Program.*

1. In recent years, the most prevalent overarching theoretical model of foreign production has been eclectic theory. It integrates other well-developed international theories, specifically locational, ownership, and internalization advantage theories (Dunning 1980).

Dunning (1988) considers location advantage the "where" question of international production. Clearly, one of the four new characteristics under investigation, "origin of foreign partner," fits within this conceptual base.

Ownership-specific advantages deal primarily with the "why" question of foreign production. The second characteristic, "use of JVs with a predetermined duration," fits here due to the structural nature of its impact.

Internalization advantage is concerned with the "how" of international production. Our focus here is on the overall use of joint ventures and the resultant tradeoff between contractual risk and economic return. Thus conceptually, the other two new characteristics, "use of joint ventures versus other modes," and "proportion of intended JVs actually implemented," are squarely positioned here.

NOTES

REFERENCES

Austin, James E. *Managing in Developing Countries.* New York: The Free Press, 1990.

Awadzi, Winston K. *Determinants of Joint Venture Performance: A Study of International Joint Ventures in the United States.* Ph.D. diss., Louisiana State University, 1987.

Baughn, C. Christopher, and Richard N. Osborn. "The Role of Technology in the Formation and Form of Multinational Cooperative Arrangements." *The Journal of High Technology Management Research* 1, no. 2 (1990): 181-192.

Beamish, Paul W. "The Characteristics of Joint Ventures in Developed and Developing Countries." *Columbia Journal of World Business* (1985): 13-19.

_____. *Multinational Joint Ventures in Developing Countries.* London and New York: Routledge, 1988.

Beamish, Paul W., and John C. Banks. "Equity Joint Ventures and The Theory of the Multinational Enterprise." *Journal of International Business Studies* 17, no. 1 (1987): 1-16.

Beamish, Paul W., and H. Y. Wang. "Investing in China via Joint Ventures." *Management International Review* 29, no. 1 (1989): 57-64.

Blodgett, Linda L. *A Resource-Based Study of Bargaining Power in U.S.-Foreign Equity Joint Ventures.* Ph.D. diss., University of Michigan, 1987.

Boisot, Max, and John Child. *The Management of Equity Joint Ventures in China.* Beijing: China-EC Management Institute, 1990.

Campbell, Nigel. *China Strategies, The Inside Story*. University of Manchester/University of Hong Kong, 1986.

_____. "Experiences of Western Companies in China." *Euro-Asia Business Review*, (July 1987): 35-38.

Canada China Trade Council Newsletters, (April 1989; September 1990).

Chen, Nai-Ruenn. *Foreign Investment in China: Current Trends*. Office of the PRC and Hong Kong, U.S. Department of Commerce, International Trade Administration, March 1986.

China Trade and Investment (15 August 1989): 21-23.

Contractor, F. J., and P. Lorange. *Cooperative Strategies in International Business*. Lexington, MA: Lexington Books, 1988.

Contractor, Farok J. "Ownership Patterns of US Joint Ventures Abroad and the Liberalization of Foreign Government Regulations in the 1980s: Evidence from The Benchmark Surveys." *Journal of International Business Studies* 21, no. 1 (1990): 55-73.

Cory, Peter F. "Industrial Cooperation, Joint Ventures and the MNE in Yugoslavia," In *New Theories of the Multinational Enterprise*, ed. Alan M. Rugman. London: Croom Helm, 1982.

Country Report - China, *The Economist Intelligence Unit*, no. 3 (1990).

Daniels, John D., Jeffrey Krug, and Douglas Nigh. "U.S. Joint Ventures in China: Motivation and Management of Political Risk." *California Management Review* (Summer 1985).

Davidson, W.H. "Creating and Managing Joint Ventures in China." *California Management Review* 29, no. 4 (Summer 1987): 77-94.

Dunning, J.H. "Toward an Eclectic Theory of International Production: Some Empirical Tests." *Journal of International Business Studies* 11, no. 2 (1980): 9-31.

_____. *Explaining International Production*. London: Unwin Hyman, 1988.

Engholm, Christopher. *The China Venture: America's Corporate Encounter with the People's Republic of China*. Glenview, Illinois: Scott, Foresman and Company, 1989.

Franko, Lawrence G. *Joint Venture Survival in Multinational Corporations*. New York: Praeger, 1971.

_____. "Use of Minority and 50-50 Joint Ventures by U.S. Multinationals During the 1970s: The Interaction of Host Country Policies and Corporate Strategies." *Journal of International Business Studies* 20, no. 1 (1989): 19-41.

Ganitsky, Joseph, and Gerard E. Watzke. "Implications of Different Time Perspectives for Human Resource Management in International Joint Ventures." *Management International Review* 30 (1990): 37-49.

Gao, Zailang. "Sino-Foreign Joint Ventures in China." Unpublished dissertation, University of International Business and Economics, Beijing, 1989.

Geringer, J.M., and L. Hebert. "Measuring Performance of International Joint Ventures." *Journal of International Business Studies* 22, no. 2 (1991): 249-264.

Gerlach, Michael. "Business Alliances and the Strategy of the Japanese Firm." *California Management Review* (Fall 1987): 126-142.

Harrigan, Kathryn R. "Joint Ventures and Competitive Strategy." *Strategic Management Journal* 9, no. 2 (1988): 141-158.

Hennart, J.F. "A Transaction Costs Theory of Equity Joint Ventures." *Strategic Management Journal* 9, no. 4 (1988): 361-374.

Hergert, M., and D. Morris. "Trends in International Collaborative Agreements." In *Cooperative Strategies in International Business*, ed. F. Contractor and P. Lorange. Lexington, MA: Lexington Books, 1988.

Killing, J. Peter. *Strategies for Joint Venture Success*. New York: Praeger, 1983.

Kogut, Bruce. "Joint Ventures: Theoretical and Empirical Perspectives." *Strategic Management Journal* 9, no. 4 (1988): 319-332.

Lee, Chol. *The Characteristics and Performance of Korean Joint Ventures in LDCs*. Unpublished working paper, Hong Ik University, Seoul, 1990.

National Council for US-China Trade. *US Joint Ventures in China: A Progress Report*, Washington, D.C.: Department of Commerce, March 1987.

Paloheimo, Annukka, and K.L. Inn Lee. *Behind The Bamboo Curtain: The Williamsonian Approach to Joint Venture Negotiations in China*. Unpublished working paper, National University of Singapore, 1988.

Park, Eui-Burm. *The Characteristics and Performance of International Joint Ventures in Korea*. Unpublished doctoral dissertation, Seoul National University, 1990.

Pisano, Gary, and David J. Teece. "Collaborative Arrangements and Global Technology Strategy: Some Evidence From The Telecommunications Equipment Industry." *Research on Technological Innovation, Management and Policy* 4 (1989): 227-256.

Punnett, B.J., and Ping Yu. "Attitudes Toward Doing Business with the PRC." *International Studies of Management and Organization* 20, nos. 1-2 (1990) : 149-160.

Schaan, Jean Louis. *Joint Venture Control: The Case of Mexico*. Unpublished doctoral dissertation, University of Western Ontario, 1983.

Shenkar, Oded. "International Joint Ventures' Problems in China: Risks and Remedies." *Long Range Planning* 23, no. 3 (1990): 82-90.

Teagarden, Mary B. *Sino-U.S. Joint Venture Effectiveness*. Unpublished doctoral dissertation, University of Southern California, Los Angeles, 1990.

The Characteristics of Joint Ventures in the People's Republic of China

Teagarden, Mary B., and Mary Ann Von Glinow. "Sino-Foreign Strategic Alliance Types and Related Operating Characteristics." *International Studies of Management & Organization* 20, nos. 1-2 (1990): 99-108.

Vernon-Wortzel, H., and L. H. Wortzel. "Globalization Strategies for Multinationals from Developing Countries." *Columbia Journal of World Business* (Spring 1988): 27-35.

Von Glinow, Mary Ann, and Mary B. Teagarden. "The Transfer of Human Resource Management Technology in Sino-U.S. Cooperative Ventures: Problems and Solutions." *Human Resource Management* 27, no. 2 (Summer 1988): 201-229.

Wells, Christopher. "Brazilian Multinationals." *Columbia Journal of World Business* 23, no. 4 (Winter 1988): 13-23.

Wells, Louis T., Jr. *Third World Multinationals.* Cambridge, Massachusetts: MIT Press, 1983.

Williamson, O. E. *Markets and Hierarchies.* New York: Macmillan, The Free Press, 1975.

[4]

EQUITY JOINT VENTURES AND THE THEORY OF THE MULTINATIONAL ENTERPRISE

Paul W. Beamish*
University of Western Ontario

John C. Banks**
Wilfrid Laurier University

Abstract. This paper extends the internalization approach to the theory of the multinational enterprise (MNE) to include an expanded role for equity joint ventures. Using the transaction cost paradigm of Williamson, this paper explains why joint ventures may sometimes be preferred over wholly owned subsidiaries. Also presented is empirical work on joint-venture performance in developing countries which demonstrates that under certain conditions joint ventures can be the optimal mode of foreign direct investment.

Joint ventures are the dominant form of business organization for multinational enterprises in the developing countries (Vaupel and Curhan 1973), and are frequently being used by Fortune 500 companies in the developed countries (Janger 1980; Harrigan 1985). In fact, for U.S.-based companies, all cooperative arrangements (involving such things as licences or local shareholders) outnumber wholly owned subsidiaries by a ratio of 4 to 1 (Contractor and Lorange 1987).

MNEs often prefer joint ventures over wholly owned subsidiaries regardless of whether or not they are required by a host country as a condition of entry (Beamish 1984). Nevertheless, fairly limited consideration has been given to the rationale for equity joint ventures in the theory of the multinational enterprise. While recent theoretical contributions utilizing the internalization approach have significantly advanced our understanding of MNEs (Buckley and Casson 1976; Casson, 1979, 1982; Rugman 1979), the theory offers only partial explanations of the ownership preferences of MNEs for other than wholly owned subsidiaries (Davidson and McFetridge 1985; Teece 1985; Thorelli 1986; Horstmann and Markussen 1986; Wells 1973). The purpose of this paper is to further extend the internalization approach by providing an economic rationale for joint ventures

---

* Paul W. Beamish is Assistant Professor of Business Policy and International Business at the University of Western Ontario. He received his Ph.D. degree in Business Administration from Western, and was winner of the Barry M. Richman Dissertation Award in International Management for the Academy of Management (1986).

** John C. Banks is Assistant Professor of Business Policy and International Business at Wilfrid Laurier University in Waterloo, Ontario and a Ph.D. candidate in International Business at York University (Canada).

Received: November 1985; Revised: August & November 1986; Accepted: December 1986.

1

2 JOURNAL OF INTERNATIONAL BUSINESS STUDIES, SUMMER 1987

within the framework provided by the transactions cost paradigm.[1] In the next section, the main features of internalization theory are reviewed. This is followed by a discussion of how the theory can be extended to joint ventures using the transactions cost paradigm developed by Williamson (1975). In the final section empirical evidence supporting some of the predictions of this expanded notion of internalization theory will be examined.

THE THEORY OF INTERNALIZATION

Internalization theory was developed to provide an economic rationale for the existence of MNEs. By definition these firms establish local operations as a means of serving a foreign market rather than engaging in arms-length transactions with market intermediaries. The theory posits that due to the transaction costs which must be borne as a result of conducting business in imperfect markets it is more efficient (less expensive) for the firm to use internal structures rather than market intermediaries to serve a foreign market. According to Williamson's (1975) reasoning these market imperfections arise from two environmental conditions: uncertainty and a small number of market agents. When these conditions coexist with two sets of human factors, opportunism and bounded rationality, he argues that the costs of writing, executing and enforcing arms-length complex contingent claims contracts with market intermediaries are greater than the costs of internalizing the market.[2] In other words, a firm facing a complex, unpredictable business environment and having few potential channel members to utilize would be more profitable performing the distribution function itself if: (i) there was a strong likelihood market agents would try to take advantage of the firm's lack of complete knowledge; and (ii) the firm was unable to specify all possible future transaction contingencies.

Researchers in international business have been very successful in providing an economic rationale for the establishment of a MNE as a response to imperfect markets utilizing transactions cost logic (Buckley and Casson 1976; Caves 1982; Dunning 1981; Hennart 1982; Rugman 1981; Teece 1981, 1985). In extending this logic to international markets they have found it useful to distinguish between strategies of vertical integration and horizontal diversification since the nature of the market failures is different in each situation. The economic reasoning supporting the internalization of markets in the case of vertical integration is concerned with the failure of markets in intermediate goods. In the case of horizontal diversification the concern is with the failure of markets in intangible assets for such things as management know-how, trade name or proprietory technology. Although the elegance and comprehensiveness of transactions cost reasoning has provided the internalization approach with a powerful logic (Rugman 1980, 1985), it is still deficient in some respects as a general theory of the MNE. In our view the major limitation is that the theory in its current form focuses primarily on one mode of hierarchy or organization. It therefore provides the firm with only one fully developed solution to the problem of imperfect international markets—the establishment of a wholly owned subsidiary (WOS). Yet, both conceptually and practically, there are a number of other modes which firms can and do adopt to deal with imperfections in international markets including licensing, management contracts, subcontracting, joint ventures and consortia. Moreover, firms often employ several different modes simultaneously in addressing the needs of a particular foreign market (Contractor 1985; Davidson and McFetridge 1985). Thus, for the internalization approach to be regarded as a general theory of the MNE it will have to provide an economic rationale for these other modes (Hennart 1985) and specify the conditions under which each would provide efficiency gains over WOSs and the market. The purpose of this paper is to provide a rationale for equity JVs within the internalization framework.

JOINT VENTURES AND INTERNALIZATION THEORY

In order to justify the utilization of international JVs within the internalization framework two necessary conditions must be shown to exist: the firm possesses a rent-yielding asset which would allow it to be competitive in a foreign market; and joint-venture arrangements are superior to other means for appropriating rents from the sale of this asset in the foreign market (Teece 1985). A detailed explanation for the possession of a sustainable competitive advantage regardless of the means employed for exploiting it in international markets has already been provided by Dunning and Rugman (1985). Likewise, the conditions within which JVs provide a superior means of exploiting these assets for firms pursuing international vertical integration has been extensively considered by Stuckey (1983) using the transaction cost paradigm. However, a similarly extensive consideration of JVs in the context of international horizontal diversification strategies is currently lacking in the literature. Thus the focus of this paper will be on the latter case.

Following Teece (1983) we would argue that the attractiveness of joint ventures is a function of both the revenue-enhancing and cost-reducing opportunities they provide the MNE. However, according to internalization theory in its present formulation, firms would have a strong economic incentive to always avoid joint-venture arrangements since these are regarded as being inferior to WOSs in allowing the firm to maximize the returns available on it ownership-specific advantages (Caves 1982; Rugman 1983; Killing 1983; Poynter 1985; Harrigan 1985). The value of the foreign local partners' assets would apparently not be sufficient in any conceivable situation to offset the strategic risks and transactions costs faced by the MNE in exploiting its ownership-specific assets. Yet this solution to the problem of imperfect markets assumes that management has the ability to organize an internal market and that a joint venture cannot be structured in such a way as to maintain both the bargaining and maladaption costs inherent in such arrangements at acceptable levels. Thus, in its current state of development, internalization theory focuses primarily on the situation where WOS and arms-length transactions are the only alternatives available to deal with Williamson's (1975) market disabling factors of opportunism, bounded rationality, uncertainty and small numbers.[3]

However, we would suggest that JVs which conform to certain preconditions and structural arrangements can actually provide a better solution to the problems of opportunism, small numbers dilemma and uncertainty in the face of bounded rationality than wholly owned subsidiaries. Although there would be costs

4   JOURNAL OF INTERNATIONAL BUSINESS STUDIES, SUMMER 1987

associated with writing, executing and enforcing pricing agreements and use restrictions regarding the transfer of the MNE's intangible assets these will be more than offset by the enhanced revenue potential of its assets as a result of forming a JV. As well, rents can exceed those available through wholly owned subsidiaries due to the potential synergistic effects of combining the MNEs assets with those of the local partner. The following section will identify the conditions under which we feel market failure due to opportunism, the small numbers dilemma and uncertainty can be efficiently addressed through joint-venture arrangements. Although discussed in detail in the section on empirical evidence, most of the following illustrations and examples of how market failure can be efficiently addressed are drawn from Beamish (1984).

One of the most significant transactional contingencies faced by MNEs considering a joint venture would apparently arise due to the problem of opportunism. Yet even Williamson (1975, 1983) allows that opportunistic behavior is not necessarily an inevitable aspect of interfirm behavior although he suspects such situations would be uncommon. We would suggest that in situations where a joint venture is established in a spirit of mutual trust and commitment to its long-term commercial success opportunistic behavior is unlikely to emerge. This is similar to the concept of mutual forbearance (Buckley and Casson 1987), where agents on a reciprocal basis, deliberately pass up short-term advantages. With a foundation of trust, the partner, and particularly the MNE, would be more willing to exercise the tolerance and perseverance necessary to see the joint venture through its difficult times. Problems could be effectively dealt with by the MNE without damaging the long-run viability and efficiency of the joint-venture arrangement. In these circumstances the effective management of opportunism would depend far more on managerial perspicacity and persistence than company lawyers masterminding complete contingent claims contracts.[4] Furthermore, if these positive attitudes are reinforced with supporting inter-organizational linkages such as mechanisms for the division of profits, joint decision-making processes and reward and control systems, the incentives to engage in self-seeking preemptive behavior could be minimized (Williamson 1983). Under such circumstances, then, opportunism would likely not obtain as the parties would be able to pursue their own self-interest without a need to resort to guile. They could negotiate a shared perception of the relative value of their respective contributions over time and establish a mutually acceptable division of profits in a vigorous yet open fashion (Berg and Friedman 1980). Their attention could be directed toward long-term joint profit maximization since there would be no need to make preemptive claims on profit streams. Consequently the partners could take the long view for investment purposes while simultaneously adjusting to changing market circumstances in an adaptive sequential manner.

A small numbers situation particularly when combined with opportunism would normally result in serious transactional difficulties for the firm (Williamson 1975). In the case of joint ventures, even if initially there are several local firms from which to select a suitable partner, a small numbers condition could obtain if the firm wished to change the terms of the agreement at a later date and seek a new partner. Having had some experience with the MNE, the initial local partner will clearly enjoy cost advantages over firms not selected at the outset. The option of switching partners is, therefore, not optimal for the MNE. However, in the absence of local partner opportunism, this small numbers situation could present much less serious transactional difficulties than normally might be expected. Moreover, by establishing those inter-organizational linkages referred to earlier, it is possible to manage many of the types of difficulties associated with exchange between bilateral monopolists regarding individual or joint maximization of profits (Contractor 1985). There will be much less incentive to secure gains by strategic posturing and the interests of the joint venture can be promoted. Thus, under certain conditions, the small numbers dilemma can be effectively dealt with in a joint venture.

The problem of uncertainty can also be handled efficiently within some international joint ventures. In the absence of opportunism and small numbers disabilities there are strong incentives for the parties to pool their respective resources. By doing so it is possible for the MNE to economize on the information requirements of foreign investment (Caves 1982; Beamish 1984; Rugman 1985). The MNE can provide firm-specific knowledge regarding technology, management and capital markets while the local partner can provide location-specific knowledge regarding host-country markets, infrastructure and political trends. By pooling and sharing information through the mechanism of a joint venture the MNE is able to reduce uncertainty at a lower long-term average cost than through pure hierarchical or market approaches.[5] Because the parties would have little incentive to behave opportunistically the derivative condition of information impactedness due to uncertainty and opportunism would not arise. Although bounded rationality would continue to be a problem, a pure hierarchical mode of transacting would not represent a superior solution to this problem alone. The low costs associated with opportunism, small numbers, uncertainty and information impactedness in joint ventures under the conditions specified above would render this mode of transacting the most efficient means of serving a foreign market.

Theoretically, although they have advantages over the market and wholly owned subsidiaries in certain circumstances, there are limits to the relative efficiency gains provided by joint ventures. First, they can suffer from the same goal distortions of hierarchies. The MNE can become biased toward the maintenance of its initial arrangements with the joint-venture partner without considering the long-term profit or cost implications. However, several approaches to ensuring that profitability goals are not subordinated to other considerations or that the joint-venture mode of transaction is not uncritically preserved can be taken. For instance, profitability goals can be maintained by giving the general manager an equity position in the joint venture. This provides a strong incentive for him to ensure that profits are earned in the joint venture itself and are not unequally siphoned to one partner over the other. Mechanisms can also be established that prevent either partner from having total control over distribution or final selling price.[6] As well, management fees (usually paid to the MNE) can be tied to the productivity/profitability of the joint venture and the length of management contracts can be held to a relatively short time period. Not tying the joint venture to a single source of supply, particularly if it is one of the partners, can help ensure that procurement biases are minimized. Finally, a conscious effort can be made to ensure that the total income derived from the joint venture by each partner, even if the mechanisms for doing so differ, are approximately equal (Contractor 1985).[7] Approaches to ensuring the joint-venture arrangement is not uncritically maintained include explicit recognition by both parties that: a partner may resort to guile at some point even if this was absent in his behavior at the outset; while the foreign partner may possess the requisite knowledge about the local economy, politics and culture at the outset he may not continue to put forth the effort[8] necessary to maintain this knowledge; and if the absolute number of locally available managers increases, the need for a foreign partner and his ability to supply management resources may be reduced.

The risk of leakage of proprietary knowledge also serves to limit the efficiency gains available through joint-venture arrangements. Leakage can occur in one of two major ways: a local employee may decide to resign and use the knowledge acquired in the joint venture to establish a competing firm (Type 1); or the local partner may decide to dissolve the arrangement and use the knowledge gained through the joint venture as a basis for continuing to serve the local (and possibly a foreign) market through his own organization (Type 2). Type 1 leakages are especially hard to prevent particularly if the employee concerned recognizes the personal trade-offs involved and is willing to live with some limitations such as being forced to serve a single market. Type 2 leakages are often easier to control because the negative consequences for the local partner can be quite significant. Pirating the MNE's existing technology will normally mean that the local partner loses access to export markets, ongoing technological developments, trademarks, marketing skills and possibly specialized raw materials. Moreover depending on how the original agreement was structured, this pirating of technology might even be construed as a form of industrial espionage. Presumably the threat of lawsuits would act as a disincentive. Certainly there is, however, a dilution of complete control with industrial espionage (Buckley 1985: 46). Leakage, therefore, is a problem in joint ventures and its costs do serve to limit the efficiency gains joint ventures offer over markets and hierarchies (Parry 1985; Rugman 1985).

EMPIRICAL EVIDENCE

This section reviews recent joint venture studies by Beamish (1984), Wells (1983) and Stuckey (1983) as they relate to internalization theory. The review of Beamish (1984) is the most extensive since it constitutes new empirical evidence. It also attempts to incorporate supporting evidence from other joint-venture researchers, including Artisien and Buckley (1985), Schaan (1984), Killing (1983), Janger (1980) and Tomlinson (1970) and was the source of many of the previously cited examples.

The Performance of Joint Ventures in LDCs

Data was collected by Beamish (1984) in three stages on a total of 66 joint ventures located in 27 different LDCs. Within the third stage, particular emphasis was placed on 12 comparative core cases. The distinction used for developed/ less developed countries was 1978 per capita GNP over/under U.S. $3,000. Joint ventures were defined as shared-equity undertakings between two or more parties, each of whom held at least five percent of the equity. The research was concerned with joint ventures that had been formed between a company, group, or individual from a developed country with a similar entity in a less developed country. While such groups could and did include local governments as partners, the focus of the research was on joint ventures in which the local government was not a shareholder. None of the core ventures involved government partners. Other partner combinations were not included in the sample because they were either less typical (i.e., two MNE partners in an LDC) or because the partners might not share the same profit motivation (i.e., government partners being more concerned with employment than profitability). Also excluded from the study were one-shot, project-oriented ventures (sometimes known as fade-out joint ventures) and ventures in which the parent company viewed its involvement purely as a portfolio-like investment. Although interviews were conducted with, and questionnaires administered to, the local partner, MNE partner, and joint-venture general manager (where possible) in each of these core ventures, for the purpose of this analysis primarily only MNE partner observations are reported. This attempt to solicit information from both partners and the general manager for each venture represented a major point of departure from many previous works on joint-venture performance. This was important because it provided a more balanced picture of the actual operation of the joint venture and increased confidence in the research findings.

The questionnaires administered in the core ventures lent themselves to non-parametric statistical analysis of data. Although questionnaire findings from the 12 core ventures were emphasized, they were supplemented by interview comments from 46 senior executives in the 66 joint ventures.

Interviews were conducted in five countries—Canada, the United States, England and two Caribbean nations. The 46 interviews averaged more than three hours in length each, and were, with five exceptions, conducted in person. The other five interviews took place by telephone.

Over 100 executives were contacted in obtaining the 46 interviews. A larger original pool was required because of the need to find joint ventures that satisfied methodological constraints. Companies agreed to participate in the research in approximately ninety percent of cases where the interviewer was able to establish that the companies' venture fit the sample design. These core ventures were all between either American, British, or Canadian MNEs and local, private firms. Ten of the 12 joint ventures were located in the Caribbean, with most of these in a single country. All of the core ventures were manufacturers. Non-manufacturing ventures were excluded because mixing joint ventures in a sample where the scale of investment is commonly much higher (mining) or lower (distribution) could potentially affect the joint-venture decision process. The core ventures were concentrated in two sectors. There were both high- and low-performing ventures in each sector. Even though this required a longer search for companies, holding industry and country constant was considered an important step in reducing the number of rival explanations of joint-venture performance.

8   JOURNAL OF INTERNATIONAL BUSINESS STUDIES, SUMMER 1987

All of the joint ventures in these industries were sampled. The research used structured interviews and a self-administered questionnaire. These questionnaires were administered with the researcher present, and any questions could be immediately clarified. This also permitted the checking of responses to ensure consistency with comments made earlier in the interview.

The sample of joint ventures was not a random sample of the joint ventures in the region. A stratified sample of joint ventures between foreign private and local private firms, primarily in one country, was used.

For inclusion in the sample, joint ventures had to have been in operation for at least three years. Because many joint ventures never get off the ground, those firms which had been fully operating businesses for less than three years were excluded to increase the comparability of the sample. Average sales for the ventures were US $4.5 million, and all of the 12 ventures had sales between US $1.0 and $10.0 million. There was no correlation between sales and performance. Five of the ventures sold to both industrial customers and consumers; two, to industrial customers only; and five, to consumers only. Half of the joint ventures exported, with no correlation between exporting and performance.

Average market share for the core ventures was forty-two percent, with a high standard deviation. There was no correlation between market share and joint-venture performance. The joint ventures had been formed between 1959-1978 and had been in operation an average of 11.5 years. There was no correlation between age and performance.

None of the core ventures had effective monopoly positions. Either local manufacturing competition existed, or tariffs were low enough to allow competitive import. The MNE held a minority equity share in 5 of the 12 ventures. Half of the core ventures exported (up to twenty-five percent of sales), with no correlation between exporting and performance.

The basis for the measure of success used in this study was the long-term viability of the joint venture. Performance of the joint ventures was measured by a managerial assessment in which only when both partners were satisfied was the venture considered successful. If one or both partners were dissatisfied with the performance, the venture was considered unsuccessful. This measure had been previously used in joint-venture research by Schaan (1983). In every case in which the venture was assessed by management as successful, both partners were also earning a fifteen percent or higher return on equity. Overall, 7 of the 12 ventures were classed as successful and 5 as unsuccessful.

While it may be possible to operate a joint venture for a short period with a dissatisfied partner, Beamish (1984) found that refusing to recognize differences is ultimately costly in terms of the long-term viability of the JV. MNE partners who are satisfied with their own returns and yet ignore their partner's dissatisfaction with performance are ultimately sowing the seeds of destruction of the joint venture. Local partners will not tolerate unsatisfactory performance indefinitely, particularly if they perceive differences in the returns earned by the other partner. Beamish (1984) observed that when the MNE partner had two more sources of income (irrespective of type) than did the local partner, poor performance resulted. When there was a closer balance in the numbers of sources of income for each partner, more satisfactory performance was observed. This is generally consistent with Contractor's (1985: 44) point that "in some cases the optimum for the local partner is to try to disallow a royalty or component supply agreement altogether and negotiate only on an equity sharing basis."

If the MNE partner is satisfied or complacent about his own performance, and the local partner is not, the local partner has numerous ways in which to express his dissatisfaction. If, for example, the local partner loses trust in the foreign partner (i.e., perceives that the MNE partner is operating opportunistically), he may move toward the formalization or enforcement of various contracts surrounding the operations of the venture. As noted earlier, the costs of such actions would negate much of the rationale[9] behind the establishment of the joint venture in the first place.

Beamish (1984, 1985) observed that the characteristics of joint ventures in less developed countries differed from those in developed countries. Differences were noted in stability,[10] autonomy, ownership, reasons for creating the venture, and management control. This issue of control has been particularly important in joint-venture research. From his joint-venture research in developed countries Killing (1983), like Kolde (1974), concluded that one partner should assume dominant control and operate the venture as if it were a wholly owned subsidiary.[11] On the other hand, Janger (1980) found in his study of joint ventures in developed and developing countries that one control structure could not be identified as more successful than the others. Tomlinson's (1970) study of joint ventures lead him to conclude that the MNEs should not insist on dominant control over the major managerial decisions in joint ventures located in LDCs. He felt that the sharing of responsibility with local associates would lead to a greater contribution from them and, in turn, to a greater return on investment. The control questionnaire developed by Killing for use with developed country joint ventures was administered by Beamish (1984) to the MNE partners in the core ventures in his LDC sample. There was a significant relationship between unsatisfactory performance and overall foreign-dominant control, and between satisfactory performance and shared or local-dominant control. In fact, the MNE partners in the unsuccessful ventures preferred to operate without a partner as much as possible. Unlike the MNE partners in the successful ventures, they were unwilling to share control in exchange for access to local managers and their local knowledge. In the successful shared control ventures, both partners had placed significant value on the others' contributions over time. The perception of a mutual long-term need between the partners reduced the propensity to act opportunistically.

As well, Artisien and Buckley (1985: Table 12) found that where the MNEs motive for preferring a joint venture (over other forms of trade and industrial cooperation with Yugoslav enterprises) was 'to achieve greater participation in decision making,' the mean success rating for the JV was 'very successful.' This correlation between shared decision-making control and joint-venture success is similar to that observed in LDCs. In both LDCs and socialist market economies, such as Yugoslavia (see also Cory 1982), MNEs from developed countries may well be confronted with higher adaptation and information requirements than they are accustomed, thus reinforcing the appropriateness of joint ventures.

Local Knowledge and Performance

Beamish's (1984) examination of the importance attached by the MNE to the local partner's ownership-specific assets also provided data regarding the determinants of joint-venture success. Interviewees were asked to assess the importance of the partner's contribution to the venture of 16 different items. These potential partner needs were divided into five groups (items readily capitalized, human resource needs, market-access needs, government/political needs, and knowledge needs) of three (or in one case, four) items each. The relative importance of each item was measured at three times: entry, the present, and a forecast of three years hence.

Needs of long-term importance was defined as those that were steadily important or increasingly important, at a minimum significance level of .05 or lower (using Kolmogorov-Smirnov one-sample test). Needs of short-term importance were those which were important, but decreasingly so. Needs were unimportant if they were steadily unimportant at a statistical significance level of .05 or lower. The pattern of results observed when the importance of the local-partner contributions to the MNE were compared in the successful and unsuccessful ventures tended to provide support for internalization theory. Differences in the value attached to the importance of the local partner's contribution were observed between the successful and unsuccessful ventures in terms of human resource needs, government/political needs and knowledge needs. Significantly, the MNE partners in the successful ventures deemed their local partner's contributions of general managers, functional managers, general knowledge of the local economy, politics, and customs, and knowledge of current business practice, as important. Not only were none of these local-partner contributions important to the MNE partners in the unsuccessful ventures, but also these MNE partners went so far as to class the local partner's contribution of general and functional managers as unimportant. Of significance here is the association between success and obtaining access to local knowledge, and the association between lack of success and not attaching importance to this local-partner contribution. In transaction cost terms, the partnership economized on the information requirements of foreign investment and reduced uncertainty by pooling their resources.

The only areas in which the MNE partners in the unsuccessful ventures felt their local partners made important contributions were in the areas of satisfying existing or forecast government requirements for local ownership. In such cases, any local partner would suffice since it was only access to the local partner's nationality (as opposed to knowledge) that was desired. With any national sufficing as a partner, there would obviously be no small numbers constraint. Yet, when a partner was chosen simply for his nationality, poor performance resulted. Although the MNE imposes the small numbers condition on itself by choosing a partner who can contribute knowledge, such a condition does not necessarily become a dilemma. As discussed earlier, if the likelihood of opportunistic behavior has already been reduced (as it is here where each partner acknowledges the significant contribution(s) of the other), small numbers transactional difficulties are also lower.

As noted earlier, where joint ventures are established in a spirit of mutual trust and commitment to long-term success, opportunism was believed unlikely to emerge. To measure commitment and its relationship to joint-venture performance, the general managers of 12 JVs were asked to complete a questionnaire, the purpose of which was to assess how characteristic a total of 16 statements were of the foreign (MNE) parent-company's attitudes and activities vis-à-vis joint ventures and/or the particular joint venture. Commitment was conceptualized along two major dimensions: commitment to a course of action (which in turn was subdivided into commitment to international business and commitment to the joint-venture structure) and commitment to the particular project (subdivided into commitment to the particular venture and commitment to the particular partner).

Ratings on each statement were over a five-point scale (uncharacteristic (1); somewhat uncharacteristic (2); average (3); somewhat characteristic (4); and characteristic (5)). The hypothesis governing all statements was that the more characteristic a statement, the greater the level of commitment, and the better the performance of the joint venture.

Based on their performance the joint ventures in the sample were classified as either high or low performers. For each group, the Kolmogorov-Smirnov one-sample test was applied to see if the distribution of responses to each of the 16 commitment statements could have come from a random distribution. In the case of the seven high performers, the responses to six statements significantly (at .05 or better) differed from a random distribution, with statements being scored heavily toward the "characteristic" end of the scale. In the case of low-performing ventures, the responses to one of the 16 items significantly differed from random, with the statement scoring toward the "uncharacteristic" end of the scale.

Two of the characteristic statements in the high-performing ventures were: management from the parent company is quite willing regularly to visit and offer assistance to the joint venture, and we try to ensure that through regular meetings, each partner knows what to expect from the joint venture. These statements in particular were consistent with a sense of commitment—the antithesis of opportunism.

Not surprisingly, there was a strong correlation between the commitment results and several other constructs — specifically need and control. Those firms exhibiting a willingness to be flexible and undertake a particular activity while controlling their opportunistic behavior (commitment) were likely to be the same firms favouring a sharing of decision-making (control) and looking for greater contributions (need) from their partners.

Other Contexts

Observations from joint-venture studies in slightly different contexts are reported in this section. Ninety percent of the manufacturing subsidiaries established by Third World multinationals in Wells' (1983) recent study were joint ventures. Most of this investment took place in other developing countries. Wells noted that the competitive advantage which the Third World investors could offer

12   JOURNAL OF INTERNATIONAL BUSINESS STUDIES, SUMMER 1987

derived from technologies enabling them to manufacture at low cost. These technologies involved small-scale flexible plants and considerable use of local inputs. Due to a lack of data about the contributions that a local partner could make to a developing country foreign investor, Wells speculated that the same contributions important to developed country investors would exist. Consequently, Third World MNEs are considered similar to the MNEs from the developed countries in Beamish's (1984) study in that presumably they could benefit equally well from the local market knowledge their partners could provide.

Wells expects the life cycles of many manufacturing subsidiaries of developing country firms to be short because the MNE is not able to provide a sustainable competitive advantage. While the MNE may continue to require knowledge of the local economy, politics and culture from the local partner, the local partner will be able to copy the MNEs contribution much faster. Third World MNEs were found to be rarely building trade names, undertaking research and development, or concentrating their efforts on activities from which they could build a sustainable advantage. While the Third World MNEs did seem to be benefitting from what we have called Type 2 leakages of proprietary technology, these benefits were generally not long term. The benefits of what Wells calls partial internalization would seem to be shorter for Third World MNEs than for the MNEs from developed countries in Beamish's study (1984).

Stuckey's (1983) research indicated that vertically integrated firms in the aluminum industry shared one of the motivations for forming joint ventures with horizontally integrated firms. He found a primary reason for creating joint ventures was because technical know-how and management expertise (intangible assets) are not easily exchanged via markets to the satisfaction of both suppliers and buyers. Stuckey feels the need for "nation-specific" knowledge typically arises when an established firm decides to invest in a country where it has had limited previous experience. Local firms or groups possess specialized information on the country's economy, politics, customs, and so on, information that is costly and time-consuming for the multinational enterprise to gather. This information is more accessible and is synthesized and used more efficiently within the relatively cooperative atmosphere of a joint venture, enabling the MNE to better deal with the problem of uncertainty. In summary, Stuckey feels the joint venture firm can be more efficient because it allows some of the economically important relationship between otherwise separate partners to be internalized by one organization (1983: 152).

Cory (1982), in his research on industrial cooperation agreements and joint ventures between Yugoslav enterprises and Western MNEs, provides empirical support that such intermediate mechanisms can, and occasionally do, represent viable intermediate, or what he calls quasi-internalized mechanisms, for resource allocation. As in this paper, Cory (1982: 167) notes that joint-venture arrangements can incorporate the essential elements of internalized relationships between the partners.

CONCLUSIONS

Internalization theory, as it is presently formulated, provides limited consideration of the efficiency and revenue gains available through joint-venture arrangements.

Although the notion that local firms may have resources which could be useful is not precluded, the theory posits that it would be less expensive for the MNE to develop these resources internally than to acquire them by establishing a joint venture. Due to transactions disabilities which are assumed to be inherent in such interfirm arrangements, whatever the MNE might gain in terms of knowledge of the local market, customs, business practices, contracts and government, it would apparently lose because of the costs associated with protecting its intangible assets from exploitation by the local partner. Thus, according to internalization theory, a rational profit-maximizing MNE would tend to use wholly owned subsidiaries. Yet this view presupposes that none of Williamson's (1975) transactional disabilities — opportunism, bounded rationality, uncertainty and small numbers condition can be efficiently dealt with in a JV. By demonstrating this assumption need not hold in all circumstances we have attempted to provide a theoretical justification for joint ventures within the context of internalization theory. Under particular arrangements the potential threats posed by opportunism and a small numbers condition can be reduced to a point where JVs become a more efficient means of dealing with environmental uncertainty even in the face of bounded rationality.

Previous research on joint-venture performance reviewed in this paper provides support for our view. Not all joint ventures are necessarily unstable or unprofitable arrangements for MNEs. Beamish (1984) has shown that not only are there clearly discernable differences in the characteristics of successful and unsuccessful joint ventures but also that these characteristics are consistent with the predictions of internalization theory in its expanded form. Forming a joint venture in an LDC is not without its cost. Nevertheless, the research we have conducted and reviewed has shown that joint ventures were more efficient than wholly owned subsidiaries for the MNE in LDC markets under certain circumstances and are consistent with Dunning's (1981) rationale for the appropriateness of joint ventures in place of wholly owned subsidiaries.

Further research is required to determine if one element of local knowledge — economic, political, or cultural — is more significant than others to MNEs. Also, because only an LDC-based sample of joint ventures was used, further research is required to determine if the theory is applicable in joint ventures between partners from two developed countries with significantly different cultures, and to joint ventures between partners from two planned economies.

There are a wide range of international industrial cooperation modes now being studied in the context of internalization. This paper provides an expanded role for one of these modes, joint ventures, in the theory of the multinational enterprise.

NOTES

1. When examining their economic rationale, it is important to distinguish between equity and contractually-based joint ventures. In the case of the former, the explicit intention of the partners is to manage the JV as a going concern over the long term. Contractual JVs, however, are established for a fixed time period with the explicit intention of the partners at the outset to dissolve the relationship at a specified date. For a discussion of contractual joint ventures, see Wright (1981, p.500). In this paper we are concerned only with equity JVs.

2. Although the terminology developed by Williamson (1975) can be somewhat turgid for the uninitiated, it contains a preciseness which we find useful for our present purposes. For definitions of these terms see note 3.

14   JOURNAL OF INTERNATIONAL BUSINESS STUDIES, SUMMER 1987

3. Williamson (1975) defines these terms as follows: uncertainty/complexity—an environmental condition where specification of the full decision tree is infeasible; small numbers—an environmental condition where only one or two market agents are available to perform the required tasks; opportunism—a human condition manifested by the strategic manipulation of information or the misrepresentation of intentions including self-interest-seeking behavior with guile; bounded rationality—a human condition characterized by a limited capacity in terms of knowledge, foresight and skill which places limits on the individual's ability to comprehend complexity: information impactedness—a derivative condition in which the underlying circumstances relevant to the transaction, or related set of transactions, are known to one or more parties but cannot be costlessly discerned or displayed for others.

4. In game situations analogous to MNE-local firm joint ventures, it has been shown that the development of cooperation can be promoted by a non-myopic player. By adopting a strategy based on trust and foresight the MNE could therefore convey its commitment to the joint venture and teach the local partner to respond in a cooperative fashion. See Alexrod (1984) and Brams and Kilgour (1985).

5. What seems to often be overlooked by management in the overall economic evaluation of joint ventures is that even though the start-up costs of wholly owned subsidiaries may be substantially lower, the long-term average costs may be much higher than joint ventures due to the very significant cost associated with independent efforts to overcome a lack of knowledge about the local economy, politics and culture.

6. Clearly, the lower the price to the distributor, the greater the profit that the distributing partner does not have to share.

7. Contractor (1985) has noted that many overseas ventures are being formed as a mix of direct investment, licensing and trade. He adds that the joint-venture partner may be compensated by a package involving some return on equity investments, plus royalties, plus technical service and management fees, plus margins on components or finished product traded with the joint venture.

   Both Schaan (1983) and Beamish (1984 p.39) provide empirical support. In both their LDC-based samples, virtually none of the foreign partners relied solely on dividends for compensation—in fact on average they had nearly two additional sources. In contrast, about one-third of the local partners relied solely on dividends, with the balance having one other source of income.

8. Commitment to the success of joint ventures often varies over time. From the MNE's perspective the level of ongoing commitment may be a function of who in the firm helped set up the joint venture and his current status with the company. See Aharoni (1966) and Beamish (1984).

9. Caves (1982) provides two positive reasons — both of which are consistent with the observations and transactions approach in this study — that cause MNEs to seek out joint ventures. The first of these is the MNE's lack of some capacity or competence needed to make the investment succeed. An obvious case is the MNE diversifying geographically and lacking in managerial know-how for competing in the new market. Another reason lies in the MNE's need for specific resources possessed by local joint-venture partners. These needs include knowledge about local marketing or other environmental conditions. In fact, Stopford and Wells (1972) observed that the major contribution to the MNE of local partners at the time of formation of joint ventures was local knowledge. Joint ventures economize on the information requirements of foreign investment and are thus likely to appeal when these information requirements are most burdensome. Caves adds that joint ventures seem to be prevalent as MNEs proceed toward more unfamiliar host countries, citing Saham's (1980: 150-51) finding that joint ventures are uncommon in culturally familiar LDC settings.

10. In a recent study of joint ventures in the U.S.A., Kogut (1987) found an instability rate as high as that which until now was only observed in LDCs.

11. Concluding that control of the joint venture should not be shared, Killing implies that wholly owned subsidiaries may be more appropriate than joint ventures in the developed countries. That these LDC observations differ from those in developed countries is not inconsistent with the earlier hypothesis. Killing's results suggest that there are relatively lower requirements for adaptation and information for the MNE when it invests in other developed (versus developing) countries. In such a case, the MNE's advantage—firm-specific knowledge of production/marketing—is sufficient. Although not the focus of this paper, it may be that internalization theory can be reconciled to the view that joint ventures by MNEs are less appropriate in developed countries than in LDCs.

REFERENCES

Aharoni, Yair. 1966. *The foreign investment decision process.* Boston: Harvard University.

Alexrod, R.M. 1984. *The evolution of cooperation.* New York: Basic Books.

Artisien, Patrick F.R. & Peter J. Buckley. 1985. Joint-ventures in Yugoslavia: Opportunities and constraints. *Journal of International Business Studies*, Spring 1:111-136.

Beamish, Paul W. 1984. Joint venture performance in developing countries. Unpublished doctoral dissertation, The University of Western Ontario.

———— 1985. The characteristics of joint ventures in developed and developing countries. *Columbia Journal of World Business,* Fall: 13-19.

Berg, Sanford V. & Philip Friedman. 1980. Corporate courtship and successful joint ventures. *California Management Review,* 22 (2): 85-91.

Brams, S.J. & Marc D. Kilgour. 1985. Optimal deterrence. *Social Philosophy and Policy,* 3 (1): 118-135.

Buckley, Peter J. 1985. New forms of international industrial cooperation. In Peter J. Buckley and Mark Casson, eds., *The economic theory of the multinational enterprise.* New York: St. Martin's Press.

———— & Mark Casson. 1976. *The future of the multinational enterprise.* Basingstoke and London: Macmillan.

———— 1985. *The economic theory of the multinational enterprise.* New York: St. Martin's Press.

———— 1987. A theory of co-operation in international business. In Farok J. Contractor & Peter Lorange, *Cooperative strategies in international business.* Lexington, MA: D.C. Heath, forthcoming.

Calvet, A.L. 1981. A synthesis of foreign direct investment theories and theories of the multinational firm. *Journal of International Business Studies,* Spring/Summer, 43-59.

Casson, Mark. 1979. *Alternatives to the multinational enterprise.* London: Macmillan.

———— 1982. Transaction costs and the theory of the multinational enterprise. In Alan M. Rugman, ed., *New theories of the multinational enterprise.* London: Crown Helm. New York: St. Martin's Press.

Caves, Richard E. 1982. *Multinational enterprise and economic analysis.* Cambridge, MA: Cambridge University Press.

Coase, Ronald H. 1952. The nature of the firm. *Economica* (1937): 386-405. Reprinted in G. Stigler and K. Boulding, eds.,*Readings in price theory.* Homewood, IL: Richard D.Irwin.

Contractor, Farok. 1985. A generalized theorem for joint-venture and licensing negotiations. *Journal of International Business Studies,* Summer, 2:23-50.

———— and Peter Lorange. 1987. *Cooperative strategies in international business.* Lexington, MA: D.C. Heath, forthcoming.

Cory, Peter F. 1982. Industrial cooperation, joint ventures and the MNE in Yugoslavia. In Alan M. Rugman, ed., *New theories of the multinational enterprise.* London: Croom Helm.

Davidson, William H. & Donald G. McFetridge. 1985. Key characteristics in the choice of international technology transfer mode. *Journal of International Business Studies,* Summer, 2:5-21.

Dunning, John H. 1958. *American investment in British manufacturing industry.* London: George Allen and Unwin.

———— 1981. *International production and the multinational enterprise.* London: George Allen and Unwin.

———— 1985. The eclectic paradigm of international production: An up-date and a reply to its critics. Department of Economics, University of Reading (mimeo).

———— & Alan M. Rugman. 1985. The influence of Hymer's dissertation on the theory of foreign direct investment. *American Economic Review,* 228-232.

Harrigan, K.R. 1985. *Strategies for joint ventures.* Lexington, MA: D.C. Heath.

Hennart, Jean-Francois. 1982. *A theory of multinational enterprise.* Ann Arbor: University of Michigan Press.

———— 1985. What is internalization? (mimeo).

Hills, Stephen M. 1978. The search for joint venture partners. *Academy of Management Proceedings.*

Horstmann, Ignatius & James R. Markussen. 1986. Licensing versus direct investment: A model of internalization by the multinational enterprise. Department of Economics, University of Western Ontario, London, March (mimeo).

Hymer, Stephen H. 1976. *The international operations of national firms: a study of direct foreign investment.* Cambridge, MA: M.I.T. Press.

———— 1973. Comment by Stephen Hymer (on 'Effects of policies encouraging foreign joint ventures in developing countries' by Wells). In E. Ayal, ed., *Micro aspects of development.* New York: Praeger: 180.

Janger, Allen R. 1980. *Organization of international joint ventures.* New York: The Conference Board.

Killing, J. Peter. 1982 How to make a global joint venture work. *Harvard Business Review,* May-June: 120-127.

———— 1983. *Strategies for joint venture success.* New York: Praeger.

Kogut, Bruce. 1987. Joint ventures: a review and preliminary investigation. In Farok J. Contractor & Peter Lorange, eds., *Co-operative strategies in international business.* Lexington, MA: D.C. Heath, forthcoming.

Kolde, E.J. 1974. *The multinational company.* Toronto: Lexington Books.

Newbould, Gerald D., Peter J. Buckley, & Jane C. Thurwell. 1978. *Going international.* Toronto: John Wiley & Sons.

Parry, Thomas G. 1985. Internalization as a general theory of foreign direct investment: A critique. *Weltwirtschaftliches Archiv,* September.

Poynter, Thomas A. 1985. *Multinational enterprise and government intervention.* New York: St. Martin's Press.

Rugman, Alan M. 1979. *International diversification and the multinational enterprise.* Lexington, MA: D.C. Heath.

_____ 1981. *Inside the multinationals: the economics of internal markets.* London: Croom Helm. New York: Columbia University Press.

_____ 1983 The comparative performance of U.S. and European multi-national enterprises, 1970-79. *Management International Review,* 23: 4-14.

_____ 1985. Internalization is still a general theory of foreign direct investment. *Weltwirtschaftliches Archiv,* September.

Saham, J. 1980. *British industrial investment in Malaysia, 1963-1971.* Kuala Lumpur: Oxford University Press.

Schaan, Jean Louis. 1983. Parent control and joint venture success: The case of Mexico. Unpublished doctoral dissertation, University of Western Ontario.

Stopford, John M. & Louis T. Wells, Jr. 1972. *Managing the multinational enterprise.* New York: Basic Books.

Stuckey, John A. 1983. *Vertical integration and joint ventures in the aluminum industry.* Cambridge, MA: Harvard University Press.

Teece, David J. 1983. Multinational enterprise, internal governance, and industrial organization. *The American Economic Review,* 75 (2), May: 233-238.

_____ 1981. The multinational enterprise: Market failure and market power considerations. *Sloan Management Review,* Spring: 3-17.

Thorelli, Hans B. 1986. Networks: Between markets and hierarchies. *Strategic Management Journal,* 7:37-51.

Tomlinson, James W.C. 1970. *The joint venture process in international business: India and Pakistan.* Cambridge, MA: M.I.T. Press.

Vaupel, James W. & Joan P. Curhan. 1973. *The world's multinational enterprises.* Boston: Harvard University Press.

Wells, Louis T., Jr. 1973. Effects of policies encouraging foreign joint ventures in developing countries. In E. Ayal, ed., *Micro aspects of development.* New York: Praeger.

_____ 1983. *Third world multinationals: The rise of foreign investment from developing countries.* Cambridge, MA: M.I.T. Press.

Williamson, Oliver E. 1975. *Markets and hierarchies: Analysis and antitrust implications — a study in the economics of internal organizations.* New York: Free Press, Macmillan.

_____ 1983. Credible commitments: Using hostages to support exchange. *The American Economic Review,* 73, (4), September: 519-540.

Wright, R.W. 1981. Evolving international business arrangements. In K.C. Dhawan, H. Etemad & R.W. Wright, eds., *International business: A Canadian perspective.* Don Mills, Ontario: Addison-Wesley.

[5]

° *Academy of Management Review*, 1989, Vol. 14, No. 2, 234–249.

Hybrid Arrangements as Strategic Alliances: Theoretical Issues in Organizational Combinations

BRYAN BORYS
Stanford University
DAVID B. JEMISON
University of Texas at Austin

Hybrid organizational arrangements, in which two or more sovereign organizations combine to pursue common interests, raise significant questions for both scholars and managers. A review of previous research yields four key issues—breadth of purpose, boundary determination, value creation, and stability mechanisms—that form the core of a theory of hybrid arrangements. This theory is then used to generate researchable propositions that explore differences among types of hybrids and to offer insights for managers of hybrid organizations.

Observers of the corporate landscape are witnessing an increase in the variety and complexity of organizational forms, many of which represent strategic alliances between organizations, for example, acquisitions, joint ventures, license agreements, research and development (R & D) partnerships, and so forth. These alliances result from strategic and operating moves by firms that have adapted to emerging opportunities as well as those that are repositioning themselves within existing industrial frameworks.

The hybrid arrangements represented by these strategic alliances command our attention for several reasons. From a managerial perspective they are important because they represent alternative ways of expanding a firm's capabilities or bringing about strategic renewal, yet they present different management challenges than those found in a conventional organization. From a theoretical perspective, hybrids are of interest because they have unique characteristics that challenge the capabilities of extant theory to both describe and explain their causes and operation. The purpose of this paper is to explore the uniqueness of these organizational arrangements and to construct a theoretical basis for analyzing them.

First, we define hybrids, illustrating this definition by identifying some common forms and uses and outlining how the unique characteristics of hybrids raise difficult issues for both scholars and managers. Next we present a model that avoids the shortcomings of existing organizational theories by incorporating the common dimensions of hybrids that make them unique organizational forms: This allows us to build a theory of hybrids sui generis. This is followed by a discussion of differences among different hybrid forms that suggest some implications for managers of hybrid organizations.

The Nature of Hybrids

Hybrids are organizational arrangements that use resources and/or governance structures from more than one existing organization. This definition encompasses a broad range of organizational combinations of various sizes, shapes, and purposes, some of which are formal organizations (e.g., mergers), whereas others are formalized relationships that are not properly organizations (e.g., license agreements). The recent proliferation of these organizational forms appears to be more than a minor and temporary change in the organizational landscape. Powell (1988) claimed that simultaneous pressures toward efficiency and flexibility are pushing more and more firms to experiment with hybrid arrangements. Because these pressures are unlikely to abate, researchers and managers need a more solid analytical framework as they study and use hybrids.

This broad definition allows us to examine the multiple purposes of hybrids while focusing on their common elements, a necessity in building a theoretical framework for hybrids (Kaplan, 1964). Although they arise for many reasons, a generic goal of hybrids is to avoid the disadvantages of conventional (unitary) organizations. Unitary organizations often suffer from, among other things, operational inefficiency, resource scarcity, lack of facilities to take advantage of economies of scale, or risks that are more appropriately spread across several business units. Hybrids offer a wide range of solutions to such problems because they draw upon the capabilities of multiple, independent organizations.

Of the universe of hybrid types, we will, for purposes of illustration, focus on five major ones: *Mergers* are the complete unification of two (or more) organizations into a single organization. *Acquisitions* involve the purchase of one organization by another, such that the buyer assumes control over the other. *Joint ventures* result in the creation of a new organization that is formally independent of the parents; control over and responsibility for the venture vary greatly among specific cases. *License agreements* involve the purchase of a right to use an asset for a particular time and offer rapid access to new products, technologies, or innovations. *Supplier arrangements* represent contracts for the sale of one firm's output to another.

Hybrids as Theoretical Orphans

In order to adequately address hybrids, a theory should analyze them in a way peculiar to themselves alone without resorting to theories of particular types (e.g., a theory of mergers, a theory of licensing agreements). The importance of hybrids in competitive strategies demands that a theory identify the qualities that contribute to hybrid survival/success. More generally, a theory should address the multiplicity of issues raised by hybrids, and it should integrate previous research in these areas into a theoretical whole. Existing theory fails on these counts.

The richness of hybrid forms, combined with their distinctive duality, makes them particularly difficult to analyze. A hybrid is simultaneously a single organizational arrangement and a product of sovereign organizations. This conjunctive nature of hybrids and the possibility for multiple levels of analyses call for an open systems approach (Scott, 1987), which allows the researcher to simultaneously address relations among and within organizations. At the same time, however, theories cast at a sufficient level of generalization, for instance, transaction cost analysis (Williamson, 1985), interorganizational relations theory (e.g., Lehman, 1975), and general systems theory (e.g., Boulding, 1956), achieve generality at the expense of the richness of explanation that is required by the variety of issues raised by hybrids. On the other side of the coin is the literature on hybrids, which is sparse (Astley, 1984) and mostly confined to analyses of particular types or isolated disciplinary perspectives (e.g., Killing, 1983).

In one perspective hybrids are viewed as organizational networks—arrangements that are "between markets and hierarchies" (Thorelli, 1986, p. 37). In this view hybrids are seen as networks of relationships of power and trust through which organizations either exchange influence and resources (Thorelli, 1986) or take advantage of economic efficiencies (Jarillo, 1988). In such analyses the network is viewed as an organizational actor, implying that strategic management of the network yields benefits to be distributed among the network members (Astley, 1984).

Network analysis, however, contributes little to our understanding of the determinants of membership in the network, taking for granted the existence of interorganizational fields (Warren, 1967), organizational communities (Astley & Fombrun, 1983), or non-zero-sum market relationships (Jarillo, 1988) that naturally evolve over time (Aldrich & Whetten, 1981). Yet hybrids often are formed to disrupt such naturally occurring industry groups and to gain a competitive advantage over their members, rather than to reinforce them.

More important for hybrid analysis, however, is the failure in network theory to recognize that the hybrid-environment boundary is not the only issue. The boundary between the partners and the hybrid is just as important. Thus, we need to understand not only which organizations will become partners but also which part(s) of each partner will belong to the hybrid.

Setting boundaries for hybrids also raises the issue of how to maintain the resulting relationship over time. Powell's (1988) analysis of the historical factors leading to increased use of hybrids suggests that hybrid stability mechanisms are central to using hybrids to reap the benefits of flexibility and efficiency that give them their competitive advantage. Astley and Fombrun (1983) explored organizational analogues to the biological processes that generate stable cooperative dynamics. Their work focused on the environmental conditions that favor cooperative strategies, and it assumed that organizational self-interest will bind partners in such environments. Much of the early work on interorganizational relations focused on mechanisms that maintain orderly relations among competitive organizations, such as coordinating agencies (Litwak & Hylton, 1962) or industrywide norms (Macaulay, 1963) (see also Benson, 1975; Lehman, 1975; Levine & White, 1961; Pfeffer, 1972). Researchers typically look outside the hybrid for stability mechanisms because hybrid partners often lack the common history necessary to generate such mechanisms internally. Yet because of partner opportunism and the fact that many hybrids are created with short life expectancies, a more robust characterization of hybrid stability is required.

Another perspective on hybrids focuses on the factors that bring two or more organizations together in the first place. Pfeffer, for example, viewed mergers and acquisitions as strategic responses to resource dependencies among organizations (1972; Pfeffer & Nowak, 1976). In a transaction cost perspective (Teece, 1982; Williamson, 1985) hybrids are seen as a way to economize on costly market transactions by incorporating them into a hierarchical framework, or hybrid arrangement. A finance-based analysis focuses on the potential gains from increased access to capital or from diversification (Breeley & Myers, 1981). Others focus on access to technologies (Jemison, 1988) or new markets (Thorelli, 1986). Hybrid theory must, however, move from lists of concrete hybrid purposes to a theory of hybrid purpose.

Uniting around a common purpose is only part of the story; the hybrid must also find a way to achieve that purpose. General organizational theories such as resource dependence (Pfeffer, 1972) and transaction cost analysis (Teece, 1982) do not address the operational issues that often plague hybrids. The difficulties of managing value creation have been studied in certain hybrid types (e.g., acquisitions [Jemison, 1988] and joint ventures [Killing, 1983]). We need, however, to uncover the general characteristics of the process of value creation in hybrids that make achievement of purpose more or less problematic.

Interdepartmental relations theories (for a review, see McCann & Galbraith, 1981) offer some insights into the problems associated with value creation in hybrids, suggesting ways to manage differentiation among partners' attitudes, goals, and perspectives. However, in this perspective an overarching authority is simplistically assumed, and thus it is incorrectly assumed that political coordination problems can be solved through optimal organizational structures, incentives, and procedures. The lack of information and goal consensus that often prevents managers within conventional organizations from applying the insights of interdepartmental relations theory (Pondy, 1970) is magnified in the hybrid case. Moreover, in the interdepartmental relations perspective the existence of a single organizational technology that provides a guide to coordination is assumed. A central problem for hybrids, however, often is the reconciliation of heterogeneous partner operations.

Our review of extant research on hybrids suggests that this work has focused on four major areas in developing a partial understanding of this phenomenon. Even though each area makes important contributions to our understanding of hybrids, each also provides an incomplete picture. These limitations highlight the uniqueness of hybrid theory:

> First, selection of partners is important; yet it is not only the *boundary* between the hybrid and its environment that is important, but also that between each partner and the hybrid.

> Second, in contrast to unitary organizations, hybrids are composed of sovereign organizations whose continued existence may or may not depend on the hybrid's performance; this sovereignty is a constant threat to the *stability* and continuity of the hybrid.

> Third, collaboration among sovereign organizations means that different *purposes* must be reconciled and molded into a common pur-

pose; this means that we need not only a coalitional model of hybrid purpose but also one that recognizes that each partner's commitment to the hybrid's purpose affects the commitments of its own members to its own purpose.

> Fourth, the hybrid often incorporates several technologies. How the partners achieve *value creation* affects, and is affected by, the operational interdependencies among partners as well as by the other elements of the theory.

In the following section we address each of these issues in turn, bringing existing theory to bear and suggesting some propositions for further study of hybrids. This approach leads to a discussion of managing hybrids that integrates these four issues.

A Theory of Hybrids

Hybrid Purpose

Although there is necessarily a common bond that exists before any hybrid is formed, hybrids are still the product of sovereign organizations. It may be convenient to assume that hybrids embody a purpose that is shared by the partners. Yet partners often have different goals, making the resolution of conflicting interests and the maintenance of harmony central to achieving the partners' goals. This harmony and conflict resolution is difficult to achieve because partners often do not share a common environment or domain and, thus, lack a foundation for generating a set of common understandings about the purpose of the hybrid and the process by which that purpose can be achieved. Not only do partners often lack a common domain, but the purpose of the combination may be to actually create that domain. Hybrids have a special need for institutional leadership during formation; this leadership allows them to develop common purpose and understanding (Selznick, 1957).

Although the purpose(s) of organizational combinations have been addressed by scholars in both strategic management and organization theory, neither group has had much to say about the dynamics of hybrid purpose. In his work on mergers and acquisitions, for example, Pfeffer argued that the purpose of combinations is to reduce uncertainty caused by dependency relationships (1972; Pfeffer & Nowak, 1976). In transaction cost theory, it is argued that one purpose of hybrids is to economize on the costs of conducting market exchanges (Teece, 1982; Williamson, 1985). One lesson of the strategy literature, however, is that success often comes form subverting or changing these relationships over time, rather than from following their dictates (Andrews, 1980; Porter, 1985).

The concept of purpose is especially important to hybrid functioning insofar as it provides institutionalized direction that acts as a legitimating mechanism both among and within the partner organizations (Scott, 1987, p. 32). This legitimating function of hybrid purpose makes *breadth* of purpose central both to institutional leadership and to the adjudication of political conflict, and it presents a paradox: Although a broad purpose may provide sufficient "glue" for the hybrid in the face of disagreements over narrow interests, a broad purpose may not provide enough detail to adjudicate among these interests. Conversely, although a narrow and focused purpose allows partners to be clearer about what they expect from each other, it may leave many important fringe issues unaddressed. Moreover, it may prove inertial for the hybrid, preventing it from moving into fruitful, yet not-agreed-upon, areas. For example, a joint venture aimed at entering the Japanese market may become incapacitated because of disputes among partners over issues such as speed of entry, the right vehicle, or relative partner commitment. On the other hand, dedicating a joint venture to gaining a dominant share of U.S. automakers' demand for automated transfer line controls may prevent the venture from capitalizing on alternative strategies that may prove profitable.

Breadth of purpose also offers insight into the relationship between the hybrid and the partner's *internal* dynamics. A focus on hybrid purpose often simplistically assumes a stable internal political, economic, and cultural situation on the part of each partner, so that the partners can treat each other as stable, unitary actors (Allison, 1971). This raises problems for negotiation among partners because negotiators may not be able to guarantee the actions of the organizations they represent. Agency theory offers few insights because according to it the organization is viewed as a unitary actor and not a combination of actors who have the potential for dissension (Fama, 1980). Making a clear organizational commitment to a particular hybrid purpose allows top management to legitimate certain actions to its subordinates by claiming that they are required to achieve the purpose; yet this phenomenon is underresearched.

Breadth of purpose is a critical dimension for developing a theory of hybrids insofar as it affects the nature of hybrid conflict through the way it legitmates agreement among partners at the hybrid level. Moreover, it sheds light on the relations between hybrid and partner at the partner level, identifying one way in which partner management generates hybrid loyalty within the partner organization. Understanding these dynamics is a first step toward understanding hybrids. Table 1 outlines research-oriented propositions regarding hybrid purpose (Propositions 1A–1C).

Boundary Definition

Boundary issues in hybrid arrangements are unique in that not only is the hybrid-environment boundary at issue but also the point at which the partner organizations end and the hybrid begins. Decisions must be made about how much of each partner's resources can be legitimately claimed by the hybrid and to what extent each partner's governance structure has legitimate power over the hybrid. Moreover, although recently formed hybrids may be new in legal or organizational fact, they are different

Table 1
Research Propositions Regarding Hybrid Organizational Arrangements

Purpose

1A. In hybrids in which stated purpose is broader than the actual activities, partners will tend to make unnecessary claims on the hybrid; thus, hybrid resources are likely to be drained off by opportunistic partners.

1B. In hybrids in which stated purpose is narrower than the scope of actual activities, the hybrid will tend to suffer from lack of cooperation from partner employees.

1C. Breadth of hybrid purpose decreases along the following spectrum: mergers and acquisitions, joint ventures, license agreements, supplier arrangements.

Boundaries

2A. The precision of boundary determination agreements is a key factor in hybrid performance.

2B. In hybrids without well-specified boundaries, partners tend to attach some of their obligations to the hybrid, thus lowering hybrid performance by saddling the hybrid with illegitimate demands on its resources.

2C. Boundary determination problems (e.g., disagreements over access to partner's resources and allocation of hybrid resources) are least frequent in mergers and acquisitions, in which ownership creates clear claims to resources and obligations, and in license agreements and supplier arrangements, in which the origin of the hybrid is determined by the solution to boundary issues. They are most frequent in joint ventures, in which the range of potential claims on partner and hybrid resources is more ambiguous.

Value Creation

3A. In hybrids in which the value creation process is poorly understood, partner managers will have different assumptions about and understandings of the hybrid's production process, thus interfering with effective cooperation.

3B. In hybrids with pooled interdependence, value creation problems increase along the following spectrum of shared resources: financial resources, capital equipment, technology, tacit skill (know-how), and human resources.

3C. Hybrids experience more difficulty with management of the value creation process than do unitary organizations with the same type of interdependence.

3D. In hybrids with sequential interdependence, the key to management of the value creation process is the quality of technical and administrative coordination mechanisms between partners (e.g., common production philosophy, production machinery, product specifications, delivery schedules, common recordkeeping).

3E. Under conditions of reciprocal interdependence, value creation will be more likely to occur when there is organizational slack within the hybrid and a reciprocal understanding of other partner organization(s).

Stability

4A. Hybrids of any type that face high levels of uncertainty and require close cooperation (e.g., those that have a broad and evolving purpose, face reciprocal interdependence, or rely on transfer of tacit knowledge) rely more on norms (i.e., culture and socialization) than do hybrids that do not face such uncertainty or require close cooperation.

4B. Because the development of normative ties entails closeness and trust, and because contracts are seldom robust against opportunism, hybrids of any type among partners that continue to compete in some markets rely less on contracts or norms than do noncompeting hybrids.

4C. Mergers and acquisitions, insofar as they are long-term hybrids, rely on hybrid-specific norms (i.e., culture, socialization processes) for stability more than do other types of hybrids.

4D. Joint ventures, which often require cooperation in the face of uncertainty and lack of close relations, rely more on institutions such as superordinate goals or "bilateral hostages" for stability than do other types of hybrids.

4E. License agreements and supplier arrangements, insofar as partner contributions tend to be measurable and specifiable in advance, will rely more on contractual mechanisms than will other types of hybrids.

Mergers and Acquisitions

5A. Managerial issues arising from breadth of purpose, interdependence among partners, and their interactions are the key determinants of performance in mergers and acquisitions.

5B. Acquisitions with reciprocal interdependence (e.g., horizontal acquisitions) are more likely to face boundary permeability difficulties than those with sequential (e.g., vertically integrated acquisitions) or pooled interdependence (e.g., unrelated acquisitions).

5C. Acquisitions with reciprocal interdependence are more likely to use institutional and normative stability mechanisms than those with sequential or pooled interdependence.

5D. The broader the acquisition's purpose, the more legitimate is the acquiring firm's involvement in a wider range of the acquired firm's activities and, thus, the greater the boundary permeability.

Table 1 (continued)
Research Propositions Regarding Hybrid Organizational Arrangements

Joint Ventures

6A. The fit between breadth of stated purpose and actual activities is the key to joint venture performance. When stated purpose is broader than actual activities, partners are susceptible to unnecessary claims on their resources; when stated purpose is narrower than actual activities, partner managements are unable to get their members to cooperate with the hybrid.

6B. Joint ventures (and license agreements, see below) are more likely than other hybrid types to suffer from problems of boundary definition; thus, the precision of boundary definition is a stronger determinant of joint venture performance than of merger, acquisition, or supplier arrangement performance.

6C. Joint ventures involving pooled interdependencies have less permeable boundaries than do those with sequential or reciprocal interdependence.

6D. Joint ventures with less permeable boundaries use contractual stability mechanisms more than do those with greater boundary permeability.

License Agreements

7A. The key elements of performance for a license agreement are the determination of breadth of purpose and the precision of its boundary definition.

7B. Stability in new license agreements is achieved through contracts more than through other means.

7C. The key boundary determination issue for license agreements is the fit between the amount of transfer of tacit knowledge and the degree of boundary permeability.

7D. As a license agreement ages, its performance is more and more determined by its ability to generate hybrid-specific norms as stability mechanisms.

7E. The more important the transfer of tacit knowledge in a license agreement, the more permeable the boundaries of the licensor and licensee must be for the hybrid to succeed.

Supplier Arrangements

8A. The primary determinant of success in supplier arrangements is management of boundary permeability and the value creation process.

8B. The performance of supplier arrangements is determined primarily by its ability to create and manage reciprocal interdependencies between supplier and buyer.

8C. New supplier arrangements use contracts more than other mechanisms for achieving stability.

8D. As supplier arrangements age, they rely more on hybrid-specific norms than on contracts as stability mechanisms.

from start-ups because they have an immediate size and presence. Hybrid partners already have acquired assets (e.g., human, physical, and financial) and have made commitments to a variety of external constituencies. These commitments may or may not be carried into the hybrid, and they may create constraints on or offer opportunities to the hybrid.

Identification of the resources and obligations that both are and are not part of the hybrid highlights the issue of boundary *permeability*. The key question is: What is the degree and nature of the permeability of the hybrid boundary; what elements—resources, authority, obligations—are allowed to cross it? Extant theory only partly informs this question. In transactions cost analysis (Williamson, 1985) it is suggested that per-

meability is determined by, all other things being equal, the relative costs of handling a particular element through the hybrid or through one of the partners. Thus, transaction cost analysis offers a rigorous post hoc discussion of the criteria for boundary definition, yet it has little to say about how to identify important factors ex ante or about organizational dysfunctions associated with boundary permeability.

Elements of organizational culture, for example, play a role in defining boundaries by creating barriers to entry of human resources. One function of stories that illustrate the uniqueness of the organization is to allow members to differentiate themselves as a group from other organizations (Martin, Feldman, Hatch, & Sitkin, 1983). Such differentiation can encourage cohesion among hybrid members and allow them to transcend their parochial loyalties to the partner and act in concert for the good of the hybrid. Of course, human resources are not the only resource around which the hybrid must draw boundaries. Partners in joint ventures designed to achieve technology transfer, for instance, often encounter difficulty agreeing on the extent of the supplier's technological know-how to be transferred (Doz, Hamel, & Prahalad, 1986).

The key issue of boundary definition, therefore, is how the hybrid determines which resources and obligations belong to it and which do not. In this light, boundary definition has two important effects. First, it determines both the resources available to the hybrid and the legitimacy of partners' claims on those resources, thus affecting its purpose. It also affects the cohesiveness of hybrid members and, thus, the hybrid's ability to achieve a given purpose. Table 1 contains researchable propositions to explore these issues, suggesting conditions in which boundary determination is crucial for hybrid success and placing boundary determination in the context of hybrid purpose and hybrid types (Propositions 2A–2C).

Value Creation

Hybrids are established for a variety of reasons relating to the inability of one of the partners to solve an important problem. Hybrids such as marketing agreements, technology transfer agreements, and some acquisitions often face the possibility that the purpose for which the hybrid was established will be prevented by unforeseen circumstances. Hybrid management is seldom as straightforward as expected because partners often lack reciprocal understanding of the other's operations, and, therefore, resistance arises from unexpected sources (Jemison, 1988). *Value creation,* as used here, refers to the process by which the capabilities of the partners are combined so that the competitive advantage of either the hybrid or one or more of the partners is improved. Thus,

value creation is a joint effort that occurs after the hybrid is formed, and the operational problems that plague collaboration are central in both hybrid theory and management.

The common theme among these issues is that the hybrid creates value in a way that each of the partners alone could not. The need for cooperation raises the problem of how to coordinate different operations, production philosophies, administrative systems, and so forth. We use Thompson's (1967) typology of technological interdependence to highlight the key aspects of this issue.

Hybrids with *pooled interdependence* are those in which the hybrid provides a common pool of resources from which each of the partners can draw. In such cases, the requirements of fit are simply that each partner can make use of the resources in the pool. In financially motivated hybrids, for example, operational issues have little importance because in them financial resources are more easily transferable and usable in many different ways. In R & D joint ventures, on the other hand, organizations will be reluctant to join unless they can be certain that the fruits of the venture will be applicable to their operations.

In hybrids with *sequential interdependence,* one partner "hands off" to another (e.g., a supplier arrangement); the key issue is ensuring a fit between the points of contact. Here hybrids face not only technical problems, such as providing detailed enough product specifications to ensure fit among components produced by different partners, but also administrative problems, such as altering delivery schedules.

Reciprocally interdependent hybrids, in which partners exchange outputs between each other and need to learn from each other (e.g., in acquisition in which tacit skills are expected to be transferred), raise a third set of issues. The nature of the hybrid purpose that requires reciprocal interdependence generally calls for fit between a wider range of partner operations than the other types. Because this fit often cannot be

241

precisely specified ex ante, it must evolve through partner interaction, making organizational slack and flexibility during start-up key issues.

Thus, the interdependence of partners in the hybrid's value creation process determines whether normal operations management is sufficient, whether special guarantees are required (e.g., product specifications), or whether, indeed, such guarantees are specifiable ex ante or must emerge over time. This complexity is magnified in practice as hybrid managers often modify their operations to suit new purposes— or even to encourage development of new purposes. Moreover, guarantees of fit between sequentially or reciprocally interdependent units often are inseparable from boundary determination issues. Research on the value creation process in hybrids has only begun to unravel these factors.

Breakdowns of the value creation process stemming from problems in managing interdependencies must be identified because such problems often are masked by lack of familiarity with the other firm, distrust, and misunderstanding. Table 1 presents researchable propositions that suggest these contingencies wherein these problems might be found (Propositions 3A–3E).

Hybrid Stability

The problem of maintaining stability over time is a final issue that must be addressed by hybrid theory. The permanence imputed to organizations by lay observers (Zucker, 1983) is not guaranteed for hybrids; in fact, hybrid arrangements often are used because they do *not* require permanent commitments from the partners. Nevertheless, stakeholders generally demand that performance in a new hybrid be similar to that of an established, permanent organization (Jemison, 1988), and they seldom allow the sort of honeymoon period of less stringent performance requirements generally experienced in other kinds of new enterprise, such as start-ups (Selznick, 1957; Tichy, 1983). These demands

raise special problems for hybrids because the mechanisms that provide stability in conventional organizations develop slowly, and partner sovereignty provides a constant strain on hybrid unity. In addressing the question of how (or whether) to maintain the hybrid over time, we take as our starting point the well-known distinction between markets and hierarchies.

Williamson's (1975) market and hierarchies scheme provides our initial characterization of stability alternatives: market-mediated contracts versus organizationally grounded authority. Recent work has extended this notion, recognizing that some market relations have hierarchical characteristics (Granovetter, 1987; Stinchcombe, 1985), and, thus, suggesting that the distinction between contract and hierarchy in hybrids is also one of degree (Thorelli, 1986).

In applying this idea to hybrids, however, we must also recognize that recourse to hierarchical mechanisms is different for hybrids than for unitary organizations. Traditional organization theories propose that a conventional organization achieves stability by instituting rules, procedures, and roles that create expectations of stability and dependability among members and stakeholders (Weber, 1946). Organizational institutions arise from the rational adoption of routines (Nelson & Winter, 1982), from acceptance of standard operating procedures (Cyert & March, 1963), or from authority that is taken for granted (Zucker, 1977). A network of institutionalized expectations provides a stable reference point from which organizational members can coordinate their actions.

From a cultural perspective, the power of organizational institutions to provide stability is rooted in shared norms and values (Schein, 1985). However, it may be that sharing per se is not the key to stability (Martin & Meyerson, 1986). The underlying source of cultural cohesion may result from members' expectations that they will be dealt with fairly, which encourages them to submit to organizational authority (Wilkins & Ouchi, 1983, p. 476). This latter formulation suggests that legitimacy and trust are key to nonmarket mechanisms of hybrid stability (Jarillo, 1988). Hybrids, however, often cannot capitalize on such reservoirs of authority and trust because their members lack a common history. Moreover, because some hybrids are not expected to continue over time, their members do not engage in the sorts of behaviors that generate legitimate authority and trust.

A second type of stability mechanism is represented by practices that are common to an industry or economic sector. Although such practices lack the normative force of shared values and legitimate authority, they do create stable expectations among hybrid members. As such, they often are adopted by many organizations whose managers recognize their practical utility and wish to avoid violating standard practices, even though these may not be normatively binding (Macaulay, 1963).

Levine and White (1961), for example, assumed the existence of an outside organization that directs the actions of other organizations. Although applicable in certain cases, such as acquisitions and some forms of cartel, many hybrids lack a strong, central partner. Facing a common outside threat may lead to coordination among organizations (Cummings, 1984). However, we should not overestimate the power of mutual interest to generate cooperation in competitive settings (Axelrod, 1984; Schelling, 1960). Even in situations of mutual advantage, some partners may be able to profit at the expense of other partners, threatening the stability of the hybrid (Doz et al., 1986). Some partners ensure hybrid stability either by tying each partner's parochial interests to the hybrid's success or by exchanging "bilateral hostages," such as key personnel or capital equipment (Kogut & Rolander, 1984). Such practices are easier to undertake than the generation of normatively binding agreements such as organizational culture, but they lack the power of the latter mechanisms.

A third mechanism for stability is the contract, which is guaranteed by forces outside the hy-

brid (e.g., the courts). One benefit of these mechanisms is that the institutions of contract and exchange that make them possible are generalized throughout the economy and, thus, are readily available and understood by the hybrid partners—although some multicultural hybrids provide important exceptions (Granovetter, 1987). The cost of such available and simple institutions, however, is their lack of flexibility and richness; the shortcomings of contractual transactions are well known in economics (Williamson, 1975, 1985), sociology (Granovetter, 1985), and organization theory (Ouchi, 1980). Contracting problems raised by opportunism and information asymmetries are exacerbated in hybrids; moreover, contracts are problematic in mergers, acquisitions, and some joint ventures in which partner obligations are designed to change over time and, thus, cannot be predicted ex ante (Harrigan, 1985).

Thus, hybrid stability can be achieved by shared norms and expectations of justice, by the adoption of common and general practices, or by relying on extrahybrid institutions, such as the legal system, for enforcement of hybrid contracts. Each of these has disadvantages: Although hybrid-specific norms are powerful and can be quite flexible, they are difficult to develop. Hybrid-specific institutions are more readily available, but they are notoriously weak against opportunisitic partners. Contracts are difficult to specify under conditions of uncertainty for which hybrid arrangements are otherwise particularly well suited. Table 1 presents a series of propositions that explore the nature and form of hybrid stability mechanisms (Propositions 4A–4E).

Generating Insights into Hybrid Management

Our exploration of the uniqueness of hybrid organizations and the theoretical issues they raise suggests that hybrids need not be theoret-

243

ical orphans. Our theory allows both scholars and managers to consider hybrids in a class of their own and at the same time to link the model with previous research. The above discussion has shown that, although unitary organizations face the same set of four issues, hybrids face them in different ways because of the need to share resources and governance structures from sovereign organizations; extant theory falls short of addressing this problem. In this section, we extend this theoretical exploration, identifying some important managerial issues and additional propositions for research.

We have made it clear that the four issues in our model—breadth of purpose, boundary permeability, value creation, and stability mechanisms—are mutually determinant and highly interdependent. We have discussed some of the more important interrelationships in our treatment of the individual issues above. For example, we discussed how hybrid purpose can lend legitimacy to claims on partner resources, thereby increasing boundary permeability, and we have discussed how, vice-versa, boundaries determine membership, thus restricting the range of participants in debates over purpose.

Our discussion of these issues was necessarily abstract because of the prior lack of a theory of hybrids. In what follows, we show that in addition to its contribution to theory building, this model offers insights into the managerial challenges presented by different types of hybrids. We will discuss these challenges in light of the five types of hybrids we used as examples, illustrating in more detail the differences among hybrid types.

Mergers and acquisitions. The central issues in analyses of mergers and acquisitions are type of interdependence and breadth of purpose, which, in turn, determine the extent of boundary permeability and stability mechanisms. The greater the reciprocal interdependence between the firms, the more permeable their boundaries must be to facilitate this close interaction and the greater their need for institutional

forms of stability because contracts cannot guarantee the fulfillment of complex and potentially ambiguous performances. The less interdependent, the more a contractual form of stability becomes useful (e.g., a conglomerate).

The more interdependent the partners in an acquisition, the greater the need for boundary permeability. A long history of organizational research has demonstrated the importance of matching responsibility with authority. We can extend this to the hybrid case by hypothesizing that in successful acquisitions hybrid managers will have authority over those resources and obligations associated with reciprocally interdependent activities. As a corollary, we suggest that the broader the purpose of the acquisition, the more potentially permeable are the boundaries of the acquired firm because the acquirer has a claim to a broader set of capabilities (Haspeslagh & Farquahar, 1987).

We suggested above that mergers and acquisitions rely more on hybrid-specific norms than on other types of stability mechanisms. Here we add that, other things being equal, the broader the purpose, the greater the reliance on normative ties since they are more flexible and can maintain a wider set of relations than can hybrid institutions or contracts. In such close relationships, stability mechanisms and boundaries will change over time, moving toward greater reliance on normative stability and greater boundary permeability. These changes should reveal new possibilites for the merger, and they should lead managers to revise old purposes and discover new ones (March, 1978). Thus, we recognize the interaction between strategy content and strategic processes (Jemison, 1981). We also argue for development of a better understanding of the dynamics of purpose in hybrids, one that transcends simplistic and static notions of strategic fit (Jemison & Sitkin, 1986).

Acquisitions are different from mergers in several important ways, some of which make breadth of purpose particularly salient. One firm is often dominant regarding size and other dimensions. Therefore, a key issue in an acquisition is how to allocate control among the firms. In addition, the management of boundary permeability is important if the purpose of the acquisition is to transfer capabilities and the capability must be preserved (Haspeslagh & Farquahar, 1987). Table 1 presents several propositions regarding acquisitions in light of our theory (Propositions 5A–5D).

Joint ventures are the most difficult of all hybrid arrangements to characterize because they are simultaneously contractual agreements between two or more organizations and a separate legal (and usually organizational) entity with its own purpose. Despite the inherent necessity for collaboration, joint venture partners retain organizational sovereignty, thus maintaining differentiation within the hybrid that may hamper cooperation. This problem, combined with the wide range of forms of joint ventures, prevents a simple characterization of the key analytic issues. Here, we indicate the major interconnections among the four elements of hybrid theory, illustrating what effects purpose and value creation have on boundaries and how boundaries and the difficulties of managing them make stability mechanisms important.

Because joint ventures typically are formed by partners that remain independent, partner managers often face difficulties in motivating their employees to cooperate with hybrid management. In response, hybrid managers invoke the hybrid's purpose to legitimate their claims upon partner employees. We can contrast this case with that of mergers and acquisitions, in which hybrid management often has greater organizational authority to back up such claims than it does in a joint venture; whereas in a license agreement or supplier arrangement, the need for collaboration often is not as high as in a joint venture. Thus, the ability of hybrid management to make legitimate claims on partner employees and resources is particularly salient for joint ventures, and it provides an important motivational force.

Purpose clearly affects boundary permeability, as well. The relationship between each partner and the joint venture is not bound by clear-cut institutions of ownership, as in mergers and acquisitions, or by contract, as in license agreements and supplier arrangements. Moreover, a joint venture often is an evolving collaboration. Thus, the nature of its hybrid-partner boundaries is constantly open to debate, and the legitimating effects of hybrid purpose are key to proper determination of these boundaries.

Hybrid boundaries also are affected by the partner interdependencies involved in the value creation process. Although joint ventures often are created with the intent of keeping the venture separate from the partner organizations, those with more complex forms of interdependence (sequential or reciprocal) require greater boundary permeability in order to ensure proper coordination.

Yet this degree of permeability is very difficult to specify contractually ex ante. Moreover, the close collaboration typically found in joint ventures requires that the joint venture develop its own identity and institutions. In fact, partner involvement intended either to help the venture or to restrict its activities often threatens its ability to accomplish its purpose.

Thus, the joint venture's purpose and the nature of its value creation affect its boundaries, the determination of which is a key issue for such a flexible organizational form. This dynamic process, as well as the nature of the partner-joint venture relationship, makes institutionalized forms of stability prominent. Table 1 contains propositions that explore these insights into joint ventures (Propositions 6A–6D).

License agreements, that is, agreements by which one firm buys the right to use an asset for a period of time (e.g., a particular production process, a patent on a device), typically involve a narrow purpose and limited time frame, and are enforced by a contract. The licensor receives a source of royalties and revenues with little additional investment and a return on prior R & D expenditures. Likewise, the licensee is able to lever its activities (e.g., increase its market coverage or overcome a weakness by using someone else's R & D or product development). Licensors often manipulate the boundaries of the agreement to their own advantage by allowing certain innovations to cross the boundary, thereby encouraging the licensee to continue the agreement, and by withholding others.

Interdependence is usually pooled (both parties using the same asset), rather than reciprocal, in such hybrids, leading to little need for extensive operational fit. Some license agreements, however, do allow the licensor access to any technology developed by the licensee through use of the asset (e.g., using a particular production process may generate new capabilities), raising significant operational issues, and in turn, affecting determination of hybrid-partner boundaries.

License agreements may lead to other forms of collaboration, as firms increase their knowledge of each other through interaction. But initially, the central issue is specification of purpose through contractual terms (after the initial process of selecting a licensee with the capability to exploit the right once it is licensed). Because license agreements tend to be unstable due to competition, changing technology, and relative rates of partner learning (Doz et al., 1986), the importance of stability mechanisms increases over time. Despite the relative inflexibility of contracts, license agreements tend to rely on them in the absence of the close and broad collaboration required to make other mechanisms feasible. Table 1 presents propositions regarding license agreements based on the previous discussion (Propositions 7A–7E).

Supplier arrangements can be characterized as contractual agreements to provide a particular type or line of goods or services within a specific time frame. Interdependence is usually sequential, with the supplier fitting its piece into the production process of the buyer. Typically, boundary permeability of the supplier must allow inspection of processes to ensure product quality, manufacturing capability, and delivery reliability. In addition, the buyer's boundary must allow the supplier to develop the product to fit the appropriate technical specifications and delivery schedule.

Over time, though, many firms develop more sophisticated supplier arrangements in which reciprocal interdependence becomes strategically important, purpose broadens, and stability mechanisms become institutionally based as well as contractual. Examples of this are Marks and Spencer in the United Kingdom, Benetton in Italy, and many Japanese firms. In these situations, the suppliers have become an integral part of the firm's entire production process, and they work closely with the firm to make suggestions about improving product quality, new materials, new production processes, and so forth. Although contracts still guide production, product specification, and delivery schedules, suppliers in these arrangements have adopted institutional norms that encourage action on behalf of the entire hybrid. Table 1 presents propositions designed to explore these insights (Propositions 8A–8D).

Conclusion

The pressures firms face to renew their capabilities, to enter new product-market arenas, to deal with resource constraints, and to develop internationally often are well met by hybrid arrangements. These arrangements, in turn, pose new and important challenges to researchers and managers alike. For managers, hybrids are becoming more important as strategic options, yet they are a phenomenon for which managers' past experiences and cognitive maps have not adequately prepared them. For researchers, hybrids challenge existing theory to explain the peculiar dynamics of hybrid purpose, boundaries, value creation, and stability.

Traditional organizational and strategic management theories offer some insights, but they are limited in their applicability to the case of hybrids because they deal with unitary organizations and, therefore, do not address the unique problems raised by an organizational entity composed of two or more sovereign organizations. Although previous attempts at characterizing hybrids have generated some powerful ideas, organizational research has lacked a systematic theoretical framework for hybrid analysis.

Our response to this problem has been to develop a model capable of exploring these issues, and to demonstrate some of the insights it generates. These are centered on four concepts: the breadth of hybrid purpose and the claims and plans that it legitimates, the permeability of hybrid-partner boundaries and the resources and obligations allowed to cross them, the interde-

pendence of partner operations in the value creation process and the complexity of the arrangements required to manage it, and the nature of the hybrid's stability mechanisms. Not only is each of these issues significant in its own right, but we have also demonstrated that understanding the interactions among them offers insights into hybrids. The ambiguity and complexity of the issues raised by hybrid organizations should not deter scholars from pursuing the important questions they raise. We hope that the perspective presented in this paper has provided a first step toward generating a deeper understanding of this increasingly pervasive organizational phenomenon.

References

Aldrich, H. E., & Whetten, D. A. (1981) Organization-sets, action sets, and networks: Making the most of simplicity. In P. C. Nystrom & W. H. Starbuck (Eds.), *Handbook of organizational design* (Vol. 1, pp. 345–408). New York: Oxford University Press.

Allison, G. T. (1971) *Essence of decision.* Boston: Little, Brown.

Andrews, K. R. (1980) *The concept of corporate strategy.* Homewood, IL: Irwin.

Astley, W. G. (1984) Toward an appreciation of collective strategy. *Academy of Management Review,* 9, 526–535.

Astley, W. G., & Fombrun, C. J. (1983) Collective strategy: Social ecology of organizational environments. *Academy of Management Review,* 8, 576–587.

Axelrod, R. M. (1984) *The evolution of cooperation.* New York: Basic Books.

Benson, J. K. (1975) The interorganizational network as a political economy. *Administrative Science Quarterly,* 20, 229–249.

Boulding, K. E. (1956) General systems theory: The skeleton of science. *Management Science,* 2, 197–208.

Breeley, R., & Myers, S. (1981) *Principles of corporate finance.* New York: McGraw-Hill.

Cummings, T. G. (1984) Transorganizational development. *Research in Organizational Behavior,* 6, 367–422.

Cyert, R. M., & March, J. G. (1963) *A behavioral theory of the*

firm. Englewood Cliffs, NJ: Prentice-Hall.

Doz, Y., Hamel, G., & Prahalad, C. K. (1986) *Strategic partnerships: Success or surrender?* Unpublished manuscript, INSEAD, Fountainebleau, France.

Fama, E. F. (1980) Agency problems and the theory of the firm. *Journal of Law and Economics,* 88, 288–307.

Granovetter, M. (1985) Economic action and social structure: The problem of embeddedness. *American Journal of Sociology,* 91, 481–510.

Granovetter, M. (1987) *Society and economy.* Unpublished manuscript.

Harrigan, K. R. (1985) *Strategies for joint ventures.* Lexington, MA: Lexington Books.

Haspeslagh, P. C., & Farquahar, A. (1987) *Managing acquisition integration: The gatekeeping role.* Working Paper, INSEAD, Fountainebleau, France.

Jarillo, J. C. (1988) On strategic networks. *Strategic Management Journal,* 9, 34–41.

Jemison, D. B. (1981) The contributions of administrative behavior to strategic management. *Academy of Management Review,* 6, 633–642.

Jemison, D. B. (1988) Value creation in acquisition integration: The role of strategic capability transfer. In G. Liebcap (Ed.), *Corporate restructuring through mergers, acquisitions and leveraged buyouts* (pp. 191–218). Greenwich, CT: JAI Press.

Jemison, D. B., & Sitkin, S. B. (1986) Corporate acquisitions:

A process perspective. *Academy of Management Review*, 11, 145–163.

Kaplan, A. (1964) *The conduct of inquiry*. New York: Chandler.

Killing, J. P. (1983) *Strategies for joint venture success*. New York: Praeger.

Kogut, B., & Rolander, D. (1984) *Stabilizing cooperative ventures: Evidence from the telecommunications and auto industry*. Working Paper WP 84–11, The Wharton School, University of Pennsylvania.

Lehman, E. W. (1975) A paradigm for the analysis of interorganizational relations. In E. W. Lehman (Ed.), *Coordinating health care: Explorations in interorganizational relations* (Vol. 17, pp. 24–30). Beverly Hills, CA: Sage.

Levine, S., & White, P. E. (1961) Exchange as a conceptual framework for the study of interorganizational relationships. *Administrative Science Quarterly*, 5, 583–601.

Litwak, E., & Hylton, L. F. (1962) Interorganizational analysis: A hypothesis on coordinating agencies. *Administrative Science Quarterly*, 6, 395–420.

Macaulay, S. (1963) Non-contractual relations in business: A preliminary study. *American Sociological Review*, 28, 55–69.

March, J. G. (1978) Bounded rationality, ambiguity, and the engineering of choice. *Bell Journal of Economics*, 9, 578–608.

Martin, J., Feldman, M. S., Hatch, J. J., & Sitkin, S. B. (1983) The uniqueness paradox in organizational stories. *Administrative Science Quarterly*, 28, 438–453.

Martin, J., & Meyerson, D. (1986) *Organizational cultures and the denial, channeling, and acceptance of ambiguity*. Working Paper 807R, Graduate School of Business, Stanford University.

McCann, J., & Galbraith, J. R. (1981) Interdepartmental relations. In P. Nystrom & W. Starbuck (Eds.), *Handbook of organizations* (Vol. 2, pp. 60–84). New York: Oxford University Press.

Nelson, R. R., & Winter, S. G. (1982) *An evolutionary theory of economic change*. Cambridge, MA: Belknap Press.

Ouchi, W. G. (1980) Markets, bureaucracies and clans. *Administrative Science Quarterly*, 25, 129–141.

Pfeffer, J. (1972) Merger as a response to organizational interdependence. *Administrative Science Quarterly*, 17, 382–394.

Pfeffer, J., & Nowak, P. (1976) Joint ventures and interorganizational interdependence. *Administrative Science Quarterly*, 21, 398–418.

Pondy, L. R. (1970) Toward a theory of internal resource allocation. In M. Zald (Ed.), *Power in organizations* (pp. 270–311). Nashville, TN: Vanderbilt University.

Porter, M. E. (1985) *Competitive advantage: Creating and sustaining superior performance*. New York: Free Press.

Powell, W. W. (1987) Hybrid organizational arrangements. *California Management Review*, 30(1), 67–87.

Schein, E. (1985) *Organizational culture and leadership*. San Francisco: Jossey-Bass.

Schelling, T. C. (1960) *The strategy of conflict*. Cambridge, MA: Harvard University Press.

Scott, W. R. (1987) *Organizations: Rational, natural and open systems*. Englewood Cliffs, NJ: Prentice-Hall.

Selznick, P. (1967) *Leadership in administration*. New York: Harper & Row.

Stinchcombe, A. L. (1985) Contracts as hierarchical documents. In A. L. Stinchcombe & C. A. Heiner (Eds.), *Organization theory and project management* (pp. 121–170). London: Oxford University Press.

Teece, D. J. (1982) Towards an economic theory of the multiproduct firm. *Journal of Economic Behavior and Organization*, 3, 39–63.

Thompson, J. D. (1967) *Organizations in action*. New York: McGraw-Hill.

Thorell, H. B. (1986) Networks: Between markets and hierarchies. *Strategic Management Journal*, 7, 37–51.

Tichy, N. M. (1983) *Managing strategic change: Technical, political and cultural dynamics*. New York: Wiley-Interscience.

Warren, R. L. (1967) The interorganizational field as a focus for investigation. *Administrative Science Quarterly*, 12, 396–419.

Weber, M. (1946) *From Max Weber: Essays in sociology*. London: Oxford University Press.

Wilkins, A. L., & Ouchi, W. G. (1983) Efficient cultures: Exploring the relationship between culture and organizational performance. *Administrative Science Quarterly*, 28, 468–481.

Williamson, O. E. (1975) *Markets and hierarchies, analysis and antitrust implications: A study in the economics of internal organization*. New York: Free Press.

Williamson, O. E. (1985) *The economic institutions of capitalism*. New York: Free Press.

Zucker, L. G. (1977) The role of institutionalization in cultural persistance. *American Sociological Review*, 42, 726–743.

Zucker, L. G. (1983) Organizations as institutions. *Research in the Sociology of Organizations*, 2, 1–47.

Bryan Borys is a doctoral candidate in Organizational Behavior at the Graduate School of Business, Stanford University.

David B. Jemison (Ph.D., University of Washington) is Associate Professor of Management at the Graduate School of Business, University of Texas. Correspondence regarding this paper should be sent to him at the Department of Management, Graduate School of Business, University of Texas at Austin, Austin, TX 78712.

We would like to thank Jerry Davis and Sim Sitkin for helpful comments on earlier drafts of this paper. A version of this paper was presented at the 1988 Academy of Management Meeting in Anaheim.

[6]

P. J. Buckley / M. Casson*

A Theory of Co-Operation in
International Business**

The Concept of Cooperation

To what extent are "cooperative ventures" really cooperative? What exactly is meant by cooperation in this context? In international business, the term cooperative venture is often used merely to signify some alternative to 100 per cent equity ownership of a foreign affiliate: it may indicate a joint venture, an industrial collaboration agreement, licensing, franchising, subcontracting, or even a management contract or counter-trade agreement. It is quite possible, of course, to regard such arrangements as cooperative by definition, but this fudges the substantive issue of just how cooperative these arrangements really are.

If not all cooperative ventures are truly cooperative, the what distinguishes the cooperative ones from the rest? To answer this question it is necessary to provide a rigorous definition of cooperation. This paper, attempts to distill, from the common-sense notion of cooperation, those aspechts which are of the greatest economic relevance. It is not intended, however, to pre-empt the use of the word "cooperation" for one specific concept. There is a spectrum of concepts – variously known as cooperation, collaboration, copartnership, and so on – and a diversity of fields of application – employee-ownership of firms, inter-governmental collaboration in economic policy, and so on; several different concepts will be needed to do full justice to the complex issues raised by cooperative behaviour in the broadest meaning of that term.

Because the manifestations of cooperative behaviour are so wide-ranging, it is desirable, within the scope of a single paper, to restrict attention to a single case. The 50-50 equity joint venture (JV) has been chosen. It is argued that while genuine cooperation is a feature of some JVs, adversarial elements can be present too, and in some cases can dominate. The factors which govern the degree of cooperation are delineated. The organisational structure of the venture and the extent and nature of the other ventures in which the participants are involved turn out to be crucial. It is potentially misleading to analyse a joint venture in isolation from other ventures, for the extent of cooperation in

---

*Professor Peter J. Buckley, Management Centre, University of Bradford, Bradford, Professor Mark Casson, Department of Economics, University of Reading, Reading, England. Manuscript received March 1987.

any one venture is strongly influenced by the overall configuration of the ventures in which the parties are involved.

Coordination

The definition of cooperation advocated here is "coordination effected through mutual forbearance". This identifies cooperation as a special type of coordination. Coordination is defined as effecting a Pareto-improvement in the allocation of resources, such that someone is made better off, and no-one worse off, than they would otherwise be. Coordination is an appropriate basis upon which to build a concept of cooperation, for it articulates the idea that cooperation is of mutual benefit to the parties directly involved (Casson, 1982).

Coordination sounds as if it must always be a good thing, but the following points should be noted about the way that the concept is applied in practice.

The externality problem. Coordination is defined with respect to all parties who are in any way affected by a venture, and not just those who join in voluntarily. Those who join presumably expect to benefit, but others who do not join may lose as a result. Sometimes the losers have legal rights which can be used to block the venture, or they can organise themselves into a club to compensate the beneficiaries for not going ahead. But when there are many non-privileged losers, who have difficulty organising themselves, it is quite possible that a venture may go ahead even though the losers, as a group, suffer more than the beneficiaries gain.

Coordination under duress. Coordination is defined with respect to an alternative position – namely what would otherwise happen – so that what is assumed about this alternative position is crucial in determining whether coordination occurs. A voluntary participant may decide to join a venture simply because he is in such an adverse position that the alternative to joining would be absolute disaster.

In some cases the adversity may be deliberately contrived by others – in particular, by other participants anxious to increase their bargaining power. Even where the adversity has not been contrived, other participants may still seek to take advantage of the unattractive nature of the alternatives available to the party concerned. A related point is that where adversity stems from a recent set-back, the party may expect coordination to return him to a position as good as his original one, and he may regard as exploitative any terms which fail to do this.

Empty threats and disappointments. It is a party's perception of the outcome of a venture, and of the alternative position, that governs his decision whether or not to join. These perceptions are subjective, in the sense that they depend upon the information available to the participant, and can vary, within the same situation, between one person and another. Expectations can be erroneous, so that a venture which effects coordination *ex ante* may turn out not to do so *ex post*. Astuté individuals or managements may be able to influence the expectations of others to their own advantage. One participant may threaten another participant that if he does not join in on onerous terms he will act to make the other participant's alternative position considerably worse than it would otherwise be. It is quite possible, therefore, for a participant to join a venture under a threat which subsequently turns out to have been empty and, either for this reason of for some other, to later regret having joined at all.

Autonomy of preferences. In conventional applications of the concept of coordination, it is assumed that a party's objectives are unchanged by involvement in a coordinating venture. This assumption is relaxed when introducing the concept of commitment later on.

Many economists consider it methodologically unsound to introduce endogeneity of preferences in this way, but in the present context there are good reasons for doing so. Not everyone is likely to be convinced of its necessity, however.

Inter-firm coordination

Coordination applies first and foremost to people rather than to firms. In certain cases, however, a firm can be regarded as a person, as when it consists of a single individual who acts as owner, manager and worker. In large firms, of course, these various functions are specialised with different individuals. The firm then becomes an institutional framework for coordinating the efforts of different people working together. This exemplifies *intra-firm* coordination. The focus of this paper, however, is on *inter-firm* coordination, in which one firm coordination, in which one firm coordinates with another. It is analytically useful to separate the intra-firm and inter-firm aspects of coordination by assuming that inter-firm coordination takes place between single-person firms of the kind described above. Subject to this qualification, inter-firm coordination may be defined as an increase in the profits of some firms that is achieved without a reduction in the profits of others.

It is also important to distinguish inter-firm coordination from *extra-firm* coordination, which is coordination effected between firms on the one hand and households on the other. Extra-firm coordination is exemplified by trade in final product markets and factor markets. Because of externalities of the kind described above, certain types of inter-firm coordination can damage extra-firm coordination to the point where coordination within the economy as a whole is reduced. It is well known, for example, that when firms collude to raise the price within an industry to a monopolistic level, the additional profit accruing to the firms is less than the loss of consumer welfare caused by the higher prices and the associated curtailment of demand. Because the consumers are usually more numerous than the firms, it is difficult for them to organise effective opposition to this. Thus when inter-firm coordination is motivated by collusion, even though the firms gain, the economy as a whole may be a loser.

Forbearance

All the parties involved in a venture have an inalienable *de facto* right to pursue their own interests at the expense of others. It is one of the hall-marks of institutional economics – and transaction cost economics in particular – that it recognises the widespread implications of this. It can manifest itself in two main ways: *aggression* and *neutrality*. An aggressive party perpetrates some act that damages another party's interests, whilst a neutral party behaves more passively: he simply refrains from some act that would benefit someone else. In either case, the party is deemed to *cheat*; if he refrains from cheating he is said to *forbear*. Often both options are available: the party can either *commit* a damaging act, or merely *omit* to perform a beneficial one. Under such conditions, neutrality is regarded as *weak cheating* and aggression as *strong cheating*.

Forbearance and cheating can take place between parties that have no formal connection with each other. They also occur in the establishment of a venture. To fix ideas, this paper focuses on the problem of sustaining a venture once operations have commenced. It is assumed that at this stage each participant has accepted certain specific obligations. Typically, a minimal set of obligations will have been codified in a formal agreement, whilst a fuller set of obligations has been made informally. Failure to honour minimal obligations represents strong cheating, honouring only minimal obligations represents weak cheating, whilst honouring the full obligations represents forbearance. In the special case where the obligations relate to the supply of effort, strong cheating involves disruption, weak cheating involves supplying a minimal amount of effort, and forbearance involves providing maximum effort.

The incentive to forbear

When only the immediate consequences of an action are considered, it often seems best to cheat. But when the indirect "knock on " effects are considered, forbearance may seem more desirable. This means, intuitively, that forbearance appeals most to those agents who take a long term view of the situation.

A short-term view is likely to prevail when the agent expects the venture to fail because of cheating by others. The risk of prejudicing the venture through his *own* cheating is correspondingly low, and there may be considerable advantages in being the firs to cheat because the "richest pickings" are available at this stage.

Knock on effects arise principally because of the repsonses of others. Their perceived importance depens upon the *vulnerability* of the party. A party is vulnerable if some course of action that might be chosen by another party would significantly reduce his welfare. Vulnerability encourages a party to think through how his own actions affect the incentives facing others. The more vulnerable his is, the more imporant it is to avoid stimulating an adverse response from other agents. Each party can, to some extent, induce long term thinking in other parties by threats that emphasise their vulnerability to his own actions. Partly because of this, the likely pattern of response by others, in many cases, is to match forbearance with forbearance, but to punish cheating. Confronted with this pattern of response, the optimal strategy in most cases is to do the same. Specifically, it is to forbear at the outset and to continue forebearing as long as others do. The situation in which all parties forbear on a reciprocal basis is termed *mutual forbearance*. According to the earlier definition, coordination effected through this mechanism is the essence of cooperation.

If other parties cheat the victim has a choice of punishment strategies. These strategies differ in both the nature of the evidence required and the severity of the punishment inflicted.

Recourse to the law has very limited scope because many forms of cheating are perfectly legal. This is particularly true where weak cheating is concerned. Even where the law has been breached, the principle that the defendant is "guilty until proven innocent", coupled with controls over what evidence is admissible in court, makes it costly, in many legal systems, for the victim to translate circumstantial information about cheating into convincing evidence.

Do-it-yourself punishment is often much cheaper. The victim can rely upon his own assessment of the situation: he does not need to convince others of his case. There are two main problems with this strategy. First, the victim may have far more limited sanctions than the law and, indeed, in some cases, such as punishing theft, the victim may have lost, as a direct consequence of the crime, the very resources he needed to inflict the punishment. Secondly, there may be a credibility problem. If the potential victim threatens to withhold promised bonuses, the threat will have little force is he is not trusted to pay them when they are deserved anyway. If he threatens to perform some seriously damaging action instead, it is possible that he may damage his own interests too – as when he threatens to undermine the entire venture – and this may create the belief that he will not actually do it. Despite these difficulties, do-it-yourself punishment is widely used. A common strategy is tit-for-tat, which matches acts of cheating with similar acts in kind. It has an appropriate incentive structure, is simple to implement, not too costly, and easily intelligible to other parties (Axelrod, 1981, 1984).

Residual risk sharing. In some cases punishment is semi-automatic, as when each participant requires each of the others to hold a share in the residual risks of the venture. If anyone cheats, the venture as a whole suffers, and the value of their equity stake diminishes as a result. This device is particularly appropriate in ventures calling for teamwork, when it is difficult to pin-point the individuals who are cheating. This means that incentives must be based, not on the inputs – because they are difficult to observe – but upon the joint output instead. This principle works well for small teams, but not for large ones, where the link beween individual performance and the share of the team rewards is relatively weak. It is also dependent on there being less likelihood of cheating in the sharing out of residual rewards than in the supply of inputs – which is a reasonable assumption in many cases.

Although these three methods are substitutes in dealing with any one type of cheating, most ventues provide opportunities for various types of cheating, and in this respect the methods complement one another quite nicely. Formal agreements between participants are often drafted by professional lawyers to make them easy to enforce through the courts. The formalities typically refer to readily observable aspects of behaviour on which convincing evidence is easy to collect. The law provides an appropriate punishment mechanism in this case. But the formal aspect of a venture cannot usually guarantee much more than its survival. True success can only come if informal understandings between the parties are honoured as well (Williamson, 1985). In this context, legal processes are seriously deficient. A system of shared equity ownership provides a suitable icentive framework, but almost invariably needs to be supplemented by do-it-yourself rewards and punishments too.

Reputation effects

It was noted above that do-it-yourself arrangements often suffer from a credibility problem. One way of resolving this problem is for the potential victim to gain a reputation for always carrying out threatened reprisals. Reputations can have other benefits too. A party with a reputation for never being first to abandon forbearance gives his partners a greater incentive to forbear themselves, for it increases the likelihood that if they too forbear then the venture as a whole will reach a successful conclusion. A reputation for forbearance also facilitates the formation of ventures in the first place; it makes it easier for the reputable party to find partners because prospective partners anticipate fewer problems in enforcing the arrangements (Blois, 1972, Richardson, 1972).

A reputation is an investment. It requires a party to forego certain short term gains in order to save on future transactions costs. The most valuable repuation appears to be a reputation for reciprocating forbearance: never being the first to abandon it, but always taking reprisals against others who do. The factors most conducive to investment in reputation are as follows.

(1) The prospect of many future ventures in which the party expects to have an opportunity of being involved. The number of ventures will be larger, the greater the party's range of contacts, the longer his remaining life expectancy, and the higher his expectation of the frequency with which new economic opportunities occur.

(2) The conspicuous demonstration of forbearance in a public domain. A high-profile venture, with a large number of observers, and a dense network of contacts spreading information about it, facilitates reputation-building. Conspicuous forbearance is favoured by a cultural environment that is open rather than secretive. A dense network of contacts is most likely within a stable social group, in which few parties enter or leave.

(3) A propensity for observers to predict the furture behaviour of a part by extrapolating his past pattern of behaviour. This governs the extent to which a party can "signal" his future intentions through his current behaviour. If peoples' attitudes are governed by prejudice based on superfical appearance rather than upon actual behaviour, acquiring a reputation that is at variance with prejudice may prove very difficult.

Co-Operation, Commitment and Trust

To what extent can it be said that one contractual arrangement is more cooperative than another? To answer this question, it is necessary to distinguish between cooperation as an input to a venture, and cooperation as an output from it. An arrangement which gives all parties a strong incentive to cheat requires a great deal of mutual forbearance if it is to be successful. Loosely speaking, it requires a large input of cooperation, in one respect, this is a weakness rather than a strength of the arrangement, since it menas that in practice the arrangement is quite likely to fail. This is important when considering joint ventures later, for it does seem that joint ventures which begin by being hailed extravagantly as a "symbol" of cooperation have a high propensity to fail.

Cooperation may be regarded as an output when an arrangement leads to greater trust between the parties, which reduces the transaction costs of subsequent ventures in which they are involved. Focussing on cooperation as an output gives a perspective which is closest to the common sense view that cooperative ventures are a "good thing".

There is a connection, however, between input and output. This is because an arrangement which calls for a considerable input of cooperation, and turns out successfully, enhances the reputations of the parties. First and foremost, it enhances their reputations with each other but, if there are spectators to the arrangement, then it enhances their reputations with them too.

The connection between input and output suggests that some arrangements may be more efficient than others in transforming an input of cooperation into an output. More precisely, cooperation is efficient when a given amount of mutual forbearance generates the largest possible amount of mutual trust. Efficiency is achieved by devising the arrangement of the venture so as to speed up the acquisition of reputation. One reason why reputation building may be slow is that cheating is often a covert practice – it is more viable if it goes undetected – and so it may be a long time before parties can be certain whether an agent has cheated or not. The importance of this factor varies from one venture to another, depending upon how easy it is for agents to make their own contribution and monitor and supervise their partners at the same time.

To speed up reputation building, it may be advantageous to create, within the arrangement itself, additional opportunities for agents to forbear reciprocally. Thus a venture may provide for a sequence of decisions to be taken by different parties, in each of which the individual agent faces a degree of conflict between his own interests and those of others. Each agent (except the first-mover) has an opportunity to respond to the earlier moves of others. The essence of this reputation-building mechanism is that, first, the decisions are open and overt, rather than secretive and covert, and secondly, that there is some connection between the overt decisions made by agents and their covert ones. In other words, the mechanism rests on the view that what the agent does when he is observed is a reflection of the way he behaves when he is not observed. Because of bounded rationality, and the persistence of habits, it is difficult for most agents to adjust their behaviour fully according to the conditions of observation. A sophisticated arrangement can set traps to catch agents "off guard", and provided agents do not face similar sequences of decisions too often, all but the cleverest and most alert are likely to unintentionally reveal something about the pattern of their unobserved behaviour as a result.

This device has certain dangers, however, not least of which is that it increases the amount of discretion accorded to each party. For it is the essence of the deferred decisions that agents have discretion over how they use in information at their disposal. If they were instructed to follow a decision rule prescribed at the outset, then their only discretionary decision would be whether to cheat on the rule. The situation would revert to one that encouraged covert rather than overt behaviour. To avoid creating excessive risks for the other parties, however, it is necessary to carefully control the amount of discretion by focussing the earliest decisions in the sequence upon issues which do not rally matter. As the venture procedes, and trust grows, so the degree of real discretion can be increased. To start with, therefore, the situation may resemble a game in which only token gains and losses are made, and only as time passes does the game become fully integrated into the "real world".

There are certain types of venture which naturally create game-playing situations. In long term ventures in a volatile environment, for example, there is a very sound logic for deferring certain decisions until after the venture has begun – namely that new information may subsequently become available that is relevant to how later parts of it are carried out. It may well be appropriate to delegate these decisions to the individuals who are most likely to have this information to hand. It then becomes possible to "fine tune" the degree of discretion to the amount of trust already present. Thus it is quite common to observe that when a number of parties work together for the first time, a tight discipline is imposed to begin with, which is then progressively relaxed as the parties begin to trust each other more.

Commitment

Up to this point, it has been assumed that cooperation is encouraged by appealing to the agents' enlightened self-interes – his incentive to cooperative is strengthened by reducing the cost to him to building up a reputation for reciprocity. It is also possible, however, to encourage cooperation by changing an agent's preferences so that the successful completion of the venture receives a higher priority than it did before. One way of doing this is to encourage the agent to perceive cooperation not as a means but as an end in itself. Cooperation then ceases to be based on strategic considerations – i.e. considerations which recommend cooperation as an appropriate means – and becomes based on commitment to cooperation in its own right.

It is worth noting, in this connection, that many everyday situations call for forbearance to be shown to people whom it is unlikely that one will ever meet again, and where there is, as a result, little incentive to forbear so far as self-interest alone is concerned. A typical situation arises in connection with unanticipated congestion in the use of a facility. When there is insufficient time to negotiate agreements between the users, and when there is either no system of priorities, or the system in force is an inappropriate one, co-odination may depend upon spontaneous forbearance. Examples include moving out of other people's way when shopping, and giving way to traffic entering from by-roads. The reason many people forbear in these situations, it seems, is that they derive welfare directly from their constructive role in the encounter.

It is likely that participation in certain types of venture can affect parties in a similar way. Indeed, participation in a venture may leave an individual far more oriented towards spontaneous cooperation than he was before. The main reason for this is the role of information-sharing in a venture. It is characteristic of many ventures that agents are asked to agree to share certain types of information with their partners. This is principally because the agents who possess certain types of information, or are in the best position to obtain it, are not necessarily those with the best judgement on how to use it. Another reason is that information provided by an agent may act as an early warning that, due to environmental changes, he (and perhaps others too) has a strong incentive to cheat, which can be reduced, in everyone's interests, by a limited renegotiation of their agreement.

In asking people to share information, however, it is likely that the response will divulge some of their more general beliefs, and their moral values too. Thus the sharing of information provides those who stand to gain most from the successful completion of the venture with an opportunity to disseminate – whether deliberately or quite subconsciously – a set of values conducive to cooperation. In this case, a venture can promote cooperation simply by providing a forum for the preaching of the cooperative ethic.

The degree of commitment to a venture is likely to be conditional upon certain characteristics of the venture. The commitment of the partners is likely to be higher, for example, the more socially meritorious or strategically important the output is deemed to be. Commitment will also tend to be higher if the distribution of rewards from the venture, when it is successfully completed, is deemed equitable by all parties. Envy of the share of gains appropriated by another partner can not only diminish motivation, but can encourage cheating – which may be "justified" as a means of generating a more equitable outcome. It is one of the characteristics of the JVs analysed in the next section that, superficially at least, the distribution of rewards seems fair because it is based on a 50 : 50 principle. As subsequent discussion indicates, however, such equity may be illusory, and once any such illusion is recognised, the degree of commitment may fall dramatically.

The psychology of commitment, if understood correctly, can be used by one party to manipulate another. But securing commitment through manipulation is a dangerous strategy for, once it is exposed, some form of reprisal or revenge is likely. The commitment previously channelled into the venture by the victim of manipulation may be transferred, and channelled into punishing the manipulator instead.

From the standpoint of economic theory, these propositions are equivalent to a postulate that an agent's preferences depend not only upon material consumption (or profit) but also upon the characteristics of the ventures in which he is involved. These characteristics relate both on the nature of the venture itself, and also to the extent of mutual commitment shown by the parties concerned. This postulate provides the basis for further developments of the theory of cooperation, which lie beyond the scope of the present paper.

The Economic Theory of Joint Ventures

Analysis of the cooperative content of "cooperative ventures" must be based upon a rigorous therory of non-equity arrangements. Because non-equity arrangements can take so many different forms, it is useful to focus upon one particular type. The 50 : 50 equity joint venture (JV) seems appropriate because it is very much symbolic of the cooperative ethos. The main focus is on arrangements involving two private firms, for although arrangements involving state-owned firms and government agencies are very important in practice (particularly in developing countries) they raise issues which lie beyond the scope of this paper. To the extent, however, that the state sector is primarily profit-motivated, the analysis below will still apply.

It is assumed that each partner in the JV already owns other facilities. It is also assumed that the JV is pre-planned, and that the equity stakes are not readily tradeable in divisible units. This means, in particular, that the joint ownership of the venture cannot be explained by a "mutual fund" effect – in other words, it is not the chance outcome of independent portfolio diversification decisions undertaken by the two firms. Working under these assumptions, theory must address three key issues.

(1) Why does each partner wish to own part of the JV rather than simply trade with it on an arm's length basis? The answer is that there must be some net benefit form internalising a market in one or more intermediate goods and services flowing between the JV and the parties' other operations. A *symmetrically motivated* JV is defined as one in which each firm has the same motive for internalising. This is the simplest form of JV to study, and is the basis for the detailed discussion presented later (see also Buckley and Casson, 1985, chapters 2,3,4).

(2) Why does each firm own half of the JV rather than all of another facility? The force of this question rests on an implicit judgement that joint ownership poses managerial problems of accountability that outright ownership avoids. To the extent that this is true, there must be some compensating advantage is not splitting up the jointly-owned facility into two (or possible more) separate facilities. In other words there must be an element of "economic indivisibility" in the facility. The way this indivisibility manifests itself will depend upon how the JV is linked into the firms' other operations.

   (a) If the JV generates a homogeneous output which is shared between the partners, or uses a homogeneous input which is sourced jointly by them, then the indivisibility is essentialy an economy of scale.

   (b) If the JV generates two distinct outputs, one of which is used by one partner and the other by the other, then the indivisibility is essentially an economy of scope.

   (c) If the JV combines two different inputs, each of which is contributed by just one of the parties, then the indivisibility manifests itself simply as a technical complemantarity between the inputs (i.e. a combination of a diminishing marginal rate of technical substitution and non-decreasing returns to scale).

(3) Given that, in the light of (1) and (2), each partner wishes to internalise the same indivisible facility, why do the partners not merge themselves, along with th JV, into a single corporate entity? The answer must be that there is some net disadvantage to such a merger. It may be managerial diseconomies arising from the scale and diversity of the resultant enterprise, legal obstacles stemming form anti-trust policy or re-

strictions on foreign acquisitions, difficulties of financing because of stock market scepticism, and so on.

It is clear, therefore, that JV operation is to be explained in terms of a combination of three factors, namely internalisation economies, indivisibilites, and obstacles to merger. As noted in the introduction, there are many contractual alternatives to JV operation, but for policy purposes particular interest centres on the question of when a JV will be preferred to outright ownership of a foreign subsidiary. Given that location factors, such as resource endowments, result in two interdependent facilities being located in different countries, the first of the three factors mentioned above – internalisation economies – militates in favour of outright ownership. It is the extent to which it is constrained by the other two factors – indivisibilities and obstacles to merger – that governs the strength of preference for a JV. The larger are indivisibilities, the greater the obstacles to merger, and the smaller are internalisation economies (relative to the other two factors) the more likely it is that the JV will be chosen (Casson, 1987, chapter 5). The interplay between these factors in governing the choice of contractual arrangements is illustrated by examples below.

The configuration of a JV operation

The configuration of a JV operation is determined by whether it stands upstream or downstream with respect to each partner's other operations, and by the nature of the intermediate products that flow between them. A JV arrangement is said to be *symmetrically positioned* if each partner stands in exactly the same (upstream or downstream) relation to the JV operation as does the other. Figure 1a illustrates symmetric forward integration, and Figure 1b symmetric backward integration. Sometimes an operation may be integrated both backwards and forwards into the same partner's operations. Figure 1c illustrates a symmetric buy-back arrangement in which each partner effectively subcontracts the processing of a product to the same jointly-owned facility.

Some writers seem to suggest that JVs are inherently symmetrical – presumably because of the 50 : 50 symmetry in the pattern of ownership – but this is far from actually being the case. JVs may, for a start, be asymmetrically positioned with respect to the partners' operations. Figure 1d illustrates a multi-stage arrangement in which one partner integrates forward into the JV and the other integrates backwards; such an arrangement is quite common in JVs formed to transfer proprietary technology to a foreign environment.

Even if a JV is symmetrically positioned, it does not follow that it is symmetrically configured, for the intermediate products flowing to and from the resepctive partners may be different. It is only when both the positioning is symmetrical, and the products are identical, that the configuration is fully symmetrical in the sense defined above.

The fact that the configuration is symmetrical does not guarantee that the motivation for internalisation is symmetrical too. If each partner, for example, re-sells the JV output within a different market structure, then the motivation for internalisation may differ in spite of the fact that the configuration is symmetric.

The symmetry properties illustrated in Figures 1a – 1c refer only to the immediate connections between the JV and the rest of the partners'operations. Each partner's operations may be differently configured from the others. This means that while the activities directly connected with the JV are symmetrically configured, the operations when considered as a whole may be asymmetric. Thus the symmetry concept used above was essentially one of local symmetry, and not of global symmetry. While global symmetry implies local symmetry, the converse does not apply.

Figure 1

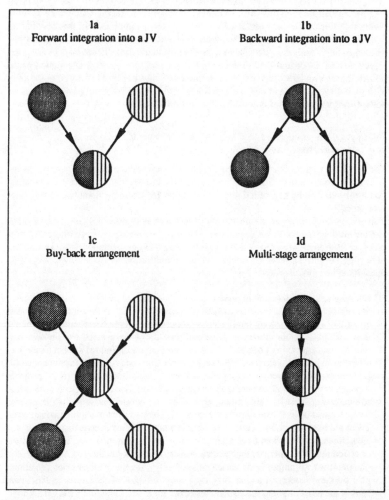

1a
Forward integration into a JV

1b
Backward integration into a JV

1c
Buy-back arrangement

1d
Multi-stage arrangement

The distinction between local and global symmetry has an important bearing on the question of the distribution of economic power between the parties. It is important to appreciate that local symmetry does not guarantee that there is a balance of economic power between the parties to the JV. It is quite possible, for example, that one of the partners may own facilities which are potential substitutes for the jointly-owned facility, whilst the orher partner does not. This becomes important if the other partner could not easily gain access to an alternative facility should the first partner place some difficulty in his way. It may be, for example, that the first partner holds a monopoly of alternative facilities. This means that in bargaining over the use of the jointly-owned facility, the first partner is likely to have the upper hand. He can use his power either to secure priorities for himself through non-price rationing, or to insist on trading with the JV at more favourable prices. The fact that the JV is 50 : 50 owned implies only that residual income is divided equally between the partners; it does not guarantee that total income is divided equally. And, as argued above, a locally symmetrical configuration does not guarantee that total income will be divided equaly. It is the symmetry of substitution possibilities that is crucial in this respect. Symmetry of substitution is likely to occur only with global symmetry, and this is a much less common type of configuration. One important consequence of this is considered in section 18 below.

JV operations motivated by lack of confidence in long-term arm's-length contracts

The next four sections illustrate how different motives for internalisation manifest themselves in various contexts. Readers familiar with the most recent literature on internalisation theory may prefer to proceed directly to section 16, where the main line of argument is resumed.

This section presents three simple examples in which both the configuration of the JV, and the motivations for it, are symmetric. The examples are designed to illustrate a progression from internalisation which involves no day-to-day operational integration between the JV and the partners' operations to internalisation which involves very close operational integration indeed.

(1) *Hedging against intermediate product price movements in the absence of a long-term futures market.* Consider the construction industry, in which main contractors have to quote fixed prices for long term projects, some of which require a large input of cement, which is liable to vary in price over the life of the project. For obvious reasons the cement cannot be stored, and there is no organised futures market either. Cement has to be purchased locally for each project, and because the sites are geographically dispersed, there is no one supplier that can economically supply all the projects. Nevertheless, prices of cement at different sites tend to vary in line with each other, so that ownership of a cement-making facility at any one location will still help to hedge against price fluctuations in the many different sources of supply that are used. There are two major contractors of equal size who specialise in cement-intensive projects. Because of economies of scale in cement production, however, a cement plant of efficient scale generates much more cement that either contractor uses. There is one plant whose output price varies most closely with the average price of cement paid by the contractors, and so they each acquire a half of the equity in this plant. This is the most efficient mechanism abailable for diversifying their risks relating to the price of cement. It involves no operational integration whatso ever between the cement facility and the site activities.

(2) *Avoiding recurrent negotiation under bilateral monopoly over the price of a differentiated intermediate product.* Suppose there are two frims which are the only users of an intermediate product which is produced with economies of scale. It is difficult for

either firm to switch away from the product, since it has no close substitutes. Upstream, therefore, there is natural monopoly, whilst downstream there is duopsony. Before any party incurs non-recoverable set-up costs through investment in specific capacity, it would be advantageous to negotiate once and for all long-term supply contracts for the product. Because of the difficulty of enforcing such contracts, however, the duopsonists may prefer to jointly acquire the upstream facility. This insures both of them against a strategic price rise initiated by an independent natural monopolist. The fact that both share in the residual risks also helps to discourage them from adversarial behaviour towards each other. A modest degree of operational integration is likely in this case.

(3) *Operational integration between upstream and downstream acitvities in the absence of efficient short term forward markets.* Extending the construction industry example, suppose that the two firms have long term projects in hand at adjacent sites, and require various types of form-work to be supplied to mould the concrete foundations. The form-work is customised and each piece has to be in place precisely on time. Both firms are sceptical about devising enforceable incentives for prompt supply by a subcontractor, as arm's length forward contracts are difficult to enforce in law. Because of the small scale of local demand relative to the capacity of an efficient-size team of workers, the two contractors may decide to secure quality of service through backward integration into a JV. Unlike the previous arrangements, this involves close day to day management of an intermediate product flow between the owners and the JV.

Quality uncertainty

Quality uncertainty can manifest itself in many different contexts. Four examples are given below to demonstrate the ubiquity of this phenomenon.

(1) *Insuring against defecitive quality in components.*
This example relates to forward integration involving two distinct flows of materials. Consider two components which are assembled to make a product. The quality of the components is difficult to assess by inspection, and other methods of assessment, such as testing to destruction, are expensive – not least in terms of wasted product. Reliable performance of the final product is crucial to the customer, and failure of the final product is often difficult to diagnose and attribute to one particular component. Because of legal impediments, it is impossible to comprehensively integrate the assembly with the production of both components, and an independent assembler would lack confidence in subcontracted component supplies. If two independent component producers form a joint venture, however, then each can enjoy a measure of confidence in the other, since each knows that the other bears half the penalty incurred by the venture if he supplies a defective product to it. This is the JV analogue of the "buyer uncertainty" argument emphasised in the internalisation literature.

(2) *Adapting a product to an overseas market*
This example involves the combination of two distinct but complementary types of know-how in the operation of an indivisible facility. The first type of know-how is technological, and is typically embodied in the design of a sophisticated product developed in an industrialised country. The other is knowledge of an overseas market possessed by an indigenous foreign firm. The complementarity concerns their use in

adapting the design and marketing strategy of the product to overseas conditions. The indivisible facility is the plant used to manufacture it overseas. Together these elements make up the classic example of the use of a JV to commence overseas production of a maturing product.

(3) *Management training and the transfer of technology*

In some cases a JV may be chosen as a vehicle for training (Kojima, 1978). Employees of technologically-advanced firm are seconded to a JV to train other employees who will remain with the venture when it is later spun off to the currently technologically-backward partner. Training involves two inputs, rather than just the one that is usually assumed. It requires not only the knowledge and teaching ability of the tutor, but also the time, attention and willingness to learn of the tutee. The tutee may be uncertain of the quality of the tutor's knowledge and ability, and may demand that the tutor bears all the commercial risks associated with the early stages of the venture. The tutor, on the other hand, may be uncertain of the effort supplied by the tutee, which could jeopardise the performance of the venture if it were poor, and so may require the tutee to bear some of the risks as well. These conflicting requirements are partially reconciled by a JV which requires both to bear some of the risks and thereby gives each an incentive to maintain a high quality of input. Those incentives can be further strengthened, in some cases, by a buy-back arrangement – or production-sharing arrangement as it is sometimes called – which encourages each party to use the output that the newly trained labour has produced and thereby gives an additional incentive to each party to get the training right.

(4) *Buy-back arrangements in collaborative R and D*

Buy-back arrangements, which combine backward and forward integration, are particularly common in collaborative research. In the research context, both the inputs to, and the outputs from the JV are services derived from heterogeneous intangible assets (i. e. they are flows of knowledge).

Consider two firms, each with a particular area of corporate expertise, who license their patents, and second personnel, to a joint research project (the indivisible facility). The planned output – new knowledge – is a proprietary public good, which is licensed back to the two firms. Each firm may be suspicious of the quality of the input supplied by the other firm, but the fact that the other firm not only holds an equity stake in the project but also plans to use the product of the research for its own purposes serves to reassure the first firm that the quality will be good (though there still remains a risk that personnel and ideas of the very best quality will be held back). Likewise, the fact that the firm itself has partially contributed to the production of the new knowledge is a reassuring factor when it comes to implementing this knowledge in downstream production.

Collusion

The role of indivisibility facilities in the previous discussion can, in fact, be taken over by any arrangement which either reduces the costs of two plants by coodinating their input procurement, or enhances the value of their outputs by coordinating their marketing. The former is relevant to backward integration by firms into a JV, whilst the latter pertains to forward integration instead. The forward integration case, discussed below, shows the JV to be an alternative to a cartel.

Consider two firms which have identified an opportunity for colluding in their sales policy. They may have independently discovered a new technology, territory, or mineral deposit and wish to avoid competition between them in its exploitation. They may, on the other hand, be established duopolists operating behind an entry barrier, who would benefit from fixing prices or quotas to maximise their joint profis from the industry. (The nature of the entry barrier is irrelevant to the argument – it may be based on technological advantage, or brand names, statutory privilege, exclusive access to inputs, and so on.)

The main problem with a sales cartel is the mutual incentive to cheat by undercutting the agreed price – for example, by selling heavily discounted items through unofficial outlets. This poses an acute monitoring problem for each party. Channelling sales through a JV reduces the incentive to cheat, since the gains from cheating are partially outweighed by the reduction in profits earned from the JV. Economies in monitoring costs may also be achieved if both parties specialise this function with the JV.

Hostages: internalising the implementation of counter-threats

In an atmosphere of mutual distrust, an imbalance in the vulnerability of two parties to a breakdown of the venture can further undermine confidence in it. This suggests the possibility that instead of collaborating on a single ventrue they should collaborate on two ventures instead. The function of the second venture is to counter-act the imbalance in the first ventrue by giving the least vulnerable party in the first ventrue the greatest vulnerability to in the second venture. Suppose, for example, that the two firms wished to collude in a product market where one firm has a much larger market share, coupled with much higher fixed costs, than the other. This is the firm that is most vulnerable to cheating by the other. To redress the balance, it may be advantageous for the two firms to agree on some other venture – say collaborative research – to run in parallel with a collusive JV to give the weaker firm an effective sanction against the stronger one. In such a case, the primary motive for the second JV concerns nothing intrinsic to the ventrue itself, but simply its ability to support the other venture.

It should be clear from the preceding examples that there are an enormous number of different forms that JV operation can take. Each of the three main factors – the internalisation motive, the indivisibility and the obstacle to merger – can take several different forms. The internalisation motive may differ between the firms. Add to this the considerable diversity of global configurations, and it can be seen that the permutations to which these aspects lend themselves make any simple typology of JV operations out of the question. While the economic principles governing the logic of JV operation are intrinsically quite straightforward, the way that environmental influences select the dominant factors in any one case is extremely complex.

Building Reputation and Commitment

It was established in the first part of the paper that almost all coordinating activity calls for some degree of mutual forbearance and that therefore most ventures – even simple trade, or team activities – involve an element of cooperation. It was also established that extensive reliance on mutual forbearance was not necessarily a good thing. The essence of cooperative efficiency, it was suggested, is that as a result of a ventrue, a small amount of mutual forbearance is transformed into a large amount of trust. Cooperatively efficient ventures will tend to accord all parties an opportunity to reciprocate forbearance within a sequence of decisions, observable to the others, calling for increasing levels of loyalty. Ventures of this kind are likely to be followed by a succession of other ventures involving the same parties – perhaps in the same grouping, or perhaps on other group-ings involving other parties with whom the original participants have established a repu-tation. (Propositions of this kind are certainly testable, even if the propositions ragarding "quantities" of forbearance and trust, from which they derived, are not.)

Some ventures lend themselves naturally to an internal organisational structure which encourages participation. These ventures call for widespread decentralisation of decision-making, afford decisions of varying degrees of responsibility, and call for the sharing of information. They provide ample opportunity for overt behaviour, and only limited op-portunity for covert behaviour. These considerations suggest than certain motives for JV operation are far more conducive to cooperation than are others. It is, in fact, the combi-nation of the motive and the main acitivity performed by the JV that seems to be crucial in this respect.

In the production sector, JVs which involve very little operational integration with the partners' other activities provide little opportunity for the partners to meet and interact on a regular basis. The greater the degree of operational integration, the greater is the re-gularity with which forbearance may have to be exercised when short-term hold-ups oc-cur in production, and the greater are the opportunities for sharing information in the planning of production. Quality uncertainty provides a motive for both parties to open up their wholly-owned operations to their JV partner once a certain degree of trust has been established, and so provides a natural route through which cooperation could progress to a point where it embraces production, product development and basic re-search.

Joint R and D is naturally cooperative because it is based upon the sharing of informa-tion and, for reasons already noted, the sharing of information often leads to the emer-gence of shared values too. This may, perhaps, partly explain why collaborative R and D seems to enjoy a special mystique all of its own.

Of the various functional areas in which JV operations can occur, sales and procurement are the least promising so far as true cooperation is concerned. A dominant motive for JV operations in this area is collusion. Collusion affords large incentives to cheat and therefore requires a major input of cooperation. The maintenance of a high price in a sta-tic market environment – so characteristic of many collusive arrangements – does not, however, create much need for meetings at which open forbearance and reciprocity can be displayed. Collusion emphasises the covert rather than overt dimension of behaviour. It therefore generates little output of trust. The most promising area for cooperation in marketing arises when a proprietary product is transferred to a new country, for then both the source firm and the recipient firm need to share information. Since the demand is un-certain, but has considerable growth potential, the market environment is dynamic rather than static, and so, unlike the case of collusion, it provides opportunities for deferring key decisions and delegating in a way that allows both parties to demonstrate forbear-ance.

The International dimension

So far nothing has been said specifically about the international aspects of JV operation. To a certain extent this is deliberate, since there are no reasons to believe that the familiar factors of international cost differentials, tariffs, transport costs, and variations in the size of regional markets are any different for JVs than they are for other international operations. It can, however, be argued that the political risks of expropriation, the blocking of profit repatriation, and so on, are lower in the case of a JV than in the case of a wholly-owned operation, though empirical support for this view is bery limited, to say the least. Tax-minimising transfer pricing, though not impossible with JVs, is more difficult to administer because of the need to negotiate the prices with the partner, and to find a subterfuge for paying any compensation involved.

So far as the general concept of cooperation is concerned, the international dimension is much less important that the inter-cultural dimension. In purely conventional analysis of transaction costs the focus is on the legal enforcemant of contracts, and so the role of the nation state is clearly paramount, in respect of both its legislation and its judicial procedures. The mechanism of cooperation, however, is trust rather than legal sanction, and trust depends much more on the unifying influence of the social group than on the coercive power of the state. Trust will normally be much stronger between members of the same extended family, ethnic group or religious group, even though it transcends national boundaries, than between member of different groups within the same country.

This means that in comparing the behaviour of large firms legally domiciled in different countries, differences in behaviour are just as likely to reflect cultural differences in the attitudes of senior management as the influence of the fiscal and regulatory environment of the home country. Cultural attitudes are certainly likely to dominate in respect of the disposition to cooperate with other firms. In this context, it may be less important to know whether a corporation is British or Italian, say, than to know whether its senior management is predominantly Quaker or Jewish, Protestant or Catholic, Anglo-Saxon or Latin, and so on. National and cultural characterisitics are correlated, but not perfectly so. In some instances, such as Japanes firms, it has proved extremely problematic to disentangle them.

In the light of these remarks, it is clear that JV operations involving firms with different cultural backgrounds are of particular long-term significance. Once established, they provide a mechanism for cultural exchange, particularly as regards attitudes to cooperation. The success of this mechanism will depend upon how receptive each firm is to ideas emanating form an alien culture. Where the firm is receptive, participation in international JVs may have lasting effects on its behaviour, not only in international operations, but in many other areas too.

Networks of interlocking JVs

The recent proliferation of international JVs means that many firms are now involved in several JVs. Two JVs are said to interlock when the same firm is a partner in both. It is not always recognised as clearly as it should be that a set of interlocking JVs is an extremely effective way for a firm to develop monopoly power at minimal capital cost. By taking a part-increst in an number of parallel ventures, producing the same product with a different partner in each case, the firm can not only establish a strong market position against buyers of the product, but it can also create a strong bargaining position against each partner as well.

Once an individual partner is committed to a venture, he is vulnerable if the monopolist threatens to switch production to one of his other JCs instead. The partner has no similar option because the remaining facilities are all partly controlled by the monopolist. In the terminology of section 2, the vulnerable firm may be obliged to renegotiate terms under duress. Although the monopolist may stand to lose by withdrawing production from one JV, he will be able to recover most of these losses from enhanced profits arising from the JVs to which production is switched.

Figure 2

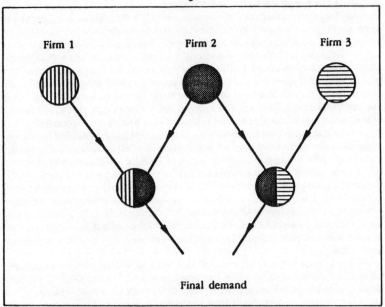

A situation of this kind is illustrated in Figure 2. Firm 2 has the ability to switch production between the two downstream plants, but neither firm 1 nor firm 3 has this option because the only other plant is partly controlled by firm 2. Although each JV is symmetrically configured in a local sense, the overall situation is globally asymmetric. Superficially, it may seem that firm 2 is a "good cooperator" because it is involved in more JVs than either of the other firms, but in reality its claim to cooperate may simply be a subterfuge. Firm 2 can, in fact, not only exercise monopoly power against the buyers of downstream output, but also play off its partners against each other. In this case it is conflict, not cooperation, and deception, not trust, that is the driving force in firm 2's choice of JV operation.

Conclusion

Joint ventures are, first and foremost, a devise for mitigating the worst consequences of mistrust. In the language of internalisation theory, they represent a compormise contractual arrangement which minimises transaction costs under certain environmental constraints. But some types of joint venture also provide a suitable contect in which the parties can demonstrate mutual forbearance, and thereby build up trust. This may open up possibilities for coordination which could not otherwise be entertained. The prospect of this encourages partners to take an unusally open-ended view of JV partnerships, and gives JVs their political and cultural mystique.

An important role of JVs, from the limited perspective of internalisation economics, is to minimise the impact of quality uncertainty on collaborative research and training. From the more open-ended perspective of long term cooperation, however, JVs designed to cope with quality uncertainty are also well adapted to help partners to reciprocate, and also to learn the values which inspire the other partner to unreserved commitment to a venture. Without doubt, JVs of this type offer a way forward to genuine cooperation in international economic relations in the future.

The analysis also suggests, however, that a degree of cynicism may be warranted in respect of the claims advanced for JVs of certain kinds. A JV may be merely a subterfuge, luring partners into making commitments which leave them exposed to the risk of renegotiation under duress. It may be a device for enhancing collusion – a practice that may be warranted if it is necessary to recover the costs of technological or product innovation, but not otherwise. It may represent a pragmatic response to regulatory distortion – as when a misguided national competition policy outlaws a merger between the partners that would afford considerable efficiency gains; the JV, in this case, is better than nothing at all, but is only second best to a policy of removing the distortion itself.

One of the most topical applications of the theory of the JV is to industrial cooperation and production-sharing arrangements involving Japanes firms. To what extent, for example, can quality uncertainty in the training process support the argument that the Japanese is an appropriate vehicle for tutoring partners in developing countries? Are Japanese JV networks in south East Asia merely agglomerations of independent JV operations, or are they part of a wider strategy to play off one partner against another in an effort to maintain low prices for Japanese imports and thereby assure the competitiveness of Japanese re-exports?

Other questions may be asked, for example, of Western corporations that seem anxious to cooperate with the Japanese. Are they really interested in long-term collaboration in the development of leading edge technologies, or is it their hope that token research collaboration with the Japanese can open the door to short term cartel-like restrictions on international trade? Do Western collaborators really hope to learn something of a cooperative ethic, and perhaps even a new system of values, from the Japanese, or are they merely interested in cooperation as a mask to disguise the replacement of competition by collusion?

There do not seem to be any easy anwers to these questions. More empirical evidence is required. It is hoped that the analysis presented in this paper affords a framework within which such evidence can be interpreted. So far, it is only possible to clarify the questions, but eventually it should be possible to answer them.

References

Axelrod, R. (1981) The Evolution of Cooperation among Egoists, *American Political Science Review*, 75, 306 – 18.

Axelrod, R. (1984) *The Evolution of Cooperation*, New York : Basic Books.

Blois, K. J. (1972) Vertical Quasi-Integration, *Journal of Industrial Economics*, 20, 253-72.

Buckley, P. J. and M. C. Casson (1985) *Economic Theory of the Multinational Enterprise: Selected Papers*, London : Macmillan.

Casson, M. C. (1982) *The Entrepreneur : An Economic Theory*, Oxford : Blackwell

Casson, M.C. (1987) *The Firm and the Market*, Cambridge, Mass : MIT Press

Kojima, K. (1978) *Direct Foreign Investment*, London : Croom Helm

Richardson, G. B. (1972) The Organisation of Industry, *Economic Journal*, 82, 883-96.

Williamson, O. E. (1985) *The Economic Institutions of Capitalism : Firms, Markets, Relational Contracting*, New York : Free Press.

** A preliminary version of this paper was presented to the joint seminar of the Swedish School of Business Administration, Helsinki, The Finnish School of Economics and the University of Helsinki, kindly arranged by H. C. Blomqvist, T. Bergelund and I. Menzler-Hokkanen, and to the staff workshop at the University of Reading. Steve Nicholas provided considerable encouragement, mixed with healthy scepticism. A revised version was presented to the Joint Research Colloquium of the Wharton School and Rutgers Graduate School of Management on Cooperative Strategies in International Business held at Rutgers University in October 1986. We are grateful to Farok Contractor, Peter Lorange, Peter Gray, Kathryn Harrigan, Ingo Walter and others for their constructive comments.

[7]

AN ECONOMIC MODEL OF INTERNATIONAL JOINT VENTURE STRATEGY

Peter J. Buckley*
University of Leeds

Mark Casson**
University of Reading

Abstract. The strategic choice between joint ventures, licensing agreements and mergers is analysed using eight key factors suggested by internalisation theory. The model explains the increasing role of international joint ventures in the 1980s in terms of the accelerating pace of technological innovation and the globalisation of markets. It offers a range of predictions about the formation of joint ventures within industries, across industries, across locations, and over time. It exploits a powerful modelling technique that has many other applications in international business strategy.

ECONOMIC METHODOLOGY

Over the last twenty years, the application of economic theory to international business studies has sharpened the analysis of key issues. Economists aim to ask the right questions and to answer these questions in a rigorous way. This means making their assumptions explicit, for a start. The set of strategies available to the firms that they are studying is clearly specified and the details of each strategy are spelt out.

In a global environment, participation in an international joint venture (IJV) is an important strategic option [Beamish and Banks 1987]. Explicit assumptions are particularly crucial when studying IJVs. No IJV, however configured, performs perfectly, and so to understand why an IJV is chosen, it is also necessary to understand the shortcomings of the alternatives. Moreover, IJVs are configured in many different ways, and different configurations are associated with different kinds of behaviour [Tallman 1992].

Economists invoke the principle of rational action to predict the circumstances (if any) under which a firm will choose a given strategy. When the firm's objective is profit-maximisation, the choice of any strategy, such as an IJV, is driven by the structure of revenues and costs. This structure is determined by

---

*Peter J. Buckley is Professor of International Business and Director of the Centre for International Business, University of Leeds, United Kingdom.

**Mark Casson is Professor of Economics, University of Reading, United Kingdom.

850 JOURNAL OF INTERNATIONAL BUSINESS STUDIES, SPECIAL ISSUE 1996

the firm's environment. By identifying the key characteristics of this environment, the firm's behaviour can be modelled in a very parsimonious way. The predictions of the model emerge jointly from the profit maximisation hypothesis and the restrictions imposed by the modeller on the structure of revenues and costs. Predictive failure of the model is addressed by reexamining these restrictions and not by discarding the maximisation principle that is at the core of the theory [Buckley 1988].

This methodology may be contrasted with the more usual approach in international business studies of leaving the assumptions implicit and deriving propositions from a discursive literature review [Parkhe 1993]. This dispenses with formal analysis and relies instead on synthesis. But a synthesis is no better than the analytical components from which it is built. This point is particularly salient to the study of IJVs. For the more complex the synthesis, the more important it is that each component is sound. The economic logic of rational action provides just the kind of check on analytical consistency that is required.

A further implication of this method is that the variables entering into the theory do not have to be of a strictly economic nature. The criterion for inclusion is that they are analysed from a rational action point of view. The modelling of IJVs illustrates this very well. A wide range of factors impact upon IJVs [Geringer and Hébert 1989]: not just traditional economic factors, such as market size, but also technological, legal, cultural and psychological factors. Variables of all these kinds appear in the model developed below.

A final point about economic models is that they permit judgements about efficiency to be made. While IJVs may be commended on social and political grounds, they could be criticised as inefficient for, say, large firms that are leaders in their industries. An economic model can address this issue head on. Since no firm, however large, can be completely self-sufficient, it is readily shown that participation in IJVs is efficient provided that the conditions are right. The main objective of this paper is to set out these conditions in full. It is because these conditions are now more widely satisfied than they were in the past that IJVs have become such an important aspect of international business.

THE TYPOLOGY OF IJVs

IJVs can take many forms. This paper focuses on a representative equity-based joint venture between two private firms. Its rationale is to combine complementary resources. These resources comprise firm-specific knowledge, and the combination is effected by each firm sharing its knowledge with the other. The knowledge provided by a firm may relate to technology, or to market conditions, or both. The firm does not normally share all its knowledge through an IJV, but only a subset of it.

The geographical scope with which technology is exploited is normally wider than that of marketing expertise, which tends to be of a more localised nature.

This has important implications for the structure of the IJV, and for the degree of symmetry between the partner firms [Harrigan 1988]. It means that the combination of two technologies through R&D collaboration is normally geared from the outset to global market exploitation. The partner firms are in a symmetric situation in the sense that the assets that they each contribute to the IJV are of global application.

By contrast, the combination of a new technology with marketing expertise usually involves market access of a more local nature. There is an asymmetry between the globally oriented asset contributed by the high-technology firm and the locally oriented asset contributed by its partner. In the course of globalising the exploitation of its technology, the high-technology firm may make a series of market-access alliances with firms in different localities. This gives the high-technology firm more experience of joint ventures, and may also allow it to play off one partner against another later.

A final possibility is that each of the firms contributes marketing expertise in a different locality. This restores the symmetry of the first case, but does not restore the global dimension unless the partners' skills, when combined, span the whole of the global market place. The principal motive for such colla-boration is the coordination of prices in different geographical segments of the world market. Such collusion is potentially significant when the product is easily traded and there are barriers to entry or over-capacity in the industry (for example, the steel industry).

These possibilities are summarised in the first two rows and columns of Table 1 and are illustrated schematically in Figure 1. The two firms are indexed 1 and 2, with Firm 1 based in Country A and Firm 2 in Country B. The figure employs the conventions introduced in Buckley and Casson [1988], refined in Casson [1995] and extended in Casson [1996]. Two physical activities are identified – production, represented by a square, and distribution, represented by a diamond. Physical activities are linked by product flow, which is indicated by a double line; the direction of flow is shown by an arrow. Two knowledge-based activities are distinguished – R&D, indicated by a triangle, and marketing, indicated by a circle. Knowledge flow is represented by a single line; to differentiate technology from marketing expertise, an asterisk is applied to lines that represent technology flow. It is assumed that technology flows from R&D to production, whilst marketing expertise coordinates production and distribution, and therefore flows to both. In practice, of course, R&D and marketing are linked as well, but this is not directly relevant to the analysis in this paper, and so in the interests of simplicity is omitted from the figure.

Ownership of an activity by Firm 1 is indicated by horizontal shading, whilst ownership by Firm 2 is indicated by an unshaded area. Jointly owned facilities are partly shaded and partly not, the proportion that is shaded indicating the share of the equity held by Firm 1. Unless otherwise stated it is assumed that

852   JOURNAL OF INTERNATIONAL BUSINESS STUDIES, SPECIAL ISSUE 1996

TABLE 1

Typology of IJVs According to the Kind of Knowledge Shared

Firm 1	Firm 2		
	Technology	Marketing	Both
Technology	1. R&D collaboration	2. Market access by Firm 1 to Country B	7. R&D collaboration with access to market B (Firm 2 'buys back')
Marketing Expertise	3. Market access by Firm 2 to Country A	4. Collusion in markets of A and B	9. Firm 2 supplies technology for use in both markets (Firm 2 'buys back')
Both	6. R&D collaboration with access to market A (Firm 1 'buys back')	8. Firm 1 supplies technology for use in both markets (Firm 1 'buys back')	5. R&D collaboration with access to both markets (both firms 'buy back')

FIGURE 1
Schematic Illustration of Four IJV Configurations Generated by the Sharing of Technology and Marketing Expertise Contributed by Two Firms

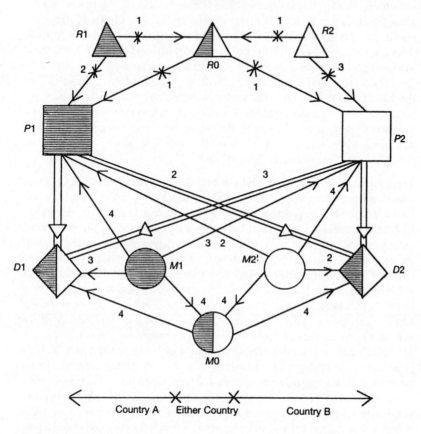

Key: See text and Table 1.

the equity is owned 50:50, as reflected in Figure 1, where exactly half the area is shaded and half is not. The IJV facilities are the laboratory R0 and the marketing headquarters M0. These can be based in either A or B, or in a third country, C, as circumstances warrant.

Table 1 identifies nine types of IJV configuration altogether. Four of them, shown in the top left-hand block of the table, combine one type of knowledge from each firm, whilst the other five involve at least one of the firms contributing both types of knowledge. The four simple types are distinguished

854   JOURNAL OF INTERNATIONAL BUSINESS STUDIES, SPECIAL ISSUE 1996

by the numerical labelling of the linkages in Figure 1. Pure research collaboration (type 1) is represented by the links from the partners' own laboratories $R1$ and $R2$ to the IJV laboratory $R0$, and the feedback of new technology to the partners' production plants $P1$ and $P2$. Market access by Firm 1 to Country B (type 2) is represented by the flow of exports from the production plant $P1$ to the IJV distribution facility $D2$. Technology from laboratory $R1$ is embodied in the product, and marketing expertise from $M2$ is used to coordinate the export flow. Conversely, market access by Firm 2 to Country A (type 3) is represented by the flow of exports from the plant $P2$ to the distribution facility $D1$. This combines technology from the laboratory $R2$ with marketing expertise from $M1$. Finally, collusion in the distribution of the products (type 4) is represented by the synthesis of marketing expertise from $M1$ and $M2$ effected by the jointly owned facility $M0$, which coordinates the jointly owned distribution facilities $D1$ and $D2$.

The simplest case to analyse, and the one that has therefore attracted most attention from economists, is pure R&D collaboration (type 1) [Veugelers and Kersteloot 1994]. The practical difficulty with this case is that when the results of R&D are shared, competition between products exploiting the same technology can dissipate partner's rents. This encourages collusion in the marketing of the final product, and such collusion is likely to be most effective if the partners share their marketing expertise as well. This combination of R&D collaboration (type 1) and shared marketing expertise (type 4) generates type 5 in the figure. Because of its practical significance, this case forms the main focus of this paper. Other cases are possible too, however. Studying the third row and third column of Table 1 reveals cases where both firms contribute technology but only one contributes marketing expertise (types 6 and 7). Such cases can arise where a new technology controlled by one firm has to be adapted to local production conditions and local customer requirements in an idiosyncratic market controlled by another firm. Alternatively, both firms may contribute marketing expertise but only one of them may contribute technology (types 8 and 9). This can occur where a new technology generates a new product that requires a distinctive approach to retailing, which is familiar to the innovating firm, but where a knowledge of the local customer base is possessed only by the partner firm.

So far, nothing has been said about joint ownership of production. This issue is highly relevant to globalisation. It is well known that many new products are nowadays developed with global markets in mind. The lower are transport costs and tariffs, the greater is the opportunity for exploiting economies of scale in production. If the existing plants of the partner firms exhibit economies of scope – for example, they have flexible equipment with unused capacity – then it may be possible to achieve economies of scale without investing in a production facility dedicated to the new product. But even if such plants exist, they may not be in an ideal location, given the specific input requirements of the product and the geographical distribution of its demand. If a new dedicated facility is indeed required, then it is natural that it should be jointly owned, particularly in a type 5 IJV where each firm is contributing both technology and marketing expertise. In fact, globalisation affords a particular stimulus to joint ventures of type 5: the development of a product with global appeal usually requires a synthesis of technical expertise, whilst the realisation of sales potential requires a synthesis of marketing expertise as well. The greater the fixed costs of R&D, and the greater the economies of scale in production, the more important is the marketing synthesis in achieving the critical level of global sales.

A joint-owned production facility $P0$ is illustrated in Figure 2. While the wholly owned facilities $P1$ and $P2$ continue to be used for other products, the product developed and marketed by the IJV is now produced in $P0$. The distribution facilities, $D1$, $D2$ may be jointly owned as well, but to avoid too many complications it is assumed instead that when production is jointly owned, the distribution facilities are not. This assumption can easily be relaxed if required. The figure is used to illustrate the types 5–9 which appear in the third row and third column of Table 1. The only symmetric type is number 5, in which both firms combine their technologies in the research laboratory $R0$ and coordinate their distribution using the marketing headquarters $M0$. A useful feature of this configuration is that each of the firms 'buys back' some of the output to which it has contributed a technological input. This gives each firm a strong incentive to ensure that its input is of high quality. It also gives it a strong incentive to ensure that the production facility $P0$ is operated in an efficient way. Buy-back from a joint facility occurs with types 6–9 as well (as Table 1 makes clear) but the incentives are not as strong because only one of the firms is involved.

THE ALTERNATIVE STRATEGIES

Not only are there many different configurations of IJV, but there are many contractual alternatives to each particular configuration. It is impossible to discuss IJV strategy rigorously unless both the particular IJV configuration and the alternatives to it are clearly specified. The alternatives considered here are those suggested by internalisation theory [Buckley and Casson 1976]: namely a merger and a licensing agreement. All three of these strategic options involve combining both the technology and the marketing expertise of the two firms, but they combine them in different ways.

The focus is on a type 5 IJV configuration, i.e., a symmetric globally oriented kind of IJV. It is assumed that production takes place in a dedicated plant owned by the IJV. Location factors are not explicitly considered: it is simply assumed that production is based in a country that has ready access for its exports (through free trade and low transport costs) to the major centres of

856 JOURNAL OF INTERNATIONAL BUSINESS STUDIES, SPECIAL ISSUE 1996

FIGURE 2
Schematic Illustration of IJV Configurations 5–9 Based on a Single Shared Production Facility

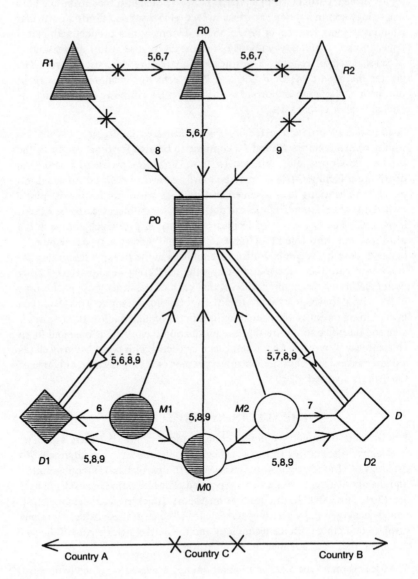

global demand. To preserve the symmetry of the configuration, this location is assumed to be a third country, C, as indicated in Figure 2.

All three options require the consent of both the firms. If no consent is achieved then no collaboration occurs (this is the null option, strategy 0). To simplify the analysis it is assumed that Firm 1 takes the initiative in promoting inter-firm collaboration and that Firm 2 plays an entirely passive role. The consequences of relaxing this assumption are considered later. It is Firm 1 that evaluates the profits from merger, IJV and licensing and compares them to each other. Firm 2 agrees to any proposed arrangement, provided that the terms leave it no worse off than before (i.e., than under the null strategy). Under these conditions the private gains to Firm 1 coincide with the overall gains from each strategy, and so in economic terms Firm 1's decision is Pareto-efficient even though to an outsider the distribution of rewards may seem unfair.

A merger could in principle be effected either by Firm 1 acquiring Firm 2, or by Firm 2 acquiring Firm 1, or by a third firm acquiring them both. It is assumed that because Firm 1 takes the initiative, it is Firm 1 that acquires Firm 2. Note, however, that even though Firm 1 may be better at spotting opportunities, Firm 2 may be better at managing a large organisation, and so it might, in fact, be more profitable for Firm 1 to arrange a reverse takeover instead. Likewise with licensing: it is possible for Firm 1 to license in Firm 2's technology (and the associated marketing expertise) or for Firm 1 to license its own technology out to Firm 2. It is assumed that Firm 1 licenses in Firm 2's technology, so that it retains its full independence, as in the case of acquisition. If, however, Firm 1's technology was much easier to value than Firm 2's then it might be easier for it to license out its own technology instead. This is another complication that will not be considered here.

It is assumed that Firm 1 extracts its rewards from collaboration through the terms on which its deals with Firm 2 are made, and not through the proportion of equity which it holds. If the equity stake were the sole consideration, then acquisition of Firm 2 would always be more profitable than a joint venture, which in turn would be more profitable than licensing, which is clearly absurd. In the context of an acquisition, it is the price at which Firm 2's equity is valued which is crucial; in the case of an IJV, it is the management fees that the IJV must pay to Firm 1, whilst in the case of licensing it is the royalty rate offered to Firm 2.

The configuration of the merger is illustrated in Figure 3. The horizontal shading throughout indicates that Firm 1 has acquired all the facilities previously owned by Firm 2. R&D and marketing have been rationalised too: the laboratories $R1$ and $R2$ have been eliminated and all research concentrated on $R0$. Similarly, the local marketing activities $M1$ and $M2$ have been eliminated in favour of global marketing through $M0$. Such rationalisation is

858   JOURNAL OF INTERNATIONAL BUSINESS STUDIES, SPECIAL ISSUE 1996

FIGURE 3
Configuration after Firm 2 Has Been Acquired and Rationalised by
Firm 1

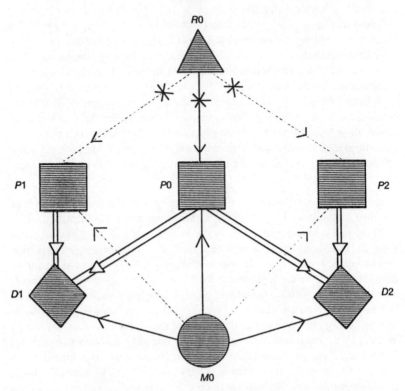

not an inevitable consequence of merger, but it is undoubtedly one of the advantages of merger that it is easier to do.

To illustrate the relationship between the new activity centred on $P0$ and the established activities centred on $P1$ and $P2$, all the activities of the firm are shown in the figure. Flows of established goods that were previously internal to the partner firms are indicated by broken double lines, whilst the flows of information that support them are indicated by broken single lines. The solid lines refer to flows involving the product that was previously generated in the IJV.

The same conventions are used in Figure 4 to illustrate the licensing option. Under licensing, Firm 2's laboratory $R2$ supplies technology direct to its 'opposite number' $R1$, which combines it with its own technology and transfers the resulting package internally to plant $P0$. The resulting product is supplied internally to $D1$, and externally to $D2$, both flows being coordinated

FIGURE 4
Configuration When Firm 1 Licenses in Technology from Firm 2

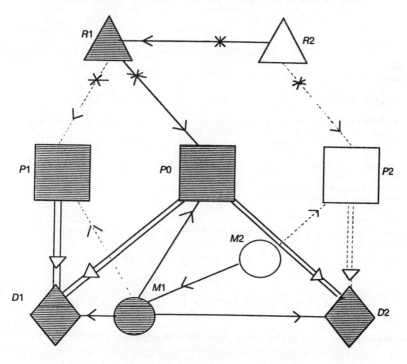

by $M1$ using information supplied to it under the licensing agreement by $M2$. This particular configuration of licensing has been chosen because it affords the most direct comparison with the configurations assumed for the other options discussed above.

INTERNALISATION FACTORS IN STRATEGIC CHOICE

The rationale of the joint venture is that it allows both of the partner firms to acquire some of the benefits of internalising knowledge flow without incurring the full set-up costs of a merger. By contrast, licensing affords no benefits of internalisation, but it avoids the more modest set up costs of an IJV.

There are many internalisation factors that potentially impact on IJVs [Buckley and Casson 1988]. Some of the most important ones are listed on the left-hand side of Table 2, together with their notation, which is used in the section, *A Formal Model of IJV Selection*. The column entries indicate the impact of each factor on the costs of each strategy.

The best known factor is the general security of property rights and, in particular, the existence of patent rights on technology. It is far easier to sell access

TABLE 2
Key Determinants of the Costs of Alternative Strategies

Determinant	Notation	Strategy		
		1. Licensing	2. IJV	3. Merger
Obstacles to licensing				
Lack of patent rights	p	+	0	0
Uncertainty about technological competence	t	+	0	0
Obstacles to IJV				
Cultural distance leading to misunderstanding and distrust	d	0	+	+
Obstacles to merger				
Protection of firm's independence	n	0	0	+
Scope economies in technology unrelated to other technologies of acquiring firm	s	0	0	+

Note: A positive sign indicates that costs increase whilst a zero sign indicates that costs are unaffected.

to a technology at arm's length when it is patented than when it is not. Thus patent coverage encourages licensing at the expense of both mergers and IJVs.

A more subtle point concerns the uncertainty that firms experience about their own degree of technological competence. A key feature of a joint venture contract, in contrast to a licensing agreement, is that it does not specify in detail exactly what technological expertise each partner will contribute to the venture. While neither partner normally commits itself to supplying all it knows, it does not attempt to restrict what it supplies under an IJV as explicitly as it would under a licensing agreement. Each firm generally agrees to contribute, within reason, whatever is necessary to achieve the agreed objective, such as the solution to a technical problem or the development of a new product. This arrangement provides mutual insurance to the partners under conditions where they are unsure, not only about their partner's technological competence, but about their own as well. If each partner firm knew exactly what it was capable of, and understood fully the requirements of the project, then it would be able to specify exactly what it required from its partner. At the same time, it would be perfectly clear as to what it was able to supply itself. Licensing would therefore involve no risk that either firm would lack the competence to fulfil its specific commitments. The more uncertain the partners are about their competence relative to the technical goal, however, the greater are the risks of specifying exactly what is required from their partner to complement their own skills, and conversely the greater are the risks of accepting an obligation to supply specific skills themselves.

This is evidently related to the tacitness of the knowledge involved [Polanyi 1966]. Although tacitness is normally discussed in terms of the costs of communicating knowledge to other people, a related, and indeed more fundamental, issue is whether people can actually communicate what they know to themselves. In other words, do managers understand where their competencies really lie before they get to put them into practice? It would seem that the concept of uncertainty about own-competence is a useful way of conceptualising this difficult issue.

The lack of specificity of the joint venture agreement therefore provides each firm with the flexibility to modify what it requires of its partner in the light of what it discovers about its own expertise. The same flexibility of response can be achieved by merger, as the top line of Table 2 makes clear. The greater the firm's uncertainty about its own technological competence, therefore, the stronger the preference for a merger or an IJV is likely to be.

It is possible to construct a number of variations on this theme – for example, where the partners discover one another's shortcomings rather than discovering their own – but the basic principle remains the same. The lack of specificity in the IJV arrangement affords a degree of mutual insurance through flexible response that is missing in an ordinary licensing agreement.

Mutual insurance only works, however, if the other partner can be trusted to make the appropriate response [Casson 1991; Ring and Van de Ven 1994]. Insuring people against their own incompetence creates a 'moral hazard' problem. They may plead incompetence merely to demand support from the other party, whilst claiming to be unable to deliver support themselves. Licensing requires less trust than an IJV because the contract, being more explicit in detail, is easier to enforce in law. This advantage of licensing depends, however, on the effectiveness of international law, which in turn depends upon the sanctions available, the rules of evidence, access to an impartial judiciary, and so on.

While IJVs are less dependent upon the law for their success, they are more dependent upon culture. From an economic perspective, culture may be defined as shared values and beliefs. Cultural homogeneity, acting through shared beliefs, reduces transactions costs by avoiding misunderstandings, whilst shared values – notably integrity and loyalty – underpin the willingness to share knowledge which is crucial to an IJV. Prudence requires that knowledge is shared only with those who can be trusted to reciprocate, which favours partnership with members of the same cultural group. This is reflected in the third line of Table 2, where cultural distance is identified as an obstacle to an IJV. Cultural distance may also be an obstacle to merger, though, contrary to popular opinion, the obstacle may not be as great as in the case of an IJV. This is because a merger permits hierarchical monitoring to be substituted for socially mediated trust, and in the long run allows corporate leadership to engineer a high-trust culture internal to the firm itself.

The last two factors in the table are classified as obstacles to merger. There is the well-known problem that some 'national champions' are protected from foreign takeover by their governments, whilst others are family firms whose shareholders value independence more than they value their profit stream. Such constraints can raise the cost of merger to a prohibitive level. Competition policy and antitrust policy can also protect firms from take-over, and in some cases antitrust policy may inhibit IJVs as well.

Then there is the nature of the acquired technology. If the acquired technology has many applications besides the particular application for which it is required, then the acquiring firm may need to diversify into these applications, or to license such applications out to other firms. In either case, it may be more advantageous for the acquiring firm to leave the original owner to do this, rather than to attempt this in addition to all the other things it has to do. The disadvantages of acquisition are greater the more unrelated is the acquired technology to the other technologies (if any) possessed by the acquiring firm.

THE DYNAMICS OF INNOVATION IN A GLOBAL ECONOMY

The choice of strategy can be analysed either as a one-off decision made afresh every time an opportunity for collaboration arises, or in terms of a commitment to handling a succession of opportunities of a given type using the same strategy. When technological innovation is spasmodic, then the first approach is the most appropriate, but in industries where innovation is a regular occurrence the second has more to recommend it. It is the second approach that is followed here.

Suppose that each firm is committed to combining one of its technologies with those of another firm, but that the firm it partners with keeps changing as new innovations continually occur. This is because innovative ability is dispersed across a number of potential partners in the industry, and indeed some major innovations may originate with entirely new entrants. When subsequent innovation renders an existing partner's technology obsolete, a change of partner is required. At any one time the firm has only one partner, but the identity of the partner changes with a frequency that reflects the rate of innovation in the industry.

Switching partners incurs considerable costs where merger is concerned, because of the expense of the legal reconstruction of the firms and their subsequent rationalisation (as indicated in Figure 3). Whilst commitment to merger affords significant internalisation benefits, its costs are large as well. Thus rapid innovation which leads to frequent partner switching considerably increases the average recurrent cost of the merger strategy. The formation of an IJV also incurs significant set up costs, though not as large as those of a merger. Correspondingly, the internalisation gains are lower too. At the opposite extreme to a merger is the licensing option, which involves low setup costs but offers no internalisation economies at all. Licensing is therefore much cheaper than merger, and somewhat cheaper than an IJV, when technological change is rapid.

The costs of switching to a new partner are normally incurred at the outset of an arrangement, whilst the benefits are deferred: they are distributed continuously over time. There is, therefore, an element of interest cost in switching, and this must be allowed for when calculating the costs and benefits of alternative strategies.

Unlike the costs of internalisation, the benefits of internalisation are continuing ones. Moreover they normally vary directly with the size of the market in a way that setup costs do not. The greater the value of the market for the product that the partner firms produce, the greater the gains from internalisation. One reason for this is that internalisation enhances the proportion of the rents from the marketing of the product that the firms can appropriate for themselves.

A FORMAL MODEL OF IJV SELECTION

There is a subtle interplay between the different factors mentioned above that requires a formal model for its elucidation. Let the three strategies be indexed in ascending order of internalisation: $k=1$ for licensing, $k=2$ for an IJV and $k=3$ for a merger. In addition there is a null strategy ($k=0$) which involves no collaboration between firms. As indicated at the outset, the firms maximise profit, subject to the constraints imposed by family ownership or 'national champion' status. It is assumed that these constraints do not apply to Firm 1, the decisionmaker, although they may well apply to its partner, Firm 2. The strategy is chosen by Firm 1 to maximise its overall profit, π.

Profit has three components: the basic gains from collaboration, which are independent of the chosen strategy but vary with the size of the market; the benefits of internalisation, which vary according to the strategy and according to market size; and the costs of internalisation, which are independent of market size but vary according to the chosen strategy, the frequency of partner change and a number of other factors described below.

Let π_k be the profit per period generated by the consistent pursuit of strategy k through a succession of collaborations with innovative partner firms. Let c_k be the set up costs incurred by strategy k when switching to a new partner firm. All of the costs identified in Table 2 may be construed as costs of this kind. Reading down the right-hand columns of the table shows that the setup cost of a licensing arrangement, c_1, is an increasing function of missing patent rights, p, and uncertainty about the firm's technological competence, t. The setup cost of an IJV, c_2, is an increasing function of cultural distance, d, whilst the setup

864   JOURNAL OF INTERNATIONAL BUSINESS STUDIES, SPECIAL ISSUE 1996

cost of a merger, c_3, is an increasing function of cultural distance, d, the degree of protection of the independence of the partner firm, n, and the scope economies of the technology, s:

$$c_1 = c_1 (p,t) \tag{1.1}$$

$$c_2 = c_2(d) \tag{1.2}$$

$$c_3 = c_3(d, n, s) . \tag{1.3}$$

Let $f \leq 1$ be the frequency with which a change of partner occurs. This frequency may be interpreted as the probability that a change will occur in any given period. The value of f reflects the pace of innovation in the global economy. Let $r \geq 0$ be the rate of interest in the international capital market. When interest charges associated with the setup costs are allowed for by summing the relevant geometric series, the average recurrent expense equivalent to a unit setup cost turns out to be

$$v=(r / (1+r)) \sum_{n=0}^{\infty} (1 / (1+r)n / f)=(f+r) / (1+r) , \tag{2}$$

provided that r is suitably small. It is readily established that v is an increasing function of the frequency f and the rate of interest r,

$$\delta v/\delta f=1/(1+r)>0 \tag{3.1}$$

$$\delta v/\delta r=(1-f)/(1+r)^2>0 . \tag{3.2}$$

Let b_k be the benefit from internalisation accruing when strategy k is applied to a market of unit size. It is assumed that the total benefit is directly proportional to the market size, x. As indicated above, the internalisation benefit of merger exceeds that of an IJV, which in turn exceeds that of licensing – which is, of course, zero; thus

$$b_3>b_2>b_1=0 . \tag{4}$$

Since profit is by definition the excess of benefit over cost,

$$\pi_0=0$$

$$\pi_k=(a+b_k)x-c_k v \qquad (k=1,2,3) , \tag{5}$$

where $a>0$ is the basic gain from collaboration per unit market size. The chosen strategy k satisfies the inequality constraint

$$\pi_k \geq \pi_i \qquad (i \neq k) . \tag{6}$$

The choice of k is unique when the inequality (6) is strictly satisfied.

All of the factors shown in equation (5) affect the choice of k, as do the factors which in turn determine them; thus

$$k = (a, b_2, b_3, d, p, n, s, t, f, r, x) . \tag{7}$$

Not all of these factors impact on IJV strategy all of the time. They only affect the choice when it is marginal, and there are three different margins that are involved. The marginal choice between an IJV and licensing depends on all of these factors except b_3, n and s, which are specific to a merger, and a, which is common to both. The marginal choice between an IJV and a merger depends on all of these factors except p and t, which are specific to licensing, and a, which is again common to both. The marginal choice between an IJV and the null strategy depends on all the factors except b_3, n and s, which are specific to mergers, and t, which is specific to licensing. In principle, all of these margins can be relevant, though only in exceptional circumstances will two or more of them be relevant at the same time.

THE INTERACTION OF MARKET SIZE AND VOLATILITY

Discrete choice models of this kind have many applications in international business. Indeed, Buckley and Casson [1981] use a variant of the present model to analyse entry through Foreign Direct Investment (FDI) to a foreign market. Their model excludes IJVs, but includes exporting as an alternative to foreign direct investment and licensing. Exporting is already included in the present model, as a component of all three strategies, and so does not need to be treated separately as in the previous model. The previous model also excludes volatility; it takes only a short-run view of technological change compared to the present paper. The formal similarities can be seen by examining the influence of market size on strategic choice, as illustrated in Figure 5.

The figure measures profit vertically and market size horizontally. The zero-profit axis is A_0A_0', corresponding to the null strategy; the bottom axis is used purely to clarify the labelling of the figure. The variation of profitability with market size under licensing is indicated by the line A_1A_1'; since licensing affords low setup costs, but no internalisation benefits, the intercept is only slightly below that of A_0A_0', whilst the slope (measured by a) is fairly modest. The situation under an IJV is indicated by A_2A_2'; the intercept is lower, because the setup costs are higher, but the slope (measured by $a+b_2$) is steeper because internalisation benefits are available. Finally the schedule A_3A_3' shows the situation under merger; the intercept is very low because the setup costs are very high, but the slope (measured by $a + b_3$) is the steepest of all because the full benefit of internalisation is being obtained.

The envelope $A_0B_0B_1B_2A_3'$, indicated by the heavy line, indicates the maximum profit generated at each market size. The strategy that generates this profit is determined by which of the schedules forms the envelope at the appropriate point. The corresponding strategy can be read off along the horizontal axis, as indicated in the figure. The figure has been drawn so that all of the strategies have a role to play – no one strategy is dominated by the others. Under these

Strategic Alliances

FIGURE 5
Influence of Market Size on Strategic Choice

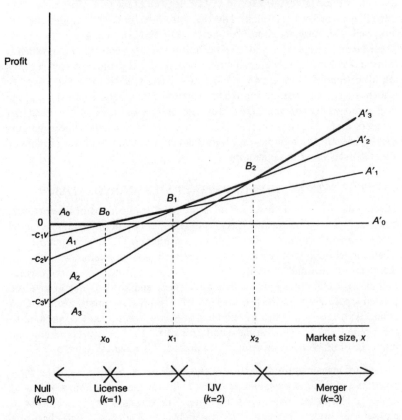

conditions there is a steady progression, as market size increases, from no collaboration, to licensing, to an IJV and finally to a merger. This is because as the size of the market grows the setup costs of internalisation, which are fixed costs independent of market size, can be spread more thinly and so greater investment in internalisation becomes worthwhile.

This is a very partial picture of the situation, however. While it is the size of the market that governs the benefits of internalisation, it is the factor v that governs costs. The factor v may be termed the volatility factor; it reflects the impact of both the pace of technological progress and the cost of capital.

A complementary view to Figure 5 is presented in Figure 6, which shows how the profitability of the different strategies varies with volatility for a given market size. The profits of licensing, IJV and merger are indicated by the respective schedules D_1D_1', D_2D_2' and D_3D_3'. The envelope of maximum profit

FIGURE 6
Impact of Volatility Factor on Strategic Choice

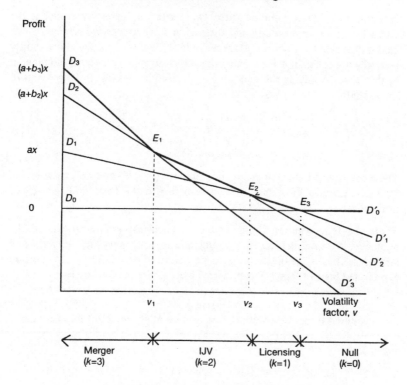

is $D_3E_1E_2E_3D_0'$. It can be seen that as volatility increases so internalisation becomes less attractive. There is first a switch from merger to IJV, then from IJV to licensing, and finally collaboration is abandoned altogether.

This diagram provides a simple explanation of joint venture instability. Compared to a merger, the advantage of an IJV stems from the ability to switch partners as technology evolves. It is intrinsic to an IJV that the arrangement is not as long lasting as a merger would be. Indeed, if an IJV turned out to be very long lasting, it would suggest that management had made a strategic error, and that a merger would have been better instead. For example, a merger would have allowed for a more thorough rationalisation of activities than an IJV. The fact that many IJVs lead to a subsequent merger confirms this view, as it shows that such strategic errors can be corrected later. It also confirms the recent view that short-lived IJVs are not necessarily a failure. Indeed, it goes further than this, and shows that a firm that participates in a succession of short-lived IJVs, far from being a poor performer, may be

868   JOURNAL OF INTERNATIONAL BUSINESS STUDIES, SPECIAL ISSUE 1996

sticking consistently to a successful strategy that affords flexibility under conditions of rapid technological change.

It seems natural to combine these two partial analyses by studying the interaction between volatility and the size of the market. An exercise of this kind is illustrated in Figure 7. Market size is plotted horizontally and volatility vertically. Once again it is assumed that no strategy is completely dominated by the others. Applying this condition to the inequalities (6), and invoking (4), shows that

$$k= \begin{cases} 0 & \textit{if } v>a/c_1 \\ 1 & \textit{if } b_2(c_2-c_1)<v\leq a/c_1 \\ 2 & \textit{if } (b_3-b_2)\,/\,(c_3-c_1)<v\leq b_2\,/\,(c_2-c_1) \\ 3 & \textit{if } v<b_2\,/\,(c_2-c_1)\,. \end{cases} \qquad (8)$$

These conditions indicate how the boundaries OF_1, OF_2 and OF_3 between the regimes shown in the figure vary in response to the costs and benefits of internalisation.

There are four regimes in the figure, each corresponding to one of the strategies. If the market size is very small and volatility very high, then the null strategy is chosen. As the market size increases and/or volatility falls, licensing is preferred instead. The IJV is preferred when either market size and volatility

FIGURE 7
Combined Impact of Market Size and Volatility on Strategic Choice

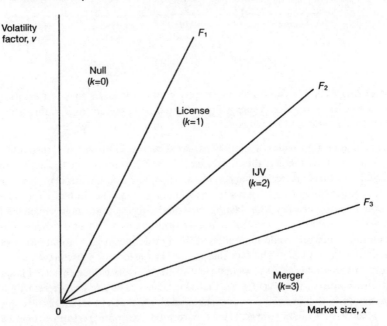

TABLE 3
Impact of Market Size and Volatility on Strategic Choice

	Volatility	
Market Size	Low	High
High	Merger	IJV
Low	IJV	Licensing

are both low – i.e., the market, though small, is subject to little innovation, or both high – i.e., there is a large market with considerable innovation. Finally, merger is selected when the market is very large but volatility is very low.

The major implications of these results are summarised in Table 3. IJVs are favoured in the symmetric situations where market size and volatility are either both low or both high. Licensing is favoured in the asymmetric situation where the market is small but volatile, and merger in the opposite situation where the market is large but stable.

Given the dependence of volatility on both the pace of technological change and the rate of interest, the results can also be summarised by saying that IJVs are favoured under the following conditions:

(a) limited innovation, low rate of interest and small market;

(b) moderate innovation, moderate rate of interest and moderate size of market; and

(c) rapid innovation, high rate of interest and large market.

(d) limited innovation, high rate of interest and moderate size of market; and

(e) rapid innovation, low rate of interest and moderate size of market.

It is suggested below that it is scenario (c) that is most relevant to the increase of IJV activity in the 1980s. Scenario (b) is also interesting, though, because it shows that IJVs can also occur under conditions of 'moderation in all things'. Other variants of this moderation theme can be generated by allowing one factor to increase whilst there is a compensating decrease in another factor; for example, 'size of market'.

The impact of the other factors can be analysed by examining their effects on each of the four regimes. Figure 8 illustrates how the effects described in Table 2 are reflected in the directions in which the various boundaries rotate in response to changes in cultural distance, d, the degree of protection of the independence of the partner firm n, missing patent rights, p, the scope economies of the technology, s, and the uncertainty about technological competence, t. It can be seen that in addition to the results reported above, IJVs are

FIGURE 8
Impact of Cultural Heterogeneity, Protection of Independence,
Economies of Scope and Technological Uncertainty on Strategic Choice

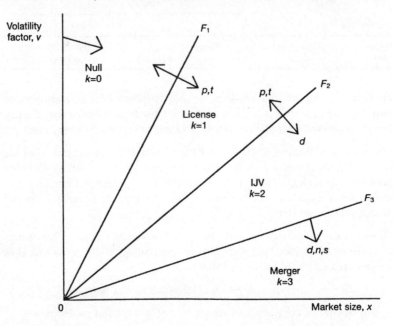

favored by a high degree of protection of the independence of the partner firm (which inhibits merger), n, and by major uncertainty about technological competence, t. The effect of cultural distance d is ambiguous: although it may encourage IJVs at the expense of mergers it also encourages licensing instead of IJVs. IJVs are definitely encouraged by economies of scope in technology, s, because such economies are difficult to exploit through a merger. Finally, IJVs are favored by uncertainty about technological competence, t, because this makes licensing a relatively inflexible arrangement.

APPLICATION OF THE MODEL – IJVs IN THE GLOBAL ECONOMY

The model can be used to explain the increasing use of IJVs in international business during the 1980s [Dunning 1993, pp. 250–55] in terms of:

- reductions in trade barriers and improvements in freight transportation, which have 'globalised' markets and so increased market size;

- rapid increases in national income, particularly in the Asian-Pacific region, which have also increased market size, particularly for consumer durables;

- accelerated technological innovation which has increased volatility;

- the emergence of new technologies, combining ideas from different scientific traditions, which has increased firms' uncertainties about their own technological competences, and

- new technologies such as information technology, biotechnology and genetic engineering which seem to exhibit greater economies of scope than the dominant engineering technologies of the 1960s.

In terms of Figure 9, factors (a)-(c) represent a shift from area Z_0-moderate market size and low volatility, in the 1960s, to Z_1-large market size and high volatility, in the 1980s. Factor (d) corresponds to the anti-clockwise rotation of the boundary OF_2 to OF_2', whilst factor (e) corresponds to the clockwise rotation of the boundary OF_3 to OF_3'. As a result, some collaborations that would have been effected by merger are now effected by IJVs. Moreover, some collaborations that would have been effected by IJVs and might now be effected by licensing because of greater volatility are still effected by IJVs because technological uncertainty has increased as well.

IJVs have not had matters entirely their own way, however. Barriers to merger

FIGURE 9
Comparative Analysis of the International Business Environment in the 1960s and 1980s

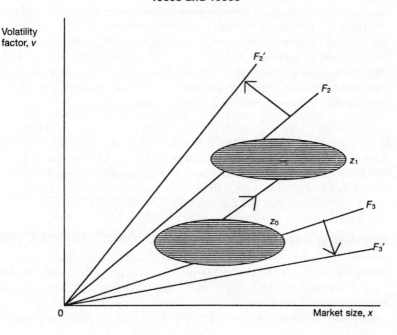

872   JOURNAL OF INTERNATIONAL BUSINESS STUDIES, SPECIAL ISSUE 1996

caused by the existence of 'national champions' have tended to diminish, allowing more foreign acquisitions to take place in high technology industries. The speculative boom in the 1980s reduced the effective cost of capital to large firms and so reduced the interest burden of financing mergers and acquisitions. Moreover, the combination of expanding market size and a degree of 'technological protectionism' in the European Union has produced a combination of large market size and more moderate volatility which is conducive to mergers between 'protected' firms. Indeed, such mergers have sometimes been favoured by the industrial policymakers on the grounds that they will help to create not national but 'European' champions.

EXTENSIONS OF THE MODEL

The scope of every economic model is restricted by the nature of the assumptions that the modeller is required to make, and the present case is no exception. Because it is such a simple model, however, it is a straightforward matter to extend it. Greater relevance can be obtained at little cost in terms of analytical complexity.

It is not difficult, for example, to augment the set of strategies. One possibility worth considering is that the firm could 'go it alone' and attempt to replicate its partner's expertise for itself. Another is that the firm could license out its own technology rather than license in its rival's technology. Economies of scope and technological uncertainties introduce some complications here, though. Suppose that both firms have other technologies besides the ones that they plan to combine in the IJV. If the other technologies of Firm 2 have greater complementarity (or 'synergy') with the technology offered by Firm 1 than have the technologies of Firm 1 with the technology offered by Firm 2, then it is appropriate for Firm 1 to license out to Firm 2 instead of the other way round. This ensures the complementaries between the different technologies within the firms' portfolios are used to greatest effect.

Firm 2 will be willing to license in the technology, though, only if it is sure that the technology will match its own competence. If Firm 2 is more uncertain of its own competence than is Firm 1 then it may be reluctant to license in, so that Firm 2 may still finish up licensing out as a response to this difficulty. It is only when Firm 2 is reasonably certain of its competence that it will be willing to act on the basis that the greatest complementarities lie between its own technologies and the technology on offer from Firm 1.

This leads to a further point, concerning the passive role that has been imputed to Firm 2 up till now. The possibility that Firm 2 will license Firm 1's technology suggests a more active role for Firm 2. In particular, it suggests that Firm 2 may attempt to bargain with Firm 1 over the distribution of the rewards from collaboration. It will no longer be the case, therefore, that all the gains from collaboration accrue to Firm 1. If the two firms have similar information about the total gains to be generated by the different strategies then they may as well dispense with negotiations and agree right away upon the strategy that maximises their total gain. They can then divide this gain amongst themselves in some equitable way, such as a 50:50 split.

When the gains are always divided in some fixed proportion then the choice of strategy will be the same as when only one of the firms takes an active role. This is because the ordering of the strategies by the active firm in any given situation is unchanged when the profits of all the strategies are reduced by the same fixed proportion. Unfortunately, however, this condition is not always satisfied in practice.

It is also possible to augment the list of exogenous variables both by addressing wholly new issues, such as the impact of tax incentives, and by refining the treatment of existing ones. Consider, for example, the impact of the pace of technological change on switching costs. When established firms are good at 'learning by doing' [Nelson and Winter 1982], future technological improvements are likely to accrue to existing partners. It is mainly when established partners are poor at learning by doing that improvements are more likely to originate with entrants to the industry. The capability of established firms to maintain their leadership is, in turn, likely to be stronger when technological change is incremental, within an existing paradigm, rather than radical, involving the emergence of a new paradigm. This suggests that it is not just the overall pace of technological change that needs to be incorporated into the model, but, more specifically, the pace of incremental change and the pace of radical change. Rapid incremental change may be perfectly compatible with the merger strategy because the enduring value of the other firm's competence is reasonably assured; but rapid radical change is likely to subvert the merger strategy and favour the IJV, or licensing, instead.

GENERALISATION OF THE RESULTS

The application of the model has focused on the growth of innovation-driven and rationalisation-driven IJVs of the kind that predominate in high-technology industries. The emergence of such IJVs has been associated with the downsizing and delayering of some large multinationals. These firms have been restructured in a more entrepreneurial and flexible form as a network of alliances. At the same time, however, a more traditional kind of IJV, concerned with market access, has continued to flourish. Such IJVs are favoured by Japanese firms seeking to consolidate their share in the European market. How far do the results derived above apply to these type 2 and type 3 IJVs, and indeed to other types of IJV as well?

The short answer is that many of the results remain unchanged, but some do not. Factors such as missing patent rights, government protection against foreign acquisition and cultural distance continue to affect IJV decisions in the

874   JOURNAL OF INTERNATIONAL BUSINESS STUDIES, SPECIAL ISSUE 1996

same way as before. This reflects the generality of the internalisation theory from which they derive. The rate of interest and market size are basic economic variables that remain important too. Other factors, though, are more specific to the type 5 IJV.

Where other types of IJV are concerned, the interplay of technological expertise and marketing expertise takes a slightly different form. For example, where market access is concerned, the speed of learning becomes more important than the pace of technological change. The faster the high-technology firm can acquire the local expertise of the market-oriented firm, and the slower the market-oriented firm is to acquire technology, the more beneficial is the IJV as a transitional method of market entry to the high-technology firm. Uncertainty about the quality of marketing expertise becomes more important too.

CONCLUSIONS

The development of an economic model is often stimulated by the desire to explain certain 'stylised facts'. In the present case the stylised fact has been the increasing number of IJVs in high-technology global industries. Economic models offer a simple yet rigorous explanation of facts which other disciplines sometimes explain in more complicated and more heuristic terms. If economic models did no more than rationalise what everyone already knows, however, then their value would be rather limited. Fortunately, the way that economic models are constructed means that they do not merely explain the facts they were designed to explain but provide new predictions as well. It is their ability to draw attention to phenomena that have not been noticed, and to integrate the explanation of these phenomena with the explanations of already known phenomena, that is the true measure of their success.

The model developed in this paper explains the formation of IJVs in terms of eight distinct but related factors. These factors are listed on the left-hand side of Table 4. They govern the margins of strategic interaction between IJVs and licensing on the one hand, and IJVs and mergers on the other. The impact of each factor on each of these strategies is indicated by the entries in the table.

The model shows that the impact of any given factor can only be understood by controlling for the seven other factors in the analysis. It is also necessary, in addition, to control for the levels of some of the factors; in particular, the effects of market size, the pace of innovation, and the rate of interest reverse direction as their level increases.

The gist of the results can be summarised by saying that IJVs represent a strategy of moderation. Just as the equity participation in an IJV is inter-mediate between that in a licensing agreement and that in a full-scale merger, so the IJV emerges as intermediate in strategic terms as well. This may help to explain why the empirical evidence on IJVs is so difficult to interpret in terms

TABLE 4
Impact of Key Explanatory Factor on Strategic Choice

Explanatory Factor	Notation	Strategy		
		Licensing	IJV	Merger
Market size	x	−	X	+
Pace of technological change	f	+	X	−
Rate of interest	r	+	X	−
Cultural distance	d	+	?	?
Protection of independence	n	+	+	−
Missing patent rights	p	−	+	+
Economies of scope	s	+	−	−
Technological uncertainty	t	−	+	+

Note: X indicates positive at a low value and negative at a high value.

of models that seek to relate IJV activities to extreme values of particular factors, such as the sunk costs of R&D.

The results summarised in Table 4 generate detailed predictions about how IJV formation will vary within industries, between industries, across countries, and over time. Factors such as technological uncertainty are firm-specific and can therefore explain why firms in the same industry adopt different strategies. The pace of technological change is industry-specific and can therefore explain differences in the frequency with which IJVs are encountered in various industries. Cultural distance is specific to pairwise combinations of countries and can therefore account for differences in the international distribution of IJVs within an industry. With globally integrated capital markets, the rate of interest tends to be uniform across industries and countries and is therefore mainly a time-specific factor.

The other factors mentioned also vary with time, of course, though some (such as the pace of technological innovation) may vary more than others (such as cultural differences). Despite the apparently restrictive nature of the assumption of profit-maximisation applied to a representative pair of firms, therefore, a wide variety of relevant results can be obtained.

REFERENCES

Beamish, Paul W. & John C. Banks. 1987. Equity joint ventures and the theory of the multinational enterprise. *Journal of International Business Studies*, 19(2): 1–16.

Buckley, Peter J. 1988. The limits of explanation: Testing the internalization theory of the multinational enterprise. *Journal of International Business Studies*, 19(2): 181–93.

—— & Mark C. Casson. 1976. *The future of the multinational enterprise.* London: Macmillan.

——. 1981. The optimal timing of a foreign direct investment. *Economic Journal*, 91: 75–87.

——. 1988. A theory of cooperation in international business. In F. J. Contractor & P. Lorange, editors, *Cooperative strategies in international business*, 31–53. Lexington, Mass.: Lexington Books.

Casson, Mark C. 1991. *The economics of business culture: Game theory, transaction costs and economic performance.* Oxford, U.K.: Clarendon Press.

——. 1995. *The organisation of international business.* Aldershot, U.K.: Edward Elgar.

——. 1996. *Information and organisation: A new perspective on the theory of the firm.* Oxford, U.K.: Clarendon Press.

Dunning, John H. 1993. *Multinational enterprises and the global economy.* Wokingham, Berkshire, U.K.: Addison-Wesley.

Geringer, J. Michael & Louis Hébert. 1989. Control and performance of international joint ventures. *Journal of International Business Studies,* 20(2): 235–54.

Harrigan, Kathryn. 1988. Strategic alliances and partner asymmetries. In F. J. Contractor & P. Lorange, editors, *Cooperative strategies in international business,* 205–26. Lexington, Mass.: Lexington Books.

Nelson, Richard R. & Sidney G. Winter. 1982. *An evolutionary theory of economic change.* Cambridge, Mass.: Belknap Press of Harvard University Press.

Parkhe, Arvind. 1993. 'Messy' research, methodological predispositions, and theory development in international joint ventures. *Academy of Management Review,* 18: 227–68.

Polanyi, Michael. 1966. *The tacit dimension.* New York: Anchor Day.

Ring, Peter Smith & Anthony H. Van der Ven. 1994. Developmental processes of cooperative interorganisational relationships. *Academy of Management Review,* 19: 90–118.

Tallman, Stephen B. 1992. A strategic management perspective on host country structure of multinational enterprise. *Journal of Management,* 18: 455–71.

Veugelers, Reinhilde & Katrien Kesteloot. 1994. On the design of stable joint ventures. *European Economic Review,* 38: 1799–1815.

[8]

F. J. Contractor / P. Lorange*

Competition vs. Cooperation: A Benefit/Cost Framework for Choosing Between Fully-Owned Investments and Cooperative Relationships

Introduction

How should a company choose between the options of investing in a fully-owned operation versus entering into a cooperative arrangement involving another international firm? The basic intent of this paper is to develop a framework for answering this question. The framework can be used in either a strategic planning sense or in a project cash flow sense, to enable the analyst to select one of the options.

In the last few years, there appears to have been a proliferation of international joint ventures, licensing, co-production agreements, joint research programs, exploration consortia, and other cooperative relationships between two or more potentially competitive firms. Contrast this with the traditional preference of international executives to enter a market or line of business alone. The latter seems to have been particularly true for larger multinationals, especially those based in the United States although for firms based in Japan, Europe and developing nations there has always been a somewhat higher propensity to form cooperative relationships (United Nations, 1978; Stopford and Haberich, 1976). Traditionally, cooperative arrangements were often seen as second best to the strategic option of going-it-alone in the larger firms. Licensing, joint ventures, co-production, management service agreements, etc., have been viewed as options reluctantly undertaken under external mandates such as government investment laws, or to cross protectionist entry barriers in developing and regulated economies.

What makes the recent spate of cooperative associations different is that they are being formed between firms in industrial free-market economies where there are few external regulatory pressures mandating a link up. Instead of the traditional pattern of a large "foreign" firm trying to access a market by associating itself with a "local" partner, many recent partnerships involve joint activities in several stages of the value-added chain, such as production, sourcing and R&D. These associations often involve firms of comparable rather than unequal size, both may be international in scope, and each may make similar rather than complimentary contributions. Further, the territorial scope of these new cooperative ventures is global, rather than restricted to a single country market as in the traditional pattern of joint ventures and contractual agreements.

Before we discuss the main issue treated in this paper, namely a model to assess the relative benefits and costs of cooperative arrangements over fully-owned subsidiaries, let us take a brief look at data on how common cooperative agreements are, and at at their various forms.

*Professor Farok J. Contractor, Graduate School of Management, Rutgers University, Newark, NJ; Professor Peter Lorange, Wharton School, University of Pennsylvania, Philadelphia, U.S.A. Manuscript received March 1987.

The Incidence of Cooperative Arrangements

How important are cooperative arrangements such as joint ventures and licensing, compared with fully-owned foreign subsidiaries? For U.S.-based companies, arrangements involving overseas "partners," licensing or local shareholders, outnumber fully-owned subsidiaries by a ratio of 4 to 1. Compared with the approximately 10,000 fully-owned foreign affiliates, there are 14 to 15 thousand affiliates in which the U.S. parent's share is *less* than 100 percent. Of the latter, in about 12 thousand affiliates, the U.S. parent has a 10 to 50 percent equity position, i.e., minority affiliates roughly equal majority and fully-owned affiliates put together.[1] In addition, there are at least 30,000 overseas licensees who have received American technology but where U.S. firms have negligible or no equity stake. (See U.S. Department of Commerce, 1981 and 1985). The fact remains that many of the cooperative ventures, particularly those in which the U.S. company has a minority stake, are rather small affairs. Hence, the above picture can be misleading. By indexes such as assets or number of employees, the fully-owned foreign subsidiaries of U.S.-based multinationals continue to account for over two-thirds of the *value* of American foreigs investment, even if these subsidiaries are vastly outnumbered by the shared equity arrangements. Companies based in Europe and Japan are said to have a higher propensity than U.S. firms to enter joint ventures and licensing agreements. But the data remain fragmentary and incomplete, making it hard to verify global patterns of cooperative activities. They are ubiquitous however and are being increasingly factored into global strategy.

Types of Cooperative Arrangements

Between the extremes of spot transacitons undertaken by two firms, on the one end, and their complete merger, on the other hand, lie several types of cooperative arrangements. These arrangements differ in the formula used to compensate each partner, i.e., the legal form of the agreement, as well as the strategic impact on the global operations of each partner. Table 1 ranks these arrangements in order of increasing inter-organizational dependence which is generally, but not necessarily, correlated with strategic impact (Pfeffer and Nowak, 1976).

For instance, technical training and "start-up" assistance agreements are usually of short duration. The company supplying the technology and training is typically compensated with a lump-sum amount, and will thereafter have minimal links with the start-up company, unless, of course, there is an additional licensing agreement. Similarly, patent licensing involves a one-time transfer of the patent right. Compensation, however, is often in the form of a running royalty expressed as a fraction of sales value. In component-supply, contract assembly, "buy-back" and franchising agreements, the principal form of compensation for both partners is the mark-up on the goods supplied, although there could be a royalty arrangement as well, as in the case of franchising. The interdependence between the partners is thus becoming somewhat greater because of delivery, quality control and transfer pricing issues associated with the supply of materials, as well as due to the global brand recognition in franchising.

Know-how licensing and management service agreements assume a closer degree of continuing assistance and organizational links. Studies show that most licensing involves the transfer of know-how and proprietary information (Contractor, 1984). It is not simply a matter of transferring a patent right or providing start-up training. It involves extended links between the two firms and ongoing interactions on technical or administrative issues. Payment in these cases will typically be in the form of a lump-sum fee plus running royalties.

Table 1: Types of Cooperative Arrangements

	Typical Compensation Method	Extent of Inter-organizational Dependence
• Technical Trainings/Start-Up Assistance Agreements	L	Negligible
• Patent Licensing	r	
• Production/Assembly/"Buy-back" Agreements	m	Low
• Franchising	r; m	
• "Know-how" Liscensing	L; r	
• Management/Marketing Service Agreement	L; r	
• Non-Equity Cooperative Agreements in		Moderate
- Exploration	$\pi_i = f(C_v \times P_v)$	
- Research Partnership	$\pi_i = f(C_v \times R_i)$	
- Development/Co-production	$\pi_i = f(C_i \times R_j)$	
• Equity Joint Venture	α	High

Key: α = Fraction of Shares/Dividends; r = Royalty as % of Turnover; L = Lump-Sum Fee; m = Markup on Components Sold, or Finished Output Brought Back; π_i = Profit of Firm L in Non-Equity Joint Venture; C_v, R_v = Costs and Revenues of the Venture; C_i, R_i = Losts and Revenues of the Firm i; R_j = Revenues of Dominant Partner.

The term "joint venture" usually connotes the creation of a separate corporation, whose stock is shared by two or more partners, each expecting a proportional share of dividends as compensation. But many cooperative programs between firms involve joint activities without the creation of a new corporate entity. Instead, carefully defined rules and formulae govern the allocation of tasks, costs and revenues. Table 1 gives three examples. Exploration consortia often involve the sharing of the venture's costs and revenue from a successful find, by formula. By comparison, the costs of a research partnership may be allocated by an agreed upon formula, but the revenue of each partner depends on what each company independently does with the technology created. In co-production agreements, such as the Boeing 767 project involving Boeing and Japan Aircraft Development Corporation (itself a consortium of Mitsubishi, Kawasaki and Fuji), each partner is responsible for manufacturing a particular section of the aircraft. Each partner's costs are therefore a function of its own efficiency in producing their part. However, revenue is a function of the successful sales of the 767 by the dominant partner Boeing (Moxon and Geringer, 1985). Each of these examples involves different risk/return tradeoffs for the parties.

Choosing between a Cooperative Arrangement and a Wholly-Owned Operation

The decision of whether to enter into a cooperative arrangement or whether to expand via a wholly-owned operation is often a critical issue in international strategy. We now introduce a framework for a cost/benefit analysis comparing the two options.

A cooperative venture may have the effect of increasing the project's revenues and/or decreasing costs over what could have been earned by a fully-owned subsidiary; on the other hand certain drawbacks endemic to cooperative relationships might decrease revenues and/or increase costs over the level of a fully-owned operation. We assume that a company has made projections for the revenues, costs and profitability of a fully-owned operation and a cooperative mode alternative. Using this as a base of reference, we make the following axiomatic statement:

A Cooperative Venture (CV) is Preferred over Fully-owned subsidiary when

$$[(R_1+R_2) + (C_1 + C_2)] - [(R_3+R_4) + (C_3+C_4)] > (1-\alpha)\pi_{CV}$$

Incremental	− Incremental	> Share of
Benefit of	Cost of a	Other Partner's
a CV	CV	Profit in Venture

and / or

if risk is reduced significantly through cooperation

where α = Profit share of firm doing the analysis

$1-\alpha$ = Profit share of other partners, $(0 < \alpha < 1)$.

That is to say, a cooperative mode is preferred over the go-it-alone option when the net benefit of the former over the latter is greater than the share of profit of the other partners. Our firm is then better off by cooperating, especially if in so doing, risk is reduced. (We will discuss how operating risks are reduced by cooperation in a later section).

The terms are defined as under: *A cooperative venture, compared with the fully-owned subsidiary will create Incremental Benefits and Costs.* These are defined in more detail in Tables 2 to 6.

By "direct" is meant the revenue and cost increments directly impinging on the project itself. By "indirect" is meant the effect of undertaking the cooperative venture on the *rest* of the global enterprise, i.e. on other divisions of the company, on affiliates in other countries, and on overall strategy. The "direct" and the "indirect" revenues and costs do not always have the same directional effect. A licensing agreement or a joint venture for instance, may in itself be directly profitable, but it can be indirectly harmful if it creates a *future* competitor, perhaps in a third country.

The analytical framework applies to all types of cooperative arrangements. We now examine the incremental benefits and costs of cooperation in more detail.

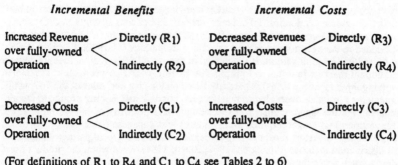

Incremental Benefits   *Incremental Costs*

Increased Revenue over fully-owned Operation — Directly (R_1) / Indirectly (R_2)

Decreased Revenues over fully-owned Operation — Directly (R_3) / Indirectly (R_4)

Decreased Costs over fully-owned Operation — Directly (C_1) / Indirectly (C_2)

Increased Costs over fully-owned Operation — Directly (C_3) / Indirectly (C_4)

(For definitions of R_1 to R_4 and C_1 to C_4 see Tables 2 to 6)

Benefits of Cooperative Ventures

Increased Revenues from Cooperation (R_1 and R_2)

The benefits of cooperative ventures are summarized in Tables 2 and 3. Among the reasons why cooperative project revenues can be greater than a single-owner operation are the other partner's market knowledge, technology, market access, ties to important buyers and government, and faster entry and payback. Besides there is the obvious, but sometimes important, fact that market share is larger because now there is one less competitor.

Table 2: Increased Revenue From Cooperative-Venture (CV) Mode

Direct (R1)	Indirect (R2)
• Other Partner's Knowledge of Market	• More Complete Product Line helps overall Sales
• Other Partner's Intangible Assets such as Technology, Patents, Trademark	• Technical or new Product Ideas Learned from other Partner, Diffused to other Parts of Company
• Other Partner's ties to Government or important Buyers	• Markups on Components, or Product
• One less Competitor; Hence Larger Market Share	
• Faster Entry improves NPV	
• Access to Market otherwise Foreclosed	

Market access, or the other partner's market knowledge remain important factors in both socialist, developing and industrial country markets. In weapons systems NATO encourages or requires tie-ups among defense firms, so that arms purchasing nations get some value added in their economies as well as receive technology (Mariti and Smiley, 1983). The AT&T/Philips joint venture is predicated in part on AT&T's relative inexperience in international markets familiar to Philips. The Boeing-JADC co-production agreement (involving three Japanese firms) is partially based on the idea that sales of the 767 would be augmented in Japan over what may have been possible had Boeing produced the airplan alone. For the Japanese market, even though MITI (Ministry of International Trade and Investment) no longer requires joint ventures with Japanese firms as a precondition of entry, foreign investors most often find it expedient to take a local partner who knows local distribution methods (Abegglen, 1982; Reich, 1984). Even when the product itself is simple, such as a commodity or chemical, distribution practices and industrial buying methods appear arcane to non-Japanese. This is an important reason for nearly a thousand joint ventures formed between U.S. and Japanese companies.

The market access motivation is often paramount in patent licensing, since a patent is a territorial monopoly. This right is conveyed to the licensee. As Telesio (1977) and Contractor (1985) show, the territory-allocation issue is very important in licensing in the pharmaceutical and chemical industries.

For small-sized companies lacking international experience, their initial overseas expansion is often more likely to be a joint venture especially when the firm is from a middle-income or developing country. Dunning and Cantwell (1983) show that the lower the GDP per capita of the host nation orginating a multinational firm, the more likely will it use joint ventures in its initial international expansion. Firms often have production capability, but lack knowledge of foreign markets for which they depend on their partners. Embraer is a successful Brazilian aircraft manufacturer, helped by its joint venture with Piper. It makes small commercial jets as well as fighters: Initially intended for the Brazilian market, Embraer is now a strong exporter, landing orders even in the most critical market, the United States. Another example is the practice of allying with a prominent retail chain in a new country targeted for expansion, or licensing a well-known trade name in order to enter a new market. When Japanese companies like Casio lacked experience in the U.S. market, they formed a cooperative promotional campaign with established U.S. retail chains. When Murjani, a Far-East based apparel manufacturer first entered the U.S., it was by licensing the Gloria Vanderbilt label. Intriguingly, over time, the Murjani name increased in type size, in the advertisements. Today, they go-it-alone in many markets.

Strategic alliances in the pharmaceutical and bio-technology fields, also have a technological synergy rationale. Contractor (1985) describes cross-licensing agreements. By pooling patents, a superior product is expected. In general, it is important to consider joint ventures as vehicles to bring together complementary skills and talents which cover different aspects of state-of-the-art know-how needed in high technology industries. Such creations of "eclectic atmospheres" can bring out significant innovations not likely to be achieved in any one parent organization's "monoculture" context.

A patent however is not merely a right to a process or design, it is also a right to a *territory*. Often, the marketing or territorial right is as important an issue as technological synergy. Research partnerships have a similar intent.

Faster entry into a market may be possible if the testing and certification done by one partner are accepted by the authorities in the other partner's territories. One partner may cede the rights to a partially developed process to another firm able to commercialize the technology faster, the fruits of the development to be shared in a joint venture. This is a typical pattern among smaller and larger firms (Doz, 1986). A medium-sized company that has invested heavily in developing a new technological break-through may not have on its own, production or global marketing resources to secure a rapid, global dissemination of its use, to achieve a quick or adequate payback for its investmen. A joint venture or licensing approach can thus be an important vehicle in achieving such dissemination and realistically getting the necessary payback quickly. This is especially true for smaller firms lacking the internal financial or managerial resources to make their own investments, and important for industries with short product cycles, or rapid technology turnover.

Paradoxically, this is also true in giant firms which are diversified. Take GE as an example, with scores of foreign affiliates, but with several hundred licensing or production contracts an minority joint ventures. The potential country/product combinations for a company with the number of products GE has, run to over ten thousand. Not even a giant firm can invest in all of these. Direct investment in fully-owned subsidiaries is reserved for the most interesting combinations; many of the rest are handled by cooperative ventures. Stopford and Wells (1972) confirm in their study that the propensity to form joint ventures is higher when the entry entails product diversification. Berg, Duncan and Freidman (1982) indicate that large average firm size and rapid growth in an industry correlate positively with joint venture formation.

Indirect benefits (R_2) of a cooperative ventur (over a single owner operation) include technical or new product ideas learned from other partner and diffused to other parts of the company (Lyles, 1986). This is likely to have been one motive for General Motors to associate with Toyota–the hope that more productive methods and better quality control could be learned from the Japanese partner. Another GM motive may have been a fuller or more complete product line. Instead of abdicating the smaller-sized end of the automobile business, joint ventures provide American producers with a means of offering a complete range of cars in the showroom. (This is important not only for the conventional marketing reason of overall impact on consumers, but because trading-up as family incomes rise is an established fact of the business.) Pharmaceutical cross-licensing agreements whereby two companies swap patented drugs and territories, are partially predicated on the same idea. Each company is able to offer a fuller range of drugs, in their country, often using the same distribution and marketing fixed costs. Or at least, to each partner, the incremental cost of adding the extra drugs plus the net royalty cost is less than the incremental revenue, so derived.

Another indirect benefit of cooperation is the possibility of having other divisions of the company handle (for a markup) products from the partner organization. While the international division of a company which formed the partnership accounts for only the direct revenues and costs, it may be the product division which derives this indirect benefit. Hence the importance of an overall framework of strategic assessment, which looks at the situation for the whole company. Seen in isolation, a cooperative venture may only be a simple start-up, technical training agreement or a standart patent license. But if the effect of this cooperative move is that it creates a long-term customer for a part or active ingredient, the stategic impact goes beyond the arrangement itself. Examples of this kind are frequently found, in the pharmaceutical industry's licensing practices or in automotive assembly agreements, where the nominal royalty accruing to the headquarters technology licensing group typically will be vastly exceeded by the profit margin earned by the division that supplies the active ingredient for the drug, or the automotive parts (Contractor, 1985).

Reduced Costs From Cooperative Venture Mode (C_1 and C_2)

Important benefits of a cooperative form over a go-it-alone option are reduction in costs, directly and indirectly. (See Table 3)

Among the reasons why project costs may be lower under a cooperative form are economies of larger scale and rationalization; government incentives available to joint ventures

Table 3: Decreased Costs from Cooperative-Venture (CV) Mode

Direct (C_1)	Indirect (C_2)
• Economies of Scale from Larger Market Shape	• Productivity and Technical Improvements Diffused to other Parts of Company
• Rationalization Based on Each Partner Nation's Corporative Advantage	
• Government Incentives/ Subsides Given to CV's only	
• Using Slack/Underutilized Equipment or Design Capabilities in each Partner Lowers Capital Cost and Overheads	
• Fewer Headquarter Personnel Deputed	
• Access trough Partner to Cheaper Inputs	
• More Productive Technology or Administrative Methods Contributed by one Partner	

and licensing (but not to fully-owned subsidiaries); lower capital investment and over-heads by utilizing slack capacity in the partner firms; and finally, cheaper inputs and more productive methods acquired through the partner. Indirectly, other parts of the company might gain cost advantages from productivity gains and other efficiency improvements learned from the other partner. This was probably an important consideration for GM when it linked up with Toyota.

Joint ventures lower the total capital cost of a project and reduce the slack production and administrative capacity of each partner. This is similar to the cost sub-additivity factor in the economics of cooperative advertising or electric utility pools (Herriott, 1986). To serve a region, electric companies get together in power-sharing arrangements which enable *each* company to install a lower maximum capacity than it would have installed independently. In our analysis, production rationalization can occur when two companies in an industry cooperate. This means that components or sub-assemblies are no longer made in two locations with unequal costs. Production of this item is transferred to the lower cost location in one of the partner firms. But there is an added advantage. Because volume in the other location is now higher, *further* reduction in average unit cost is possible due to economies of larger scale. Many international joint ventures in the automobile business are based on this cost-reduction factor.

Another example is a licensing/franchising operation for the servicing of marine engines and boats in ports over the world. Ships are drawn to the internationally recognized "brandname" for the service facility so that they can enjoy an identically high standard of service anywhere. Moreover, there are important economies of scale in centralized engine rebuilding, parts inventories and training, savings which are passed on to the franchise holder, and thence to the customer.

The synergistic effect of joint ventures was confirmed by McConnell and Nantell (1985) who show that the value of the shares of over 200 firms listed in the New York and American stock exchanges, was increased for those companies that had undertaken joint ventures.

The "Costs" of Cooperation

Decreased Revenues From Cooperative Venture Mode (R_3 and R_4)

We now examine the possible detrimental effects of cooperative modes as compared with fully-owned investments. The incremental costs of cooperative ventures are summarized in Tables 4 and 5.

Table 4: Decreased Revenue from Cooperative-Venture (CV) Mode

Direct (R_3)	Indirect (R_4)
• CV Associated does not allow Firm to Expand into Certain Lines of Business in the Future	• Partner's Desire to Export Decreases Sales made by other Affiliates in International Markets
• Partner Reaps the Benefit of Future Business Expansion, not Proportional to their Future Contribution	• Partner becomes more formidable Competitor in the Future
• Setting Lower Price at Behest of Partner	

As opposed to fully-owned investments, the firm may be constrained by its association and suffer a relative decline in revenues becauce it does not have the freedom to expand into certain lines of business, or because end-product prices set in collaboration with the partner may be lower than they would like them to be. Contractor (1983; 1985) shows in an algebraic negotiations model that the optimum price for the end-product is different for the two partners in a joint venture or license, in many conditions. This is also observed in practice.

In general, as joint ventures evolve, the relative benefits derived by the partners is frequently not commersurate with their original contributions. According to Hamel, Prahalad and Doz (1986), Japanese firms plan ahead to increase the benefits they extract from an alliance across the "collaborative membrane," leaving the European or American partner in a worse strategic position. In their view the Japanese often look upon partnerships as a cynical competitive move, based on tactical expediency.

Indirectly, global revenues frequently decline because the partner's desire to have the venture export cuts into the sales of the firm in other countries. In general, revenue declines could occur in the future if the partner turns into a global competitor, having learnt the technology or skills.

The worry of "creating a future competitor" is often overblown, but must be considered when entering into any venture or transferring technology to another firm. Much depends on the industry and the circumstances. Let us consider two opposite examples. One is a chemical company helping to set up a PVC-plastic plant for a Korean firm. The technology is mature, if not widely known in its most efficient production form. The PVC industry is globally decentralized. Delivery to customers from lacal sources is a more common pattern than imports. Hence there is little reason to fear that the company receiving the assistance will become a global competitor, or otherwise impinge upon the strategy of the firm supplying the technology (except in that one country).

The opposite case of the "junior" partner turning evenutally into a global competitor is well documented (but only for Japanese firms). Reich (1985) or Abegglen (1982) relate many examples, including the celebrated stories of Western Electric licensing transistor technology to Sony for $25,000 in 1953 and RCA assisting Japanese companies to make color-television receivers. Apart from Japan, there is no empirical evidence to show how significant this problem is in cooperative agreements. One has to assess whether the partners are mutually inter-dependent and vulnerable later on. Much depends on the duration of the arrangement, the ability of each partner to "go-it-alone" on its expiration, and independently keep up with technical changes in the industry; the territorial or other constraints written into the agreement; and whether the industry is characterized by global production-integration efficiences or characterized by decentralized adaptation at the country level.

In industries which are "configured" to be country-based or globally decentralized (Porter, 1986), cooperative ventures are less dangerous in terms of creating global competition; but this is true only if the partner is a "local" firm inlikely to make their own direct investments in other countries. Otherwise, even if the industry is territorially fragmented or "multi-domestic", an improved technology can be easily spread by a partner already global in scope. It may take time though. Competition from a former joint venture partner or licensee is likely to be felt sooner, and in greater intensity, in geographically concentrated industries.

Overall, the opinion of the Office of Technology Assessment or of authors such as Contractor (1985) is that U.S. technology transferred to overseas licensees or joint-venture partners does not induce a pervasive competitive threat, barring a few notable cases. The technology receiving organization is often local in orientation, or remains one-step behind; the rate of technical change may be rapid enough to diminish the danger from one transfer; or the terms of the agreement itself may limit the other partner via patents or other restrictive clauses. The potential threat can be dealt with through careful creation of a "black box position" for one-self, emphasizing not only legal and patent protection, but also maintaining control over the venture through staffing, maintaining one's strong independent research momentum, and through linking the partner up through a complex system of relationships.

Increased Costs From The Cooperative Mode (C_3 and C_4)

Costs of a cooperative venture may exceed that of a fully-owned, internalized operation because of the the extra elements of having to negotiate and transfer technology and administer an enterprise jointly with another firm. This is, in brief, the "transaction costs" and "governance cost" argument, pioneered by Williamson (1975). Buckley and Casson (1976) and Rugman (1982) place considerable emphasis on the raltive efficiencies of "internalized" expansion of the multinational firm, unencumbered by partners.

For a multinational firm, costs rise when global optimization is not possible with respect to sourcing, finance, tax, transfer-pricing and distribution because of the divergent objectives of the partner. A large literature describes these disadvantages. This is typified by Stopford and Wells (1972), Killing (1983), Gullander (1976) and Reich (1985).
Indirectly, a cooperative venture can increase costs to corporate headquarters in legal and administrative overheads for the extra costs of negotiating and monitoring agreements. Many firms with extensive licensing and joint venture agreements need to support larger legal departments than they would otherwise.

Table 5: Increased Costs from Cooperative Venture (CV) Mode

Direct (C3)	Indirect (C4)
• Cost of Transferring Technology/ Expertise to Partner	• Slight Increase in Headquarters Administrative, Legal and Other Overheads
• Increased Coordination/ Governance Costs	• Opportunity Costs of Executives or Technicans Deputed to CV
• Pressures from Partner to Buy From Designated Sources. Or Sell Through their Distribution Channel.	
• Global Optimization of MNC Partner may not be possible for - Sourcing - Financial Flows - Tax - Transfer Pricing - Rationalization of Production	

Risk Reduction Benefits of Cooperative Ventures

Cooperative ventures reduce a partner's risk by (a) diversifying or spreading the risk of a large project over more than one firm, (b) enabling diversification in a product portfolio sense, (c) enabling faster entry and payback, (d) cost sub-additivity: the cost to the partnership is less than the cost of an equivalent investment undertaken by each firm alone, and (e) reducing political risk in some cases.
A large project such as a new car or airplane is a multi-billion dollar undertaking. Joint production such as the Boeing 767 Project spreads the risk of failure (and the potential gains) over more than one party. This applies also to exploration consortia. We have seen how product portfolio diversification via partnerships such as the GM/Toyota venture reduces market risk; how the total capital investment of a project can be reduced by rationalization and scale economies from a joint venture; and how the experience of both partners, sharing of markets and test results make for quicker entry and payback. All of these reduce risk, besides reducing costs.
The risk sharing function of coalitions is especially important in research-intensive industries like computers where each successive generation of technology costs much more to develop, while at the same time product cycles shrink, leaving less time to amortize the development costs.

Another dimension of risk reduction has to do with containing some of the political risk by linking up with a local partner. Such a partner may have sufficient poitical clout to steer the joint venture clear of local governmental action or interference (Stopford and Wells, 1972; United Nations, 1978).

Table 6: Risk Reduction

- ● Lower Capital Investment At Stake
  - Partial Investment
  - Excess Capacity Utilization
  - Economies of Scale
  - Economies of Rationalization and
    Quasi-Integration

- ● Faster Entry/Certification

- ● Use CV as Guinea-Pig

- ● For Large Risky Projects
  - Limit Risk Per Venture
  - Diversify Risk Over Several

- ● Lower Political Risk

- ● Medium and Small Sized Firms

Multiple partnerships for risk-diversification purposes are found in many high-tech areas; companies have a stake in many ventures with several potential competitors, in several technologies at various stages of development-almost like dancing with multiple partners, or a loose network (Miles and Snow, 1986). The strategy is to maintain a stake and potential payoff from several (sometimes speculative) projects. This limits risk per venture, while diversifying it over several. The cooperative venture is, in many instance, viewed as a "guinea-pig", perhaps to be brushed aside should it come up with an interesting discovery or market success. Especially for medium and small size firms, cooperative ventures may be the only way to reduce risk to tolerable levels, in such industries.

Conclusions: The Value and Limitations of the Analytical Framework

This paper presented a benefit/cost framework to enable a firm to choose between competing on a "go-it-alone" basis, versus cooperating with another company in a joint venture, licensing, or other negotiated agreement. The framework detailed direct and indirect, incremental benefits and costs of a cooperative association over a fully-owned investment. The incremental net benefit of a cooperative venture over a go-it-alone alternative has to be not only positive, but moreover, be large enough to cover the other partners'share of the profits in order for the cooperative alternative to be chosen. Or the risk of the cooperation alternative has to be so substantially below the go-it-alone option that the former will be chosen. This must occur in a large number of cases, judging from the prevalence of joint venture, licensing, franchising, management, joint exploration, research partnerships and other contracts in international business.

The above approach can be used to analyze any cooperative venture. In some cases, actual cash flow calculations have been made for the comparison (Contractor, 1985), but at the least, the framework provides a useful strategic planning exercise, which helps to plan negotiation terms with prospective partners. It helps to focus attention not merely on the direct effects of the cooperative venture, but on its indirect and future effects on other parts of the company, so that the overall picture emerges.

The present analysis compares only two options at a time, such as a fully-owned subsidiary or a joint venture *ex ante*. It cannot predict success or failure; it is simply a planning tool. Quantification of every factor may be difficult and tenuous, except in simple cases; but much the same drawback applies to capital budgeting exercises involved in project planning and projecting future cash flows. At a minimum, the framework provides a useful strategy checklist.

International executives need to acquire a new set of skills since they already negotiate and run far larger numbers of cooperative arrangements with other firms, than fully-owned subsidiaries. In a closed global administrative system, efficiency and optimization require centralized control over fully-owned operations. Some industries, with homogeneous products or technological standardization may be moving in that direction (Levitt, 1983). In other industries, because of local mandates, marketing and cultural variation, entrenched competitors, and high development risk, among several factors discussed in this paper, cooperative forms of international business organization can frequently be superior. The educated executive must therefore know both arts, of centralized control as well as external negotiation and cooperation.

Footnotes

1 These estimates are drawn from U.S. Department of Commerce (1981). In the latest benchmark survey of the Commerce Department (U.S. Department of Commerce, 1985) the numbers of all foreign affiliates and U.S. parents appear to have dropped dramatically from the five years previous survey. But this is a statistical data collection anomaly rather than a fact. For further details on this issue see the appendix to Chapter 1 in Contractor, F., and Lorange, P., *Cooperative Strategies In International Business* (Lexington, Mass.: Lexington Books, 1987 forthcoming).

References

Abblegen, J., "U.S.-Japanese Technological Exchange in Perspective, 1946-1981," in Uehara, C. (ed.), *Technological Exchange: The US-Japanese Experience* (New York: University Press, 1982).

Berg, S., Duncan, J., and Friedman, P., *Joint Venture Strategies and Corporate Innovation* (Cambridge, Mass.: Oelgeschlager, Gunn and Hain, 1982).

Boston Consulting Group, *"Strategic Alliance"*, Working Paper #276, 1985.

Buckley, P.J. and Casson, M. *The Future of the Multinationl Enterprise*, (New York: Holmes & Meir, 1976).

Contractor, F.J., *Licensing in International Strategy: A Guide for Planning and Negotiations*, (Westport, CT: Greenwood Pess, 1985).

Contractor, F.J., "Technology Licensing Practice in U.S. Companies: Corporate and Public Policy Implications of an Empirical Study," *Columbia Journal of World Business*, Fall 1983, pp. 80-88.

Contractor, F.J., "Technology Importation Policies in Developing Countries: Some Implications of Recent Theoretical and Empirical Evidence", *Journal of Deveoping Areas*, July 1983, pp. 499-520.

Doz, Y., "Technology Partnerships Between Larger and Smaller Firms", (draft paper, August 1976).

Dunning, J. and Cantwell, J., "Joint Ventures and Non-Equity Foreign Involvement by British Firma with Particular Reference to Developing Countries: An Exploratory Study," working paper, University of Reading (Economics Deparment), 1983.

Gullander, S., "Joint Venture and Cooperative Strategy," *Columbia Journal of World Business*, Winter 1976, pp. 104-114.

Hamel, G., Doz, Y. and Prahalad, C., "Strategic Partnerships: Success or Surrender?" paper presented at the Rutgers/Wharton Colloquium on *Cooperative Strategies in International Business*, October 1986.

Herriott, S. R., "The Economic Foundations of Cooperative Strategy: Implications for Organization and Management," working paper, University of Texas, 1986.

Killing, J. P., *Strategies for Joint Vernture Success*, (New Jork: Praeger, 1983).

Levitt, T., "The Globalization of Markets," *Harvard Business Review*, May-June, 1983, pp. 92-102.

Lyles, M. A., "Learning Among Joint Venture Sophisticated Firms," paper presented at the Rutgers/Wharton Colloquium on *Cooperative Strategies in International Business*, October 1986.

Mariti, P., and Smiley, R. H., "Cooperative Agreements and the Organization of Industry," *Journal of Industrial Economics*, June 1983, pp. 437-451.

McConnell, J., and Nantell, J. R., "Common Stock Returns and Corporate Combinations: The Case of Joint Ventures," *Journal of Finance*, Vol. 40, pp. 519-536.

Miles, R. F., and Snow, C. C., "Network Organizations: New Concepts for New Forms," *California Management Review*, Vol. 28, No. 3, Spring 1986.

Moxon, R. W. and Geringer, J. M., "Multinational Ventures in the Commercial Aircraft Industry," *Columbia Journal of World Business*, Summer 1985, pp. 55-62.

Pfeffer, J., and Nowak, P., "Joint Ventures and Interorganizational Interdependence," *Administrative Science Quarterly*, Vol. 21, September 1976, pp. 398-418.

Porter, M. E., "The Changing Patterns of International Competition," *California Management Review*, Vol. 28, No. 2, Winter 1986.

Reich, R. B., "Japan Inc., U.S.A." *The New Republic*, November 26, 1984, pp. 19-23.

Stopford, J. M., and Wells, L., *Managing the Multinational Enterprise*, (New York: Basic Books, 1972).

Telesio, P., *Foreign Licensing Policy in Multinational Enterprises*, D.B.A. dissertation, Harvard University, 1977.

United Nations (Economic and Social Council), *Transnational Corporations in World Development: A Re-Examination*, (New York: United Nations, 1978).

United States Department of Commerce, *U.S. Direct Investment Abroad, 1977* Washington D.C.: U.S. Government Printing Office, 1981).

United States Department of Commerce, U.S. *Direct Investment Abroad, 1982: The Benchmark Survey* (Washington D.C.: U.S. Government Printing Office, 1985).

Williamson, O. E., Markets and Hierarchies: *An Analysis and Antitrust Implications*, (London: Free Press, 1975).

[9]

REAPPRAISING THE ECLECTIC PARADIGM
IN AN AGE OF ALLIANCE CAPITALISM

John H. Dunning*
Reading and Rutgers Universities

Abstract. This article discusses the implications of the advent of alliance capitalism for our theorizing about the determinants of MNE activity. In particular, it argues that, due to the increasing porosity of the boundaries of firms, countries and markets, the eclectic, or OLI, paradigm of international production needs to consider more explicitly the competitive advantages arising from the way firms organize their inter-firm transactions, the growing interdependencies of many intermediate product markets, and the widening of the portfolio of the assets of districts, regions and countries to embrace the external economies of interdependent activities.

INTRODUCTION

Over the last decade or so, a number of events have occurred that, viewed collectively, suggest that the world economy may be entering a new phase of market-based capitalism – or, at least, changing its trajectory of the past century. These events recognize no geographical boundaries; and they range from changes in the way in which individual firms organize their production and transactions, to a reconfiguration of location-specific assets and the globalization of many kinds of economic activity.

The preeminent driving force behind these events has been a series of systemic technological and political changes, of which a new generation of telecommunication advances and the demise of central planning in Eastern Europe and China are, perhaps, the most dramatic. But, no less far reaching has been the economic rejuvenation of Japan and the emergence of several new industrial powers – especially from East Asia – whose approach to market-based capitalism – both at a socio-institutional and a techno-economic level [Freeman and Perez 1988] – is very different from that long practiced by Western nations.

The inter-related and cumulative effects of these phenomena have compelled scholars to reexamine some of their cherished concepts about market-based

---

*John H. Dunning is Emeritus Professor of International Business at the University of Reading, U.K., and State of New Jersey Professor of International Business at Rutgers University, New Jersey, U.S.A. Professor Dunning has been researching into the economics of international direct investment and the multinational enterprise since the 1950s. He has authored, co-authored, or edited thirty-two books on the subject and on industrial and regional economics.

Received: February 1995; Revised: August 1995; Accepted: August 1995.

462   JOURNAL OF INTERNATIONAL BUSINESS STUDIES, THIRD QUARTER 1995

capitalism, and to do so in two major respects. The first is that the growing acceptance that, by themselves, competitive market forces do not necessarily ensure an optimum innovation-led growth path in a dynamic and uncertain world. This is partly because technology is an endogenous variable – not an exogenous one as assumed in the received literature – and partly because the pressures of frequent and unpredictable technological and political changes do not permit a Pareto optimal allocation of resources [Pigou 1932]. With the acceleration of technological change, and a growing emphasis on institutional learning and continuous product improvement, both the concepts and the policy prescriptions of our forefathers are becoming less relevant each day.

The second revered concept that is now under scrutiny is that the resources and competencies of wealth-creating institutions are largely independent of each other; and that individual enterprises are best able to advance their economic objectives, and those of society, by competition, rather than co-operation. Unlike the first idea, this concept has only been severely challenged over the last decade, although, for more than a century, scholars have acknowledged that the behavior of firms may be influenced by the actions of their competitors [Cournot 1851], while Marshall [1920] was one of the first economists to recognize that the spatial clustering or agglomeration of firms with related interests might yield agglomerative economies and an industrial atmosphere, external to the individual firms, but internal to the cluster.

It is the purpose of this paper to consider some of the implications of the changes now taking place in the global marketplace for our understanding of the determinants of multinational enterprise (MNE) activity; and especially the eclectic paradigm of international production.[1] The main thrust of the paper is to argue that, although the autonomous firm will continue to be the main unit of analysis for understanding the extent and pattern of foreign-owned production, the OLI configuration determining trans-border activities is being increasingly affected by the collaborative production and transactional arrangements between firms; and that these need to be more systematically incorporated into the eclectic paradigm. But, prior to subjecting this idea to closer examination, we briefly outline the underlying assumptions of the extant theory of MNE activity in the mid-1980s.

HIERARCHICAL CAPITALISM

For most of the present century, the deployment of resources and capabilities in market oriented economies has been shaped by a micro-organizational system known as Fordism and a macro-institutional system known as hierarchical capitalism.[2] The essential characteristic of both these systems is that the governance of production and transactions is determined by the relative costs and benefits of using markets and firms as alternative organizational modes. In conditions of perfect competition, where exchange and coordination costs are zero and where there are no externalities of production or consumption, all transactions will be determined by market forces. Business entities will buy their inputs at arm's-length prices from independent firms and households, and sell their outputs at arm's-length prices to independent purchasers.

In practice, such a governance structure has rarely existed; to some degree, all markets contain some impurities. Such impurities are of two kinds. The first is structural market failure, which arises from the actions of participants in or outside the market to distort the conditions of demand or supply. The second is endemic or natural market failure, where either, given the conditions of supply and demand, the market qua market is unable to organize transactors in an optimal way, *or* it is difficult to predict the behavior of the participants. Such endemic market failure essentially reflects the presence of uncertainty, externalities, and the inability of producers to fully capture increasing returns to scale in conditions of infinite demand elasticity. It also accepts that bounded rationality, information asymmetries and opportunism are more realistic principles governing economic conduct [Williamson 1985, 1993] than perfect cognition and profit- or utility-maximizing behavior on the part of the transactions in the market.

It is partly to avoid or circumvent such market imperfections, and partly to recoup the gains of a unified governance of interrelated activities, that single activity firms choose to internalize intermediate product markets and, in so doing, become diversified firms. To coordinate these different activities, the administrative system takes on the guise of a hierarchy; and as Chandler [1962, 1990] has well demonstrated, as U.S. firms internalized more markets in the last quarter of the 19th century, so hierarchical capitalism came to replace 'arm's-length' capitalism.

Throughout most of the present century, as economic activity has become increasingly specialized and more complex, and as technological advances and political forces have created more endemic market imperfections, the role of large hierarchies, relative to that of markets, as an organizational modality has intensified. At the firm level, the fully integrated production facilities of enterprises such as the Ford Motor Company[3] in the 1960s epitomized the raison d'etre for, and the extreme form of, hierarchical capitalism; hence the coining of the term 'Fordism'. At a sectoral level, the proportion of output from most industrial countries supplied by vertically integrated or horizontally diversified firms rose throughout most of the 20th century.[4] Until the late 1970s, scholars usually considered cooperative forms of organizing economic activity as *alternatives* to hierarchies or markets, rather than as part and parcel of an organizational *system of firms*, in which inter-firm and intra-firm transactions complement each other. This, in part, reflected the fact that, in the main, economists viewed the boundary of a firm as the point at which its owners relinquished de jure control over resource harnessing and usage; and, to a large extent, this boundary was thought to be coincident with a loss of majority equity ownership. It is not surprising, then, that, for the most part, minority joint ventures were regarded as a second best alternative to full ownership. At the same time, most contractual arrangements were considered as market transactions – even in situations in which there was some element of a continuing and information sharing relationship between the parties to the exchange.

We would mention two other important features of 20th century hierarchical capitalism. The first is that it implicitly assumes that the prosperity of firms depends exclusively on the way in which their management internally organizes the resources and capabilities at their disposal. These include the purchased inputs from other firms and the marketing and distribution of outputs. Admittedly, the behavior of such firms might be affected by the strategies of other firms, e.g., oligopolistic competitors, monopolistic suppliers, large customers, and labor unions. But, with these exceptions, in hierarchical capitalism, the external transactions of firms are assumed to be *exogenous*, rather than *endogenous*, to their portfolio of assets and skills, and to the way in which these assets and skills are combined with each other to create further value-added advantages.

The second characteristic of hierarchical capitalism is that firms primarily react to endemic and structural market failure by adopting 'exit'-, rather than 'voice'-type strategies. Hirschman [1970] first introduced this concept of exit and voice to explain the responses of firms and states to threats to their economic sovereignty. He postulated two such responses, viz. 'exit' to a better alternative, and 'voice,' which he defined as any attempt at all to change, rather than escape from, an objectionable state of affairs (p. 30). Borrowing from Hirschman's terminology, we might identify two reactions of firms to the presence of market failure. These are: (i) to 'exit,' where the response is to replace the market by internal administrative fiat, and (ii) to 'voice,' where the response is to work with the market (in this case the buyers of its products or the sellers of its purchases) to reduce or eliminate market failure.

Our reading of the raison d'être for hierarchical capitalism, particularly its U.S. brand, is that it was (and still is) an 'exit' reaction to market failure.[5] To a limited extent, 'voice' strategies are evident in joint equity ventures and contractual agreements and in compensatory institutional instruments – e.g., futures and insurance markets. But, in general, collaborative production, marketing or innovatory projects or problem solving are eschewed. Contract disputes are usually resolved by litigation procedures rather than by propitiating attempts to remove the cause of the disputes. Competition and adversarial relations, rather than cooperation and synergistic affinities, are the hallmarks of hierarchical capitalism, and this is evident in the conduct of both inter-firm and intra-firm coordination procedures and transactions. Hierarchical capitalism rarely interprets the roles of firms and governments as being complementary to each other [World Bank 1992].

It is beyond the scope of this paper either to trace the factors that led to hierarchical capitalism and the scale system of production, or to describe its characteristics in any detail. Suffice to mention that, between the mid-1870s and the early 1970s, a series of technological, organizational and financial events occurred that helped reduce the transaction and coordination costs of multi-activity hierarchies relative to those of arm's-length intermediate product markets. Moreover, in contrast to the craft system of production which preceded it, the main impact of the mass production system was felt in the fabricating or assembling, rather than in the processing sectors. And, it was in the former sectors where – in order to better coordinate the stages of production, to reduce the risks of supply irregularities, and to ensure quality control over downstream operations – firms began to internalize intermediate product markets and to engage in vertical integration and horizontal diversification in order to capture the economies of scope and scale.

We have already asserted that mainstream economic and organizational theorists paid only scant attention to this phenomenon until the post-War II period,[6] and that much of the credit for such work as was done must go to scholars interested in the explanation of the growth of MNEs.[7] In the 1950s, both Penrose [1956] and Bye [1958] sought to explain the extension of a firm's territorial boundaries in terms of the perceived gains to be derived from vertical and horizontal integration. Later, Penrose formulated a more general theory of the growth of firms [Penrose 1959]; but, her penetrating insights into the advantages of internalized markets (although she never used this term)[8] had to wait many years before they were adequately acknowledged.[9]

Since the mid-1970s, there has been a plethora of academic papers and monographs that have tried to interpret the existence and growth of MNEs in terms of the benefits that such firms are perceived to derive from internalizing cross-border intermediate product markets.[10] Although several scholars have considered cooperative arrangements as alternatives to fully owned affiliates, and as forms of quasi internalization,[11] for the most part, they have been accommodated in a market/hierarchies transaction costs model, with such arrangements being perceived as a point on a continuum between arm's-length markets and complete hierarchies.

The eclectic paradigm, first put forward by the present author at a Nobel Symposium in 1976, is different from internalization theory[12] in that it treats the competitive (so called O-specific) advantages of MNEs, apart from that which arise from the act of cross-border internalization, as *endogenous* rather than as *exogenous* variables. This means that the paradigm is not just concerned with answering the question of why firms engage in FDI, in preference to other modes of cross-border transactions. It is also concerned with why

466   JOURNAL OF INTERNATIONAL BUSINESS STUDIES, THIRD QUARTER 1995

these firms possess unique resources and competencies – relative to their competitors of other nationalities – and why they choose to use at least some of these advantages jointly with a portfolio of foreign-based immobile assets.

At the same time, as so far enunciated, the eclectic paradigm is embedded within a socio-institutional framework of hierarchical capitalism, which, as stated earlier, presumes that the wealth creating and efficiency enhancing properties of an MNE are contained within the jurisdiction of its ownership. Thus, using the OLI nomenclature, except where they are acquired by M&As, the O advantages of firms are presumed to be created and organized quite independently of their dealings with other firms; the L advantages of countries are assumed to reflect the scope and character of their unconnected immobile assets, and the way in which hierarchies and markets determine their use; and, the propensity of firms to internalize intermediate product markets is based primarily on the presumption that most kinds of market failure[13] faced by firms are generally regarded by them as immutable, i.e., exogenous. Currently, the eclectic paradigm only peripherally embraces the ways in which the participation of firms in collaborative arrangements, or in networks of economic activity, affect the configuration of the OLI variables facing firms at a given moment of time, or on how this configuration may change over time. Partly, one suspects, this is because the value of such arrangements is difficult to quantify; and, partly because inter-firm transactions have been perceived to be of only marginal significance to the techno-economic production system of Fordism and to the socio-institutional paradigm of hierarchical capitalism.

ALLIANCE CAPITALISM

As suggested in the introduction, a series of events over the last two decades has led several scholars to suggest that the world is moving to embrace a new trajectory of market capitalism. This has been variously described as alliance, relational, collective, associate and the 'new' capitalism.[14] A critical feature of this new trajectory – which is essentially the outcome of a series of landmark technological advances and of the globalization of many kinds of value-added activity – is that it portrays the organization of production and transactions as involving both cooperation and competition between the leading wealth creating agents.[15] This view is in marked contrast to that which has dominated the thinking of economists since Adam Smith, whereby collaboration among firms is viewed as a symptom of *structural* market failure,[16] rather than as a means of reducing *endemic* market failure. And, it would be a bold scholar who would argue that most agreements concluded between firms over the last hundred years have been aimed at facilitating rather than inhibiting competition.

But, our reading of the literature suggests that, both the raison d'être for concluding inter-firm alliances, and their consequences for economic welfare, have significantly changed over the last two decades. We would at least hypothesize that a powerful contemporary motive for concluding such arrangements is to reduce the transaction and coordinating costs of arm's-length market transactions, and to leverage the assets, skills and experiences of partner firms. Another motive is to create or extend hierarchical control, which may also prompt firms to engage in M&As. However, cooperative arrangements differ from M&As in three respects. First, the former usually involve only a part – and sometimes a minor part – of the collaborating firms' activities. Second, they may entail no change in the ownership structure of the participating firms; and third, whereas the hierarchical solution implies an 'exiting' by firms from the dictates of the marketplace, the alliance solution implies a 'voice' strategy of working within these dictates to maximize the benefits of the joint internalization of inter-related activities.

The choice between a hierarchical and alliance modality as a means of lessening arm's-length market failure clearly depends on their respective costs and benefits. The literature on the rationale for joint ventures and non-equity transactions – vis à vis markets and hierarchies – is extensive and well known, and will not be repeated here.[17] It is, however, generally accepted that the choice rests on a trade-off between the perceived benefits of sharing risks and capital outlays on the one hand, and the costs of a loss of control associated with a reduced (or no) ownership on the other. Partly, the outcome will be influenced by the success of the 'voice' between the participants, as illustrated, for example, by the exchange of information, the division of managerial and financial responsibility, and the distribution of profits. But, in the main, most scholars view the choice as being determined by the most cost-effective way of organizing a portfolio of resources and capabilities.

Another reason for collaborative arrangements, however, has less to do with reducing the coordinating and transaction costs of alternative organizational modalities, and more to do with protecting existing – or gaining new – proprietary, or O-specific, advantages. Cooperative alliances have a parallel with strategic asset acquiring FDI: and, according to several researchers, over the past decade, the principal incentives for alliance formation have been to lower transaction costs, develop new skills and to overcome or create barriers to entry in national or international markets.[18] Sometimes, these alliances take the form of shared ownership, i.e., the merging of firms, or the setting up of greenfield joint ventures. But, since the early 1980s, the great majority of inter-firm associations have tended to be less formal in structure and more specific in scope and purpose. According to research undertaken at MERIT [Hagedoorn 1993a], the goals of most strategic alliances have been to gain access to new and complementary technologies, to speed up innovatory or learning processes and to upgrade the efficiency of particular activities – e.g., research and development (R&D), marketing and distribution, manufacturing methods, etc. – rather than to enhance the overall prosperity of the participating firms.

It is, perhaps, worth rehearsing some of the reasons for the spectacular growth of competitiveness-enhancing alliances since 1980. Essentially, these reduce to the impact that technological advances and the globalization of the market economy have had on the organization of economic activity. The consequences of the former – a supply-side phenomenon – have been fivefold; first, to raise the fixed – and particularly the learning and innovatory – costs of a wide range of manufacturing and service activities; second, to increase the interdependence between distinctive technologies that may need to be used jointly to supply a particular product;[19] third, to enhance the significance of multipurpose, or core, technologies, such as robotization, informatics and biotechnology; fourth, to truncate – and sometimes dramatically so[20] – the product life-cycle of a particular product; and fifth, which is partly a consequence of the other four characteristics, and partly a result of the changing needs of consumers to focus on the upgrading of core competencies of firms, and on the way these are organized as a means of improving their global competitive advantages.

One of the main consequences of the globalization of economic activity described earlier has been to force firms to be more dynamically competitive. This is particularly the case for firms from advanced industrial countries, and it is demonstrated in two main ways: first, a more determined effort to raise the efficiency with which they produce their existing products, and second, by the successful innovation of new products and the upgrading of assets and skills throughout their value chains.

This combination of global supply and demand pressures on competitiveness has caused firms – and particularly large hierarchies – to reconsider both the scope and organization of their value-added activities. In particular, the 1980s and early 1990s have seen three major responses. First, there has been a fairly general movement by firms towards the shedding or disinternalization of activities both along and between value chains; and towards the specialization on those activities that require resources and capabilities in which firms already have (or can acquire) a perceived competitive advantage. This is a *'concentrate on critical competency'* response. At the same time, because of the interdependence of technological advances, e.g., computer-aided design and manufacturing techniques, firms find that they need to assure access to the products over which they have now relinquished control. Firms may also wish to exercise some influence over the quality and price of these products, and over the innovation of new products. This means that disinternalization is frequently replaced, not by arm's-length transactions, but by controlled inter-firm cooperative arrangements. Such agreements are particularly noticeable between firms and their subcontractors in the more technologically advanced and information-intensive sectors [Hagedoorn 1993b].[21]

Second, because of competitive pressures, the huge and rising costs of R&D and speedier rates of obsolescence, firms – particularly in high technology sectors – have been increasingly induced to engage in cross-border alliances. Freeman and Hagedoorn traced 4,192 of these alliances between 1980 and 1989. They found that 42% were organized through R&D pacts; that 90% were between companies from the Triad; and that 63% were formed during the second half of the 1980s. The majority of the alliances involved large firms competing as oligopolies in global markets.[22] The need, on the one hand, for operational participation and, on the other, for complementarity, shared learning and an encapsulation of the innovation time span has combined to make the 'voice' strategy of cooperative ventures a particularly suitable mode for sustaining and advancing competitive advantage.[23] At the same time, to be successful, an *'asset-seeking alliance response'* does have implications for governance structures, a point we will take up later in this paper.

The third response of firms to recent events has been to try to widen the markets for their core products, so as to benefit fully from the economies of scale. This is, itself, a cost-reducing strategy. It serves to explain much of market-seeking and strategic asset-acquiring FDI – especially between firms servicing the largest industrial markets – as well as those of minority-owned foreign joint ventures and non-equity arrangements that are intended to gain speedy entry into unchartered and unfamiliar territories. Thus, of the 4,192 alliances identified by Freeman and Hagedoorn, 32% were geared towards improving access to markets. As might be expected, such alliances were particularly numerous among firms with Japanese partners. Such a 'voice' strategy might be termed a *'market-positioning alliance response.'*

Each of the three responses identified has widened the sphere of influence of the firms participating in external partnerships. Such actions have also caused a heightened degree of dependence on firm partners for their own prosperity. Thus, the resources and capabilities of companies such as Philips, IBM and Toyota – each of which has several hundred inter-firm alliances – cannot be considered in isolation. Gomes-Casseres and Leonard-Barton [1994] have identified some eighty recently established learning, supply, and positioning partnerships in the personal digital assistants (PDA) sector alone.[24] One must also consider the impact that these alliances have had on their internally generated O-specific advantages. The design and performance of the next generation of autos, microchips and computers critically depend on not only the advances in innovatory and manufacturing capabilities of the leading assembling companies, but also on the way these capabilities interact with those of their suppliers. Boeing's competitive advantages in producing the next breed of large passenger aircraft are likely to rest as much on the interaction it has with its suppliers and its customers – e.g., the airlines – as it does on its own technological and commercial strengths. Siemens – a leading producer of mainframe computers – relies heavily on cutting-edge technology supplied by

470   JOURNAL OF INTERNATIONAL BUSINESS STUDIES, THIRD QUARTER 1995

Fujitsu. In its venture to explore the seabed, Kennecott's mining consortium brings together a large number of firms supplying very different, but inter-related, technologies from many different sectors. Lorenzoni and Baden Fuller [1995] give several examples of organizations which view their subcontractors as partners in innovation and skill development.[25]

Of course, inter-firm cooperation is not a new phenomenon. What is, perhaps, new is its relative significance as an organizational form, whereby the success of the firms involved is being increasingly judged by each party's ability to generate innovation-led growth; by the range, depth and closeness of the interaction between themselves and their alliance or networking parties; and by the effect that such alliances are having upon overall industrial perform-ance. It is the combination of these factors, taken together with the twin forces of the disinternalization of hierarchical activities and the impressive growth of M&As to gain access to complementary assets,[26] which lead us to suggest – along with Gerlach [1992] – that the term *alliance* capitalism might be a more appropriate description of the features of innovation-led capitalism now spreading through the globalizing economy, than the term *hierarchical* capitalism.

A distinctive feature of alliance capitalism is its governance structure. Within a hierarchy, decisions rest on a pyramid of delegated authority. In establishing and strengthening relationships with other firms, customers and labor unions, success is usually judged by the extent to which the hierarchy is able to obtain its inputs at the least possible cost, and to sell its output at the most profitable price. Relationships between firms and within firms are normally defined by a written contract.

In alliance capitalism, decisions are more likely to rest on a consensus of agreement between the participating parties, and there is rarely any formal structure of authority. Such an agreement is based upon a commitment, on the part of each party, to advance the interests of the alliance; and upon mutual trust, reciprocity and forbearance between the partners. In the modern factory practicing flexible manufacturing or Toyota-like production methods, labor is not thought of as a cog in the wheel, as it is in traditional Fordism, but as a partner in the wealth-producing process. Suppliers are not just expected to produce goods to agreed specifications, but to actively work with the purchasing firms to continually upgrade the quality and/or lower the price of their outputs. Even within the hierarchical firm, technological and organiz-ational imperatives are requiring each function, activity or stage of production to be closely integrated with the other. Thus, for example, the purchasing and R&D departments may be expected to work with the manufacturing depart-ments on the design and development of new products and production methods. The personnel, finance and production departments each need to be involved in the introduction of new working procedures and incentive arrangements. At the same time, industrial customers and large wholesale and retail outlets may be expected to play an increasingly significant role in determining the direction and pattern of product improvement.

The growing significance of inter-firm cooperative transaction arrangements would suggest that 'voice,' relative to 'exit,' strategies are becoming more cost effective. This, of course, could be either due to the 'push' factor of the increasing net costs of hierarchical control, or to the 'pull' factor of the reduced costs of alliances. It is likely that both factors have been at work in recent years; but, it can surely be no accident that the thrust towards alliance capitalism first originated in Japan, whose culture especially values such qualities as teamwork, trust, consensus, shared responsibility, loyalty, and commitment, which are the essential ingredients of any successful partnership. These qualities – together with the recognition that, by improving quality control throughout the value chain and cutting inventories to the minimum – essentially enabled Japanese producers, particularly in the fabricating sectors, to break into their competitors' markets, and to adopt the production strategies and working practices that conformed to the resource and institutional advantages of their home countries. Indeed, most researchers are agreed that the two most significant competitive advantages of Japanese firms that evolved during the post-World War II period were, first, the way they restructured their production and intra-firm transactions, and second, the way they managed and organized their vertical and horizontal relationships with other firms.[27]

Before considering the implications of the new trajectory of market-based capitalism for our theorizing about MNE activity, we would mention three other trends in economic organization that are also favoring more, rather than less, inter-firm cooperation. The first concerns the renewed importance of small- and medium-size firms in the global economy.[28] This has led some commentators, notably Naisbitt [1994], to assert that yesterday's commercial behemoths are tomorrow's dinosaurs. The reasoning behind this assertion that 'small is beautiful' is that modern production methods, accelerating techno-logical advances, more demanding consumers and the growing importance of services, are all eroding the advantages of large plants based on a continuous, scale-friendly and relatively inflexible production system.

While accepting that there is some evidence for this contention (for example, much of the growth in employment now taking · place in the advanced industrial countries is in small- to medium-size firms) we, like Harrison [1994], are not convinced that the strategic influence of large firms is diminishing. We would prefer to suggest that any restructuring of the activity of large firms reflects their preferences for replacing hierarchical with alliance relationships; and, that an increasing number of small firms are, in fact, part of keiretsu-like networks, which, more often than not, are dominated by large, lead or flagship firms, or as Lorenzoni and Baden Fuller [1995] put it, "strategic centers"

[D'Cruz and Rugman 1992, 1993]. Many small firms, too, are either spin-offs of large firms, or owe their prosperity to the fact that the latter are frequently their main clients and suppliers of critical assets. The kinds of example one has in mind are the hundreds of second- or third-tier suppliers to the large Japanese automobile companies;[29] the intricate web of horizontal relationships between the various associated companies of the Japanese 'soga shosa'; the extensive outsourcing of both hardware and software development by the Japanese video game producer Nintendo; the network of knitwear firms in the Modena region of northern Italy; the many hundreds of Asian subcontractors to the giant footwear and apparel firms, e.g., Nike and Benetton.[30] The competitive advantages of the firms in these and similar groups are closely dependent on the exchange of skills, learning experiences, knowledge, and finance between the firms in the network; and on the example and lead given by the flagship firms.

The second trend is related to the first. It is the growth of spatial clusters of economic activities that offer external or agglomerative economies to firms located within the cluster. The idea, of course, is not new. Marshall paid much attention to it in his study of U.K. industry in the early 20th century [Marshall 1920]. Recently, it has been given a new lease of life by Porter [1990], who considers the presence of related industries as one of the four key determinants of a country's competitive assets; and, by Krugman [1991] who believes that such economies largely explain the geographical specialization of value-added activities. While the evidence on the subnational spatial concentration of particular activities is still fragmentary, such as we have suggests that, in the technology and information-intensive sectors, not only are MNEs creating multiple strategic centers for specialized activities, but such clusters are becoming an increasingly important component of competitiveness [Enright 1994]. The form and extent of the clusters may differ.[31] Sometimes, they relate to a range of pre-competitive innovatory activities, e.g., science parks; sometimes to very specific sectors, e.g., auto assemblers and component suppliers;[32] and, sometimes, to entrepreneurial or start-up firms, and cooperative research organizations, e.g., SEMITECH. Sometimes the local networks are contained in a very small geographical area, e.g., financial districts in London and New York; sometimes they spread over a whole region, e.g. the cluster of textile firms in north Italy.

The third trend is the growth of industrial networks. Inter-firm alliances can, range from being simple dyadic relationships to being part of complex, and often overlapping, networks consisting of tens, if not hundreds, of firms. The literature on industrial networks is extensive;[33] but, up to now, the subject has been mainly approached from a marketing or an organizational, rather than from an economic, perspective. This is, perhaps, one reason why internalization theory and the eclectic paradigm of international production have sometimes been portrayed as alternative approaches to network analysis. But to the economist, a network is simply a web of interdependent dyadic relationships. One must admit, this makes theorizing about the behavior of the participants very difficult, but no more so than theorizing about the behavior of oligopolists. It is also true that the economist is primarily concerned with the firm as a unit of analysis; but, this in no way should inhibit him (or her) from considering the implications for the firm when it is a part of a network of related firms.

What is clear, however, is that, as networks of alliances become more important, the composition and behavior of the group of firms becomes a more important determinant of the foreign production of the individual firms comprising the network. Nowhere is this more clearly seen than in the role played by the keiretsu in influencing both the competitive advantages of its member firms, and in the way in which these advantages are created, upgraded and used.

REAPPRAISING THE ECLECTIC PARADIGM

We now turn to consider the implications of alliance capitalism for our theorizing about the determinants of MNE activity, and, more particularly, for the eclectic paradigm. In brief, the implications are threefold. First, the concept of the competitive, or O-specific, advantages of firms, as traditionally perceived, needs to be broadened to take *explicit* account of the costs and benefits derived from inter-firm relationships and transactions (both at home and abroad), and particularly those that arise from strategic alliances and networks. Second, the concept of location (or L) advantages of countries, as traditionally perceived, needs to give more weight to the following factors: (1) the territorial embeddedness of interdependent immobile assets in particular geographical areas;[34] (2) the increasing need for the spatial integration of complex and rapidly changing economic activities; (3) the conditions under which inter-firm competitive enhancing alliances may flourish; and, (4) the role of national and regional authorities in influencing the extent and structure of localized centers of excellence.

Third, the idea that firms internalize intermediate markets, primarily to reduce the transaction and coordination costs of markets, needs to be widened to encompass other – and, more particularly, dynamic and competitiveness enhancing – goals, the attainment of which may be affected by micro-governance structures. The incorporation of external alliances into the theory of internalization presents no real problems, other than semantic ones. Either one treats a non-equity alliance as an extension of intra-firm transactions, and accepts that the theory is concerned less with a de jure concept of hierarchical control and ownership, and more with the de facto ways in which inter-dependent tangible and intangible assets are harnessed and leveraged; or, one treats the inter-firm alliance as a distinctive organizational mode, and more specifically one which is complementary to, rather than a substitute for, a

474   JOURNAL OF INTERNATIONAL BUSINESS STUDIES, THIRD QUARTER 1995

hierarchy. Partly, of course, the choice will depend on the unit of analysis being used. Is it the alliance or the network, per se, in which case the idea of 'group internalization' may be a relevant one? Or, is the unit of analysis the individual enterprises that comprise the alliance or network? For our purposes, we shall take the individual enterprise as the unit of analysis.[35]

Let us now be more specific about the modifications that alliance capitalism seems to require of the eclectic paradigm. We consider each of its components in turn. On the left-hand side of Table 1, we set out some of the more important OLI variables that scholars traditionally have hypothesized to influence the level and structure of MNE activity. Research has shown that the composition and significance of these determinants will differ according to the value of four contextual variables, viz. (1) the kind of MNE activity being considered (*market, resource, efficiency* or *strategic asset seeking*), (2) the portfolio of location-bound assets of the countries from which the FDI originates, and in which it is concentrated, (3) the technological and other attributes of the sectors in which it is being directed, and (4) the specific characteristics (including the production, innovatory and ownership strategies) of the firms undertaking the investment.

The variables identified in Table 1 are more than a checklist. They are chosen because a trilogy of extant economic and behavioral theories – viz. *the theory of industrial organization and market entry, the theory of location*[36] and *the theory of the firm*[37] – suggests that they offer robust explanations of the ownership structure of firms, the location of their activities, and the ways in which they govern the deployment of resources and capabilities within their control or influence. However, until very recently, none of these theories have paid much attention to the role of cooperative agreements in influencing MNE activity.

On the right-hand side of Table 1, we identify some additional OLI variables, which we believe, in the evolving era of alliance capitalism, need to be incorporated into our theorizing about MNE activity. The table shows that not all of the OLI variables listed require modification. Thus, of the Oa-specific variables, we would not expect the formation of strategic partnerships to greatly influence the internal work processes of the participating firms, although technological advances, and the need for continuous product improvement, is likely to demand a closer interaction between related value-adding activities, and may well enhance the contribution of shop-floor labor to raising process productivity. Nor would we expect the proprietary rights of brand ownership, favored access to suppliers, or the financial control procedures of firms to be much affected by cooperative agreements.

By contrast, Oa advantages stemming from a firm's ability to create and organize new knowledge, to maintain and upgrade product quality, to seek out and forge productive linkages with suppliers and customers, especially – in

TABLE 1
A Reconfiguration of the Eclectic Paradigm of International Production

1. Ownership-Specific Advantages
(of enterprise of one nationality (or affiliates of same) over those of another)

Hierarchical-Related Advantages	Alliance or Network-Related Advantages
a. Property right and/or intangible asset advantages (Oa).	a. *Vertical Alliances*
Product innovations, production management, organizational and marketing systems, innovatory capacity, non-codifiable knowledge: "bank" of human capital experience; marketing, finance, know-how, etc.	(i) Backward access to R&D, design engineering and training facilities of suppliers. Regular input by them on problem solving and product innovation on the consequences of projected new production processes for component design and manufacturing. New insights into, and monitoring of, developments in materials, and how they might impact on existing products and production processes.
	(ii) Forward access to industrial customers, new markets, marketing techniques and distribution channels, particularly in unfamiliar locations or where products need to be adapted to meet local supply capabilities and markets. Advice by customers on product design and performance. Help in strategic market positioning.
b. Advantages of common governance, i.e., of organizing Oa with complementary assets (Ot).	b. *Horizontal Alliances*
(i) Those that branch plants of established enterprises may enjoy over de novo firms. Those due mainly to size, product diversity and learning experiences of enterprise, e.g., economies of scope and specialization. Exclusive or favored access to inputs, e.g., labor, natural resources, finance, information. Ability to obtain inputs on favored terms (due, e.g., to size or monopsonistic influence). Ability of parent company to conclude productive and cooperative inter-firm relationships e.g., as between Japanese auto assemblers and their suppliers. Exclusive or favored access to product markets. Access to resources of parent company at marginal cost. Synergistic economies (not only in production, but in purchasing, marketing, finance, etc., arrangements).	Access to complementary technologies and innovatory capacity. Access to additional capabilities to capture benefits of technology fusion, and to identify new uses for related technologies. Encapsulation of learning and development times. Such inter-firm interaction often generates its own knowledge feedback mechanisms and path dependencies.
	c. *Networks*
	(i) of similar firms Reduced transaction and coordination costs arising from better dissemination and interpretation of knowledge and information, and from mutual support and cooperation between members of network. Improved knowledge about process and product development and markets. Multiple, yet complementary, inputs into innovatory developments and exploitation of new markets. Access to embedded knowledge of members of networks. Opportunities to develop 'niche' R&D strategies; shared learning and training experiences, e.g., as in the case of cooperative research associations. Networks may also help promote uniform product standards and other collective advantages.
(ii) Which specifically arise because of multinationality. Multinationality enhances operational flexibility by offering wider opportunities for arbitraging, production shifting and global sourcing of inputs. More favored access to and/or better knowledge about international markets, e.g., for information, finance, labor etc. Ability to take advantage of geographic differences in factor endowments, government intervention, markets, etc. Ability to diversify or reduce risks, e.g., in different currency areas, and creation of options and/or political and cultural scenarios. Ability to learn from societal differences in organizational and managerial processes and systems. Balancing economies of integration with ability to respond to differences in country-specific needs and advantages.	(ii) business districts As per (i) plus spatial agglomerative economies, e.g., labor market pooling. Access to clusters of specialized intermediate inputs, and linkages with knowledge-based institutions, e.g., universities, technological spill-overs.

476   JOURNAL OF INTERNATIONAL BUSINESS STUDIES, THIRD QUARTER 1995

TABLE 1 (continued)
A Reconfiguration of the Eclectic Paradigm of International Production

2. Internalization Incentive Advantages (i.e., to circumvent or exploit market failure).

Hierarchical-Related Advantages	Alliance or Network-Related Advantages
Avoidance of search and negotiating costs.	While, in some cases, time limited inter-firm cooperative relationships may be a substitute for FDI; in others, they may add to the I incentive advantages of the participating hierarchies, R&D alliances and networking which may help strengthen the overall competitiveness of the participating firms. Moreover, the growing structural integration of the world economy is requiring firms to go outside their immediate boundaries to capture the complex realities of know-how trading and knowledge exchange in innovation, particularly where intangible assets are tacit and need to speedily adapt competitive enhancing strategies to structural change.
To avoid costs of moral hazard, information asymmetries and adverse selection; and to protect reputation of internalizing firm.	
To avoid cost of broken contracts and ensuing litigation.	
Buyer uncertainty (about nature and value of inputs (e.g., technology) being sold).	
When market does not permit price discrimination.	
Need of seller to protect quality of intermediate or final products.	
To capture economies of interdependent activities (see b. above).	Alliances or network related advantages are those which prompt a 'voice' rather than an 'exit' response to market failure; they also allow many of the advantages of internalization without the inflexibility, bureaucratic or risk-related costs associated with it. Such quasi-internalization is likely to be most successful in cultures in which trust, forbearances, reciprocity and consensus politics are at a premium. It suggests that firms are more appropriately likened to archipelagos linked by causeways rather than self-contained 'islands' of conscious power. At the same time, flagship or lead MNEs, by orchestrating the use of mobile O advantages and immobile advantages, enhance their role as arbitragers of complementary cross-border value-added activities.
To compensate for absence of future markets.	
To avoid or exploit government intervention (e.g., quotas, tariffs, price controls, tax differences, etc.)	
To control supplies and conditions of sale of inputs (including technology).	
To control market outlets (including those which might be used by competitors).	
To be able to engage in practices, e.g., cross-subsidization, predatory pricing, leads and lags, transfer pricing, etc. as a competitive (or anti-competitive) strategy.	

3. Location-Specific Variables (these may favor home or host countries)

Hierarchical-Related Advantages	Alliance or Network-Related Advantages
Spatial distribution of natural and created resource endowments and markets.	The L-specific advantages of alliances arise essentially from the presence of a portfolio of immobile local complementary assets, which, when organized within a framework of alliances and networks, produce a stimulating and productive industrial atmosphere. The extent and type of business districts, industrial or science parks and the external economies they offer participating firms are examples of these advantages which over time may allow foreign affiliates and cross-border alliances and network relationships to better tap into, and exploit, the comparative technological and organizational advantages of host countries. Networks may also help reduce the information asymmetries and likelihood of opportunism in imperfect markets. They may also create local institutional thickness, intelligent regions and social embeddedness [Amin and Thrift 1994].
Input prices, quality and productivity, e.g. labor, energy, materials, components, semi-finished goods.	
International transport and communication costs.	
Investment incentives and disincentives (including performance requirements, etc.).	
Artificial barriers (e.g. import controls) to trade in goods.	
Societal and infrastructure provisions (commercial, legal, educational, transport, and communication).	
Cross-country ideological, language, cultural, business, political, etc. differences.	
Economies of centralization of R&D production and marketing.	
Economic system and policies of government: the institutional framework for resource allocation.	

unfamiliar markets – to externalize risk, to successfully manage a complex portfolio of core assets and value-creating disciplines, and to internalize the skills and learning experiences of other organizations, may be strongly influenced by some kinds of cooperative arrangements. Moreover, each of these advantages may better enable a firm both to engage in transborder activities, and to seek out appropriate agreements to strengthen and consolidate its competitive competencies.

The literature identifies two groups of competitive Ot advantages arising from the way in which a firm combines its own resources and capabilities with those of other firms. The first are those which a firm gains from being a multi-activity enterprise, independently of where these activities are located. Such economies of common governance may enable an established firm of one nationality to penetrate a foreign market more easily than a single activity competitor of the same or of another nationality. The second type of Ot advantage arises as a direct consequence of foreign production.[38] The impact of alliance capitalism is to offer an additional avenue for firms to acquire and build up both types of advantages – and, normally, to do so with less financial outlay and risk than hierarchical capitalism might require.[39]

It is, however, the second kind of Ot advantage that is the quintessence of both the multiactivity and the multinational firm. The implication is, then, that any decline in hierarchical activity reflects a diminution in the net benefits of internalized markets, which may lead to a '*concentrate on core competency strategy.*' It is also implied that other ways of obtaining the advantages are becoming more attractive (for example, as a result of a reduction of other kinds of market failure). In our present context, the switch in organizational form is a reflection of a shift in the techno-economic system of production. As we have already argued, this tends to favor a 'voice,' rather than an 'exit,' response to the inability of markets to cope with the externalities of interdependent activities in the first place.

It is too early to judge the extent to which the economies of synergy (and operational flexibility) are being realized in a more cost-effective way by external partnerships, rather than by hierarchical control. In any event, as we have already stated, many – indeed, perhaps, the majority of – strategic business alliances identified by scholars should not be regarded as substitutes for FDI, as they are directed to achieving very specific purposes.

Turning next to the internalization advantages (I) of MNE activities, it is perhaps here where the cooperative interaction between Japanese firms is most clearly demonstrated as a viable alternative to the full ownership and control favored by U.S. firms. Here, too, it is not so much that inter-firm agreements add to the internalization incentives of firms. It is rather that they may help to achieve the same objective more effectively, or spread the capital and other risks of the participating firms. In other words, inter-firm agreements may

478   JOURNAL OF INTERNATIONAL BUSINESS STUDIES, THIRD QUARTER 1995

provide additional avenues for circumventing or lessening market failure where the FDI route is an impractical option.

Clearly, the impact of alliance capitalism on the organization of economic activity will vary according to the type of market failure being considered; it is also likely to be highly industry and country specific. Institutional structures, learning paths, the extent of social and territorial embeddedness, cultural values, and national systems of education and innovation are likely to play an especially important role. In some countries, such as Japan, there is less incentive by firms to internalize markets in order to avoid the costs of broken contracts, or to ensure the quality of subcontracted products. The reason is simply because these types of market failure are minimized by the 'voice' strategies of buyers and sellers, which are built upon mutual interest, trust and forbearance. The keiretsu network of inter-firm competitive interaction – sometimes between firms in the same sector and sometimes across sectors – is perhaps one of the most frequently quoted alternatives to hierarchical internalization. Although there is frequently some minority cross-ownership among the networking firms, the relationship is built upon objectives, values and strategies that negate the need for the internalization of some kinds of market failure. At the same time, the extent and pattern of keiretsu ties is likely to vary between industrial sectors. It is, for example, most pronounced in the fabricating sectors (where the number and degree of complexity of transactions are the most numerous) and the least pronounced in the processing sectors. And, it is, perhaps, not without interest that Japanese FDI in Europe – relative to its U.S. counterpart – is concentrated in those sectors in which inter-firm, rather than intra-firm, transactions are the preferred modality of counteracting market failure in Japan [Dunning 1994b].

While it would be inappropriate to generalize from this example, it is nevertheless the case that – again due to the adoption of new and flexible production techniques – American firms in the auto and consumer electronic sectors are disinternalizing parts of their value chains. At the same time, they are reducing the number of major suppliers and delegating more design and innovatory functions to them.[40] Moreover, Japanese-owned auto assemblers in the U.S. are replicating or modifying the keiretsu-type relationships of their parent companies as more Japanese suppliers have been setting up subsidiaries, or engaging in cooperative agreements with U.S. firms to supply components to the assemblers [Banjerji and Sambharya 1994].

Most certainly, a 'voice' response to market failure is raising the profile of strategic partnerships in the organizational strategies of MNEs. Nevertheless, it is the case that some kinds of benefits of cross-border value-added activity can only be effectively realized through full hierarchical control over such operations. Examples include situations in which path dependency, learning experience and the global control over financial assets and key technologies and competencies bring their own O-specific advantages, which, because of possible conflicts of interest, would not be realizable from inter-firm agreements. Such agreements, then, would probably be confined to very specific areas of a firm's value-added activities; and, noticeably, those that are outside its core competencies, need specialized proficiencies, can be closely monitored for quality control, and are too costly to produce internally [Quinn and Hilmer 1994]. But, to achieve and sustain many of the most valuable O-specific advantages of multinational operations, hierarchical control probably will remain the principal mode of internationalization, and this applies as much to the Japanese as it does to U.S.- and European-based MNEs.

We finally consider how the advent of alliance capitalism is affecting the location-specific variables influencing international production. We have already indicated that the received literature generally assumes these variables to be exogenous to individual firms, at least at a given moment of time; although, over time, such firms may affect the L advantages of particular countries or regions.

There are essentially two main ways in which alliance capitalism may affect, or be affected by, the presence and structure of immobile assets. The first is that it may introduce new L-specific variables, or modify the value of those traditionally considered by location theory. The second is that the response of firms to economic geography may be different because of the impact that external alliances may have upon their competitive strengths and global strategies.

Let us first deal with the first type of effect. Chief among the L variables affecting MNE activity – and that surveys have revealed have become more significant in the past decade – is the availability of resources and capabilities that investing firms believe are necessary to both upgrade and make best use of their core O-specific advantages. In some cases, these complementary assets, or the rights to their use, can be bought on the open market (e.g., power supplies and transport and communication facilities); but, in others, and noticeably in regimes of rapid technological progress [Teece 1992], the 'continuous handshake' of an alliance relationship, rather than the 'invisible hand' of the market is favored [Gerlach 1992]. Since frequently a foreign direct investment requires the establishment of several of these bilateral relationships, it follows that the positioning of a constellation of related partners becomes a prime locational factor. Where part or all of the constellations are sited in close proximity to each other, then additional benefits may arise. These include not only the static agglomerative economies earlier identified, but also the dynamic externalities associated with the gathering and dissemination of information, and the cross-fertilization of ideas and learning experiences.

The attention given by governments of host countries – or of regions in host countries – to the building of a critical mass of inter-related activities, which is consistent with the perceived dynamic comparative advantage of their location-bound assets, and to the use of FDI in order to create or upgrade core competences to advance this goal, is just one illustration of the growing benefits to be derived from inter-firm linkages.[41] These serve as an L-pull factor. Casual empiricism, both past and present, provides ample examples of how the presence of spatially related business networks attract new investors, and recent evidence unearthed by Wheeler and Mody [1992], Harrison [1994], Lazerson [1993], Herrigel [1994], Audretsch and Feldman [1994], and Enright [1994] confirms these impressions. It also reveals that an innovation-driven industrial economy, which seeks to be fully integrated into world markets, needs to focus more attention on the development of clusters of inter-firm linkages, of intelligent regions and of local institutional thickness [Amin and Thrift 1994].

The new trajectory of capitalism has other implications for the locational requirements of MNE investors. Some of these are set out in Table 1. As a generalization, while traditional production-related variables generally are unaffected or becoming less important, those to do with minimizing transaction and coordination costs of markets or the dysfunctioning of hierarchies, those specific to being part of a group or cluster of related activities, and those that help protect or upgrade the global competitiveness of the investing firm, are becoming more important.[42]

Turning now to the second type of effect that alliance capitalism has on L advantages, we ask the following question: How far, and in what ways, are the responses of MNEs to the L advantages of countries themselves changing because of the growing pluralism of corporate organizations? The answer is that such pluralism allows firms more flexibility in their locational strategies, and that the immobile assets of countries will not only affect the extent and pattern of foreign participation, but also its organizational form. Thus, on the one hand, the opportunities for networking in a specific country may increase FDI. This is particularly the case when an MNE acquires a firm that is already part of a network. On the other hand, the potential to network may also reduce FDI, as it may allow a foreign firm to acquire the complementary assets it needs without making an equity stake.

Of the two scenarios, the one which is more likely to occur will, of course, depend on a host of industry, firm and country-specific considerations. But, our point will have been made if it is accepted that the hypothesis of scholars about the response of firms to at least some L-specific variables may need to be modified in the light of the growing significance of non-equity-based cooperative arrangements, and of networks of firms with related interests. We also believe that the ways in which MNEs choose to leverage and use a portfolio of interrelated location-bound assets, with those of their own O-specific advantages and the complementary competencies of external partners, are, themselves, becoming an increasingly important core advantage of such firms.

CONCLUSIONS

This paper has suggested that the socio-institutional structure of market-based capitalism is undergoing change. The catalyst is a new wave of multi-purpose generic technological advances and the demands of innovation-led production, which are compelling more cooperation among economic agents. Though part of that cooperation is 'bought' by firms through M&A activity, the growing significance of inter-firm partnering and of networking is demanding a reexamination of traditional approaches to our understanding of the extent and form of international business activity.

Our discussion has concentrated on only one of these approaches, viz., the eclectic paradigm of international production, and has suggested that this explanatory framework needs to be modified in three main ways. First, the role of innovation in sustaining and upgrading the competitive advantages of firms and countries needs to be better recognized. It also needs to be more explicitly acknowledged that firms may engage in FDI and in cross-border alliances in order to acquire or learn about foreign technology and markets, as well as to exploit their existing competitive advantages. Inter alia, this suggests a strengthening of its analytical underpinnings to encompass a theory of innovation – as, for example, propounded by Nelson and Winter [1982], and Cantwell [1989, 1994] – that identifies and evaluates the role of technological accumulation and learning as O-specific advantages of firms, and the role of national education and innovation policies affecting the L advantages of countries.

Second, the paradigm needs to better recognize that a 'voice' strategy for reducing some kinds of market failure – and particularly those to do with opportunism and information impactness by participants in the market – is a viable alternative to an 'exit' strategy of hierarchical capitalism; and that, like hierarchies, strategic partnerships are intended to reduce endemic market failure, and may help to advance innovatory competitiveness rather than inhibit it. Among other things, this suggests that theories of inter-firm cooperation or collective competition, which tend to address issues of static efficiency [Buckley 1994], need to be widened to incorporate questions of dynamic efficiency, e.g., market positioning.

Third, the eclectic paradigm needs to acknowledge that the traditional assumption that the capabilities of the individual firm are limited to its ownership boundaries (and that, outside these boundaries, factors influencing the firms competitiveness are exogenous to it) is no longer acceptable whenever the quality of a firm's efficiency-related decisions is significantly influenced by the collaborative agreements they have with other firms. The concept of decision taking has implications that go well beyond explaining FDI and international production; indeed, it calls into question some of the fundamental underpinnings of the theory of industrial organization.

Much of the thrust of this paper has been concerned with suggesting how these three evolving concepts – innovation-led growth, a 'voice' reaction to market failure, and cooperation as a competitiveness-enhancing measure – affect the OLI configuration facing firms engaging, or wishing to engage, in cross-border transactions. In doing so, it has thrown up a number of casual hypotheses as to the kinds of O-specific advantages that are most likely to be affected by inter-firm alliances and networks, and about how the opportunities to engage in such alliances or networks may affect, and be affected by, the portfolio of inter-related location-specific assets. Our analysis has also sought to identify some of the implications of the gathering pace of innovation-led production, and of alliance capitalism, for the organization of economic activity. In doing so, it has suggested that the internalization paradigm still remains a powerful tool of analysis, as long as it is widened to incorporate strategic-asset-acquiring FDI and the dynamic learning activities of firms, and to more explicitly take account of the conditions under which a 'voice' strategy of inter-firm cooperation may be a preferable option to an 'exit' strategy for reducing the transaction and coordination costs of arm's-length markets, and building inter-active learning-based competitiveness.[43]

There has been some exploratory empirical testing, using both field and case study data, of the impact of alliances and networks on the performance of locational and organizational strategies of participating firms. Studies by Gomes-Casseres [1994, 1995] on the global computer and electronics industries; by Gomes-Casseres and Leonard-Barton [1994] on the multimedia sector; by Mowery [1991] on the commercial aircraft industry; by Brooks, Blunden and Bidgood [1993] on the container transport industry; by Shan and Hamilton [1991] and Whittaker and Bower [1994] on the pharmaceutical industry; by Peng [1993] on the role of network and alliance strategies in assisting the transition from a collectivist to a market-based economy; by Helper [1993] on the 'exit' and 'voice' sourcing strategies of the leading auto-assemblers; by Enright [1993], Glaismeier [1988], Henderson [1994], Lazerson [1993], Piore and Sabel [1984], Saxenian [1994] and Scott [1993] on the rationale for regional clusters and specialized industrial districts in Europe and the U.S.; and, multiple case studies by a number of authors on the roles of keiretsu-based transactions and relational contracting as alternatives to hierarchies (e.g., Lincoln [1990]) are just a few examples.

But, much more remains to be done. Indeed, it is possible that the basic contention of this paper, viz. that innovation-led production systems and co-operative inter-firm agreements are emerging as the dominant form of market-based capitalism, is incorrect. At the same time, it would be difficult to deny that important changes – and, for the most part, irreversible technological changes – are afoot in the global economy; and, that these changes are requiring international business scholars to reexamine at least some of the concepts and theories that have dominated the field for the last two decades or more.

NOTES

1. As set out, most recently, in Dunning [1993a, Ch. 4].

2. See, e.g., Dunning [1994a] and Gerlach [1992] for a more extensive analysis of this proposition.

3. Especially at River Rouge (U.S.), where its empire included ore and coal mines, 70,000 acres of timberland, saw mills, blast furnaces, glass works, ore and coal barges, and a railway [Williamson 1985].

4. As, for example, is shown by data published in the U.S. Census of Manufacturers and the U.K. Census of Production (various issues).

5. For full details, see Chandler [1962] and Dunning [1994a].

6. At the time it was published [1937], Coase's article on *The Nature of the Firm* was treated as an 'aberration' by his fellow economists [Williamson 1993]. As Coase himself acknowledged [1993], in the 1980s there was more discussion of his ideas than during the whole of the preceding forty years.

7. I do not know for sure which particular scholar first used the concept of market failure to explain the existence and growth of the MNE. I first came across the concept of internalization in the early 1970s in a chapter by John McManus entitled, 'The Theory of the Multinational Firm,' in an edited volume by Pacquet [McManus 1972].

8. It is also of some interest that Penrose did not cite Coase in any of her work.

9. There were, I think, two reasons for this. The first was that mainstream microeconomists were strongly influenced (one might almost say hidebound) by the static equilibrium models of Chamberlin [1933] and Robinson [1933]; and the second was that Penrose had not formalized her theory in a manner acceptable to her colleagues.

10. Among the most frequently quoted scholars are Buckley and Casson, Hennart, Rugman, and Teece. A summary of the views of the internalization school are contained in Dunning [1993a]. See also Rugman [1981], Hennart [1982], Buckley and Casson [1985], and Casson [1987].

11. See, for example, the contributions to Buckley's edited volume [1994].

12. Elsewhere [Dunning 1993b], we have suggested paradigm is a more appropriate term to apply to explain the reactions of firms to cross-border market failure.

13. Exceptions include structural market failure deliberately engineered by firms and the extent to which they may be able to influence the content and degree of market failure, e.g., by lobbying for particular government action, and by the setting up of compensating institutions, e.g., insurance and future markets, to reduce risk.

14. See especially Best [1990], Gerlach [1992], Lazonick [1991 and 1992], Michalet [1991], Dunning [1994a] and Ruigrok and Van Tulder [1995].

15. Here, we think it appropriate to make the point that the expression *alliance capitalism* should be perceived partly as a sociocultural phenomenon and partly as a techno-organizational one. The former suggests a change in the ethos and perspective towards the organization of capitalism, and, in particular, towards the relationships between the participating institutions and individuals. The latter embraces the formal structure of the organization of economic activity, including the management of resource allocation and growth. Alliance capitalism is an eclectic (sic) concept. It suggests both cooperation and competition *between* institutions (including public institutions) and between interested parties *within* institutions. De facto, it is also leading to a flattening out of the organizational structure of decisiontaking of business enterprises, with a pyramidal chain of command being increasingly replaced by a more heterarchical inter-play between the main participants in decisiontaking. Finally, we would emphasize that we are not suggesting that alliance capitalism means the demise of hierarchies, but rather that the rationale and functions of hierarchies requires a reappraisal in the socioeconomic climate of the global marketplace now emerging.

484   JOURNAL OF INTERNATIONAL BUSINESS STUDIES, THIRD QUARTER 1995

16. In the words of Adam Smith [1776] 'people of the same trade seldom meet together, even for merriment and diversion, but the conversation ends in a conspiracy against the public, or in some contrivance to raise prices'.

17. See especially Buckley and Casson [1988], Contractor and Lorange [1988], Kogut [1988], Hennart [1988, 1989] and Hagedoorn [1993a and 1993b].

18. The facts are documented in various publications, e.g., Freeman and Hagedoorn [1992], Hagedoorn [1990, 1993a,b], Gomes-Casseres [1993] and UNCTAD [1993, 1994].

19. Some examples are set out in Dunning [1993a], p. 605 ff. "Optoelectronics, for example, is a marriage of electronics and optics and is yielding important commercial products such as optical fibre communication systems [Kodama 1992]. The latest generation of large commercial aircraft, for example, requires the combined skills of metallurgy, aeronautical engineering and aero-electronics. Current medical advances often need the technological resources of pharmacology, biotechnology, laser technology, and genetic engineering for their successful commercialization. The design and construction of chemical plants involves innovatory inputs from chemical, engineering and materials sectors. New telecommunication devices embrace the latest advances in carbon materials, fibre optics, computer technology, and electronic engineering. Modern industrial building techniques need to draw upon the combined expertise of engineering, materials and production technologies. In its venture to explore the sea-bed, Kennecott's consortium brings together a large number of technical disciplines and firms from many different industrial sectors [Contractor and Lorange 1988]. Since both the consumption and the production of most core technologies usually yield externalities of one kind or another, it follows that one or the other of the firms involved may be prompted to recoup these benefits by integrating the separate activities, particularly those which draw upon the same generic technology."

20. Examples include the rapid obsolescence of successive generations of computers and the information-carrying power of micro-chips.

21. One particularly good example is the pharmaceutical industry, where the large drug companies are increasingly internalizing the most novel and risky types of biotechnology innovations to small specialist firms. In the words of two British researchers [Whittaker and Bower 1994] "The large pharmaceutical companies no longer view themselves as the primary innovators in the industry. . . . The biotechnology companies take on the role of supplier of innovatory activity." The authors go on to illustrate the symbiotic supplier/buyer relationship that is developing between the two groups of firms. "The large drug company needs technologically novel products to market and the biotechnology company needs finance, sometimes some ancillary technical expertise in later-stage process development and formulation, skill in handling regulatory agreements and marketing forces (p. 258).

22. For example, of the alliances identified by Freeman and Hagedoorn, 76.3% were accounted for by 21 MNEs, each of whom had concluded 100 or more alliances.

23. At the same time, MNEs have increased the R&D intensity of their foreign operations, and have set up technological listening posts in the leading innovating countries.

24. The authors assert that such alliances result from the fusion of technologies from computer communications and consumer electronics; and that because no single firm had (or has) the internal capabilities or the time needed to produce a PDA, that it was necessary to form a cluster of 'matching' alliances.

25. In their words "Competitive success requires the integration of multiple capabilities (e.g., innovation, productivity, quality, responsiveness to customers) across internal and external organizational boundaries" (p. 151).

26. Not to mention to preclude competition from gaining such assets.

27. See, for example, several chapters in an edited volume by Encarnation and Mason [1994].

28. As shown by a variety of indices.

29. See, for example, Banjerji and Sambharya [1994].

30. For further illustrations, see Hamel [1991], Harrison [1994], Stopford [1995], Whittaker and Bower [1994] and Lorenzoni and Baden Fuller [1995].

31. For an interesting discussion of the differing nature of business districts both in the U.S. and in other countries, see Markusen, Hall, Deitrick and Campbell [1991].

32. It is estimated that 70% of all Toyota's suppliers are within 100 miles of the Toyota's main assembling complex in Tokyo.

33. See particularly, Forsgren and Johanson [1991], Håkansson and Johanson [1993], Johanson and Mattsson [1987, 1994] and Johanson and Vahlne [1977].

34. In the words of Amin and Thrift [1994], and in the context of the globalizing economy, "centers of geographical agglomeration are centers of representation, interaction and innovation within global production filieres." . . . It is their "unique ability to act as a pole of excellence and to offer to the wide collectivity a well consolidated network of contacts, knowledge, structures and institutions underwriting individual entrepreneurship which makes a center a magnet for economic activity" (p. 13)

35. For an examination of the alliance as a unit of analysis, see Gomes-Casseres [1994].

36. Where country-specific characteristics are regarded as endogenous variables, then the theory of international economics becomes relevant. This is the position of Kojima [1978, 1990], who is one of the leading exponents of a trade-related theory of MNE activity.

37. In particular, the transaction cost theories of Coase and Williamson. The resource-based theory of the firm [Wernerfelt 1984; Barney 1991; Peteraf 1993] is much broader and, in many respects, is closer in lineage to industrial organization theory, as it is concerned with explaining the origin of a firm's sustainable competitive advantages in terms of resource heterogeneity, limits to competition, and imperfect resource immobility.

38. It is these latter advantages that internalization economists claim *follow* from foreign owned production, rather than *precede* it; although, of course, once established, these advantages may place the MNE in a more favored position for sequential investment.

39. Of course, in some instances, e.g., jointly funded R&D projects, the resulting economic rents may also have to be shared.

40. Stopford [1995], drawing upon the World Automotive Components supplement published by the *Financial Times* on the July 12, 1994, gives several examples of this phenomenon.

41. As is amply realized by the national governments of foreign investment agencies in their attempts to attract foreign firms to locate in their territories.

42 .We accept that it may be difficult to separate the specific effect of alliance capitalism from the other forces influencing the L advantage of countries. This, indeed, is a fertile area for empirical research.

43. According to Storper [1994] those firms, sectors, regions and nations that are able to learn faster and more efficiently become competitive because knowledge is scarce and, therefore, cannot be imitated by new entrants or transferred by codified and formal channels to other firms, regions or nations.

REFERENCES

Amin, Ash & Nigel Thrift, editors. 1994. *Globalization, institutions and regional development in Europe*. Oxford: Oxford University Press.

Audretsch, David B. & Maryann P. Feldman. 1994. External economies and spatial clustering. A. In P. R. Krugman & A. Venables, editors, *The location of economic activity: New theories and evidence*. London: Center of Economic Policy Research, CPER.

Banjerji, K. & R. B. Sambharya. 1994. Vertical keiretsu and international market entry: The case of the Japanese automobile industry. Mimeo. Virginia & New Jersey: West Virginia and Rutgers Universities.

Barney, Jay B. 1991. Firm resources and sustained competitive advantage. *Journal of Management,* 17: 99–120.

Bartness, Andrew & Keith Cerny. 1993. Building competitive advantage through a global network of capabilities. *California Management Review*: 78–103.

Best, Michael. 1990. *The new competition: Institutions of restructuring.* Cambridge, Mass.: Harvard University Press.

Brooks, M. R., R. G. Blunder & C. I. Bidgood. 1993. Strategic alliances in the global container transport industry. In R. Culpan, editor, *Multinational strategic alliances*, 221–50. New York & London: Haworth Press.

Buckley, Peter J., editor. 1994. *Cooperative forms of the TNC activity.* UNCTC Library on Transnational Corporations. London: Routledge.

_____ & Mark C. Casson. 1985. *The economic theory of the multinational enterprise.* London: Macmillan.

_____ 1988. A theory of cooperation in international business. In F. J. Contractor & P. Lorange, editors, *Cooperative strategies in international business*, 31–53. Lexington, Mass.: D. C. Heath.

Bye, Maurice. 1958. Self-financed multiterritorial units and their time horizon. *International Economic Papers,* 8: 147–78.

Cantwell, John A. 1989. *Technological innovation and multinational corporations.* Oxford, U.K.: Basil Blackwell.

_____, editor. 1994. *Transnational corporations and innovatory activities.* United Nations Library on Transnational Corporations. London: Routledge.

Casson, Mark C. 1987. *The firm and the market.* Oxford, U.K.: Basil Blackwell.

Chamberlin, Edward. 1933. *The theory of monopolistic competition.* Boston: Harvard University Press.

Chandler, Alfred D., Jr. 1962. *Strategy and structure.* Boston: Harvard University Press.

_____. 1990. *Scale and scope: The dynamics of industrial capitalism.* Cambridge, Mass.: Harvard University.

Coase, Ronald H. 1937. The nature of the firm. *Economica* 4 (November): 386–405.

_____. 1988. *The firm, the market and the law.* Chicago & London: University of Chicago Press.

_____. 1993. The nature of the firm: meaning and influence. In O. E. Williamson & S. G. Winter, editors, *The nature of the firm*, 34–74. New York & Oxford: Oxford University Press.

Contractor, Farok J. & Peter Lorange. 1988. *Cooperative strategies in international business.* Lexington, Mass.: D. C. Heath.

Cournot, Antoine A. (trans. N. T. Bacon). 1851. *Researches into mathematical principles of the theory of wealth.* New York: Macmillan.

D'Cruz, Joseph R. & Alan M. Rugman. 1992. Business networks for international business. *Business Quarterly,* 54 (Spring): 101–107.

_____. 1993. Business networks for global competitiveness. *Business Quarterly,* 57 (Summer): 93–98.

Dunning, John H. 1977. Trade, location of economic activity and the multinational enterprise: A search for an eclectic approach. In B. Ohlin, P. O. Hesselborn & P. M. Wikman., editors, *The international allocation of economic activity*, 395–418. London: Macmillan.

_____. 1993a. *Multinational enterprises and the global economy*. Wokingham, Berkshire, U.K.: Addison Wesley.

_____. 1993b. *Globalization of business*. London & New York: Routledge.

_____. 1994a. *Globalization, economic restructuring and development* (The Prebisch Lecture for 1994). Geneva: UNCTAD.

_____. 1994b. The strategy of Japanese and US manufacturing investment in Europe. In M. Mason & D. Encarnation, editors, *Does ownership matter? Japanese multinationals in Europe*, 59–86. Oxford, U.K.: Clarendon Press.

Enright, Michael J. 1993. Organization and coordination in geographically concentrated industries. In D. Raff & N. Lamoreaux, editors. *Coordination and information: Historical perspectives on the organization of enterprise*. Chicago: Chicago University Press.

_____. 1994. Geographic concentration and firm strategy. Paper presented to Prince Bertil Symposium on The Dynamic Firm: The Role of Regions, Technology, Strategy and Organization, Stockholm, June.

Forsgren, Mats & Jan Johanson, editors. 1991. *Managing networks in international business*. Philadelphia: Gordon and Breach.

Freeman, Christopher. 1991. Networks of innovators: A synthesis of research issues. *Research Policy*, 20: 499–514.

_____ & John Hagedoorn. 1992. Globalization of technology. Working Paper 92.013. Maastricht, The Netherlands: Maastricht Research Institute on Innovation and Technology (MERIT).

Freeman, Christopher & C. Perez. 1988. Structural crises of adjustment, business cycles, and investment behavior. In G. Dosi, C. Freeman, R. Nelson, G. Silverberg & L. Soete, editors, *Technical change and economic theory*. London: Pinter Publishers.

Gerlach, Michael L. 1992. *Alliance capitalism: The social organization of Japanese business*. Oxford, U.K.: Oxford University Press.

Glaismeier, Amy. 1988. Factors governing the development of high tech industry agglomeratives: A tale of three cities. *Regional Studies*, 22: 287–301.

Gomes-Casseres, Benjamin. 1993. Computers, alliances and industry evolution. In D. B. Yoffie, *Beyond free trade: firms, governments and global competition*. Boston: Harvard Business School Press.

_____. 1994. Group versus group: How alliance networks compete. *Harvard Business Review*, July–August: 62–74.

_____. 1995. *Collective competition: International alliances in high technology*. Boston: Harvard University Press.

_____ & Dorothy Leonard-Barton. 1994. Alliance clusters in multimedia: Safety net or entanglement? Mimeo. Harvard Business School.

Hagedoorn, John. 1990. Organizational modes of inter-firm cooperation and technology transfer. *Technovation*, 10(1): 17–30.

_____. 1993a. Understanding the rationale of strategic technology partnering: Interorganizational modes of cooperation and sectoral differences. *Strategic Management Journal*, 14: 371–85.

_____. 1993b. Strategic technology alliance of cooperation in high technology industries. In G. Grabher, editor, *The embedded firm*, 116–37. London & Boston: Routledge.

_____ & Joseph Schakenraad. 1993. Strategic technology partnering and international corporate strategies. In K. S. Hughes, editor, *European competitiveness*, 60–86. Cambridge, U.K.: Cambridge University Press.

488   JOURNAL OF INTERNATIONAL BUSINESS STUDIES, THIRD QUARTER 1995

Håkansson, Lars & Jan Johanson. 1993. The network as a governance structure. In G. Grabher, editor, *The embedded firm*, 35–51. London & Boston: Routledge.

Hamel, Gary. 1991. Competition for competence and inter-partner learning with international strategic alliances. *Strategic Management Journal*, 12: 82–103.

Harrison, Bennett. 1994. *Lean and mean: The changing landscape of power in the age of flexibility*. New York: Basic Books.

Helper, S. 1993. An exit-voice analysis of supplier relations: The case of the US automobile industry. In G. Grabher, editor, *The embedded firm*, 141–60. London & Boston: Routledge.

Henderson, V. 1994. Externalities and industrial development. In P. Krugman & A. Venables, editors, *The location of economic activity: New theories and evidence*. London: Centre of Economic Policy Research (CPER).

Hennart, Jean-François. 1982. *A theory of the multinational enterprise*. Ann Arbor, Mich.: University of Michigan Press.

———. 1988. A transaction costs theory of equity joint ventures. *Strategic Management Journal*, 9: 361–74.

———. 1989. Can the 'new forms of investment' substitute for the 'old forms': A transaction costs perspective. *Journal of International Business Studies*, 20(2): 211–33.

Herrigel, G. B. 1994. Power and the redefinition of industrial districts: The case of Baden Württemberg. In G. Grabher, editor, *The embedded firm*, 227–52. London & Boston: Routledge.

Hirschman, Albert, O. 1970. *Exit, voice and loyalty*. Cambridge, Mass.: Harvard University Press.

Johanson, Jan & Lars G. Mattsson. 1987. Internationalization in industrial systems – network approach. In N. Hood & J.-E. Vahlne, editors, *Strategies in global competition*. Chichester & New York: John Wiley.

———. 1994. The markets-as-networks tradition in Sweden. In G. Laurent, G. L. Lilien & B. Pras, editors, *Research traditions in marketing*, 321–46. Dordrecht, Boston: Kluwer.

Johanson, Jan & Jan-Erik Vahlne. 1977. The internationalization process of the firm – A model of knowledge development and increasing foreign market commitments. *Journal of International Business Studies*, 8(1): 23–32.

Kobrin, Stephen J. 1993. Beyond geography: Inter-firm networks and the structural integration of the world economy. Working Paper 93–10. Philadelphia: Centre for International Management Studies, University of Pennsylvania.

Kodama, Fumio. 1992. Japan's unique capability to innovate: Technology, fusion and its international implications. In T. S. Arrison, C. F. Bergsten & M. Harris, editors, *Japan's growing technological capability: Implications for the US economy*. Washington, D.C.: National Academy Press.

Kogut, Bruce. 1988. Joint ventures: Theoretical and empirical perspectives. *Strategic Management Journal*: 319–22.

———, Weijian Shan & G. Walker. 1993. Knowledge in the network and the network as knowledge. In G. Grabher., editor, *The embedded firm*, 67–94. London & New York: Routledge.

Kogut, Bruce & Sea Jin Chang. 1991. Technological capabilities and Japanese direct investment in the United States. *Review of Economics and Statistics*, 73(3): 401–13.

Kojima, Kiyoshi. 1978. *Direct foreign investment: A Japanese model of multinational business operations*. London: Croom Helm.

———. 1990. *Japanese direct investment abroad.* Social Science Research Institute Monograph Series 1. Mitaka, Tokyo: International Christian University.

Krugman, Paul R. 1991. *Geography and trade.* Leuven, Belgium: Leuven University Press & Cambridge MIT Press.

Lazerson, M. 1993. Factory or putting out? Knitting networks in Modena. In G. Grabher, editor, *The embedded firm.* London & Boston: Routledge.

Lazonick, William.1991. *Business organization and the myth of the market economy.* Cambridge, U.K.: Cambridge University Press.

———. 1992. Business organization and competitive advantage: Capitalist transformation in the twentieth century. In G. Dosi, R. Giannelti & P. A. Toninelli, editors, *Technology and enterprise in a historical perspective*, 119–63. Oxford, U.K.: Clarendon Press.

Lincoln, James R. 1990. Japanese organization and organizational theory. *Research and Organizational Behavior,* 12: 255–94.

Lorenzoni, G. & Charles Baden Fuller. 1995. Creating a strategic center to manage a web of partners. *California Management Review,* 37(3): 146–63.

Malecki, Edward J. 1985. Industrial location and corporate organization in high technology industries. *Economic Geography,* 61(4): 345–69.

Markusen, Ann, Peter Hall, S. Deitrick. & S. Campbell. 1991. *The rise of the gunbelt: The military remapping of industrial America.* New York & Oxford: Oxford University Press.

Marshall, Alfred. 1920. *Principles of economics.* London: Macmillan.

Mason, Mark & Dennis Encarnation, editors. 1994. *Does ownership matter? Japanese multinationals in Europe.* Oxford, U.K.: Clarendon Press.

McManus, John. C. 1972. The theory of the multinational firm. In G. Paquet, editor, *The multinational firm and the nation state.* Toronto: Collier Macmillan.

Michalet, Charles-Albert. 1991. Strategic partnerships and the changing international process. In L. K. Mytelka, editor, *Strategic partnerships: States, firms and international competition.* London: Pinter Publishers.

Mody, Ashoka. 1993. Learning through alliances. *Journal of Economic Behavior and Organization,* 20: 151–70.

Mowery, David C. & David J. Teece. 1993. Japan's growing capabilities in industrial technology: Implication for US managers and policy makers. *California Management Review,* Winter: 9–34.

Mytelka, Lynne K. 1991. *Strategic partnerships: States, firms, and international competition.* London: Pinter Publishers.

Naisbitt, John. 1994. *Global paradox: The bigger the world economy, the more political its smallest players.* New York: William Morrow.

Nelson, Richard R. & Sidney G. Winter. 1982. *An evolutionary theory of economic change.* Cambridge, Mass.: Harvard University Press.

Peng, M. W. 1993. *Blurring boundaries: The growth of the firm in planned economies in transition.* Mimeo. Washington Center for International Business Education and Research, University of Washington.

Penrose, Edith T. 1956. Foreign investment and growth of the firm. *Economic Journal,* 60: 220–35.

———. 1959. *The theory of the growth of the firm.* Oxford, U.K.: Basil Blackwell.

490   JOURNAL OF INTERNATIONAL BUSINESS STUDIES, THIRD QUARTER 1995

Perez, C. 1983. Structural changes and the assimilation of new technologies on the economic and social system. *Futures,* 15: 357–75.

Peteraf, Margaret. 1993. The cornerstones of competitive advantage: A resource based view. *Strategic Management Journal,* 14: 179–91.

Pigou, Arthur C. 1932 (fourth edition). *The economics of welfare.* London: Macmillan.

Piore, Michael J. & Charles. F. Sabel. 1984. *The second industrial divide: Possibilities for prosperity.* New York: Basic Books.

Porter, Michael. 1990. *The competitive advantage of nations.* New York: Free Press.

Powell, William W. 1990. Neither market nor hierarchy: Network forms of organization. *Research in Organizational Behavior,* 12: 245–336.

Quinn, James B. & F. G. Hilmer. 1994. Strategic outsourcing. *Sloan Management Review,* Summer: 43–55.

Robinson, Joan. 1933. *The economics of imperfect competition.* London: Macmillan.

Ruigrok, Winfried & Rob van Tulder. 1995 (forthcoming). *The logic of international restructuring.* London & New York: Routledge.

Rugman, Alan M. 1981. *Inside the multinationals: The economics of internal markets.* London: Croom Helm.

Saxenian, Anna Lee. 1991. The origins and dynamics of production networks. In *Silicon Valley Research Policy,* 20: 423–37.

———. 1994. *Regional advantage: Culture and competition in Silicon Valley and Route 128.* Cambridge, Mass.: Harvard University Press.

Scott, Allen J. 1993. *Technologies: High-technology industry and regional development in Southern California.* Berkeley & Los Angeles: University of California Press.

———. 1994. The geographic foundations of industrial performance. Paper presented to the Prince Bertil Symposium on The Dynamic Firm, the Role of Regions, Technology, Strategy and Organization, Stockholm, June.

Shan, Weijian & William Hamilton. 1991. Country-specific advantage and international cooperation. *Strategic Management Journal,* 12(6): 419-32.

Smith, Adam. 1776. *An inquiry into the nature and clauses of the wealth of nations,* Vol. 1 (1947 edition published by J. M. Dent & Sons, London).

Stopford, John M. 1995. *Competing globally to create and control resources,* Mimeo. London Business School.

Storper, M. 1994. *Institutions of a learning economy.* Los Angeles: School of Public Policy and Social Research, UCLA.

Teece, David J. 1992. Competition, cooperation and innovation. *Journal of Economic Behavior and Organization,* 18: 1–25.

UNCTAD. 1993. *World investment report 1993.* Transnational corporations and integrated international production. Geneva: UNCTAD Program on Transnational Corporations.

———. 1994. *World investment report 1994.* Transnational corporations, employment and the workplace. Geneva: UNCTAD Program on Transnational Corporations.

Weiermar, Karl. 1991. Globalization and new forms of industrial organization. In I. H. Rima, editor, *The political economy of global restructuring,* Vol. II, 159–71. Aldershot, U.K. & Brookfield, Vt.: Edward Elgar.

Wernerfelt, Birger. 1984. A resource-based view of the firm. *Strategic Management Journal* 5(2): 171–80.

Wheeler, K. & A. Mody. 1992. International investment and location decisions: The case of US firms. *Journal of International Economics,* 33: 57–76.

Whittaker, E. & D. Jane Bower. 1994. A shift to external alliances for product development in the pharmaceutical industry. *R&D Management,* 24(3): 249–60.

Williamson, Oliver E. 1985. *The economic institutions of capitalism.* New York: Free Press.

———. 1993. The logic of economic organization. In O. E. Williamson & S. E. Winter, editors, *The nature of the firm.* New York & Oxford: Oxford University Press.

World Bank. 1992. *The World Development Report.* New York & Oxford: Oxford University Press.

[10]

CONTROL AND PERFORMANCE
OF INTERNATIONAL JOINT VENTURES

J. Michael Geringer* and Louis Hebert**
University of Western Ontario

Abstract. Control is a critical concept for successful management and performance of international joint ventures (IJVs). This paper reviews and synthesizes prior studies addressing the conceptualization and operationalization of control within IJVs, as well as the IJV control-performance relationship. The paper also presents a new conceptualization of IJV control, as well as a conceptual framework for studying control of IJVs.

THE IMPORTANCE OF CONTROL
IN INTERNATIONAL JOINT VENTURES

With continued globalization of the world's economies, joint ventures (JVs) have become an important element of many firms' international strategies. These ventures involve two or more legally distinct organizations (the parents), each of which actively participates in the decisionmaking activities of the jointly owned entity [Geringer 1988]. If at least one parent organization is headquartered outside the JV's country of operation, or if the venture has a significant level of operations in more than one country, then it is considered to be an international joint venture (IJV).

An alternative to wholly-owned subsidiaries, IJVs are commonly used by firms as a means of competing within multidomestic or global competitive arenas [Porter & Fuller 1986; Harrigan 1988]. Increasingly, they are perceived as strategic weapons, as one of the elements of an organization's business units network [Harrigan 1987]. Joint ventures also represent an

---

*J. Michael Geringer (Ph.D., University of Washington) is an Assistant Professor of Policy at the University of Western Ontario. Besides the *Journal of International Business Studies,* his articles have appeared in such journals as the *Columbia Journal of World Business, Business Quarterly*, and the *Strategic Management Journal.* His research interests include formation and management of international alliances, MNE diversification strategies, and strategic management of technology.

**Louis Hebert (M.Sc., University of Quebec at Trois Rivieres) is a Ph.D. candidate in Business Policy at the University of Western Ontario. His current research interests center on the strategic management and control of technology, particularly within international joint ventures.

This research was sponsored by the Plan for Excellence, School of Business, University of Western Ontario, and the Quebec Fonds pour la formation de chercheurs et l'aide a la recherche (F.C.A.R.). Of the many people who provided contributions to this research, the authors would like to acknowledge Paul Beamish, Rod White, Colette Frayne, and the anonymous reviewers.

Received: June 1988; Revised: November & December 1988; Accepted: December 1988.

effective way of coping with the increasing competitive and technological challenges of today's environment [Perlmutter & Heenan 1986].

However, despite their potental contributions, IJVs are not without their drawbacks. The presence of two or more parents can make IJVs difficult to manage and often characterized by poor performance [Drucker 1974; Young & Bradford 1977; Janger 1980; Killing 1983; Geringer 1986]. A critical determinant of IJV performance appears to be the control exercised by parents over a venture's activities [Rafii 1978; Killing 1983; Schaan 1983]. Yet, particularly in comparison to wholly-owned subsidiaries, the exercise of effective control over IJVs may represent a more difficult proposition for the parent organizations because they are often unable to rely solely on their ownership position to determine the IJV's behavior and management, instead requiring recourse to other modes of influence.

Furthermore, a firm that agrees to participate in an IJV inevitably complicates its life. Although each partner must, by definition, relinquish some control over an IJV's activities, such a move is often accompanied by great consternation. A firm may avoid relinquishing control over some or all of its activities for reasons intimately related to its corporate strategy and objectives. Attainment of a firm's objectives over the long term is contingent on its ability to implement a strategy which exploits its distinctive competencies along one or several critical dimensions of corporate activity. Insufficient or ineffective control over an IJV can limit the parent firm's ability to coordinate its activities, to efficiently utilize its resources and to effectively implement its strategy [Stopford & Wells 1972; Lorange, et al. 1986; Anderson & Gatignon 1986]. In turn, exercising control over some or all of the activities of an IJV helps protect the firm from premature exposure of its strategy, technological core or other proprietary components to outside groups. Even if its products or processes are protected by patents or copyrights, a firm may nonetheless fear damaging "leakage" of unprotected innovations or know-how if shared with partners. Such disclosures, between the partners or to organizations outside the venture, may have serious effects on the competitive position of a parent or the IJV, possibly creating new competitors or otherwise limiting the IJV's or parent's overall efficiency [Parry 1985; Rugman 1985; Reich & Mankin 1986].

It is from this perspective that we will present a review and synthesis of the principal research addressing the issue of the control of IJVs. The discussion's emphasis will be on the similarities and differences in prior conceptualizations and operationalizations of IJV control, and in the approaches used to examine the control-performance relationship for IJVs. The paper will conclude with the presentation of a new conceptualization of IJV control and a conceptual framework for studying control of IJVs.

CONCEPTUALIZATION AND OPERATIONALIZATION OF JOINT VENTURE CONTROL

Control refers to the process by which one entity influences, to varying degrees, the behavior and output of another entity [Ouchi 1977] through the use of power, authority [Etzioni 1965] and a wide range of bureaucratic, cultural and informal mechanisms [Baliga & Jaeger 1984]. Control plays an important role in the capacity of a firm to achieve its goals. Typically, as organizations expand in size, there are concurrent increases in the complexity and differentiation of their structures [Lawrence & Lorsch 1967], as well as in the risks of conflicts, opportunistic behavior and competing goals between units. As a result, top management are confronted by the increasingly crucial need to monitor, coordinate and integrate the activities of the organization's business units, including IJVs [Child 1977; Mintzberg 1979].

The importance of the issue of control explains why, for many years, scholars have devoted attention to this concept's role in the management of organizations [Etzioni 1961; Tannebaum 1968; Child 1972a, 1972b; Lorange & Scott Morton 1974; Ouchi & Maguire 1975; Edstrom & Galbraith 1977; Ouchi 1978; Vancil 1979]. Nevertheless, many researchers have felt that the essence of the concept had not yet been adequately captured [Giglioni & Bedeian 1974; Miner 1982], resulting in numerous recent attempts to provide more thorough and explicit frameworks, definitions and conceptualizations of control [Green & Welsh 1988; Schreyogg & Steinmann 1987; Merchant 1982]. Several authors have shown particular concern for the exercise of control within large organizations, particularly multinational corporations [Skinner 1968; Franko 1971; Stopford & Wells 1972; Brooke & Remmers 1978]. In particular, they have examined the different degrees of control multinationals exercise over their subsidiaries [Cray 1984; Anderson & Gatignon 1987], as well as the mechanisms, systems and procedures used and the variables influencing the recourse to them [Doz & Prahalad 1981, 1984; Baliga & Jaeger 1984; Egelhoff 1984].

In contrast, the issue of control of IJVs has received relatively scant attention. The topic of IJV control was first raised by West [1959], who recognized the potential inter-partner conflicts which could result from this form of organization. According to West, without effective control efforts, firms were likely to experience great difficulty in managing JVs. Yet, despite this early observation regarding its importance, the issue of control has received only fragmented and unsystematic attention in the JV literature. More than ten years passed between West's initial observations and the re-emergence of the issue of control within the JV literature. Moreover, as discussed below, these subsequent research efforts have largely examined very different dimensions of IJV control, and no explicit attempts have been made to provide an integrative approach to the issue.

The first dimension of IJV control which researchers have examined is the *mechanisms* by which control may be exercised. Initial studies showed that firms frequently relied on majority ownership or on voting control (in turn, largely determined by majority equity shareholdings) to achieve effective management control of an IJV's activities [Tomlinson 1970; Friedman & Beguin 1971; Stopford & Wells 1972]. Although these studies showed that a majority position in equity or votes could ensure some degree of control over the venture, the same argument might not be valid for IJVs where the equity was equally divided between parents or in which a firm had only a minority participation role. This latter situation especially concerned firms that, over time, were unable to demand full or dominant ownership positions in many international investments. With continued diffusion of technology, increased scale and risk accompanying new projects, increased globalization of many industries and host government policies promoting local equity participation in order to obtain resources or market access, the option of implementing wholly-owned or dominant ownership ventures has often been constrained [Moxon & Geringer 1985; Porter & Fuller 1986].

In addressing such concerns, Behrman [1970] as well as Friedman and Beguin [1971] suggested that control was not a strict and automatic consequence of ownership. According to these studies, a variety of mechanisms were available to firms for exercising effective IJV control: right of veto, representation in management bodies and special agreements related to either technology (e.g., licensing) or management (e.g., management services). Companies might also be able to rely on their technical superiority and managerial skills as a means of guaranteeing participation in the management of day-to-day operations. The nomination of one of a firm's managers as the IJV general manager [Rafii 1978], as well as employment of different ownership structure arrangements [Gullander 1976], could represent further means of exercising managerial control.

In extending this stream of research, Schann [1983] demonstrated the breadth of mechanisms available to parent firms for exercising control over their IJVs (Table 1). Among these control options, the JV board of directors, formal agreements, the appointment of key personnel, the JV planning process, the reporting relationships and a variety of informal mechanisms appeared to be particularly important for Schaan's sample. He also made a significant contribution to knowledge of IJV control by categorizing control mechanisms into two main types. Schaan distinguished positive control mechanisms, which parent firms employed in order to promote certain behaviors, from negative control mechanisms, which were used by a parent to stop or to prevent the IJV from implementing certain activities or decisions. Positive control was most often exercised through informal mechanisms, staffing, participation in the planning process and reporting relationships. In contrast, negative control relied principally on formal agreements, approval by parents and the use of the JV board of directors. These latter, negative forms of control exemplified what Child [1973] described as bureaucratic mechanisms.

In addition to the *mechanisms* by which control may be exercised, a second dimension examined by scholars was the *extent* of control exercised over an IJV. Borrowing from organizational behavior research, most studies examining this latter dimension have conceptualized control as being dependent upon the centralization or the locus of the decisionmaking process. One such study was Dang's [1977] research on the autonomy of U.S. multinationals' subsidiaries in the Philippines and Taiwan. Undoubtedly influenced

TABLE 1
Positive and Negative Control Mechanisms

Positive	Negative
Ability to make specific decisions	Board
Ability to design:	Executive committee
1) Planning process	Approval required for:
2) Appropriation requests	1) Specific decisions
Policies and procedures	2) Plans, budgets
Ability to set objectives for JVGM	3) Appropriation requests
Contracts:	4) Nomination of JVGM
management	Screening/No objection of parent before
technology transfer	ideas or projects are discussed with other
marketing	parent
supplier	
Participation in planning or budgeting process	
Parent organization structure	
Reporting structure	
Staffing	
Training programs	
Staff services	
Bonus of JVGM tied to parent results	
Ability to decide on future promotion of JVGM (and other JV managers)	
Feedback; strategy/plan budgets, appropriation requests	
JVGM participation in parent's worldwide meetings	
Relations with JVGM; phone calls, meetings, visits	
Staffing parent with someone with experience with JV	
MNC level in Mexico	
Informal meetings with other parent	

Source: J. L. Schaan, *Parent control and joint venture success: The case of Mexico*, 249. Unpublished doctoral dissertation, University of Western Ontario, 1983.

by the Aston Group studies and the stream of research on centralization/decentralization/autonomy in large organizations and multinationals, Dang defined control as the autonomy of a subsidiary and measured the construct with a decentralization index based on seventeen key decisions. Executives from parent companies and their subsidiaries were asked to evaluate the subsidiaries' degree of autonomy for these decisions along a three-point scale. Non-parametric tests failed to reveal any differences in control based on ownership, or between complete or joint ownership. As a result, Dang concluded that the tendency and degree of multinationals' control over their subsidiaries could not be explained by equity ownership and, thus, that wholly-owned subsidiaries were not more tightly controlled than JVs. Nevertheless, he observed a more frequent presence of multinationals' expatriate managers in JVs and, therefore, suggested that the control exercised over the JVs might be more important than indicated by his control index.

Using a similar perspective, Killing [1983] studied control in thirty-seven JVs from developed countries. Building in part on the work of Tomlinson [1970], Killing employed interviews of parent company executives and JV general managers to examine parent firms' influence on nine types of decisions: pricing policy, product design, production scheduling, manufacturing process, quality control, replacement of managers, sales targets, cost budgeting and capital expenditures. More specifically, he inquired whether each decision was made (1) by the JV general manager alone, (2) by the local parent alone, (3) by the foreign parent alone, (4) by the JV general manager with input from the local parent or (5) from the foreign parent or (6) from both parents. Using this scale, Killing classified each sample venture as either a dominant partner JV (where only one of the parents played a dominant role in decisionmaking), a shared management JV (where each parent played an active role in decisions), or an independent JV (where the JV general manager enjoyed extensive decisionmaking autonomy). Beamish [1984] subsequently employed this same scale in an examination of JVs in less developed countries.

A significant contribution of the locus of decisionmaking perspective to the JV literature was conceptualizing control as a continuous variable, rather than merely an absolute, dichotomous variable representing parents' exercise of either total control or no control over the IJV. However, despite this contribution, several scholars have criticized the locus of decisionmaking perspective for presenting a very limited and incomplete view of IJV control [Skinner 1968; Brooke & Remmers 1978]. For example, several studies discussed above demonstrated the existence of means other than decisionmaking for exercising effective control over IJVs. Another criticism of this perspective is its implicit suggestion that parent firms seek to control the overall IJV, rather than targeting specific activities or processes perceived as crucial for achievement of the IJV's or the parent's strategic objectives. Concern with this implicit conceptualization of control constituted one of the bases for Schann's [1983] examination of ten IJVs in Mexico. Explicitly defining control as "the process through which a parent company ensures that the way a JV is managed conforms to its own interest" (p. 57), Schaan demonstrated that firms tended to seek control over specific "strategically important activities" rather than over the whole IJV.

Schaan's finding that control also had a *focus* dimension, i.e., that parents may choose to exercise control over a relatively wider or narrower scope of the IJV's activities, was supported by Geringer's [1986] study of ninety developed country JVs. These findings support the notion of parent firms' parsimonious and contingent usage of resources for controlling IJVs. This suggests that the exercise of effective control should emphasize selective control over those dimensions a parent perceives as critical, rather than attempting to control the entire range of the IJV's activities. This notion of selective control efforts raises the prospect of a split control IJV, one in which a parent firm may exercise dominant control over only a few dimensions of the venture. A split control IJV might be distinct from either of Killing's [1983] categories of an overall dominant control JV or a shared control JV, if all or most of the IJV's activities were dominated by a single parent firm but if no individual parent controlled a clear majority of the venture's activities.

As demonstrated by the preceding review, IJV control is a complex and multidimensional concept. Control is a much more subtle phenomenon than a proxy like centralization of decisionmaking is liable to capture, and it can be quite distinct from mere consideration of relative equity ownership or relative overall control of an IJV. In fact, as suggested by the above discussion, it is possible to distinguish three dimensions or parameters which comprise IJV control: (1) the *focus* of control, i.e., the scope of activities over which parents exercise control; (2) the *extent* or degree of control achieved by the parents; and (3) the *mechanisms* the parents use to exercise control. Contrary to initial appearances, these three parameters are not incompatible, but rather complementary and interdependent. They each examine a different aspect of IJV control.

The main problem remains that most studies on IJV control have had a limited perspective of the control concept or have only looked at one of its dimensions. Only a few studies, in particular ones by Schaan [1983] and Geringer [1986], have considered more than one parameter. However, it appears necessary to consider all three dimensions of control in order to obtain a thorough understanding of the control phenomenon for IJVs, although this integration has yet to be accomplished.

In addition to simultaneously addressing control's three dimensions, another important step toward improved understanding of parent control of IJVs lies in the identification of the different types of control mechanisms, similar to Schaan [1983]. Researchers need to broaden the range of control mechanisms which managers may employ, as well as refining the operationalization of these various mechanisms. In pursuing this task, it may be valuable to acknowledge the differences in the orientation of control mechanisms. Borrowing Bartlett's [1986] terminology, the "mechanism" dimension may be broken down into three components. First, control mechanisms may be *context-oriented*. These mechanisms encompass a wide variety of informal and culture-based mechanisms and their essential purpose is to establish an organizational context appropriate for the achievement of parent company objectives. For example, firms frequently emphasize the IJV's development of a teamwork culture, rather than an "us-them" culture. This might be promoted by designating all personnel as employees of the IJV, rather than individual parent firms, and by promoting a set of policies that evidences consistency between individuals' motivations and the IJV's well-being. Such a culture may represent a very effective substitute to more formal or *content-oriented* mechanisms. In the case of this second dimension of control mechanisms, rather than relying on the organizational setting, parents rely on more direct interventions, either by top managers or by the IJV's board of directors. These mechanisms are typically bureaucratic in nature, or what Schaan [1983] termed "negative" control mechanisms. They include specification in the IJV agreement of veto rights or the assignment of selected responsibilities to each parent. The final dimension may be termed *process-oriented* mechanisms, in which parent firms exercise control through reporting relationships or influence on IJV planning and decisionmaking processes. For instance, parent firms may require the participation of their corporate staff in the IJV's strategic planning process.

Future research should also emphasize greater depth of probing regarding the critical considerations and implications associated with each control mechanism, as well as the interrelationships between control mechanisms and both the extent and the focus of IJV control. For instance, staffing may represent a crucial strategic control mechanism for an IJV parent [Frayne & Geringer 1987; Pucik 1988]. A parent may be able to influence the relative allocation of control over a venture by influencing staffing of the IJV's top management positions. The IJV general manager's position, in particular, can affect an IJV's operations [Schaan & Beamish 1988] since the general manager is responsible for maintaining relationships with each of the parents, as well as running the venture. The means of selecting, training, evaluating and rewarding the performance of IJV general managers can significantly affect not only the venture itself, but also its relationship with each parent. The relative power of the IJV general manager's position is influenced by the governance structure established by the parents, and can range from autocratic (individual dominant control) to democratic (sharing of control among many managers). Given the importance of this and other control mechanisms, more extensive examination of these variables is necessary to enhance understanding of IJV control.

THE JOINT VENTURE
CONTROL-PERFORMANCE RELATIONSHIP

To the extent that scholars have devoted attention to control in IJVs, the ultimate objective should not be limited to the study of the control concept itself. Rather, the underlying rationale should be improved understanding of the relationship of control to IJV performance. Thus, this section will review the approaches that have been employed in examining this critical relationship, as well as the studies' findings.

Tomlinson [1970], often considered the first scholar to empirically study the control-performance relationship for IJVs, did not directly examine parent control, but rather the "attitude of parents toward control." From a sample of seventy-one IJVs in India and Pakistan, Tomlinson found that IJVs evidenced higher levels of profitability when their U.K. parents assumed a more relaxed attitude toward control. However, the validity of these results may be questionable, since Tomlinson used return on investment as the measure of profitability. Utilization of this measure for a multi-industry sample does not appear adequate and may have produced bias in the results. Variations in the financial performance of IJVs could be caused, for example, by industry differences rather than differences in the attitude toward control.

Although Franko [1971] also studied the control-performance relationship, his work, which was related to Stopford and Wells' research [1972] on multinational corporations (MNCs), has received limited attention by researchers in the "IJV control" field because it focused on the parent (the MNC) and its strategy rather than on the IJV and its control. Using a sample of 169 U.S. MNCs involved in more than 1100 JVs, Franko examined how parent control over JVs as well as the JVs' stability or instability (measured by the liquidation or significant changes in ownership of a JV) varied according to the MNC parent's strategy. Franko's main argument was that different strategies had different organizational and control requirements, thereby influencing the stability of JVs. From his sample data, Franko concluded that JVs were more stable when the MNC parent followed a product-diversification strategy (roughly equivalent to Doz' [1986] national responsiveness strategy), which usually demanded less control over subsidiaries. In contrast, JVs evidenced greater instability when the parent's strategy emphasized product concentration (roughly equivalent to Doz' [1986] global product strategy), which usually relied on centralization of decisionmaking and strong control. Moreover, Franko demonstrated that JV stability tended to vary with the evolution of the MNC parent's organizational structure and strategy.

Nevertheless, Franko's results embody serious limitations. The author never clearly defined his concept of control, nor did he propose a genuine and direct measure of this construct. To evaluate control, he relied on the importance given by MNC parent firms to standardization and to the centralization of decisionmaking, particularly for marketing policy issues. Furthermore, the author's dependent variable, changes in JV ownership structure, fails to provide a clear sense of the JV's absolute or relative success or of the achievement of the JV's objectives, and therefore of the performance of the JVs. Because ownership may also be a control mechanism, utilization of this construct may result in confusion regarding the meaning of ownership changes. It is open to conjecture whether these changes are indicative of modifications in the control of the JV, or of its poor performance. Despite these concerns, Franko made a significant contribution by examining the JV control-performance link using the "strategy-structure" conceptual framework. Within this perspective, the degree of parental control as well as the JV's performance (or its stability) is presumed to be contingent on the MNC's strategy and structure. Unfortunately, despite the potential insights from employing this framework, no researchers have yet attempted to extend Franko's work in studying the control-performance relationship for IJVs.

The studies that constitute the "mainstream" of research on control and performance of IJVs have adopted a different, but not necessarily incompatible, approach than that employed by Franko [1971]. For example, Killing [1983] asserted that, among his three JV categories, dominant partner JVs are more likely to be successful, at least compared to shared management ventures. His argument was essentially as follows: since the presence of two (or more) parents constitutes the major source of management difficulties in JVs, dominant partner JVs, in which the venture's activities are dominated by a single parent, will be easier to manage and consequently more successful. This argument is especially easy to interpret within a transaction cost analytical framework, where transaction costs are defined as the costs assumed by firms for the enforcement, monitoring and administration of a transaction [Williamson 1981]. According to Williamson, firms tend to choose structural arrangements for transactions (markets or hierarchies) that minimize these costs. Coordination of and conflicts between parents, as well as the potential unintended disclosures of proprietary know-how discussed earlier, can generate transaction costs associated principally with uncertainty, opportunistic behavior and asset-specificity [Williamson 1975; Ouchi 1977; Anderson & Gatignon 1987] that can limit the potential gains from cooperating in an IJV [Beamish & Banks 1987; Buckley & Casson 1988]. Viewed from this perspective, dominant control is a mechanism for reducing the risks associated with coordination, potential conflicts and dis-closures and, consequently, for minimizing transaction costs and stabilizing the IJV.

To test this hypothesis, Killing measured performance via management's assessment of the JV's performance (ranging from poor to good), as well as evaluating the liquidation or reorganization of the JV as a sign of failure. To justify use of these variables rather than financial indicators, Killing [1983], like Rafii [1978], explained that the profitability of the JV for a parent firm is not based solely on the JV's profits, but also on transfer prices, royalties and management fees not included in traditional financial performance measures. Due to this deficiency, traditional financial measures were, consequently, judged to be inadequate for use within a JV context.

Consistent with his hypothesis, Killing found that dominant partner JVs tended to be more successful, on both measures, than were shared manage-ment ventures. Independent JVs also exhibited superior levels of perform-ance. In this latter case, Killing suggested that the JVs' autonomy was more a result than a cause of their performance. However, the evidence presented in support of this assertion was inconclusive. It did not completely rule out that autonomy, or the absence of parental control, was the stimulus rather than the response to higher JV performance. Furthermore, no formal statistical tests were used to support the assertion.

Similar to Killing [1983], Anderson and Gatignon [1986] proposed that entry modes offering greater control, as measured via the relative level of owner-ship, would be more efficient for highly proprietary products or processes. However, the work of other researchers has not provided much evidence to support Killing's [1983] contention that JVs dominated by one parent exhibited superiority in performance. For instance, Janger [1980] used a classification schema similar to Killing's, yet did not find that one type of JV tended to be more successful than another. Similarly, Awadzi, et al., [1986] failed to find any relationship between extent of parent control and the performance of IJVs.

Beamish [1984] also attempted to test Killing's hypothesis. Using Killing's [1983] data, he used a chi-square test to examine the relationship between type of JV and its performance, but found no significant relationships evident at the 0.05 level. Beamish subsequently utilized Killing's control scale and performance measures for twelve JVs in less developed countries (LDCs). Unsatisfactory IJV performance was found to be correlated (significance$=0.067$) to dominant foreign control, while dominant local control (control by LDC partner) and shared control JVs were judged unsatisfactory in only a few cases. Further analysis also demonstrated that dominant foreign control was significantly associated with unsatisfactory performance in four decisions (production scheduling, production process, quality control and replacement of managers) involving mainly production issues.

Using the notion that parent firms seek control over specific activities as a conceptual starting point, Schaan [1983] extended that argument as well as identifying several subtleties regarding the phenomenon. In particular, Schaan concluded that venture success, or the extent to which parental expectations for the IJV were met, was a function of the fit among three variables: the parent's criteria for success, the activities or decisions it controlled and the control mechanisms which were utilized. He concluded that IJVs in which parents achieved this "fit" would evidence better performance. Schaan failed to provide details regarding the underlying rationale for his conclusions. However, one can imagine that a parent firm not adequately exercising control over activities judged as critical for the achievement of its objectives could ultimately suffer from ineffective strategy implementation and strategic inflexibility.

Thus, despite its conceptual appeal, the relationship between dominant control and IJV performance appears to be far more complex and less direct than scholars may have originally perceived. Janger [1980] suggested that the organization of a JV has only a small direct influence on its performance. According to him, it would not be "the structure alone that makes for a successful organization, but how well the structure fits the strategy and power situation in the venture" (p. 32). Despite such comments, most prior research has been limited to a direct test of the IJV control-performance relationship without taking account of or controlling for other variables such as the parents' strategy and structure, as Franko [1971] did. Subsequent inconsistencies in results may therefore be an outgrowth of this situation.

Furthermore, the tendency of prior research to evidence differences both in the object of study and in the operationalization of performance may also help explain the conflicting results found in the literature. On one hand, scholars have focused either on developed country JVs [Killing 1983; Geringer 1988], on less developed country JVs [Tomlinson 1970; Friedman & Beguin 1971; Renforth 1974; Raveed 1976; Dang 1977; Rafii 1978; Schaan 1983; Beamish 1984], or on both types of JVs [Franko 1971; Janger 1980]. As demonstrated by Beamish [1985], less developed country JVs typically have purposes and dynamics quite different from those of developed country JVs. For instance, the motives underlying their formation have often been tactical in nature, or limited to the desire either to obtain knowledge about the local environment or respond to foreign ownership legislation.

On the other hand, no consensus on the appropriate definition of IJV performance has yet emerged. A variety of objective measures for IJV performance have been used, ranging from financial indicators [Tomlinson 1970; Good 1972; Dang 1977; Renforth 1974], to the survival or liquidation of the venture [Franko 1971; Raveed 1976; Killing 1983], its duration [Harrigan 1988; Kogut 1988a], and instability of (or significant changes in) its ownership [Franko 1971; Gomes-Casseres 1987]. However, these objective measures may not adequately reflect the extent an IJV has achieved its objectives. Despite poor financial results, liquidation, or instability, an IJV may nevertheless have attained the objectives of its parents—for example, of transferring a technology—and thus be considered "successful" by one or all of the parents. Likewise, IJVs may be viewed as "unsuccessful," despite achieving good financial results or continued stability in ownership or governance structures. Because of such concerns, Killing [1983], and later Schaan [1983] and Beamish [1984] used a perceptual measure based on a single-item scale measuring the parent's satisfaction vis-a-vis the performance of an IJV. The main advantage of this type of measure is its ability to provide information regarding the extent to which the IJV has achieved its objectives. Moreover, by collecting data from *each* parent regarding their level of satisfaction, as done by Schaan [1983] and Beamish [1984], researchers can help overcome methodological limitations associated with the use of such perceptual measures. The measure's reliability may also be enhanced if data is collected from multiple time periods, or from more than one respondent per firm, although such efforts may confront a myriad of logistical and cost barriers.

In short, the above review suggests that the empirical evidence regarding the control-performance relationship in IJVs is still limited. The importance and direction of this relationship have yet to be established, tested, and clarified.

CONCEPTUAL FRAMEWORK FOR STUDYING CONTROL OF INTERNATIONAL JOINT VENTURES

As previously discussed, prior research has been highly fragmented on the basis either of the conceptualization of IJV control, the object of study or the attention devoted to IJV performance (Table 2). In addition, clear understanding of the IJV control-performance relationship is constrained by apparent inconsistencies in results.

As a first step toward solving these problems, we have previously proposed a conceptualization of control that takes into account its three different dimensions. The next step involves the development of an integrative approach for studying control in IJVs. To address this latter issue, two conceptual frameworks appear to be particularly useful. The first framework is the transaction cost approach. Several works, mainly conceptual in nature, have already used their theoretical framework to explain the formation and dynamics of JVs [Beamish & Banks 1987; Harrigan 1988; Hennart 1988; Kogut 1988b]. Other studies that do not directly refer to transaction costs, including most of the recent studies of IJV control, also employ rationales that are compatible with this framework. Although the

TABLE 2
Summary of Research on JV Control

Conception of Control	Authors	Type of JVs[1]	Measure of Performance	JV Control-Performance Relationship
Mechanisms	Tomlinson (1970)	LDC	Profitability	Indirect
	Friedman & Beguin (1971)	LDC	—	—
	Stopford & Wells (1972)	both	—	—
	Gullander (1976)	LDC	—	Direct
	Rafii (1978)	LDC	Cost efficiency	Contingent on fit among criteria of success, activities controlled and mechanisms
	Schaan (1983)	LDC	Perceptual measure of satisfaction	—
Extent	Franko (1971)	both	Instability (change in ownership structure)	Contingent on MNC[2] parent's strategy
	Dang (1977)	LDC	Not provided	Supposed as contingent
	Janger (1980)	both	Survival & perceptual measure of satisfaction	Dominant control associated with performance
	Killing (1983)	DC		
	Beamish (1984)	LDC	Same as Killing (1983)	No solid evidence for Killing's (1983) hypothesis
	Geringer (1986)	DC	—	—
	Awadzi et al (1986)	DC	Composite Index including financial, non-financial and industry-oriented measures	Non-significant relationship
Focus	Schaan (1983)	LDC	See above	See above
	Geringer (1986)	DC	—	—

[1]LDC refers to Less Developed Country; DC refers to Developed Country.
[2]MNC refers to multinational corporation.

transaction cost framework seems particularly valuable for providing a general theoretical base for analyzing control in IJVs, this perspective's potential usefulness may be limited by the difficulties and complexity associated with its empirical verification and operationalization. Further work aimed at operationalizing the measurement and evaluation of transaction costs is needed before the usefulness of this conceptual schema can be fully appreciated, particularly for studying IJV control.

The second conceptual framework with potential applications for studying control of IJVs is the strategy-structure approach. Although its potential usefulness was suggested by Franko's research [1971], and despite extensive use in examinations of parent-subsidiary relationships, the strategy-structure schema has not been employed subsequently for research on IJV control or the control-performance relationship. In fact, with the exception of Franko's, there have not been any studies which have explicitly considered the role of parent firm strategy in influencing the control parents subsequently exercise over their IJVs. This situation seems particularly surprising considering the importance attributed to organizational strategy-structure fit within the strategic management literature.

An especially promising avenue for future research lies in the integration of these two frameworks, which are not fundamentally incompatible but rather complementary. As shown by Jones and Hill [1988], transaction cost analysis provides the theoretical underpinnings absent in the strategy-structure paradigm. Thus, to better understand the relationship linking control and performance of IJVs, we must consider on one hand that there can be benefits from the exercise of IJV control. Without such control, parent firms may encounter difficulties in achieving the full potential of their strategies and in attaining their objectives. Control therefore can enable the firm to reduce transaction costs that could limit a strategy's benefits.

On the other hand, the exercise of IJV control is not without drawbacks; it indeed has a cost [Hulbrut & Brandt 1976; Jaeger 1982; Wilkins & Ouchi 1983; Vernon 1983]. Control often implies a commitment from a firm in terms of both responsibility and resources, and may lead to increased overhead costs [Anderson & Gatignon 1986]. It can also increase the risks to which a firm is exposed [Davidson 1982]. Consequently, the exercise of extensive control over an IJV's activities and decisions can generate important coordination and governance costs and limit the efficiency of an alliance [Contractor & Lorange 1988]. This may be especially true for control efforts oriented toward activities and decisions having little importance for performance of either the IJV or the parent firm.

Therefore, the critical issue for a parent firm is to exercise control, in terms of mechanisms, extent and focus, over an IJV in such a manner that will enable it to successfully implement its strategy without incurring a level of administrative or organizational inefficiencies which outweighs the gains from its cooperative endeavor. In other words, there is a strategy-structure "fit" when the benefits outweigh the costs of control, and this "fit" is best when the margin between benefits and costs is optimized. This rationale is readily illustrated by Franko's [1971] results. In the case of a product diversification (or national responsiveness) strategy, the foreign parent may perceive the need to exercise at least a moderate level of control over the IJV in order to protect its interests and to ensure effective strategy implementation. However, the extent of control that the foreign partner attempts to exercise may limit the autonomy and flexibility of the IJV and its local management, hindering the venture's ability to respond to local market demands and generating a level of transaction costs that may offset the strategy's potential benefits.

It is from this perspective that we propose a model for the study of IJV control (Table 3). Among its major characteristics, this model relies on an integrative concept of IJV control that takes into account its different dimensions. Furthermore, it is organized around the concept of strategy, more specifically the parents' international competitive strategies and the IJV's strategy. On one hand, Porter and Fuller [1986] have advocated the importance of looking at coalitions, such as IJVs, within the context of a firm's overall strategy for competing internationally in an industry. This approach is consistent with the stream of research on the relationship between strategy (at the corporate as well as the business level), structure and performance [Chandler 1962; Stopford & Wells 1972; Rumelt 1974; White 1986]. On the other hand, several authors have recently suggested that subsidiaries could have very different strategic roles depending on their parent's strategy, their environment and their competencies [White & Poynter 1984; Bartlett & Ghoshal 1986; Ghoshal 1987]. In addition, Gupta [1987] indicated that different strategic roles had different organizational requirements and that, consequently, subsidiaries' strategies had a relevant effect on how a parent managed its subsidiaries. Therefore, we believe that a thorough examination of the ways parents manage or control their subsidiaries, jointly or wholly-owned, must include consideration of strategy.

In the proposed model, IJV performance is mainly a function of the fit between the international strategy of the parents, the IJV strategy, and the parameters of control. It thus marks a net departure from traditional or most-used models where IJV performance is viewed as a direct outcome either of the mechanisms used or of the extent of control. In our model, strategy and control are also expected to have a direct influence, but to a much smaller extent. This raises the possibility that some combinations of strategy and control may be associated with superior performance. However, this issue has not yet been addressed in the literature, and space and focus limitations prevent us from addressing it here. Furthermore, among its advantages, our approach helps to emphasize what functions would be most critical to an organization's overall success. This type of research perspective could enhance understanding of the decisions parent firms make about which IJV activities to control, the extent of control to exercise, and the control mechanisms to employ. It can help clarify the nature of the linkages between these three basic parameters of control and IJV performance, and also permit recommendations to managers on what and how to control in order to promote achievement of IJV goals.

TABLE 3
A Strategy-Control Model of JV Performance

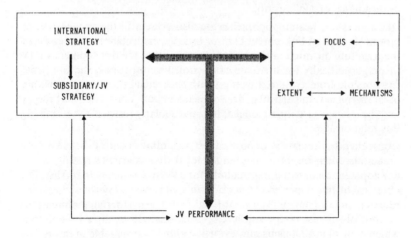

CONCLUSIONS

As corporations increasingly utilize alliances such as IJVs as tools for attaining strategic objectives, the issue of IJV control is experiencing a corresponding increase in attention from academics and practitioners alike. Yet, understanding of IJV management lags behind the demands of practice. Although a wide variety of control mechanisms have been identified, managers have received minimal guidance about when and how to use them, as well as about the potential tradeoffs between alternative control options. As a result, many firms have chosen to bypass the IJV option or have entered ventures ill-prepared. These firms may not only be missing potentially valuable opportunities, they may ultimately be eliminating themselves as viable contenders within entire industries. This concern is particularly critical when it affects participation within highly competitive global (or globalizing) industries.

In addressing control of IJVs, this paper has attempted to bring into focus a critical variable influencing venture development and performance, and to provide a base for improved understanding and management of IJVs. Review of the literature leaves no doubt that control is a crucial organizational process, for IJVs as well as for any other organizational form. It is also a complex and multidimensional concept. This feature may help explain why researchers have used different approaches to study control in IJVs. These differences, as shown in this paper, are particularly evident in the conceptualization and operationalization of control. In addition, due to variations among, and weaknesses of, prior measures of IJV performance, many conclusions from these previous studies have to be interpreted with some degree of caution. Furthermore, the empirical component of many studies is not without its shortcomings. Methodological issues such as differences in the object of study and in dependent variables may constitute potentially serious threats to the external validity of many, if not all, prior studies of IJV control.

Differences in research approaches are also evident in the frameworks or rationales used to link parent control to IJV performance. The review of the literature provided in this paper illustrates that the development of JV theory, specifically for the issue of control, has not reaped the full benefits possible from cross-fertilization with theoretical developments within other disciplines. In particular, developments in both transaction cost theory and the strategy-structure model appear particularly relevant for examining this relationship.

Consequently, research opportunities regarding control in IJVs are numerous. Many opportunities remain for further research stressing theory development and testing, particularly for JVs in developed countries. The objective of this paper was to assist in this endeavor by synthesizing prior research on IJV control. The identification of three underlying dimensions of control—focus, extent and mechanisms—as well as three orientations which control mechanisms may evidence, should be valuable in improving the design of future research. Similarly, discussion of a conceptual framework of IJV control should further enhance development of JV theory, specifically as it concerns control and performance of IJVs.

REFERENCES

Anderson, E. & H. Gatignon. 1986. Modes of foreign entry: A transaction cost analysis and propositions. *Journal of International Business Studies*, Fall: 1-26.

Awadzi, W., B.L. Kedia & R. Chinta. 1986. Performance implications of locus of control and complementary resources in international joint ventures—An empirical study. Presented at Academy of International Business Conference, London.

Baliga, B.R. & A.M. Jaeger. 1984. Multinational corporation: Control systems and delegation issues. *Journal of International Business Studies*, Fall: 25-40.

Bartlett, C.A. 1986. Building and managing the transnational: The new organization challenge. In M. Porter, ed., *Competition in global industries*, 367-404. Boston: Harvard Business School Press.

_____ & S. Ghoshal. 1986. Tap your subsidiaries for global reach. *Harvard Business Review*, November-December: 87-94.

Beamish, P.W. 1984. Joint venture performance in developing countries. Unpublished doctoral dissertation, University of Western Ontario.

_____. 1985. The characteristics of joint ventures in developed and developing countries. *Columbia Journal of World Business*, 20(3): 13-19.

_____ & J.C. Banks. 1987. Equity joint ventures and the theory of the multinational enterprise. *Journal of International Business Studies*, Summer: 1-16.

Behrman, J. 1970. *National interest and the multinational enterprise*. New York: Prentice Hall.

Brooke, M. & H. Remmers. 1978. *The strategy of multinational enterprise*. London: Pitman.

Buckley, P. & M. Casson. 1988. A theory of cooperation in international business. In F. Contractor & P. Lorange, eds., *Cooperative strategies in international business*, 31-53. Toronto: Lexington.

Chandler, A.D. 1962. *Strategy and structure: Chapters in the history of the American industrial enterprise*. Cambridge, Mass: MIT Press.

Child, J. 1977. *Organization: A guide to problems and practice*. New York: Harper & Row.

_____. 1972a. Organizational structure, environment and performance—The role of strategic choice. *Sociology*, January: 1-22.

_____. 1972b. Organization structure and strategies of control: A replication of the Aston study. *Administrative Science Quarterly*, 17: 163-77.

_____. 1973. Strategies of control and organizational behavior. *Administrative Science Quarterly*, 18: 1-17.

Contractor, F. & P. Lorange. 1988. The strategy and economics basis for cooperative venture. In F. Contractor & P. Lorange, eds., *Cooperative strategies in international business*, 1-28. Toronto: Lexington Books.

Cray, D. 1984. Control and coordination in multinational corporations. *Journal of International Business Studies*, Fall: 85-98.

Dang, T. 1977. Ownership, control and performance of the multinational corporation: A study of U.S. wholly-owned subsidiaries and joint ventures in the Philippines and Taiwan. Unpublished doctoral dissertation, University of California, Los Angeles.

Davidson, W.H. 1982. *Global strategic management*. New York: Wiley.

Doz, Y. 1986. *Strategic management in multinational companies*. Oxford: Pergamon.

_____ & C.K. Pralahad. 1981. Headquarters influence and strategic control in MNCs. *Sloan Management Review*, Fall: 15-29.

_____ & C.K. Prahalad. 1984. Patterns of strategic control within multinational corporations. *Journal of International Business Studies*, Fall: 55-72.

Drucker, P. 1974. *Management: Tasks, responsibilities, promise*. New York: Harper & Row.

Edstrom, A. & J.R. Galbraith. 1977. Transfer of managers as a coordination and control strategy in multinational organizations. *Administrative Science Quarterly*, 22: 248-63.

Egelhoff, W.G. 1984. Patterns of control in U.S., U.K., and European multinational corporations. *Journal of International Business Studies*, Fall: 73-84.

Etzioni, A. 1965. Organizational control structure. In J. G. March, ed., *Handbook of organization*, 650-77. Chicago: Rand McNally.

_____. 1961. *The comparative analysis of complex organizations*. New York: Free Press.

Franko, L.G. 1971. *Joint venture survival in multinational corporations*. New York: Praeger.

Frayne, C.A. & J.M. Geringer. 1987. Self-management: A key to improving international joint venture performance. *Proceedings*. Conference on International Personnel and Human Resource Management, Singapore.

Friedmann, W.G. & J.P. Beguin. 1971. *Joint international business ventures in developing countries*. New York: Columbia University Press.

Gatignon, H. & E. Anderson. 1987. The multinational corporation's degree of control over foreign subsidiaries: An empirical test of a transaction cost explanation. Report *87-03. Cambridge: Marketing Science Institute.

Geringer, J.M. 1986. Criteria for selecting partners for joint ventures in industrialized market economies. Ph.D. dissertation, University of Washington, Seattle.

_____. 1988. *Joint venture partner selection: Strategies for developed countries*. Westport, Conn.: Quorum Books.

Ghoshal, S. 1987. Global strategy: An organizing framework. *Strategic Management Journal*, 8(5): 425-40.

Giglioni, G.B. & A.G. Bedeian. 1974. A conspectus of management control theory: 1900-1972. *Academy of Management Journal*, 17: 292-305.

Gomes-Casseres, B. 1987. Joint venture instability: Is it a problem? *Columbia Journal of World Business*, Summer: 97-107.

Good, L. 1972. United States joint ventures and manufacturing firms in Monterrey, Mexico: Comparative styles of management. Unpublished doctoral dissertation, Cornell University.

Green, S.G. & M.A. Welsh. 1988. Cybernetics and dependence: Refining the control concept. *Academy of Management Review*, 13(2): 287-301.

Gullander, S. 1976. Joint ventures and corporate strategy. *Columbia Journal of World Business*, Spring: 104-14.

Gupta, A.K. 1987. SBU strategies, corporate-SBU relations, and SBU effectiveness in strategy implementation. *Academy of Management Journal*, 30: 477-500.

Harrigan, K.R. 1987. Strategic alliances: Their new role in global competition. *Columbia Journal of World Business*, Summer: 67-9.

_____. 1988. Strategic alliances and partner asymmetries. In F. Contractor & P. Lorange, eds., *Cooperative strategies in international business*, 205-26. Toronto: Lexington.

Hennart, J.F. 1988. A transaction costs theory of equity joint venture. *Strategic Management Journal*, 9(4): 361-74.

Hulbrut, J.M. & W.K. Brandt. 1976. Patterns of communication in the multinational corporation: An empirical study. *Journal of International Business Studies*, Spring: 57-64.

Jaeger, A.M. 1982. Contrasting control modes in the multinational corporation: Theory, practice and implications. *International Studies of Management and Organization*, 12(1): 59-82.

Janger, A.R. 1980. *Organization of international joint ventures*. New York: Conference Board.

Jones, G.R. & C.W.L. Hill. 1988. Transaction cost analysis of strategy-structure choice. *Strategic Management Journal*, 9(2): 159-72.

Killing, J.P. 1983. *Strategies for joint venture success*. New York: Praeger.

Kogut, B. 1988a. A study of the life cycle of joint ventures. In F. Contractor & P. Lorange, eds., *Cooperative strategies in international business*, 169-85. Toronto: Lexington.

_____. 1988b. Joint ventures: Theoretical and empirical perspectives. *Strategic Management Journal*, 9(4): 319-32.

Lawrence, P. & L. Lorsch. 1967. *Organization and environment: Managing differentiation and integration*. Homewood, Ill.: Irwin.

Lorange, P. & M.F. Scott Morton. 1974. A framework for management control systems. *Sloan Management Review*, Fall: 41-56.

_____, M.F. Scott Morton & S. Ghoshal. 1986. *Strategic control*. St. Paul: West.

Merchant, K. A. 1982. The control function of management. *Sloan Management Review*, Summer: 43-55.

Miner, J. 1982. The uncertain future of the leadership concept: Revisions and clarifications. *Journal of Applied Behavioural Sciences*, 18(3): 293-307.

Mintzberg, H. 1979. *The structuring of organization*. New York: Prentice-Hall.

Moxon, R.W. & J. M. Geringer. 1985. Multinational consortia in high technology industries: Commercial aircraft manufacturing. *Columbia Journal of World Business*, Summer: 55-62.

Ouchi, W.G. 1977. The relationship between organizational structure and organizational control. *Administrative Science Quarterly*, 22: 92-112.

_____. 1978. The transmission of control through organizational hierarchy. *Academy of Management Journal*, 21: 173-92.

_____ & M.A. McGuire. 1975. Organizational control: Two functions. *Administrative Science Quarterly*, 20: 559-69.

Parry, T.G. 1985. Internationalization as a general theory of foreign direct investment: A critique. *Weltwirtschaftliches Archiv*, September: 564-69.

Perlmutter, H.V. & D.A. Heenan. 1986. Cooperate to compete globally. *Harvard Business Review*, March-April: 136+.

Porter, M.E. & M.B. Fuller. 1986. Coalitions and global strategy. In M. E. Porter, ed., *Competition in global industries*, 315-44. Boston: Harvard Business School Press.

Pucik, V. 1988. Strategic alliances with the Japanese: Implications for human resource management. In F. Contractor & P. Lorange, eds., *Cooperative strategies in international business*, 487-98. Toronto: Lexington.

Rafii, F. 1978. Joint ventures and transfer of technology to Iran: The impact of foreign control. Unpublished doctoral dissertation, Harvard University.

Raveed, S. 1976. Joint venture between U.S. multinational firms and host governments in selected developing countries: A case study of Costa Rica, Trinidad and Venezuela. Unpublished doctoral dissertation, Indiana University.

Reich, R.B. & E.D. Mankin. 1986. Joint ventures with Japan give away our future. *Harvard Business Review*, March-April: 78-86.

Renforth, W.E. 1974. A comparative study of joint international business ventures with family firm of non-family firm patterns: The Caribbean Community experience. Unpublished doctoral dissertation, Indiana University.

Rugman, A.M. 1985. Internalization is still a general theory of foreign direct investment. *Weltwirtschaftliches Archiv*, September: 570-75.

Rumelt, R.P. 1974. *Strategy, structure and economic performance*. Boston: Harvard Business School.

Schaan, J.L. 1983. Parent control and joint venture success: The case of Mexico. Unpublished doctoral dissertation. University of Western Ontario.

———— & P.W. Beamish. 1988. Joint venture general managers in LDCs. In F. Contractor & P. Lorange, eds., *Cooperative strategies in international business*, 279-99. Toronto: Lexington.

Schreyogg, G. & H. Steinmann. 1987. Strategic control: A new perspective. *Academy of Management Review*, 12(1): 91-103.

Skinner, W. 1968. *American industry in developing countries*. New York: Wiley.

Stopford, J.M. & L.T. Wells. 1972. *Managing the multinational enterprise*. New York: Basic Books.

Tannebaum, A.S. 1968. *Control in organization*. New York: McGraw-Hill.

Tomlinson, J.W.C. 1970. *The joint venture process in international business: India and Pakistan*. Cambridge, Mass.: MIT Press.

Vancil, R.F. 1979. *Decentralization: Managerial ambiguity by design*. Homewood, Ill.: Irwin.

Vernon, R. 1983. Organizational and institutional responses to international risk. In R.G. Herring, ed., *Managing international risk*, 191-216. Cambridge: Cambridge University Press.

West, M.W. 1959. Thinking ahead: The jointly-owned subsidiary. *Harvard Business Review*, July-August: 31-32.

White, R.E. 1986. Generic business strategies, organizational context and performance: An empirical investigation. *Strategic Management Journal*, 7: 217-31.

———— & T.A. Poynter. 1984. Strategies for foreign-owned subsidiaries in Canada. *Business Quarterly*, Summer: 59-69.

Wilkins, A.L. & W.G. Ouchi. 1983. Efficient cultures: The relationship between culture and organizational performance. *Administrative Science Quarterly*, 32: 468-81.

Williamson, O.E. 1981. The economics of organization: The transaction cost approach. *American Journal of Sociology*, 87(3): 548-77.

————. 1975. *Markets and hierarchies: Analysis and antitrust implications*. New York: Free Press.

Young, G.R. & S. Bradford, Jr. 1977. *Joint ventures: Planning and action*. New York: Financial Executives Research Foundation.

[11]

FIRM OWNERSHIP PREFERENCES AND HOST GOVERNMENT RESTRICTIONS: AN INTEGRATED APPROACH

Benjamin Gomes-Casseres*
Harvard University

Abstract. Two approaches may explain how multinational enterprises (MNEs) select ownership structures for subsidiaries. The first argues that MNEs prefer structures that minimize the transaction costs of doing business abroad. The second argues that ownership structures are determined by negotiations with host governments, whose outcomes depend on the bargaining power of the firm. This paper presents a framework integrating these two approaches and uses statistical methods to separate their effects empirically.

The statistical analysis supports an important hypothesis of the bargaining school—that attractive domestic markets increase the relative power of host governments. But it finds no support for other hypotheses of this school, such as those predicting that firms in marketing- and R&D-intensive industries have more bargaining power than others. These latter factors were apparently more important in determining firm ownership preferences. Futhermore, the paper measures when government ownership restrictions deter firm entry, concluding that relatively large firms, and those with high intra-system sales are deterred more than others.

In recent years, there has been a renewed interest in the determinants of ownership structures of foreign subsidiaries. The basic question of when and why multinational enterprises (MNEs) form joint ventures abroad is being addressed with a refined set of tools and with new theories. This

---

*Benjamin Gomes-Casseres is Assistant Professor of Business Administration at the Graduate School of Business Administration, Harvard University. He holds the B.A. degree from Brandeis University, the M.P.A. degree from Princeton University, and the D.B.A. degree from Harvard University. His related articles on joint ventures have appeared in the *Journal of Economic Behavior and Organization* and the *Sloan Management Review*. His current research and consulting focus on the management of international transfers of technology and their effects on competitiveness.

I received valuable comments on this research from Louis T. Wells, Jr., Donald R. Lessard, Robert Schlaifer, Dennis J. Encarnation, Stephen J. Kobrin and three anonymous referees. The research was funded by the Harvard Business School's Division of Research. Harvard's Multinational Enterprise Project and the Strategic Planning Institute in Cambridge, Massachusetts, gave me access to their data. The views presented here are mine.

Received: August 1988; Revised: December 1988 & March & May 1989; Accepted: May 1989.

1

renewed interest is partly due to two developments: (1) a new conception of the role of ownership in international business; and (2) a better understanding of the process of negotiation between MNEs and host country governments. These two new developments, however, have not been integrated into one framework. This article attempts to do that.

In the last decade, numerous authors have successfully used transaction cost ideas to analyze the role of ownership in international business (for example, Buckley & Casson [1976]; Hennart [1982]; and a recent review in Teece [1986]). This approach has also been applied specifically to MNEs' choice between whole and joint ownership in foreign subsidiaries [Gomes-Casseres 1989b; Anderson & Gatignon 1986; Hennart 1988]. Almost without exception, however, this stream of research has ignored the effects of host government ownership restrictions on MNE choices. None of these authors would deny, of course, that such restrictions can make an MNE form a joint venture even where transaction cost analysis would predict a wholly-owned subsidiary. But the tendency in this literature has been to focus on only one of these two effects at a time.

Another school of thought, using the bargaining power approach, has made the opposite omission. In an effort to explain the outcome of negotiations between MNEs and host country governments, virtually all the authors in this school have downplayed the factors that influence MNE ownership preferences (for example, Fagre & Wells [1982]; Grieco [1982]; Lecraw [1984]; and a recent review in Kobrin 1987). Again, most of them have acknowledged that firms may prefer something other than whole ownership, and that somehow this had to be taken into account. But they, too, have tended to focus on only one side of the equation.

This pattern of academic specialization would not have been surprising were it not for the complementarity of the two approaches. These two theories are not competing explanations of the same phenomenon, but address two distinct questions. To put it simply, the transaction cost model answers the question: What ownership structure *does the firm want*? The second approach, the bargaining power model, answers the question: What ownership structure *can the firm get*?

These two questions are not only distinct in substance, but usually also in time. At the risk of oversimplifying the decisionmaking process, one can visualize an MNE first deciding what it wants, and then seeking the host government's agreement. Conceptualizing the decision as a sequential process is the first step in integrating the two approaches.

The second step in integrating the two models lies in separating their predictions empirically. Kobrin recently recognized the complementarity of the two approaches in his study of bargaining power, but lamented that "it is difficult to determine whether differences in observed ownership stem from differences in preferences or bargaining power" [1987, p. 624]. The difficulty, of course, is that firm preferences are not directly observable. But without separating the effects, one cannot hope to test either theory.

This paper has four purposes, First, it discusses a conceptual synthesis of the transaction cost and bargaining models. Second, it presents a method for separating their effects in empirical tests. Third, it applies these methods and discusses results of new tests of the bargaining power model. Fourth, it extends existing tests of the bargaining approach by measuring the conditions under which host government policies deter entry by the MNE. A detailed discussion of my tests of the transaction cost model appears in Gomes-Casseres [1989b].

OWNERSHIP TRADE-OFFS AND NEGOTIATION

Ownership Preferences

Even when host governments do not impose restrictions on foreign ownership, an MNE choosing the ownership structure for a new subsidiary must make some key trade-offs. Take the example of an MNE venturing into a new country where there are established competitors. A joint venture may be an effective way to acquire local expertise, but there may be significant costs to shared management. In Stopford & Wells [1972], the MNE's choice would depend on a trade-off between the firm's "need for resources," and its "need for control." It will prefer a joint venture when the first is larger than the second, and a wholly-owned subsidiary otherwise.

In the transaction cost model, the problem is formulated slightly differently. Here the trade-off is between the costs of using market or internal channels for transferring organizational capabilities. In the example above, the MNE could get the needed local expertise either by hiring the services of a local firm (e.g., to supply market research and represent the MNE in negotiations with government), or by forming a joint venture with a local firm. In the first case it would be acquiring an organizational capability by using the market; in the second it would be using an internal channel, because the capabilities would be transferred from a party with an ownership share in the venture.[1] This distinction—between internal and market channels for transferring firm capabilities—is also critical to the transaction cost theory of the multinational enterprise [Hennart 1982].

In the transaction cost approach, too, the benefits of using ownership channels would be reduced by the cost of sharing equity. Foremost among these are "shirking" by the joint venture partners—each of which has less than a full stake in the venture—and conflicts of interest between them. Note also that this model relies not only on transaction costs, but also on arguments about firm capabilities and strategies. The latter determine when the MNE needs contributions from local firms; transaction costs then determine whether ownership channels will be used for these transfers. This model is discussed further in Gomes-Casseres [1989b]; similar arguments appear in Hennart [1988].

This process of weighing costs and benefits of various ownership structures results in the MNE's preference, i.e., what it *wants*. But two firms that both prefer wholly-owned ventures may do so to different degrees, i.e., one may want it more intensely that the other.[2] It is therefore more useful to think of the firm's preferences as being a ranking among ownership options with varying distances between them. The MNE's capabilities and the transaction costs of different ownership structures can then be thought of as determining these distances.

Ownership Concessions

MNEs facing host government ownership restrictions[3] can be expected to go through a similar process to derive their preference rankings. In addition, however, the relative power of firm and government helps determine in these cases what ownership structure the firm *can get*. It is critical to realize that the firms will make concessions on ownership based on their preference rankings. In other words, a firm ranking whole ownership significantly higher than a joint venture will be less likely to give in on the ownership issue than a firm that, while still preferring whole ownership, sees a joint venture as a close second choice.

As a result, the ownership structure that the MNE actually ends up with is a function of: (1) the intensity with which it prefers whole ownership (if at all); and (2) its bargaining power relative to the government's. Excluding the calculation of firm preferences from this synthesis is just as misleading as ignoring the bargaining power of the parties.

This framework recognizes that ownership is not an all-important issue to firms, or to governments for that matter. Both parties might be willing to accept something less than their top ownership preference in return for gains on other issues. Thus, the government might drop its insistence on a joint venture in return for increases in the MNE's contribution to other national goals.[4] Or the firm might settle for its second choice in return for access to a lucrative market.

In this context, therefore, the slippery concept of "bargaining power" does not indicate how the total economic benefits of an investment are distributed. Rather, it refers simply to the ability of one party to skew the outcome of negotiations in the direction of the ownership structure it prefers [Lax & Sebenius 1986]. That ability depends not only on what the government has to offer the MNE, but also on how badly the MNE wants whole ownership.

Deadlocked Negotiations

The synthesis proposed above allows analysis of a phenomenon not adequately dealt with in either the transaction cost or the bargaining power model. Authors using the latter framework have pointed out that sometimes host government ownership restrictions seemed to deter entry by MNEs [Fagre & Wells 1982]. But when does this happen: when the firm has relatively more power than the government, or vice versa? These authors do

FIRM PREFERENCES & HOST GOVERNMENT RESTRICTIONS   5

not answer this question, partly because the concept of bargaining power itself is misleading in this context.

In my framework, entry deterrence occurs when: (1) the MNE has a preference schedule where the joint venture form ranks below not investing at all; and (2) the government's ranking places whole ownership below the no-investment alternative. It is not a question of bargaining power at all, but one of comparing the cost-benefit calculations of the two parties. Each party considers not only the various ownership options, but also the alternative of foregoing investment. That alternative sets the "reservation value" for each party; an agreement will not be reached unless its net benefits exceed this value [Lax & Sebenius 1986].

One party's no-agreement alternative may, in turn, affect its bargaining power in ownership negotiations. When an MNE can go elsewhere with its investment, it is less likely to give in to government demands than otherwise. Similarly, if a restrictive government can find other firms that would accept a forced joint venture, it may not give in to one MNE's insistence on whole ownership. Host government ownership restrictions can thus have both *ownership effects* and *entry effects*. Because these two sets of effects are interrelated, tests of the bargaining model should attempt to estimate both, as is done below.

SEPARATING EFFECTS ON PREFERENCES AND BARGAINING

The statistical methods used here attempt to estimate how the ownership and entry effects of restrictive policies vary with characteristics of the MNE, its subsidiary, the industry, and the host country.

Estimating Ownership Effects

The main problem in estimating the separate ownership effects of transaction and MNE-government bargaining models is that they share a number of explanatory factors. For example, both models predict that the R&D-intensity of a subsidiary's business should affect ownership choice, but for different reasons. The first model claims that R&D intensity leads to whole ownership because MNEs prefer internal channels over contracts when transferring technological capabilities. The second model predicts the same final outcome, but credits the MNE's increased bargaining power with the result.

Recognizing this problem, previous researchers have tested bargaining hypotheses by comparing ownership patterns in countries whose governments restricted foreign ownership with patterns elsewhere [Fagre and Wells 1982; Lecraw 1984; Kobrin 1987]. But this introduces a different problem. The ownership patterns in a restrictive host may be due to other features of the country's environment, or to systematic differences in the types of firms investing in each group of countries. Although most of these researchers recognized these possibilities, they were not able to deal with them in satisfactory ways.

6 JOURNAL OF INTERNATIONAL BUSINESS STUDIES, FIRST QUARTER 1990

The method used here resolves both these problems.[5] It, too, makes a distinction between groups of "restrictive" and "open" countries, but it controls for differences in firm and country characteristics between the two groups. The method is analogous to that used in testing for structural change in time-series models [Johnston 1984]. Assuming only one explanatory variable, X, the regression model is:

$$Y = A_0 + (A_1 - A_0)D + B_0 X + (B_1 - B_0)DX \qquad (1)$$

where

Y = observed ownership level of subsidiary,

D = dummy variable equal to 1 if subsidiary is in a restrictive country, and 0 otherwise,

X = independent variable that is hypothesized to effect both bargaining power and firm preferences.

In this model, the terms A_0 and B_0 represent, respectively, the intercept and the effect of X on ownership level in non-restrictive countries, because $D = 0$ for these observations. These coefficients can thus be interpreted as reflecting a model of firm preferences alone, because MNE-government bargaining plays no role in these countries. The terms A_1 and B_1 then represent, respectively, the intercept and the effect of X on ownership level in restrictive countries, because $D = 1$ for these observations. These coefficients, therefore, can be interpreted as reflecting *both* firm preferences and bargaining power, because both processes are at work in these countries.

One can then test whether X affects either firm preferences, or bargaining power, or both, by considering whether the coefficients in the regression model are statistically significantly different from zero. If B_0 is zero, then X has no effect in open countries; this implies that X has no effect on firm preferences. If $(B_1 - B_0)$ is zero, then X has the same effect in open countries as it does in restrictive countries (i.e., $B_1 = B_0$). Because the ownership levels in restrictive countries appear to be affected by X in the same way whether or not bargaining takes place, X can be said to have no effect on bargaining power. If X affects both firm preferences and bargaining power, the coefficients on X as well as on DX should be significantly different from zero.

In the data set used here, Y was defined as a binary variable, which was equal to 1 if the subsidiary was a joint venture. This does not affect the interpretation of the model, but it required the use of a binary regression technique. In the binomial logit model used, the effects of the independent variables are assumed to be linear in the logarithm of the odds that the dependent variable is equal to one. As in ordinary least-square regressions, the one-tailed significance levels of the estimated effects represent the probabilities that the true effects have signs opposite those of the estimates; these are reported below. Similarly, the standardized beta coefficients give the estimated amount, in standard deviations, that the dependent variable changes

FIRM PREFERENCES & HOST GOVERNMENT RESTRICTIONS   7

with one standard deviation change in the independent variable; these, too, are reported below.[6]

Estimating Entry Effects

The degree to which restrictive policies deter entry can also be expected to depend partly on characteristics of the MNE or of the proposed venture. For example, MNEs seem to prefer whole ownership of subsidiaries that trade extensively with other members of their global systems, because conflicts of interest are likely to arise between the partners in these situations.[7] Consequently, an MNE can be expected not to place such subsidiaries in restrictive countries, unless, of course, it can gain an exception to the ownership rules through the bargaining process.

The methods used here attempt to measure the impact of a number of firm, industry, and subsidiary variables on the entry effect of ownership restrictions.[8] One simple way to do this would be to compare the means of these variables in open and restrictive countries. The problem with this method is that this difference between means may be due to other factors. For example, the groups of open and restrictive countries may also differ systematically in economic terms, and this might be the reason behind the variance in subsidiary characteristics. The following regression model controls for such effects:

$$X = A + B_1 D + B_2 Z + B_3 V \tag{2}$$

where
- X = firm or subsidiary variable hypothesized to affect the degree of entry deterrence,
- D = dummy variable equal to 1 if subsidiary is in a restrictive country, and 0 otherwise,
- Z = other host country characteristic,
- V = other firm or subsidiary characteristic.

In this model, the coefficient on the dummy variable indicating host country policy (B_1) measures the difference between the level of X in open and restrictive countries, while controlling for the effects of other country, firm, and subsidiary variables on X. If the coefficient is positive, then entry by subsidiaries with low levels of X are deterred more than entry by subsidiaries with higher levels of X. The reverse is true for negative coefficients. There can, of course, be several Z and V variables, but their coefficients are of no interest here.

The Sample and Variables

Sources of Data. The data used here came from several sources. The bulk of it was collected by the Harvard Multinational Enterprise Project. The 187 parent firms in this project were all U.S. *Fortune 500* companies with at least six foreign investments. Among other variables, the database contains for each subsidiary the host country, ownership structure, industry (at 4-digit SIC level), and characteristics such as size of assets and extent of intra-system sales [Curhan, Davidson & Suri, 1977].

A select sample of the data collected in this project was used here. First, the sample includes only subsidiaries that did at least some manufacturing. Second, the sample is limited to subsidiaries that were still active in 1975, the last year for which there are data.[9] These cross-sectional data thus contain ownership "corrections" that the MNEs might have made after initial entry [Gomes-Casseres 1987], and are therefore more likely to represent a long-run, stable pattern. Third, the sample excludes joint ventures between two or more MNEs.

A number of variables derived from the Profit Impact of Marketing Strategies (PIMS) project were added to the Harvard data. This project, administered by the Strategic Planning Institute, collected detailed business information on over 2,000 domestic strategic business units (SBUs) of some 200 large U.S. firms [Schoeffler, Buzzell & Heany 1974; Clark 1984]. Industry averages (4-digit SIC) of selected variables from these data were used as proxies for the characteristics of the subsidiaries in the Harvard data. As usual in this type of work, it would have been better to use the actual characteristics of the subsidiaries, as was indeed done whenever possible. But subsidiary-level information was not available on key variables like R&D and marketing intensity, so that proxies had to be used. Among available proxies, the PIMS data seem more appropriate than others, as they are based on information from SBUs of firms very similar to those in the Harvard data. Furthermore, the proxies used here were at the 4-digit SIC level, and so are more likely to reflect subsidiary characteristics than more aggregate proxies commonly used in the literature.

To measure the effects of the subsidiary's environment, the analysis uses economic information on host countries gathered by the World Bank [1978], and data on host government ownership policies from the U.S. Department of Commerce [1981]. Finally, a measure of how familiar U.S. firms were with different countries was derived from Davidson [1980].

Definitions of Variables. Following Franko [1971] and Stopford & Wells [1972], a joint venture is defined here as any subsidiary where the MNE owned less than 95% of the equity.[10] Actual ownership level was not used because the difference, say, between 100% foreign ownership and 80% was likely to be perceived differently by firms and government than that between 80% and 60%. Separate tests with another qualitative dependent variable using a 50%-of-equity cutoff point yielded substantially the same results [Gomes-Casseres 1985].

This and all other variables used in the analyses below are defined in Table 1. The independent variables are numbered to facilitate comparison across tables. Each definition also gives the variable's source, and its sample mean and standard deviation (sd).

RESULTS AND DISCUSSION

Results of logit analyses to estimate the ownership effects of restrictive policies are shown in Table 2. Because the binary dependent variable is equal to one when the subsidiary is a joint venture, a negative coefficient in this table implies that the variable discouraged joint ventures (and encouraged whole ownership), while a positive coefficient implies that the variable encouraged joint ventures. The first analysis (shown in column 2.1) contained a series of independent variables thought to influence firm preferences, but without the interaction terms that would separate these effects from those of bargaining. In other words, only the Xs from equation (1) above were included, in addition to the restrictive-country dummy D, but the interaction terms between these two (the DXs) were excluded. The other analysis (shown in column 2.2) included these interaction terms (DXs above) to estimate separately the effects of bargaining. These results are discussed in the next three sections.

Because all the interaction terms in column 2.2 are based on the *Restrictive Host Gov* dummy variable, one might expect some multicollinearity problems. But only two of the pairwise correlations between these interaction terms (no. 13 through no. 23) and the dummy variable (no. 12) are over .80 and four are over .60. Furthermore, the results in the two cases with high correlations—the *Familiarity* and *GDP Growth* terms—are still statistically significant at the .005 level (Table 2, discussed below), implying that the collinearity did not lead to high standard errors on the estimates. Elsewhere in the data there were few correlations over .50; most were well below .20. In each of the cases where the coefficients in Table 2 were statistically insignificant, this did not seem due to collinearity problems.

Firm Ownership Preferences

Elsewhere I discussed at length the results of tests of a model of firm ownership preferences [Gomes-Casseres 1989b]. The base regression in that paper contained the first seven variables in column 2.1 and the restrictive-country dummy.[11] The results were essentially the same as shown here, and were consistent with the arguments above on how firm strategies, capabilities, and transaction costs influence ownership preferences. They suggest that MNEs prefer whole ownership when they have a lot of experience in an industry or a country, when intra-system sales of the subsidiary are high, or when the subsidiary was in a marketing-intensive industry. But MNEs preferred joint ventures when they relied on local inputs of raw material and when local firms could contribute skills to a joint venture. Rather than discuss these conclusions in more detail here, it will be more useful to test some of the arguments about firm preferences using the results of the four additional variables not discussed in my previous paper (nos. 8-11).[12]

Stopford & Wells [1972] and Franko [1987] found that relatively *small firms* in an industry tended to favor joint ventures more than leading firms. This is consistent with the arguments above and in Gomes-Casseres [1989b].

TABLE 1
Definitions of Variables

Dependent Variable	
MNE Owns <95%	Dummy variable equal to 1 if the parent MNE owned less than 95% of the subsidiary's equity in 1975. From Harvard MNE database. (mean=0.29; sd=0.46)
Independent Variables	
1. *R&D/Rev Sub Ind*	Average percentage share that R&D expenses represented in revenues of PIMS SBUs in the subsidiary's principal 4-digit SIC industry. Based on PIMS. (mean=2.6; sd=2.3)
2. *MNE's #Subs In Ind*	Number of foreign manufacturing subsidiaries that the parent MNE had in 1975 in the same 3-digit SIC industry as the subsidiary's principal product. From Harvard MNE database. (mean=14; sd=13)
3. *>10% Sales Intrasystem*	Dummy variable equal to 1 if more than 10% of the subsidiary's sales in 1975 were to other members of the parent MNE's system. From Harvard MNE database. (mean=0.18; sd=0.38)
4. *Resource-Based Sub*	Dummy variable equal to 1 if the subsidiary's main product was in one of the following 2-digit SIC groups, which can be considered "resource-based" industries: food and beverage (SIC 20), tobacco (SIC 21), textile mills (SIC 22), wood except furniture (SIC 24), pulp and paper (SIC 26), petroleum (SIC 29), rubber (SIC 30), leather (SIC 31), stone and glass (SIC 32), and primary metals (SIC 33). Subsidiary's product from Harvard MNE database. (mean=0.25; sd=0.43)
5. *Marketing/Rev Sub Ind*	Average percentage share that marketing expenses represented in revenues of PIMS SBUs in the subsidiary's principal 4-digit SIC industry. Based on PIMS. (mean=11.8; sd=9.9)
6. *Industrial GNP of Host*	Size of the host country's industrial sector in 1976, in millions of U.S. dollars. From World Bank (1978). (mean=69,300; sd=73,600)
7. *Familiarity with Host*	Index (from 0 to 16) of how "familiar" foreign host countries were to U.S. MNEs, based on how often these MNEs entered one country before another during 1900-1976. From Davidson [1980]. (mean=9.5; sd=5.5)
8. *Parent Assets <Indavg*	Dummy variable equal to 1 if the parent's assets in 1975 were less than the average for firms in the same principal 3-digit SIC industry as the parent. Based on Harvard data. (mean=0.39; sd=0.49)
9. *Sub Assets >$10M*	Dummy variable equal to 1 if the subsidiary's assets in 1975 were greater than $10 million. Based on Harvard data. (mean=0.34; sd=0.47)

TABLE 1
(continued)

10. *#MNEs in Industry*	Number of parent firms with at least one foreign subsidiary in the same 4-digit SIC industry as the subsidiary's main product. Based on Harvard data. (mean=14; sd=11)
11. *GDP Growth of Host*	Average annual percentage growth rate of the host country's real per capita GDP in 1960-76. From World Bank (1978). (mean=3.6; sd=1.5)
12. *Restrictive Host Gov*	Dummy variable equal to 1 if the subsidiary was in one of the following host countries, which in 1975 had policies restricting foreign ownership or encouraging joint ventures: Australia, Brazil, Colombia, Ecuador, France, Japan, India, Indonesia, Iran, Malaysia, Mexico, New Zealand, Nigeria, Pakistan, Peru, Philippines, South Korea, Spain, Sri Lanka, and Venezuela. (mean=0.45; sd=0.50)

Interaction terms between independent variables

13. *RSTR×R&D/Rev*	Product of *Restrictive Host Gov* and *R&D/Rev Sub Ind* variables.
14. *RSTR×MNEs #Subs*	Product of *Restrictive Host Gov* and *MNEs #Subs in Ind* variables.
15. *RSTR×Intrasys>10%*	Product of *Restrictive Host Gov* and *>10% Sales Intrasystem* variables.
16. *RSTR×Res Based*	Product of *Restrictive Host Gov* and *Resource-Based Sub* variables.
17. *RSTR×Mktng/Rev*	Product of *Restrictive Host Gov* and *Marketing/Rev Sub Ind* variables.
18. *RSTR×Indstr GNP*	Product of *Restrictive Host Gov* and *Industrial GNP of Host* variables.
19. *RSTR×Familiarity*	Product of *Restrictive Host Gov* and *Familiarity with Host* variables.
20. *RSTR×Par Assets<Indavg*	Product of *Restrictive Host Gov* and *Parent Assets <Indavg* variables.
21. *RSTR×Sub Assets>$10M*	Product of *Restrictive Host Gov* and *Sub Assets> $10M* variables.
22. *RSTR×MNEs in Industry*	Product of *Restrictive Host Gov* and *#MNEs in Industry* variables.
23. *RSTR×GDP Growth*	Product of *Restrictive Host Gov* and *GDP Growth of Host* variables.

Because of oligopolistic competition [Knickerbocker 1973], small firms can be expected to be pressed to expand abroad even though this stretched their organizational capabilities to the limit. In these situations, local partners might make valuable contributions to new ventures. Indeed, the coefficient on the variable measuring whether the MNE's assets are smaller than average for its industry (*Parent Assets < Indavg*) is positive and statistically significant at the .05 level in column 2.1. It remains positive, but declines in significance in column 2.2, which incorporates bargaining effects (see below).

TABLE 2
Logit Analyses: Ownership Effects of Firm, Country, and Industry Variables (standardized beta coefficients with *t*-statistics) (*N*=1,877)

| | Dependent Variable: *MNE Owns*<95% | | | |
| | Column 2.1 | | Column 2.2 | |
Independent Variables	Betas	*t*-stats	Betas	*t*-stats
1. *R&D/Rev Sub Ind*	-0.031	-0.97	-0.039	-0.75
2. *MNE's #Subs in Ind*	-0.135***	-4.22	-0.132**	-2.75
3. *>10% Sales Intrasystem*	-0.075***	-2.59	-0.083**	-2.08
4. *Resource-Based Sub Ind*	0.116***	4.00	0.153***	3.83
5. *Marketing/Rev Sub Ind*	-0.214***	-5.94	-0.229***	-3.82
6. *Industrial GNP of Host*	0.161***	4.74	0.185***	3.70
7. *Familiarity with Host*	-0.291***	-8.82	-0.400***	-7.84
8. *Parent Assets<Indavg*	0.052**	1.93	0.058*	1.38
9. *Sub Assets>$10M*	0.075***	2.68	0.130***	3.25
10. *#MNEs in Industry*	0.061**	2.18	0.064*	1.56
11. *GDP Growth of Host*	0.114***	4.07	-0.035	-0.67
12. *Restrictive Host Gov*	0.266***	9.50	-0.041	-0.35
13. *RSTR×R&D/Rev*	—		0.012	0.20
14. *RSTR×MNE's #Subs*	—		-0.004	-0.07
15. *RSTR×Intrasys>10%*	—		0.015	0.43
16. *RSTR×Res Based*	—		-0.062**	-1.59
17. *RSTR×Mktng/Rev*	—		0.021	0.30
18. *RSTR×Indstr GNP*	—		-0.061	-1.07
19. *RSTR×Familiarity*	—		0.214***	3.06
20. *RSTR×Par Assets<Indavg*	—		-0.007	-0.16
21. *RSTR×Sub Assets>$10M*	—		-0.081**	-2.03
22. *RSTR×MNEs in Industry*	—		-0.011	-0.21
23. *RSTR×GDP Growth*	—		0.315***	3.03
R^2	0.185		0.201	

Note: Because the dependent variable is equal to one when the subsidiary is a joint venture, positive effects indicate variables that encourage joint ownership and negative effects indicate those that encourage whole ownership.

*Statistically different from zero at .10 level (one-tailed)
**Statistically different from zero at .05 level (one-tailed)
***Statistically different from zero at .005 level (one-tailed)

Similar arguments would predict that MNEs investing in relatively *large subsidiaries* should prefer joint ventures. In pursuit of scale economies, firms may be forced to set up larger plants than they can support and manage by themselves. The coefficient on the variable measuring whether the subsidiary's assets exceed $10 million (*Sub Assets>$10M*) is indeed positive and statistically significant at the .005 level in the regression.

Another factor that can be expected to lead MNEs to prefer joint ventures may be a high *degree of competition* in the subsidiary's industry. Two separate arguments suggest that the costs of a joint venture may decline as the number of competitors rises. First, the incentive for internalization may decline as the opportunity for monopolistic pricing falls [Buckley & Casson 1976]. Second, transaction costs for transferring technology through contractual means may decline with a rise in the number of competitors [Stobaugh

FIRM PREFERENCES & HOST GOVERNMENT RESTRICTIONS   13

1984], thus lowering the benefits of using ownership channels and reducing the costs of joint ventures. The coefficient on the variable measuring the number of MNEs in an industry (*#MNEs in Industry*) is indeed positive and statistically significant at the .05 level in column 2.1. It remains positive, but declines in significance in column 2.2, which incorporates bargaining effects (see below).

A fourth variable that appears to influence the ownership choice in column 2.1, serves as an excellent example of how bargaining effects can become entangled with firm preferences in a mis-specified statistical model. The coefficient on the variable measuring the *host country's growth rate* (*GDP Growth of Host*) is positive and significant at the .005 level in column 2.1, but the other regression shows that this is entirely due to the effect that this variable has in restrictive countries. In column 2.2, the coefficient on the interaction term with the restrictive-country dummy (*RSTR × GDP Growth*) is positive and significant at the .005 level, but that on the main variable is not significant. In open countries, therefore, this variable seems to have no effect on ownership patterns. (This result is discussed further below.)

Ownership Effects of Restrictive Policies

Comparison with Previous Studies. This last example illustrates why the specification in column 2.1 cannot distinguish between the independent variables' effects on ownership preferences and on bargaining. Yet this is essentially the specification used in Kobrin [1987]. The results discussed next suggest that, because of this mis-specification, many of the factors that Kobrin concluded affected the bargaining process, in fact influenced firm preferences. The adjustments that Fagre & Wells [1982] and Lecraw [1984] made to attempt to control for firm preferences also seemed to have been incomplete. Many of the results that they attributed to MNE-government bargaining seem also to be due to the process by which firms select their preferred ownership structures.

Overall, it is striking that the variables included in this study seem to affect firm preferences much more than they do relative bargaining power. Seven of the twelve main variables[13] in 2.2 are statistically significant at the .05 level, compared to only three of the twelve interaction terms. As discussed above, the test of whether any variable affects bargaining power depends on the statistical significance of its interaction with the restrictive-country dummy. In other words, column 2.2 suggests that eight of the twelve independent variables in this study do *not* affect the relative power of MNEs and governments.[14]

What is remarkable is that many of the variables that here do not seem to affect bargaining over ownership are precisely those that previous researchers found did just that. For example, Fagre & Wells [1982] and Lecraw [1984] found that the extent of intra-system sales, the R&D- and marketing-intensity of the subsidiary's business, and the degree of competition in the industry all affected bargaining over ownership. None of the coefficients

on the corresponding interaction terms in column 2.2 are statistically significant even at the .10 level (*RSTR* × *Intrasys* > 10%, *RSTR* × *R&D/Rev*, *RSTR* ×
Mktng/Rev, and *RSTR* × *MNEs in Industry*).

In interpreting these differences, some of the limitations of this study should
be kept in mind. Many of the proxies used here are crude, even though
most are identical or similar to those used in previous studies. In particular,
the measure of what constitutes a restrictive host government policy—which
is central in this analysis—is binary and based on aggregate studies. Furthermore, although multicollinearity does not seem to have been a problem, it
might still have inflated the standard errors, leading to low *t*-statistics. As
a result, some of the insignificant coefficients may well be due to the
methods and proxies used.

Factors Affecting Ownership Outcome. A substantial body of literature
argues that technology, market power, and other factors affect MNE-
government bargaining. How can these views be reconciled with the results
in Table 2? It is best to examine this question separately for each factor.

This study did find support for one of Fagre & Wells's hypotheses that
failed their own tests. They expected that MNEs making relatively *large
investments* would have greater bargaining power than others, but could find
no conclusive evidence of this. The coefficient on *RSTR* × *Sub Assets* > $10M
in Table 2 is indeed negative and statistically significant at the .05 level.
This implies that when making major investments abroad, MNEs in restrictive countries were less likely to form joint ventures than those in open countries, as implied by Fagre & Wells's hypothesis.

The estimate of the effect of *R&D intensity* is perhaps one of the most
surprising. In Gomes-Casseres [1989b] I described how R&D can have two
opposing influences on ownership preferences.[15] Firms exploiting their own
technology prefer whole ownership in industries with high R&D spending,
but firms acquiring technology prefer joint ventures. These opposing effects
seem to cancel each other out to yield a coefficient on *R&D/Rev Sub Ind*
that is not significantly different from zero (Table 2). As a result, the effect
on bargaining (measured with *RSTR* × *R&D/Rev*) can also be expected to be
statistically insignificant.

Furthermore, substantial case evidence suggests that bargaining power of
R&D-intensive firms varies within their industries. Grieco's [1982] study of
the computer industry in India, for example, shows that while IBM refused
to give in to the government's demand for local participation, other firms
did. Similarly, Franko's [1987] study of a large group of countries found that
"insider" firms refused joint ventures while "outsider" firms gave in to
government demands in both the computer and pharmaceutical industries.
Recently, IBM gained an exception to Mexico's ownership policies, but
Apple and DEC did not.[16] Such effects, of course, cannot be measured with
an industry average such as used here.

A number of variables that were included to try to capture the effects of
intra-industry differences in bargaining power also did not yield statistically

significant results. The *relative size of the MNE* affected ownership preferences as discussed above, but not bargaining power (*RSTR × Par Assets <
Indavg*). The same was true for the *international experience* of the MNE
(*RSTR × MNE's #Subs*), and the *degree of competition* in each industry
(*RSTR × MNEs in Industry*).[17] All of these proxies may have been too crude
to measure the kinds of effects described by Franko [1987]. Fagre & Wells
[1982] reported similar problems with their measure of industry competition.

Two variables included to measure the effect of vertical integration yielded
somewhat mixed results. The extent of a subsidiary's intra-system sales
seemed not to affect bargaining power in Table 2 (*RSTR × Intrasys > 10%*),
contrary to expectations and earlier results [Fagre & Wells 1982; Lecraw
1984; Reuber 1973]. However, as discussed below, this variable affected
entry deterrence significantly.

The other indicator of vertical integration, this time between the MNE and
local raw material producers, did seem to affect the bargaining power of
the MNEs. Two conflicting hypotheses might be reasonable in this case. On
the one hand, MNEs depending on local raw materials might yield to government pressure in order to gain access to the inputs. On the other hand,
governments seeking to develop and exploit their country's natural resources
might yield to the firms' demands. In fact, investment in *resource-based
industries generally led MNEs to prefer a joint venture*.[18] But when, due
to other circumstances, they chose whole ownership, MNEs investing in
resource-based industries had greater bargaining power than others. The
coefficient on *RSTR × Res Based* is negative and statistically different from
zero at the .05 level, supporting the second hypothesis above.[19] In other
words, it appears that government reliance on MNEs for the development
and export of resources increased the bargaining power of the firms.

While many of the results above are surprising, it is somewhat easier to
understand why *marketing intensity* does not seem to affect the bargaining
process. The coefficient on *RSTR × Mktng/Rev* is not statistically different
from zero at the .10 level.[20] Here, too, there may be differences within industries. But, in addition, there are fewer reasons why host governments should
be expected to give in to MNE demands. Unlike with high-technology industries, most governments do not set out to develop industries that create value
through advertising. Some governments even argue that royalties paid to
foreign firms for use of trademarks is a net loss to the country, unlike royalties for imported technology.

It seems more reasonable to assume that host governments have greater
bargaining power than MNEs in such industries.[21] In return for ownership
concessions, host governments can grant consumer good firms protection
against imports or restrict the number of domestic competitors. This seems
to have been the pattern in India [Encarnation & Vachani 1985], and
perhaps today in China. These countries, in effect, use the attraction of
their domestic markets to gain concessions from MNEs.

There is strong evidence that the *attraction of the domestic market* increases the government's bargaining power across a broader range of countries, as suggested by previous researchers [Reuber 1973; Lecraw 1984; Kobrin 1987]. The more attractive a host country market, the more an MNE will be willing to trade away its ownership preferences for access to the market. But market attractiveness might be measured in various ways. The results in Table 2 suggest that the sheer size of a country's market does not affect bargaining, but that its growth rate does. The former was measured by *Industrial GNP of Host*, which appears to encourage joint ventures equally in both open and restrictive countries.[22] Economic growth, on the other hand, seems to encourage joint ventures only in restrictive countries: the coefficient on the interaction term (*RSTR* × *GDP Growth*) is positive and significant at the .005 level, but that on the main variable (*GDP Growth of Host*) is not significant. One reason for this result may be that the large number of competitors likely to be present in large markets might reduce the attractiveness of entry, while the capacity constraints likely in a rapidly growing market will increase it.

Another country variable also seems to affect bargaining over ownership. When countries are arranged according to their relative *familiarity* to U.S. firms [Davidson 1980], governments of the least familiar countries appear to have less bargaining power than others. Firms generally prefer whole ownership in familiar countries, as indicated by the negative coefficient on *Familiarity with Host*. One reason for this is that U.S. firms would have less to learn about these host environments [Gomes-Casseres 1989b]. But, MNEs can be expected to yield to the ownership demands of governments of familiar countries more often than to the demands of governments of less familiar countries. One reason for this is that familiarity with the environment is likely to result in better working relationships with local partners, and thus lower risks in "forced" joint ventures. This expectation is consistent with the positive coefficient on *RSTR* × *Familiarity*, which is statistically significant at the .005 level.

It is striking that these two country factors—economic growth and familiarity—seem to have the greatest impact on bargaining than the other variables considered here. In the simple regression in column 2.1, the restrictive-country dummy (*Restrictive Host Gov*) had a positive coefficient, but in the regression with interaction terms it is effectively zero. This suggests that ownership policies do not have any *across-the-board effect* on ownership structure.[23] Rather, their effect depends completely on the characteristics of the industry, the subsidiary, and, especially, the host country. This broad conclusion affirms the thrust of the bargaining model, even though other results lead me to discount specific variables reported as significant by previous authors.

Entry Effects of Restrictive Policies

MNEs have two choices if their ownership preferences conflict with those of the government: (1) negotiate a compromise; and (2) decline to invest.

The results in Table 2 discussed above suggest that the ability of MNEs to gain ownership concessions did not vary much with firm characteristics. But their decisions of when to decline to invest did. Thus, some types of firms turned away more easily when faced with restrictive policies than other types. Such differential effects of ownership restrictions have received little attention in the literature.

The results of tests to measure the effect of restrictive policies on entry deterrence are shown in Table 3. The firm characteristics listed in this table were independent variables in separate OLS or Logit regressions. The independent variables were country and firm factors, as well as the dummy variable indicating a restrictive country (*Restrictive Host Gov*). As a result, the coefficients on this dummy variable measure the difference in the dependent variable between open and restrictive countries. This is model (2) described above.

Among the variables with strong effects on entry patterns, the proxies for vertical integration stand out. Subsidiaries in restrictive countries were much less likely to have high *intra-system sales* (>10% *Sales Intrasystm*) than those in open countries; this difference was statistically significant at the .005 level. On average, 12% of the subsidiaries in restrictive countries had intra-system sales exceeding 10%, compared to 22% in open countries. This result is consistent with other findings on the effect of this variable. MNEs investing in subsidiaries that were highly integrated into their global system preferred whole ownership [Gomes-Casseres 1989b]. Because they failed to gain concessions from host country governments (Table 2), they may have decided to avoid investing in restrictive countries. Where they did give in to government demands for a joint venture and went ahead with the investment, they could be expected to modify the subsidiary's strategy to reduce the extent of intra-system sales. That, too, would lead to the result observed here.

Vertical integration between the subsidiary and local firms also seemed to have had important effects on entry decisions. Firms investing in *resource-based* subsidiaries (*Resource-Based Sub*) were also more likely to invest in open countries than in restrictive ones; this effect was statistically significant at the .05 level. On average, 22% of all subsidiaries in restrictive countries were resource-based, compared to 27% in open countries. It appears that firms seeking resources abroad were concerned with the government intervention implied by the restrictive policies. This fear may have been accentuated by the fact that resource-based subsidiaries faced a relatively greater risk of expropriation than others [Bradley 1977]. This pattern may have contributed to the MNEs' ability to gain ownership concessions from host governments, as shown in Table 2. The governments' goal of exploiting national resources, combined with the MNEs' willingness to go elsewhere for raw materials, could well have tipped the balance of power in ownership negotiations.

Restrictive ownership policies also seemed to have deterred firms with relatively little *international experience*. The MNEs investing in restrictive

TABLE 3
Effects of Firm Characteristics
on Deterrent Effects of Restrictive Policies

Firm Characteristics (Dependent Variable)	Coefficients on *Restrictive Host Gov* Controlling for Effects of Country and Other Firm Variables		Regression Method Used
	Coefficient	*t*-statistic	
1. *R&D/Rev Sub Ind*	0.04	0.40	OLS
2. *MNE's #Subs in Ind*	1.51***	2.57	OLS
3. *>10% Sales Intrasystem*	−0.17***	−4.83	Logit
4. *Resource-Based Sub Ind*	−0.06**	−2.29	Logit
5. *Marketing/Rev Sub Ind*	0.26	0.58	OLS
8. *Parent Assets <Indavg*	0.05**	1.96	Logit
9. *SUB Assets >$10M*	−0.03	−1.00	OLS
10. *#MNEs in Industry*	0.30	0.63	OLS

Notes: The regression analyses include variables 1 through 12. Natural coefficients are shown for the OLS regressions, and standardized coefficients for the Logit regressions. Because variable *Restrictive Host Gov* is equal to one in restrictive countries, positive coefficients indicate that the average of the firm characteristic is higher in restrictive countries than in open countries; the reverse is true for negative coefficients. For example, the results on variable 3 above indicate that subsidiaries in restrictive countries have lower intra-system sales than those in open countries.

*Statistically different from zero at .10 level (one-tailed)
**Statistically different from zero at .05 level (one-tailed)
***Statistically different from zero at .005 level (one-tailed)

countries had more subsidiaries worldwide than those investing in open countries, as shown by the positive coefficient on *MNE's #Subs in Ind*, which is statistically significant at the .005 level. There might be two explanations for this result. First, the experience of operating in a variety of environments might have helped these firms deal with restrictive host governments, even though they could not win ownership concessions (Table 2). For example, they may have learned how to manage relations with host governments, or how to manage joint ventures effectively. Second, while restrictive countries may not be locations of choice for a firm just beginning expansion abroad, they may offer positive marginal returns to a firm that is already active in all the choice locations.

But while the firms that refused to be deterred by restrictive policies had extensive international networks, they were typically not the largest in their industries. The positive coefficient on *Parent Assets <Indavg* suggests that the *largest firms* in an industry stayed away from restrictive countries more than smaller firms; this effect was statistically significant at the .05 level. On average, 47% percent of MNEs in restrictive countries had assets below their industry's average, compared to 37% in open countries. The smaller, second-tier firms were more likely to form joint ventures voluntarily than others (Table 2), and were also more likely to give in to government demands in order to gain market access [Franko 1987].

Along a number of *other dimensions,* the MNEs investing in restrictive countries were similar to those in open countries; in other words, the restrictive policies here had little deterrent effect. In particular, this deterrent effect did not vary with the R&D or marketing intensity of the subsidiary, with the number of firms in an industry, or with the size of the investment. Excepting this last factor, all of these also seemed to have little effect on ownership outcomes (Table 2), contrary to some arguments of the bargaining school. It is therefore not surprising to find that they also had little effect on entry. Firms investing in large subsidiaries, however, did gain ownership concessions (Table 2), and so may not have needed to avoid restrictive countries.

CONCLUSION

The choice of ownership structure for a foreign subsidiary depends on factors in two different, but interacting, processes. One set of factors affects *what the firm wants,* i.e., its preferred ownership structure for a subsidiary. These factors include the capabilities of the firm, its strategic needs, and the transaction costs of different ways of transferring capabilities. Another set of factors determine *what the firm can get,* which may be different from what it wants. In particular, when the firm prefers whole ownership but the host government's policies try to encourage joint ventures, then the ownership structure of the subsidiary will be determined in negotiations between firm and government. In this process, the relative bargaining power of the parties affect the outcome.

The existence of two distinct processes led to the development of two schools of thought about the ownership decision: the transaction cost and the bargaining power approaches. But because the ownership structures that we actually observe all stem from a mixture of the two processes, previous researchers have had difficulty testing the arguments of either school of thought. As a result, there has been considerable controversy about which approach best explains ownership patterns.

This paper develops a conceptual framework that combines the arguments of both schools of thought and uses statistical methods that empirically separate the effects due to the two processes. These methods are used here primarily to test the predictions of the bargaining school. Overall, the results suggest that several factors previously thought to affect the bargaining process (e.g., R&D intensity, marketing intensity, and intra-system sales), in fact do so only to a limited extent or not all all. But other factors (e.g., market attractiveness and subsidiary size) do seem to affect the outcome of ownership negotiations. This analysis thus constitutes a partial confirmation of the overall bargaining power approach.

The paper also explores the conditions under which firms facing restrictive governments decide to forego investing altogether instead of yielding to the ownership demands. This option has been suggested in the literature on bargaining, but it has not been examined empirically. The results suggest that whether or not firms forego investing depends on their characteristics and those of the proposed subsidiary, such as the firm's size and the extent of intra-system sales of the subsidiary. Thus, some factors previously thought important in bargaining appear to affect not the ownership outcome, but the entry decision itself.

These results have important implications for international business theories and for business and government policies. They suggest that a theory about multinational enterprise behavior should consider not only the costs and benefits perceived by the firm, but also the impact of relations between firms and governments. Recognizing both these effects, managers should analyze the two aspects of global strategy, i.e., what is ideal for the firm, and what the firm can get. And government policymakers should consider that foreign investment policies may affect not only how firms organize their subsidiaries but also whether they will invest at all. Taking account of multiple processes in theory and policy is never easy, but integrated approaches such as that in this paper can help.

NOTES

1. This discussion assumes that the MNE's own capabilities, too, are best transferred through ownership channels. Otherwise, the MNE could write a licensing contract with the local firm. The example above also assumes that the MNE needs to acquire the local expertise. If it did not, it would prefer a wholly-owned venture.

2. Of course, the same may be true for one firm facing two different situations, such as subsidiaries in different countries or industries. Ownership preferences depend not only on firm factors, but also on industry and country factors. See Gomes-Casseres [1989b].

3. To use the terminology introduced above, these governments' preference is for a joint venture, although their reasons may vary, and their cost/benefit calculations on this score differ from those of the MNE.

4. In other words, in the government's preference ranking of ownership structures, 100% foreign ownership may rank close or far behind joint ventures, and the MNE's contributions may well reverse the ranking.

5. I am indebted to an anonymous referee for valuable suggestions on statistical methods.

6. Logit analysis and OLS regressions differ significantly, however, in the definition and interpretation of R^2 as a measure of goodness of fit. Amemiya [1981, pp. 1504-7] considers several definitions and finds all are flawed; but he offers no good alternative. The measure used here is that in Maddala [1983, pp. 37-8] which is defined analogous to R^2 in OLS regressions, i.e., the squared correlation between Y and $E(Y)$. Both Maddala and Amemiya report a controversy in the literature about whether the upper limit of this measure is one or less than one, and a suggestion that this R^2 may well be very low in logit models. At any rate, tests of the goodness of fit of the regressions presented here are not critical to the interpretation of the results. The paper depends much more on significance tests of the coefficients, which are analagous to tests in OLS models.

7. This hypothesis can, of course, be tested with the methods described above. See Gomes-Casseres [1989b].

8. Because the method relies on comparing characteristics of investments in open and restrictive countries, it cannot be used to estimate the impact of country factors on entry deterrence.

9. Unfortunately, there are not more recent data with the level of detail and the breadth of coverage of this database. However, there are good reasons to believe that results presented here are still valid today. Kobrin [1988] compares ownership patterns in the 1975 Harvard data with those in his more limited 1985 survey and finds no substantial differences. In Gomes-Casseres [1985] I tested whether the effects of a number of independent variables examined here changed over the years 1960-1975,

FIRM PREFERENCES & HOST GOVERNMENT RESTRICTIONS   21

and found that they did not. The relationships examined here thus seemed to have been quite stable, even though there might have been change in numbers of subsidiaries, distribution across countries and industries, and so on. Further analysis of time trends is in Gomes-Casseres [1988].

10. Actually, the Harvard data did not collect information on subsidiaries with less than 5% foreign ownership, so that the joint ventures in this analysis have between 95% and 5% MNE ownership.

11. To reduce confounding effects of bargaining, the paper's sample excluded some of the most restrictive countries that are included here, i.e., Japan, Spain, Sri Lanka, India, Mexico, and Pakistan.

12. These variables are included here because there are compelling hypotheses about their effects on the bargaining process.

13. "Main variables" is used here to refer to the X's in equation (1) above. They include all firm, industry, and country variables, except for the restrictive-country dummy (*Restrictive Host Gov*) and the interaction terms with that dummy variable.

14. Note that these variables might still affect the deterrence effect of restrictive policies, as discussed below.

15. Fagre & Wells [1982], too, reported that the relationship between technology and bargaining power was complex and non-linear. However, I found no evidence of such non-linearity in the residuals from the regressions in Table 2.

16. A comparison of IBM's bargaining with India in 1978 and Mexico in 1985 is in Gomes-Casseres [1989a].

17. Highly experienced firms were likely to prefer whole ownership, because they did not need the contribution of local firms. The coefficient on *MNE's #Subs in Ind* is negative and statistically significant coefficient at the .05 level. See also Gomes-Casseres [1989b].

18. Positive coefficient on *Resource-Based Sub Ind*. Dependence on local resources might imply a bilateral monopoly situation leading to high transaction costs that can be minimized by sharing ownership with producers of the local resources. See Gomes-Casseres [1989b].

19. Because of the two conflicting hypotheses, some might prefer to apply a two-tailed test here. In that case, the null hypothesis of no effect is rejected only at the 10% confidence level.

20. Fagre & Wells's, Kobrin's, and Lecraw's results to the contrary are almost certainly due to the strong effect of marketing intensity on firm preferences. The coefficient on *Marketing/Rev Sub Ind* is negative and statistically significant at the .005 level.

21. Using different statistical methods, I found some evidence for this. See Gomes-Casseres [1985], Chapter 7.

22. As discussed in Gomes-Casseres [1989b], the number of local firms that can contribute valuable skills to the MNE's operation is likely to be greater in countries with large industrial sectors. As a result, MNEs are more likely to prefer joint ventures in these countries than in smaller ones.

23. In terms of equation (1) above, the intercepts in open and restrictive countries are equal: $A_1 = A_0$, so that $(A_1 - A_0) = 0$.

REFERENCES

Amemiya, Takeshi. 1981. Qualitative response models: A survey. *Journal of Economic Literature*, December: 1483-1536.

Anderson, Erin & Hubert Gatignon. 1986. Modes of foreign entry: A transaction cost analysis and propositions. *Journal of International Business Studies*, Fall: 1-26.

Bradley, David G. 1977. Managing against expropriation. *Harvard Business Review*, July-August 1977.

Buckley, Peter J. & Mark Casson. 1976. *The future of the multinational enterprise*. New York: Homes and Meier.

Clark, Kim B. 1984. Unionization and firm performance: The impact on profits, growth, and productivity. *The American Economic Review*, December: 893-919.

Curhan, Joan P., William H. Davidson, & Rajan Suri. 1977. *Tracing the multinationals*. Cambridge, MA: Ballinger.

Davidson, William H. 1980. *Experience effects in international investment and technology transfer*. Ann Arbor: U.M.I. Research Press.

Encarnation, Dennis J. & Sushil Vachani. 1985. Foreign ownership: When hosts change the rules. *Harvard Business Review*, September-October: 152-60.

Fagre, Nathan & Louis T. Wells, Jr. 1982. Bargaining power of multinationals and host governments. *Journal of International Business Studies*, Fall: 9-23.

Franko, Lawrence G. 1971. *Joint venture survival in multinational corporations.* New York: Praeger.

_____. 1987. New forms of investment in developing countries by U.S. companies: A five industry comparison. *Columbia Journal of World Business*, Summer: 39-56.

Gomes-Casseres, Benjamin. 1985. Multinational ownership strategies. DBA dissertation, Harvard University.

_____. 1987. Joint venture instability: Is it a problem? *Columbia Journal of World Business*, Summer: 97-102.

_____. 1988. Joint venture cycles: The evolution of ownership strategies of U.S. MNEs, 1945-75. In Farok J. Contractor & Peter Lorange, eds., *Cooperative strategies in international business.* Lexington: Lexington Books.

_____. 1989a. Joint ventures in the face of global competition. *Sloan Management Review*, Spring: 17-26.

_____. 1989b. Ownership structures of foreign subsidiaries: Theory and evidence. *Journal of Economic Behavior and Organization*, January: 1-25.

Grieco, Joseph M. 1982. India's experience with the international computer industry. *International Organization*, Summer: 609-32.

Hennart, Jean-Francois. 1982. *A theory of multinational enterprise.* Ann Arbor: University of Michigan.

_____. 1988. A transaction cost theory of equity joint ventures. *Strategic Management Journal*, July-August: 36-47.

Johnston, John. 1984. *Econometric methods* (third edition). New York: McGraw-Hill.

Knickerbocker, F. T. 1973. *Oligopolistic reaction and the multinational enterprise.* Boston: Harvard Business School.

Kobrin, Stephen J. 1987. Testing the bargaining hypothesis in the manufacturing sector in developing countries. *International Organization,* Autumn: 609-38.

_____. 1988. Trends in ownership of U.S. manufacturing subsidiaries in developing countries: An inter-industry analysis. In Farok J. Contractor & Peter Lorange, eds., *Cooperative strategies in international business.* Lexington: Lexington Books.

Lax, David A. & James K. Sebenius. 1986. *The manager as negotiator.* Boston: Harvard Business School Press.

Lecraw, Donald J. 1984. Bargaining power, ownership, and profitability of transnational corporations in developing countries. *Journal of International Business Studies*, Spring-Summer: 27-43.

Maddala, G. S. 1983. *Limited-dependent and qualitative variables in econometrics.* Cambridge, U.K.: Cambridge University.

Reuber, Grant L. 1973. *Private foreign investment in development.* Oxford: Clarendon Press.

Schoeffler, Sidney, Robert D. Buzzell & Donald F. Heany. 1974. Impact of strategic planning on profit performance. *Harvard Business Review*, March-April: 137-45.

Stopford, John M. & Louis T. Wells, Jr. 1972. *Managing the multinational enterprise.* New York: Basic Books.

Teece, David J. 1986. Transaction cost economics and the multinational enterprise. *Journal of Economic Behavior and Organization*, 7: 21-45.

U.S. Department of Commerce. 1981. The use of investment incentives and performance requirements by foreign governments. A report prepared by the Investment Policy Division, Office of International Investment, International Trade Administration, October, mimeographed.

World Bank. 1978. *World development report: 1978.* Washington: The World Bank.

[12]

You can't run from strategic alliances.
So learn how to borrow.

Collaborate with Your Competitors – and Win

by Gary Hamel, Yves L. Doz, and C.K. Prahalad

Collaboration between competitors is in fashion. General Motors and Toyota assemble automobiles, Siemens and Philips develop semiconductors, Canon supplies photocopiers to Kodak, France's Thomson and Japan's JVC manufacture videocassette recorders. But the spread of of what we call "competitive collaboration"–joint ventures, outsourcing agreements, product licensings, cooperative research–has triggered unease about the long-term consequences. A strategic alliance can strengthen both companies against outsiders even as it weakens one partner vis-à-vis the other. In particular, alliances between Asian companies and Western rivals seem to work against the Western partner. Cooperation becomes a low-cost route for new competitors to gain technology and market access.[1]

Yet the case for collaboration is stronger than ever. It takes so much money to develop new products and to penetrate new markets that few companies can go it alone in every situation. ICL, the British computer company, could not have developed its current gener-

ation of mainframes without Fujitsu. Motorola needs Toshiba's distribution capacity to break into the Japanese semiconductor market. Time is another critical factor. Alliances can provide shortcuts for Western companies racing to improve their production efficiency and quality control.

We have spent more than five years studying the inner workings of 15 strategic alliances and monitoring scores of others. Our research (see the insert "About Our Research") involves cooperative ventures between competitors from the United States and Japan, Europe and Japan, and the United States and Europe. We did not judge the success or failure of each partnership by its longevity–a common mistake when evaluating strategic alliances–but by the

Gary Hamel is lecturer in business policy and management at the London Business School. Yves L. Doz is professor of business strategy at INSEAD, Fontainebleau, France. C.K. Prahalad is professor of corporate strategy and international business at the University of Michigan. The authors often collaborate in research and writing on international business. Professors Prahalad and Doz are the authors of The Multinational Mission *(Free Press, 1987).*

---

1. For a vigorous warning about the perils of collaboration, see Robert B. Reich and Eric D. Mankin, "Joint Ventures with Japan Give Away Our Future," HBR March-April 1986, p.78.

shifts in competitive strength on each side. We focused on how companies use competitive collaboration to enhance their internal skills and technologies while they guard against transferring competitive advantages to ambitious partners.

There is no immutable law that strategic alliances *must* be a windfall for Japanese or Korean partners. Many Western companies do give away more than they gain – but that's because they enter partnerships without knowing what it takes to win. Companies that benefit most from competitive collaboration adhere to a set of simple but powerful principles.

Collaboration is competition in a different form. Successful companies never forget that their new partners may be out to disarm them. They enter alliances with clear strategic objectives, and they also understand how their partners' objectives will affect their success.

Harmony is not the most important measure of success. Indeed, occasional conflict may be the best evidence of mutually beneficial collaboration. Few alliances remain win-win undertakings forever. A partner may be content even as it unknowingly surrenders core skills.

Cooperation has limits. Companies must defend against competitive compromise. A strategic alliance is a constantly evolving bargain whose real terms go beyond the legal agreement or the aims of top management. What information gets traded is determined day to day, often by engineers and operating managers. Successful companies inform employees at all levels about what skills and technologies are off-limits to the partner and monitor what the partner requests and receives.

Learning from partners is paramount. Successful companies view each alliance as a window on their partners' broad capabilities. They use the alliance to build skills in areas outside the formal agreement and systematically diffuse new knowledge throughout their organizations.

Why Collaborate?

Using an alliance with a competitor to acquire new technologies or skills is not devious. It reflects the commitment and capacity of each partner to absorb the skills of the other. We found that in every case in which a Japanese company emerged from an alliance stronger than its Western partner, the Japanese company had made a greater effort to learn.

Strategic intent is an essential ingredient in the commitment to learning. The willingness of Asian companies to enter alliances represents a change in competitive tactics, not competitive goals. NEC, for example, has used a series of collaborative ventures to enhance its technology and product competences. NEC is the only company in the world with a leading position in telecommunications, computers, and semiconductors – despite its investing less in R&D (as a percentage of revenues) than competitors like Texas Instruments, Northern Telecom, and L.M. Ericsson. Its string of partnerships, most notably with Honeywell, allowed NEC to leverage its in-house R&D over the last two decades.

Western companies, on the other hand, often enter alliances to avoid investments. They are more interested in reducing the costs and risks of entering

> It's not devious to absorb skills from your partner – that's the whole idea.

new businesses or markets than in acquiring new skills. A senior U.S. manager offered this analysis of his company's venture with a Japanese rival: "We complement each other well – our distribution capability and their manufacturing skill. I see no reason to invest upstream if we can find a secure source of product. This is a comfortable relationship for us."

An executive from this company's Japanese partner offered a different perspective: "When it is necessary to collaborate, I go to my employees and say, 'This is bad, I wish we had these skills ourselves. Collaboration is second best. But I will feel worse if after four years we do not know how to do what our partner knows how to do.' We must digest their skills."

The problem here is not that the U.S. company wants to share investment risk (its Japanese partner does too) but that the U.S. company has no ambition *beyond* avoidance. When the commitment to learning is so one-sided, collaboration invariably leads to competitive compromise.

Many so-called alliances between Western companies and their Asian rivals are little more than sophisticated outsourcing arrangements (see the insert "Competition for Competence"). General Motors buys cars and components from Korea's Daewoo. Siemens buys computers from Fujitsu. Apple buys laser printer engines from Canon. The traffic is almost entirely one way. These OEM deals offer Asian partners a way to capture investment initiative from Western competitors and displace customer-competitors from value-creating activities. In many cases this goal meshes with that of the Western partner: to regain competitiveness quickly and with minimum effort.

About Our Research

We spent more than five years studying the internal workings of 15 strategic alliances around the world. We sought answers to a series of interrelated questions. What role have strategic alliances and outsourcing agreements played in the global success of Japanese and Korean companies? How do alliances change the competitive balance between partners? Does winning at collaboration mean different things to different companies? What factors determine who gains most from collaboration?

To understand who won and who lost and why, we observed the interactions of the partners firsthand and at multiple levels in each organization. Our sample included four European-U.S. alliances, two intra-European alliances, two European-Japanese alliances, and seven U.S.-Japanese alliances. We gained access to both sides of the partnerships in about half the cases and studied each alliance for an average of three years.

Confidentiality was a paramount concern. Where we did have access to both sides, we often wound up knowing more about who was doing what to whom than either of the partners. To preserve confidentiality, our article disguises many of the alliances that were part of the study.

Consider the joint venture between Rover, the British automaker, and Honda. Some 25 years ago, Rover's forerunners were world leaders in small car design. Honda had not even entered the automobile business. But in the mid-1970s, after failing to penetrate foreign markets, Rover turned to Honda for technology and product-development support. Rover has used the alliance to avoid investments to design and build new cars. Honda has cultivated skills in European styling and marketing as well as multinational manufacturing. There is little doubt which company will emerge stronger over the long term.

Troubled laggards like Rover often strike alliances with surging latecomers like Honda. Having fallen behind in a key skills area (in this case, manufacturing small cars), the laggard attempts to compensate for past failures. The latecomer uses the alliance to close a specific skills gap (in this case, learning to build cars for a regional market). But a laggard that forges a partnership for short-term gain may find itself in a dependency spiral: as it contributes fewer and fewer distinctive skills, it must reveal more and more of its internal operations to keep the partner interested. For the weaker company, the issue shifts from "Should we collaborate?" to "With whom should we collaborate?" to "How do we keep our

partner interested as we lose the advantages that made us attractive to them in the first place?"

There's a certain paradox here. When both partners are equally intent on internalizing the other's skills, distrust and conflict may spoil the alliance and threaten its very survival. That's one reason joint ventures between Korean and Japanese companies have been few and tempestuous. Neither side wants to "open the kimono." Alliances seem to run most smoothly when one partner is intent on learning and the other is intent on avoidance – in essence, when one partner is willing to grow dependent on the other. But running smoothly is not the point; the point is for a company to emerge from an alliance more competitive than when it entered it.

One partner does not always have to give up more than it gains to ensure the survival of an alliance. There are certain conditions under which mutual gain is possible, at least for a time:

The partners' strategic goals converge while their competitive goals diverge. That is, each partner allows for the other's continued prosperity in the shared business. Philips and Du Pont collaborate to develop and manufacture compact discs, but neither side invades the other's market. There is a clear upstream/downstream division of effort.

The size and market power of both partners is modest compared with industry leaders. This forces each side to accept that mutual dependence may have to continue for many years. Long-term collaboration may be so critical to both partners that neither will risk antagonizing the other by an overtly competitive bid to appropriate skills or competences. Fujitsu's 1 to 5 size disadvantage with IBM means it will be a long time, if ever, before Fujitsu can break away from its foreign partners and go it alone.

Each partner believes it can learn from the other and at the same time limit access to proprietary skills. JVC and Thomson, both of whom make VCRs, know that they are trading skills. But the two companies are looking for very different things. Thomson needs product technology and manufacturing prowess; JVC needs to learn how to succeed in the fragmented European market. Both sides believe there is an equitable chance for gain.

How to Build Secure Defenses

For collaboration to succeed, each partner must contribute something distinctive: basic research, product development skills, manufacturing capacity, access to distribution. The challenge is to share enough skills to create advantage vis-à-vis companies outside the alliance while preventing a wholesale transfer of core skills to the partner. This is a very thin line to walk. Companies must carefully select what skills and technologies they pass to their partners. They must develop safeguards against unintended, informal transfers of information. The goal is to limit the transparency of their operations.

The type of skill a company contributes is an important factor in how easily its partner can internalize the skills. The potential for transfer is greatest when a partner's contribution is easily transported (in engineering drawings, on computer tapes, or in the heads of a few technical experts); easily interpreted (it can be reduced to commonly understood equations or symbols); and easily absorbed (the skill or competence is independent of any particular cultural context).

Western companies face an inherent disadvantage because their skills are generally more vulnerable to transfer. The magnet that attracts so many companies to alliances with Asian competitors is their manufacturing excellence – a competence that is less transferable than most. Just-in-time inventory systems and quality circles can be imitated, but this is like pulling a few threads out of an oriental carpet. Manufacturing excellence is a complex web of employee training, integration with suppliers, statistical process controls, employee involvement, value engineering, and design for manufacture. It is difficult to extract such a subtle competence in any way but a piecemeal fashion.

There is an important distinction between technology and competence. A discrete, stand-alone technology (for example, the design of a semiconductor chip) is more easily transferred than a process compe-

> **Alliances should establish and enforce specific performance requirements. No performance, no technology transfer.**

tence, which is entwined in the social fabric of a company. Asian companies often learn more from their Western partners than vice versa because they contribute difficult-to-unravel strengths, while Western partners contribute easy-to-imitate technology.

So companies must take steps to limit transparency. One approach is to limit the scope of the formal agreement. It might cover a single technology rather than an entire range of technologies; part of a product line rather than the entire line; distribution in a

limited number of markets or for a limited period of time. The objective is to circumscribe a partner's opportunities to learn.

Moreover, agreements should establish specific performance requirements. Motorola, for example, takes an incremental, incentive-based approach to technology transfer in its venture with Toshiba. The agreement calls for Motorola to release its microprocessor technology incrementally as Toshiba delivers on its promise to increase Motorola's penetration in the Japanese semiconductor market. The greater Motorola's market share, the greater Toshiba's access to Motorola's technology.

Many of the skills that migrate between companies are not covered in the formal terms of collaboration. Top management puts together strategic alliances and sets the legal parameters for exchange. But what actually gets traded is determined by day-to-day interactions of engineers, marketers, and product developers: who says what to whom, who gets access to what facilities, who sits on what joint committees. The most important deals ("I'll share this with you if you share that with me") may be struck four or five organizational levels below where the deal was signed. Here lurks the greatest risk of unintended transfers of important skills.

Consider one technology-sharing alliance between European and Japanese competitors. The European company valued the partnership as a way to acquire a specific technology. The Japanese company considered it a window on its partner's entire range of competences and interacted with a broad spectrum of its partner's marketing and product-development staff. The company mined each contact for as much information as possible.

For example, every time the European company requested a new feature on a product being sourced from its partner, the Japanese company asked for detailed customer and competitor analyses to justify the request. Over time, it developed a sophisticated picture of the European market that would assist its own entry strategy. The technology acquired by the European partner through the formal agreement had a useful life of three to five years. The competitive insights acquired informally by the Japanese company will probably endure longer.

Limiting unintended transfers at the operating level requires careful attention to the role of gatekeepers, the people who control what information flows to a partner. A gatekeeper can be effective only if there are a limited number of gateways through which a partner can access people and facilities. Fujitsu's many partners all go through a single office, the "collaboration section," to request information and assistance from different divisions. This way the

Competition for Competence

In the article "Do You Really Have a Global Strategy?" (HBR July-August 1985), Gary Hamel and C.K. Prahalad examined one dimension of the global competitive battle: the race for brand dominance. This is the battle for control of distribution channels and global "share of mind." Another global battle has been much less visible and has received much less management attention. This is the battle for control over key technology-based competences that fuel new business development.

Honda has built a number of businesses, including marine engines, lawn mowers, generators, motorcycles, and cars, around its engine and power train competence. Casio draws on its expertise in semiconductors and digital display in producing calculators, small-screen televisions, musical instruments, and watches. Canon relies on its imaging and microprocessor competences in its camera, copier, and laser printer businesses.

In the short run, the quality and performance of a company's products determine its competitiveness. Over the longer term, however, what counts is the ability to build and enhance core competences—distinctive skills that spawn new generations of products. This is where many managers and commentators fear Western companies are losing. Our research helps explain why some companies may be more likely than others to surrender core skills.

Alliance or Outsourcing?

Enticing Western companies into outsourcing agreements provides several benefits to ambitious OEM partners. Serving as a manufacturing base for a Western partner is a quick route to increased manufacturing share without the risk or expense of building brand share. The Western partners' distribution capability allows Asian suppliers to focus all their resources on building absolute product advantage. Then OEMs can enter markets on their own and convert manufacturing share into brand share.

Serving as a sourcing platform yields more than just volume and process improvements. It also generates low-cost, low-risk market learning. The downstream (usually Western) partner typically provides information on how to tailor products to local markets. So every product design transferred to an OEM partner is also a research report on customer preferences and market needs. The OEM partner can use these insights to read the market accurately when it enters on its own.

A Ratchet Effect

Our research suggests that once a significant sourcing relationship has been established, the buyer becomes less willing and able to reemerge as a manufacturing competitor. Japanese and Korean companies are, with few exceptions, exemplary suppliers. If anything, the "soft option" of outsourcing becomes even softer as OEM suppliers routinely exceed delivery and quality expectations.

Outsourcing often begins a ratchetlike process. Relinquishing manufacturing control and paring back plant investment leads to sacrifices in product design, process technology, and, eventually, R&D budgets. Consequently, the OEM partner captures product-development as well as manufacturing initiative. Ambitious OEM partners are not content with the old formula of "You design it and we'll make it." The new reality is, "You design it, we'll learn from your designs, make them more manufacturable, and launch our products alongside yours."

Reversing the Verdict

This outcome is not inevitable. Western companies can retain control over their core competences by keeping a few simple principles in mind.

A competitive product is not the same thing as a competitive organization. While an Asian OEM partner may provide the former, it seldom provides the latter. In essence, outsourcing is a way of renting someone else's competitiveness rather than developing a long-term solution to competitive decline.

Rethink the make-or-buy decision. Companies often treat component manufacturing operations as cost centers and transfer their output to assembly units at an arbitrarily set price. This transfer price is an accounting fiction, and it is unlikely to yield as high a return as marketing or distribution investments, which require less research money and capital. But companies seldom consider the competitive consequences of surrendering control over a key value-creating activity.

Watch out for deepening dependence. Surrender results from a series of outsourcing decisions that individually make economic sense but collectively amount to a phased exit from the business. Different managers make outsourcing decisions at different times, unaware of the cumulative impact.

Replenish core competences. Western companies must outsource some activities; the economics are just too compelling. The real issue is whether a company is adding to its stock of technologies and competences as rapidly as it is surrendering them. The question of whether to outsource should always provoke a second question: Where can we outpace our partner and other rivals in building new sources of competitive advantage?

company can monitor and control access to critical skills and technologies.

We studied one partnership between European and U.S. competitors that involved several divisions of each company. While the U.S. company could only access its partner through a single gateway, its partner had unfettered access to all participating divisions. The European company took advantage of its free rein. If one division refused to provide certain information, the European partner made the same request of another division. No single manager in the U.S. company could tell how much information had been transferred or was in a position to piece together patterns in the requests.

Collegiality is a prerequisite for collaborative success. But *too much* collegiality should set off warning bells to senior managers. CEOs or division presidents should expect occasional complaints from their counterparts about the reluctance of lower level employees to share information. That's a sign that the gatekeepers are doing their jobs. And senior management should regularly debrief operating personnel to find out what information the partner is requesting and what requests are being granted.

Limiting unintended transfers ultimately depends on employee loyalty and self-discipline. This was a real issue for many of the Western companies we studied. In their excitement and pride over technical achievements, engineering staffs sometimes shared information that top management considered sensitive. Japanese engineers were less likely to share proprietary information.

There are a host of cultural and professional reasons for the relative openness of Western technicians. Japanese engineers and scientists are more loyal to their company than to their profession. They are less steeped in the open give-and-take of university research since they receive much of their training from employers. They consider themselves team members more than individual scientific contribu-

> When a foreign partner houses, feeds, and looks after your managers, there is a danger they will "go native."

tors. As one Japanese manager noted, "We don't feel any need to reveal what we know. It is not an issue of pride for us. We're glad to sit and listen. If we're patient we usually learn what we want to know."

Controlling unintended transfers may require restricting access to facilities as well as to people. Companies should declare sensitive laboratories and

factories off-limits to their partners. Better yet, they might house the collaborative venture in an entirely new facility. IBM is building a special site in Japan where Fujitsu can review its forthcoming mainframe software before deciding whether to license it. IBM will be able to control exactly what Fujitsu sees and what information leaves the facility.

Finally, which country serves as "home" to the alliance affects transparency. If the collaborative team is located near one partner's major facilities, the other partner will have more opportunities to learn—but less control over what information gets traded. When the partner houses, feeds, and looks after engineers and operating managers, there is a danger they will "go native." Expatriate personnel need frequent visits from headquarters as well as regular furloughs home.

Enhance the Capacity to Learn

Whether collaboration leads to competitive surrender or revitalization depends foremost on what employees believe the purpose of the alliance to be. It is self-evident: to learn, one must *want* to learn. Western companies won't realize the full benefits of competitive collaboration until they overcome an arrogance borne of decades of leadership. In short, Western companies must be more receptive.

We asked a senior executive in a Japanese electronics company about the perception that Japanese companies learn more from their foreign partners than vice versa. "Our Western partners approach us with the attitude of teachers," he told us. "We are quite happy with this, because we have the attitude of students."

Learning begins at the top. Senior management must be committed to enhancing their companies' skills as well as to avoiding financial risk. But most learning takes place at the lower levels of an alliance. Operating employees not only represent the front lines in an effective defense but also play a vital role in acquiring knowledge. They must be well briefed on the partner's strengths and weaknesses and understand how acquiring particular skills will bolster their company's competitive position.

This is already standard practice among Asian companies. We accompanied a Japanese development engineer on a tour through a partner's factory. This engineer dutifully took notes on plant layout, the number of production stages, the rate at which the line was running, and the number of employees. He recorded all this despite the fact that he had no manufacturing responsibility in his own company, and that the alliance didn't encompass joint manufacturing. Such dedication greatly enhances learning.

Collaboration doesn't always provide an opportunity to fully internalize a partner's skills. Yet just acquiring new and more precise benchmarks of a partner's performance can be of great value. A new benchmark can provoke a thorough review of internal performance levels and may spur a round of competitive innovation. Asking questions like, "Why do their semiconductor logic designs have fewer errors than ours?" and "Why are they investing in this technology and we're not?" may provide the incentive for a vigorous catch-up program.

Competitive benchmarking is a tradition in most of the Japanese companies we studied. It requires many of the same skills associated with competitor analysis: systematically calibrating performance against external targets; learning to use rough estimates to determine where a competitor (or partner) is better, faster, or cheaper; translating those estimates into new internal targets; and recalibrating to establish the rate of improvement in a competitor's performance. The great advantage of competitive collaboration is that proximity makes benchmarking easier.

Indeed, some analysts argue that one of Toyota's motivations in collaborating with GM in the much-publicized NUMMI venture is to gauge the quality of GM's manufacturing technology. GM's top manufac-

> "Our Western partners approach us with the attitude of teachers. We have the attitude of students."

turing people get a close look at Toyota, but the reverse is true as well. Toyota may be learning whether its giant U.S. competitor is capable of closing the productivity gap with Japan.

Competitive collaboration also provides a way of getting close enough to rivals to predict how they will behave when the alliance unravels or runs its course. How does the partner respond to price changes? How does it measure and reward executives? How does it prepare to launch a new product? By revealing a competitor's management orthodoxies, collaboration can increase the chances of success in future head-to-head battles.

Knowledge acquired from a competitor-partner is only valuable after it is diffused through the organi-

zation. Several companies we studied had established internal clearinghouses to collect and disseminate information. The collaborations manager at one Japanese company regularly made the rounds of all employees involved in alliances. He identified what information had been collected by whom and then passed it on to appropriate departments. Another company held regular meetings where employees shared new knowledge and determined who was best positioned to acquire additional information.

Proceed with Care – But Proceed

After World War II, Japanese and Korean companies entered alliances with Western rivals from weak positions. But they worked steadfastly toward independence. In the early 1960s, NEC's computer business was one-quarter the size of Honeywell's, its primary foreign partner. It took only two decades for NEC to grow larger than Honeywell, which eventually sold its computer operations to an alliance between NEC and Group Bull of France. The NEC experience demonstrates that dependence on a foreign partner doesn't automatically condemn a company to also-ran status. Collaboration may sometimes be unavoidable; surrender is not.

Managers are too often obsessed with the ownership structure of an alliance. Whether a company controls 51% or 49% of a joint venture may be much less important than the rate at which each partner learns from the other. Companies that are confident of their ability to learn may even prefer some ambiguity in the alliance's legal structure. Ambiguity creates more potential to acquire skills and technologies. The challenge for Western companies is not to write tighter legal agreements but to become better learners.

Running away from collaboration is no answer. Even the largest Western companies can no longer outspend their global rivals. With leadership in many industries shifting toward the East, companies in the United States and Europe must become good borrowers – much like Asian companies did in the 1960s and 1970s. Competitive renewal depends on building new process capabilities and winning new product and technology battles. Collaboration can be a low-cost strategy for doing both. ▯

[13]

Strategic Management Journal, Vol. 12, 83–103 (1991)

COMPETITION FOR COMPETENCE AND INTER-PARTNER LEARNING WITHIN INTERNATIONAL STRATEGIC ALLIANCES

GARY HAMEL
London Business School, London, U.K.

Global competition highlights asymmetries in the skill endowments of firms. Collaboration may provide an opportunity for one partner to internalize the skills of the other, and thus improve its position both within and without the alliance. Detailed analysis of nine international alliances yielded a fine-grained understanding of the determinants of inter-partner learning. The study suggests that not all partners are equally adept at learning; that asymmetries in learning alter the relative bargaining power of partners; that stability and longevity may be inappropriate metrics of partnership success; that partners may have competitive, as well as collaborative aims, vis-à-vis each other; and that process may be more important than structure in determining learning outcomes.

THE RESEARCH QUESTION

A skills-based view of the firm

It is possible to conceive of a firm as a portfolio of core competencies on one hand, and encompassing disciplines on the other, rather than as a portfolio of product-market entities (Prahalad and Hamel, 1990). As technology bundles, core competencies make a critical contribution to the unique functionality of a range of end-products. An example is Honda's expertise in powertrains, which is applied to products as diverse as automobiles, motorcycles, generators, and lawn mowers. Encompassing disciplines include total quality control, just-in-time manufacturing systems, value engineering, flexible manufacturing systems, accelerated product development, and total customer service. Such disciplines allow a product to be delivered to customers at the best possible price/performance trade-off. Core competencies and value-creating disciplines are precisely the kinds of firm-specific skills for which there are only imperfect external markets, and hence form the *raison d'etre* for

the multinational enterprise (Buckley and Casson, 1985; Caves, 1971; Teece, 1981).

Conceiving of the firm as a portfolio of core competencies and disciplines suggests that interfirm competition, as opposed to inter-product competition, is essentially concerned with the acquisition of skills. In this view global competitiveness is largely a function of the firm's pace, efficiency, and extent of knowledge accumulation. The traditional 'competitive strategy' paradigm (e.g. Porter, 1980), with its focus on product-market positioning, focuses on only the last few hundred yards of what may be a skill-building marathon. The notion of competitive advantage (Porter, 1985) which provides the means for computing product-based advantages at a given point in time (in terms of cost and differentiation), provides little insight into the process of knowledge acquisition and skill building.

Core competencies and value-creating disciplines are not distributed equally among firms. Expansion-minded competitors, exploiting such firm-specific advantages, bring the skill deficiencies of incumbents into stark relief. The present

0143–2095/91/050083–21$11.50

study was unconcerned with why such discrepancies in skill endowments exist, but was very concerned with the role international strategic alliances might play in effecting a partial redistribution of skills among partners. While 'globalization' has been widely credited for provoking a shift to collaborative strategies (Ghemawat, Porter and Rawlinson, 1986; Hergert and Morris, 1988; Ohmae, 1989; Perlmutter and Heenan, 1986), the ways in which strategic alliances either enhance or diminish the skills which underlie global competitiveness have been only partially specified. *The goal of the present research was to understand the extent to which and means through which the collaborative process might lead to a reapportionment of skills between the partners.*

While skills discrepancies have been recognized as a motivator for international collaboration (Contractor and Lorange, 1988; Root, 1988), the crucial distinction between acquiring such skills in the sense of gaining *access* to them—by taking out a license, utilizing a subassembly supplied by a partner, or relying on a partner's employees for some critical operation—and actually *internalizing* a partner's skills has seldom been clearly drawn. This distinction is crucial. As long as a partner's skills are embodied only in the specific outputs of the venture, they have no value outside the narrow terms of the agreement. Once internalized, however, they can be applied to new geographic markets, new products, and new businesses. For the partners, an alliance may be not only a means for trading access to each other's skills—what might be termed *quasi-internalization*, but also a mechanism for actually acquiring a partner's skills—*de facto internalization*.

A conception of strategic alliances as opportunities for *de facto* internalization was suggested during a major research project on 'competition for competence' in which the author participated (Prahalad and Hamel, 1990). In that study managers often voiced a concern that, when collaborating with a potential competitor, failure to 'out-learn' one's partner could render a firm first dependent and then redundant within the partnership, and competitively vulnerable outside it. The two premises from which this concern issued seemed to be that (1) few alliances were perfectly and perpetually collusive, and (2) the fact that a firm chose to collaborate with a present or potential competitor could not be

taken as evidence that that firm no longer harbored a competitive intent *vis-à-vis* its partner. Indeed, when it came to the competitive consequences of inter-partner learning, the attitudes of some managers in the initial study had shifted from naiveté to paranoia within a few short years. This seemed to be particularly true for managers in alliances with Japanese partners. What was lacking was any systematic investigation of the determinants of inter-partner learning.

METHODOLOGY

Thus the research objective was theory development rather than theory extension. The parameters which controlled the choice of research design were: (1) a belief that existing theoretical perspectives illuminated only a small part of the collaborative phenomenon; (2) a desire to identify the determinants of a certain class of collaborative outcomes, i.e. inter-partner learning; and (3) the consequent need for observation that was administratively fine-grained, multi-level and longitudinal. These considerations made inevitable the choice of a research design based on the principles of grounded theory development (Glaser and Strauss, 1967; Mintzberg, 1978; Pettigrew, 1979; Seyle, 1964). Because patterns of causality are extremely complex in most real-world administrative systems, traditional deductive–analytic methodologies force the researcher to declutter the phenomenon by: (1) substituting crude proxies for difficult-to-measure determinants or outcomes; (2) assuming away some of the multidimensionality in causal relationships; and/or (3) narrowing the scope of research. In doing so, much of the potential value of the research is lost. The problem is not that the resulting theories are under-tested (i.e. they fail a test of rigor), but that they are under-developed (i.e. they are so partial in coverage that they illuminate only a fragment of the path between choice, action and outcome). For the purposes of this study a decision was made not to prematurely prune the collaborative problem into a shape that would fit within the constraints of a deductive methodology.

Grounded theory development proceeded in two stages. In the first stage the goal was to illuminate the basic dimensions of a theory of inter-partner learning. To this end an attempt was made to maximize underlying differences among cases in order to discover those concepts or theoretical categories that were most universal (where the data across cases were most similar), and those that were entirely idiosyncratic (where the data across cases were most divergent). Interviews were initially conducted with 74 individuals across 11 companies concerning nine international alliances. The number of individuals interviewed within each company ranged from three to 11, with six the average. Interviews were typically 2 hours in length, though a few consumed an entire day. Given concerns over confidentiality on the part of participating firms, several of the participating firms requested anonymity. The 11 firms in the study ranged in size from under $500 million in sales to more than $50 billion. Four of the companies were domiciled in the United States, four within the European Community, and three in Japan. Each firm derived at least 30 percent of its revenue from outside its domestic market. Industries covered included aerospace, chemicals, semiconductors, pharmaceuticals, computers, automobiles, and consumer electronics. In every company managers with responsibility for strategic alliances from both divisional and business unit levels were interviewed. Approximately 40 percent of the interviews were with functional supervisors or first-line employees who worked regularly across the collaborative membrane. Seven of the participating firms had a partner within the sample of 11 firms; in this way both 'sides' of three on-going partnerships were observed. Thus inter-case diversity was achieved along the dimensions of partner nationality and industry affiliation, and agreement type (equity-based joint ventures versus long-term co-marketing, design and supply relationships).

The anxiety over asymmetric learning expressed by managers in the earlier study was confirmed in the first stage interviewing process. Concerns were of three broad types: (1) concern over the *intent* of partners (collaborative versus competitive, internalization of partner skills versus mere access); (2) concern over the 'openness' of the firm to its partner—what came to be termed *transparency*; and (3) concern over firm's ability to actually absorb skills from its partner, i.e. *receptivity*. As the core categories that came to constitute the formal internalization

model, *intent*, *receptivity*, and *transparency* were identified as prospective determinants of inter-partner learning. Also emerging from the first round of interviewing was a proposed linkage between learning and inter-partner bargaining power, and, consequently a notion of collaboration as a 'race to learn.'

Having illuminated an overarching formal model, the second stage of research aimed at understanding in detail the processes and mechanisms through which intent, receptivity, and transparency impacted on learning outcomes. This was accomplished through a second round of case-based research, termed 'theoretic sampling' (Glaser and Strauss, 1967: 45–77), because the choice of which cases to compare is directed by the emerging theory. By selecting cases where the researcher hoped to find both maximum and minimum variance along the dimensions of the core model, it was possible to amplify the core model. A further criterion to be satisfied was the need to gain even deeper, more extensive access to the individuals involved in the process of collaborative exchange than had been achieved in first stage interviewing, and to ensure that access was gained to both sides of the collaborative membrane. This was deemed necessary if the researcher was to have any hope of measuring, however crudely, the migration of skills between partners, the criticality of those skills (and hence the extent to which they should be valued and protected or sought by each partner), and ultimately, the competitive consequences of those skill transfers.

These requirements were met in the following ways. Two partnerships, involving five firms (one partnership was triadic), were selected for intensive study. Inter-case differences were minimized to the extent that both partnerships comprised a European firm (or firms) on one side, and a Japanese firm on the other. Thus it was possible to compare the behavior of the European firms, one with another, and the behavior of the Japanese partners, one with another. Both alliances were more than 5 years old at the time the study commenced, both had received substantial media attention, and were regarded as two of the most important and 'successful' Euro-Japanese alliances. Both partnerships were set within the electronics industry.

At the same time there were potentially significant differences between the cases: one centered around professional products with a 3–5-year life cycle, and the other around a consumer product with a 6–12-month life-cycle. One of the European partners had a clear corporate strategy for core competence building, the others did not. The locus of activity for one partnership was based in Europe, the other in Japan. One partnership involved regular and intensive collaboration across the membrane, the other periodic inter-working. One partnership was a joint equity venture, the other a mixture of long- and short-term development and supply contracts. And of course there was the opportunity to compare the behavior of partners based in very different national contexts. The first stage interview process, as well as much of the anecdotal evidence (e.g. *Business Week*, 1989), suggested this difference in national origin might be crucial to learning outcomes.

Each of the five partners agreed to provide access to facilities as well as to key managers and operating employees. Each of the partners also agreed to submit to a minimum of 40 hours of interviewing. While single, week-long research visits were made to the Japanese partners, repeated research visits, extending over 2 years, were made to the European partners. Interviewing continued until saturation of core categories—intent, transparency, and receptivity—was achieved, i.e. new properties of the categories were no longer emerging. Relying on archival data, as well as interviews with industry analysts, two detailed industry briefing notes were prepared. The detailed research reports which summarize the output of the second stage interviewing are contained in Hamel (1990).

FINDINGS

The six major propositions which grew out of the data are summarized in Table 1. They will be discussed in turn, and the evidence which produced them briefly summarized.

Competitive collaboration

Though not always readily admitting it, several partners clearly regarded their alliances as transitional devices where the primary objective was the internalization of partner skills. As one Japanese manager put it:

We've learned a lot from [our partner]. The [foreign] environment was very far from us—we didn't understand it well. We learned that [our partner] was very good at developing. Our engineers have learned much from the relationship.

A European manager stated that:

[Our partner] was passionately hungry to find out the requirements of the users in the markets they wanted to serve. We were priming the market for them.

A manager in a Japanese firm that had to contend with a persistently inquisitive European partner believed that:

The only motivation for [our European partner] is to get mass manufacturing technology. They see [the alliance] as a short circuit. As soon as they have this they'll lose interest.

This manager believed that the partner would see eventual termination of the agreement as evidence of successful learning, rather than of a failed collaborative venture.

While no manager in the study claimed a desire to 'deskill' partners, there were several cases in which managers believed this had been the outcome of the collaborative process. In these cases the competitive implications of unanticipated (and typically unsanctioned) skill transfers were clearly understood, albeit retrospectively. The president of the Asia-Pacific division of an American industrial products company was in no doubt that his firm's Japanese partner had emerged from their 20-year alliance as a significant competitor:

We established them in their core business. They learned the business from us, mastered our process technology, enjoyed terrific margins at home, where we did not compete in parallel, and today challenge us outside of Japan.

The divisional vice-president of a Western computer company had a similar interpretation of his firm's trans-Pacific alliance:

A year and a half into the deal I understood what it was all about. Before that I was as naive as the next guy. It took me that long to see that [our partner] was preparing a platform to come into all our markets.

Table 1. A theory of inter-partner learning: Core propositions

1. *Competitive collaboration*
   (a) Some partners may regard internalization of scarce skills as a primary benefit of international collaboration.
   (b) Where learning is the goal, the termination of an agreement cannot be seen as failure, nor can its longevity and stability be seen as evidence of success.
   (c) Asymmetries in learning within the alliance may result in a shift in relative competitive position and advantage between the partners outside the alliance. Thus some partners may regard each other as competitors as well as collaborators.

2. *Learning and bargaining power*
   (a) Asymmetries in learning change relative bargaining power within the alliance: successful learning may make the original bargain obsolete and may, *in extremis*, lead to a pattern of unilateral, rather than bilateral, dependence.
   (b) The legal and governance structure may exert only a minor influence over the pattern of inter-partner learning and bargaining power.
   (c) A partner that understands the link between inter-partner learning, bargaining power, and competitiveness will tend to view the alliance as a race to learn.

3. *Intent as a determinant of learning*
   (a) The objectives of alliance partners, with respect to inter-partner learning and competence acquisition, may be usefully characterized as internalization, resource concentration, or substitution.
   (b) An internalization intent will be strongest in

firms which conceive of competitiveness as competence-based, rather than as product-based, and which seek to close skill gaps rather than to compensate for skills failure.
   (c) A substitution intent pre-ordains asymmetric learning; for systematic learning to take place, operators must possess an internalization intent.

4. *Transparency as a determinant of learning*
   (a) Asymmetry in transparency pre-ordains asymmetric learning: some firms and some skills may be inherently more transparent than others.
   (b) Transparency can be influenced through the design of organizational interfaces, the structure of joint tasks, and the 'protectiveness' of individuals.

5. *Receptivity as a determinant of learning*
   (a) Asymmetry in receptivity pre-ordains asymmetric learning: some firms may be inherently more receptive than others.
   (b) Receptivity is a function of the skills and absorptiveness of receptors, of exposure position, and of parallelism in facilities.

6. *The determinants of sustainable learning*
   Whether learning becomes self-sustaining—that is, whether the firm eventually becomes able, without further inputs from its partner, to improve its skills at the same rate as its partner—will depend on the depth of learning that has taken place, whether the firm possesses the scale and volume to allow, in future, amortization of the investment needed to break free of dependence on the partner, and whether the firm possesses the disciplines of continuous improvement.

Yet another manager felt a partner had crossed the line distinguishing collaboration from competition:

> If they were really our partners, they wouldn't try to suck us dry of technology ideas they can use in their own products. Whatever they learn from us, they'll use against us worldwide.

Recognizing the potential danger of turning collaborators into competitors, a senior executive in a Japanese firm hoped his firm's European partners would be 'strong—but not too strong.'

The proposition that partners possessing parallel internalization and international expansion goals would find their relationships more conten-

tious than partners with asymmetric intents arose, in part, from observing the markedly different relationships that existed between three partners in a triadic alliance. The British firm in the alliance, possessing neither an internalization intent nor global expansion goals, enjoyed a placid relationship with its Japanese partner. However, the French and Japanese firms in the alliance, each possessed of ambitious learning and expansion goals, were often at loggerheads. A technical manager in the Japanese firm remarked that:

> The English were easier to work with than the French. The English were gentlemen, but the French were [not]. We could reach decisions

very quickly with the English, but the French wanted to debate and debate and debate.

This seemed to be a reaction to the difficulty of bargaining with a partner who possessed equally ambitious learning goals.

In general, whenever two partners sought to extract value in the same form from their partnership—whether in the form of inter-partner learning benefits or short-term economic benefits, managers were likely to find themselves frequently engaged in contentious discussions over value-sharing. The relationships where managers were least likely to be troubled by recurring arguments over value appropriation were those where one partner was pursuing, unequivocably, a learning intent and the other a short-term earnings maximization intent. In such relationships—there were three—one partner was becoming progressively more dependent on the other. That the British firm mentioned above ultimately withdrew from the business on which the alliance was based suggested a fundamental proposition: just as contentiousness does not, by itself, indicate collaborative failure (some managers recognized they had to accept a certain amount of contentiousness as the price for protecting their core skills and gaining access to their partner's), an abundance of harmony and good will does not mean both partners are benefiting equally in terms of enhanced competitiveness. Collaborative success could not be measured in terms of a 'happiness index.'

Learning and bargaining power

The link between learning and bargaining power emerged clearly in several cases, one of which is briefly summarized here. A European firm in the study had entered a sourcing agreement with a Japanese partner in the mid-1970s, and later, partly through the use of political pressure, had succeeded in enticing the Japanese partner into a European-based manufacturing joint venture to produce a sophisticated electronics product that had, heretofore, been sourced by the European firm from Japan. At the time the joint venture was entered, the European firm established a corporate-wide goal to gain an independent, 'worldclass,' capability to develop and manufacture the particular product. This was seen as part of a broader corporate-wide effort

to master mass manufacturing skills that were viewed as crucial to the firm's participation in a host of electronics businesses. Over the next 7 years, the European firm worked assiduously to internalize the skills of its Japanese partner. By the late 1980s the firm had progressed through six of the seven 'steps' it had identified on the road from dependence to independence—where the journey began with a capability for assembling partner-supplied sub-assemblies using partner-specified equipment and process controls, and ended with a capability for simultaneous advance of both product design and manufacturing disciplines (i.e. design for manufacturability, component miniaturization, materials science, etc), independent of further partner technical assistance.

In interviews with both the European firm and its Japanese partner, it became clear that the bargaining power of the Continental firm had grown as its learning had progressed. For the European firm, each stage of learning, when complete, became the gateway to the next stage of internalization. Successful learning at each stage effectively obsolesced the existing 'bargain,' and constituted a *de facto* query to the Japanese partner: '*Now* what are you going to do for us?' As the firm moved nearer and nearer its goal of independence, it successively raised the 'price' for its continued participation in the alliance. The Japanese partner also learned through the alliance. Managers credited the venture with giving them insight into unique customer needs and the standards-setting environment in Europe. However, the Japanese firm could not easily obsolesce the initial bargain; this due not to any learning deficiency on its part, but to the difficulty of unwinding a politically visible relationship.

The notion of collaboration as a race to learn emerged directly from the interview data. As one Western manager put it:

If they [our partner] learn what we know before we learn what they know, we become redundant. We've got to try to learn faster than they do.

Several Western firms in the study seemed to have discovered that where bargaining power could not be maintained by winning the race to learn, it might be maintained through other means. In a narrow sense managers saw collaboration as a race to learn, but in a broader sense they saw it as a race to remain 'attractive' to their partners. A European manager stated:

> You must continually add to the portfolio of things that make you desirable to your partner. Many of the things that [our partner] needed us for in the early days, it doesn't need now. It needed to establish a base of equipment in Europe and we have done this for them. You must ensure that you always have something to offer your partner—some reason for them to continue to need you.

Managers in a Japanese firm whose European partner had shown a high propensity to learn, believed that ultimate control came from being ahead in the race to create next-generation competencies. Leadership here brought partial control over standards, the benefits of controlling the evolution of technology, and the product price and performance advantages of being first down the experience curve. One senior manager put it succinctly:

> Friendship is friendship, but competition is competition. Competition is about the future and that is R&D.

Here was a suggestion that partners in competitive alliances may sometimes be more likely to view collaboration as a race to get to the future first, rather than a truly cooperative effort to invent the future together. Again, this provided evidence of a subtle blending of competitive and collaborative goals.

The greater the experience of interviewees in administering or working within collaborative arrangements, the more likely were they to discount the extent to which the formal agreement actually determined patterns of learning, control, and dependence within their partnerships. The formal agreement was seen as essentially static, and the race for capability acquisition and control essentially dynamic. As the interviewing progressed it became possible to array the factors which interviewees typically associated with power and control. Power came first from the relative pace at which each partner was building new capabilities internally, then from an ability to out-learn one's partner, then from the relative contribution of 'irreplaceable' inputs by each partner to the venture, then from relative share of value-added, then from the operating structure (which partner's employees held key functional posts), then from the governance structure (which partner was best represented on the board and key executive committees), and finally from the legal structure (share of ownership and legally specified terms for the division of equity and profits). On this basis it was possible, for several of the alliances, to construct a crude 'relative power metric.' For the triadic partnership mentioned above (British, French, and Japanese), relative power was apportioned as per Table 2.

While the legal and managerial power of the British partner was at least equal to that of its counterparts, it failed almost totally to exploit other potential sources of power and control. The British firm's failure to keep pace with its partners in learning and competence-building made its acquisition by one of its partners, or some other ambitious firm, almost inevitable. By way of contrast, the French firm, with no advantage in terms of ownership or executive authority, was able to substantially increase its control of the relationship through a rapid pace of learning. The French firm had substantially increased its R&D budget, hoping eventually to counterbalance its Japanese partner's faster pace of new product development and competence-building. Although the French firm's equity stake remained at 33 percent through most of the 1980s, it continued to enhance its bargaining power by internalizing the skills of its Japanese partner and gaining an ever-increasing share of value-added. From the very different experiences of the British and French firms in this alliance came the proposition that power vested in a particular firm through the formal agreement will almost certainly erode if its partners are more adept at internalization or quicker to build valuable new competencies.

The perspectives on bargaining power and learning which emerged from the case analysis also gave rise to propositions regarding the longevity of rivalrous alliances. In general, it appeared that competitively oriented partners would continue to collaborate together so long as they were: (1) equally capable of inter-partner learning or independent skills development, and/or (2) both substantially smaller, and mutually vulnerable, to industry leaders.

Three broad determinants of learning outcomes emerged during the study and constitute the core of the internalization model. *Intent* refers to a firm's initial propensity to view collaboration as

90   G. Hamel

Table 2.   Relative power of partners in a triadic alliance[1] (ranked by perceived importance as determinants of bargaining power)

	British	French	Japanese
1. Relative pace of competence building[2]		+++	+++++
2. Relative success at inter-partner learning		++++	++
3. Relative criticality of inputs[3]		++	+++
4. Relative share of value-added[4]	+	++	++++
5. 'Possession' of key operating jobs[5]	++	++	+
6. Representation on governing bodies[6]	++	+	+
7. Legal share of ownership[7]	+	+	+

[1] The number of plus signs indicates the relative power within the joint venture that each partner gained from each factor.
[2] Managers in the Japanese partner believed their firm was innovating more rapidly than its European partners in the areas of miniaturization, production engineering, and advanced technologies.
[3] For most of the venture's early history product designs, process equipment, and high-precision components were supplied exclusively by the Japanese partner.
[4] By 1985 European content was approximately 50 percent. The French partner supplied a greater share of the European content than the British partner.
[5] The Managing Directors of the two European plants were Europeans. At each plant a Japanese employee held the Deputy Managing Director's post.
[6] Each partner was responsible for appointing two representatives to the Supervisory Board and one representative to the Management Board. The agreement stipulated that a European was to be President of the Supervisory Board. An executive seconded from the British partner occupied this position.
[7] Each of the three partners held 33.33 percent of the joint venture's equity.

an opportunity to learn; *transparency* to the 'knowability' or openness of each partner, and thus the potential for learning; and *receptivity* to a partner's capacity for learning, or 'absorptiveness.' While there was much a firm could do to implant a learning intent, limit its own transparency, and enhance its receptivity, there seemed to be some inherent determinants of inter-partner learning, more or less exogenous to the partnership itself, that either predisposed a firm to positive learning outcomes, or rendered it unlikely to successfully exploit opportunities to learn. These are outlined in Table 3, and will be discussed below, along with more 'active' determinants or learning outcomes.

Intent as a determinant of learning

The only collaborative intent that was consistent across all firms in the study was *investment avoidance*. In some cases this seemed to be a partner's sole objective. Five of the seven Western firms in the study that had alliances with Japanese partners, had not possessed an internalization intent at the time they entered their Asian alliances. Possessing what came to be called a

substitution intent, these firms seemed satisfied—at least in the beginning—to substitute their partner's competitiveness in a particular skill area for their own lack of competitiveness. Insofar as it could be ascertained, the Japanese counterparts in these alliances seemed to possess explicit learning intents—with one possible exception. This apparent asymmetry in collaborative goals between Western and Japanese partners is deemed significant because in no case did systematic learning take place in the absence of a clearly communicated internalization intent.

In cases where one partner had systematically learned from the other, great efforts had been made to embed a learning intent within operating-level employees. One project manager recalled that at the outset of the alliance his divisional vice president had brought together all those with organization-spanning roles and told them:

> I wish we didn't need this partnership. I wish we knew how to do what our partner knows how to do. But I will be more disappointed if, in three years, we have not learned to do what our partner knows how to do.

In one firm where learning did not take place, the blame was put on a failure to clearly

Table 3.   Inherent determinants of inter-partner learning: A comparison of prototypes

	Factors associated with positive learning outcomes	Factors associated with negative learning outcomes
Strength of internalization intent		
1. Competitive posture *vis-à-vis* partner	Co-option now, confrontation later	Collaboration instead of competition
2. Relative resource position versus corporate ambitions	Scarcity	Abundance
3. Perceived pay-off—capacity to exploit skills in multiple businesses	High; alliance entered to build corporate-wide core competencies	Low; alliance entered to 'fix' problems in a single business
4. Perspective on power	Balance of power begets instability	Balance of power begets stability
Transparency (organizational)		
5. Social context	Language and customs constitute a barrier	Language and customs not a barrier
6. Attitude towards outsiders	The clan as an ideal: exclusivity	The 'melting pot' as ideal: inclusivity
Transparency (skills)		
7. Extent to which skills are context-dependent	Skills comprise tacit knowledge embedded within social systems	Skills comprise explicit knowledge held by a few 'experts'
8. Relative pace of skills enhancement	Fast	Slow
Preconditions for receptivity		
9. Sense of confidence	Neither under-confidence nor over-confidence in its own capabilities	Either under-confidence or over-confidence in its own capabilities
10. Need to first unlearn	As a newcomer, little that must be forgotten before learning can begin	As a laggard, much that must be unlearned before new skills drive out old
11. Size of skills gap with industry leaders	Small	Substantial
12. Institutional vs. individual learning	Capacity for 'summing up' and transferring individual learning	Fragmentation (vertical and horizontal) frustrates learning

communicate learning objectives to those with inter-organizational roles:

> Our engineers were just as good as [our partner's]. In fact, their's were narrower technically, but they had a much better understanding of what the company was trying to accomplish. They knew they were there to learn; our people didn't.

A manager in a company with a record of successful learning from partners described what had been done to embed a learning intent:

> We wanted to make learning an automatic discipline. We asked the staff every day, 'What did you learn from [our partner] today?' Learning was carefully monitored and recorded.

While several Western firms had adopted defensive learning intents, as they came to understand the internalization goals of their Japanese partners, none of these firms could demonstrate that systematic learning had taken place. That the alliance could be a laboratory for learning seemed to be a difficult message to convey, once the alliance had become widely viewed as simply an alternative to internal efforts, as one manager commented:

> When the deal was put together some of us were skeptical, but we were told this was the wave of the future and we'd have to learn to rely on [our partner]. So we relied on them; boy, did we rely on them. Now we're hearing [from senior management] that we shouldn't rely on them *too* much; we have to keep some kind of 'shadow' capability internally. Well, I think we've gotten this message a bit late. Letting [our partner] do the tough stuff has become second nature to us.

To summarize the argument thus far, learning took place by design rather than by default, and skill substitution or surrender by default in the absence of design. In situations where there was a marked asymmetry in intent, the migration of skills between partners could not be accurately characterized as merely 'leakage' (Harrigan, 1986). The competitive consequences of skills transfers, as well as the actual migration of skills, was often unintended, unanticipated, and unwanted by at least one of the partners. This seems to be the fate that befell Varian Associates, a U.S. producer of advanced electronics including semiconductors. Reflecting on its joint venture with NEC, one of Varian's senior executives concluded that 'all NEC had wanted to do was to suck out Varian's technology, not sell Varian's equipment' (Goldenberg, 1988: 85).

What factors might account for observed differences in intent? Whether or not a firm possessed an explicit internalization intent seemed to be a product of: (1) whether it viewed collaboration as a more or less permanent alternative to competition or as a temporary vehicle for improving its competitiveness *vis-à-vis* its partner; (2) its relative resource position *vis-à-vis* its partner and other industry participants; (3) its calculation of the pay-off to learning; and (4) its preference for balanced vs. asymmetric dependence within the alliance. Taking these proposed determinants in turn, it was mentioned earlier that several partners had developed defensive internalization intents upon discovering the learning goals of their partners. The majority of Western firms in the study appeared to have initially projected their own substitution intents onto their partners. These firms tended to describe the logic of their collaborative ventures in terms of 'role specialization,' 'complementarity,'

'centers of excellence,' and so on. Such descriptors evinced a view of collaboration as a stable division of roles based on the unique skill endowments of each partner, rather than as a potentially low-cost route to replicating partner skills and erasing initial dependencies.

With one exception, those Western partners that had lacked an initial internalization intent had all been substantially larger than their Japanese partners at the time their alliances were formed. The assumption seemed to be that relative size was a good proxy for relative skill levels. A U.S. manager summarized the attitude that had prevailed a decade earlier when the firm entered its first major Japanese alliance: 'We invented the industry. What could we possibly learn from an up-start in Japan?' An executive in their Japanese partner reflected on difference in the two partner's attitudes toward learning:

> When we saw [our larger Western partner] doing something better, we always wanted to know why. But when they come to look at what we are doing, they say, 'Oh, you can do that because you are Japanese,' or they find some other reason. They make an explanation so they don't have to understand [what we are doing differently].

An abundance of resources, and a legacy of industry leadership, whether real or perceived, made it difficult for a firm to admit to itself that it had something to learn from a smaller partner.

The intent to learn also appeared to be a function of the firm's calculation about the pay-off to learning. In those firms where the internalization intent was strongest and most deeply felt, the skills to be acquired from the partner were seen as critical to the growth of the entire company, and not just the competitiveness of a single product or business. This was in contrast to firms where competitiveness was defined solely in end-product terms, and where top management had no explicit plans for building corporate-wide skills. Here alliances were viewed as short cuts to a more competitive product line (by relying on a partner for critical components or perhaps entire products), rather than as short cuts to the internalization of skills that could be applied across a range of businesses. Without clear corporate goals for competence building, and a deep appreciation for the critical contribution of core competence leadership to long-term competitiveness, individual businesses appeared unlikely to devote resources to the task of learning.

The perceived pay-off to learning was also influenced, in some cases, by a partner's calculation of the cost of continued dependence. Managers in the study identified a range of potential costs that could be associated with dependency in a core skill area: an inability to thwart a partner intent on entering the firm's prime markets; or the obverse—being constrained from entering an emerging market, or having one's entry slowed by a powerful partner; the risk of being 'stranded' by a collaborator who pre-emptively ended the relationship; or being disadvantaged when the financial terms of the agreement are re-negotiated. Japanese partners, in particular, seemed to view strategic alliances as second-best options. A group of managers interviewed in one firm expressed an opinion, quite vehemently, that their company would never accept a situation in which it was, over the long term, dependent on a Western partner for an important aspect of its product-based competitiveness—this despite the fact that several of that firm's foreign partners were in just such a dependency position. Not surprisingly, this firm possessed a strong internalization intent.

There may be a reason why Japanese firms, in particular, seemed adverse to the very notion of symmetrical dependency between partners. Nakane (1970) has shown that social organization in Japan is based on the notion of dependence. The parent–child analogy is applied to the government and its public, employers and employees, managers and subordinates, and large firms and their suppliers. In this view a 'balance of power' brings indeterminateness and instability to a relationship, while a clearly disproportionate allocation of power, that is, dependence, brings cohesion and consistency. The preference of Japanese managers for unequivocable decision-making power in foreign subsidiaries and joint ventures has been well documented (Ballon, 1979; Ouchi and Johnson, 1974). Indeed, when asked to consider a hypothetical American–Japanese joint venture located in the U.S., Japanese managers felt that future trust would be highest if Japanese, rather than American, managers occupied the most powerful positions, and if Japanese managers, rather than Americans,

had responsibility for initiating key decision processes such as capital budgeting (Sullivan and Peterson, 1982).

It seems unlikely that many Japanese managers would disagree with Harrigan's (1986: 148) assertion that:

> Managers can be as crafty as they please in writing clauses to protect their firm's technology rights, but the joint venture's success depends on trust.

But when Japanese managers list 'trust' as one of the most important conditions for a successful joint venture (Block and Matsumoto, 1972), they may be speaking not of the trust that comes from what Buckley and Casson (1988) term 'mutual forbearance,' but from unequivocal dependence. If knowledge is power, and power the father of dependence, one can expect Japanese firms to strive to learn from their partners.

Transparency as a determinant of learning

Whereas intent established the desire to learn, transparency determined the potential for learning. Some partners were, for a variety of reasons, more transparent—more open and accessible—than others. Of course, every partner intended to share some skills with its opposite number. Even in firms with an inherently 'protective' stance *vis-à-vis* their partner, some degree of openness was accepted as the price for enticing the partner into the relationship and successfully executing joint tasks. Yet many managers drew a distinction between what might be termed 'transparency by design,' and 'transparency by default.' The concerns managers expressed were over unintended and unanticipated transfers.

Such concerns arose in cases where managers believed their partner's learning had gone far beyond what was deemed essential for the successful performance of joint tasks, to encompass what was necessary to internalize skills. A partner's learning could be both more intensive than foreseen in the formal agreement, and more extensive. The greatest sense of 'unfairness,' and the greatest sense of failure in managing transparency, was observed in those firms where a partner's learning had extended to skill areas that were not explicitly part of the formal agreement. This often seemed to be the cases in OEM sourcing arrangement where an up-stream partner had used the alliance to gain insights into customer needs and market structure. A European-based manager described the process thus:

> Anytime we demanded unique features for the European market [in a product sourced from Japan, our Japanese partner] wanted a complete justification for each item. They wanted to understand why we wanted certain product features, competitors' product information, customer perceptions, all the market-based things. You can get fifteen years of accumulated wisdom across the table in two hours.

Broadly, there appeared to be at least five inherent, *ex ante* determinants of transparency: (1) the penetrability of the social context which surrounded the partner; (2) attitudes towards outsiders, i.e. clannishness; (3) the extent to which the partner's distinctive skills were encodable and discrete; and (4) the partner's relative pace of skill-building.

While this exploratory study cannot provide an answer to the question, 'Are Japanese partners inherently less transparent than their Western counterparts?' what can be said is that nearly all the Western partners in the study believed this to be the case. The study suggested that there were indeed systematic, though not irreversible, asymmetries in transparency between Western and Japanese partners. Typical was the comment of one Western manager:

> Despite the fact that we were [in Japan] for training, I always felt we were revealing more information about us than [our Japanese partners] were about themselves.

Interestingly, no Japanese manager expressed an opinion that Western partners might be inherently less transparent than Japanese partners. Peterson and Schwind (1977) found similar evidence of asymmetry in transparency between Japanese and Western alliance partners. In their study of international joint ventures located in Japan, 'communication' was the problem mentioned most often by both expatriate and Japanese managers. However, for expatriate managers 'difficulty in receiving exact information and data' from their Japanese partners ranked a close second, mentioned by 87 percent of U.S.

expatriate respondents. The next most noted problems, 'reluctance to report failures,' and 'no open discussion of problems,' further reflect the frustration these managers felt in extracting information from their Japanese partners. However, no Japanese manager mentioned access to information as a major annoyance in dealing with Western partners.

It seems plausible to propose that this asymmetry in perceptions of relative opaqueness rests at least in part on the extent to which a firm's knowledge base is context-bound (Terpstra and David, 1985). Contextuality refers to the 'embeddedness' of information in social systems. In general, knowledge in Oriental cultures is more contextual than information in Occidental cultures (Benedict, 1946). Form and content, ritual and substance cannot easily be disentangled. Context dependent knowledge (for example, principles of industrial relations in Japan) is inherently less transparent than context-free knowledge (e.g. the principles of the transistor).

Japanese employees working within Western partners seemed to more easily gain acceptance by peers, and more quickly become insiders than was the case in reverse. For example a divisional vice president managing a joint European–Japanese design effort within Europe remarked that:

> we were conscious of [our partner's employees] on-site and did try to keep information exchange on a need-to-know basis. However, after a while, they ceased to be different. We played badminton together, we went to the same parties and restaurants. They became close friends.

While several Western managers, with employees working in Japanese-based alliances, expressed concerns over the fact that their staff might 'go native,' no Japanese manager expressed such concern in the reverse case. Several managers both Western and Japanese, expressed the opinion that the 'openness' of Western culture and organizational contexts facilitated the assimilation of partner employees, while the sense of 'clan' possessed by Japanese staff made them sensitive to the risk of revealing competitively useful information to a partner. The same European manager who commented on the easy social integration of Japanese team members also recalled that:

Once the contract was signed, [the Japanese partner] had a view of what we needed to know to complete the project. They were totally open in this regard, but totally closed on all other issues. They had well-defined limits in terms of what they would tell us. The junior guys would tell us nothing unless a senior person was there.

The point here is not that Japanese organizations are clannish. That point has been made before (Ouchi, 1980). Instead, it is that where clannishness is high, opportunities for access will be limited, and transparency low. As a member of a clan, an employee involved in a partnership can be expected to retain a sense of identity with, and loyalty to, the parent. When conflicts arise which reflect an incongruity between parent and partner goals, a clan member will search for solutions consistent with the parent's goals.

An asymmetry in language skills often exacerbated inherent constraints on transparency such as clannishness and complexity. That operating employees in Western firms almost universally lacked Japanese language skills and cultural experience in Japan served to limit the transparency of their Asian hosts. One engineer from a European company recalled his frustration in working with a partner in Japan:

Whenever I made a presentation [to our partner] I was one person against ten to twelve. They'd put me in front of a flip chart, then stop me while they went into a conversation in Japanese for ten minutes. If I asked them a question they would break into Japanese to first decide what I wanted to know, and then would discuss options in terms of what they might tell me, and finally would come back with an answer.

Not only did it appear that some organizations were more penetrable than others, it appeared that some types of knowledge were inherently more deeply buried in the social context of the firm than others. Explicit knowledge was more encodable than tacit knowledge—it could be transferred in engineering drawings, extracted from patent filings, etc., and discrete knowledge was more easily extracted from a partner than systemic knowledge. In general, it appeared that specific technologies (e.g. a microprocessor chip design), were more transparent than deep-seated competencies (e.g. value-engineering skills), and that market intelligence flowed more easily than knowledge of leading edge manufacturing know-

how. Thus an asymmetry in the nature of the skills contributed by each partner to the venture could, *ceteris paribus*, preordain asymmetric learning. In partnerships where one firm brought product designs and market experience to the table, and the other (typically Japanese) manufacturing competence, the partner contributing production skills seemed to benefit from an inherently lower level of transparency. For while it did not appear that a firm could transfer product designs to its partner without revealing, perhaps inadvertently, a great deal of implicit market information, it was possible for the producing partner to ship back finished products without revealing much of what comprised its manufacturing competence.

The pace of a firm's innovation also seemed to determine its transparency to its partner. In some cases one partner's speed of innovation out-ran the other's pace of absorption. One fast-moving partner believed it could afford to be very open in terms of access, and yet remain essentially opaque, given its rapid pace of product development. Managers in this Japanese firm believed that their rate of new product introduction was between four and five times faster than that of their partner. Despite their partner's avowed learning intent, managers in this firm felt relatively unconcerned:

We are very convinced that our R&D speed is faster than [our partner's]. This is our ultimate protection [against partner encroachment].

The researcher was reminded of the old adage about the difficulty of drinking from a fire hose.

Partners employed a wide variety of active measures to limit transparency. In one firm, all partner requests for information and access were processed through a small 'collaboration department.' Staff from this department attended virtually all meetings between managers and staff of the two partners. In this way they were able to control the 'aperture' through which the partner gained access to people and facilities. Out of this case grew the notion of a 'gatekeeping' role: one or more individuals charged with monitoring knowledge flows across the collaborative membrane.

Another determinant of relative transparency position appeared to be the number of people from each partner seconded to the other, or, more generally, the extent to which the nature of joint tasks required regular and intensive intermingling of staff from the two partners. At one extreme was the task of jointly designing a car, where the need to mate together powertrain, body, and suspension required intensive cross-membrane interaction, and made both partners highly transparent to each other. At the other extreme was the much simpler task of specifying single 'plug-in' components to be supplied by a partner.

Firms in the study also sought to limit their transparency to ambitious partners by restricting the collaborative agreement to a narrow range of products or markets. One manager argued that:

> If you source the *entire* product in, there is a lot greater transfer of design skills—your partner gets to see everything. What you should do is design components, source from multiple places, and then do integration and manufacturing yourself.

Another firm saw site selection and control as key issues in limiting transparency:

> It helps to have a joint company in a third location; this helps to protect you. You don't let your partner do joint work on your site. And if you have a third site you can decide what you put in and what you don't.

Given the fact that the process of collaborative exchange took place not at senior management levels, but at operating levels, the management of transparency depended, ultimately, on the ability and willingness of operators to sometimes say 'no' to a partner's requests for information or access. The extent to which operating employees had an explicit sense of the need to protect information from bleeding through to a partner varied widely across the sample firms. One project manager was surprised by how close-mouthed his partner's engineers were:

> Everyone I met within [our partner] seemed to operate with well-defined limits on what they would tell us. Their engineers were very guarded with technical details. Sometimes I had to appeal to higher level managers to get information critical to the project's success.

In one firm senior managers explicitly recognized the tensions that could arise when operating

employees were asked to work in a collegial way to make the alliance a success, and at the same time had a responsibility for limiting the partner's access to core skills. One way out of this dilemma was to give operators the right to escalate partner requests for information.

It appeared that firms which could rely on passive or 'natural' barriers to transparency had an inherent advantage over partners that could not. This was not only because natural barriers to transparency seemed to be the most difficult to overcome, but also because active measures were sometimes regarded by partners as provocative. When U.S. firms have relied on contractual clauses and other active means to limit transparency, they have often been accused of acting in bad faith, or undermining trust (Ballon, 1979). To the extent that passive barriers can substitute for active measures, a partner may be able to claim for itself the high ground of trust and openness, and yet still benefit from almost unassailable barriers to partner encroachment.

Receptivity as a determinant of learning

If intent establishes the desire to learn, and transparency the opportunity, receptivity determines the capacity to learn. Just as there were active and passive determinants of transparency, so there were of receptivity. In several cases, when questioned as to why they had apparently learned more than their Western partners Japanese managers answered, in essence, 'We had the attitude of students, and our Western partners the attitude of teachers.' Ballon would no doubt accept such a generalization:

> When looking at the West from outside the Western Hemisphere, one attitude stands out. It is just how anxious Americans and Europeans are to *teach* the rest of the world (1979: 27).

Humility may be the first prerequisite for learning. However, the distinction between teachers and students rested on more than just cultural stereotypes.

Generating an enthusiasm for learning, that is an attitude of receptivity, among operating employees seemed to depend largely on whether the firm entered the alliance as a *late-comer*, or as a *laggard*; i.e. whether the alliance was seen by the majority of employees as a proactive choice to support ambitious growth goals (the perspective of late-comers), or as an easy 'way out' of a deteriorating competitive situation (the perspective of laggards). Where a firm had become a laggard, and had come to think of itself as such, middle-level managers and operators appeared more likely to adopt an acquiescent attitude towards dependency and learning opportunities. While they sometimes saw learning as a laudable goal, they possessed little enthusiasm for the task. Perhaps not surprisingly, in firms that had struggled to maintain their competitiveness in a particular product/market, and had failed, alliances tended to be seen by operating-level employees as confirmation of their failure, and not as a means to rebuild skills. A sense of resignation was not conducive to receptivity.

The stigma of failure did not attach itself to firms using alliances to build skills in new areas, i.e. closing skills 'gaps' as opposed to compensating for a skills failure. The European partner mentioned earlier could not have claimed to possess world-class manufacturer skills at the time it entered its alliance with a Japanese partner. Yet it had succeeded, through its own efforts, in dramatically improving the productivity of its color television manufacturing in the 5 years preceding the joint venture, and had come close to Japanese productivity levels. It had also doubled its share of the European color television market in the decade preceding the alliance. Thus it was not difficult for employees to regard the partnership as a multiplier, rather than as a substitute, for internal efforts.

Organization learning theory suggests that laggards may confront two cruel paradoxes. First, learning often cannot begin until unlearning has taken place (Burgleman, 1983b; Hedberg, 1981; Nystrom and Starbuck, 1984). This is particularly true where the behaviors that contributed to past success have been deeply etched in the organization's consciousness. The problem of unlearning is not only a cognitive problem—altering perceptual maps—but a problem of driving out old behavior with new behavior. The link between changed cognition and changed behavior is probably more direct in individuals (Postman and Underwood, 1973; Watzlawick, Weakland and Fisch, 1974) than it is in large multinational companies (Prahalad and Doz, 1987). Current patterns of behavior in large organizations are typically 'hard-wired' in struc-

ture, in information systems, incentive schemes, hiring and promotion practices, and so on (Argyris and Schon, 1978). The implication here is that unlearning will be a significant hurdle for a laggard attempting to compensate for past skill failure. For a late-comer using an alliance to build skills in a new area, unlearning is not a prerequisite. Receptivity will not be impaired by employees clinging to past practices.

Second, while a reduction in organizational slack typically precipitates the search for new knowledge (Cyert and March, 1963), the complete absence of slack just as surely frustrates learning (Burgelman, 1983a). Some slack is necessary if the organization is to search for new approaches, experiment with new methods, and embed new capabilities. Learning is a luxury which can be afforded by those with some minimum complement of time and resources. A small crisis abets learning, a big crisis limits learning. Of course it has been argued that collaboration may be a timely and low-cost mechanism for acquiring new skills. But even here, as learning progresses from knowledge-gathering to capability-building, investment needs escalate. A firm may understand how its partner achieves a certain level of performance, but not have the resources needed to embed that understanding through staff development and investment in new facilities. Again, the results of the study support the contention that learning is most likely to occur in the middle ground between abundance and arrogance on one side, and deprivation and resignation on the other.

To these two paradoxes may be added a third: the greater the need to learn, i.e. the farther one partner is behind its counterpart, the higher the barriers to receptivity. Simply put, to replicate the skills of a partner, a firm must be able to identify, if not retrace, the intermediate learning 'steps' between its present competence level and that of its partner. After visiting the most advanced manufacturing facility of a Japanese partner, a manager in one Western firm remarked:

> It's no good for us to simply observe where they are today, what we have to find out is how they got from where we are to where they are. We need to experiment and learn with intermediate technologies before duplicating what they've done.

If the skills gap between partners is too great, learning becomes almost impossible.

The notion of receptivity was seen to apply to the corporate body, as well as to individual receptors. Individual learning became collective learning when (1) there existed a mechanism for 'summing up' individual learning, i.e. first recording and then integrating the fragmentary knowledge gained by individuals, and (2) learning was transferred across unit boundaries to all those who could benefit in some way from what had been learned. It was evident in the study that firms with a history of cross-functional teamwork and inter-business coordination were more likely to turn personal learning into corporate learning than were firms where the emphasis was on 'individual contributors' and 'independent business units.' A senior manager in a Japanese partner commented on the internal relationships that had aided its learning, and hindered, it believed, its partner's learning:

> Within [my firm] there is a great deal of mutual responsibility. Responsibility is a very grey area in Japan; many people are involved. There is much more overlap in responsibility than in [our Western partner] where information seems to be compartmentalized. [Our partner] thought we asked too many questions, but in [my company] information is shared with many people even if they are not directly involved. Engineers in [one department] want to know what is happening in design [in another department] even if that is not related to their direct responsibilities.

On the other side of the relationship a Western manager offered a similar perspective:

> [In joint meetings, staff] groups [from our Japanese partner] would almost always be multi-disciplinary, even for technical discussions. [They] clearly wanted to understand the implications of our technology. You had the feeling that most of the [their] people who were sitting in the [joint] meetings were there only to learn. We would have never taken anyone into such a meeting without a direct interest in what was being discussed.

In terms of active determinants, receptivity depended upon, above all else, the diligence with which those with greatest access to the partner approached the task of learning. One firm in particular appeared to conceive of inter-partner learning as a rigorous discipline. This firm's success in internalizing partner skills suggests that such a conception may be a prerequisite for systematic learning. A senior executive in the company described its 'inch-by-inch' efforts to learn from its partner:

> You need to be incredibly patient, but eventually you would get what you wanted. In the event of the slightest breakdown, you had to ask [our partner], 'What now?' We acquired the know-how very slowly in this way, by finding out all the little mistakes [we were making], by repeatedly asking questions, and by forcing them, little by little, to yield technical information.

In this case receptivity seemed to thrive as long as top management continued to express an active interest in what was being learned. Top management's commitment to learning was exhibited first through a clear intent to establish a world-class consumer electronics manufacturing competence, secondly through the hiring of a wholly new executive group, and thirdly through a constant stream of investment to build up a physical plant as closely parallel to that of the partner as possible. Given initial estimates that it would take between 3 and 5 years for the firm to 'catch up' with its Japanese partner, top management believed its unwavering enthusiasm for, and attention to, the partnership was critical to a positive learning outcome. Internalizing new skills via an alliance would seem to require a reasonably long attention span on the part of top management.

The personal skills of receptors also influenced receptivity. The European partner referred to above had assembled a collaborative team with the necessary skills to observe, interpret, apply, and improve upon partner skills. One member of the team came from the watch-making industry, and others from successful precision-engineering firms. The average age of team members was estimated to be 35 years. The relatively young age of the team, and the fact that few were tainted with the burden of past failure, reduced the need for 'unlearning.' The team also benefited from a liberal training budget. For this company it was not enough to embed, through goal setting and daily reinforcement, a learning discipline, receptors had to be competent to receive. This meant that their skills had to parallel, as closely as possible, those from whom they were learning.

Determinants of sustainable learning

Whether a skills gap closed through inter-partner learning later re-opened seemed to depend on several factors, all of which can be summarized under the general heading of a *capacity for self-sustaining learning*. The critical point here is that intercepting a partner's skills at a point in time appeared to be a lesser challenge than matching a partner's underlying rate of improvement over time. To break free of dependence a firm had, first, to match its pace of absorption to its partner's pace of innovation, and then to equal or better its partner's capability for autonomously and continuously improving those skills. NEC, when it formed its alliance with Honeywell in the earlier 1960s, was much smaller than its partner. Nonetheless, NEC ultimately reversed its initial dependency. Those few firms in the study that were committed to turning the tables of dependency appeared to agree that matching a partner's pace of autonomous improvement depended on: (1) capturing know-why as well as know-what from their partners, (2) mastering the disciplines of continuous improvement, and (3) achieving global scale.

Two firms in the study recognized that, as long as they operated at regional scale, they could not fully apply the lessons learned from partners operating at global scale. Both firms made large international acquisitions with the express goal of amortizing investment in world-scale facilities that paralleled those of their partners. Both firms found that as their learning agendas shifted from technology to competence, from discrete skills to systemic skills, and from know-how to know-why, their pace of learning had slowed. It was clear to both partners that building a foundation for autonomous improvement demanded insight into the underlying dynamic which drove their partner's pace of innovation. Again, this was a substantial challenge, particularly for Western firms, as at least some of the impetus behind the innovative pace of their Japanese counterparts appeared to be culturally idiosyncratic (Baba, 1989; Imai, 1986; Itami, 1987).

DISCUSSION

Though this research grew out of an interest in skills-based competition (Nelson and Winter, 1982; Dierickx and Cool, 1989; Quinn, Doorley and Paquette, 1990; Prahalad and Hamel, 1990; Barney, 1990; Teece, Pisano and Shuen, 1990), it is also important to set it within the context of existing research on the management of

strategic alliances. The way in which the present study both complements and challenges prior research on collaboration is now discussed.

Collaboration as a transitional stage

Joint ventures and other non-market inter-firm agreements have typically been pictured as an intermediate level of integration between arm's-length contracts in open markets and full ownership (Nielsen, 1988; Thorelji, 1986). But where the goal of the alliance is skills acquisition, an alliance may be seen, by one or both partners, not as an optimal compromise between market and hierarchy, to use Williamson's (1975) nomenclature, but as a half-way house on the road from market to hierarchy. In this sense the alliance is viewed not as an alternative to market-based transactions or full ownership, but as an alternative to other modes of skill acquisition. These might include acquiring the partner, licensing from the partner, or developing the needed skills through internal efforts. There are several reasons collaboration may in some cases be the preferred mode of skills acquisition.

For some skills, what Itami (1987) terms 'invisible assets,' the cost of internal development may be almost infinite. Complex skills, based on tacit knowledge, and arising out of a unique cultural context may be acquirable only by up-close observation and emulation of 'best in class.' Alliances may offer advantages of timeliness as well as efficiency. Where global competitors are rapidly building new sources of competitive advantage, as well as enhancing existing skills, a go-it-alone strategy could confine a firm to permanent also-ran status. Alliances may be seen as a way of short-circuiting the process of skills acquisition and thus avoiding the opportunity cost of being a perpetual follower. Motorola's reliance on Toshiba for re-entry to the DRAM semiconductor business seems to reflect such a concern. Internalization via collaboration may be more attractive than acquiring a firm in total. In buying a company the acquirer must pay for non-distinctive assets, and is confronted with a substantially larger organizational integration problem.

Capturing value vs. creating value

There are two basic processes in any alliance: *value creation* and *value appropriation*. The extent of value creation depends first on whether the market and competitive logic of the venture is sound, and then on the efficacy with which the two partners combine their complementary skills and resources; that is, how well they perform joint tasks. Each partner then appropriates value in the form of monetary or other benefits. In general, researchers have given more attention to the process of value creation than the process of value appropriation. The primary concern of both the transactions cost (Hennart, 1988) and strategic position (e.g. Harrigan, 1985) perspectives is the creation of joint value. Transactional efficiency gained through quasi-internalization is one form of value creation; improvement in competitive position is another. Both perspectives provide insights into why firms collaborate; neither captures the dynamics which determine collaborative outcomes, and the individual monetary and long-term competitive gains taken by each partner. Making a collaborative agreement 'work' has generally been seen as creating the preconditions for value creation (Doz, 1988; Killing, 1982, 1983). There is much advice on how to be a 'good' partner (Goldenberg, 1988; Perlmutter and Heenan, 1986)—firms are typically urged to build 'trust' (Harrigan, 1986; Peterson and Shimada, 1978)—but little advice on how to reap the benefits of being a good partner.

There appear to be two mechanisms for extracting value from an alliance: bargaining over the stream of economic benefits that issues directly from the successful execution of joint tasks, and internalizing the skills of partners. These 'value pools' may be conceptually distinct, but they were shown to be related in an important way. Bargaining power at any point in time within an alliance is, *ceteris paribus*, a function of who needs whom the most. This, in turn, is a function of the perceived strategic importance of the alliance to each partner and the attractiveness to each partner of alternatives to collaboration. Depending on its bargaining power a partner will gain a greater or lesser share of the fruits of joint effort. An important issue then is what factors prompt changes in bargaining power. Some factors will be exogenous to the partnership. A change in strategic priorities may suddenly make a partnership much more or much less vital for one of the partners (Franko, 1971). Likewise, a shift in the market or competitive environment

could devalue the contribution of one partner and revalue the contribution of the other. Rapid change in technology might produce a similar effect (Harrigan, 1985). However, there is one determinant of relative bargaining power that is very much within the firm's control: its capacity to learn.

While Westney (1988) and Kogut (1988) recognize that learning may be an explicit goal in an alliance, they do not specify the critical linkages between learning, dependency, and bargaining power. Conversely, while Pfeffer and Nowak (1976) and Blois (1980) correctly view alliances as mechanisms for managing inter-organizational dependence, they do not take a dynamic view of interdependence, and hence miss the linkage between learning and changes in relative dependency. If bargaining power is a function of relative dependence it should be possible to lessen dependency and improve bargaining power by out-learning one's partner. Most bargains obsolesce with time (Kobrin, 1986); by actively working to internalize a partner's skills it should be possible to accelerate the rate at which the bargain obsolesces. This seems to have been the motivation for Boeing's Japanese partners in recent years (Moxon, 1988). It was clearly the motivation of two of the Japanese partners in the study.

The process of collaborative exchange

Researchers have tended to look at venture and task structure when attempting to account for partnership performance. An equally useful perspective might be that of a *collaborative membrane*, through which flow skills and capabilities between the partners. The extent to which the membrane is permeable, and in which direction(s) it is permeable determines relative learning. Though researchers and practitioners often seem to be preoccupied with issues of structure—legal, governance and task (Harrigan, 1988; Killing, 1983; Schillaci, 1987; Tybejee, 1988) the study suggests that these may be only partial determinants of permeability. Conceiving of an alliance as a membrane suggests that access to people, facilities, documents, and other forms of knowledge is traded between partners in an on-going process of *collaborative exchange*. As operating employees interact day-by-day, and continually process partner requests for access,

Table 4. Distinctive attributes of a theory of competitive collaboration

	Traditional perspective	Alternative perspective
Collaborative logic	Quasi-internalization	*De-facto* internalization
Unit of analysis	Joint outcomes	Individual outcomes
Underlying process	Value creation	Value appropriation
Success determinants	Form and structure (macro-bargain)	Collaborative exchange (micro-bargains)
Success metrics	Satisfaction and longevity	Bargaining power and competitiveness

a series of *micro-bargains* are reached on the basis of considerations of operational effectiveness, fairness, and bargaining power. Though these bargains may be more implicit than explicit, out-learning a partner means 'winning' a series of *micro-bargains*. The simple hypothesis is that the terms of trade in any particular micro-bargain may be only partially determined by the terms of trade which prevailed at the time the macro-bargain was struck by corporate officers. A firm may be in a weak bargaining position at the macro level, as NEC undoubtedly was when it entered its alliance with Honeywell in the computer business in the early 1960s, but may be able to strike a series of advantageous micro-bargains if, at the operational level, it uniquely possesses the capacity to learn. Restating the bargaining power argument advanced earlier, the cumulative impact of micro-bargains will, to a large extent, determine in whose favor future macro-bargains are resolved.

Success metrics

Where internalization is the goal, the longevity and 'stability' of partnerships may not be useful proxies for collaborative success. Nevertheless, they have often been used as such (Beamish, 1984; Franko, 1971; Gomes-Casseres, 1987; Killing, 1983; Reynolds, 1979). A long-lived alliance may evince the failure of one or both partners to learn. It was interesting to note in the study that, despite collaborative agreements in Japan with Japanese firms spanning several decades, several Western partners were still unable to 'go it alone' in the Japanese market. By way of contrast, there were few cases in

which Japanese firms had remained dependent on Western partners for continued access to Western markets (though in one case the Japanese partner ultimately acquired its European partner). Likewise, an absence of contention in the relationship is not, by itself, an adequate success metric. A firm with no ambition beyond investment avoidance and substitution of its partner's competitiveness for its own lack of competitiveness may be perfectly content not to learn from its partner. But where a failure to learn is likely to ultimately undermine the competitiveness and independence of the firm, such contentedness should not be taken as a sign of collaborative success. The theoretical perspective on collaboration developed in this paper is summarized in Table 4.

ACKNOWLEDGEMENT

The author would like to thank the Gatsby Charitable Foundation for funding the research on which this article is based. In addition, thanks are due the two referees for their constructive suggestions.

REFERENCES

Argyris, C. and D. A. Schon. *Organizational Learning*, Addison-Wesley, Reading, MA, 1978.
Baba, Y. 'The dynamics of continuous innovation in scale-intensive industries,' *Strategic Management Journal*, **10**, 1989, pp. 89–100.
Ballon, R. J. 'A lesson from Japan: Contract, control, and authority,' *Journal of Contemporary Business*, **8**(2), 1979, pp. 27–35.

Barney, J. B. 'Firm resources and sustained competitive advantage.' Unpublished manuscript, Department of Management, Texas A&M University, 1990.

Beamish, P. W. 'Joint venture performance in developing countries.' Unpublished doctoral dissertation, University of Western Ontario, 1984.

Benedict, R. *The Chrysanthemum and the Sword*, reprint (1974), New American Library, New York, 1946.

Block, A. and H. Matsumoto. 'Joint venturing in Japan.' *Conference Board Record*, April 1972, pp. 32-36.

Blois, K. J. 'Quasi-integration as a mechanism for controlling external dependencies,' *Management Decision*, 18(1), 1980, pp. 55-63.

Buckley, P. J. and M. Casson. *Economic Theory of the Multinational Enterprise: Selected Papers*, Macmillan, London, 1985.

Buckley, P. J. and M. Casson. 'A theory of cooperation in international business.' In F. J. Contractor and P. Lorange (eds), *Cooperative Strategies in International Business*, D.C. Heath, Lexington, MA, 1988, pp. 31-53.

Burgelman, R. A. 'A model of the interaction of strategic behavior, corporate context and the concept of strategy,' *Academy of Management Review*, 8(1), 1983a, pp. 61-70.

Burgelman, R. A. 'A process model of internal corporate venturing in the diversified major firm,' *Administrative Science Quarterly*, 28(2), 1983b, pp. 223-244.

Business Week. 'When U.S. joint ventures with Japan go sour,' 24 July 1989, pp. 14-16.

Caves, R. E. 'International corporations: The industrial economics of foreign investment,' *Economica*, February 1971, pp. 1-27.

Contractor, F. J. and P. Lorange. 'Why should firms cooperate: The strategy and economic basis for cooperative ventures.' In F. J. Contractor and P. Lorange (eds), *Cooperative Strategies in International Business*, D.C. Heath, Lexington, MA, 1988, pp. 3-28.

Cyert, R. M. and J. G. March. *A Behavioral Theory of the Firm*. Prentice-Hall, Englewood Cliffs, NJ, 1963.

Dierickx, I. and K. Cool. 'Asset stock accumulation and sustainability of competitive advantage,' *Management Science*, December 1989, pp. 1504-1514.

Doz, Y. 'Technology partnerships between larger and smaller firms: Some critical issues.' In F. J. Contractor and P. Lorange (eds), *Cooperative Strategies in International Business*, D.C. Heath, Lexington, MA, 1988, pp. 317-328.

Franko, L. G. *Joint Venture Survival in Multinational Corporations*, Praeger, New York, 1971.

Ghemawat, P., M. E. Porter and R. A. Rawlinson. 'Patterns of international coalition activity.' In M. E. Porter (ed.), *Competition in Global Industries*, Harvard University Press, Boston, MA, 1986, pp. 345-365.

Glaser, B. G. and A. L. Strauss. *The Discovery of Grounded Theory: Strategies for Qualitative Research*. Aldine, New York, 1967.

Goldenberg, S. *International Joint Ventures in Action: How to Establish, Manage and Profit from International Strategic Alliances*, Hutchinson Business Books, London, 1988.

Gomes-Casseres, B. 'Joint venture instability: Is it a problem,' *Columbia Journal of World Business*, Summer 1987, pp. 97-102.

Hamel, G. 'Competitive collaboration: Learning, power and dependence in international strategic alliances.' Unpublished doctoral dissertation, Graduate School of Business Administration, University of Michigan, 1990.

Harrigan, K. R. *Strategies for Joint Ventures*. Lexington Books, Lexington, MA, 1985.

Harrigan, K. R. *Managing for Joint Venture Success*. Lexington Books, Lexington, MA, 1986.

Harrigan, K. R. 'Joint ventures and competitive strategy,' *Strategic Management Journal*, 9, 1988, pp. 141-158.

Hedberg, B. L. T. 'How organizations learn and unlearn.' In P. C. Nystrom and W. H. Starbuck (eds), *Handbook of Organizational Design*, Oxford University Press, London, 1981.

Hergert, M. and D. Morris. 'Trends in international collaborative agreements.' In F. J. Contractor and P. Lorange (eds), *Cooperative Strategies in International Business*, D.C. Heath, Lexington, MA, 1988, pp. 99-109.

Hennart, J. 'A transaction cost theory of equity joint ventures,' *Strategic Management Journal*, July-August, 9, 1988, pp. 36-74.

Imai, M. *Kaizen: The Key to Japan's Competitive Success*, Random House, New York, 1986.

Itami, H. with T. W. Roehl. *Mobilizing Invisible Assets*. Harvard University Press, Cambridge, MA, 1987.

Killing, J. P. 'How to make a global joint venture work,' *Harvard Business Review*, May-June 1982, pp. 120-127.

Killing, J. P. *Strategies for Joint Venture Success*. Praeger, New York, 1983.

Kobrin, S. J. 'Testing the bargaining hypothesis in the manufacturing sector in developing countries,' Unpublished manuscript, 1986.

Kogut, B. 'Joint ventures: Theoretical and empirical perspectives,' *Strategic Management Journal*, 9(4), 1988, pp. 319-322.

Mintzberg, H. 'Patterns in strategy formulation,' *Management Science*, 24(9), 1978, pp. 934-948.

Moxon, R. W., T. W. Roehl and J. F. Truitt. 'International cooperative ventures in the commercial aircraft industry: Gains, sure, but what's my share.' In F. J. Contractor and P. Lorange (eds), *Cooperative Strategies in International Business*, D.C. Heath, Lexington, MA, 1988, pp. 255-278.

Nakane, C. *Japanese Society*. University of California Press, Berkeley, CA, 1970.

Nelson, R. R. and S. G. Winter. *An Evolutionary Theory of Economic Change*, Belknap Press, Cambridge, MA, 1982.

Nielsen, R. P. 'Cooperative strategy,' *Strategic Management Journal*, 9, 1988, pp. 475-492.

Nystrom, P. C. and W. H. Starbuck.; 'To avoid

organizational crises, unlearn,' *Organizational Dynamics*, **12**(4), 1984, pp. 53–65.

Ohmae, K. 'The global logic of strategic alliances,' *Harvard Business Review*, March–April 1989, pp. 143–155.

Ouchi, W. G. 'Markets, bureaucracies, and clans,' *Administrative Science Quarterly*, **25**, 1980, pp. 129–141.

Ouchi, W. C. and R. T. Johnson. 'Made in America (under Japanese management),' *Harvard Business Review*, September–October 1974, pp. 61–69.

Perlmutter, H. V. and D. H. Heenan. 'Cooperate to compete globally,' *Harvard Business Review*, March–April 1986, pp. 136–152.

Peterson, R. B. and H. F. Schwind. 'A comparative study of personnel problems in international companies and joint ventures in Japan,' *Journal of International Business Studies*, **8**(1), 1977, pp. 45–55.

Peterson, R. B. and J. Y. Shimada. 'Sources of management problems in Japanese–American joint ventures,' *Academy of Management Review*, **3**, 1978, pp. 796–804.

Pettigrew, A. M. 'On studying organizational cultures,' *Administrative Science Quarterly*, **24**(4), 1979, pp. 570–581.

Pfeffer, J. and P. Nowak. 'Joint ventures and interorganizational interdependence,' *Administrative Science Quarterly*, **21**, 1976, pp. 398–418.

Porter, M. E. *Competitive Strategy: Techniques for Analyzing Industries and Competitors*, Free Press, New York, 1980.

Porter, M. E. *Competitive Advantage*, Free Press, New York, 1985.

Postman, L. and B. J. Underwood. 'Critical issues in interference theory,' *Memory and Cognition*, **1**, 1973, pp. 19–40.

Prahalad, C. K. and Y. Doz. *Multinational Mission*, Free Press, New York, 1987.

Prahalad, C. K. and G. Hamel. 'The core competence and the corporation,' *Harvard Business Review*, May–June 1990, pp. 71–91.

Quinn, J. B., T. L. Doorley and P. C. Paquette. 'Building leadership in high technology industries: Focus technology strategies on services innovation.' Unpublished paper presented at the Second International Conference on Managing the High Technology Firm, University of Colorado, Boulder, CO, 10 January 1990.

Reynolds, J. I. *Indian–America Joint Ventures: Business Policy Relationships*. University Press of America, Washington, DC, 1979.

Reich, R. B. and E. D. Mankin. 'Joint ventures with Japan give away our future,' *Harvard Business Review*, March–April 1986, pp. 78–86.

Root, F. R. 'Some taxonomies of cooperative arrangements.' In F. J. Contractor and P. Lorange (eds), *Cooperative Strategies in International Business*, D.C. Heath, Lexington, MA, 1988, pp. 69–80.

Schillaci, C. E. 'Designing successful joint ventures,' *Journal of Business Strategy*, **8**(2), 1987, pp. 59–63.

Seyle, H. *From Dream to Discovery: On Being a Scientist*, McGraw-Hill, New York, 1964.

Sullivan, J. and R. B. Peterson. 'Factors associated with trust in Japanese–American joint ventures,' *Management International Review*, **22**(2), 1982, pp. 30–40.

Teece, D. J. 'The multinational enterprise: Market failure and market power considerations,' *Sloan Management Review*, **22**(3), 1981, pp. 3–17.

Teece, D. J., G. P. Pisano and A. Shuen. 'Firm capabilities, resources, and the concept of strategy,' CCC Working Paper No. 90–8, Center for Research in Management, University of California at Berkeley, 1990.

Terpstra, V. and K. David. *The Cultural Environment of International Business*, South-Western, Cincinnati, OH, 1985.

Thorelli, H. B. 'Networks: Between markets and hierarchies,' *Strategic Management Journal*, **7**, 1986, pp. 37–51.

Tybejee, T. T. 'Japan's joint ventures in the United States.' In F. J. Contractor and P. Lorange (eds), *Cooperative Strategies in International Business*, D.C. Heath, Lexington, MA, 1988, pp. 457–472.

Watzlawick, P., J. H. Weakland and R. Fisch. *Change*. Norton, New York, 1974.

Westney, D. E. 'Domestic and foreign learning curves in managing international cooperative strategies.' In F. J. Contractor and P. Lorange (eds), *Cooperative Strategies in International Business*, D.C. Heath, Lexington, MA, 1988, pp. 339–346.

Williamson, O. E. *Markets and Hierarchies: An Analysis and Antitrust Implications*. Free Press, New York, 1975.

[14]

Strategic Management Journal, Vol. 9, 361–374 (1988)

A TRANSACTION COSTS THEORY OF EQUITY JOINT VENTURES

JEAN-FRANCOIS HENNART
The Wharton School, University of Pennsylvania, Philadelphia, Pennsylvania, U.S.A.

This paper presents a transaction costs theory of equity joint ventures. It distinguishes between 'scale' and 'link' JVs. Scale JVs arise when parents seek to internalize a failing market, but indivisibilities due to scale or scope economies make full ownership of the relevant assets inefficient. Link JVs result from the simultaneous failing of the markets for the services of two or more assets whenever these assets are firm-specific public goods, and acquisition of the firm holding them would entail significant management costs.

American multinational enterprise (MNEs) used to be known for their rigid insistence on wholly-owned subsidiaries. No longer. Today joint ventures (JVs) are 'in'. AT&T and Olivetti, General Motors and Toyota, Honeywell and Ericsson, United Technologies and Rolls Royce, Hercules and Montedison, General Electric and SNECMA, even the largest American firms are joining forces with foreign rivals, setting up cooperative research, manufacturing, or distribution ventures.

The increasing importance taken by domestic and international JVs has spawned some new theoretical and empirical work which has increased our knowledge of these cooperative arrangements. Harrigan (1985), for example, has shown that JVs take a variety of forms and are used for a wide range of purposes. The goal of this paper is to show that the transaction cost framework (Williamson, 1975, 1985) can provide a unifying paradigm which accounts for the common element among these seemingly dissimilar JVs.

My aim is to use the insights of transaction-costs theorists to sketch a static theory of equity JVs. I do not claim that the minimization of transaction costs is the sole reason behind JVs. Collusion, for example, is an important motive which is ignored by the model. Similarly, no attempt will be made to critically evaluate the assumptions underlying transaction costs theory, nor to compare the explanatory power of such a framework to that of alternative approaches. Supporting evidence will be adduced where available to ground the theory, and show that the argument is plausible, but I do not pretend to have shown conclusive support. The model seeks to explain why equity JVs are chosen as a first-best strategy: it may not be applicable to equity JVs which are created as a result of government pressure. It accounts for both domestic and international equity JVs, although much of the discussion will focus on the latter.

The literature distinguishes between equity and non-equity JVs. Equity JVs arise whenever two or more sponsors bring given assets to an

0143–2095/88/040361–14$07.00
© 1988 by John Wiley & Sons, Ltd.

Received 2 February 1987
Revised 9 July 1987

362   *J.-F. Hennart*

independent legal entity and are paid for some or all of their contribution from the profits earned by the entity, or when a firm acquires partial ownership of another firm. The term 'non-equity JV' describes a wide array of contractual arrangements, such as licensing, distribution, and supply agreements, or technical assistance and management contracts. Non-equity JVs are thus contracts. Consequently, we will restrict the use of the term JV to describe equity JVs, while the term 'contract' will be used to describe non-equity JVs and other types of contractual arrangements.

It is useful to contrast two types of equity JVs. 'Scale' JVs are created when two or more firms enter together a contiguous stage of production or distribution or a new market. The main characteristic of these ventures is that they result from similar moves by all the parents: forward or backward vertical integration, horizontal expansion, or diversification. Examples include the drilling consortia routinely used by integrated oil companies, the iron-ore JVs established by steel producers, or the component JVs created by automobile producers. In all these ventures the partners are pursuing strategies of backward vertical integration. Banking consortia, such as the European American Bank, formed by a group of European banks to jointly enter the U.S. market, can also be classified as scale JVs.

Here the strategy is one of horizontal expansion.

In 'link' JVs, on the other hand, the position of the partners is not symmetrical. The JV may, for example, constitute a vertical investment for one of the parties, and a diversification for the other. One example of such JV would be Dow-Badische, a JV of Dow Chemical and BASF, a German chemical company. BASF set up the venture to exploit is proprietary technology in the U.S. market, while for Dow, which took responsibility for marketing the JV's output, the JV was a way to fill in its product line. Similarly, Philips/Du Pont Optical, a JV recently established by these two firms to manufacture and sell compact disks, represents a horizontal investment for Philips, which already produces compact disks in Europe, and a way for Du Pont to diversify into electronic products (Freeman and Hudson, 1986).

Figure 1 contrasts scale and link JVs in the aluminum industry. Aluminium Oxide Stade, a scale JV, represents a vertical forward investment for both parents. They provide their own bauxite to the JV and take a share of the alumina which is proportional to their equity. Queensland Alumina, on the other hand, is a link JV. Comalco, one of the partners, is following a strategy of vertical forward integration: it provides all of the bauxite used in the plant, but only takes part of the alumina output. For the other

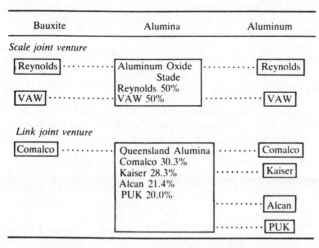

(...) denotes market sales or purchases of bauxite and alumina.

Figure 1.   Link and scale joint ventures in the aluminum industry

partners the venture is a vertical backward investment in alumina.

Both scale and link JVs have two main characteristics. First, the relationship between the parent(s) and the JV is an equity, or hierarchical one. This equity link suggests that hierarchical coordination has been found preferable to coordination through spot markets or contracts. A JV thus represents a particular type of internalization. Second, hierarchical control over the firm is shared with other firms. This is in contrast to an exclusive link, as in a wholly owned subsidiary.

The following sections of this paper seek to explain those two characteristics. We will set out the conditions under which JVs will be preferred to spot markets or contractual agreements and then show when shared equity will be chosen over exclusive ownership. But before we develop a transaction costs theory of JVs, it is important to show why some of the explanations given so far for JVs have been inadequate.

RECEIVED THEORY

Long before JVs and other cooperative strategies caught the attention of business strategists, they had been studied by industrial economists because of their potential impact on competition. Pate (1969), for example, found that most U.S. JV parents belonged to the same industry, and deduced that U.S. JVs were undertaken to reduce competition. Berg and Friedman (1980) showed, however, that other motives besides collusion could explain JVs. The following discussion will concentrate on these other motives.

JVs have been seen as achieving four main objectives: (1) taking advantage of economies of scale and diversifying risk; (2) overcoming entry barriers into new markets; (3) pooling complementray bits of knowledge; (4) allaying xenophobic reactions when entering a foreign market. As will be shown, each of these four reasons constitutes a necessary, but not a sufficient condition for the existence of JVs.

Economies of scale

It is often argued that increases in the minimum efficient scale (MES) of a number of economic activities have led firms to enter into JVs. For example, the desire to reduce costs through economies of scale in automobile manufacturing is usually given as a cause for the spate of JVs in component production in that industry. This analysis implies that the optimal scale is larger at the component than at the assembly level, thus forcing two or more assemblers to join forces to produce components. That differences in MES across stages provide a necessary, but not a sufficient condition for JVs is made clear by looking at two fairly similar mineral industries, tin and aluminum. Today, the MES of a bauxite mine or of an alumina refinery is larger than that of an aluminum smelter. Only the largest aluminum firms have enough downstream capacity to absorb the output of an efficiently sized upstream facility. As a result, most recent bauxite mines and alumina refineries have been built by consortia of aluminum producers, and JVs account today for more than half of the world's bauxite and alumina capacity.

The case of tin shows, however, that the presence of divergences between the MES of successive stages is not a sufficient reason for the emergence of JVs. In tin as well, the production process is characterized by large differences in MES across stages, the MES of a tin smelter being much larger than that of an alluvial tin mine. Yet tin smelters are not operated by JVs of tin mining firms, but are run by specialist firms, with minimal equity in tin mining. There must therefore be more to JVs than scale economies.

Increasing global environment

The recent proliferation of JVs has also been explained by the need of firms, in an increasingly global competitive environment, to be present in all main world markets. Building local distribution networks, however, is both very expensive and time-consuming. JVs are said to be a way to enter a maximum number of markets with minimum investment. Although it is difficult to fault such a statement, it is also true that one can enter markets with even less investment. Distribution and licensing agreements allow firms to obtain a global presence with a limited resource commitment. Heublein, for example, has achieved a global market share for its Smirnoff vodka by licensing in 27 countries its production to local firms.

Pooling knowledge

Some authors have seen JVs as devices to pool or exchange knowledge. Yet, here as well, alternatives exist. Licensing is widely used to combine technical knowledge with that of local conditions, while cross-licensing allows firms to exchange complementary information. A theory of JVs must therefore show when and why JVs are preferred to licensing.

Reducing political risk

Lastly, JVs have been explained by the desire of multinational enterprises (MNEs) to share the ownership of their foreign subsidiaries with local firms, in order to defuse xenophobic reactions in host countries. It is not obvious, however, that a partly foreign-owned firm will, everything else constant, be necessarily better treated than a wholly-owned subsidiary. In any case, a MNE can totally reduce its visibility and still exploit its advantages if it licenses or franchises a local firm. In that respect, JVs are a second best compared to contractual modes. Why they would be used remains unclear.

In conclusion, each of these four commonly described reasons provides a necessary, but not a sufficient, condition for the emergence of JVs. To explain why JVs are formed one must show convincingly: (1) why an equity link is sometimes preferred to other means of acquiring intermediate inputs; (2) why the firm chooses to share the ownership of the JV with other parents. Although those two aspects of JV are interrelated, they will be dealt with separately to simplify the exposition.

WHY EQUITY?

This section argues that all JVs can be explained as a device to bypass inefficient markets for intermediate inputs. The presence of inefficiencies in intermediate markets is thus a necessary condition for JVs to emerge.[1]

---

[1] The argument that JVs are used to bypass inefficient markets was first made explicitly by Stuckey (1983) in the context of the aluminum industry. Much in the discussion that follows is inspired by this pathbreaking work.

Whether a market fails or not depends on a number of technological, political, and social factors. Analyzing the transaction cost properties of specific markets requires a thorough study of the technology used at both the upstream and downstream stages, and of its impact on the potential number of parties at each stage (see, for example, Globerman and Schwindt, 1986; Joskow, 1985 at the industry level, and Monteverde and Teece, 1982; Walker and Weber, 1984, at the firm level). Nevertheless, a certain number of generalizations can be made. Intermediate inputs sold in narrow, imperfect markets are likely to include some raw materials and components, some types of knowledge and, in some instances, loan capital and distribution services. Some of the points argued below have been made by others to explain why firms internalize transactions within wholly-owned networks. Here I argue that the presence of high transaction costs can also, in specific circumstances outlined in the next section, lead to internalization between parents and JVs.

Raw materials and components

The characteristics of the markets for raw materials and intermediate inputs explain why, given significant differences in MES across stages, JVs are used in some industries but not in others. This point is best made by returning to our previous discussion of the tin and aluminum industries, and by looking at the market for intermediate inputs, here bauxite and tin concentrates.

The market for bauxite is narrow, as efficient bauxite refining requires that the bauxite refinery be designed around the characteristics of the ore. Since bauxites are heterogeneous, each refinery obtains its bauxite from a particular mine. Switching costs are high. To organize such a bilateral relationship through spot markets would be hazardous, because after investments have been made, one party could hold up the other by unilaterally changing the price of bauxite.

One way for traders to protect themselves is to write long-term contracts fixing *ex ante* the price of bauxite over a period of time which corresponds to the life of the plant. Because mining and refining bauxite require very large investments—an efficiently sized mine costs half a billion dollars and a refinery between 500 million and a billion—such contracts typically run for 20–25 years. Over such a long time span they cannot effectively protect the parties against changes in the environment, as it is difficult to specify *ex ante* all possible contingencies. Contracts thus remain incomplete, exposing parties to opportunistic renegotiations (Stuckey, 1983). Aluminum firms must therefore use equity to control their supply of bauxite. Equity control reduces the problem of opportunism because it aligns the incentives of buyers and sellers of bauxite. Both can now be paid in proportion to the firm's global profits, thus attenuating incentives for bargaining and opportunism.

Similarly, the presence of JVs in the oil industry derives in part from high transactions costs in the market for crude. Oil refining is a capital-intensive flow process, requiring a constant throughput. Storing crude oil is costly. As in the case of bauxite, refineries are custom-built to handle a particular type of crude. The market for crude tends therefore to be thin, and oil refiners have found it necessary to integrate backward into crude exploration and production (Greening, 1976; Teece, 1976).

By contrast, coordination between stages is, in the case of alluvial tin, efficiently performed by spot markets. Alluvial tin concentrates are nearly pure tin, and can be handled by any smelter. Because tin is a semi-precious metal its transportation costs are low relative to its value. These two conditions have favored the emergence of an efficient market for tin concentrates, allowing smelters to acquire feed, and mines to sell their output, without the fear of opportunistic exploitation. Consequently, miners have not entered smelting through JVs (Hennart, 1986).

The same considerations explain the need to JV the supply of parts or components. When the MES of some components is very large relative to a single firm's demand, JVs will be used if the component is specific to the purchaser, while independent suppliers will be used for standard parts, which are sold in a relatively broad market. Automobile assemblers, for example, JV the supply of parts which are specific to their models (engines), but purchase standard parts from large independent suppliers (Monteverde and Teece, 1982; Walker and Weber, 1984). Here also, JVs arise whenever relying on independent suppliers would involve excessive transaction costs.

Knowledge

The second factor of production that is often sold in inefficient markets is knowledge (Casson, 1979; Rugman, 1981; Teece, 1981; Hennart, 1982). The connection between JVs and knowledge is twofold. Link JVs are used to combine different types of knowledge. The Dow-Badische JV mentioned earlier linked BASF's technological expertise with Dow's marketing know-how. Scale JVs serve to pool similar types of knowledge. For example, CFM International, a JV between General Electric and SNECMA of France, merges the two parents' experience to develop and manufacture a new fuel-efficient jet engine.

Why is knowledge transferred through JVs in those cases, and not by licensing or cross-licensing? To answer this question one must focus on the transactional characteristics of knowledge. Knowledge *per se* is costly to exchange because of buyer's uncertainty: the buyer of knowledge cannot be told prior to the sale the exact characteristics of what he is buying. If the seller were to provide that information in order to educate the buyer on the value of know-how for sale, he would, by revealing the information, be transfering the know-how free of charge (Arrow, 1962: 615). The patent system is an institution which has been devised to solve this problem. In exchange for disclosing his knowledge, the inventor is granted a monopoly on its use.

The efficiency of the patent system thus depends crucially on the power and willingness of public authorities to establish and enforce monopoly rights on the sale of goods and services embodying the knowledge. Only if the inventor can be assured of an exclusive right to produce his invention will he consent to disclose it. If he has reasons to believe his rights will not be protected, he will keep his invention secret and exploit it himself, for by not disclosing it he secures a *de facto* monopoly for at least as long as it takes for others to market imitations.

Patents suffer from another type of limitation. Recall that patents lower the high information costs faced by buyers of knowledge by revealing it and simultaneously establishing exclusive property rights in its use. To reduce market transaction costs the patent must therefore contain the totality of the information necessary to produce the commodity. Some types of knowledge, however, are difficult to put on paper. Such is the case for a firm's experience in manufacturing and marketing a product, and for country-specific knowledge, the intimate knowledge of local customs, markets, politics, and people which comes from having lived in a particular country, or more generally for what Polanyi (1958) has called 'tacit' knowledge. Such knowledge cannot be embodied in designs, specifications, and drawings, but instead is embedded in the individual possessing it. When knowledge is tacit, it cannot be effectively transferred in codified form; its exchange must rely on intimate human contact. A sole exchange of patents is then insufficient. Instead, the patent must be accompanied by transfer of personnel from the patenting firm (Teece, 1981).

The problem with transferring tacit knowledge is that it is impossible for either party to know *ex ante* what the cost and the value of the transfer will be. The buyer does not know, by definition, what he is buying. He fears that the information he will be sold will be obsolete, or inappropriate. The seller does not know how much it will cost him to effect the transfer. New technical or human problems are likely to arise which could not be foreseen when the contract was drafted.[2] It is often difficult for both parties to distinguish *ex post* between poor luck or poor performance. In those circumstances, parties may exploit contract incompleteness and the difficulty of assessing performance to their own advantage. Once he has been paid, the seller has little incentive to provide continuous support, and may provide less than promised. The buyer may have misrepresented his needs, or his capacity to absorb the information, in order to get better terms. He may then use the resulting difficulties as a pretext to withhold payment. Hierarchical coordination is then advantageous, because the parties to the exchange are no longer rewarded by the quantity of information transferred, but by their obedience to managerial directives. They

have therefore fewer incentives to cheat (Hennart, 1982: 97–121).

The cost of transferring know-how by contract, i.e. the cost of licensing, will therefore depend on the type of knowledge to be transferred and on the protection given to property rights in knowledge. Some types of knowledge, such as chemical formulae for the manufacture of new compounds whose production requires no careful adjustments, are patentable; and the patent conveys all of the necessary information to produce the product. The sale or rental of such know-how will incur low market transaction costs. Tacit knowledge, on the other hand, is difficult to codify, and often non-patentable. Even if patented, the patent will provide only a small part of the information necessary to market the new product or to use the new process. Tacit knowledge will be more efficiently transferred if the transferor and the recipient are linked through common ownership.

There is empirical support for the notion that equity links are chosen to transfer non-codified technological know-how. In alumina production the crucial know-how is how to adapt that basic process to the characteristics of the bauxite. That knowledge, obtained by experience, is held by the 'majors', the six aluminum producers which have long been active in the industry. Because it is tacit, it is never licensed, but is transferred through JVs between the 'majors' and entrants into the industry (Stuckey, 1983: 163).

There is also a good deal of evidence that JVs are used to transfer a different technology package than licensing. JVs are chosen to communicate both patent rights and tacit knowledge, while licensing is usually limited to patent rights. This point was highlighted in Davies' (1977) study of the transfer of knowledge from British to Indian firms. He found that while 60 percent of the licensing agreements only transferred designs, specifications and drawings, JVs were used to transfer a much wider range of know-how, including tacit knowledge. Technology suppliers often sent technical and managerial personnel to their JV to transfer tacit know-how, while this was rarely done by licensors. Killing's 1980 study of licensing agreements and JVs between Canadian, American and Western European firms also found that the transfer of knowledge to JVs relied much more heavily on personal contact than in the case of licensing. In

---

[2] An interesting example of some of the problems inherent in transferring tacit knowledge through licensing comes from the experience of Honda in licensing the production of its Ballade to British Leyland. Honda expected BL to send a few design engineers and foremen to Japan for training. But because of the compartmentalized British trade unions, and the narrowness of the tasks assigned to each employee, effective transfer required inviting 300 foremen and engineers to Japan, at a cost of over a hundred times what Honda had budgeted. See Ohmae, 1985: 71–72.

19 of the 30 JVs, but only in one of the 74 license agreements he surveyed, a permanent employee had been assigned by the technology supplier to facilitate the transfer.[3]

Two other types of tacit knowledge which are difficult to transfer through contracts are marketing and country-specific knowledge. Both types of know-how have similar characteristics: they are acquired by firms in a given industry and country as a by-product of operating in that industry and country, yet they are costly for a new entrant to obtain. Both are not patentable and difficult to codify, and their sale would be subject to high transaction costs.

We would therefore expect firms which are entering new industries or new countries to establish hierarchical links with local producers. The strength of this motivation for JVs will vary with the extent to which knowledge of local conditions is required for successful operation, and with the degree to which entrants are familiar with conditions in the market they wish to enter. In the case of country-specific knowledge, for example, the greater the cultural distance between the investor's home and the host country, the greater the need to acquire country-specific knowledge.

The preceding considerations account for the strong relationship between diversification and JVs. Stopford and Wells (1972: 126) found, for example, that diversified firms had a larger percentage of JVs among their overseas manufacturing affiliates than the firms with a narrow product line. Diversifying firms must acquire skills in marketing their new products and, given the difficulty of licensing such marketing knowledge, they must establish equity links with the firms owning it.

There is also a great deal of evidence showing the importance of local knowledge acquisition as a *raison d'etre* for international JVs. Both Stopford and Wells (1972) and Franko (1973) found that U.S. firms that engage in JVs abroad ranked 'general knowledge of local economy, politics, and customs' the most important contribution of the local partner to the JV. It is also striking to note that, when free to choose their mode of entry, MNEs rarely use JVs to enter

culturally similar countries (Stopford and Haberich, 1978). Kogut and Singh (1985) found that, for a sample of foreign firms investing in the United States, the probability to JV rather than acquire a U.S. company was higher the greater the cultural distance between the investor's country of origin and the United States.

That JVs serve to acquire country-specific knowledge is also clear from the fact that in many JVs the local partner assumes management. A 1974 survey of JVs in Japan found that 85 percent were managed by the Japanese partner, and only 2 percent by the foreign partner (*Economist*, 1977). Yoshahira (1984: 112) also found a clear correlation between the percentage of parent ownership in Japanese foreign affiliates and the degree of parent control, thus supporting the view that JVs are a way for Japanese companies to buy management skills for their foreign subsidiaries.

Distribution

The distribution of a product in a given area requires both physical facilities (such as warehouses, stocks of finished products and components, repair facilities, offices or retail stores) and an investment in knowledge. The distributor must establish a reputation through advertising or direct selling, adapt the product to local tastes and conditions of use, find out how to price it, and learn to demonstrate and service it. Distribution thus involves set-up costs, which vary from small to substantial, depending on the type of products sold. In some cases these investments are specific to a particular product, with low resale value in alternative uses.

There are three cases where arm's-length distribution agreements suffer from high transaction costs. The first one arises when distribution is subject to economies of scale or scope, a rather common occurrence. This tends to reduce the number of potential distributors in any given area. An equity participation in the distributor allows the manufacturer to avoid the resulting bargaining stalemates.

In other cases there are many potential distributors facing a manufacturer, but effective distribution requires substantial up-front investments. The distributor may then fear that, having developed the market in the expectation of a long-lived relationship, he will find himself

---

[3] Harrigan (1985: 351) also documents the loan by parents of their best technological personnel to their JVs.

squeezed by the manufacturer. One solution is to obtain exclusive distribution rights for a period which is long enough to fully depreciate his investments. Such a contract could, in theory, reduce the problems of opportunistic recontracting. The more uncertain the environment, and the greater the value of the investments the distributor must dedicate to the manufacturer's products, the greater the chances, however, that such a long-term contract will break down.[4] In practice the distributor's defense will often be to minimize the investments dedicated to pushing, supporting, and servicing the sale of the manufacturer's products, so as to reduce his loss should the manufacturer behave opportunistically.

Vertical integration into distribution solves these contractual difficulties. The higher the optimal level of dedicated investments to be made by the distributor, and the greater the degree of uncertainty, the more efficient it will be for the manufacturer to own all or a part of his distributor. Thus we would expect integration into distribution to prevail in the case of products requiring specialized distribution facilities (for example, refrigeration), or in that of new shopping goods. The sale of these goods requires a substantial up-front investment in adapting the product to the needs of the public, and in demonstrating and advertising it to the customer (Williamson, 1985: 75–84).

Another problem inherent in subcontracting distribution is that of quality control. Whenever a good's quality cannot be evaluated before its purchase, the use of a trademark will economize on a customers' search costs, and buyers will be willing to pay a premium for such trademarked goods and services. All the sellers of goods bearing a trademark are interdependent, in the sense that the quality of the goods and services sold by anyone using the trademark will affect the profits of all that share in that trademark. Independent distributors of trademarked goods therefore have weak incentives to maintain the quality of the trademarked goods they carry. If consumers are mobile, a distributor of trademarked goods will capture most of the savings from debasing quality (for example selling stale merchandise), while the losses from this reduction

in quality will be shared by all others using the trademark through the fall in its global value. Franchised distribution contracts attempt to control such free-riding by having the franchisee agree to a set of constraints that prevent him from debasing quality. The larger the number of contractual stipulations that are needed to achieve that end, and the greater the difficulty of defining and enforcing contractual rules, the stronger the manufacturer's incentive to own his distributor.

Several empirical studies support this explanation of vertical integration into distribution. In a study of the channels used to sell electronic components, Anderson and Schmittlein (1984) found that firms integrated into direct selling when sales required the salesperson to make substantial firm-specific investments. Historical evidence from Chandler (1977), Porter and Livesay (1971) and Nicholas (1983) shows that manufacturers sought equity control of distribution when (1) products required expensive, dedicated investments in distribution assets and (2) it was difficult to control quality debasement by distributors.

The importance of access to distribution as a motive for both international and domestic JVs is apparent from even a cursory reading of the literature. Kogut and Singh's (1985) data base shows that 42 percent of the JVs entered by foreigners in the U.S. over the 1971–83 period are for marketing and distribution, while Jacque (1986) found that close to 60 percent of U.S. joint ventures in Japan were of that type.

Loan capital

Capital markets are also characterized by significant transaction costs. Lending involves making funds available to the debtor, to be paid back later with interest. The risk is that the debtor might be unable to meet his obligations, either because he has willfully spent the funds with no intention to repay, or because he has been unsuccessful in his investments. The easiest way for the lender to protect himself is to obtain some collateral, whose value to the borrower is greater than the value of the loan. The next-best thing is to carefully monitor the way the lender is spending the borrowed funds.

Credit markets are likely to be especially imperfect for young firms with no track record and for investments in risky projects with no

---

[4] Note that it is not uncertainty *per se* which causes problems, but uncertainty *joined* with small-number conditions. See Williamson (1985).

collateral, such as R&D. Monitoring the borrower from the outside is likely to be difficult. A banker is strictly limited in the quantity, quality, and timeliness of the information he can obtain on his client. Hierarchical control is a much more efficient method to reduce risk, because a boss is entitled to much more information from his subordinates, and has the power to intervene much earlier than a banker could (Williamson, 1975: 159). In those cases a JV with the borrower can be an efficient method of funding risky projects. There is some evidence that a number of small R&D-intensive firms use JVs with larger firms as a way of financing projects that could not be funded either internally or through the capital market (Berg and Friedman, 1980; Harrigan, 1985).

WHY SHARED EQUITY?

JVs and the internalization of intermediate inputs

The preceding section has argued that equity JVs constitute a way to bypass some inefficient markets in intermediate inputs. This explains why a firm may want to establish an equity link with another firm. JVs are, however, operations where equity in that firm is shared with other firms. A theory of JVs must therefore explain why a firm chooses a JV as opposed to a wholly owned greenfield investment or acquisition.

Here it is useful to distinguish between scale and link JVs. Scale JVs allow firms to reconcile the need to bridge a failing market with the presence of large differences in MES across successive stages. In aluminum, for example, where the MES of bauxite mining and refining

is much higher than that for smelting and fabricating, a bauxite mining firm establishing a wholly owned, captive alumina refinery of efficient size would face the problem of disposing of the bulk of the alumina produced, since its needs are likely to be only a fraction of the output. Because the market for alumina is very narrow, selling the output on the spot market or through contracts would cause difficult marketing problems. The alternative of setting up a captive downstream network of sufficient size to absorb all of the alumina would involve a tremendous investment. The solution lies in a JV with other vertically integrated aluminum companies. Each member of the JV will take a share of the output. This allows the bauxite firm to build an efficiently sized refinery while solving the problem of disposing of the alumina (Stuckey, 1983). Similarly, drilling consortia allow integrated oil companies to take part in a number of scattered drilling programs, each of them with a limited probability of success, rather than in a few wholly owned drilling ventures of efficient size. Were it not for high transaction costs in the market for crude, drilling would be undertaken by a small number of independent crude producers, each of them holding a widely diversified portfolio of potential properties.

Link JVs are created to remedy the simultaneous failure of at least two markets. Assume that efficient production requires the combination of two types of knowledge held by firms A and B. As shown in Figure 2, if A's know-how is marketable, but B's is not, A will license B. If B's knowledge is marketable, but A's is not, B will license A. If both types of know-how are difficult to sell, A and B will form a JV. This last case is that of Dow-Badische, the JV of Dow

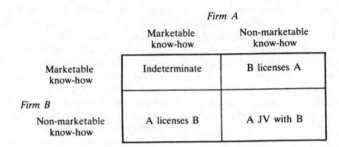

Figure 2. A model of link joint ventures

and BASF described earlier. Absent failure in the market for production know-how, BASF would have licensed Dow. If the market for country-specific knowledge and distribution services was competitive, BASF would have contracted with Dow to obtain those services. A JV was chosen because both of those markets were experiencing high transaction costs.

Although I have focused on the main failings in intermediate markets which give rise to JVs, the list is not meant to be comprehensive. Nevertheless, Figure 3 shows how our model of link JVs as created by the simultaneous failing of at least two intermediate goods markets can account for a wide variety of commonly observed JVs. For simplicity it is assumed that only two intermediate goods are traded in each JV. Scale JVs are on the diagonal, as they involve two firms internalizing together the same markets: raw materials JV, such as those in bauxite and alumina, are in cell 6F; R&D JVs between competitors where both parties bring similar research capacities in cell 3C; and distribution JVs which have been entered to overcome scale economies, such as the banking consortia set up by European firms to enter the United States, in cell 4D. Because situations are symmetrical along the diagonal, only the lower half of the table has been filled in.

Cell 3B describes 'market entry' JV such as Dow-Badische. Cell 3A, entitled 'sugar-daddy'

JVs', refers to those JVs mentioned earlier in which small R&D firms pair with older-established companies to obtain financing. Cell 3C describes R&D link JVs in which two or more firms bring complementary knowledge. The JVs set up in Southeast Asia by Japanese trading companies would fit in cells 4B and 4C. These are often tripartite JVs, in which equity is shared by a *sogo-shosha*, a Japanese manufacturer, and a local firm (Kojima and Ozawa, 1984). The trading company procures the inputs and sometimes markets the output, the Japanese manufacturer provides the tacit technology, while the local partner brings in country-specific knowledge and the advantage of nationality. Japanese Trading Companies own equity in these ventures to guarantee a return on their extensive investment in trading and distribution networks.

Cell 5C describes those JVs in which the local partner brings its nationality as principal contribution. Nationality cannot be obtained through equity, as acquisition of a local firm immediately changes its status to that of a foreign-owned entity. While a contractual exchange between the foreign firm and the local firm would be the best way to allay xenophobic reactions, a JV will be chosen when the markets for the intermediate goods to be exchanged, for example tacit know-how, are subject to high transaction costs. An example of such a JV is Marine Resource, a JV between Bellingham Cold Storage

		Capital A	Marketing/ country–specific knowledge B	Tacit technology C	Distribution D	Nationality E	Intermediate inputs F
1.	Capital						
2.	Country knowledge						
3.	Tacit technology	'Sugar-daddy'	'Market entry'	R&D scale R&D link			
4.	Distribution		Triparite	Japanese	Distribution scale and link		
5.	Nationality			Nationality-based			
6.	Intermediate inputs		Downstream vertical		Downstream vertical		Raw materials scale

Figure 3.   Joint ventures and markets for intermediate inputs

and Sovrybflot, the Soviet fishing monopoly (Contractor, 1986). Sovrybflot has a long experience in marketing fish species which are not consumed in the U.S., a tacit type of know-how which is difficult to sell. Bellingham Cold Storage lacks this expertise, but, as a U.S. firm, has fishing rights on the U.S. 200-mile economic zone, from which foreigners are excluded. The JV thus pools two assets which are difficult to exchange through markets or contracts.

Cell 6B accounts for the downstream JVs which are common in vertically integrated industries. These ventures link firms with knowledge and access to local markets, and vertically integrated concerns which provide them with intermediate inputs not traded on competitive markets. They are found, for example, in the downstream stages of the petroleum, copper, and aluminum industries (Stopford and Wells, 1972: 132–138). In aluminum, JVs between local firms and aluminum majors are common in the downstream fabrication stage, a stage that is characterized by wide variations in product needs between countries. JVs allow the majors to obtain that expertise which, because it is tacit, cannot be obtained from consultants, while guaranteeing the local firm's access to aluminum ingot, a product traded in narrow markets.

JVs vs. acquisitions or greenfield investments

It would appear at this point that we have established necessary and sufficient conditions for the emergence of link JVs, but this is not so. We have shown that these JVs result from the pooling of complementary assets which cannot be efficiently combined on spot markets or through contracts. But pooling could be effected by other means: one of the firms could buy out its potential JV partner. Another possibility would be to hire away its key personnel. In both cases the firm would end up with a wholly owned subsidiary. We must therefore explain the choice between acquisition and greenfield investment on the one hand, and JV on the other.

Excluding the case where acquiring the firm owning the complementary assets is illegal, or would incur the ire of government authorities or of potential customers, the answers seems to lie in the fact that JVs are used to acquire assets which have two main characteristics: they are (1) firm-specific and (2) public goods. By firm-

specific we mean that, even though they often constitute a small part of the firm's assets, they cannot be dissociated from the firm itself; public goods assets are assets that can be shared at low marginal cost.

If assets can be shared at low marginal cost, replication is more expensive than acquisition. The owner of these assets should be willing to sell the services produced from those assets at a low price, since providing these additional services does not increase his costs. Setting up a greenfield operation will therefore be inherently more costly than obtaining the use of existing assets through takeover or JV. A JV or a takeover will be preferred to a greenfield investment in this case.

Whenever assets can be shared at low marginal costs, and hence the efficient choice is between a takeover or a JV, a JV will be chosen if the assets which each party needs are a subset of those held by their partner. In this case, purchasing the whole firm would force the acquirer to enter unrelated fields or to suddenly expand in size, with the attendant management problems. Selling off the unusable assets is precluded by the fact that the assets are firm-specific, a point developed below.

The preceding argument can be made clearer with one example. Consider distribution systems. Distribution is often a public good, as it has zero or low marginal cost: once a channel is organized the additional cost of using it for similar or complementary products is small, or even negative if the new products 'fill in' a line. In some cases distribution assets are also firm-specific, in the sense that they could not be sold independently from the rest of the firm's operations: if vertical integration between manufacturing and distribution is efficient, then the distribution assets of the firm to be acquired will be linked to its manufacturing plants, and the two must be bought as a package.[5] Purchasing such assets would propel the buyer into new, unfamiliar markets, thus raising management costs. Selling off the unneeded manufacturing plants would increase the costs of running the distribution

---

[5] One example might be a firm, such as Dole, which owns banana plantations and operates a fleet of specialized ships and of refrigerated warehouses. Dole could not sell its distribution network separately from its plantations since, for reasons explained in Reid (1983), banana firms find it necessary to integrate banana growing, shipping, and distribution.

system by reducing potential economies of scope since, given the need for vertical integration into distribution, the new buyer of the manufacturing facilities would switch the distribution of the plant's output to his own channel. A JV in this case offers distinct advantages, since it allows vertical integration into distribution without the need to acquire the linked manufacturing assets.

Some types of knowledge have the same characteristics. Production or marketing know-how is a public good and a firm-specific asset. Like all types of knowledge it is a public good: sharing it with an additional party incurs zero marginal costs.[6] It is firm-specific, in the sense that it cannot be acquired separately from the firm. A full takeover of the firm holding the know-how will involve substantial management costs if the firm to be acquired is large, if it operates in a different industry than the acquiror, or if it is foreign-based.

In summary, whenever the needed assets are public goods it is more expensive to replicate than to acquire them. If these assets are also firm-specific, acquiring them by taking over the firm owning them will sometimes mean buying a collection of other businesses and a labor force which is foreign and/or employed in fields unknown by the buyer. In that case a JV is desirable, as it reduces management costs.[7] Taking over a firm involves transforming personnel into employees. As employees, the top executives of the acquired firm will have less incentives to perform than when they were running their own firm. If the acquiring firm believes it will experience significant problems in supervising these employees, it will opt for a JV in preference to a wholly owned subsidiary. For example, many firms entering foreign markets do not take over their local partner because they do not want to attenuate the incentives that the local firm's personnel has to transfer its know-how to the foreign partner. If the firm supplying marketing or country-specific know-how is paid from the future profits of the venture then it will have an incentive to supervise its employees so that they perform efficiently. Since it is more

costly to manage foreign than domestic employees, it is often efficient to let the local partner manage local operations. Similarly, one of the reasons why large, cash-rich firms which take an equity in small entrepreneurial R&D companies do not buy them out is apparently the difficulty of managing the new employees, given the usual differences in company culture.[8]

CONCLUSION

Much of the literature on JVs has failed to identify the conditions that are both necessary and sufficient for their existence. This paper has sketched a transaction costs theory of the choice between contracts, full ownership, and JVs. It distinguishes between scale and link JVs. Scale JVs arise when parents seek to internalize a failing market, but indivisibilities due to scale or scope economies make full ownership of the relevant assets inefficient. Link JVs result from the simultaneous failing of the markets for the services of two or more assets whenever these assets are firm-specific public goods, and acquisition of the firm owning them would entail significant management costs. JVs will thus represent a first-best strategy in a limited number of specific circumstances.

The paper provides a clear framework which explains a number of known characteristics of JVs and accounts for a wide variety of JV types. It gives a new explanation of why JVs transfer particular types of know-how; why they are widely used by diversifying firms; and why they are the preferred way to enter new countries and industries.

One limitation of the theory is that it is static, while the JV process is inherently dynamic, since the mean life of a JV is quite short on average. One way to make it dynamic would be to focus on the speed and predictability of the rate of decay of some of the advantages traded in JVs, particularly knowledge.

While this paper has outlined the benefits of JVs, a complete theory should also discuss their

---

[6] Although transfer costs may be positive (Teece, 1977).
[7] This point is supported by Kogut and Singh (1985), who found that the probability that a foreign firm would choose a JV with a U.S. company over an acquisition was higher the greater the cultural distance and the size of the U.S. firm.

[8] A General Motors executive thus explained the firm's purchase of 11 percent of Teknowledge: 'If we purchased such a company outright, we would kill the goose that lay the golden egg.' See *Business Week*, 25 June 1984: 41 quoted in Williamson, 1985: 159.

costs. These have, however, been dealt with at length elsewhere (Stopford and Wells, 1972). Because a JV is a contractural pooling of complementary assets belonging to different parents, a contract will usually be drawn to harmonize the interests of both parties. Such a task is easier in scale than in link JVs, for in scale JVs the parents follow similar strategies. In many scale aluminum JVs, for example, each party supplies its own feedstock and takes its share of output, usually proportional to its equity. This arrangement avoids conflicts about the pricing of inputs or outputs (Stuckey, 1983). Link JVs, on the other hand, involve the transfer of intermediate goods which, by definition, do not have clear arm's-length prices. Yet the pricing of these goods determines how profits will be divided between the parents, and is therefore a frequent source of contractual difficulties.

Clearly, JVs are often the product of multiple factors, and any theory must necessarily abstract from some of them. This paper has attempted to show that transactions costs theory can provide new insights into this complex phenomenon.

ACKNOWLEDGEMENTS

Earlier versions of this paper were presented at the Academy of Management meetings in Chicago in August 1986 and at the Conference on Cooperative Strategies in International Business, New Brunswick, NJ, in October 1986. I thank Erin Anderson, Peter Buckley, Bruce Kogut, Peter Lorange, Jose de la Torre, Gordon Walker, and two anonymous referees for valuable comments, and the Wharton Center for International Management Studies for financial support.

REFERENCES

Anderson, E. and D. Schmittlein. 'Integration of the sales force: an empirical examination', *The Rand Journal of Economics*, **15**, 1984, pp. 383–395.
Arrow, K. 'Economic welfare and the allocation of resources for invention'. In K. Arrow (ed.), *The Rate and Direction of Inventive Activity*, Princeton University Press, Princeton, 1962.
Berg, S. and P. Friedman. 'Causes and effects of joint venture activity: Knowledge acquisition vs. parent horizontality', *Antitrust Bulletin*, Spring, 1980, pp. 143–168.

Casson, M. *Alternatives to the Multinational Enterprise*, Macmillan, London, 1979.
Chandler, A. *The Visible Hand*, Belknap Press, Cambridge, MA, 1977.
Contractor, F. 'Strategic considerations behind international joint ventures', *International Marketing Review*, **3**, 1986, pp. 74–85.
Davies, H. 'Technology transfer through commercial transactions', *Journal of Industrial Economics*, **26**, 1977, pp. 161–175.
Economist. 'Joint-venture problems in Japan', 14 May 1977, p. 100.
Franko, L. *Joint Venture Survival in Multinational Corporations*, Praeger, New York, 1973.
Freeman, A. and R. Hudson. 'Du Pont and Philips plan joint venture to make, market laser-disk products', *Wall Street Journal*, 30 October 1986.
Globerman, S. and R. Schwindt. 'The organization of vertically related transactions in the Canadian forest products industries', *Journal of Economic Behavior and Organization*, **7**, 1986, pp. 199–212.
Greening, T. 'Oil wells, pipelines, refineries and gas stations: a study of vertical integration, Ph.D. dissertation, Harvard University, 1978.
Harrigan, K. *Strategies for Joint Ventures*, Lexington Books, Lexington, MA, 1985.
Hennart, J. F. *A Theory of Multinational Enterprise*, University of Michigan Press, Ann Arbor, MI, 1982.
Hennart, J. F. 'The tin industry'. In M. Casson and associates, *Multinationals and World Trade*, George Allen and Unwin, London, 1986.
Jacque, L. 'The changing personality of U.S.-Japanese joint ventures: a value-added chain mapping paradigm'. Department of Management, The Wharton School, 1986.
Joskow, P. L. 'Vertical integration and long-term contracts'. *Journal of Law, Economics and Organization*, **1**(1), 1985, pp. 33–80.
Killing, P. 'Technology acquisition: license agreement or joint venture'. *Columbia Journal of World Business*, Fall 1980, pp. 38–46.
Kogut, B. and H. Singh. 'Entering the United States by acquisition or joint venture: Country patterns and cultural characteristics', Working paper, Reginald Jones Center, The Wharton School, 1985.
Kojima, K. and T. Ozawa. *Japan's General Trading Companies: Merchants of Economic Development*. OECD, Paris, 1984.
Monteverde, K. and D. Teece. 'Supplier switching costs and vertical integration in the automobile industry', *Bell Journal of Economics*, **13**, 1982, pp. 206–213.
Nicholas, S. 'Agency contracts, institutional modes, and the transition to foreign direct investment by British manufacturing multinationals before 1935', *Journal of Economic History*, **48**, 1983, pp. 675–686.
Ohmae, K. *Triad Power: The Coming Shape of Global Competition*, Free Press, New York, 1985.
Pate, J. 'Joint venture activity, 1960–1968', *Economic Review, Federal Reserve Bank of Cleveland*, 1969, pp. 16–23.

Polanyi, M. *Personal Knowledge: Towards a Post-critical Philosophy*, University of Chicago Press, Chicago, IL, 1958.

Porter, G. and H. C. Livesay. *Merchants and Manufacturers*, Johns Hopkins, Baltimore, 1971.

Reid, R. 'The growth and structure of multinationals in the banana export trade'. In M. Casson (ed.), *The Growth of International Business*, George Allen and Unwin, London, 1983.

Rugman, A. *Inside the Multinationals*. Columbia University Press, New York, 1981.

Stopford, J. and K. Haberich. 'Ownership and control of foreign operations'. In Ghertman, M. and J. Leontiades (eds), *European Research in International Business*, North-Holland, Amsterdam, 1980.

Stopford, J. and L. Wells. *Managing the Multinational Enteprise*, Basic Books, New York, 1972.

Stuckey, J. *Vertical Integration and Joint Ventures in the Aluminum Industry*, Harvard University Press, Cambridge, MA, 1983.

Teece, D. *Vertical Integration and Vertical Divestiture in the U.S. Oil Industry*. Institute for Energy Studies, Stanford, CA, 1976.

Teece, D. 'Technology transfer by multinational firms', *Economic Journal*, **87**, 1977, pp. 246–261.

Teece, D. 'The market for know-how and the efficient international transfer of technology', *Annals of the American Academy of Political and Social Science*, **458**, 1981, pp. 81–96.

Walker, G. and D. Weber. 'A transaction cost approach to make-or-buy decisions', *Administrative Science Quarterly*, **29**, 1984, pp. 373–391.

Williamson, O. *Markets and Hierarchies*. Free Press, New York, 1975.

Williamson, O. *The Economic Institutions of Capitalism*, Free Press, New York, 1985.

Yoshahira, N. 'Multinational growth of Japanese manufacturing enterprises'. In Okochi, A. and T. Inoue (eds), *Overseas Business Activities*, University of Tokyo Press, Tokyo, 1984.

[15]

Academy of Management Review
1997, Vol. 22, No. 1, 177–202.

KNOWLEDGE, BARGAINING POWER, AND THE INSTABILITY OF INTERNATIONAL JOINT VENTURES

ANDREW C. INKPEN
Thunderbird
PAUL W. BEAMISH
University of Western Ontario

Although the high rate of instability of international joint ventures (IJVs) has been well documented, the underlying reasons for the instability need clarification. In this article, we develop a theoretical framework for instability of IJVs grounded in a bargaining power and dependence perspective. *Instability* is defined as a major change in partner relationship status that is unplanned and premature from one or both partners' perspectives. The core argument is that the instability of IJVs is associated with shifts in partner bargaining power. Shifts in the balance of bargaining power occur when partners of an IJV acquire sufficient knowledge and skills to eliminate a partner dependency and make the IJV bargain obsolete. Our primary focus is on the acquisition of local knowledge by the foreign partner and the impact that this acquisition of knowledge has on the stability of the IJV.

As competition increasingly becomes more global, many firms are using alliances to enter new markets, obtain new skills, and share risks and resources. Despite the surge in their popularity, international alliances are often described as inherently unstable organizational forms. Porter (1990), for example, observed that alliances involve significant costs in terms of coordination, reconciling goals with an independent entity, and creating competitors. Porter suggested that these costs make many alliances transitional rather than stable arrangements and, therefore, alliances are rarely a sustainable means for creating competitive advantage. Supporting this argument, authors of several empirical studies of alliances have found instability rates of close to 50% (e.g., Bleeke & Ernst, 1991; Kogut, 1988). Based on the finding that 24 of the 49 international alliances they studied were considered failures by one or both partners, Bleeke and Ernst (1991) suggested that most alliances will terminate, even successful ones.

Alliances also have been described as a *race to learn*, and the partner that learns the fastest dominates the relationship (Hamel, 1991). According to this scenario of inevitable instability, there are clear winners and

The authors thank Steve Currall, Charles Hill, and *AMR*'s five anonymous reviewers for their help in developing this article.

losers. However, some international alliances survive and prosper for many years, and both sides become more competitive through a win-win relationship. This example raises the issue of why some international alliances are more stable than others. We address this issue by examining equity-based international joint ventures (IJVs). An equity-based JV is an alliance that combines resources from more than one organization to create a new organizational entity (the "child"), which is distinct from its parents. Equity-based JVs are considered hierarchical because they more closely replicate some of the features associated with organizational hierarchies than do other alliances (Gulati, 1995). Siecor, an alliance between Siemens and Corning, provides an example. In this JV, the partners brought together their complementary capabilities in telecommunications and glass technology to build an independent organization with its own headquarters, CEO, board of directors, and staff. An IJV is a JV with two or more parents of different nationality. Our focus is on IJVs based in the home country of one of the partners, which we call the *local partner*. The partner operating outside its country of domicile is referred to as the *foreign partner*.

A variety of strategic objectives have been suggested to explain firms' motives for the formation of IJVs (Contractor & Lorange, 1988; Hennart, 1991; Kogut, 1988). A firm that enters a foreign market for the first time is likely to use a joint venture; this is also true for the foreign firm that seeks to obtain access to resources controlled by local firms (Hennart, 1991). In both situations, IJVs are often chosen because the alternatives of replicating a complete operation via full acquisition or greenfield investment are too costly and because the local partner controls resources deemed useful to the foreign partner. An IJV may be designed to market a product in the local market, or it may be involved in the sourcing of materials, components, or technology, possibly for use in the foreign partner's home market. IJVs are widely used as a mode of direct foreign investment. For example, Makino (1995) found that almost 70% of Japanese direct investments in manufacturing in Asia as of 1991 were via IJVs.

Regardless of the specific venture objective, our primary interest, like that of Yan and Gray (1994) and Parkhe (1991), is IJVs in which the foreign partner seeks a viable long-term presence in a country via direct investment. In this type of IJV, it would be unusual for the local partner not to contribute some local knowledge. The primary knowledge contribution of foreign partners generally involves technology, management expertise, and global support (Yan & Gray, 1994). Note that we are not suggesting that the only contribution of a local partner is local knowledge. In another section of this article, we suggest that if local partners take steps to ensure that their roles encompass more than a one-time contribution of local knowledge, instability may be controllable. Nevertheless, even when technology sourcing or risk sharing are important objectives of the foreign partner, if the venture is international, it is likely that the local partner possesses important local knowledge.[1]

Unlike alliances such as R&D partnerships or licensing agreements, contracts between IJV partners are often executed under conditions of high uncertainty, and, therefore, it is highly unlikely that all future contingencies in an IJV can be anticipated at the outset. As IJVs grow, they may develop an identity and a culture distinct from that of the partners, adding to problems of coordination. Also, the collaborative motives for IJVs are often different from other alliances; therefore, statements generalizing about the instability of alliances should be interpreted carefully.[2] The factors associated with instability of IJVs are not necessarily the same as those for all types of alliances.

In the literature on JV instability, various factors have been identified as causes of instability, including changes in partners' strategic missions (Harrigan & Newman, 1990), changes in importance of the JV to the parents (Harrigan & Newman, 1990), increases in the competitive rivalry between partners (Kogut, 1989), the foreign investment climate of the host country (Blodgett, 1992), and the existence of prior relationships between the partners (Blodgett, 1992). Although these factors may be associated with instability, and in some cases provide a strong indication that instability is imminent, they provide incomplete explanations for the instability of IJVs.

Our interest is instability that results from factors endogenous to the IJV relationship. Figure 1 illustrates the boundaries of the article and the conceptual orientation. Factors creating instability as a result of reasons exogenous to IJVs (e.g., changes in foreign country investment or ownership regulations; shifts in political regimes) are for the most part not controllable by managers of IJVs and are outside the scope of this article. We argue that the primary factor contributing to instability, and a factor that can be controlled by firms in IJVs, is a shift in partner bargaining power associated with the acquisition of knowledge and skills that allows a firm to eliminate a partner dependency. With a few exceptions (Hamel, 1991; Parkhe, 1991; Yan & Gray, 1994), the literature on IJVs has not addressed this issue in detail. Thus, the departure in this article is the focus on factors that *enable* firms to make the IJV bargain obsolete. We explore the question of how IJV firms, and in particular foreign partners, are able to create an unstable environment.

---

[1] When government legislation prohibits wholly owned subsidiaries, silent partners that contribute little more than a means to bypass legislation may be used. Also, if a foreign partner cannot legally become sole owner of the JV, our stability arguments do not hold. However, as trade and investment opportunities have become more liberal, particularly in developing countries, few countries continue to mandate the use of JVs for foreign investment.

[2] For example, licensing agreements and arrangements for sharing technology have gained notoriety as vehicles for licensee firms to build their own skill base and shift the alliance of power in their favor. An article that describes the competitive implications of sharing technology with a potential competitor was written by Reich and Mankin (1986). These authors focused on high-technology agreements in which the U.S. partner acquired and distributed Japanese products (in effect, outsourcing relationships). Note that these are not JVs according to our definition.

Firms contribute various types of knowledge and skills to their IJVs. For local partners, a critical knowledge contribution revolves around an understanding of local market, cultural, and environmental conditions. Although the foreign partner does not necessarily enter the IJV with the specific objective of knowledge acquisition, access to knowledge originating in the local country is an important factor in motivating the foreign partner to choose an IJV investment rather than full ownership. We propose that as the foreign partner's local knowledge and its commitment to acquire local knowledge increase, the probability of the instability of the IJV also increases because of changes in partner dependency. We also argue that the acquisition of technology-based knowledge by the local partner, although possible, is less likely to be a factor in creating instability than is the foreign partner's acquisition of knowledge.

The local knowledge argument complements the well-developed theme in the international management literature concerning the frequent conflict between global and local optimization of strategy (e.g., Bartlett & Shoshal, 1989; Franko, 1971). Given these conflicting demands, two closely related questions are addressed in this article. First, when a multinational enterprise (MNE) involved in an IJV as a foreign partner decides to pursue a localization strategy (i.e., a strategy of operating autonomously in the local environment), how can it happen? We argue that the MNE's acquisition of local knowledge *enables* the MNE to make the transition from an IJV to a subsidiary. We also suggest that an important distinction has to be made between the effect that local knowledge has on stability and the decision to acquire the knowledge. For example, an MNE may decide that its IJV should be a wholly owned subsidiary. Unless the MNE has acquired the local knowledge necessary to manage the venture autonomously, a wholly owned subsidiary is not a viable option. Thus, the acquisition of local knowledge can facilitate the transition to a subsidiary, and it is a necessary factor in the decision.

The second and equally important question involves the factors that influence the foreign partner's decision and ability to acquire local knowledge. In some IJVs, the foreign partner may choose not to pursue a localization strategy. In other IJVs, localization may not be possible because the local partner outlearns the foreign partner, which becomes the basis for an obsolete bargain. An examination of these questions requires an analysis of the dynamics of collaborative relationships, so that we can develop a comprehensive framework of the instability of IJVs.

DEFINITIONS AND THEORETICAL UNDERPINNINGS

Local Knowledge

To establish an operational presence in a country, a firm must access local knowledge as a means of overcoming market uncertainties (Stopford & Wells, 1972). IJVs provide low-cost, fast access to new markets by "borrowing" a partner's already-in-place local infrastructure (Doz, Prahalad, &

Hamel, 1990). This infrastructure includes sales forces, local plants, market intelligence, and the marketing presence necessary to understand and serve local markets. Local knowledge also relates to cultural traditions, norms, values, and institutional differences. For example, when Kentucky Fried Chicken entered China, a local partner was considered essential because of the complexities associated with obtaining operating licenses and leases, negotiating employment contracts, and interpreting investment regulations. When a foreign firm does not have local knowledge, as in the case of Kentucky Fried Chicken, an IJV can be used to gain quick access to a local partner's knowledge base. Yan and Gray (1994: 1492) quoted a U.S. manager in a U.S.-China IJV: "We have the technology and certain know-how. The Chinese partner knows how to make things happen in China. You put the two together right, it works."

Instability of IJVs

As indicated previously, the primary factor contributing to instability is a shift in partner bargaining power. Several definitions of instability have been used in the JV literature. Franko (1971) defined a JV as *unstable* when parent holdings changed to include 50% or 95% ownership, a parent sold its JV interest, or the venture was liquidated. Killing (1983) considered both a shift in JV control and venture termination as evidence of instability. Other researchers have adopted a narrower view. For example, Kogut (1989) used venture termination as the sole indicator of instability. However, as Kogut indicated, a JV cannot be considered unstable simply because its lifespan is short. All relationships between firms face challenges that threaten to change or terminate the basis for cooperation. Sometimes terminations are planned and anticipated by the involved parties. Ventures also may be terminated as a matter of policy when there is a change in the ownership or management of the parent. In other cases, difficulties associated with ending a relationship may create a rationale for maintaining an existing JV that would otherwise be terminated.

We maintain that instability should be linked with *unplanned* equity changes or major reorganizations. Usually, instability will result in premature termination of a JV, either when one partner acquires the JV business or the venture is dissolved. A complicating factor is that termination of a JV will not always be a mutual decision (Hamel, 1991; Parke, 1991). The premature termination of a JV may be precipitated by the actions of one partner. For example, when one firm is trying to learn from its partner in order to reduce its dependency, the partner that is doing the learning may have very different longevity objectives than the partner that is providing the knowledge. In this scenario, a terminated relationship would be classified as unstable, because termination was premature from the perspective of the partner that is providing the knowledge. Thus, if at least one of the partners anticipates a long-term relationship, premature termination of the venture would constitute instability. When both partners plan for termination at the time the JV is formed, instability will not be an issue unless termination occurs prematurely.

In keeping with the previous arguments, JV *instability* is defined as a major change in relationship status that was *unplanned* and *premature* from the perspective of either one or both partners. In most JVs, the partners do not have a specific plan for the termination of their ventures.[3] The premature termination of a JV can be traumatic for the venture partners. However, it is important to emphasize that we do not equate JV longevity with JV success. Many firms view JVs as intentionally temporary and recognize that their ventures will not last indefinitely. If a JV termination is an orderly and mutually planned event, the JV may well be evaluated as extremely successful. In fact, a JV that is prematurely terminated also may be evaluated as successful, depending on the criteria used to evaluate its performance.[4]

If an unstable JV involves changes in relationship status, a stable JV, by definition, must be one without unplanned changes in relationship status. However, stable JVs may be terminated when the strategic needs of the partners change. For example, in 1995, Chrysler announced that it was winding down its 25-year alliance with Mitubishi Motors (Templin, 1995). One of Chrysler's objectives in the relationship was access to a source of small cars for the U.S. market. Because Chrysler developed an internal supply of cars, the rationale for the relationship with Mitsubishi was no longer present.

A further consideration is that stability carries a positive connotation. In fact, in the opening section of this article, we linked stability with a win-win relationship. In our view, a stable JV is one in which the partners believe the benefits to the relationship exceed the costs of termination. Nevertheless, a JV may have the outward appearances of stability; however, one partner may view it as unsuccessful because the balance of power has shifted to a degree that is undesirable. In another section of this article, we discuss how the acquisition of knowledge by one partner in what looks like a stable JV can create the potential for instability.

Theoretical Underpinnings

Our framework is conceptually grounded in a bargaining power and dependence perspective. This perspective was developed by Emerson (1962), and it was generalized to the organizational level in Pfeffer and Salancik's (1978) resource dependence model. The essence of the model is

---

[3] A seldom used option is to incorporate "fade-out" provisions in the JV agreement. This type of venture has been used in China, but it has been largely discontinued. If longevity is not a goal, another option is "contractual" JVs that include a specific termination date. Also, JV agreements sometimes include a specific period of time during which the partners have the option to either renegotiate or modify their agreement.

[4] This definition of instability raises some interesting methodological questions. Specifically, how can the pre-JV motives of the JV partners be measured accurately? A longitudinal approach beginning at, or ideally before, the time of JV formation would provide the richest insights into the collaborative process.

that the possession or control of key resources by one entity may make other organizations dependent on that entity. According to this notion of resource fit, relationships are terminated for the inverse of the reasons for which they were formed (Seabright, Levinthal, & Fichman, 1992). Young and Olk (1994) found support for this argument in a study of U.S.-based R&D consortia. In this study, alliance firms that had gained knowledge as a result of membership in the consortium were more likely to leave the alliance.

In a cooperative relationship, dependence can be a source of power for the firm controlling key resources, because, to some degree, each firm can increase or withhold resources that are attractive to its partner (Bacharach & Lawler, 1980). When one firm controls an "irreplaceable" JV resource or input, a dependency situation is created (Hamel, 1991). Although dependency is voluntary when firms choose to form JVs, once the JV is operational, firms depend on their partners for specific resources and inputs. A firm that has the option to contribute or withhold an important resource or input can use that option as leverage in bargaining with its partner (Pfeffer, 1981).

The notion of "cooperative" may seem at odds with dependence and power. However, the key point is that at the time an IJV is formed, each partner is dependent on the other(s) for critical inputs. Thus, the firms must cooperate to ensure that these critical inputs are transformed into a productive entity (i.e., the IJV). Over time, the dependence may change, and as a result, the bargaining power of one partner may be enhanced. When that happens, the JV partner with the increased bargaining power has access to more partners and options, including terminating the venture, compared to the partner with limited bargaining power (Yan & Gray, 1994).

The bargaining power perspective is particularly appropriate for the examination of the stability of JVs, because all JVs involve a negotiated bargain between the partners. At a general level, bargaining power in JVs is based on the relative urgency of cooperation, available resources, commitments, other alternatives, and the strengths and weaknesses of each partner (Schelling, 1956). Focusing mainly on domestic JVs, Harrigan and Newman (1990) adopted the view that the relative bargaining power of potential JV partners is determined primarily by what each partner brings to the venture. Rarely will these contributions be symmetrical, because each partner views the potential costs and benefits of cooperating differently. As partners' strategic missions, expectations, loyalties, and resource mixes change, the balance of bargaining power in the JV shifts (Harrigan & Newman, 1990). When the balance of power shifts, and inevitably it will, the need for cooperation between the partners may diminish or disappear. At this point, the parent may decide to undertake all activities that were previously performed by the JV (Harrigan, 1986).

Yan and Gray's (1994) inductive study, perhaps the most systematic exploration of the concept of bargaining power in IJVs to date, identified both resource-based and context-based components of bargaining power. The context-based components, although important, are only indirectly related to the dynamics of the IJV relationship. Given our primary interest in shifts in partner bargaining power associated with the acquisition of knowledge, the resource-based components are of particular interest. The resources and capabilities committed by the partners to the JV were a major source of bargaining power. Expertise in areas such as local sourcing, domestic distribution, and personnel management was the main resource contributed by the local partners (Yan & Gray, 1994). For the foreign partners, resource contributions included expertise and technology for production management and global support.

To link the partner resource contributions directly to bargaining power and to understand the process of bargaining power shifts, concepts of organizational knowledge management must be incorporated in the framework. The pace of knowledge acquisition by one IJV partner is an important process dimension, because, as Hamel (1991) argued, this dimension is very much within the firm's control. Therefore, Hamel identified learning as the most important element in determining relative bargaining power. Substantial knowledge acquisition by one partner over time can erode the value of the knowledge contributed by the other partner, breaking down the bargaining relationship between the partners. This argument forms the fundamental conceptual premise of this article: The acquisition of knowledge and skills can shift an IJV partner's bargaining power and may enable the firm to eliminate its dependency on its partner.

Partners in IJVs acquire knowledge and skills through a process of knowledge management and creation. Although still rather small, there is a growing body of theoretical (Kogut, 1988; Parkhe, 1991; Pucik, 1991; Westney, 1988) and empirical studies (Dodgson, 1993; Hamel, 1991; Inkpen, 1995a; Inkpen & Crossan, 1995; Simonin & Helleloid, 1993) addressing the issue of JVs and alliances as mechanisms for gaining access to partners' knowledge and skills. When a JV is created, organizational boundaries become permeable. This permeability provides firms with a "window on their partners' broad capabilities" (Hamel, Doz, & Prahalad, 1989: 134). Consequently, knowledge creation and learning should be viewed as potential strategic benefits of joint venturing.

By forming a JV, partner firms may gain access to the embedded knowledge of other organizations and, therefore, to new organizational skills and capabilities. Through their involvement in the operation of the JV, firms can learn from their partners. Huber (1991) called this *grafting*, the process by which firms internalize knowledge not previously available within the organization. Knowledge perceived as potentially useful for the organization may be acquired by individual managers or organizational subunits, such as a JV (Inkpen, 1995b). This knowledge has the potential to be shared and distributed within the organization, and through processes of amplification and interpretation, the knowledge is

FIGURE 1

Boundaries of the Article: Partner Knowledge, Bargaining Power, and the Instability of International Joint Ventures (IJVs)

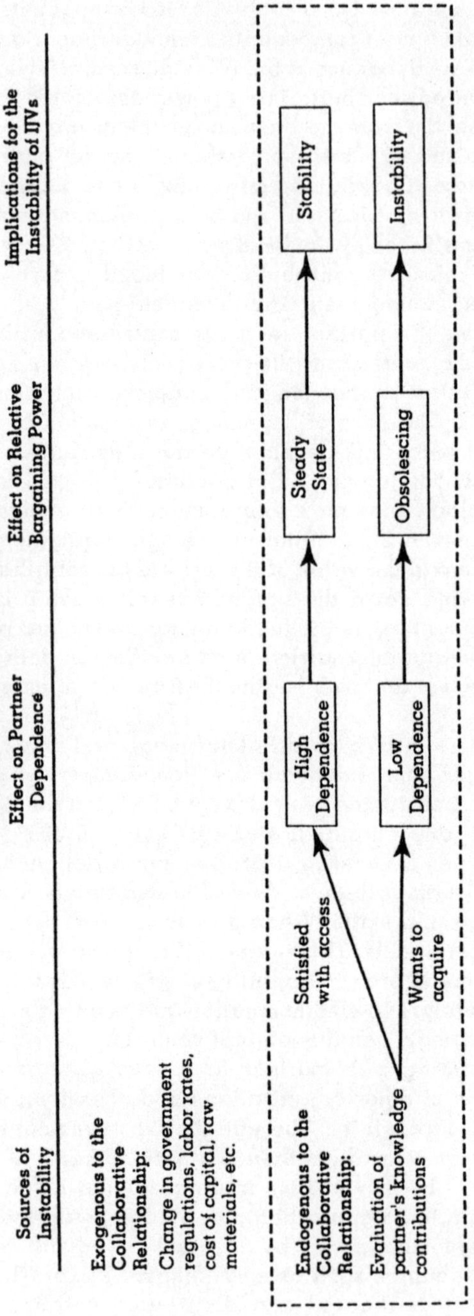

Sources of Instability	Effect on Partner Dependence	Effect on Relative Bargaining Power	Implications for the Instability of IJVs

Exogenous to the Collaborative Relationship:

Change in government regulations, labor rates, cost of capital, raw materials, etc.

Endogenous to the Collaborative Relationship:

Evaluation of partner's knowledge contributions

Satisfied with access

Wants to acquire

High Dependence → Steady State → Stability

Low Dependence → Obsolescing → Instability

FIGURE 2
Instability of the International Joint Venture (IJV) and the Foreign Partner's Bargaining Power

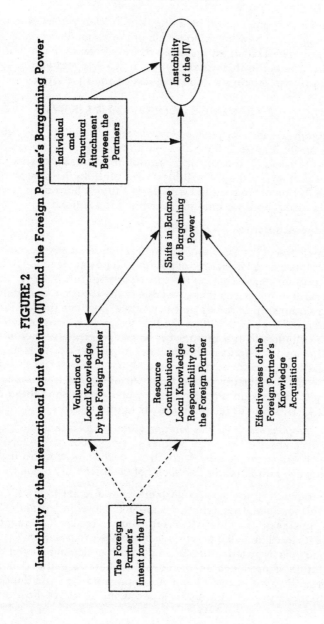

given shared organizational meaning (Daft & Weick, 1984; Nonaka, 1994). The translation of new knowledge into organizational action is the basis for creating new skills that underpin a firm's competitive advantage. Of particular interest in this article is the knowledge that enables firms involved in IJVs to eliminate dependencies on their partners.

A FRAMEWORK OF INSTABILITY IN IJVs

Through a focus on partner knowledge acquisition that shifts bargaining power, Figure 2 illustrates the framework of the instability of the IJV. As discussed in the previous section, the initial balance of power between partners of the IJV will inevitably shift. In the next sections, we examine the factors associated with these shifts in bargaining power, and from this discussion, we generate specific propositions.

Knowledge Acquisition by the Foreign Partner

Knowledge of the local environment is usually a key resource of local partners; it is also a key source of bargaining power, because it makes the foreign partner dependent on the local partner (Yan & Gray, 1994). As a foreign partner increases its knowledge of the local market, instability of the IJV relationship becomes more probable, because the foreign partner gains bargaining power. When the JV was formed, local knowledge may have contributed to the mutual needs of the partners (Beamish, 1988). When the need dissipates, and the foreign partner acquires local knowledge, the foreign partner may view a JV as unnecessary. In effect, over time, the unique domain of the local partner shifts from being complementary to the foreign partner to being undistinguished (Ring & Van de Ven, 1994). This line of reasoning leads to the following proposition:

> Proposition 1: As the foreign partner's local knowledge increases, the foreign partner's dependence on the local partner decreases, leading to a shift in bargaining power and greater likelihood of the instability of the IJV.

A reduction in the foreign partner's commitment to the IJV and need for its partner need does not always mean the foreign partner will acquire the IJV business or establish a subsidiary. As the foreign partner increases its local knowledge, various outcomes are possible. For example, an increase in knowledge that erased a partner dependency plus a desire to maintain a presence in the local market were the circumstances prompting Ralston Purina, Bayer AG, Monsanto Co., and Sandoz to convert alliances to subsidiaries in Japan (Ono, 1991).[5] In Ralston Purina's

---

[5] A popular stereotype is that of a "naive" U.S. firm contributing technology and a Japanese firm contributing local knowledge to a Japan-based JV. After several years of operation, the Japanese company is familiar with the technology and no longer needs the JV, whereas the U.S. firm has gained nothing in the local market. There is no systematic

FIGURE 3
Knowledge Acquisition and Instability

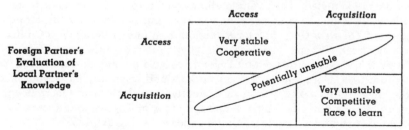

Local Partner's Evaluation of
Foreign Partner's Knowledge

case, the firm ended its 20-year venture with Taiyo Fishery Company and established a wholly owned Japanese subsidiary. After gaining experience in Japan, Ralston Purina's management apparently decided that a Japanese partner was no longer necessary.

Alternatively, as the foreign partner learns about local market realities, it may decide to withdraw from the market. In contrast, the foreign partner may seek a more prominent role in the management of the JV, leading to conflict over the division of control, which in turn could lead to an unstable relationship. Finally, as we discuss in another section, the embedded history of prior relationships between the partners may be a stabilizing factor that counterbalances shifts in bargaining power.

Knowledge Acquisition by the Local Partner

In contrast to the foreign partner's building of a local knowledge base, the local partner may acquire the skills of its foreign partner, making the IJV redundant, because the foreign partner's skill-based resource contributions are no longer needed. In their study of U.S.-China JVs, Yan and Gray (1994) found that for Chinese firms in IJVs, the overwhelming goal in cooperating with Western firms was to learn the more advanced Western technology. The Chinese partners fully expected that management would shift from the foreigners to them. However, Yan and Gray (1994) concluded that the Chinese partners did not significantly gain bargaining power through knowledge, because the U.S. partners protected

---

evidence to support this argument. Many technology-licensing arrangements in Japan have ended this way, but these were not JVs designed to enter the Japanese market. As the Purina, Monsanto, Bayer, and Sandoz cases suggest, foreign firms in Japan are capable of making their local partners obsolete. According to Jones and Shill (1993), the survival record of Western-Japanese alliances in Japan is very good. These authors studied 200 alliances that were terminated and found that, on average, the alliances lasted 20 years.

their technologies. Also, the U.S. partners were able to maintain the original balance of bargaining power by making additional resource commitments to their technological capabilities.

Even if local partners have unhindered access to the foreign partner's skills, the knowledge required to eliminate a foreign dependency is usually more difficult to acquire for the local partner than for the foreign partner. The New United Motor Manufacturing Inc. (NUMMI) JV in California between General Motors and Toyota illustrates this point. Because NUMMI had been managed by Toyota, Toyota's managers were forced to learn how to work with American workers and labor unions. Toyota has deployed its new knowledge in a wholly owned plant in Georgetown, Kentucky. As described by a senior manager at Toyota, that knowledge came directly from Toyota's NUMMI experience (Sasaki, 1993).

Hedlund (1994) distinguished among three forms of knowledge: (a) cognitive knowledge in the form of mental constructs, (b) skills, and (c) knowledge embodied in products and well-defined services. Hedlund suggested that embodied knowledge was the easiest to transfer, followed by cognitive knowledge, and skills were most difficult to transfer. Skills, such as complex engineering processes, are highly embedded in organizational routines (Nelson & Winter, 1982) and, therefore, are difficult to extract from another firm. Also, the foreign partner can take explicit measures to protect the transparency of its skills, particularly if the skills comprise explicit knowledge held by a few "experts" (e.g., Kentucky Fried Chicken's secret recipe of herbs and spices). Local knowledge, such as investment regulations, supplier practices, labor laws, and cultural traditions, can be classified primarily as cognitive knowledge. Cognitive knowledge is usually easier to transfer than are skills, because it is not as sensitive to team embeddedness (Zander, 1991, cited in Hedlund, 1994). In many cases, it is tacit knowledge (Polanyi, 1966) that is highly contact dependent; for IJVs, the context is the local environment. Because this knowledge often comes packaged in the form of individuals (Hedlund, 1994), foreign partners can gain access to the knowledge through active managerial involvement in the IJV process. In other words, the experience of the managers in an IJV is the key to acquiring this type of knowledge (Nonaka & Takeuchi, 1995).

The skills provided by the foreign partner, such as how to manufacture high-precision products, will consist of a combination of both tacit and explicit, or codifiable, knowledge. The explicit knowledge that can be expressed in schemata, diagrams, and charts is relatively easy to transfer, although as Zander (1991) found, codifiability does not necessarily lead to faster competitor imitation. Because tacit and explicit knowledge are mutually complementary (Nonaka & Takeuchi, 1995), there will be a strong tacit dimension associated with how to use and implement the explicit knowledge. This tacit and difficult dimension is the "glue" that holds together the organizational routines associated with the foreign partner's skills.

Empirical evidence supports the previous arguments. Hamel (1991) found that market intelligence was transfered between alliance partners more easily than knowledge of leading-edge manufacturing skills. The local partners in Yan and Gray's (1994) study encountered significant difficulty in learning from their U.S. partners. When successfully implementing a local strategy in the United States, Toyota's executives needed only to learn how to transfer an existing management process to North America. For General Motors to reduce its dependency on Toyota, changes in very fundamental operating philosophies were required (Badaracco, 1991; Sasaki, 1993). The local knowledge that Toyota needed was more accessible and easier to internalize than the knowledge base that General Motors had to build. Finally, Hennart, Roehl, and Zietlow (1995) studied Japanese JVs in the United States and found that when JVs were terminated, the more common scenario involved the Japanese partner acquiring the JV business, and by implication, the local knowledge necessary to run the business.

In summary, knowledge acquisition by either partner has the potential to shift the balance of bargaining power that, in turn, could lead to the initiation of changes in the partner relationship. This is illustrated in Figure 3. To the extent that the balance of power shifts sufficiently to lead to instability, it is more likely that the underlying cause is knowledge acquisition by the foreign partner compared to knowledge acquisition by the local partner. We also expect that the "skilling" of the local partner (leaking the foreign partner's skills to the local partner) should be less likely in IJVs than in other types of alliances, most notably technology-sharing relationships or R&D alliances. This is because a JV is a separate entity, in which the local partner may have difficulty penetrating the venture's boundaries to gain access to the foreign partner's skills. The foreign partner may put up barriers to keep the local partner outside specific skill areas. In contrast, there are fewer boundaries in a technology-sharing relationship, which increases the risk that organizational skills may be appropriated by a partner (for a discussion of learning in R&D alliances from a domestic perspective, see Young & Olk, 1994). There is little question that particularly in the 1960s, many Japanese firms used licensing arrangements as a source for learning their partner's skills (Reich & Mankin, 1986).

The Value of Local Knowledge

The preceding discussion focused on the *effect* of IJV stability posed when partner knowledge acquisition leads to changes in partner dependency. An equally important issue is why, in some IJVs, foreign partners aggressively seek to acquire local knowledge, but in other IJVs, they do not. We examine this question by starting with a key assumption: When an IJV is formed, the contribution of local knowledge by the local partner has strategic value to the foreign partner (Yan & Gray, 1994). Until the foreign partner acquires sufficient local knowledge to operate autonomously, the foreign partner will continue to depend on its local partner.

The foreign partner's valuation of local knowledge involves two stages. The first stage occurs prior to the formation of the IJV when the foreign partner considers the value associated with gaining access to a potential partner's local knowledge. If gaining access to a partner's local knowledge satisfies the foreign partner's resource requirements, an IJV may result. The second stage occurs after the formation of the IJV, when the foreign partner gains access to local knowledge. The question for the foreign partner now becomes: Is access sufficient, or should the knowledge be acquired?

A foreign firm involved in an IJV can choose what resources and how much it can devote to gaining local knowledge acquisition. Acquiring local knowledge *enables* a foreign partner to reduce its commitment to collaboration. If a foreign partner places high strategic value on access to and acquisition of local knowledge, shifts in bargaining power become more likely, because it is likely that the foreign partner will not be content with access alone. Thus, Figure 2 shows a direct relationship between the valuation of local knowledge and shifts in the balance of the bargaining power.

> Proposition 2: *The strategic value of local knowledge to the foreign partner will be positively related to shifts in IJV bargaining power.*

Proposition 2 is a refinement of Proposition 1. Proposition 1 suggests that the foreign partner's knowledge of local conditions will inevitably increase over time, simply because the foreign partner is in the host country. This process represents passive knowledge acquisition. Proposition 2 implies active knowledge acquisition by the foreign partner that can shift the JV bargaining power away from the local partner.

Why would a foreign partner actively seek to acquire local knowledge? The critical factor is the strategic intent of the foreign partner. Firms often utilize IJVs as an entry mode in an effort to balance their desire for international product/market diversification and growth with their perceived need for control. The subsequent desire to acquire local knowledge will be driven by various strategic factors. The decision to acquire local knowledge may reflect a desire to increase control over the IJV because of a shift in the strategic importance of the venture (Harrigan & Newman, 1990) or because of the increased importance of the local market. Alternatively, a foreign partner's increased concerns about leaking proprietary technology to the local partner may result in its acquiring local knowledge.

A partner's decision not to acquire local knowledge may reflect the cost of this acquisition. Previously, we used the example of Kentucky Fried Chicken. In order for Kentucky Fried Chicken to eliminate a dependency in China, the firm would have to learn many complex investment regulations, local operating laws, and so on. Although this knowledge was possible, it could be very expensive, and there was no guarantee of success. Finally, acquiring local knowledge may be in response to the foreign partner's recognition that the original IJV agreement was an obsolescing bargain (Vernon, 1977), because the local partner has little to contribute on an ongoing basis.

Factors Influencing Acquisition of Local Knowledge

When a foreign partner has a strategic objective of acquisition and proprietary control over local knowledge, the speed of knowledge acquisition that is necessary to shift bargaining power will be influenced by two key factors: (a) the foreign partner's effectiveness in acquiring local knowledge and (b) the initial resource contributions of the partners.

Effectiveness in acquiring local knowledge. Although a foreign partner's acquisition of local knowledge can occur passively over time, explicit efforts to acquire this knowledge are of greater interest. This leads to the premise that knowledge acquisition is an organizational process that can be managed by the foreign partner (Hedlund & Nonaka, 1993; Nonaka, 1994). The process of acquiring knowledge that originates with an IJV partner is, in effect, the process of creating organizational knowledge (Nonaka, 1994). Creating organizational knowledge is not simply a matter of learning from others or acquiring knowledge from outside (Nonaka & Takeuchi, 1995). It is a complex organizational process involving various organizational levels and actors. Through this process, specific knowledge becomes amplified throughout the organization. To capture the dynamic movement of knowledge across various organizational levels, Nonaka (1994) developed the concept of a spiral of knowledge creation. In the spiral, knowledge moves upward in an organization; it begins at the individual level, moves to the group level, and finally moves to the firm level. As the knowledge spirals upward in the organization, individuals interact with each other and with their organizations.

In an IJV, managers assigned to the venture from the foreign parent will be exposed to various aspects of local knowledge. Clearly, these managers will develop new ideas about conducting business in the local environment. However, in order for that local knowledge to be internalized at the parent organizational level, there must be knowledge connections among the various organizational levels to create the potential for individuals to share their observations and experiences (Von Krogh, Roos, & Slocum, 1994). These knowledge connections provide a basis for transforming individual knowledge into organizational knowledge. An organization's set of internal managerial relationships facilitates the sharing and communicating of new knowledge.

Although the process of knowledge creation is nonlinear and interactive, specific organizational conditions can be identified that promote this process (Nevis, DiBella, & Gould, 1995; Nonaka & Takeuchi, 1995). Drawing on Nonaka and Takeuchi's (1995) work, empirical researchers using the JV context have identified several key factors that contribute to the ability of firms to acquire knowledge associated with their IJVs (Inkpen, In press). These factors include partner intention, top management commitment, and tolerance for information redundancy. The absence of these factors creates obstacles to knowledge creation. Although a detailed examination of these factors is beyond the scope of this article, it is important to recognize that the foreign partner's effectiveness in acquiring knowledge will influence its bargaining power. If a foreign partner is ineffective at knowledge creation (and more specifically at acquiring local knowledge), it will not be able to reduce its dependency on the local partner.

> *Proposition 3: There will be a positive relationship between the foreign partner's effectiveness in acquiring local knowledge and shifts in bargaining power.*

Resource contributions of the partners. When a JV is formed, the partners must allocate responsibility for various decision areas (Geringer & Hebert, 1989; Killing, 1983). This allocation of responsibility is the basis for determining the resources and capabilities committed by the partners to the JV (Yan & Gray, 1994). These resource contributions are negotiated by the partners, and they are an important factor in determining the initial balance of power.

In an IJV, the local partner is usually expected to contribute important local knowledge. However, this does not mean that the foreign partner cannot contribute resources associated with local management. For example, in many of the Japanese-American JVs formed to supply U.S.-based automotive transplants, the Japanese partners controlled local marketing functions (Womack, 1988). Therefore, the American partners contributed local knowledge confined to areas such as legal process, workforce management, and some supplier management. Without control over local marketing, American partners were in a vulnerable position should their Japanese partners seek to acquire further local knowledge.

Initial resource contributions of the partners, as determined by the allocation of strategic responsibilities, will play an important role in stability of the IJV, because of their influence on the complexity of the foreign partner's knowledge acquisition task. By relinquishing local responsibilities to the foreign partner when the venture is formed, the local partner provides the foreign partner with an incentive to gain complete local knowledge and, hence, to increase its bargaining power. The acquisition of local knowledge by the foreign partner also is simplified if the JV starts out with the responsibility for key local knowledge belonging to the foreign partner.

Thus, we predict that initial resource contributions made to an IJV will influence subsequent shifts in bargaining power. It has already been established that firms will differ in how effective they will be at acquiring knowledge. The foreign partner's responsibility for local knowledge at the time the IJV is formed will determine the nature of the knowledge-acquisition task necessary to reduce a partner dependency. If the foreign partner views the task as complex, it may be dissuaded from acquiring additional knowledge. In contrast, if the foreign partner views the task as relatively simple, it is likely that it will acquire more knowledge, and likelihood for shifts in bargaining power will be greater. Thus, the foreign partner's responsibility for local knowledge will be related to the likelihood of shifts in bargaining power.

> Proposition 4: The greater the responsibility for local knowledge initially allocated to the foreign partner, the more likely that the foreign partner will seek additional local knowledge from the local partner and the more likely that bargaining power will shift.

Regardless of the speed of local knowledge acquisition, it is important to emphasize that when a foreign partner has the explicit intent to gain knowledge, the local partner is in a vulnerable position. In IJVs in developing countries, the vulnerability of the local partners can be high if the local partner is not a competitive threat to the foreign partner outside the IJV's country of domicile. In this case, the foreign partner is usually larger and has greater international scope; therefore, local partners may not be able to prevent a foreign partner from increasing its local knowledge. It is also unrealistic to expect foreign partners to complacently ignore the opportunity to increase their local knowledge. However, as Dymsza (1988) noted, the foreign firm's contribution may become less important over time if the firm from the developing country is committed to increasing its skills.

Furthermore, if the value of local knowledge declines, in terms of either access or acquisition, the foreign partner may choose to end the venture. For example, local knowledge may decline in value if changes in local regulations open up a previously closed economy to greater competition.

Attachment Between the Partners

Attachment is the binding of one party to another (Salancik, 1977). Attachment between partners develops through experience in the collaborative relationship and through investments the partners make in the relationship over time (Seabright et al., 1992). When the partners have developed a strong attachment, inertial forces may block the pressures for change in the relationship (Blau, 1964; Salancik, 1977). If firms have worked together in the past, they will have a basic understanding about each other's skills and capabilities (Heide & Miner, 1992). The partners may have developed commitments to each other because of a relationship that existed prior to forming the JV. According to Parkhe (1993a: 803), "The older a relationship, the greater the likelihood it has passed through a critical shakeout period of conflict and influence attempts by both sides."

Because of prior relationships, firms often form JVs with firms with whom they have transacted in the past. For example, in a study of 40 IJVs, Inkpen (1995a) found that in 24 cases, the partners had previously worked together. An MNE's knowledge about its local partner, generated through previous interactions, also can play an important role in determining its equity position in the host country (Sohn, 1994).

Attachments in collaborative relationships may be the result of individual or structural ties that reflect the prior history of the relationship (Seabright et al., 1992). Individual attachment reflects the socialization by individuals during their involvement in exchange activities. Seabright and colleagues (1992) suggested that individual attachments are important early in a relationship but that they diminish in significance as the relationship persists. In IJVs, individual attachment may be represented by personal relationships between partners' managers. Such managers may initiate a relationship based on personal knowledge and trust that in the early years of the JV provides a buffer against the normal pressures of collaboration. It is common in IJVs for a partner's senior managers to take an active interest in the JV process and make a commitment to working with top managers from the other partner(s). Ring and Van de Ven (1994) suggested that personal bonds of friendship can lead to norms of group inclusion and escalate the commitment by parties to a cooperative relationship. They proposed that the likelihood of termination of interorganizational relationships decreased over time, because economic exchanges become transformed into socially embedded relationships.

Individual attachments are closely related to the tenure of individual boundary-spanning managers involved in the IJV (Seabright et al., 1992). A high turnover of managers can lead to a loss of relationship continuity and a reduction of individual attachment. Structural attachment reflects the history of organizational investments made since the formation of the IJV (Seabright et al., 1992). Structural attachments should increase with the duration of the relationship as formalized procedures replace some of the coordination of IJV activities through personal contact (Van de Ven, 1976).

Continuing business relationships often become overlaid with social content that generates strong expectations of trust and forbearance (Granovetter, 1985). Thus, attachment can lead to the formation of JVs that have an existing stock of "relationship assets" (Fichman & Levinthal, 1991) and a high degree of interpartner trust (Gulati, 1995). Parkhe (1991) suggested that the unplanned termination of an IJV is more likely when firms are working together for the first time. Kogut (1989) found that structural ties between JV partners were negatively related to JV dissolution. Kogut's variable for structured ties was a composite of three types of relationships: supply, other JVs, and licensing agreements. Thus, we predict that attachment exerts a main effect on the likelihood of instability.

> *Proposition 5: The greater the individual or structural attachment between the IJV partners, the lower the likelihood of IJV instability.*

The central theme of this article is that shifts in partner bargaining power are the underlying cause of instability in IJVs. As a firm acquires knowledge that reduces its dependency on its IJV partner, the likelihood of instability increases. As we argued previously in the case of the foreign partner, knowledge of local conditions will inevitably increase over time, simply because the foreign partner is now located in the host country. An IJV partner also may actively engage in acquiring knowledge, which results in reduced partner dependency and a shift in bargaining power. However, because of attachment, the shift in bargaining power associated with knowledge acquisition will not necessarily lead to instability in IJVs.

Blau (1964) and Cook (1977) argued that attachment can lead to maintaining a relationship that provides fewer of the needed resources than it originally did. Seabright and colleagues (1992: 123) suggested that attachment "constitutes a counterforce to change rather than a pressure for change.... In this manner, attachment may attenuate the effects of changes affecting resource fit on the likelihood of a relationship dissolving." This discussion suggests that attachment can moderate the effects of shifts in bargaining power. Thus, the effect of shifts in bargaining power on the likelihood of instability decreases as attachment increases.

> *Proposition 6: The greater the individual and structural attachment between IJV partners, the lower the effect of shifts in bargaining power on the likelihood of IJV instability.*

The argument that relationship investments and attachments can moderate the forces of shifts in bargaining power may appear counter to the previous discussion on resource fit and the termination of relationships for the inverse of the reasons for which they were formed. IJVs involve many layers of interfirm complexity (Harrigan & Newman, 1990). Our view is that in any IJV, there will be both resource fit and attachment implications, which may exert opposing forces on the stability of the relationship. The forces may lead to what we term *dormant instability*.[6] When the foreign partner acquires sufficient local knowledge to destabilize the IJV, a situation of dormant instability (or superficial stability from the opposite perspective) results. Thus, the foreign partner may choose to reorient or restructure the relationship, or, because of attachment, it may be willing to let the potential instability lie dormant. In any event, once the local knowledge is acquired by the foreign partner, the balance of power between the partners has shifted. This dormant instability may ultimately have a destabilizing impact on the IJV, because both partners

---

[6] Our thanks to an anonymous reviewer for suggesting this point.

now understand that the foreign partner's voluntary dependence on the local partner's knowledge contributions may not last. This situation also may lead to resentment by the local partner, which in itself is a source of instability.

Attachment and the valuation of knowledge. Our proposed framework incorporates the dynamic nature of IJVs. A foreign partner's valuation of local knowledge will be influenced by both strategic factors and by the strength of the partner relationship. This valuation is represented in Figure 2 by the feedback loop from attachment to the valuation of local knowledge by the foreign partner. Attachment is the result of an evolving history of partner interactions. When an IJV is formed, attachments may be present that may have developed either through prior interfirm relationships or during the negotiation stage. As the duration of an IJV increases, structural attachments will likely continue to develop. Individual attachments may increase or decrease, depending on the continuity of managers involved in the IJV. As the level of attachment changes, we predict that this shift will influence the foreign partner's evaluation of the strategic value associated with its partner's local knowledge.

> Proposition 7: Changes in individual and structural attachment between IJV partners will lead to updating of the foreign partner's valuation of local knowledge.

Managerial Implications

For a foreign firm that is interested in maintaining a stable, long-term IJV relationship, this article has several implications. First, explicit attempts to build knowledge of the local country by capitalizing on the local partner's experience are usually transparent and may be interpreted by local partners as competitive rather than collaborative in nature. Second, IJV partners may have to let their IJV develop its own culture and systems. General Electric has followed this strategy with its successful Japanese JVs. GE has leveraged its Japanese partners' names to recruit personnel for its JVs and allowed its JVs to develop into independent companies without interference from the parents in day-to-day management (Turpin, 1993). Third, continuity in the personal relationships between the top management of both partners can be an important source of attachment between the partners. Without continuity, there is the risk of "corporate amnesia," whereby managers in the parent companies forget their original motivation for this alliance and the past lessons from their relationship (Turpin, 1993).

Toppan Moore, a JV between Toppan Printing of Japan and Moore Corporation (Moore) of Canada, provides a good example of a stable, long-lasting collaboration (Beamish & Makino, 1994). With 1994 revenues of more than $1.5 billion and more than 3,000 employees, Toppan Moore was Japan's largest company that produced business forms and its third largest printing company. In this, Moore contributed manufacturing and product technologies, and the Japanese partner assumed initial responsibility for sales, distribution, and local marketing support.[7] Over time, the JV modified products to meet the requirements of Japanese customers and developed its own production capabilities, reducing its day-to-day dependence on Moore. Moore maintained its bargaining power by continuing to make technological and marketing contributions. Although the Japanese partner's immediate operational need for Moore lessened, access to future technological developments remained an important aspect of the relationship. Consequently, the advantages of collaboration for Moore and Toppan Printing continued to outweigh the need for competition.

Local partners and the control of instability. When a local partner is interested in stability, it should consider several ideas associated with controlling IJV stability and minimizing the foreign partner's acquisition of local knowledge. First, the local partner can discourage the foreign partner from sending large numbers of managers to the venture. As we indicated previously, knowledge creation in organizations begins with individuals. The greater the number of foreign managers at the IJV, the greater the foreign partner's access to local knowledge. Second, the local partner can continue to actively invest in local knowledge. In other words, the local partner should not treats its knowledge contributions passively, but it should continue to upgrade the value of the knowledge to the foreign partner. Third, the local partner can consider the track records of potential partners, particularly how long other IJVs that they were a part of have survived. This record should provide an indication of the foreign partner's expectations regarding the role of the local partner. Finally, the local partner can bargain for greater responsibility in managing the JV and, in effect, increase the importance of its role in the venture's success.

CONCLUSION

When JVs are formed to exploit interfirm differences in skills, there is always the risk that one partner may acquire knowledge that it lacked when the alliance was formed (Parkhe, 1993b). In fact, many firms enter JVs with the objective to gain explicit knowledge (Hamel, 1991; Inkpen, 1995a). When knowledge acquisition shifts the balance of bargaining power between partners, the cooperative basis for the JV may erode, and venture instability may result. Even though this argument applies to any JV in which partner knowledge contributions create a dependency, the focus in this article was on IJVs and the specific nature of local knowledge. When a JV is international and the foreign partner seeks to expand

---

[7] Given the difficulty in penetrating Japanese markets, it is unlikely that Moore was in a position to control sales and distribution in the JV when it was formed. However, the examples of Ralston Purina, Bayer AG, and Monsanto Co. suggest that foreign firms can acquire local marketing knowledge over time.

its geographic scope of operations, the local partner's knowledge of local economic, political, and cultural environments will be a key contribution to the JV. Our main argument is that once the venture is formed, if the foreign partner attaches a high value to the acquisition of local knowledge and has the ability to acquire the knowledge, the probability of JV instability increases. Once the foreign partner has acquired local knowledge, unless the local partner is contributing other valuable and nonimitable skills to the JV, the rationale for cooperation will be eliminated. Instability may be the result, although attachment between the partners may moderate the shifts in bargaining power. Thus, the acquisition of local knowledge is an enabling device for the foreign partner to operate autonomously.

Although some ventures are formed in which the partners agree on a termination plan, this article was focused on instability as an undesirable event for one or all partners. Given its undesirability, if a local partner takes steps to ensure that its role encompasses more than simply contributing local knowledge, instability may be controllable. A foreign partner also may choose as a viable strategy access of local knowledge rather than acquisition of the knowledge. Consequently, IJVs can be stable and sustainable arrangements for creating competitive advantage.

REFERENCES

Badaracco, J. 1991. *The knowledge link.* Boston: Harvard Business School Press.

Bacharach, S., & Lawler, E. J. 1980. *Power and politics in organizations.* San Francisco: Jossey-Bass.

Bartlett, C. A., & Ghoshal, S. 1989. *Managing across borders: The transnational solution.* Boston: Harvard Business School Press.

Beamish, P. W. 1988. *Multinational joint ventures in developing countries.* London: Routledge.

Beamish, P. W., & Makino, S. 1994. Toppan Moore. In P. W. Beamish, J. P. Killing, D. Lecraw, & A. Morrison (Eds.), *International management* (2nd ed.): 388-402. Burr Ridge, IL: Irwin.

Blau, P. M. 1964. *Exchange and power in social life.* New York: Wiley.

Bleeke, J., & Ernst, D. 1991. The way to win in cross-border alliances. *Harvard Business Review,* 69(6): 127-135.

Blodgett, L. L. 1992. Factors in the instability of international joint ventures: An event history analysis. *Strategic Management Journal,* 13: 475-481.

Contractor, F. J., & Lorange, P. 1988. Why should firms cooperate: The strategy and economics basis for cooperative ventures. In F. Contractor & P. Lorange (Eds.), *Cooperative strategies in international business:* 3-30. Lexington, MA: Lexington Books.

Cook, K. 1977. Exchange and power in networks of interorganizational relations. *Sociological Quarterly,* 18: 62-82.

Daft, R. L., & Weicke, K. E. 1984. Toward a model of organizations as interpretation systems. *Academy of Management Review,* 9: 284-295.

Dodgson, M. 1993. Learning, trust, and technological collaboration. *Human Relations,* 46: 77-95.

Doz, Y., Prahalad, C. K., & Hamel, G. 1990. Control, change, and flexibility: The dilemma of transnational collaboration. In C. Bartlett, Y. Doz, & G. Hedlund (Eds.), *Managing the global firm:* 117-143. London: Routledge.

Dymsza, W. A. 1988. Successes and failures of joint ventures in developing countries: Lessons from experience. In F. Contractor & P. Lorange (Eds.), *Cooperative strategies in international business:* 403-424. Lexington, MA: Lexington Books.

Emerson, R. M. 1962. Power dependence relationships. *American Sociological Review,* 27(February): 31-41.

Fichman, M., & Levinthal, D. A. 1991. Honeymoons and the liability of adolescence: A new perspective on duration dependence in social and organizational relationships. *Academy of Management Review,* 16: 442-468.

Franko, L. 1971. *Joint venture survival in multinational companies.* New York: Praeger.

Geringer, J. M., & Hebert, L. 1989. Control and performance of international joint ventures. *Journal of International Business Studies,* 20: 235-254.

Granovetter, M. 1985. Economic action and social structure: The problem of embeddedness. *American Journal of Sociology,* 78: 481-510.

Gulati, R. 1995. Does familiarity breed trust? The implications of repeated ties for contractual choice in alliances. *Academy of Management Journal,* 38: 85-112.

Hamel, G. 1991. Competition for competence and inter-partner learning within international strategic alliances [Special Issue]. *Strategic Management Journal,* 12: 83-104.

Hamel, G., Doz, Y. L., & Prahalad, C. K. 1989. Collaborate with your competitors—and win. *Harvard Business Review,* 67(1): 133-139.

Harrigan, K. R. 1986. *Managing for joint venture success.* Lexington, MA: Lexington Books.

Harrigan, K. R., & Newman, W. H. 1990. Bases of interorganizational cooperation: Propensity, power, persistence. *Journal of Management Studies,* 27: 417-434.

Hedlund, G. 1994. A model of knowledge management and the N-form corporation. *Strategic Management Journal.* 15: 73-90.

Hedlund, G., & Nonaka, I. 1993. Models of knowledge management in the West and Japan. In P. Lorange, B. Chakravarthy, J. Roos, & A. Van de Ven (Eds.), *Implementing strategic processes: Change, learning, and cooperation:* 117-144. Oxford: Basil Blackwell.

Heide, J. B., & Miner, A. S. 1992. The shadow of the future: Effects of anticipated interaction and the frequency of contact on buyer-seller cooperation. *Academy of Management Journal,* 35: 265-291.

Hennart, J. F. 1991. The transactions cost theory of joint ventures: An empirical study of Japanese subsidiaries in the United States. *Management Science,* 37: 483-497.

Hennart, J. F., Roehl, T., & Zietlow, D. S. 1995. *"Trojan horse" or "workhorse"? The evolution of U.S.-Japanese joint ventures in the United States*—Revised. CIBER Working paper 95-103, College of Commerce and Business Administration, University of Illinois, Urbana-Champaign, IL.

Huber, G. P. 1991. Organizational learning: The contributing processes and a review of the literatures. *Organization Science,* 2: 88-117.

Inkpen, A. C. 1995a. *The management of international joint ventures: An organizational learning perspective.* London: Routledge.

Inkpen, A. C. 1995b. Organizational learning and international joint ventures. *Journal of International Management,* 1: 165-198.

Inkpen, A. C. In press. An examination of knowledge management in international joint ventures. In P. W. Beamish & J. P. Killing (Eds.), *Cooperative strategies: North American perspectives.* San Francisco: New Lexington Press.

Inkpen, A. C., & Crossan, M. M. 1995. Believing is seeing: Joint ventures and organization learning. *Journal of Management Studies,* 32: 595–618.

Jones, K. K., & Shill, W. E. 1993. Japan: Allying for advantage. In J. Bleeke & D. Ernst (Eds.), *Collaborating to compete: Using strategic alliances and acquisitions in the global marketplace:* 115–144. New York: Wiley.

Killing, J. P. 1983. *Strategies for joint venture success.* New York: Praeger.

Kogut, B. 1988. Joint ventures: Theoretical and empirical perspectives. *Strategic Management Journal,* 9: 319–322.

Kogut, B. 1989. The stability of joint ventures: Reciprocity and competitive rivalry. *Journal of Industrial Economics,* 38: 183–198.

Makino, S. 1995. *Joint venture ownership structure and performance: Japanese joint ventures in Asia.* Unpublished doctoral dissertation, University of Western Ontario, London, ON.

Nelson, R. R., & Winter, S. G. 1982. *An evolutionary theory of economic change.* Cambridge, MA: Harvard University Press.

Nevis, E. C., DiBella, A., & Gould, J. M. 1995. Understanding organizations as learning systems. *Sloan Management Review,* 23(2): 73–85.

Nonaka, I. 1994. A dynamic theory of organizational knowledge. *Organization Science,* 5: 14–37.

Nonaka, I., & Takeuchi, H. 1995. *The knowledge-creating company: How Japanese companies create the dynamics of innovation.* New York: Oxford University Press.

Ono, Y. 1991. Borden's breakup with Meiji Milk shows how a Japanese partnership can curdle. *Wall Street Journal,* February 21: B1, B6.

Parkhe, A. 1991. Interfirm diversity, organizational learning, and longevity in global strategic alliances. *Journal of International Business Studies,* 22: 579–602.

Parkhe, A. 1993a. Strategic alliance structuring: A game theoretic and transaction cost examination of interfirm cooperation. *Academy of Management Journal,* 36: 794–829.

Parkhe, A. 1993b. "Messy" research, methodological predispositions, and theory development in international joint ventures. *Academy of Management Review,* 18: 227–268.

Pfeffer, J. 1981. *Power in organizations.* New York: Pitman.

Pfeffer, J., & Salancik, G. R. 1978. *The external control of organizations: A resource dependence perspective.* New York: Harper and Row.

Polanyi, M. 1966. *The tacit dimension.* London: Routledge & Kegan Paul.

Porter, M. E. 1990. *The competitive advantage of nations.* New York: Free Press.

Pucik, V. 1991. Technology transfer in strategic alliances. Competitive collaboration and organizational learning. In T. Agmon & M. A. Von Glinow (Eds.), *Technology transfer in international business:* 121–138. New York: Oxford University Press.

Reich, R., & Mankin, E. 1986. Joint ventures with Japan give away our future. *Harvard Business Review,* 64(2): 78–86.

Ring, P. S., & Van de Ven, A. 1994. Developmental processes of cooperative interorganizational relationships. *Academy of Management Review,* 19: 90–118.

Salancik, G. R. 1977. Commitment and the control of organizational behavior and belief. In B. M. Staw & G. R. Salancik (Eds.), *New directions in organizational behavior:* 1–54. Chicago: St. Clair Press.

Sasaki, T. 1993. What the Japanese have learned from strategic alliances. *Long Range Planning,* 26(6): 41–53.

Schelling, T. C. 1956. An essay on bargaining. *American Economic Review,* 46: 281–306.

Seabright, M. A., Levinthal, D. A., & Fichman, M. 1992. Role of individual attachments in the dissolution of interorganizational relationships. *Academy of Management Journal,* 35: 122–160.

Simonin, B. L., & Helleloid, D. 1993. Do organizations learn? An empirical test of organizational learning in international strategic alliances. In D. Moore (Ed.), *Academy of Management Best Paper Proceedings:* 222–226.

Sohn, J. H. D. 1994. Social knowledge as a control system: A proposition and evidence from the Japanese FDI behavior. *Journal of International Business Studies,* 25: 295–324.

Stopford, J. M., & Wells, L. T. 1972. *Managing the multinational enterprise.* New York: Basic Books.

Templin, N. 1995. Strange bedfellows: More and more firms enter joint ventures with big competitors. *Wall Street Journal,* November 1: A1, A6.

Turpin, D. 1993. Strategic alliances with Japanese firms: Myths and realities. *Long Range Planning,* 26(5): 11–16.

Van de Ven, A. H. 1976. On the nature, formation, and maintenance of relations among organizations. *Academy of·Management Review,* 1: 24–36.

Vernon, R. 1977. *Storm over multinationals.* Cambridge, MA: Harvard University Press.

Von Krogh, G., Roos, J., & Slocum, K. 1994. An essay on corporate epistemology. *Strategic Management Journal,* 15: 53–71.

Westney, D. E. 1988. Domestic and foreign learning curves in managing international cooperative strategies. In F. Contractor & P. Lorange (Eds.), *Cooperative strategies in international business:* 339–346. Lexington, MA: Lexington Books.

Womack, J. P. 1988. Multinational joint ventures in motor vehicles. In D. Mower (Ed.), *International collaborative ventures in U.S. manufacturing:* 301–348. Cambridge, MA: Ballinger.

Yan, A., & Gray, B. 1994. Bargaining power, management control, and performance in United States-China joint ventures: A comparative case study. *Academy of Management Journal,* 37: 1478–1517.

Young, C., & Olk, P. 1994. Why dissatisfied members stay and satisfied members leave: Options available and embeddedness mitigating the performance commitment relationship in strategic alliance. *Academy of Management Best Papers Proceedings:* 57–61.

Zander, U. 1991. *Exploiting a technological edge—Voluntary and involuntary dissemination of technology.* Unpublished doctoral dissertation, Institute of International Business, Stockholm.

Andrew C. Inkpen received his Ph.D. from the University of Western Ontario. He is an assistant professor of management at Thunderbird, The American Graduate School of International Management. His current research interests include the management of knowledge in strategic alliances, trust in international joint ventures, and knowledge transfer in multinational corporations.

Paul W. Beamish received his Ph.D. from the University of Western Ontario. He is the Royal Bank Professor of international business at the Richard Ivey School of Business, University of Western Ontario. He currently serves as Editor-in-Chief of the *Journal of International Business Studies.* His current research focuses on various aspects of international cooperative strategies.

How to make a global joint venture work

*Learning to live with
two parents
is harder than managers think*

J. Peter Killing

*Despite the great potential for conflict,
many companies routinely – and successfully – use joint ventures. With the increasing use of this form of management,
business leaders must think about the
more effective way of managing: shared
management or dominant parent. This
author, drawing from his research with 37
joint ventures involving mostly North
American and Western European companies, explores the different ways executives
can tailor their management approach to
the specific needs of the enterprise. How
fast should the joint venture grow? What
constitutes good or bad management of it?
The answers to these questions and others
are critical to venture success, as is management flexibility.*

*J. Peter Killing is associate professor of
business administration at the University
of Western Ontario, where he teaches business policy. He has taught management
programs in Brazil and Canada and has
consulted with companies there, as well as
with Canadian governments. He is currently involved in the start-up of an
Ontario manufacturing company.*

Illustrations by Geoffrey Moss.

In the 1960s and early 1970s, a number of U.S. and foreign companies, spurred by tales of great wealth lying on the seabed, were independently look-ing for mine sites and evaluating techniques for raising manganese nodules to the ocean surface. By 1980 all of these independent efforts had coalesced into five major ventures. Four of these were international, headed by U.S. Steel, INCO, Lockheed, and Kennecott; the fifth was an all-French venture. At least one U.S. company voiced strong opposition to the notion of bringing in partners, but in view of the technical, economic, and political risks involved, a joint venture partnership was the only means of continuing.

The managers of these undersea enter-prises and others are discovering that they have a lot to learn about the design and management of joint ven-tures. Managers often disparage joint ventures as losing propositions – too complex, too ambiguous, too inflexi-ble. But as projects get larger, technology more expen-sive, and the costs of failure too large to be borne alone, managers in many businesses must learn to accept and work with joint ventures. In addition, nationalistic governments such as those of India and Mexico are demanding that joint ventures replace autonomous corporate subsidiaries.

Joint ventures, however, do have a high overall failure rate, and many of the failures are very costly for the partner companies. According to a study done by the Boston Consulting Group, more than 90 ventures in Japan collapsed between 1972 and mid-1976. Many of these were large ventures that involved prominent U.S. companies such as Avis, Sterling Drug, General Mills, and TRW. And a Harvard Business School study reveals that 30% of a sample of 1,100 joint ventures formed before 1967 between American companies and partners in other developed countries proved unstable because of strategic and organizational changes made by a venture's parents. These ventures were either liquidated or taken over by one partner, or control passed from one partner to the other.[1]

The 37 experiences on which I base this article provide further evidence of poor joint venture performance: 7 collapsed and 5 were drastically reor-ganized. The majority of the 37 were run by North American and Western European companies, and all included a local partner. I will examine the causes of joint venture difficulties and present evidence that not all joint ventures are prone to failure. If the problem types can be avoided – or managed very carefully – joint ventures can be highly successful.

1 These data were collected
as part of the Harvard Business School's
"Multinational Enterprise and the Nation
State" project,
under the direction of Raymond Vernon.
The study was reported by
John M. Stopford and Louis T. Wells, Jr. in
Managing the Multinational Enterprise
(New York: Bowie Books, 1972)
and by Lawrence G. Franko in
*Joint Venture Survival in
Multinational Corporations*
(New York: Praeger, 1971).

The difficulties of double parenting

The problems in managing joint ventures stem from one cause: there is more than one parent. The owners, unlike the shareholders of a large, publicly owned corporation, are visible and powerful. They can – and will – disagree on just about anything: How fast should the joint venture grow? Which products and markets should it encompass? How should it be organized? What constitutes good or bad management?

This last issue flares up when one parent believes that short-term performance is crucial while the other thinks that building a solid base for the future is more important. At the board level differences in priorities, direction, and perhaps values often emerge, for the board of directors contains representatives from each parent. The result can be confusion, frustration, and slowness in making decisions. Some typical examples of conflicts illustrate this problem:

☐ The board of directors of one American-British joint venture continually disagreed about the amount of data required before a decision could be made. The British could not understand why the Americans wanted all those numbers. The Americans, on the other hand, believed the British were flying blind.

☐ An American-German venture, located in the United States, featured board meetings in which the Americans continually wanted to change some of the German operating procedures, which had been imported along with the product design. This request, made in English, was followed by a long discussion in German among the German board members. Their invariable response was negative: "The joint venture will continue to operate the way we do in Germany."

☐ One very successful joint venture manager, who had taken his American venture from $4 million to $60 million in annual sales, had to decide where to locate a new plant. The manager and his American board members felt that the plant should not be put in the same European country as the existing one since they would then both fall under the same union jurisdiction, thus risking simultaneous strike action. The European board members, however, wanted the plant built near one of the existing plants in order to absorb laid-off workers. Finally, after the manager persuaded each side to make concessions, the two partners reached an agreement.

In such cases, an apparently straightforward decision becomes long and complex. The general manager, summoning all his negotiating skills, has to persuade each parent that the other is not getting preferential treatment. The slowness and the confusion of the decision-making process at the board level can place a joint venture at a distinct competitive disadvantage.

Dominant parent vs. shared management

In spite of the great potential for conflict, companies in several industries routinely – and successfully – depend on joint ventures. In the land development and construction business, for instance, they are often used to obtain sufficient financing to assemble large land tracts or to undertake major building projects. Joint ventures are also common in oil and gas exploration.

These kinds of projects are all *dominant parent* enterprises – that is, they are managed by one parent like wholly owned subsidiaries. The dominant parent selects all the functional managers for the enterprise. And the board of directors, although made up of executives from each parent, plays a largely ceremonial role as the dominant parent executives make all the venture's operating and strategic decisions.

In *shared management* ventures, of course, both parents manage the enterprise. In 12 of the 20 such partnerships in this study, both parents contributed functional personnel. The board of directors, also consisting of executives from each parent, has a real decision-making function. While shared management ventures can arise in any industry, they are most common in manufacturing situations in which one parent is supplying technology and the other knowledge of the local market.

The *Exhibit* shows managements' assessment of performance, suggesting that dominant ventures outperform shared management ventures. (*Independent* ventures, which I shall not go into in this article, are free of interference from either parent and perform well; but since freedom in part results from good performance, their high performance ratios are not surprising.)

The difference in failure rates between dominant parent ventures and shared management ventures is striking. Since shared management ventures are not consistently used for riskier business tasks, their higher failure rate is a strong indication that they are more difficult to operate than dominant parent ventures. For this reason, corporate executives should know when dominant parent ventures are feasible and use them whenever possible.

Exhibit	Managements' assessment of joint venture performance

Type	Number of ventures	Poor	Satisfactory	Good	Liquidated or reorganized
Dominant parent	13	23 %	23 %	54 %	15 %
Shared management	20	55	20	25	50
Independent	4	25	0	75	0
Weighted average	37	36 %	22 %	42 %	31 %

When can dominant ventures work?

The trade-off between using shared management and dominant joint ventures is clear-cut: Will the extra benefit of having a partner who is helping to run the joint venture outweigh the resulting disadvantages?

That the amount and type of help needed from a partner changes over time complicates the choice. Usually, a manager will require the partner's managerial expertise in, say, technology or market-related matters for a few years but will soon learn enough so that such help is no longer needed. If, however, the technology or market in question continues to change quickly, the partner's permanent help may be needed. Many companies prefer to start with a shared management venture that they can later convert to a dominant venture. Once both parents have become accustomed to operating the venture, however, such transitions are difficult to make.

Thus, if a partner is chosen for reasons other than managerial input—financial backing, access to resources, patents, or because it consumes a large amount of the product to be made—a dominant parent venture provides the best fit. The president of one Canadian passive venture partner viewed his company's participation simply as a financial investment, offering a good return at an acceptable level of risk. Dominant parent joint ventures are also appropriate when a company takes on a partner solely in response to pressures from a host government. In such a situation, foreign companies often prefer to find a passive local company that (1) has no knowledge of the product, (2) is willing to be a passive investor, and (3) is neither a government agency nor controlled by the government. If the local partner never learns the joint venture's business, the dominant parent's bargaining position with the host government will remain strong.

The passive partner, which may be supplying large sums of money or important technology to a venture over which it will exert very little influence, must trust the competence and honesty of the dominant parent. This partner's representatives on the board of directors cannot be expected to play a large role, especially if the board meets infrequently and perfunctorily.

Using shared management

Dominant parent rather than shared management joint ventures are more likely to be successful. As previously stated, however, shared management is critical in ventures where both partners' continuing managerial involvement is needed. And while half of the shared ventures in this study had to be liquidated or reorganized, the others worked well.

Given the problems that a board with representatives from each parent can create, it is not surprising that autonomy plays an important role in the achievements of shared ventures. The veteran manager of one venture cited a critical success factor for any venture: *early* success. This gives the general manager a base of credibility so that when the inevitable downturn occurs, the manager has the freedom to ask the parents for help if necessary, rather than having it thrust on him or her.

Deteriorating performance in a shared management venture, however, obliges each parent to become more involved in the details of the venture. This reduction in the manager's autonomy slows and confuses the decision-making process, and performance worsens. Such a small fluctuation thus triggers a series of events that can throw the system out of equilibrium, leading to the destruction of the venture.

The worst case of parental overinvolvement I found concerned a U.S. company where the manager made no meaningful decisions. Rather, he spent most of his time collecting information for, and making presentations to, his board of directors. He complained: "In no area was either parent willing to defer to the other's knowledge or expertise. I felt I was dragging an elephant behind me whenever I tried to do something."

It takes considerable willpower for a parent company *not* to intervene when a venture is faring poorly. One Canadian company in the study did

restrain itself, to its ultimate benefit. When performance began to falter, the Canadians allowed their British partners to become more involved but did not jump in themselves. When the British failed to rectify the situation, the Canadians approached them directly —not via the joint venture—and argued that they had had their chance and should now let the Canadians run the show. This was done and performance improved.

Ownership & dominance

Of course, majority ownership and dominance of a joint venture do not necessarily go hand in hand. The parent holding only 24% of one venture's shares was its exclusive manager. And one parent dominated four other ventures, despite the fact that they were 50-50 deals. Many companies avoid 50-50 joint ventures, although they can be managed by one parent if the passive partner agrees.

Of course, not all parents of shared management ventures own equal shares, as evidenced by 5 of the 20 shared ventures in this study. The manager of one successful 50-50 venture stated that the ownership made little difference to the general manager of a shared management venture. In his view, it was the manager's job in a 51-49 or up to a 60-40 venture to ensure that no decisions were "forced" by shareholders' vote since the goodwill of the minority partner would be lost—to the lasting detriment of the venture.

In this particular case, the eight-man board consisted of four executives from the American parent, three from the German parent, and the general manager, who was a former employee of the German company. The manager made it clear to both parents that, should any issue come to a board vote, he would vote with the German parent executives—even if he disagreed with them—thus creating a four-four deadlock. In other words, all issues would have to be negotiated. Yet in 14 years of his administration, no issue has ever been put to the board for a formal vote.

Staffing a venture

Naturally, joint ventures that draw functional managers from both parents are more difficult to manage than those that do not. Managers of international joint ventures may not only have communication problems because of language barriers; they may also have different attitudes toward time, the importance of job performance, material wealth, and the desirability of change.

Particularly troublesome are programs between partners from developed and developing countries. For example, an American-Iranian venture (one of only two in the study between the developed and developing worlds) did have problems until a new general manager sent most of the Americans back home. They could not adapt to dealing with a work force that had, on average, a grade three education. The Americans were replaced with Iranians who were first sent for short training periods with the U.S. parent. Performance improved considerably.

Of course, such differences can delay the creation of an effective, cohesive management team.[2] The ability of managers to interpret one another's estimates—the forecasts of a sales manager, the delivery promises of a production manager, the cost estimates of an engineer—can develop more rapidly in a group that shares many basic assumptions, in which everyone is seen as working toward the same objective.

The president of one Canadian venture with functional managers from three companies supported this notion:

"The differences in corporate background show up in a number of ways. In one division, I discovered I had insulted a senior manager by going directly to a subordinate to get some information. In his previous company, the hierarchy was very strictly observed, and if you wanted information you asked at the top and the request was relayed down until someone could answer. Then the answer came all the way back up. I'm used to an operation where you go directly to the man who can answer the question. Employees of another division are disgruntled with the bureaucracy they find here. They are used to a small, entrepreneurial organization. What we regard as the facts of life, like the time taken to get an approval, they look at with surprise and dismay."

Life also becomes more difficult for a joint venture general manager if the functional executives from the parents, rather than the board of directors, serve as the venture's main links to the parent. In one way, these links will be valuable assets by easing the transmission of technical and other information from the parents to the venture; but on the other hand, they can force a functional manager to pay more attention to the events in and signals coming from the parent company than in the joint venture. One West Coast manager summarized the problem of trying to create a cohesive management team in such a situation:

---

2 This argument is based on the notion of core skills developed by Leonard Wrigley in his unpublished Harvard Business School thesis,   *Divisional Autonomy and Diversification,* 1970.

Harvard Business Review   May-June 1982

"You cannot use your organizational position, because you are not sure where the loyalties of those below you really lie. The people who work for you are not necessarily appointed by you, so your hiring, firing, and promotion powers are limited."

Should both parents contribute managers?

In spite of the comments so far, joint ventures that had managers from both parents performed neither better nor worse than those that did not. (Four out of the eight shared management ventures in this study that did not use executives from both parents were successful, compared with six out of the eleven that did—not a significant difference.)

One of the dominant parent ventures had a general manager from the passive parent. Apparently, the foreign dominant parent wanted to curry favor with the local government. Partly as a result of this unusual staffing decision, the venture became one of only two dominant parent ventures in this study that failed. The general manager explained the impotence he felt:

"I was in a very peculiar and often frustrating position, since I did not control the major parameters of the business. We made most of our purchases from [the dominant parent] at a price fixed by them, and we sold nearly all our output to them, again at their price. Product mix, and even the production schedule, was beyond my control. My number two man reported to his superiors in Germany every day; but because of the language problem, I never knew exactly what was being discussed. Because of the difference in parent pay scales, he was being paid even more than I was."

Having managers from only one parent in a venture can lead to frustrations for the managers as well as parent company executives. One venture manager blamed the demise of his venture on the fact that the technology-supplying U.K. parent had not sent a full-time technical manager to the Canadian venture. Delays caused by explanations via telex, telephone, and letters to the British that their technology needed modification enabled the competition to enter the market first and ultimately prevented the venture from obtaining the market share it needed for survival.

Clearly, there are both pros and cons to using functional executives from both parents in a shared management joint venture. Research suggests no right or wrong staffing choice. But if a venture falls on hard times, mixed staffing may add to its problems.

One European venture provides a dramatic example of the disintegration that can set in.

The American and European parent companies had each supplied the venture with two functional managers, and the Europeans had also supplied its general manager. An American in the U.S. head office explained:

"We had no quarrel with the general manager. He was competent and tried to represent each side fairly; but when it came right down to it, there was no question about where his loyalties lay. As things got tough in the market, they started to make changes in the venture that we did not approve, and our functional managers reported them to us. The problem was that our managers were not supposed to be communicating directly with us; our information was supposed to come from the general manager. At a board meeting, we made the mistake of asking some very pointed questions that made it clear we knew some things they didn't want us to. As a result, our manager who had given us the information was cut off by the others, and we got nothing more. Over time, the split between the managers from the two companies grew, and the place practically became an armed camp."

Not surprisingly, this joint venture was dissolved shortly thereafter.

Guidelines for joint venture success

Knowledge of what to expect with different types of joint ventures—and even the recognition that there *are* different types—is a key to prevention of failure. Another is to plan the management process in a joint venture before it is set up. One manager in New York explained that, in establishing a European joint venture, he spent 50% of his time on legal work to ensure that each parent got a fair deal, 30% of his time selecting the products that the venture would turn out, and 20% deciding on the approach to the market. But the manager allocated no time to determining the input that each parent would make to decisions about the joint venture. At last word the venture was performing satisfactorily, despite continuing debates between its parents concerning its management.

Such an approach is particularly foolhardy since a company may end up with a shared management venture that it could have avoided with

---

3 For a further comparison between license agreements and joint ventures,

see my article, "Technology Acquisition: License Agreement or Joint Venture?" *Columbia Journal of World Business,* Fall 1980.

foresight and planning. Some important guidelines, then, on the use of dominant parent and shared management ventures are the following:

1 If one parent's operational skills are unnecessary to the success of a joint venture, the other parent should oversee the venture.

When forced by a foreign government to enter into a joint venture, then, a company should choose a local partner willing to play a passive role, which is most likely to be found in an unrelated business. Such a choice will also minimize the possibility that the local company will learn enough about the business that the foreigner's skills will become unimportant in the eyes of the local government.

2 If both parents' skills are necessary to the success of a joint venture, but those of one parent can readily be transferred on a one-time basis, the other parent should dominate the venture.

If, for instance, a foreign partner has great technical skills in a slowly changing area, it should transfer the skills to the venture and allow the local parent to make the key decisions. Many managers, however, would rather enter into a license agreement than become a passive joint venture partner because the risks are much lower. They feel uncomfortable making a substantial equity investment without having a significant decision-making role.

There are several possible responses to the dominant parent vs. license agreement situation. First, many technology-supplying companies, instead of putting up cash, ask for equity in exchange for their technology. (Of the foreign parents in this study, 47% did, in fact, receive equity in exchange for their technology.) Second, a joint venture may have a better chance of success than a licensee because technology transfer between a parent and a joint venture is usually easier than that between a licensor and licensee.[3] And third, technology-supplying parents that intend to play a passive role will be much more careful about choosing a partner than a licensee. Thus, the overall risk-return ratio for a joint venture is usually superior to that of a license agreement.

3 If the skills of both parents are crucial to the success of the venture, a shared management joint venture is appropriate.

A shared management venture will result in better decisions than either parent could have made on its own, although the process of making those decisions will almost certainly be slower than that in competing companies. For the sake of efficiency, a company should: (1) choose a partner with complementary rather than similar areas of expertise, so that each company will have separate competencies, and (2) give the joint venture general manager as much auton-

omy as possible, with the board making decisions only when necessary.

The degree of each partner's reliance on the other's skills can change dramatically over time, sometimes eliminating the need for a shared management joint venture – or for any venture at all. Representatives of 13 of the 19 parent companies in the study stated that, at the time their ventures were formed, they could not have carried out the task without the partner's help. By the time the study was completed, however, only 6 still felt that this was true. The learning process naturally weakens the desire of companies to keep their joint ventures together. And the frustrations in sharing power may no longer be balanced by the feeling that, in spite of the difficulties, the venture is worthwhile. "Why not go it alone?" becomes an increasingly powerful argument.

Thus, as circumstances change, parents should be willing to modify a venture. In two cases in this study, dominant parent ventures were converted to shared management ventures; in two others, the reverse process took place. Less drastic modifications may also be required to keep the venture in tune with its parents' needs and its environment. And as the use of joint ventures increases, flexibility to meet the inevitable challenges and changing conditions will play an ever-expanding role in their survival. ⊖

[17]

Strategic Management Journal, Vol. 9, 319–332 (1988)

JOINT VENTURES: THEORETICAL AND EMPIRICAL PERSPECTIVES

BRUCE KOGUT

The Wharton School, University of Pennsylvania, Philadelphia, Pennsylvania, U.S.A.

This paper compares the perspectives of transaction costs and strategic behavior in explaining the motivation to joint venture. In addition, a theory of joint ventures as an instrument of organizational learning is proposed and developed. Existing studies of joint ventures are examined in light of these theories. Data on the sectoral distribution and stability of joint ventures are presented.

The study of joint ventures has attracted increasing interest in the popular press and academic literature. Though joint ventures are an important alternative to acquisitions, contracting, and internal development, the literature has not been consolidated and analyzed. This article provides a critical review of existing studies and new data in order to establish current theoretical and empirical directions. In particular, a theory of joint ventures as an instrument of organizational learning is proposed. In this view a joint venture is used for the transfer of organizationally embedded knowledge which cannot be easily blueprinted or packaged through licensing or market transactions.

The paper is divided into four sections. The first section develops three theories on joint ventures from the perspectives of transaction costs, strategic behavior, and organizational theory. The subsequent section reviews the literature on the motivations for joint ventures and empirical trends in their occurrence. Where possible, the findings are related to the three theoretical perspectives. Because there has been such considerable work in the area of international joint ventures, the third section summarizes some of the major findings regarding foreign entry and

stability. The final section suggests some avenues for future research.

The theses of this article are essentially two. First, it will be argued that most statements on the motivations for joint ventures are reducible to three factors: evasion of small number bargaining, enhancement of competitive positioning (or market power), and mechanisms to transfer organizational knowledge. Second, it will be proposed that the cooperative aspects of joint ventures must be evaluated in the context of the competitive incentives among the partners and the competitive rivalry within the industry.

THEORETICAL EXPLANATIONS

Narrowly defined, a joint venture occurs when two or more firms pool a portion of their resources within a common legal organization. Conceptually, a joint venture is a selection among alternative modes by which two or more firms can transact. Thus, a theory of joint ventures must explain why this particular mode of transacting is chosen over such alternatives as acquisition, supply contract, licensing, or spot market purchases.

0143–2095/88/040319–14$07.00
© 1988 by John Wiley & Sons, Ltd.

Received 15 September 1986
Revised 23 July 1987

Three theoretical approaches are especially relevant in explaining the motivations and choice of joint ventures. One approach is derived from the theory of transaction costs as developed by Williamson (1975, 1985). The second approach focuses on strategic motivations and consists of a catalogue of formal and qualitative models describing competitive behavior. Though frequently these approaches are not carefully distinguished from one another, they differ principally, as discussed later, insofar as transaction cost arguments are driven by cost-minimization considerations, whereas strategic motivations are driven by competitive positioning and the impact of such positioning on profitability. A third approach is derived from organizational theories, which have not been fully developed in terms of explaining the choice to joint venture relative to other modes of cooperation.

TRANSACTION COSTS

A transaction cost explanation for joint ventures involves the question of how a firm should organize its boundary activities with other firms. Simply stated, Williamson proposes that firms choose how to transact according to the criterion of minimizing the sum of production and transaction costs. Production costs may differ between firms due to the scale of operations, to learning, or to proprietary knowledge. Transaction costs refer to the expenses incurred for writing and enforcing contracts, for haggling over terms and contingent claims, for deviating from optimal kinds of investments in order to increase dependence on a party or to stabilize a relationship, and for administering a transaction.

Williamson posits that the principal feature of high transaction costs between arms-length parties is small numbers bargaining in a situation of *bilateral governance*. Small number bargaining results when switching costs are high due to asset specificity; namely, the degree to which assets are specialized to support trade between only a few parties.[1] The upshot of this analysis is that a firm may choose, say, to produce a component even though its production costs are higher than what outside suppliers incur. Such a decision

may, however, be optimal if the expected transaction costs of relying on an outside supplier outweigh the production saving.[2]

Because a joint venture straddles the border of two firms, it differs from a contract insofar as cooperation is administered within an organizational hierarchy.[3] It differs from a vertically integrated activity in so far as two firms claim ownership to the residual value and control rights over the use of the assets. An obvious question is why should either firm choose to share ownership? Clearly, the answer lies in the diseconomies of acquisition due to the costs of divesting or managing unrelated activities or the higher costs of internal development. Thus, a necessary condition is that the production cost achieved through internal development or acquisition is significantly higher than external sourcing for *at least one* of the partners.

If vertical (or horizontal) integration is not efficient, then an alternative is the market or contract. As described earlier, a transaction cost explanation for why market transactions are not chosen rests on potential exploitation of one party when assets are dedicated to the relationship and there is uncertainty over redress. Leaving aside integration as economically infeasible and market transactions as too fraught with opportunistic risk, the final comparison is between a joint venture and a long-term contract.

A transaction cost theory must explain what discriminates a joint venture from a contract, and in what transactional situations a joint venture is best suited. Two properties are particularly distinctive: joint ownership (and control) rights and the mutual commitment of resources. The situational characteristics best suited for a joint venture are high *uncertainty* over specifying and monitoring performance, in addition to a high degree of asset specificity.[4] It

---

[1] Asset specificity is not a sufficient condition: uncertainty and frequency of the transactions are also necessary.

[2] For a careful analysis of this problem, see Walker and Weber, 1984; for an analysis of the downstream choice of using a direct sales agent (employee) or representative, see Anderson and Schmittlein, 1984.

[3] Subsequent to writing the earlier drafts of this paper, working papers by Hennart, and by Buckley and Casson (both forthcoming) came to my attention. The subsequent revisions have benefited from their work, though the substance of the argument has not changed.

[4] It is frequently suggested that institutional choices can be linearly ordered from market to firm. Not only is this conceptually unfounded, but the interaction of asset specificity, uncertainty, and frequency is unlikely, to say the least, to result in a linear effect.

is uncertainty over performance which plays a fundamental role in encouraging a joint venture over a contract.

To clarify why uncertainty over peformance makes the properties of joint ownership and mutual contribution particularly valuable, consider first a joint venture designed to supply one of the parties, and second a joint venture serving as a horizontal extension of one or more links of each parent's value-added chain. In the case where the joint venture represents a vertical investment for one party and a horizontal for the other, the venture replaces a supply agreement. In this case the venture is the outcome of the production advantage of the supplier coupled with the transaction cost hazards facing one or both of the parties.

These hazards pose the problem of how an agreement to divide excess profits (sometimes called the problem of 'appropriability') can be stabilized over time. Transaction cost hazards can face either the supplier or the buyer. Such hazards are likely to stem from the uncertainty in a supply contract over whether the downstream party is providing information on market conditions, over whether both parties are sharing new technologies, or over whether the supplier is performing efficiently or with the requisite quality production. Each of these cases poses the issue of whether, in the absence of the capability to specify and monitor performance, a governance mechanism can be designed to provide the incentives to perform.

A joint venture addresses this issue by creating a superior monitoring mechanism and alignment of incentives to reveal information, share technologies, and guarantee peformance. Instrumental in achieving this alignment are the rules of sharing costs and/or profits and the mutual investment in dedicated assets, i.e. assets which are specialized to purchases or sales from a specific firm. Thus, both parties gain or lose by the performance of the venture.

It is by *mutual hostage positions* through joint commitment of financial or real assets that superior alignment of incentives is achieved, and the agreement on the division of profits or costs is stabilized. Non-equity contracts can also be written to provide similar incentives by stipulating complex contingencies and bonding. A joint venture differs by having both parties share in the residual value of the venture without specifying *ex*

ante the performance requirements or behavior of each party. Instead, the initial commitments and rules of profit-sharing are specified, along with administration procedures for control and evaluation.

A more complex case is whether the joint venture represents a horizontal investment in order to supply both parties or sell in an outside market. The discriminating quality of a mutually horizontal joint venture is that the venture employs assets, such as one party's brand label reputation, which are vulnerable to erosion in their values. This latter aspect is particularly important if the joint venture has potential *externalities* which influence the value of the strategic assets of the parties, such as through a diffusion of technology, the erosion of reputation and brand labels, or the competitive effects on other common lines of business. It is, ironically, the initial complementarity between the parents' assets which both motivates joint cooperation and poses the transactional hazard of negative externalities, either through erosion or imitation of such assets as technology or reputation.

If two parties seek to resolve this dilemma by contracting to a third party, or to each other, the danger is that the agent will underinvest in complementary assets and free-ride the brand label or technological advantage. As a result the contracting party will undersupply, or mark up its price of, the inputs it contributes. A joint venture addresses these issues again by providing a superior alignment of incentives through a mutual dedication of resources along with better monitoring capabilities through ownership control rights. In summary, the critical dimension of a joint venture is its resolution of high levels of *uncertainty* over the behavior of the contracting parties when the assets of one or both parties are specialized to the transaction and the hazards of joint cooperation are outweighed by the higher production or acquisition costs of 100 percent ownership.

STRATEGIC BEHAVIOR

An alternative explanation for the use of joint ventures stems from theories on how strategic behavior influences the competitive positioning of the firm. The motivations to joint venture for strategic reasons are numerous. Though transaction cost and strategic behavior theories share several commonalities, they differ fundamentally in the objectives attributed to firms. Transaction cost theory posits that firms transact by the mode which minimizes the sum of production and transaction costs. Strategic behavior posits that firms transact by the mode which maximizes profits through improving a firm's competitive position *vis-à-vis* rivals. A common confusion is treating the two theories as substitutes rather than as complementary.

Indeed, given a strategy to joint venture, for example, transaction cost theory is useful in analyzing problems in bilateral bargaining. But the decision itself to joint venture may stem from profit motivations and, in fact, may represent a more costly, though more profitable, alternative to other choices. The primary difference is that transaction costs address the costs specific to a particular economic exchange, independent of the product market strategy. Strategic behavior addresses how competitive positioning influences the asset value of the firm.

Potentially, every model of imperfect competition which explains vertical integration is applicable to joint ventures, from tying downstream distributors to depriving competitors of raw materials and to stabilizing oligopolistic competition. Of course, not every motive for collusive behavior is contrary to public welfare. Where there are strong network externalities, such as in technological compatibility of communication services, joint research and development of standards can result in lower prices and improved quality in the final market.[5] Research joint ventures which avoid costly duplication among firms but still preserve downstream competition can similarly be shown to be welfare-improving.[6]

Many joint ventures are, on the other hand, motivated by strategic behavior to deter entry or erode competitors' positions. Vickers (1985) analyzes joint ventures in research as a way to deter entry through pre-emptive patenting. In oligopolistic industries it might be optimal for the industry if one of the firms invested in

patentable research in order to forestall entry. But given free-rider problems, encumbents would tend to underinvest collectively in the absence of collusion. Vickers shows that, for small innovations, a joint venture is an effective mechanism to guarantee the entry-deterring investment. For large innovations it is in the interest of each firm to pursue its own research, for the expected payoff justifies the costs. More generally, Vernon (1983) sees joint ventures as a form of defensive investment by which firms hedge against strategic uncertainty, especially in industries of moderate concentration where collusion is difficult to achieve despite the benefits of coordinating the interdependence among firms.

A strategic behavior perspective of joint venture choice implies that the selection of partners is made in the context of competitive positioning *vis-à-vis* other rivals or consumers. Though this area has not been investigated, the prediction of which firms will joint venture is unlikely to be the same for both transaction cost and strategic behavior perspectives. Whereas the former predicts that the matching should reflect minimizing costs, the latter predicts that joint venture partners will be chosen to improve the competitive positioning of the parties, whether through collusion or through depriving competitors of potentially valuable allies. Thus, two important differences in the implications of a transaction cost and strategic behavior analysis are the identification of the motives to cooperate and the selection of partners.

ORGANIZATIONAL KNOWLEDGE AND LEARNING

Transaction cost and strategic motivation explanations provide compelling economic reasons for joint ventures. There are, of course, other explanations outside of economic rationality. Dimaggio and Powell's depicture of mimetic processes of firms offers an interesting alternative point of view, for it is premature to rule out joint venture activity as a form of band-wagon behavior (Dimaggio and Powell, 1983). In other words, joint venture activity can be analogous to fashion trend-setting.[7]

---

[5] For an analysis of network externality, see Katz and Shapiro, 1985.

[6] See Ordover and Willig, 1985. Friedman, Berg, and Duncan (1979) found, in fact, that firms which joint venture tend to lower R&D expenditures. Their findings, therefore, support the argument that research ventures substitute for internal development and are motivated by efficiency considerations.

[7] Indeed, Gomes Casseres (1987) has found that joint venture waves exist and are difficult to predict by reasonable economic causes.

There is, however, a third rational explanation for joint ventures which does not rest on either transaction cost or strategic behavior motivations. This explanation views joint ventures as a means by which firms learn or seek to retain their capabilities. In this view, firms consist of a knowledge base, or what McKelvey (1983) calls 'comps', which are not easily diffused across the boundaries of the firm.[8] Joint ventures are, then, a vehicle by which, to use the often-quoted expression of Polanyi (1967), 'tacit knowledge' is transferred. Other forms of transfer, such as through licensing, are ruled out—not because of market failure or high transaction costs as defined by Williamson and others, but rather because the very knowledge being transferred is organizationally embedded.

This perspective is frequently identified with a transaction cost argument, even though the explanatory factors are organizational and cognitive rather than derivatives of opportunism under uncertainty and asset specificity. An example of this confusion is the explanation for joint ventures, commonly embraced as a form of transaction cost theory, that the transfer of know-how in the market place is severely encumbered by the hazards which attend the pricing of information without revealing its contents. Because knowledge can be transferred at—so it is claimed—zero marginal cost, the market fails, as sellers are unwilling to reveal their technology and buyers are unwilling to purchase in the absence of inspection.

Yet, as Teece (1977) demonstrated, the transfer of technology entails non-trivial costs, partly because of the difficulty of communicating tacit knowledge. If knowledge is tacit, then it is not clear why markets should fail due to opportunistic behavior. It would seem, in fact, that knowledge could be described to a purchaser without effecting a transfer, specified in a contract, and sold with the possibility of legal redress. In this sense tacitness tends to preserve the market.

Rather, the market is replaced by a joint venture not because tacitness is a cost stemming from opportunism, but rather from the necessity of replicating experiential knowledge which is not well understood. More generally, tacitness is an aspect of the capital stock of knowledge within a firm. In this regard there is an important distinction between capital specific to individuals, and for which there may be an external labor market, and capital specific to organizations, or what Nelson and Winter (1982) call skills and routines, respectively. For transactions which are the product of complex organizational routines, the transfer of know-how can be severely impaired unless the organization is itself replicated.[9]

In this perspective a joint venture is encouraged if neither party owns each other's technology or underlying 'comps', nor understands each other's routines.[10] Or conversely, following Nelson and Winter (1982), a firm may decide to joint venture in order to *retain* the capability (or what they call 'remember-by-doing') of organizing a particular activity while benefitting from the superior production techniques of a partner. Even if a supply agreement were to operate at lower production and transaction costs a firm may choose a more costly joint venture in order to maintain the option, albeit at a cost, to exploit the capability in the future. What drives the choice of joint ventures in this situation is the difference in the value of options to exploit future opportunities across market, contractual, and organizational modes of transacting. Thus, a joint venture is encouraged under two conditions: one or both firms desire to acquire the other's organizational knowhow; or one firm wishes to maintain an organizational capability while benefitting from another firm's current knowledge or cost advantage.

The three perspectives of transaction cost, strategic behavior, and organizational learning provide distinct, though at times, overlapping, explanations for joint venture behavior. Transaction cost analyzes joint ventures as an efficient solution to the hazards of economic transactions. Strategic behavior places joint ventures in the context of competitive rivalry and collusive agreements to enhance market power. Finally, transfer or organizational skills views joint ven-

---

[8] It could be argued that there is no more sustainable asset over which there is, to paraphrase Rumelt (1984), an uncertainty of imitation, than an organizationally embedded source of competitive advantage.

[9] Teece (1982) makes a similar point in explaining the multi-product firm.
[10] Harrigan (1985) provides an excellent description by which firms seek to benefit from technological 'bleedthrough'. For example, internal R&D facilities are sometimes created which parallel the joint venture and staff is then rotated back and forth from the parent and joint venture organizations.

tures as a vehicle by which organizational knowledge is exchanged and imitated—though controlling and delimiting the process can be itself a cause of instability.

EMPIRICAL STUDIES ON JOINT VENTURE MOTIVATIONS

Despite a relatively long history of research on joint ventures there have been only a few empirical studies of their frequency and motivations. In part the paucity of cross-sectional studies on joint ventures has been due to the difficulty of acquiring information. There have been, however, sufficient studies to date to draw a picture of joint venture activity in the United States and, to a lesser extent, overseas for the case of American multinational corporations.

A summary of the broad sectoral findings of a number of studies is given in Table 1. All of the studies rely on the publication *Mergers and Acquisitions*, though a few of the studies had access to the data used for the journal directly from the Bureau of Economics of the Federal Trade Commission.[11] All the studies show a

[11] The Pate data are for joint ventures only between American firms; the Kogut data are for joint ventures located only in the United States.

similar concentration of joint ventures in the manufacturing sector. Kogut finds, however, a higher percentage in manufacturing than the rest. Because joint venture activity appears to be cyclical, it is unclear whether his estimates are the result of the chosen period, the smaller sample, or the correction for announced ventures which were never realized. (The other estimates are based on announcements.)

A problem with the above data is that it is difficult to infer trends regarding the propensity to venture without normalizing for the size of the industry and of firms. Boyle (1968) discovered persuasive evidence that larger firms engage more frequently in joint ventures than do smaller firms. Ideally, therefore, the ratio of joint venture sales or assets to industry sales or assets would serve as a measure of intensity which would correct for size effects. Unfortunately, the data required for the calculations of this ratio are not available.

Berg and Friedman (1978a) attempt to normalize their sample by taking a ratio between the number of joint ventures in an industry and the total number of companies. The measure is conceptually faulty, as there is no reason to exclude parents outside of the industry. Moreover, as most publicly available data underreport joint ventures among small firms, the ratio tends to overstate joint venture participation of industries with large firms. On the other hand,

Table 1. Summary of results on the sectoral distribution of joint ventures

	Manufacturing industries	Natural resource development	Services	Other	Source
Pate (1960–68) (n = 520)	53.5	7.9	16.9	21.7	Federal Reserve Bank of Cleveland, FTC, Mergers and Acquisitions
Boyle (1965–66) (n = 275)	66.1	15.3	5.8	12.7	FTC, Mergers and Acquisitions
Duncan (1964–75) (n = 541)	59.1	12.8	20.7	8.1	Bureau of Economics, FTC, Mergers and Acquisitions
Harrigan (pre-1969–84) (n = 880)	54.8	11.7	15.1	18.4	Mergers and Acquisitions, Funk & Scott
Berg and Friedman (1966–70) (n = 1762)	60.4	9.5	N.A.	30.1*	Bureau of Economics, FTC, Mergers and Acquisitions
Kogut (1971–85) (n = 148)	67.1	12.8	11.3	8.7	Questionnaire based on Mergers and Acquisitions (U.S.-based only)

* Includes services
Sources: Pate (1969). Boyle (1968). Duncan and Harrigan, reported in Harrigan (1985). Berg and Friedman (1978a), and author's estimate.

they find that the ratio is correlated at 0.95 with the absolute number of joint ventures in an industry; moreover, their sample is dominated by ventures between two firms from the same industry as the joint venture. Joint venture incidence was especially predominant in mining, petroleum refining and basic chemicals, and low in textiles, paint and agricultural chemicals, specialty non-electric machinery. Electronics and computers were found to have a low ratio of joint ventures to the number of firms but a high absolute number. In general, then, their measure appears to provide a reasonable gauge of joint venture incidence except for a few industries. It is important, therefore, to check results using their measure against other ways of estimating joint venture incidence.

Another strategy to analyze joint ventures is to study one or a few selected industries in depth. Studies of this type have been specifically oriented to testing whether joint ventures increase efficiency or enhance market power. Whereas a finding which shows enhanced market power for all firms in the industry suggests strategic motivations for joint ventures, findings of efficiency are consistent with, but not confirmatory of, a transaction cost hypothesis, since strategic rivalry may reduce costs within any firm attaining a long-run competitive advantage. For this reason it has been easier to test strategic motivation explanations for joint ventures than transaction cost hypotheses.

Previous industry studies have found some support that joint ventures are a form of strategic behavior to increase market power. Fusfeld (1958) found 70 joint ventures in the iron and steel industry, 53 of which were supply agreements among firms within the industry. More strikingly, he found that the joint ventures created two industrial groups, in addition to U.S. Steel. Using a rich data set, Berg and Friedman (1977) tested for the impact of joint ventures on firm rates of return in the chemical industry. Controlling for other variables they found that firms which had engaged in one or more joint ventures earned lower rates of return. Based on this finding they argued that, since most joint ventures in this industry involved some form of technological exchange, upstream ventures did not increase the market power of the participants. On the other hand, as they admit elsewhere (1978a), they cannot reject the hypothesis that failing firms

engage in joint ventures in order to stabilize competition.

Stuckey's (1983) investigation of the aluminum and bauxite industry is a particularly valuable contribution because it specifically analyzed whether joint ventures were motivated by transaction cost or strategic motivations. Having examined 64 joint ventures among the six major firms, he found that of 15 possible linkages, eight occurred, that each major had at least one joint venture with another and five had at least two. He also found a high number of joint ventures with new entrants and other industry members. Moreover, while Stuckey noted that many of the joint ventures resulted in more efficiency through achieving optimal scale economies, the ventures between the majors occurred 'in bauxite and alumina production, the stages where coordination on expansion is most vital' (Stuckey, 1983: 201). Hence he concluded that transaction cost explanations appear more relevant to aluminum production, whereas strategic behavior was more prevalent in the upstream stages.

A third strategy is to analyze the within-sample variation across industries among variables to test for the efficiency and market power characteristics of joint ventures by relating their incidence to structural characteristics of the industry or to the characteristics of the parents. Pate (1969: 18) looked at 520 domestic joint ventures during 1960–1968 and found that over 50 percent of the parents belonged to the same two-digit SIC level and 80 percent were either horizontally or vertically related. Similar results were found by Boyle (1968) for 276 domestic ventures, and by Mead (1967) who, after examining 885 bids for oil and gas leases, found only 16 instances where the joint venture partners competed on another tract in the same sale. Thus, the Pate, Boyle, and Mead studies all conclude that joint ventures are motivated by market power objectives.

Pfeffer and Nowak (1976a) investigated more directly the motivation of market power by analyzing transaction patterns across industries and the degree of industry concentration. Out of 166 joint ventures, 55.5 percent were between parents from the same industry. They found that parents from industries which have a high exchange of sales and purchase transactions, and which are technology-intensive, tend to have more joint ventures. Interestingly, they found that joint ventures occur more frequently when the two parents are from the same industry of intermediate concentration. Since it is beneficial, though difficult, to collude in industries of intermediate concentration, they conclude that joint ventures are used to reduce uncertainty when oligopolistic rivalry is difficult to stabilize. In investigating the relationship between parents and progeny they found that again transaction frequency and technology of the venture industry were significantly related to joint venture incidence at the industry level, though no significant relationship was found for industry concentration.[12]

A second study by Pfeffer and Nowak (1976b) found further that horizontal parent pairings were correlated with concentration of the venture's industry. Both studies are, however, open to the problem that concentration and firm size are likely to be correlated; thus the result may be the outcome of the sampling bias discussed earlier. In fact, Berg and Friedman (1980) show that the correlation between concentration and joint venture incidence disappears when controlling for the size of the parent firms.

A number of studies have tried to analyze motivations by looking at the effect of joint ventures upon the profitability of the parents. McConnell and Nantell (1985) analyzed stock returns by an event study of 210 firms listed on the American and New York Stock Exchanges which entered into 136 joint ventures between 1972 and 1979. They found a significant and positive impact on the stock values of the parent firms, with an average increase of just less than 5 million dollars in equity value. Arguing that joint ventures were motivated by synergies, they concluded that the similarities in their findings to those for merger activity imply that both are carried out largely for efficiency reasons. Given, however, that they did not attempt to test further if the positive gains are related to measures of market power, their conclusion is unwarranted, especially given the evidence, as discussed earlier, that joint ventures are frequently used between parent firms in interdependent industries.

Berg and Friedman (1981) tested more explicitly the relationship between industry rates of industry returns, joint venture incidence, and potential market power. Their sample consisted of over 300 ventures (mostly at the three-digit level) and was divided into joint ventures which are and are not formed for knowledge-acquisition. Controlling for other variables, and correcting for autocorrelation in the data, they found that industry rates of return were negatively related to knowledge-acquisition joint ventures and positively related to non-knowledge-acquisition ventures. They conclude on this basis that knowledge-acquisition ventures do not enhance the market power of the firm, for the benefits of market coordination would be immediate whereas the payoff to R&D is long-term. No control was made for structural variables, such as concentration, to test for other market power effects. Their results are also consistent with the view that joint ventures are likely to be chosen to transfer organizational knowledge, as opposed to achieving market power.

In an important study, Duncan (1982) partitioned his sample as to whether the parents are from the same three-digit SIC industry and to whether the joint venture and the parents are from the same industry. He finds that, at the three-digit level, ventures with parents from different industries are more prevalent (73 percent of the sample). Thus, Duncan concludes that Pfeffer and Nowak's inference of market power for parent pairings at the two-digit level is not robust at a lower level of industry aggregation. Since two-digit SIC classifications are too broad to infer collusive motivations when parent firms are related at this level of aggregation, Duncan's findings are to be preferred over those of Pfeffer and Nowak. In addition, he found that non-horizontal pairings between parents or between parents and the venture are negatively related to industry rates of returns. However, Duncan did find support for higher industry rates of return when there is a horizontal relationship between the parents, suggesting that market power objectives may be the objective for these cases.

In summary, studies to date show that there is evidence both for a market power and efficiency argument for joint venture motivations. The Berg and Friedman (1981) study also provides support for the use of joint ventures as instruments for the transfer of organizational knowledge as

---

[12] It is hard to evaluate the results of this paper because the authors move back and forth from multiple regression to bivariate and partial correlations without stating why one test is preferred, and report in one place concentration as significant even though it only tested at 0.15 (Pfeffer and Nowak, 1976: 415).

opposed to means by which to enhance market power. However, these results must be taken as preliminary. None of the studies explicitly tested the effect of horizontal joint ventures between two firms from the same industry on firm rates of return.[13] Finally, whereas evidence of market power supports the strategic behavior perspective, the evidence of efficiency is consistent with, but not confirmatory of a transaction cost explanation. Future work should analyze directly the joint effect of joint ventures and industry structural characteristics on the valuation of the firm and specify more rigorous tests of transaction cost theories.

INTERNATIONAL JOINT VENTURES

Because the subject of how a foreign firm enters a country has been central in the literature on the international activities of the multinational enterprise, there is a longer history of studies on joint ventures in the field of international business. These studies are especially important because, unlike the domestic studies, a few have investigated the choice of joint ventures among other alternatives for entry. Many of these studies have examined the use of joint ventures as a response to governmental regulations, especially in developing countries, through an analysis of a few cases (Tomlinson, 1970; Friedman and Kalmanoff, 1961). Though the case studies are of unquestionable interest, we focus primarily upon studies statistically analyzing entry decisions.

Though, theoretically, there has been significant work in understanding entry decisions as a question of minimizing transaction costs, most studies have empirically investigated the strategic motivation hypothesis. Stopford and Wells (1972) conducted the earliest statistical analysis of the foreign entry decision for 155 American multinational corporations. They found that the use of joint ventures relative to wholly owned subsidiaries declined as the importance of technology and, especially, marketing and product standardization increased. Moreover, joint ven-

tures were particularly prevalent in extractive industries. Of particular interest is their finding that if the entry entailed a product diversification, joint ventures were more likely, ostensibly for the reasons of acquiring local expertise in new areas.

Fagre and Wells (1982) tested to see if the value of a firm's intangible assets influenced its ability to bargain with governments to acquire control, and found that the greater the technological, marketing expense, need for intra-firm coordination, and product diversity, the greater the control (i.e. equity share) of the multinational corporation. The authors explained the positive relationship of product diversity to the preference for wholly owned subsidiaries—among other factors, the superior capability of the multinational corporation to manage multi-product subsidiaries, an argument which suggests a possible contradiction of the earlier Stopford and Wells finding on the need for local cooperation in new product entry. Another interpretation of their results is that multinational corporations will only transfer important resources if they attain control. That indeed the equity percentage reflects an outcome of a negotiation is supported by Gomes-Casseres (1985), who estimated that if constraints were to be removed, equity percentage of joint ventures would stabilize at wholly owned.

Despite a few studies on the choice of acquisition or wholly owned subsidiaries, only two studies to date have analyzed statistically the selection of joint ventures against other alternative entry modes. Caves and Mehra (1986) analyzed the acquisition and greenfield (i.e. start-up investments) entry decisions of 138 foreign firms into the United States. Using joint ventures as a control they found that joint ventures and acquisitions served as subsitute, rather than as complementary, modes of entry, when controlling for other variables.[14]

Kogut and Singh (1986) analyzed explicitly the choice of acquisitions and joint ventures, focusing on country patterns.[15] They hypothesized that

---

[13] Berg and Friedman (1981) and Duncan (1982) employed industry rates of return, which can be argued to be a good measure of the public good characteristic of collusion but is a poor measure of the efficiency implications of joint ventures and for competitive rivalry within industry.

[14] It is unclear from the data whether this is the result of treating only greenfield as wholly-owned or jointly controlled.
[15] Franko (1976) had shown that Europeans have a higher frequency for the use of joint ventures than American firms and Wilson (1980) had found strong country patterns in his greenfield and acquisition study. Edstrom (1976) analyzed only Swedish joint ventures and acquisition.

entry could be influenced by the cultural characteristics of a firm's country or origin in relation
to the United States because of the difficulty of
managing the post-acquisition process. In part,
if cultural distance effects were to be found, it
could be concluded that foreign firms respond to
the *perceived* transactional costs of entry. They
found that acquisitions were positively related to
the size of the foreign firm and negatively related
to the size of the American firm and cultural
distance between the United States and the
country of origin.

Another line of research has been to investigate
the use of joint ventures when there is high need
for intra-firm coordination across borders. If
there are frequent intra-firm transfers of resources
and potential export conflict, Franko (1971)
found that joint ventures are more unstable, and
Stopford and Wells (1972) found they are used
less often. Hladik (1985) analyzed this indirectly
by testing the determinants of whether an
overseas venture would entail either R&D or
export responsibilities. She found that a number
of environmental variables (size of the market,
technical competence of the partner, technological resources of the host country) were positively
related to R&D ventures, whereas scale economies in R&D and the American firm's technological intensity were negatively related. In the case
of exports she found that a joint venture was
more likely to be allowed to export if the product
was outside of, or peripheral to, the parent's
product line.

The studies on international joint ventures
have, in summary, found:

1. Equity share is influenced by the strategic
   importance of the R&D or marketing expenditures and product diversity (Stopford and
   Wells, 1972; Fagre and Wells, 1982).
2. The choice to enter by a joint venture is
   considered against other alternatives, and is
   influenced by the size of the targeted firm
   relative to that of the foreign firm, by the
   characteristics of the industry, and by the
   cultural characteristics of the foreign and home
   countries (Caves and Mehra, 1986; Kogut and
   Singh, 1986).
3. The responsibilities assigned to the joint
   venture are influenced by the capabilities of
   the foreign country and of both partners, in
   addition to possible conflict between the
   subsidiary and the foreign partner (Stopford
   and Wells, 1972; Hladik, 1985).

A DIGRESSION ON JOINT VENTURE INSTABILITY

The international business literature has also
addressed the issue of instability. Beamish (1985)
has recently summarized the findings of several
studies regarding instability. My own findings
have been added, and are given along with his
summary in Table 2. Some care must be given
in comparing the studies. Several authors have

Table 2. Summary of results on instability of joint ventures

Sample size	Development level of country	Unstable* (%)	Unsatisfactory
1100	Primarily developed (DC)—Franko (1971)	24.1†	NA
36	Developed (DC)—Killing (1982, 1983)	30‡	36
168	Mixed (DC and LDC)—Janger (1980)	NA	37
60	Mixed (DC and LDC)—Stuckey (1983)	42‡	NA
66	Developing—Beamish (1985)	45‡	61
52	Developing—Reynolds (1984)	50	NA
149	United States—Kogut	46.3†	NA

* Franko defined a joint venture as unstable where the holdings of the MNE crossed the 50 percent or
95 percent ownership lines, the interests of the MNE were sold, or the venture was liquidated.
† Includes dissolutions and acquisitions. If major reorganizations added, instability is 28.3 percent and
51.7 percent for the Franko and Kogut samples, respectively.
‡ Includes major reorganizations
Source: Table is adapted (with alterations) from Beamish (1985). Calculations of Kogut are from
unpublished data.

defined instability in terms of attitudinal data; others have looked at the dissolution of the venture; and still others have looked at dissolution, acquisition, or any change in ownership. A more complex obstacle to making a comparison is that one of the most potent causes of instability is the age of the venture; there is no correction for age differences of the ventures in the table.

Nevertheless, the table is of interest in providing some idea of the significance of instability. Based on this table, Beamish concluded that instability rates of joint ventures in less developed countries are significantly higher, even after correcting for the higher incidence of joint ventures with governments in LDCs which show the greatest rates of instability. The data from the study by Kogut (1987) show instability rates for domestic and international joint ventures in the United States to be roughly equivalent to those for LDCs in Beamish's study. At this time, therefore, it is premature to conclude whether joint venture instability varies across regions, especially in the absence of correcting for age.

Several explanations for joint venture termination have been offered. One destabilizing source is conflict between the parents and the joint venture. Stopford and Wells (1972), Franko (1971), and Holton (1981) discuss the trade-off between autonomy and parental control, and conclude that the conflict increases with the degree of coordination desired by the parents with their other operations. In summarizing his interesting work on control in joint ventures, Schaan (1985) concludes that satisfactory performance is more likely to the degree to which parents fit control mechanisms to their criteria for success, presumably because otherwise there is likely to be confusion over how each parent can exercise power to achieve its objectives without infringing upon its partner's authority.

There have been a few studies which have methodically examined stability rates in terms of the relationship of the parents.[16] Killing (1982, 1983) found that satisfactory performance was more prevalent in ventures with a dominant parent compared to those where control was shared. However, neither Janger (1980) nor Beamish (1984) found any relationship between

dominant control and satisfactory performance. Beamish (1984, 1985) qualifies Killing's conclusion by finding that foreign majority ownership is not common in LDCs, and that shared control reveals better performance.[17]

One problem with the above studies is the failure to correct for the age distribution of the ventures. Using a hazard rate methodology, Kogut (1987) looked at the influence of cooperative and competitive incentives on instability while incorporating the age distribution directly into the estimation. The results showed that the health of the industry, the cooperative incentives among the partners, and the degree of competitive rivalry influenced stability.

A final way to examine instability among joint ventures is to analyze changes in the environment of strategy. It stands to reason that if the incidence of joint venture is related to industry characteristics or strategies, then changes in the values of these parameters should affect survival rates. Franko (1971) examined instability of foreign ventures of American firms in terms of changes in strategy, as proxied by changes in the organizational structure of the firm. He found higher instability for organizations which had divided divisions into world regional areas. Since firms organized along areas tend towards product standardization and high marketing expenses, joint ventures would obstruct. Franko concludes, the coordination of international trans-shipments of standardized goods and the control over brand labels and advertising.

CONCLUSIONS

In comparing the theoretical and empirical results, it is clear that studies have advanced further in testing strategic behavior explanations. Transaction cost and organizational knowledge explanations involve microanalytic detail which is difficult to acquire for one firm, not to mention for a cross-section of joint ventures. For this reason it is likely that case studies of industries or a few ventures will be the most appealing methodology to provide initial insight into transaction cost and transfer of organizational

---

[16] This conflict is likely to be of a cultural nature as well, if the venture or subsidiary is overseas. See, for example, Peterson and Shimada (1978) and Wright (1979).

[17] Both Killing's and Beamish's results await confirmatory statistical tests. Beamish has provided some tests in his thesis. See Beamish, 1984: 51–52 for the main results.

knowhow motivations. Less difficult, but still formidable, will be the analysis of joint venture formation and stability in terms of the strategies of the parents. It is not surprising, therefore, that more headway has been made into the relationship of joint ventures to industry characteristics.

It should be expected that the theories and their derived hypotheses will fare differently depending on contextual factors and the type of research questions being pursued. A transaction cost explanation should fit reasonably well the choice of how to cooperate when the transaction has little effect on downstream competition. Strategic behavior explanations certainly provide a more informative framework for the investigation of how joint ventures affect the competitive position of the firm. Organizational learning should apply reasonably well to explain ventures in industries undergoing rapid structural change, whether due to emergent technologies which affect industry boundaries or the entry of new (and perhaps foreign) firms.[18]

There is the danger, however, that more profound reasons for the use of joint ventures may be obscured by focusing only on theoretical explanations for joint ventures at the cost of more substantive explanations. Two alternative views are worthy of attention. The first is a reformulation of strategic behavior but only writ large—namely, that joint ventures are a response of leading members of national oligopolies to coopt foreign entrants. It is easy to forget that interpenetration of firms from different national oligopolies is a relatively recent phenomenon. Some insight into the motives of joint ventures might be gained by comparing several of the recent pairings between international firms against the international cartel agreements in oil, steel, iron and other minerals in the 1920s and 1930s.

The coordination of international competition by joint ventures raises a second perspective on joint ventures as one expression of what Dimaggio and Powell (1983) see as the growing institutionalization of markets and the bureaucratic dominance of the economy. From this point of view, joint ventures are another mode by which markets are replaced by organizational coordination. In

this sense, joint ventures are a means by which large corporations increase their organizational control through ties to smaller firms and to each other. In the need to develop a better understanding of the choice of joint ventures against other alternatives of transacting or effecting strategies, it would be a mistake to ignore the larger question of the role of joint ventures in the evolution of national institutional structures and international oligopolies.

ACKNOWLEDGEMENTS

I would like to acknowledge the helpful criticism of Erin Anderson, Dan Schendel, and the anonymous referees, as well as the research assistance of Bernadette Fox. The research for this paper has been funded under the auspices of the Reginald H. Jones Center of the Wharton School through a grant from AT&T.

REFERENCES

Anderson, E. and D. Schmittlein. 'Integration of the sales force: an empirical examination', *Rand Journal of Economics*, 1984, pp. 385–395.

Beamish, P. M. 'Joint venture performance in developing countries'. Unpublished doctoral dissertation, University of Ontario, 1984.

Beamish, P. M. 'The characteristics of joint ventures in developed and developing countries', *Columbia Journal of World Business*, 1985, pp. 13–19.

Berg, S. and P. Friedman. 'Joint ventures, competition and technological complementaries', *Southern Economic Journal*, 1977, pp. 1330–1337.

Berg, S. and P. Friedman. 'Joint ventures in American industry: an overview', *Mergers and Acquisitions*, **13**, 1978a, pp. 28–41.

Berg, S. and P. Friedman. 'Joint ventures in American industry, Part II: Case studies of managerial policy', *Mergers and Acquisitions*, **13**, 1978b, pp. 9–17.

Berg, S. and P. Friedman. 'Technological complementarities and industrial patterns of JV activity, 1964–1965', *Industrial Organization Review*, **6**, 1978c, pp. 110–116.

Berg, S. and P. Friedman. 'Joint ventures in American industry, Part III: Public policy issues', *Mergers and Acquisitions*, **13**, 1979, pp. 18–29.

Berg, S. and P. Friedman. 'Causes and effects of joint venture activity', *Antitrust Bulletin*, **25**, 1980, pp. 143–168.

Berg, S. and P. Friedman. 'Impacts of domestic joint ventures on industrial rates of return: a pooled cross-section analysis', *Review of Economics and Statistics*, **63**, 1981, pp. 293–298.

[18] For speculations along these lines, see Westney, forthcoming.

Boyle, S. E. 'The joint subsidiary: an economic appraisal', *Antitrust Bulletin*, 1963, pp. 303–318.

Boyle, S. E. 'Estimate of the number and size distribution of domestic joint subsidiaries', *Antitrust Law and Economics Review*, 1, 1968, pp. 81–92.

Buckley, P. and M. Casson. 'A theory of cooperation in international business', in Contractor, F. and Lorange, P. (eds), *Cooperative Strategies in International Business*, Lexington Books, Lexington, MA, forthcoming.

Caves, E. and K. Mehra. 'Entry of foreign multinationals into U.S. manufacturing industries', in Porter, M. E. (ed.), *Competition in Global Industries*, Harvard Business School Press, Boston, MA, 1986.

Dimaggio, J. and W. Powell. 'The iron cage revisited: institutional isomorphism and collective rationality in organizational fields', *American Sociological Review*, 48, 1983, pp. 147–160.

Duncan, L. 'Impacts of new entry and horizontal joint ventures on industrial rates of return', *Review of Economics and Statistics*, 64, 1982, pp. 120–125.

Edstrom, A. 'Acquisition and joint venture behavior of Swedish manufacturing firms', *Scandinavian Journal of Economics*, 1976, pp. 477–490.

Fagre, N. and L. Wells. 'Bargaining power of multinationals and host government', *Journal of International Business Studies*, Fall 1982, pp. 9–23.

Franko, L. G. *Joint Venture Survival in Multinational Corporations*, Praeger, New York, 1971.

Franko, L. G. *The European Multinationals*, Harper & Row, London, 1976.

Friedman, P., S. V. Berg and J. Duncan. 'External vs. internal knowledge acquisition: JV activity and and R&D intensity', *Journal of Economics and Business*, 31, 1979, pp. 103–110.

Friedman, W. and G. Kalmanoff. *Joint International Business Ventures*, Columbia University Press, New York, 1961.

Fusfeld, D. 'Joint subsidiaries in the iron and steel industry', *American Economic Review*, 48, 1958, pp. 578–587.

Gomes-Casseres, B. 'Multinational Ownership Strategies'. Unpublished DBA thesis, Harvard Business School. 1985.

Gomes-Casseres, B. 'Evolution of ownership strategies of U.S. MNEs', in Contractor, F. and Lorange, P. (eds), *Cooperative Strategies in International Business*, Lexington Books. Lexington, MA, forthcoming.

Harrigan, K. R. *Strategies for Joint Ventures*, Lexington Books, Lexington, MA, 1985.

Harrigan, K. R. *Managing for Joint Venture Success*, Lexington Books, Lexington, MA, 1986.

Hennart, J. F. 'A transaction cost theory of equity joint ventures', *Strategic Management Journal*, forthcoming.

Hladik, K. J. *International Joint Ventures: An Economic Analysis of U.S. Foreign Business Partnerships*. Lexington Books, Lexington, MA, 1985.

Holton, R. E. 'Making international JVs work', Otterbeck, L. (ed.), in *Management of Headquarters-Subsidiary Relationships in Multinational Corporations*, St. Martins Press, New York, 1981.

Janger, A. H. *Organizations of International Joint Ventures*, Conference Board Report 87, New York, 1980.

Katz, M. L. and C. Shapiro. 'Network externalities, competition, and compatibility', *American Economic Review*, 75, 1985, pp. 424–40.

Killing, J. 'How to make a global joint venture work', *Harvard Business Review*, 60, 1982, pp. 120–127.

Killing, J. *Strategies for Joint Venture Success*, Praeger, New York, 1983.

Kogut, B. 'Competitive rivalry and the stability of joint ventures', Reginald H. Jones Working Paper, Wharton School, 1987.

Kogut, B. and H. Singh. 'Entering the United States by acquisition or joint venture, country patterns and cultural characteristics', Reginald H. Jones, Working Paper, Wharton School, 1986.

McConnell, J. and J. Nantell. 'Common stock returns and corporate combinations: the case of joint ventures', *Journal of Finance*, 40, 1985, pp. 519–536.

McKelvey, B. *Organizational Systematics: Taxonomy, Evolution, Classification*, University of California, Berkeley, 1983.

Mead, W. J. 'Competitive significance of joint ventures', *Antitrust Bulletin*, 1967.

Nelson, R. and S. Winter. *An Evolutinary Theory of Economic Change*, Harvard University Press, Cambridge, MA, 1982.

Ordover, J. A. and R. D. Willig. 'Antitrust for high-technology industries: assessing research joint ventures and mergers', *Journal of Law and Economics*, 28, 1985, pp. 311–343.

Pate, J. L. 'Joint venture activity, 1960–1968', *Economic Review*. Federal Research Bank of Cleveland, 1969, pp. 16–23.

Peterson, R. B. and Shimada, J. Y. 'Sources of management problems in Japanese–American joint ventures', *Academy of Management Review*, 3, 1978, pp. 796–804.

Pfeffer, J. and P. Nowak. 'Joint ventures and interorganizational interdependence', *Administrative Science Quarterly*, 21, 1976a, pp. 398–418.

Pfeffer, J. and P. Nowak. 'Patterns of joint venture activity: implications for anti-trust research', *Antitrust Bulletin*, 21, 1976b, pp. 315–339.

Polanyi, M. *The Tacit Dimension*, Doubleday, New York, 1967.

Reynolds, J. I. 'The "pinched shoe" effect on international joint ventures'. *Columbia Journal of World Business*, 19, 1984, pp. 23–29.

Rumelt, R. 'Towards a strategic theory of the firm', in Lamb, R. B. (ed.), *Competitive Strategic Management*, Prentice Hall, New Jersey, 1984.

Schaan, J. L. 'Managing the parent control in joint ventures'. Paper presented at the Fifth Annual Strategic Management Society Conference. Barcelona, Spain, 1985.

Stopford, M. and L. Wells. *Managing the Multinational Enterprise*, Basic Books, New York, 1972.

Stuckey, A. *Vertical Integration and Joint Ventures in the Aluminum Industry*. Harvard University Press

Cambridge, MA, 1983.

Teece, D. 'Technology transfer by multinational firms', *Economic Journal*, **87**, 1977, pp. 242–261.

Teece, D. 'Towards an economic theory of the multiproduct firm', *Journal of Economic Behavior and Organization*, **3**, 1982, pp. 39–63.

Thompson, D. *Organizations in Action*. McGraw Hill, New York, 1967.

Tomlinson, J. W. L. *The Joint Venture Process in International Business*. MIT Press, Cambridge, MA, 1970.

Vernon, R. 'Organizational and institutional reponses to international risk', in Herring, R. (ed.), *Managing International Risk*. Cambridge University Press, New York, 1983.

Vickers, J. 'Pre-emptive patenting, joint ventures, and the persistence of oligopoly', *International Journal of Industrial Organization*, **3**, 1985, pp. 261–273.

Walker, G. and D. Weber. 'A transaction cost approach to make or buy decisions', *Administrative Science Quarterly*, **29**, 1984, pp. 373–391.

Westney, E. 'Domestic and foreign learning curves in managing international cooperative strategies', in Contractor, F. and Lorange, P. (eds), *Cooperative Strategies in International Business*, Lexington Books, Lexington, MA, forthcoming.

Williamson, O. E. *Markets and Hierarchies: Analysis and Antitrust Implications*, Basic Books, New York, 1975.

Williamson, O. E. 'The economics of organization: the transaction cost approach', *American Journal of Sociology*, **87**, 1981, pp. 548–577.

Williamson, O. E. *The Economic Institutions of Capitalism*, Free Press, New York, 1985.

Wilson, B. 'The propensity of multinational companies to expand through acquisitions', *Journal of International Business Studies*, **12**, 1980, pp. 59–65.

Wright, R. W. 'Joint venture problems in Japan', *Columbia Journal of World Business*, **14**, 1979, pp. 25–30.

[18]

THE EFFECT OF NATIONAL CULTURE ON THE CHOICE OF ENTRY MODE

Bruce Kogut*
Stockholm School of Economics

Harbir Singh**
University of Pennsylvania

Abstract. Characteristics of national cultures have frequently been claimed to influence the selection of entry modes. This article investigates this claim by developing a theoretical argument for why culture should influence the choice of entry. Two hypotheses are derived which relate culture to entry mode choice, one focussing on the cultural distance between countries, the other on attitudes towards uncertainty avoidance. Using a multinomial logit model and controlling for other effects, the hypotheses are tested by analyzing data on 228 entries into the United States market by acquisition, wholly owned greenfield, and joint venture. Empirical support for the effect of national culture on entry choice is found.

Foreign direct investment into the United States has grown dramatically since the early 1970s. Accompanying this increase has been a growth of academic work studying the phenomenon.[1] Whereas impressive information concerning foreign direct investment in the United States in general is available, there has been surprisingly few statistical investigations concerning the choice of entry modes.

The objective of this article is two-fold. First, original data regarding the choice of entry mode by foreign firms is described in terms of country and industry patterns. Second, the factors that influence the choice between joint ventures, wholly owned greenfield (i.e., start–up) investments, and acquisitions are analyzed statistically. In particular, the statistical investigation seeks to

---

*Bruce Kogut is a Visiting Professor at the Institute of International Business at the Stockholm School of Economics and is on leave from the Wharton School.

**Harbir Singh is an Associate Professor of Management at the Wharton School of Business. His prior research is on corporate acquisitions and on top management incentives, and has been published in the *Academy of Management Journal* and the *Strategic Management Journal*.

Of the many helpful contributions, the authors would like to acknowledge Erin Anderson, Ned Bowman, Mark Casson, Richard Caves, Wujin Chu, Hubert Gatignon, Jean Francois Hennart, Jake Jacoby, Tom Pugel, Steve Young, and the anonymous referees. The authors thank Dileep Hurry, Ommer Khaw, Eirene Chen, and Criag Stevens for their research assistance. Funding for the project was provided by the Reginald H. Jones Center of the Wharton School under a grant from AT&T.

Received: April 1986; Revised: September 1986, March 1987 & February 1988; Accepted: February 1988.

explain a striking difference among countries regarding their propensities to enter by acquisition versus other modes. These differences in country propensities towards acquisitions are examined in a framework which relates aspects of a nation's culture to preferences regarding the governance of foreign operations.[2]

This article represents the first statistical test of the relationship between culture and entry choice as an explanation of country patterns of entry modes while controlling for firm– and industry–level variables. Because our measure of culture is derived from the indices of Hofstede [1980], the results validate the usefulness of his constructs, though this was not our primary intention. Moreover, the findings suggest that transaction cost explanations for mode of entry choice must be qualified by factors stemming from the institutional and cultural context.[3]

A PREFATORY NOTE ON TERMINOLOGY

It is important at the outset to define terminology. This article looks at three kinds of entry modes: acquisitions, joint ventures, and greenfield investments. Acquisitions refer to the purchase of stock in an already existing company in an amount sufficient to confer control. All of the acquisitions in our study consist of a controlling equity share with the remaining shares dispersed across many investors. A joint venture is the pooling of assets in a common and separate organization by two or more firms who share joint ownership and control over the use and fruits of these assets.[4] A greenfield investment is a start–up investment in new facilities. Such an investment can be wholly owned or a joint venture. For purposes of simplifying the exposition, we classify all start–up investments which are wholly owned under greenfield and those which involve shared ownership under joint venture.

Many studies, as discussed later, have treated greenfield and acquisition as representing alternative entry modes, with joint ventures being only a question of the degree of ownership. This approach implies that entry and ownership involve two sequential decisions, the first deciding whether to invest in new facilities or to acquire existing ones, the second one on how ownership should be shared. Whereas such an approach is clearly defensible on both theoretical and empirical grounds, we treat joint ventures as a choice made simultaneously with other alternative modes of entry.

Our reasoning can be tersely summarized as follows. Conceptually, it could well be argued that joint ventures are not merely a matter of equity control, but represent a set of governance characteristics appropriate for certain strategic or transaction cost motivations or for the transfer of tacit organizational knowledge [Kogut 1987]. Joint ventures are vehicles by which to share complementary but distinct knowledge which could not otherwise be shared or to coordinate a limited set of activities to influence the competitive positioning of the firm. Empirically, the evidence on whether managers consider joint ventures sequential to, or simultaneous with, other entry choices is slim. It is of interest, therefore, that Gatignon and Anderson [1987], whose results are described in more detail later, find that their statistical model of entry choice discriminates well between wholly owned and shared control choice of entries, but not between wholly owned and the *degree* of shared control. This finding suggests that managers perceive the choice as between wholly owned and joint venture (and possibly other entry modes), with degree of ownership being explained by other factors, such as perhaps the bargaining power of the parties.[5] Consequently, due both to the above conceptual and empirical reasons, we frame the joint venture choice as made simultaneously in consideration with other entry alternatives.

THEORETICAL FRAMEWORK

The theory underlying our approach reflects in some ways a return to an older line of thought in the work on foreign direct investment. Since the publication of Stephen Hymer's thesis in 1960, the economic theory of foreign direct investment has been driven not by country–level variables, such as differences in interest rates, but by industry– and firm–level variables [Hymer 1960]. Industry–level variables reflect barriers to entry and patterns of oligopolistic behavior. Firm–level variables are related to the concept of transaction costs, whereby the transfer of specialized assets between firms is impeded by market failures, thus necessitating the expansion of the firm (in some cases across borders) in order to internalize the transfer. To the extent that the same variables influence whether to enter by foreign direct investment, licensing, or exporting, the choice of the mode of entry is jointly and simultaneously determined.[6]

Because our emphasis in this article is upon country patterns in the entry mode propensities, we do not seek to develop a full theory of entry choice. Rather, we concentrate on only those factors likely to affect national patterns. Observations on differences among countries in their propensities to joint venture, acquire, or invest in greenfield sites have been made by Robinson [1961], Brooke and Remmers [1972], Franko [1976], and Stopford and Haberich [1978] in relation to the lower frequency of overseas joint venture activity by American firms compared to that by European firms. In his study on foreign acquisitions, Wilson [1980] found that there were significantly different patterns of acquisition among American, British and Japanese corporations.

A number of previous studies lend theoretical and empirical support to the relationship between a firm's country of origin and the mode of entry. Two studies, in particular, isolate the influence of culture on entry mode patterns. The investigations by researchers at the University of Uppsala related foreign direct investment patterns to the "psychic distance" between countries.[7] By psychic distance, it is meant the degree to which a firm is uncertain of the characteristics of a foreign market. Psychic distance, they reasoned, would be influenced by differences in the culture and language of the home and target countries. Similarly, Puxty [1979] speculated on the relationship between cultural differences and ownership policies regarding overseas subsidiaries. Neither of these studies, however, laid out systematically how cultural differences influence entry choices, or provided large–sample statistical evidence.

We seek to explain differences in country propensities in the choice of entry modes from the point of departure that differences in cultures among countries influence the perception of managers regarding the costs and uncertainty of alternative modes of entry into foreign markets. Assuming revenues constant across alternatives, managers will choose the entry mode which minimizes the perceived costs attached to the mode of entry and subsequent management of the subsidiary. Because differences in national cultures have been shown to result in different organizational and administrative practices and employee expectations, it can be expected that the more culturally distant are two countries, the more distant are their organizational characteristics on average [Bendix 1956; Lincoln, Hanada and Olson 1981]. If cultural factors influence differentially the perceived or real costs and uncertainty of the mode of entry, there should exist country patterns in the propensity of firms to engage in one type of entry mode as opposed to others.

Due to the difficulty of integrating an already existing foreign management, cultural differences are likely to be especially important in the case of an acquisition. Indeed, empirical studies on mostly domestic acquisitions have shown that post–acquisition costs are substantial and are influenced by what Jemison and Sitkin [1986] call the organizational fit of the two firms. They define organizational fit as "the match between administrative practices, cultural practices, and personal characteristics of the target and parent firms" [Jemison and Sitkin 1986, p. 147]. Sales and Mirvis [1984] document in detail the administrative conflicts following an acquisition when both firms differ strongly in their corporate cultures.

In contrast to the integration costs of an acquisition, a joint venture serves frequently the purpose of assigning management tasks to local partners who are better able to manage the local labor force and relationships with suppliers, buyers, and governments [Franko 1971; Stopford and Wells 1972]. Thus, a joint venture resolves the foreign partner's problems ensuing from cultural factors, though at the cost of sharing control and ownership. Unquestionably, a joint venture is affected by the cultural distance between the partners. But such conflict should not obscure the original motivation to choose a joint venture because the.initial alternative of integrating an acquisition appeared more disruptive than delegating management tasks to a local partner. Of course, a joint venture may be troubled not only by the cultural distance of the partners, but also due to concerns over sharing proprietary assets. A wholly owned greenfield investment avoids both the costs of integration and conflict over sharing proprietary assets by imposing the management style of the investing firm on the start–up while preserving full ownership.[8]

For this reason, we expect that the use of acquisitions by foreign firms entering the United States should be dissuaded, the more distant the culture of the country of origin.[9] The following analysis tests the relationship of cultural factors to country patterns in entry mode choice under two different hypotheses:

1. The greater the cultural distance between the country of the investing firm and the country of entry, the more likely a firm will choose a joint venture or wholly owned greenfield over an acquisition.

2. The greater the culture of the investing firm is characterized by uncertainty avoidance regarding organizational practices, the more

likely that firm will choose a joint venture or wholly owned greenfield over an acquisition.

Hypothesis 1 is derived from the premise that firms from culturally distant countries will attach greater costs to the management of acquisitions relative to joint ventures or to wholly owned greenfield investments than firms from culturally similar countries.[10] These costs may be perceptual only or accurate appraisals of the increased difficulties of managing a foreign workforce in a culturally distant country. Hypothesis 2 is derived from the premise that acquisitions confront firms with greater uncertainty over the management of foreign operations.[11] Therefore, firms from countries characterized by relatively high uncertainty avoidance in their organizational practices will tend towards joint ventures or greenfield investments.

LITERATURE REVIEW

There have been several previous studies which have found that entry choice is influenced by the firm's uncertainty over the characteristics of the targetted countries. In this section, the central findings are reviewed. These studies differ in terms of which entry modes are being compared and are, as a result, complex to compare. The implications for the choice of entry mode are sorted out more clearly in a subsequent section when discussing the relationship of the explanatory variables.

A common theme in a number of studies has been the identification of perceived uncertainty as a function of a firm's experience in a country. In developing their theory of internationalization based on the Uppsala school's work on psychic distance, Johanson and Vahlne [1977] attributed the evolutionary process by which a firm advances from exporting to joint venturing and wholly owned subsidiaries to the reduction in perceived risk regarding the foreign market as a firm gains in experience. They did not, however, explore the implications for country patterns in entry mode behavior from psychic distances between countries, nor stipulate clearly how the experience of the firm mitigates perceived uncertainty arising from differences in cultures.

The influence of firm experience on entry choice has played a prominent role in several of the studies employing the Harvard Multinational Enterprise Data Base. In their pioneering study on the ownership structure of American multinational firms, Stopford and Wells [1972] found joint ventures, relative to wholly owned activities, were less likely to be chosen, the more central the product to the core business of the firm and more experience the firm had in the relevant country. Similarly, they found that marketing and advertising intensity, as well as research and development intensity, discouraged the use of joint ventures.

Dubin [1975] turned to an investigation of the determinants of foreign acquisitions by American firms over the period of 1948 to 1967. Using bivariate cross-tabulations without statistical testing, he found that the tendency to acquire fell with the size of the firm, its foreign experience, and if the target country was an LDC. His findings, thus, suggest an increasing use of acquisitions the lower the cultural and physical barriers between the home and host countries and the more experience the firm has in the foreign market.

Davidson [1980] analyzed a version of the Multinational Enterprise Data Base which was updated from 1967 to 1975 and traced the establishment of foreign subsidiaries from their inception. Through the identification of statistically significant correlations, he found three patterns: 1) that firms will more likely invest where they or their competitors in the same industry have invested before; 2) that countries which have reputedly similar cultures are a preferred target of investment; and 3) that previous firm–level experience in a country— no matter if licensing or joint venture—leads to an increasing likelihood of wholly owned investment for later entries.

The above studies suggest, therefore, that the choice of entry mode is influenced by cultural differences and firm experience. However, because the statistical studies by Dubin [1975] and Davidson [1980] did not test these relationships while controlling for other variables, the explanation for country patterns could be considered to be derived from two spurious relationships. The first is the relationship between the historically greater involvement of particular countries internationally and the influence of firm experience on entry choice. The second is the relationship between differences in industrial composition among countries, differences in the intensity of marketing and research expenditures across industries, and the influence of the desire of firms to control the international extension of marketing– or research–intensive assets.

In the three studies that investigated the determinants of entry mode while statistically controlling for other variables, experience has not, however, been proven to be instrumental in choice of entry mode. Analyzing entry by acquisition versus greenfield for American, British, German and Japanese firms, Wilson [1980] reported that experience did not significantly influence the decision to invest in foreign countries by a greenfield establishment over an acquisition.[12] The decision to acquire was found, instead, to co–vary positively with diversification and negatively with the proportion of recently established subsidiaries to total establishments and with whether the target country was an LDC.

Caves and Mehra [1986] analyzed 138 decisions of non–American firms to enter the United States by greenfield versus acquisition through a qualitative choice model with industry– and firm–level variables as the independent variables, while controlling for joint ventures. Their data was drawn from a listing of reported announcements for the years of 1974 to 1980. Their results disconfirmed the hypothesis that previous investments in a country influenced a foreign firm's decision to enter by greenfield over acquisition into the United States. Rather, they found that size of the foreign firm, diversity of its product range, and its degree of multinationality positively and significantly influenced the decision to acquire. In addition, industries producing durable goods were more likely to be characterized by entry through acquisition because, argue Caves and Mehra, the adaptation of durable goods to local conditions requires skills better captured through acquisition than through greenfield investment.

CHOICE OF ENTRY MODE   417

Joint ventures were found to be negatively related to the choice of acquisitions, thus supporting the premise of this paper that acquisitions and joint ventures are substitute modes of entry. No control was made for country–level variables.

In a recent study, Gatignon and Anderson [1987] reanalyzed 1267 entry decisions from the Harvard Multinational Database for the years 1960 to 1974, also using a quantal choice model. As described earlier, their analysis of entry as a three–way decision between wholly owned and various levels of joint venture control was not able to discriminate well between the chosen degree of joint venture ownership. Their binomial test of wholly owned versus joint venture, however, confirmed the Stopford and Wells [1972] bivariate results. Wholly owned subsidiaries (greenfield and acquisition) were favored over partial ownership, the greater the R&D and advertising intensity of the foreign firm. They also found support that the degree of multinationality had a negative effect on the likelihood to joint venture.[13] Their dummy variables for regions tended to show strong country patterns. Based on the positive relationships between R&D and marketing/advertising intensity to wholly owned entries, they conclude that a transaction cost theory of entry choice is supported.[14]

In summary, the literature to date has found that uncertainty over the foreign market influences managers decisions on how to invest overseas, that there are clear but unexplained country patterns in the selection of entry modes, and that both firm– and industry–level variables are related to the choice of entry mode. The previous literature has not, however, clearly extrapolated from the research on cultural traits to implications for country patterns in the relative use of different entry modes, nor has it tested the relationship between cultural factors and entry mode choice while controlling for other factors.

This paper tests explicitly the influence of country cultural characteristics, including attitudes toward uncertainty, upon the choice of the mode of entry into the United States. Though country–level economic variables are currently discounted as explaining why firms invest overseas, cultural differences among countries play a role, this article contends, in explaining how this investment is channeled.

DESCRIPTION OF ENTRY MODE PATTERNS

Because data comparing entry activities of foreign firms in the United States are not easily available, it is worthwhile to report the patterns found in our sample before turning to statistical tests of the above hypotheses. Whereas aggregated data on foreign acquisitions are routinely available from Department of Commerce publications, similar data for joint ventures are generally lacking. In part, this imbalance can be explained by the significance of acquisitions as a mode of entry for foreign firms into the United States. For the years between 1976 and 1983, acquisitions were responsible for over 50% of the foreign direct investment in the United States, rising as high as 79% of the total value in 1981.[15]

On the other hand, data on joint ventures as a mode of entry into the United States is not aggregated and published by the Department of Commerce. While

418   JOURNAL OF INTERNATIONAL BUSINESS STUDIES, FALL 1988

TABLE 1
Distribution of Modes of Entry by Industrial Sector

	Joint Ventures	Acquisitions	Greenfield	Total N
Resource	18	35	2	55
Paper	3	26	5	34
Chemical	2	15	3	20
Petroleum	25	35	17	77
Rubber	3	3	2	8
Primary Metal	2	20	6	28
Metal Fabrication	2	8	4	14
Machinery	4	7	0	11
Electrical Equipment	24	14	13	51
Transportation	25	21	13	59
Instrumentation	10	3	10	23
Other Manufacturing	3	10	0	13
Communication	1	4	2	7
Wholesale	8	17	3	28
Financial Services	4	30	0	34
Other Services	12	25	5	42
Total	147	274	85	506

it is thus impossible to have a value estimate of joint ventures, it is possible, based on the sources listed in the appendix, to describe the frequency of the mode of entry across industries and countries. This data is available for acquisitions, greenfield, and joint ventures, as well as other investments not included in this study.

Table 1 provides a breakdown of joint ventures, acquisition, and greenfield by industry for the years 1981 to 1985. There is a clear difference in industry patterns among the modes of entry. Joint ventures are relatively more frequent in pharmaceuticals/chemicals and electric and nonelectric machinery. Acquisitions occur primarily in natural resources, financial services, and miscellaneous manufacturing industries. Chemical and electrical machinery are especially attractive industries for greenfield investments. At a higher level of aggregation, acquisitions tend to be relatively more common than other modes of entry in nonmanufacturing sectors of the economy.

The country pattern is given in *Table 2*. Again, there are strong differences among the modes of entry. For Japan, 46 of its 114 entries are joint ventures.[16] Whereas Japanese acquisitions are not common, Japanese firms have a high proportion of the wholly owned greenfield investments. Scandinavia and, especially France, also lean towards joint ventures. United Kingdom represents the other extreme; 111 of its 141 entries are acquisitions, with the remainder evenly divided between joint ventures and greenfield.

The trends in our sample show clear differences in country propensities regarding the selection of the mode of entry. It is unclear, however, whether these patterns are robust when the relationship is controlled for firm– and industry–level factors. It could well be that the country pattern is generated by differences

TABLE 2
Acquisitions, Joint Ventures and Greenfield Entry by Country of Corporate Headquarters

	Joint Ventures	Acquisitions	Greenfield	Total N
United Kingdom	15	111	15	141
Japan	46	35	33	114
Scandinavia	9	5	4	18
Switzerland	4	20	3	27
Germany	6	10	8	24
France	23	6	4	33
Italy	4	3	1	8
Netherlands	6	24	7	37
Belgium	5	10	2	17
Malaysia	1	1	0	2
S. Africa	1	0	2	1
Canada	13	28	3	45
Other	14	20	5	25
Total	147	274	85	506

in the sectoral characteristics of foreign direct investment across the countries of origin. The next section gives a formal statistical test to determine the factors influencing the choice of entry.

SELECTION OF VARIABLES

The hypotheses to be treated posit that the choice of entry is significantly influenced by the cultural characteristics of the home country of the investing firm. Because of the confounding effects of the relationship of firm– and industry–level variables with country identification, it is not possible to test for country effects without controlling for other influences. Consequently, the statistical analysis will investigate the following specification:

Entry Choice = *f*(cultural characteristics; firm variables, industry variables)

In previous studies, a number of firm and industry variables have been tested and shown to be significant in explaining the mode of entry choice. These studies indicate several proxies. Because, as discussed below, acquisitions form the baseline case, we discuss the relationship of these proxies to the dependent variable in the context of choosing a joint venture or greenfield relative to acquisition. As our interest is in controlling for specification error, we merely summarize the conventional arguments of the existing literature on the expected relationships between the control variables and the choice variables.

Firm-level Variables

Diversification [Diversified].

Dubin [1975], Wilson [1980], and Caves and Mehra [1986] have found that firms following diversification strategies are more likely to enter a foreign country by acquisition over greenfield. The presumable explanation for this pattern is that diversified firms are competing on superior management and/ or production efficiencies in mature industries, and, therefore, are not concerned with a de novo transfer of a product innovation or brand level. Analogously, diversified firms should be more likely to engage in acquisitions relative to joint ventures.

Country Experience [Experience].

The effect of previous entry on subsequent entry mode in the same country has not been shown in large–sample multivariate studies to be significant.[17] Nevertheless, theoretically, we can expect that the propensity to joint venture relative to acquisition should decline as a foreign firm learns more about the local environment. It can also be expected as a firm picks up experience, it is more likely to increase its use of acquisitions relative to joint venturing with local partners.

Multinational Experience [Multinational].

Contrary to their expectation on the sign of the coefficient, Caves and Mehra [1986] found that multinationality (i.e., the number of countries in which a firm has subsidiaries) is significantly correlated with the choice of acquisition over greenfield.[18] One interpretation of this finding is that a firm with greater international experience is able to bear the risk of an acquisition and to integrate subsidiaries of diverse managerial nationality. Along these lines, the greater the multinationality, the greater a firm's ability to acquire; the lesser the multinationality, the more likely a firm will share the risks and management responsibility through a joint venture. Multinationality should, thus, favor the ability to acquire.

Asset Size [U.S. Asset Size and Non–U.S. Asset Size].

It stands to reason that the larger the investing firm, the greater its ability to acquire. Despite the logic, the empirical evidence is mixed. Dubin [1975] found that smaller firms tended to acquire relatively more frequently than large firms, though he did not control for other factors. In his cross–sectional tests, Wilson [1980] confirmed Dubin's findings. However, these studies drew upon entry data of the largest corporations of the United States and other European countries. Caves and Mehra [1986] study did not restrict their attention to entries of the larger corporations. Their results showed that the size of the entering firm is positively and significantly related to entry by acquisition over greenfield. Because acquisitions require generally more financial and managerial resources than joint ventures, size of the foreign firm's assets should be positively correlated with the tendency to acquire. Conversely, acquisitions are discouraged, the larger the assets of the American partner, target firm, or investment size.

Industry-level Variables

Industry Variables [R&D and Advertising].

One explanation for the country pattern is that countries differ in their industrial structures and that choice of entry modes will be influenced by the characteristics of the industry. Because of a substantial literature confirming their importance, industry R&D expenditures to sales and industry media and advertising expenditures to sales were chosen as control variables in the statistical investigations.[19] Data on both variables are taken from the Federal Trade Commission's Line of Business study for 1975.[20]

Conventionally, the relationship of these variables to entry choice is said to discourage joint ventures in order to preserve proprietary assets and to discourage unrelated acquisitions. The previous empirical studies have assumed, however, foreign entry was usually for the purpose of market access or low cost manufacturing. Clearly, foreign entry into the United States may be motivated in order to source technology or purchase brand labels.

The more diverse motives of investing in the American economy make it more difficult to sign the structural variables. For example, firms from R&D–intensive industries might joint venture if they possess the requisite technologies but lack the marketing depth. Or they may tend to acquire if they are investing for technology sourcing. Similarly, firms from marketing–intensive industries might engage in a joint venture if they possess the brand label but lack other resources along the value–added chain. Or they may acquire if they are investing for market penetration and lack label recognition. Stopford and Wells [1972] found that American firms pursuing an advertising–intensive strategy tend to full ownership of their overseas subsidiaries. Their data is drawn, however, from a time when American firms were investing overseas with clear strategic advantages. For our study, it is equally likely that foreign firms are investing in the United States for technology and brand label acquisition as for the exploitation of their proprietary assets. No prediction is made, therefore, on the signs of the coefficients for *R&D* and *Advertising*.[21]

Sectoral Dummies [Manufacturing and Services].

Two sectoral dummies are used in order to control for other exogenous effects not captured by the *R&D* and *Marketing* variables. These dummies are required because there are clear patterns in the modes of entry across services, extractive, and manufacturing industries and we wish to control for sectoral effects not captured by the structural variables. (See Table 1.) Because Japanese firms are active in joint ventures and manufacturing, there would be a bias towards overstating the Japanese contribution in the total number of manufacturing entries and in joint ventures. To avoid a bias, sectoral effects are controlled by using dummies for whether the entry is in manufacturing or in services.

Country-level Variables

As noted earlier, previous studies have pinpointed uncertainty as a significant influence upon the investment decision. Whereas uncertainty has been multiply interpreted, one interpretation concerns the ability of the foreign firm to manage the local operations of its subsidiary. The perceived ability to manage may be influenced by two considerations, one concerns the absolute cultural attitudes towards uncertainty avoidance, the second concerning the relative cultural distance between the country of the investing firm and the country of entry.

Both considerations are proxied in the specification of the regression equations through the use of variables entitled uncertainty avoidance and cultural distance.

The measures for uncertainty avoidance and cultural distance are derived from the work of Hofstede [1980]. Hofstede found that differences in national cultures vary substantially along four dimensions. These dimensions were labeled uncertainty avoidance, individuality, tolerance of power distance, and masculinity–femininity. Hofstede created ordinal scales for countries for each of these dimensions based on a standardized factor analysis of questionnaires administered between 1968 and 1972 to 88,000 national employees in more than 40 overseas subsidiaries of a major American corporation. Bias for differences in occupational positions among subsidiaries was controlled. As the study consisted of two questionnaires separated by a four–year interval, it was possible to test for the reliability in scores over time; only questions showing a greater than .5 correlation in scores were used to derive the scales.

The indices of Hofstede can be criticized for a number of reasons, especially regarding the internal validity of the dimensions and the method of constructing the scales.[22] Whereas the criticism has a sound basis, Hofstede's study has some appealing attributes, namely, the size of the sample, the codification of cultural traits along a numerical index, and its emphasis on attitudes in the workplace. Our use of the indices are, furthermore, conservative, for if they are poor constructs, they are less likely to be found significant and with the a priori predicted sign.

Based on these scales, the statistical analysis used two cultural variables to test the two hypotheses.

Cultural Distance [Cultural Distance].

We hypothesize that the more culturally distant the country of the investing firm from the United States, the more likely the choice to set up a joint venture. Using Hofstede's indices, a composite index was formed based on the deviation along each of the four cultural dimensions (i.e., power distance, uncertainty avoidance, masculinity/femininity, and individualism) of each country from the United States ranking. The deviations were corrected for differences in the variances of each dimension and then arithmetically averaged. Algebraically, we built the following index:

$$CD_j = \sum_{i=1}^{4} \{(I_{ij} - I_{iu})^2/V_i\}/4 \, ,$$

where I_{ij} stands for the index for the ith cultural dimension and jth country, V_i is the variance of the index of the ith dimension, u indicates the United States, and CD_j is cultural difference of the jth country from the United States. Though the scaling method imposes weights based on index variance, any resultant measurement error cannot be expected to be correlated theoretically with the other independent variables and should reduce the significance of the statistical relationships.

TABLE 3
Summary of Predicted Signs

Variable	Joint Venture	Greenfield
Diversified	−	−
Experience	−−	−
Multinational	−	−
U.S. Asset Size	+	+
Non–U.S. Asset Size	−	−
R & D	NP*	NP
Advertising	NP	NP
Manufacturing	NP	NP
Services	NP	NP
Cultural Distance	+	+
Uncertainty Avoidance	+	+

*NP − No Prediction

Uncertainty Avoidance [Uncertainty Avoidance].

Uncertainty avoidance should not be understood as referring to the individual's willingness to bear risk or as the risk profile of a firm regarding its product strategy. Rather, the elements making up the dimension are organizational and managerial in character. The construction is fortunate for our purposes, as we wish to isolate the influence of cultural attitudes towards uncertainty over organizational functions, such as employment relations. The more uncertainty avoiding a culture tends to be, the less attractive is the acquisition mode due to the organizational risks of integrating foreign management into the parent organization.

The above discussion is summarized in *Table 3*.

MODEL SPECIFICATION

The decision to enter by acquisition, joint venture, or greenfield is modeled as a qualitative choice problem. A multinomial logit model is specified to estimate the effect of the explanatory factors on the probability that each of the three alternatives would be chosen. The multinomial logit allows the explanatory variables to affect differential odds of choosing one alternative relative to another. Thus, the coefficient vector is specific to the alternative, not to the firm making the choice [Judge et al. 1985, pp. 770–72]. Consequently, the specification of the probabilities is:

$$P_{ij} = \exp(x_{ij}B_j) \left/ \sum_{j=1}^{j=3} \exp(x_{ij}B_j), \right.$$

where P_{ij} is the probability that the ith firm will choose alternative j, x_{ij} is a vector of variables representing the variables characterizing the ith firm and the jth governance mode and B_j is the vector of coefficients to the independent variables. However, since the probabilities are constrained to sum to one, the system of equations are over-identified. The parameters can be estimated by setting the Bs of one of the alternatives to 0. In our model, it stands to reason to use acquisitions as the baseline case by which to compare the estimated parameters of the other alternatives (joint venture or greenfield).

Under this condition, the specification is reduced to:

$$P_{ij} = \exp(x_{ij}B_j)/1 + \sum_{e=2}^{3} \exp(x_{ij}B_j),$$

with the baseline alternative specified as

$$P_{i1} = 1/1 + \sum_{e=2}^{3} \exp(x_{ij}B_j).$$

The parameters (*B*s) are estimated by maximizing a log likelihood function using the Newton–Raphson iteration procedure.[23]

Unfortunately, values for *R&D* and *Advertising* are only available for manufacturing. Since missing values eliminate the entire case from the sample, we follow a technique suggested by Johnston (1972, pp. 238–41).[24] We treat the manufacturing, service, and extractive as three equations with explanatory variables which are not identical. For the nonmanufacturing sectors, *R&D* and *Advertising* are recorded as 0. If we assume the disturbance terms are not correlated, we can run a single multinomial estimation. The dummy variables will pick up the sectoral differences.

RESULTS

The results are provided in *Table 4*. The estimated coefficients should be interpreted as representing the marginal utility of choosing a joint venture or wholly owned greenfield relative to an acquisition. A positive coefficient signifies that the greater the value of the independent variable, the more likely the alternative (i.e., joint venture or acquisition, as the case may be) will be chosen; the converse is true for a negative sign. *T*–test statistics are given in parentheses.

The estimated parameters for the equation using cultural distance show strong support for the first hypothesis. The effect of *Cultural Distance* is to increase the probability of choosing a joint venture over an acquisition and is significant at the .001 level. Its effect is, however, only significant at the .1 level for greenfield. (We are using a conservative two–tail test, though arguably we could apply, following Caves and Mehra, a one–tail test to the coefficients for which we have predicted signs.) The results for *Uncertainty Avoidance* are more impressive, with the coefficients correctly signed and significant at .001 and .05 for joint venture and greenfield, respectively.

The asset size variables generally are correctly signed. The effect of *U.S. Asset Size* on choosing a joint venture is significant at .001. Clearly, the larger the size of the American partner, the more likely to joint venture than acquire. The effect of *U.S. Asset Size* on choosing greenfield is negative and significant in both the uncertainty avoidance and cultural distance runs at the .1 and .05 level, respectively. It is likely, however, that this result stems from the

TABLE 4
Parameter Estimates for Multinomial Logit Model of Entry Choice

	Constant	Diversified	Experience	Multinational	U.S. Asset Size	Non-U.S. Asset Size	R & D	Advertising	Manufacturing	Services	Cultural Distance	Uncertainty Avoidance
Hypothesis 1												
Acquisition	0	0	0	0	0	0	0	0	0	0	0	—
Joint Venture	−10.3 (−4.08)[a]	.12 (.58)	−.68 (−.85)	0.009 (.42)	2.64 (4.94)[a]	.13 (.23)	.181 (1.90)[c]	−.24 (−.73)	1.06 (.95)	−.07 (−.04)	1.35 (4.7)[a]	—
Greenfield	−8.6 (−4.13)[a]	.19 (1.08)	−0.63 (−.96)	−.009 (−.58)	−.75 (−1.93)[c]	1.3 (2.78)[b]	.096 (1.37)	−.16 (−.95)	3.59 (3.15)[a]	−7.80 (−.16)	.40 (−1.84)[c]	—
Hypothesis 2												
Acquisition	0	0	0	0	0	0	0	0	0	0	—	0
Joint Venture	−10.6 (−4.62)[a]	.28 (1.33)	−.78 (−1.03)	.001 (.04)	2.42 (4.99)[a]	−.51 (−.97)	.21 (2.35)[b]	.24 (.91)	.85 (.87)	.28 (.19)	—	.73 (4.4)[a]
Greenfield	−9.11 (−4.37)[a]	.23 (1.33)	−.68 (−1.05)	−.003 (−.23)	−.73 (−1.86)[c]	1.09 (2.15)[b]	.09 (1.35)	−.16 (−.96)	3.66 (3.2)[a]	−8.6 (−.11)	—	.03 (2.23)[b]

(t-statistics in parentheses)
N = 228   [a] $p < .10$ [b] $p < .05$ [c] $p < .01$

measurement of asset size for greenfield in terms of the investment and for acquisition or joint venture in terms of the asset size of the target or partner. The effect of the *Non–U.S. Asset Size* is insignificant for the case of joint venture in the cultural distance estimation, but correctly signed, though still insignificant, for the uncertainty avoidance estimation. Interestingly, larger size of the foreign firm encourages greenfield over acquisition at the .01 level in the cultural distance run and .05 in the uncertainty avoidance run; this result confirms the finding of Dubin.

Experience and *Multinationality* are correctly signed (with the exception of the coefficient to *Multinationality* for joint venture in the *Uncertainty Avoidance* estimation.). However, the *t*–tests are not significant. Similar to earlier studies, therefore, experience effects as measured by prior entries are not shown to be robust under large–sample multiple regression estimates. Unlike some other studies (e.g., Caves and Mehra [1986], and Gatignon and Anderson [1987]), our measure for multinational experience is not found to be significant.

We also do not find diversified firms more likely to enter by acquisition. To the contrary, the variable *Diversified* is positively signed, showing that diversified firms tend to enter by joint venture or greenfield. The results are not significant and it would be premature at this time to speculate on the causes.

The industry sectoral variables are of some interest. Of the dummy variables, only *Manufacturing* is significant in both equations, indicating a preference for greenfield investment over acquisition in the manufacturing sector. As shown later, this effect is almost entirely due to Japanese investments.

The most interesting of the industry–level variables is the positive effect of *R&D* on joint venture and greenfield entry, though only significant in the former case (at .1 for the cultural distance estimation and .05 for uncertainty avoidance). Elsewhere, we have shown that joint ventures appear to be particularly encouraged in growing and R&D–intensive industries [Kogut and Singh 1987]. This result is counter to previous findings and some transaction cost arguments. A possible interpretation is that non–U.S. firms enter the United States to tap into American technology by joint ventures. At a minimum, given the positive sign to *R&D* for both joint ventures and greenfield (though not significant for the latter), acquisitions appear to be discouraged in high R&D–intensive industries.

Advertising is negatively related to joint ventures and greenfield investments. Though the results are not significant, they are consistent with Caves and Mehra's [1986] argument that acquisitions are favored for the purpose of brand label or product adaptation. This relationship is expected to be more pronounced for mature industries, which we will explore more fully in further work.

CONTROLLING FOR JAPANESE ENTRIES

It could be argued that the cultural results are driven by outliers, namely, that Japan scores highly distant in culture from the United States and scores high on uncertainty avoidance. At the same time, Japanese firms tend toward greenfield and joint venture entries. Thus, the results could be interpreted as a primarily Japanese effect.

From one point of view, Japan as an outlier is consistent with our argument and this result should be expected to hold for entries from other countries that are culturally different from the United States but whose firms have yet to establish a strong foreign investment position. Nevertheless, the effects of cultural distance and uncertainty avoidance should be expected to hold for the sample in the absence of Japanese entries. To show this, we reestimate the earlier equations on a subsample of the data, having removed the Japanese cases. These results are given in *Table 5*.

The effects of culture are indeed weaker but still correctly signed and significant in two cases. *Cultural Distance* is significant at .05 for joint ventures and just shy of .15 for greenfield. (Again, it is important to note that under a one–tail test, it is significant at .1.) The *Uncertainty Avoidance* effect is negligible in the case of joint ventures but significant at .05 for greenfield.

The other effects remain largely the same as before, except for changes in significance. Interestingly, *Multinationality* is positively signed, showing that acquisitions are discouraged for the more multinational of corporations. On the other hand, *Experience* increases in significance in the runs, and is significant in three of the runs at .1 using a one–tail test. The positive effect of *R&D* for joint ventures remains significant at the .05 level in both runs. The manufacturing dummy coefficient is highly insignificant. Clearly, then, the earlier sectoral effect is driven by the sectoral preference of Japanese firms.

In summary, the statistical estimations provide strong support that cultural distance and national attitudes towards uncertainty avoidance influence the choice of entry mode. It should be underlined that these relationships are robust despite the controls added for industry– and firm–level effects. The weaker results for the subsample when the Japanese entries are removed are partly a result of the reduced sample size (the cases drop from 228 to 173) and partly a result of the outlier effect of Japan.[25] It is impressive, therefore, that cultural effects appear to be still persistent despite the reduction in sample size and the diminishment in variance of the cultural variables.

CONCLUSIONS

The above results offer the first large–sample multiple regression test of the prevailing view that entry mode selection is influenced by cultural factors. The results have a secondary implication in terms of validating the usefulness of Hofstede's measures of cultural dimensions. Unquestionably, a scale measuring the cultural characteristics at the firm level would be preferable. Yet, the collection of such data appears formidable at this time. It is, therefore, all the more remarkable that the strength of the results were found, despite using measures of national cultural attitudes which were developed for other purposes.

The results should be interpreted with care. The variable of uncertainty avoidance is defined in the context of organizational and managerial preferences; it is not a measure of cultural attitudes towards risk in a larger sense. Furthermore,

TABLE 5
Parameter Estimates for Multinominal Logit Model of Entry Choice Excluding Japanese Entries

	Constant	Diversi-fied	Experi-ence	Multi-national	U.S. Asset size	Non-U.S. Asset Size	R&D	Adver-tising	Manufac-turing	Services	Cultural Distance	Uncertainty Avoidance
Hypothesis 1												
Acquisition	0	0	0	0	0	0	0	0	0	0	0	—
Joint Venture	−21.0 (−.25)	.13 (.41)	−1.29 (−1.20)	−0.01 (−.31)	3.44 (3.92)a	−.42 (−.63)	.32 (2.11)b	−.31 (−.70)	11. (.14)	1.45 (.009)	1.23 (2.15)b	—
Greenfield	−18.4 (−0.19)	.18 (.88)	−0.18 (−.14)	.006 (.35)	−.79 (−1.81)c	1.36 (2.41)b	−.02 (−.17)	−.18 (−.97)	13.8 (.15)	−.009 (.000)	.59 (1.48)	—
Hypothesis 2												
Acquisition	0	0	0	0	0	0	0	0	0	0	—	0
Joint Venture	−20.0 (−.23)	.13 (.42)	−1.66 (−1.46)	.001 (.03)	3.34 (3.9)a	−0.43 (−.68)	−.28 (2.24)b	−.23 (−.58)	11.1 (.13)	−0.05 (−.00)	—	.02 (0.28)
Greenfield	−19.5 (−.21)	.26 (1.24)	−0.50 (.41)	.01 (.52)	−83 (−1.89)c	1.13 (1.94)c	−.02 (−.23)	−.18 (−1.01)	13.9 (.15)	.20 (.001)	—	.04 (1.96)b

(t-statistics in parentheses)
N = 173,   a $p < .01$ b $p < .05$ c $p < .1$

the results may only have validity within a particular historical time. Since foreign direct investment has been concentrated historically between the United States and Europe, which are relatively culturally similar, there are confounding effects of cultural distance and experience. As Japan and other Asian countries continue to increase their overseas investments in the West, cultural distance may be increasingly offset by growing experience at the firm level. Though we have tried to control for such effects, it could well be that our proxy variables were insufficient.

A final consideration which deserves further exploration is a more refined analysis of entry decisions in the context of oligpolistic gaming. Competitive dynamics, such as the rush to invest, are likely to influence the entry choice. In addition, the relationship among the variables may change depending on the functional purpose of the entry. Both refinements are the subject of current work.

The results have a wider implication outside of country patterns and the choice of entry. The above study suggests that when economic choice is compared across countries, cultural characteristics are likely to have profound implications. Whereas theories of internalization and the firm may be culturally robust, their empirical application in a comparative setting appears to warrant the consideration of cultural differences on the costs and risks which managers attach to different modes of transacting.

Whether these results are interpreted as contradicting an internalization theory of entry choice is largely a question of the definition of transaction costs. To some, transaction costs are broadly defined to include communication and control costs, even if these costs are derived from cultural factors. In our view, it is theoretically and empirically interesting to distinguish between transaction costs that are independent of a firm's country of origin and those that are determined by cultural factors. The multinational corporation is the heir, to use Philip Curtin's [1984] expression, of the historical cross–cultural broker in world trade. But no matter how superior the current multinational corporation may be in replacing the skills of traders by the international extension of organizational boundaries, the management of these firms are likely to be influenced by the dominant country culture. The results of this paper suggest that further investigation into the cultural determinants of managerial decision–making is soundly warranted.

APPENDIX
DATA SOURCES

Data on joint ventures, acquisitions, and greenfield are not compiled systematically by the United States government and must, therefore, be gleaned from a number of publicly-available sources. Data on acquisitions were taken from two sources: the Department of Commerce's publication *Foreign Direct Investment in the United States* for the years 1981 to 1985 and *Mergerstat Review*, W.T. Grimm & Company, Chicago, 1984, for the years 1981, 1982 and 1983. Acquisitions valued less than $10 million were excluded. In addition to the Commerce publication cited above, sources used for joint ventures were: *Mergers and Acquisitions* and the *Yearbook on Corporate Mergers, Joint Ventures, and Corporate Policy*. For the statistical investigation, data for joint ventures were taken for the years 1981 to 1985. Data on greenfield investments were found in *Foreign Direct Investment in the United States*, again for the years 1981 to 1985.

NOTES

[1]For a review, see Ajami and Ricks [1981]; Arpan, Flowers and Ricks [1981]; McClain [1983]; and Hood and Young [1980].

[2]An exploratory investigation of strategic motives for the choice of entry is provided in Kogut and Singh [1987].

[3]For an extensive argument along these lines, see Robbins [1987].

[4]A joint venture is both legally and conceptually different from a minority equity participation investment, where a firm invests directly into a second company but does not share control with a third party.

[5]We would like to thank Jean–Francois Hennart for this observation on the Anderson–Gatignon paper, which came to our attention subsequent to submitting this article for review.

[6]Caves (1982, chap. 3) argues similarly in his discussion on the joint determination of exporting and foreign direct investment.

[7]The main findings are reported in Hornell, Vahlne and Wiedersheim–Paul [1973]. A brief English description is given in Johanson and Vahlne [1977].

[8]The numerous anecdotes on the motivations of Japanese firms to invest in greenfield sites in rural areas are consistent with this argument.

[9]It is important to note that our hypothesis is stated at the country level to represent average tendencies. We cannot make statements to the particular firm without more detailed knowledge of the correspondence of the national to corporate culture.

[10]Cultural distance is, in most respects, similar to the "psychic distance" used by the Uppsala school.

[11]A common confusion is to treat uncertainty avoidance as equivalent to risk attitudes in general. We, in agreement with Hofstede [1980], use uncertainty avoidance in the original sense of Cyert and March to refer to the way uncertainty is organizationally resolved as separate from the issue of whether an organization or firm chooses or avoids risky environments for a given return.

[12]Wilson's data also came from the Multinational Data Base on 187 U.S. multinationals for the period up to 1967, plus from the activities of 202 foreign–based multinationals through 1971.

[13]They called this variable an experience effect, but in order to be consistent with our description of similar variables in other studies, we have relabeled it as a measure of multinationality in accordance with Caves and Mehra.

[14]Another interpretation is that the results confirm that firms maintain in–house what Dunning [1977] calls "ownership advantages".

[15]R. David Belli, "U.S. Business Enterprises Acquired or Established by Foreign Direct Investors in 1983," *Survey of Current Business*, Department of Commerce, 1984.

[16]Though high, it is lower than the 73% reported by Tsurumi [1976] for Japanese overseas manufacturing subsidiaries in 1971. However, Tsurumi included subsidiaries in which Japanese firms had less than 25% share. If we take out these subsidiaries (which are better considered as minority investments), then the percentage is 60%. Caves reports Tsurumi's estimate as 82%, but we have been unable to locate the source of the figure [Caves 1982, pp. 89–90].

[17]Caves and Mehra [1985] proxied experience by whether the firm had made a previous investment in the United States. Wilson [1980] used the proportion of subsidiaries established before an arbitrarily chosen breakpoint.

[18]On the other hand, Steuber et al. [1973] found that the percentage of equity share in a United Kingdom subsidiary by a foreign firm increased with the multinationality of the parent.

[19]For a summary of studies on R&D and advertising, see Scherer [1980, chaps. 14 and 15]. For a summary of research on the relation of R&D and advertising to foreign entry choice, see Caves [1982, chap. 1].

[20]The line of business data are drawn from confidential government surveys of businesses. Though somewhat dated, the published summary statistics for R&D have been found to be reasonably stable over time. For evidence, see Scherer [1982]. We have made a parallel assumption for *Advertising* expenditures.

[21]This argument is consistent with Caves and Mehra [1986].

[22]Hofstede [1980] points out, however, that the external validity is reasonable high when tested against other variables which should be correlated with cultural differences.

[23]We would like to thank Hubert Gatignon for sharing his program and his advice with us.

[24]We are indebted to Tom Pugel for this suggestion.

[25]Attempts to avoid the loss in sample size by using a country dummy for Japan with the full sample floundered due to the collinearity between the Japan dummy and cultural measures (.81 for *Cultural Distance* and .86 for *Uncertainty Avoidance*).

REFERENCES

Abbegglen, J.C. & G. Stalk. 1984. The role of foreign companies in Japanese acquisitions. *The Journal of Business Strategy*, 4:3–10.

Ajami, R.A. & D.A. Ricks. 1981. Motives of non-American firms investing in the U.S. *Journal of International Business Studies*, 13 (Winter):25–34.

Arpan, J.S., E.B. Flowers & D.A. Ricks. 1981. Foreign direct investment in the United States. *Journal of International Business Studies*, 12 (Spring/Summer):137–54.

Bendix, Reinhard. 1956. *Work and authority in industry: Ideologies of management in the course of industrialization*. Berkeley:University of California.

Brooke, M.Z. & H.L. Remmers, eds. 1972. *The multinational company in Europe: Some key problems*. London: Longman.

Caves, Richard. E. 1982. *Multinational enterprise and economic analysis*. Cambridge, U.K.: Cambridge University Press.

_____& S. Mehra. 1986. Entry of foreign multinationals into U.S. manufacturing industries. In M. Porter, ed., *Competition in global industries*. Boston: Harvard Business School.

Curtin, Philip. 1984. *Cross–cultural trade in world history*. London: Cambridge University Press.

Davidson, William H. 1980. The location of foreign direct investment activity: Country characteristics and experience effects. *Journal of International Business Studies*, 12 (Fall):9–22.

Dubin, Michael. 1975. *Foreign acquisitions and the spread of the multinational firm*. D.B.A. thesis, Graduate School of Business Administration, Harvard University.

Dunning, John. 1977. Trade, location of economic activity and the MNE: A search for an eclectic theory. In B. Ohlin, ed., *The international allocation of economic activity*. London: Holmes and Meier.

Franko, Lawrence G. 1976. *The European multinationals*. Stanford, CT: Greylock Publishers.

Gatignon, H. & E. Anderson. 1987. The multinational corporation's degree of control over foreign subsidiaries: An empirical test of a transaction cost explanation. Report Number 87–103, Marketing Science Institute, Cambridge, Massachusetts.

Hofstede, Geert. 1980. *Culture's consequences: International differences in work-related values*. Beverly Hills: Sage Publications.

Hood, N. & S. Young. 1980. Recent patterns of foreign direct investment by British multinational enterprises in the United States. *National Westminster Bank Quarterly Review*: 21–32.

Hornell, E., J.E. Vahlne & F. Wiedersheim-Paul. 1973. *Export och utlandsetableringar*. Uppsala: Almqvist & Wiksell.

Hymer, Stephen. 1960. *The international operations of national firms: A study of direct foreign investment*. Ph.D. thesis, Department of Economics, Massachusetts Institute of Technology.

Jemison, D.B. & S.B. Sitkin. 1986. Corporate acquisitions: A process perspective. *Academy of Management Review*, 11:145–63.

Johanson, J. & J.E. Vahlne. 1977. The internationalization process of the firm—A model of knowledge development and increasing foreign market commitments. *Journal of International Business Studies*, 8 (Spring/Summer):22–32.

Johnston, J. 1972. *Econometric methods*. New York: McGraw-Hill.

Judge, G., W. Griffiths, R. Hill, H. Luetkephl & T. Lee. 1985. *The theory and practice of econometrics*. New York: John Wiley.

Kogut, B. 1987. Joint ventures: Theoretical and empirical perspectives. *Strategic Management Journal*, forthcoming.

——& H. Singh. 1987. Entering the United States by joint venture: Industry structure and competitive rivalry. In F. Contractor & P. Lorange, eds., *Cooperative Strategies in International Business*. Lexington, MA: Lexington Press.

Lincoln, J.R., M. Hanada & J. Olson. 1981. Cultural orientations and individual reactions to organizations: A study of employees of Japanese-owned firms. *Administrative Science Quarterly*, 25:93–115.

McClain, David. 1983. Foreign direct investment in the United States: Old currents, "new waves," and the theory of direct investment. In C.P. Kindleberger & D. Audretsch, eds., *The Multinational Corporation in the 1980s*. Cambridge, MA: MIT Press.

Pate, James L. 1969. Joint venture activity, 1960–1968. *Economic Review*, Cleveland: Federal Reserve Board.

Pugel, T.A. 1981. Technology, transfer and the neoclassical theory of international trade. In R.G. Hawkins & A.J. Prasad, eds., *Technology Transfer and Economic Development*. Greenwich, CT: JAI Press.

Puxty, A.G. 1979. Some evidence concerning cultural differentials in ownership policies of overseas subsidiaries. *Management International Review*, 19:39–50.

Robbins, James. 1987. Organizational economics: Notes on the use of transaction cost theory in the study of organizations. *Administrative Science Quarterly*, 32:68–86.

Robinson, Richard D. 1961. Management attitudes toward joint and mixed ventures abroad. *Western Business Review*.

Sales, A.L. & P.H. Mirvis. 1984. When cultures collide: Issues in acquisition. In *Managing organizational transitions*. Homewood, IL: Irwin.

Scherer, F.M. 1980. *Industrial market structure and economic performance*. Chicago: Rand McNally College Publishing Company.

——1982. Inter-industry technology flows and productivity growth. *Review of Economics and Statistics*, 64 (November): 627–34.

Steuber, M.D. et al. 1973. *The impact of foreign direct investment on the United Kingdom*. London: Department of Trade and Industry.

Stopford, J. & L. Wells. 1972. *Managing the multinational enterprise: Organization of the firm and ownership of the subsidiaries*. New York: Basic Books.

Stopford, J.M. & K.O. Haberich. 1978. Ownership and control of foreign operations. In M. Ghertman & J. Leontiades, eds., *European Research in International Business*, pp. 141–67. Amsterdam: North Holland.

Wilson, Brent. 1980. The propensity of multinational companies to expand through acquisitions. *Journal of International Business Studies*, 12 (Spring/Summer):59–65.

[19]

BARGAINING POWER, OWNERSHIP, AND PROFITABILITY OF TRANSNATIONAL CORPORATIONS IN DEVELOPING COUNTRIES

DONALD J. LECRAW*
University of Western Ontario

Abstract. As the bargaining power of the transnational corporations (TNCs) in the sample increased relative to the bargaining power of the host country, and as the desire of the TNCs for a high level of equity ownership increased, the percent equity ownership of the TNCs in their subsidiaries increased. The relationship between percent equity ownership and subsidiary success from the TNCs' viewpoint, however, was J-shaped. High and low levels of equity ownership were associated with high levels of success. Control of critical operational variables by the TNC was directly related to success.

INTRODUCTION

■ Over the past 20 years there has been continuing controversy over the determinants and effects of different patterns of ownership and control of the subsidiaries of transnational corporations (TNCs) in less developed countries (LDCs). Some countries such as Singapore and Hong Kong place virtually no restrictions on the percentage of equity ownership held by TNCs in most sectors of their economies; others place severe restrictions on equity ownership by TNCs and prohibit it outright in many sectors of their economy; others require that foreign ownership be reduced or phased out over time. One of the advantages of foreign direct investment (FDI) sometimes cited by TNCs based in Japan and in LDCs is the generally higher level of equity participation they have given to investors in the host country [Lecraw 1977, 1981; Wells 1983]. The reasons expressed by host governments for encouraging (or insisting on) local equity participation are complex and sometimes contradictory, ranging from better access to information, and control of payments for technology transfer and management fees, to control over pricing of output and intracompany trade, reinvestment, and remittance of profits and capital.[1] As importantly, a high level of foreign ownership may carry significant political costs for the host government quite apart from its economic impact.

Recently, Fagre and Wells [1982] have used a bargaining power framework to explore the relationship between the characteristics of a TNC (size, intrafirm transfers, advertising and R&D intensities, and product diversity) and the percent equity ownership position that TNCs achieved in their subsidiaries in the host country.[2] The first step of the analysis in this paper replicates this work using a different data set and extends the analysis to include additional characteristics of the host country and of TNCs that might influence their relative bargaining power.

Poynter [1982] has shown that a TNC may find it advantageous to bargain not for increased equity ownership, but for control over the variables critical to the success of the subsidiary from the TNC's viewpoint. The second step of the analysis relates the relative bargaining power of a TNC and of the host government (as proxied by their characteristics) to the degree of control the TNC exercised over its subsidiary in the host country.

*Donald J. Lecraw is Professor of Economics and International Trade at the School of Business Administration, the University of Western Ontario. He has published books and articles on industrial organization, choice of technology, economic development, and international trade.

This research was partially funded by the United Nations Centre on Transnational Corporations and the Centre for International Business Studies, The University of Western Ontario. The author is also grateful to Paul Beamish for suggesting that the data base that the author compiled could be used to test several of the hypotheses presented in this paper.

Finally, Killing [1982] has shown that there is a link between the profitability (success) of a TNC's subsidiary and the division of overall control between the TNC and its local partners. The third step of the analysis of the paper examines the TNC's control over several of the functions within its subsidiary—marketing, finance, technology, production, imports, exports, and so on—evaluates the importance of control over these functions to the TNC, and analyzes the relationship between the TNC's control over these critical success variables and the success of the subsidiary from the TNC's viewpoint.

The research presented here links what had previously been 3 separate areas of analysis into a more unified framework, and tests hypotheses that are generated by this framework on a common data set. In this way, this research both supports and extends the work of Fagre and Wells, Killing, and Poynter.

The conclusions in this paper are based on data gathered from 153 subsidiaries of TNCs that operated in 6 manufacturing industries in the 5 countries of the ASEAN region: Thailand, Malaysia, Singapore, Indonesia, and the Philippines. These countries vary greatly in income levels, size of the domestic market, resource base, development strategies, and policies toward FDI. The TNCs in the sample were based in the United States, Europe, Japan, and several LDCs. The sample then may give a good basis on which to reach generalizations concerning the determinants of ownership and control of the subsidiaries of TNCs in LDCs, and concerning the effects of ownership and control on the success of these investments.

The next section sets out the theoretical framework for the analysis. The third section describes the methodology and tests the hypotheses generated from the theory. The fourth section draws some implications from the analysis for policy of both TNCs and host governments.

THEORETICAL FRAMEWORK

In the pioneering work of Vernon [1971], Stopford and Wells [1972], and Franko [1971], 4 factors were seen as major determinants of the level of equity ownership of TNCs in their subsidiaries: the desired ownership level of the TNC; the bargaining power of the TNC; the desired level of local equity participation of the host country; and the bargaining power of the host government (including the bargaining power of locally-owned firms in the host country). Analysis of the determinants of equity participation in terms of the relative bargaining power and the equity ownership policies of the TNC and the host country governments has proved to be a fruitful approach and will be used in the first part of the analysis of this paper.

Over the past 10 years several authors have developed a comprehensive theory of the international activities of firms that can be used to analyze the decision of a firm on the mode of its international activity: exports, licensing, or FDI.[3] In order to operate internationally, a firm must possess firm-specific (ownership) advantages in technology, production, marketing, finance, and management that allow it to compete with firms in the market for goods and services abroad. These firm-specific advantages are often due to the country-specific advantages of the firm's home country: natural resources, market size, income level, and factor costs. The host country possesses advantages in location as well in its natural resources, markets, and factor costs.

A TNC will undertake FDI when 3 conditions are met: when its firm-specific advantages allow it to compete in the host country; when the host country has advantages that are attractive to the TNC; and when the advantages of internalizing the transaction within the firm by FDI are greater than the advantages of transferring the goods and services it possesses via the market for exports or licenses of its technology (broadly defined to include all forms of the firm's expertise, including brand names). The stronger the internalization advantages for the firm, the greater will be its desire to use FDI as the mode of its international activity and the greater its desire to retain ownership in its subsidiary abroad to appropriate the return earned on these advantages.

Placed into a bargaining framework, firm-specific advantages may give the TNC bargaining power over the host country; internalization advantages influence its desire to retain ownership and control over the appropriation of the returns of its subsidiary.[4] The desired ownership structure of a TNC for its subsidiaries in LDCs is then a function of its firm-specific advantages, internalization advantages, and host country advantages. Several of these factors have been described at length elsewhere and will be only briefly outlined here.[5]

Internalization advantages for an R&D-intensive TNC may be great if, as is often the case, the market for its technology is not perfect due to asymmetric information [Killing 1980]. R&D-intensive TNCs, therefore, often prefer to exploit their firm-specific advantages by internalizing the transaction through FDI in wholly-owned subsidiaries rather than via the market for technology. Possession of a proprietary product or technology may also increase the bargaining position of a TNC over the host government, particularly if other TNCs or local investors cannot supply technology of the same type or level of advancement.

As with technology, the external market for marketing skills and brand names is often imperfect. Faced with these imperfections, marketing-intensive TNCs often choose to exploit their firm-specific advantages by internalizing the transaction through FDI (again in wholly-owned subsidiaries in order to appropriate the return) rather than via the market for licensing brand names or products. Such firms may have the ability to develop a marketing package that is independent of the country in which they operate, may place little value on inputs from local partners in the form of marketing expertise and access to channels of distribution, and may fear loss of control over product quality [Horst 1974].

In the past, considerable emphasis has been placed on TNCs as providers of scarce capital resources at costs lower than those available to local investors in LDCs. Unless a TNC is willing to change its strategy to become a financial intermediary making portfolio loans or investments, it can only exploit this firm-specific advantage—access to relatively inexpensive capital—by internalizing the transaction via FDI.[6] The lower the cost of capital for the TNC relative to capital costs in the host country, the greater are the internalization advantages for the TNC. If capital is indeed a scarce resource that can best be provided by the TNC, its bargaining power and hence its level of equity participation might increase with the size of the investment (in terms of assets) and the investment's capital intensity.

Another source of bargaining power for the TNC may be its ability to sell the output of its subsidiary in the host country on export markets, either to other units of the TNC, to independent firms, or through its own channels of distribution in markets in other countries. The TNC's access to export markets may become an especially important bargaining chip if the host country is following a development strategy based on export-led growth. TNCs have the choice of exploiting their firm-specific advantage—access to export markets—via FDI or by serving as a trading company for exports of locally-owned firms in the host country. The decision whether to exploit proprietary expertise in international trade via the market as trading firms or to internalize it via FDI is a complex one, and not well understood. [See Moxon 1983; and Lecraw's comments on Moxon's paper, 1983b.] Moxon, writing about export platform FDI, concluded on theoretical grounds that firms will undertake FDI based on a firm-specific advantage in access to export markets "when the parent possesses a complete package of export marketing and technological advantage, and where the costs of operation and control of the subsidiary do not offset these advantages."

Management expertise is another firm-specific advantage which TNCs may provide to their subsidiaries in the host country and which may increase their bargaining power. Conversely, host governments may push for increased local equity participation in order to increase the management expertise of their entrepreneurs and managers. Quantifying the effect of "management expertise" on the bargaining power of TNCs is difficult. Host governments also have difficulty in assessing the value of this expertise for the local subsidiary and the host economy. As the complexity of the managerial technology increases, however, the advantages of internalizing the transfer via FDI may increase, thereby increasing the TNC's desire to exploit its firm-specific advantage via FDI and its desire for a high degree of equity ownership and control.

Finally, the desire of a TNC to exploit its firm-specific advantages via FDI may depend on the managerial (or other) resources the firm has available to commit to the subsidiary. For example, a small, fast-growing firm may not have excess managerial capacity or financial resources to use for the investment, operation, and control of a subsidiary in an LDC. In this case, it may find that licensing or exports are the most profitable means by which it can exploit its firm-specific advantages in proprietary technology, marketing, and management. By extension, such a firm may be more apt to be satisfied with minority equity participation rather than commit its scarce financial and managerial assets to acquire and control a higher percentage of the equity in its foreign subsidiaries.

The preceding analysis implicitly assumed that TNCs use their bargaining power to achieve their desired level of equity participation in their subsidiaries in LDCs in order to appropriate the highest possible share of the return on their firm-specific advantages by internalizing the transactions within the firm. [See Magee 1977.] There are 2 problems with this viewpoint.

First, there may be ways by which the TNC may appropriate the return on its foreign investment other than by equity participation—licensing and management fees paid by the subsidiary, sale of inputs to the subsidiary, sale of its output to other units of the TNC or on world markets, and interest on intracompany debt. The TNC may use its bargaining power not to increase its equity ownership, but to secure some other means by which to appropriate this return, possibly by manipulating the transfer price of these other payments. Despite the efforts of host governments and their local partners, control of these variables to reflect arm's-length, free-market values ("fair" values) has often been quite difficult [Lecraw 1984]. Through these and other means, the use of internalization to appropriate returns through equity ownership in a subsidiary may be reduced and the TNC may use its bargaining power to gain advantageous concessions other than equity participation if it can control the allocation of the returns from the subsidiary in other ways. The fewer the transactions between the parent TNC and its subsidiary, however, the fewer the possibilities for the TNC to appropriate the return on its firm-specific advantages except through equity participation.

Second, TNCs may bargain for increased equity participation in order to increase their control over the operations of their subsidiary, to try to ensure that the internalization advantages are in fact realized. The link between the level of equity participation and the TNC's control over its subsidiary, however, may not be straightforward. Depending on the type of technology transferred, the capabilities of the local partners, and host government policies, a TNC may be able to control the operations of its subsidiary that are critical from its viewpoint without majority ownership, or, conversely, may have little control over these operations despite majority (or even complete) ownership. A TNC may therefore be willing to trade reduced equity ownership for increased control of variables crucial to the success of the venture from its point of view, if such a trade-off is possible. In this way, TNCs have sometimes been able to reduce host-government intervention in the operations of their subsidiaries, while at the same time appropriating their desired share of the surplus generated by their firm-specific advantages.[7]

The link, therefore, between the bargaining power of the TNC, the level of its equity participation, its control of the subsidiary, and its perception of the success of the investment is complex and may be difficult to trace. One implication of this analysis, however, may be testable using the data in this study. All else equal, the desire of the TNC for a high level of equity participation should increase as the economic ties between its subsidiary and the parent (through trade in inputs and outputs, machinery, and management and technology fees) decrease, because the potential of appropriating the profits of its investment, except through return on equity, has decreased.[8] The hypotheses concerning the relationship between TNC and host-country characteristics, the level of equity ownership desired by the TNC, and the bargaining power of the TNC and host country are displayed in Table 1.

TABLE 1

Expected Signs

Independent Variables	Dependent Variables		
	Actual Equity Ownership	S^{TNC}	Effective Control
Technological leadership	+	+	+
Advertising intensity	+	+	+
Subsidiary assets	+	+	+
Capital/output	+	+	+
Exports/sales	+	+	+
TNC assets	+	?	+
TNC-subsidiary linkages	−	?	+
Host country attractiveness	−	−	−
Potential TNC investors	−	−	−
Time (1960 = 1)	−	−	−
Dummy - Japanese TNC	−	?	−
Dummy - LDC TNC	−	?	−
Dummy variable European TNC	?	?	?
Constant term	+	?	+

To this point the analysis has sketched the often tangled relationship between the bargaining power of the TNC and its desired level of equity participation, the level of participation it achieves, and its control of its subsidiary, either as a whole, or over its critical strategic variables. The bargaining power of the host country also influences this relationship as the host country uses its bargaining power to appropriate a share of the profits earned by the TNC within its country.[9] The host country may possess scarce resources or control access to markets—either of which increases its bargaining power with the TNC. If the host government controls access to its markets through tariffs or nontariff barriers to trade and if the TNC investment is designed' to serve the host-country market, the host government can bargain access to its domestic market to gain equity participation for host-country nationals. The more attractive the host-country's internal market, the less open it is to trade; and the more willing the host government is to forego the immediate gains that the TNC may be able to provide via FDI, the greater the bargaining power of the host country. Similarly, the greater the diffusion of the expertise that TNCs can provide, the greater is the opportunity for the host government to play TNCs against one another in bargaining over the level of equity ownership and the share of the surplus from the venture accruing to each partner. In general, the greater the country-specific advantages of the host country, the greater its bargaining power and the higher the level of local ownership it may gain for local investors.

Several researchers have recently analyzed the relationships between the level of a TNC's equity participation, its control of the operations of its subsidiary, the success of the investment, and the reasons for failure. [See Killing 1982; Schaan 1982; and Beamish and Lane 1982.] These researchers used intensive interviews with small samples of Canadian firms that formed joint ventures both in developed countries (the United States) and in LDCs (Mexico and Kenya). Their general conclusion was that the relationship between joint venture success and equity ownership was U-shaped, that is, joint ventures in which the TNC held a small minority share (control was with the local partner) or a large majority share (control was with the TNC) tended to be more successful than joint ventures in which the partners held roughly equal shares (control was split). Joint ventures in which control was roughly equal at the board level or divided along functional lines tended to experience splits between the TNC and its local partner when the joint venture was under pressure from its external political or economic environment. These splits between the partners often led to friction at the operating level, compromises with which neither partner was satisfied, reduced commitment to the venture, and unsatisfactory performance.[10]

Data collected as part of the present study, although considerably less detailed than those of Killing [1982] and Schaan [1982], can be used to analyze the relationship between equity ownership, the assets brought to the venture by the TNC and the local partner, the critical success variables of the venture, the division of control, and the success of the venture.[11]

The next section describes the data and methodology used to test some of these hypotheses on the determinants of the relative bargaining power of TNCs and host governments, equity ownership, control, and success of subsidiaries of TNCs in LDCs.

As part of this study, data were collected using a questionnaire during interviews with 153 subsidiaries of TNCs based in the United States (52 subsidiaries), Europe (35 subsidiaries), Japan (43), and other LDCs (23) located in the 5 ASEAN countries: Thailand (39 subsidiaries), Malaysia (31), Singapore (29), Indonesia (19) and the Philippines (35). The characteristics of the firms in the sample and the 6 light manufacturing industries in which they operated are described in Lecraw [1981, 1984]. In general, these industries were quite concentrated (average 4-firm concentration ratio of 71.2 percent), exported little of their output (exports/ industry sales averaged 5.1 percent), imported a high percentage of their inputs (imports/total inputs averaged 41 percent) and operated behind high tariffs (nominal tariffs averaged 33.4 percent). In general, the TNCs in the sample had majority ownership in their subsidiaries (71 percent), the subsidiaries were quite small (assets averaged $4.1 million), and profits were high (19.8 percent on equity). The subsidiaries generally produced for the local market (exports/sales averaged 7.1 percent) although a few subsidiaries exported more than 50 percent of their output.[12] [See Lecraw 1984, Tables 1-4.]

METHODOLOGY The analysis in the previous section developed several hypotheses concerning the relationship between the relative bargaining power of the TNC and the host government, their desires for equity participation, the level of equity participation, the level of control achieved by the TNC in its subsidiary in the host country, and the success of the subsidiary. This analysis led to the hypotheses that the bargaining power of the TNC would increase with the level of the technology the TNC initially transferred to the venture, with the venture's on-going dependence on the TNC for technology in the future, with increasing advertising intensity of the TNC, with increasing dependence of the subsidiary on the TNC for export markets, and with increased size and capital intensity of the venture. The bargaining power of the host country would increase with increasing attractiveness of its local market and the degree it controlled market access through tariffs, and with increasing availability to the host country of the TNC's proprietary assets from other sources.

There was a problem in directly observing and measuring the 4 variables which jointly determine the actual level of equity ownership (EO) in this model: TNC bargaining power (BP^{TNC}), host country bargaining power (BP^{HC}), the TNC's desired level of equity ownership (DE^{TNC}), and the host country's desired level of equity ownership (DE^{HC}). The model has 5 structural equations:

$$EO = f(BP^{TNC}, BP^{HC}, DE^{TNC}, DE^{HC}), \tag{1}$$

$$BP^{TNC} = g(X), \tag{2}$$

$$BP^{HC} = h(X), \tag{3}$$

$$DE^{TNC} = l(X), \tag{4}$$

$$DE^{HC} = m(X), \tag{5}$$

where X is a vector of the TNC and host country characteristics. The BP^{TNC}, BP^{HC}, DE^{TNC}, and DE^{HC} are unobserved variables, but the X_i and Equity Ownership are observable. This problem led to the construction of a reduced form equation:

$$EO = n(X). \tag{6}$$

If the reduced form (Equation 6) is estimated, it is incorrect to draw explicit conclusions on the link between the X_i and bargaining power and desired equity ownership, or the link between bargaining power and desired equity ownership to actual equity ownership. This is a problem with drawing conclusions from the estimation of any reduced–form equation when the structural equations contain unobserved variables and hence cannot be estimated separately. It reduces the strength of the conclusions of the analysis of this paper about the usefulness of the bargaining power framework or, at best, conclusions are left to the interpretation of the reader.

Part of this problem can be circumvented if several assumptions are made. If the TNC's desired level of equity ownership does not vary between host countries and if the TNC achieved its desired level in at least one country, then the highest level of equity ownership of the TNC in any LDC can be used as a proxy for its desired level of ownership. If the host country's desired level of equity ownership does not vary among TNCs and if it achieved this level with a subsidiary of one TNC, then the lowest level of TNC equity (the highest level of host country equity) can be used as a proxy for the host country's desired level of equity ownership. Then, the differences between actual Equity Ownership and the TNC's desired ownership, and between actual Equity Ownership and the host country's desired ownership can be observed and the ratio of these differences related directly to the characteristics of the TNC and the host country. (If $DE^{TNC} = EO$, S^{TNC} was set equal to 1,000).

$$S^{TNC} = \frac{EO - DE^{HC}}{DE^{TNC} - EO} = q(X) \tag{7}$$

S^{TNC} might be considered the success of the TNC in bargaining with the host country. (See Figure 1.) S^{TNC} depends on the 2 sets of variables which have been identified with the relative bargaining power of the TNC and the host country. This methodology follows Fagre and Wells. S^{TNC} is a combination of their 2 variables, "Firm-Corrected Ownership" and "Country-Corrected Ownership."[13] Data were

FIGURE 1

The relationship between the actual level of equity ownership (EO), the desired level of ownership of the host country (DE^{HC}), and the TNC (DE^{TNC}), and bargaining success (S^{TNC}).

Percent Equity of the TNC

100	_____
80	_____ DE^{TNC}
60	_____ EO
20	_____ DE^{HC}
0	_____

$$S^{TNC} = \frac{EO - DE^{HC}}{DE^{TNC} - EO} = \frac{60 - 20}{80 - 60} = 2$$

collected for the firms in the sample on EO, the X_i, and they were used to construct S^{TNC} under the assumptions listed above.

The bargaining power of the TNC may increase as the technological intensity of the product and process technology it brings to the subsidiary increases. Three measures might be used as proxies for the intensity of the TNC's R&D. The most often used proxy for R&D intensity has been the R&D/sales ratio of the parent TNC. The technology transferred to the subsidiary, however, may be older than the latest technology produced and used by the TNC at home. The R&D intensity of the subsidiary, as measured by local R&D/(subsidiary sales) is an even more unreliable measure since, typically, significant R&D is not performed at the subsidiary level. Licensing and technical service fees as a percent of sales is also not a satisfactory measure because the size of these fees often does not reflect the value of the technology transferred due to manipulation of transfer prices by the TNC and because some host governments control the level of these payments. A measure of technological intensity was used that might circumvent these problems. It ranked on a scale of 1 to 10 the technological leadership of the parent TNC as perceived by the firm's managers. This measure embodies not only the technology that could have been transferred with the initial investment, but also the potential for further transfer in the future, another potential source of bargaining power for the TNC.

Finding a reasonable proxy for the advertising intensity of the firm also presented problems, although they were not as severe as those for technological intensity. The advertising to sales ratio of the subsidiary relative to other firms in the industry in the host country was used.

The bargaining power of the parent TNCs may have increased as the capital requirements of the subsidiary increased. The capital intensity and capital requirements variables were straightforward to measure: total assets/output and total assets. These 2 variables were correlated, however, so that when they were entered in the regression equation together, they were significant at only the 10 percent level.

Export intensity was measured as exports/sales. The higher the export/sales ratio, the greater the bargaining power of the TNC.

The size (assets) of the parent TNC relative to the other parent TNCs in the industry was included in the regression equation to test the hypothesis that for smaller firms capital and managerial resources were a binding constraint on their ability to undertake majority equity participation in their subsidiaries abroad.

As the economic linkages between the TNC and its subsidiary increase, the TNCs may have become less reliant on subsidiary profits for earning a return on their investment. The flow of resources between the TNC and its subsidiary as a percent of sales was used to proxy this linkage effect: inputs, interest on loans and intrafirm suppliers' credit, intrafirm sales, management and technical service fees, and an imputed rental value on machinery and equipment supplied by the TNC.[14]

Finding a proxy for the "attractiveness" of the host country as a site for a subsidiary proved difficult because many variables could influence a TNC's perception of host country attractiveness. Moreover, the relative importance of the various factors could vary between TNCs and over time. The managers interviewed were asked to rank from low (1) to high (10) the attractiveness of the host country as an investment site at the time of the investment.

The number of TNCs that had already undertaken a FDI in the countries of the ASEAN region in the firm's industry at the time it made its investment was used as a proxy for the number of potential entrants into the industry in the host country. As this number increased, the relative bargaining power of the TNC should decrease.

"Time" was included as an explanatory variable because the TNCs in the sample had invested in different years. Host economics and government policies had changed over time and multinationals based in Japan and LDCs tended to be late entrants.

Finally, when the TNC was based in Europe, Japan, or an LDC, 3 dummy variables were used to pick up any residual difference between the percent ownership attained and the relative bargaining power of the TNC and the nationality of the parent TNC. These dummy variables test the hypothesis that TNCs based in different countries "give" local partners a greater share of the equity in their foreign subsidiaries. These dependent and independent variables are tabulated in Table 1 with their expected signs.

RESULTS

Table 2 displays the regression results. For the regression on Actual Equity Ownership all the coefficients had the expected sign and most were significant at the 5 percent level. Note that, everything else being equal, the TNCs in the sample based in Japan and LDCs had a lower level of Actual Equity Ownership although only by 4 percent and 7 percent, respectively. U.S.-based and European TNCs had about the same propensity for equity participation given firm and country characteristics (their relative bargaining strengths). Smaller TNCs tended to take lower equity positions than did larger ones. The regression results lend some support to the hypotheses on the determinants of the relative bargaining power of TNCs and the host countries. Actual Equity Ownership increased as the technical leadership, the advertising intensity, and the export ratio increased, and decreased as host country attractiveness and the number of potential TNC investors increased, and with time. Although the coefficients of the variables representing the capital intensity and capital requirements had the expected sign, they were only significant at the 10 percent level.[15]

The regression on S^{TNC} supports these conclusions. Notice that the variables used to proxy a TNC's desire for equity ownership—TNC assets, TNC-subsidiary linkages, and the TNC home country dummy variables—were no longer significant because S^{TNC} factors the desired level of equity ownership out of the relationship. Time was significantly negative, indicating that the 5 host countries had become more successful in their bargaining with TNCs for equity ownership over time.

TABLE 2

Regression Results

Independent Variables	Dependent Variables		
	Actual Equity Ownership, EO	TNC Bargaining Success (X100), S^{TNC}	Effective Control
Constant	50.3***	5.3	6.2***
	(5.70)	(.84)	(4.13)
Technological leadership	1.32**	2.4***	.21***
	(2.12)	(2.37)	(3.21)
Advertising intensity	1.20**	.87*	.12**
	(1.98)	(1.76)	(2.13)
Subsidiary assets	.35*	.72*	−.10*
	(1.67)	(1.72)	(1.66)
Capital/output	.42	.17	07
	(1.37)	(1.43)	(1.10)
Export/sales	3.12***	5.5***	.37***
	(2.91)	(3.25)	(2.97)
TNC assets	.63***	1.1	.10**
	(2.50)	(.73)	(1.98)
TNC-subsidiary linkages	−5.14**	−2.3	.30***
	(2.23)	(1.24)	(2.75)
Host-country attractiveness	−2.15***	−3.6***	−.14
	(3.01)	(3.12)	(1.15)
Potential TNC investors	−2.77***	−2.7**	−.12**
	(2.63)	(2.11)	(1.98)
Time (1960 = 1)	−.52**	−.74**	−.05**
	(2.55)	(2.20)	(2.02)
Dummy-Japanese TNC	−.04***	−.17	+.07**
	(3.50)	(.84)	(2.10)
Dummy-LDC TNC	−.07**	.32	−.03*
	(2.91)	(.15)	(1.92)
European TNC	+.02	+.87*	.02
	(1.10)	(1.67)	(1.61)
$\bar{R}^2$	.63	.47	.55

The t statistics are in parentheses.

*** significant at the 1 percent level
** significant at the 5 percent level
* significant at the 10 percent level

These results support and extend those of Fagre and Wells and give a more solid foundation to the hypothesis that the level of equity participation of TNCs is influenced by their relative bargaining position with host country governments.

Control Over the Subsidiary

The next issue to be considered is that of control over the operations of the subsidiary in the host country.[16] There may often be no straightforward relationship between the percentage of equity ownership of the TNC and control over its subsidiary. "Control" was broken down into 18 areas in production, finance, marketing, exports, and imports, including overall management control. (See the Appendix for a list of these areas.) The managers of the 153 subsidiaries rated the importance of control over each of these factors for the success of the investment from the parent TNC's viewpoint (1 = no importance; 10 = critical importance), and the degree of control that the TNC had over each factor (1 = no control; 10 = complete control). These data were used to construct a composite measure of the

TNC's control over its subsidiary, "Effective Control." (Details of how this measure was calculated are in the Appendix.) Effective Control essentially was a measure of the degree of control that the TNC had over the 18 variables weighted by their importance for the success of the investment from the TNC's viewpoint. Put another way, Effective Control measured the degree of control over the critical success variables retained within the TNC compared to the control lost to those outside the TNC, such as, local partners or the host government. Effective Control was scaled from 1 (no effective control) to 10 (complete effective control). For the firms in the sample, the correlation between the TNC's percent equity ownership in its subsidiary and its Effective Control over its subsidiary was .57, far from a 1 to 1 correspondence.

The next step in the analysis was to examine the relationship between Effective Control as a dependent variable and the factors that may have determined the relative bargaining power and desires for equity ownership of the TNCs and the host countries as independent variables using linear multiple regression. The expected signs of the coefficients are displayed in Table 1 based on the theory presented in the previous section. Notice that the expected signs are the same (except for "TNC-subsidiary linkages") for Effective Control as for Actual Equity Ownership since the factors that influenced Actual Ownership and Effective Control were the same. A higher degree of linkages between TNC and subsidiary may reduce the TNC's desire for equity ownership (because it can take its profits in other forms besides on its equity), but should increase its level of effective control.

The results of the regression analysis generally supported the hypotheses, although there were a few surprises (Table 2). First, although TNCs based in Japan and LDCs had generally lower actual equity ownership than U.S. and Europe-based TNCs, Japanese TNCs seem to have retained a slightly higher degree of Effective Control within the TNC (significant at the 5 percent level), given their relative bargaining power. This result may have some interesting policy implications, since one of the reasons given by host-country governments for an increased level of local equity participation has been to retain control of the activities of the subsidiaries of TNCs.[17]

The relationship between Effective Control of a TNC over its subsidiary and the success of the investment was tested using 3 measures of success: the profitability of the subsidiary; the success of the subsidiary as rated by the TNC (1 = unsuccessful; 10 = very successful); and the "corrected" success where the success rating of an individual subsidiary was scaled in relation to the average success rating of the firms in the sample in the same industry in the same country, that is, country and industry corrected success (CICS). The TNCs were asked to rate the success of their investment because profitability was not the only component of success for the TNCs in the sample, and because the reported profitability of the subsidiaries of TNCs has been found to differ from actual profitability.[18] The CICS rating was used to try to isolate the relationship between Effective Control and the success of the subsidiary independent of industry and country effects. The scatter diagram plotting CICS against Effective Control is in Figure 2. The relationship was roughly linear: the greater the Effective Control, the greater the CICS of the subsidiary from the TNCs' viewpoint. This relationship also held when success and profitability were plotted against Effective Control, although there was a much wider scatter about the trend, as expected.

The relationship between Percent Equity Ownership and CICS is displayed in Figure 3. Note that the relationship was roughly J-shaped. The lowest level of CICS occurred when equity ownership was roughly split between the TNC and its local partners. When equity ownership clearly resided with one partner or the other, the subsidiary tended to be more successful from the TNC's point of view. This J-shaped relationship also held between Overall Management Control and CICS, not surprising in light of the high correlation (.63) between Percent Equity Ownership and Overall Management Control. These results support the research

FIGURE 2

The Relationship Between Country And Industry
Corrected Success and Effective Control

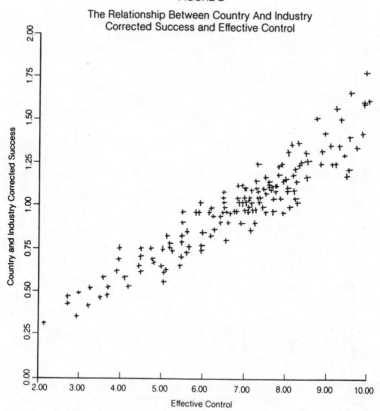

of Killing [1982] and Schaan [1982] and provide it with statistical support drawn
from a large sample of firms based in different home countries, operating in
several industries, and investing in several host countries.

CONCLUSIONS AND IMPLICATIONS
The theoretical and statistical analyses of this paper have traced the relationships
between the characteristics of TNCs and host developing countries, their desired
equity ownership in the subsidiary, control over the subsidiary, and the success of
the TNCs in attaining their goals using a bargaining power framework of analysis.
There was not a close relationship between Percent Equity Ownership and
Effective Control. Some TNCs with a low percent of the equity in their subsidiaries
had a high degree of control over the critical success variables in their subsidiaries. Conversely, some TNCs with a high level of equity ownership had a low
degree of control over these variables. Some TNCs were able to control their
subsidiaries in LDCs by means other than through their share of the equity of the
subsidiary. There was a close linear relationship between the level of control a
TNC had over the areas of operation of its subsidiaries that were critical to
success, and the success of the investment from the TNC's viewpoint. The
relationship between the TNC's overall management control and its equity
ownership position in its subsidiary and the success of the subsidiary from its

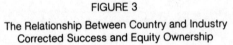

FIGURE 3

The Relationship Between Country and Industry
Corrected Success and Equity Ownership

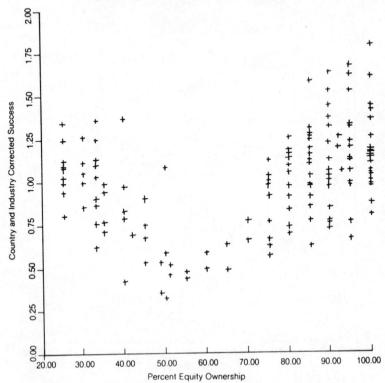

viewpoint was roughly J-shaped. Low success occurred when ownership and overall control were roughly equally divided between the TNC and its local partner. These conclusions have several implications for TNCs and host countries alike.

First, the relative bargaining power of TNCs and host LDCs, as proxied by the variables in Table 1, had a strong influence on the percent equity participation the TNCs in the sample attained in the ASEAN Region. Before investing in the LDC, TNCs might do well to assess their relative bargaining power so that they do not set unreasonable target levels of equity participation in negotiations with investors and host governments in LDCs. If the relative bargaining power of a TNC and the host government changes over time, negotiations may be initiated by either party to change the level of equity participation to reflect these changed conditions. Conversely, if a host government sets mandatory minimum levels of equity participation by its nationals, it may either discourage FDI (if the levels are higher than warranted by its relative bargaining power) or give up potential benefits of increased local ownership (if the levels set are too low).

Second, because the relationship between equity participation and effective control was not close, a TNC may be able to retain control over the factors of the operation of its subsidiary that are important to it, even though it has a low level of

FIGURE 4

The Relationship Between Effective Control and Equity Ownership

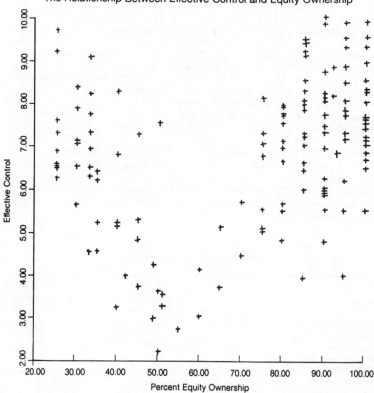

equity participation. A TNC may therefore be able to reduce the level of its equity participation in response to host country demands while retaining control over the factors that are critical to the success of its investment. If the TNC has significant linkages to its subsidiary in the LDC, it may be able to appropriate a satisfactory share of the profits earned on its firm-specific advantages in ways other than through its share of the dividends from its equity investment.

In its drive for increased equity ownership, a TNC may cause the host government to react in such a way as to reduce the TNC's control over these key factors in spite of its higher equity position, or, conversely, the TNC may not invest in a country that does not allow it its desired level of equity participation even though the TNC may be able to appropriate a satisfactory share of profits despite a reduced level of equity ownership. This trade-off between equity and control may be particularly important in countries where the host government perceives a high economic and political cost associated with foreign ownership. Conversely, host governments may have placed undue emphasis on the level of equity participation of TNCs in their economies in their desire to appropriate a share of the profits earned by TNCs operating in their economies, rather than focusing on the level of effective control and the linkages between TNCs and their local subsidiaries.

Third, there was a strong relationship between effective control and the success of the investment from the TNC's viewpoint. The relationship between Overall

Management Control (and percent equity participation) and success was J-shaped: high and low levels of Overall Management Control (and high and low levels of equity participation) led to greater success than when ownership and management control were split roughly equally. These results reinforce the previous conclusions that it may be to the TNC's advantage to trade off reduced equity participation for increased effective control, a trade-off that may be available if increased equity participation (because it is highly visible) carries a high perceived cost to the host government, but effective control does not (because it is more difficult to discern, monitor, and regulate). TNCs should be careful about reaching a situation in which the level of equity ownership and control is roughly equal between the partners. On the other hand, host governments might gain more benefits for their countries if they bargained over increased local control rather than for increased local equity participation if they are concerned about losing control over their economies to TNCs and about the effects of transfer pricing on the flow of net benefits to their economies.

Fourth, although TNCs based in Japan have typically taken a lower level of equity ownership in LDCs than U.S. or European TNCs, they managed to retain a higher level of effective control over their subsidiaries, even when the relative bargaining power (as proxied by firm and country characteristics) of the 3 groups of firms is taken into account.

Calculation of Effective Control

APPENDIX

Factors	Control(C) 1(no)-10(complete)	Importance(I) 1(none)-10(critical)
Output pricing	6	8
Output volume	4	9
Output quality	8	10
Technology transfer	10	10
Technology control	10	10
Capital expenditures	5	7
Financing source	1	2
Financing cost	2	2
Financing amount	1	1
Dividends timing	5	6
Dividends amount	7	6
Fees paid to the TNC	7	8
Advertising and marketing and expenditures	4	7
Channels of distribution	3	2
Import price	6	5
Import source	8	10
Import volume	4	3
Export price	9	3
Export destination	8	4
Export volume	7	2
Overall management	6	7

$$\text{Effective Control} = \frac{\Sigma C_i \cdot I_i}{I_i} = \frac{801}{122} = 6.6$$

FOOTNOTES

1. Ironically, one of the persistent problems in joint ventures in LDCs is often the desire of local partners for a quick payback at the expense of the continued reinvestment desired by the TNCs.

2. In this paper the term "subsidiary" is used rather loosely to refer to a direct investment by a TNC in the host country regardless of the extent of the TNC's equity position in that subsidiary.

3. See Dunning [1979], Casson [1979], Buckley and Casson [1976], Rugman [1980], and Buckley [1981].

4. The greater the advantages of internalizing the international activity via FDI relative to licensing or export, the lower the relative returns to these activities and the more the firm will strive to retain a high share of the profits of the venture abroad by a high level of equity position in its subsidiary in the host country.

5. See Stopford and Wells [1972, Chapter 8] and Fagre and Wells [1982].

6. Conglomerate diversification, especially if the parent firm acts as a holding company, may be one form of externalizing the TNC's proprietary asset of access to relatively inexpensive capital. Conglomerate diversification usually occurs within national boundaries, although with a few notable exceptions (for example, Seagrams' attempt to take over Conoco).

7. See Poynter [1982] and Bradley [1977] for analyses of the determinants of host government intervention against TNCs and the strategic alternatives available to TNCs to reduce this intervention.

8. This effect may be decreased somewhat if the TNC is concerned about the price at which intrafirm goods and services are transferred and if there is a potential conflict over transfer prices with its local partner.

9. See Stern and Tims [1975], de la Torre [1981], and Streeten [1976] for analyses of the relative bargaining power of host countries.

10. In a preliminary draft of their paper, Fagre and Wells [1982] wrote, "As a practical matter, we had to use the degree of control (as measured by equity ownership) to indicate bargaining success." But further on they wrote, "Developing nations, just as many multinational corporations, generally equate equity ownership with control. In reality, ownership and control may not be perfectly related. . . . However, there is probably a reasonable correspondence between the percentage of equity ownership held by a parent corporation and the actual degree of control exercised over the affiliates in most cases." Fagre and Wells cited previous work by several authors to support this statement.

11. See Lecraw [1981, Table 3-4] and Kumar and Kim [1982].

12. There were wide variations about these averages. See Lecraw [1983a] for further data on the firms in the sample.

13. This measure may be better than that used by Fagre and Wells in that the comparison is for subsidiaries in LDCs, not to the ownership level of the TNCs' European subsidiaries where business conditions may be radically different from those in the host LDC.

14. See Vaitsos [1974, Chapter 5] for an analysis of transfer pricing by TNCs.

15. The correlation between capital intensity and capital requirements was .43.

16. See Hayashi [1978], Puxty [1979], Sim [1977] and Welge [1980] for analyses of comparative management and control systems among U.S., British, German, and Japanese TNCs.

17. This statement makes the assumption that local joint venture partners will act in the interest of the nation in exercising their control over the subsidiary. Even if this is not true, however, at least they will use their control for their own benefit and, to the extent they are part of the nation, the nation gains. This argument is roughly similar to "I'd rather be had by someone within my group than by a stranger."

18. See Vaitsos [1974, Chapter 5].

REFERENCES   Beamish, P., and Lane, H. "Joint Venture Performance in Developing Countries." London, Canada: University of Western Ontario, 1982. Mimeo.

Bradley, D. G. "Managing Against Expropriation." *Harvard Business Review*, July–August 1977, pp. 75-83.

Buckley, P. J., and Casson, M. "The Optimal Timing of a Foreign Direct Investment." *The Economic Journal*, March 1981, p. 75-87.

_____. *The Future of the Multinational Enterprise*. London: Macmillan, 1976.

Casson, M. *Alternatives to the Multinational Enterprise*. London: Macmillan, 1979.

de la Torre, J. "Foreign Investment and Economic Development: Conflict and Negotiation." *Journal of International Business Studies*, Fall 1981, pp. 9-32.

Dunning, J. "Explaining Changing Patterns of International Production: In Defense of the Eclectic Theory." *Oxford Bulletin of Economics and Statistics*, November 1979, pp. 269-295.

Fagre, N., and Wells, L. T. Jr. "Bargaining Power of Multinationals and Host Governments." *Journal of International Business Studies*, Fall 1982, pp. 9-24.

Franko, L. G. *Joint Venture Survival in Multinational Corporations*. New York: Praeger, 1971.

Hayashi, K. "Japanese Management of Multinational Operations: Sources and Means of Control." *Management International Review 18*, No. 4 (1978), pp. 47-57.

Horst, T. *At Home Abroad: A Study of the Domestic and Foreign Operations of the American Food-Processing Industry*. Cambridge, MA: Ballinger, 1974.

Killing, P. "Technology Acquisition: License Agreements or Joint Ventures." *Columbia Journal of World Business*, Fall 1980, pp. 38-46.

_____. "How to Make a Global Joint Venture Work." *Harvard Business Review*, May/June 1982, pp. 120-127.

Kumar, K., and Kim, K. Y. "The Korean Manufacturing Multinationals." East-West Center, University of Hawaii, 1982. Mimeo.

Lecraw, D. J. "Direct Investment by Firms from Less Developed Countries." *Oxford Economic Papers*, November 1977, pp. 442-457.

_____. "Internationalization of Firms from LDCs: Evidence from the ASEAN Region." In *Multinationals from Developing Countries*, edited by K. Kumar and M. McLeod. Lexington, MA: D.C. Heath Lexington Books, 1981.

_____. "Performance of Transnational Corporations in Less Developed Countries." *Journal of International Business Studies*, Spring-Summer 1983a, pp. 15-33.

_____. "Comment on Moxon." *International Business Strategies in the Asia-Pacific Region*, edited by R. Moxon, T. Roehl, and F. Truitt. Vol. 4, Part 1. JAI Press, 1983b.

_____. "Evidence on Transfer Pricing by TNCs." In *Transfer Pricing and the MNE*, edited by Alan Rugman. Cambridge, MA: MIT Press, forthcoming, 1985.

Magee, S. "Technology and the Appropriability of the Multinational Corporation." In *The New International Economic Order*. Cambridge, MA: M.I.T. Press, 1977.

Moxon, R. "Export Platform Investment in the Asia-Pacific Region." In *International Business Strategies in the Asia-Pacific Region*, edited by R. Moxon, T. Ruehl, and F. Truitt. JAI Press, 1983.

Poynter, T. A. "Government Intervention in Less Developed Countries: The Experience of Multinational Companies." *Journal of International Business Studies*, Spring-Summer 1982, pp. 9-25.

Puxty, A. G. "Some Evidence Concerning Cultural Differentials in Ownership Policies of Overseas Subsidiaries." *Management International Review* 19, No. 2 (1979), pp. 39-52.

Rugman, A. M. "Internalization as a General Theory of Foreign Direct Investment: A Re-Appraisal of the Literature." *Weltwirtschaftliches Archiv*, Band 116, Heft 2, 1980, pp. 365-379.

Schaan, J. L. "Joint Ventures in Mexico." Ph.D. proposal, Business School, The University of Western Ontario, London, Canada, 1982. Mimeo.

Sim, A. B. "Decentralized Management of Subsidiaries and Their Performance: A Comparative Study of American, British, and Japanese Subsidiaries in Malaysia." *Management International Review* 17, No. 2 (1977), pp. 45-51.

Stern, E., and Tims, W. "The Relative Bargaining Strengths of the Developing Countries." *American Journal of Agricultural Economics*, May 1975, pp. 225-236.

Stopford, J., and Wells, L. T. Jr. *Managing the Multinational Enterprise*. New York: Basic Books, 1972.

Streeten, P. "Bargaining with Multinationals." *World Development*, Vol. 4, No. 3, March 1976.

Vaitsos, C. V. *Intercountry Income Distribution and Transnational Enterprises*. Oxford: Oxford University Press, 1974.

Vernon, R. *Sovereignty at Bay*. New York: Basic Books, 1971.

Welge, M. K. "A Comparison of Managerial Structures in German Subsidiaries in France, India, and the United States." *Management International Review* 21, No. 2 (1980), pp. 5-21.

Wells, L. T. Jr. *Third World Multinationals: The Rise of Foreign Investment from Developing Countries*. Cambridge, MA: M.I.T. Press, 1983.

[20]

*M. A. Lyles**

Learning Among Joint Venture Sophisticated Firms**

Introduction

More firms are utilizing joint ventures for the first time to increase their strategic capabilities and global competitiveness. Yet the use of cooperative alliances among firms, in particular, joint ventures, are controversial topics both to academics and practitioners (Pfeffer & Salancik, 1978; Pennings, 1981). Strategic and international management theorists have studied individual joint ventures to determine the reasons for formation, the factors for success and the cultural implications (Franko, 1971; Killing, 1982; Stopford & Wells, 1972). Economic analysis has attempted to provide economic rationales for joint ventures and the impact on research and development (Berg, Duncan, & Friedman, 1982; Harrigan, 1985; Hladik, 1985; Pfeffer & Nowak, 1976). Prior studies have not led to a greater understanding of the joint venturing process from a corporate viewpoint nor of the learning that has accumulated from past experiences. Thus, for strategic management a critical question remaining is to what extent firms have learned from this process and whether joint venturing contributes to a firm's strategic capabilities.

This study documents the learning that has occurred in firms that have been successful at operating multiple joint ventures in an international context. It seeks to determine how these firms developed new programs and structures, innovated, and created new frames of reference in order to adapt and to learn. It builds upon the work of Chandler (1962), Cyert and March (1963), and Miles (1982) who have addressed the learning process in complex organizations as they coped with environmental stress. It attempts to fill the gaps in the research on joint ventures by exploring how joint venturing experiences have increased the competitive edge of the parenting firms. For our purposes, a joint venture (JV) is considered to be an independent entity formed by two or more parent firms.

The term „learning" refers to the development of insights, knowledge and associations between past actions, the effectiveness of those actions, and future actions (Fiol & Lyles, 1985). Learning is the process in which growing insights and successful restructuring of organizational problems reflect themselves in structural elements and outcomes (Chandler, 1962; Chakravarthy, 1982; Hedberg, 1981; Miller & Friesen, 1980). Hence, learning is both action outcomes and changes in the state of knowledge. When seen in a learning context, a host of issues about joint venturing activities may be better understood by both the researcher and the practitioner.

Longitudinal studies in the strategic management field are rare. Rarer yet are research studies that aim to understand the learning that takes place as firms attempt to survive and change under dynamic environmental conditions. While organizational learning has recently been identified as important in strategic management, it has received remarkably little attention by researchers. For these reasons, this study is exploratory in nature and

* *Professor Marjorie A. Lyles, Assistant Professor, Department of Business Administration, University of Illinois at Urbano-Champaign, Illinois, U.S.A. Manuscript received March 1987.*

will attempt to allow the important issues to emerge from the data (Glaser & Strauss, 1967).

The paper addresses the issue of *whether* learning occurred in joint venture experienced firms, *how* it occurred, and *what* was learned. It represents a subset of an ongoing research project on JV sophisticated firms. Four firms, two American and two European, were chosen to participate in the study based on their extensive JV experience. Appendix I gives a summary description of the firms. The paper begins by identifying the conceptual framework used to assess the learning patterns. It then presents the results of interviews conducted with each firm on the firm's joint venturing experiences and what has been learned. Finally, implications are suggested.

The Learning Framework

Organizational adjustment is an essential element of a firm's ability to survive and to sustain competitiveness over time. Fiol and Lyles (1985) suggest that it is necessary to separate mere adjustment decisions from deeper changes, such as in the belief structures, values, and norms. They argue that learning occurs at two levels, higher- and lower-. Lower-level learning may be apparent from observing the actions that are taken and the structural changes that are made. On the other hand, higher-level learning represents changing associations, frames of reference and programs that beg a methodology that analyzes the more in-depth functioning of an organization. In order to study learning in JV sophisticated firms, it is necessary to look not only at the way the JVs were implemented but also to examine the attitudes and values of the management.

Figure 1 represents the framework for determining if learning occurred and what learning occurred as a result of these joint venturing activities. The figure shows the interrelatedness of lower-level and higher-level learning and the roles that unlearning and experimentation play in creating new learning. Each of these will be discussed below.

Levels of Learning

Lower-level learning. Lower-level learning is a result of repetition and routine and involves association building. Cyert and March (1963) identify standard operating procedures or success programs, goals, and decision rules as illustrative of learning based on routine. It occurs in contexts that are well understood and where management thinks it can control the situation (Duncan, 1974). Two types of lower-level learning will be discussed below: success programs and management systems.

Success programs. Organization that exist for any length of time develop standard methods for handling repetitive decisions that become standard operating procedures. These are successful methodologies that have worked in the past, and organizations resist changing them. They can be quickly utilized rather than reassessing the decision situation each time it arises (Cyert & March, 1963).

Management systems. Galbraith (1973) suggests that firms will also develop management systems to handle their information processing needs in repetitive, unchanging situations. The management systems include the policies, hierarchies, rewards, and administrative systems that reflect how the organization has learned to handle reoccurring situations. It is generally traumatic for the organization to restructure or to implement new management systems (Cyert & March, 1963).

Higher-level learning. The adjustment of overall missions, beliefs and norms is higher-level learning. These have long term effects and impact the whole organization, not just the joint venture or a division. Over time, every organization faces the need for renewal

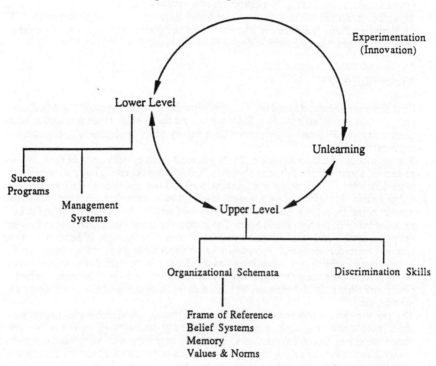

Figure 1: Learning Framework

and for reanalysis of its mission and basic capabilities. Evidence suggests that higher-level learning often results in new frames of reference, new skills for problem formulation or agenda setting, new values, or unlearning of past success programs (Lyles & Mitroff, 1980; Miller & Friesen, 1980; Starbuck, 1983). Three types of higher-level learning will be discussed next: discrimination skills, unlearning, and innovation.

Discrimination skills. An organization that can utilize different success programs and management systems for different situations has learned to discriminate. In other words, higher-level learning includes the ability to discriminate among different decision situations and to choose appropriate behaviors or actions for each situation.

Unlearning. Firms that can unlearn and reframe their past success programs to fit with changing environmental and situational conditions will have a greater likelihood of survival and adaptation (Hedberg, 1981; Starbuck, 1983). Unlearning is particularly important at the strategic level where each decision situation may be unique and where past success may not be an indication of future success. Miles (1982) argues that negative performance feedback precipitates the search for new methods for handling decisions and problems. Hence, unlearning is triggered by mistakes, failures, or poor performance.

Innovation or experimentation. The ability to develop fresh approaches to situations or problems indicates a new dimension to higher-order learning. Experimentation may generate conceptual leaps in the development of associations and may result in the changing of the old success programs or norms. It represents a disassociation with the reinforcement of past behaviors and a reaction to the momentum that builds up (Starbuck, 1983).

Innovation or experimentation may be closely tied to unlearning and is necessary for organizational renewal and the development of new capabilities.

This study describes the learning that is reported by the upper management of four JV sophisticated firms. It determines whether lower- and higher-level is reported and what patterns emerged. Next the methodology will be discussed.

Methodology

Four firms were selected based on their long histories with joint venturing and their current involvement in multiple JVs. Each has at least thirty years JV experience, at least twenty ongoing JVs, and experiences with a variety of JV configurations in numerous locations.

A triangulation of data collection methods was used to query each firm about its JV experiences, about specific JVs, and about the learning that occurred. In-depth interviews were conducted with corporate management, staff and line management and with the JV management. At least eight people were interviewed at each firm, with the maximum number being about forty. The interviews were conducted in the United States and in Europe and lasted an average of two hours. The companies and the individual managers were very cooperative and allowed the researcher to return for multiple interviews. In this manner, the researcher had the opportunity to raise additional questions, to clarify certain events, or to probe deeper regarding an event. To verify the verbal reports, two other kinds of data were necessary: publicly available information (such as annual reports, newspaper clippings), and company archival data (such as minutes from board meetings, memos, etc.).

The interviews were semi-structured, asking each participant to reconstruct his/her personal involvement in JVs, the historical evolutions of the firm's JV strategies, and the factors affecting future JV decisions. Questions regarding past joint ventures were straightforward such as asking about the reporting or management structures, the amount of involvement of the parent firm in the JV, and the successes/failures.

Data from the interviews were coded and were verified by the archival data, the person interviewed, or other informants. Alternative viewpoints about events were identified and served as probes for later interviews or were verified by the other data.

This methodology is appropriate because information about a firm's learning is not available outside that firm, it requires an in-depth analysis, and learning is a lagged phenomenon. Although the sample size of four firms is small, an in-depth analysis of each firm was possible. The interviews built statements based on reconstructed logic, but the events could be verified by checking them in the formal reports or external documents. Statements of learning were perceptual and subject to individual biases and judgments; however, the use of multiple informants helps to minimize this bias.

Results

Each firm was analyzed to determine its JV approach based on the interviews, the detailed information about specific JVs, and the archival data (Table 1). The firms varied between allowing the JV decentralized control versus centralized control from the parent. Three of the four firms licensed their technology with the JVs, but one firm licensed its technology but also received technologies from its partners. Three frims were willing to take minority positions, and all of the firms wanted their partners to have an active part in the management of the JVs. Each also said that they would prefer wholly-owned subsidiaries to JVs. However, JVs were a necessary component of their global competitiveness. Next the analysis of the learning framework is presented.

Table 1: Profile of JV Approaches

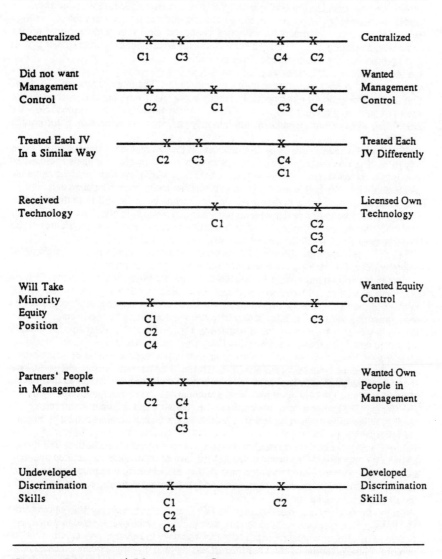

Decentralized		Centralized
X X	X X	
C1 C3	C4 C2	

Did not want Management Control		Wanted Management Control
X X	X X	
C2 C1	C3 C4	

Treated Each JV In a Similar Way		Treated Each JV Differently
X X	X	
C2 C3	C4	
	C1	

Received Technology		Licensed Own Technology
X	X	
C1	C2	
	C3	
	C4	

Will Take Minority Equity Position		Wanted Equity Control
X	X	
C1	C3	
C2		
C4		

Partners' People in Management		Wanted Own People in Management
X X		
C2 C4		
C1		
C3		

Undeveloped Discrimination Skills		Developed Discrimination Skills
X	X	
C1	C2	
C2		
C4		

Success Programs / Management Systems

The two types of lower-level learning represent ways of doing things that were successful in the past. The research looked for decision rules or ways of handling JVs that are repeated and worked well and for structures, reporting systems, management methods, etc., that were repeated across the JVs.

Two firms said there was an usual way of handling JVs and two firms said there was not. Of the two „yes" firms, each had different approaches to its success program. C1`s approach was decentralized, allowing each JV to make important decisions about its operations but to provide guidance from the parent corporation. C1 provides the technology but no management contracts. It maintains control of the JV through informal means such as socialization of the management and low turnover among the management. „Get good people and give them freedom" was the rule.

On the other hand, C2's usual way is to have 50% equity, not to participate in the management, and to maintain control over the technology. The management of C2 claim that this is changing. One person said, „There was a usual way, but it is changing. We were not ready to place our people in a JV. We wanted our 50% equity position. Now we are willing to place our technology into minority positions wherever new opportunities are coming."

Both firms who have a usual way also said that in the future, there were not going to be any rules. The two other firms said they have no hard and fast rules in their approaches, except that they do require the use of their financial reporting systems. All four firms indicate that what they had learned over time is that flexibility is the best approach.

Discrimination skills. One higher-level learning technique is the ability to discriminate when a certain behavior or action is appropriate and when it is not. This is situational analysis. The researcher looked for certain decision rules for defining the attributes of the JVs that meant they would be treated one way versus another.

Three firms said they are flexible. One respondent said, „I would say that it's a case of being realistic. I think we are realistic in adjusting to the local situations."

Although the respondents indicate that the firms are becoming better at changing their management techniques based on the situation, the researcher found little evidence of this in three of the firms. The JV data and the interviews did not indicate any decision rules for segmenting the JVs into situations where one method would be used versus another. In C2, however, where there was a usual way for handling JVs, discrimination skills were required to determine when this usual way was appropriate.

Unlearning. Part of learning is unlearning and reframing past behaviors or success programs that are no longer appropriate. To determine if unlearning occurs, one must look for environmental jolts, mistakes or failures, critical incidents, or changes in the success programs or management systems. Table 2 summarizes the events mentioned by the respondents. Two categories, future conflicts and partner rapport, were identified within three firms as influencing their learning. Both of these concern maintaining a good partner relationship.

Future Conflicts acknowledge that at formation, there may be mixed motives and hidden agendas by both firms. One firm formed a JV to have its products manufactured and marketed in a particular country. As time passed, the parent company acquired the skills necessary to market the product themselves–and they thougt their skills were better than the JV's. This created a conflict.

What the firms learned is to accept that the JV's reasons-for-being may change over time and to recognize that they want to acquire their partner's skills over a period of time. One person said, „The only general learning is that you have to be very, very careful that you think of all the potential conflicts of interest. It's more likely in your core business, core countries, than on the fringe." It appears that when the firms had less JV experience, they believed that a JV was forever and that there would be minimal conflicts.

Issues relating to maintaining partner rapport were frequently mentioned. These were verbalized as „lessons" such as „You should treat your partners with 49% as if they were yourself," „Have the firm's president meet with top partners when he is travelling," and „The ventures have got to satisfy the real desires of both parties to be successful." These were seen as important as the firms learned to deal with the ambiguity of the JV's futures.

Table 2: Unlearning/Mistakes

Types	Firms			
	C1	C2	C3	C4
Building in Future Conflicts	X		X	X
Partner Rapport Issues	X	X		X
Technology Transfer Issues		X	X	
Cultural Issues				
Human Resource			X	
Futuristic Issues	X	X		
Equitiy Issues				X
Partner Choice				X

Partner Choise is important because of the potential for conflict. The firms would not choose a partner with the same international aspirations as theirs because they would then meet them head-on somewhere. Also they have learned not to form a JV with people who want the JV as a way to save their own company, as a life buoy.

The two American firms view Technology Transfer as an area in which they made mistakes. They said that it takes experience to recognize that once you license your mature or stable technology, you sell your business and create a new competitor.

Cultural differences has been discussed in the literature as a problem in JVs because of country differences and firm differences (Wright, 1979). None of the firms mention this as a reason for a mistake or failure, although it was mentioned as important for getting along with your partner.

Innovativeness. Innovativeness indicates an ability to move away from the learned responses of the success programs and to experiment with new approaches. Table 3 summarizes the responses.

It was expected that as firms gain JV experience, they would become more risk-taking as they grew comfortable with joint venturing. Three firms indicated that they were more risk-taking now. One respondent from the fourth firm said: „You take the decision that has the most pro's and con's and the best risk profile. So in this respect, we look at JV's like any other alternative." This last firm is also the firm that had the most flexible approach to JVs.

From analysis of the interviews, it became clear that two different kinds of risk were being discussed. The first was financial risk and indicates whether the firms would be willing to forego financial returns. Managerial risk, the second, represents giving up control over the JV decision-making or the technology. Taking a smaller equity position, licens-

Table 3: Innovations: Taking Risks

More Risk-Taking	Firms			
	C1	C2	C3	C4
Yes No	X	X	X	X
Taking Financial Risks	C1	C2	C3	C4
Yes No	X	X	X	X
Taking Managerial Risks	C1	C2	C3	C4
Yes No	X	X	X	X

ing the technology, or participating in management were indications of this kind of risk. This analysis shows that three frims would *not* forego financial returns or sacrifice profitability. If they foresaw that the JV might be a financial risk, they would not be involved. One person said , „Early on we didn't go into JVs because of profitability. I think today, we will not go into them unless they are going to be profitable. Early on we went for market share."

On the other hand, two firms indicate that they would take managerial risks. One person said, „We are willing to take risks by starting with a small equity position and expecting to increase our share over time." Another person from the same firm said, „As a large company, you must be willing sometimes to take a minority interest with a smaller partner." With the right partner, it is possible to take risks on the amount of the equity position.

The JV experienced firms reconfirm the importance of profitability since there is no reason to sacrifice profitability because you are in a JV. However, it is possible to take risks when you are referring to the management systems. Three firms are trying new ways of doing things. The new ways are such things as developing lateral communication links, being more open to different kinds of partner firms, licensing a technology that had been closely protected, or foregoing some control in order to get their „name" utilized.

Transference of learning. The respondents unanimously agreed that there was a transference of learning from multiple JV experiences, although some of it was indirect and informal. For example, the single-business firm, C4, found that „We were finding out, from experiences elsewhere in the world, that our partners are less interested in our business than we are: they had many other operations in other business areas. We slowly started to understand that we had to contribute much more to the management."

The transference takes place through the people and is influenced by the organizational structure. One respondent said: „The type of people you need in managerial/operational positions in a JV is different from the type of people you need in a wholly-owned subsidiary because they need more diplomatic qualities." These same people develop networks that serve to disseminate their experiences.

Table 4: Transference of Learning

Methods of Transference	Firms			
	C1	C2	C3	C4
Top Management overseeing Process	X	X	X	X
International Operations			X	
Training and Socialization			X	X
Direct Management JV Experience		X	X	X
Management Networks	X	X		
Topics	C1	C2	C3	C4
Geographic / Cultural Knowledge			X	X
Development of Partner Relations	X	X	X	X
Management Systems		X		
Interrelatedness of JVs		X	X	X
JV Negotiations / Management Skills				X
Time Orientation (long/short)	X			X

The firms use their joint venture experiences as a credential which makes it easier for them to form new joint ventures. They are viewed as better partners and they have experienced people. One person said, „We now have a cadre of people well qualified to enter JV negotiations, well qualified to handle problems in JVs and that is the result of experiences that began in the 1950's."

Table 4 summarizes the methods used for the transference of learning, and it lists the topics that emerged from the interviews. The respondents recognize that top management in its role of overseeing all the joint ventures play an active role in sharing the lessons learned. Communication and socialization of managers become important methods for the transference of these lessons and norms.

Learning Patterns

The learning within the four firms was demonstrated in several ways. These firms have a high frequency of joint ventures and place importance on them as a means for implementing the firm's overall strategic direction. Joint ventures are recognized by each of the firms as a necessary condition for maintaining global competitveness. Hence, these firms identify that JVs help them to reach their goals. The evidence of continued JV usage and of meeting strategic goals provides insight into the experiences gained and into the learning that occurred.

The organizational histories and statements by the management reveal how the firms learned. They are transmitted by the people, by the sharing of experiences, by the development of organizational stories, and by the development of management systems. The backgrounds of the individual managers reveal the extensive direct experience in the forming, managing, negotiating, and problem-solving with the JV partners and management. The upper-level management of these firms provide the medium for the transference of the learning.

What the firms learned from their JV experiences is somehow both unique and general. It is unique in the sense that each firm has its own unique characteristics and histories, and it is general in the sense that there exists some pattern to the learning that is generalizable across the firms. Listed below are several learning patterns that were gleaned from the interviews.

1. Routine success programs and management systems can be used successfully for joint venturing if the firm enacts its environment.

   Firms that joint venture operate in the most complex of environments: not only are they dealing with environmental complexity in their home markets but also with cultural complexity and the environmental stress of multiple markets. Strategic management researchers appear to argue that in environments of high uncertainty and complexity, firms should attempt to operate with flexibility and in a decentralized mode (Lawrence & Dyer, 1983; Meyer, 1982). In this study we find that three of the firms are doing just that, namely, operating in a very flexible, decentralized manner.

   Yet the fourth firm presents an alternative to this approach. It has maintained the use of its usual way of handling JVs by enacting the environment. It has chosen to set up JVs only in environments that meet certain criteria and then to use its success programs. It is operating under the same environmental conditions as the other firms but sets constraints on the elements that it considers as most important, namely, the partner firms, technology and extent of management involvement.

2. Initial decisions about licensing, equity position and management relations, although appropriate at the time they were made, frequently constrained choices and created conflicts later.

   Since the firms were among the first to use JVs, they began cautiously without prior knowledge or experience or the ability to learn from their peers' experiences. Consequently, each developed comfortable ways or success programs for handling the JV management. These reflect the cultures and norms of the parent firms which were accepting of new cultures and management approaches.

   Nonetheless, the initial reasons for the JVs and the original management systems became obsolete over time (Harrigan, 1985). Lyles (1986) documents how the desire for involvement and the desire for control change over time. The initial contracts, legal statements, or agreements focused attention on the wrong set of issues. This came as a surprise to the parent firms' management. It also created conflicts in their relationships with their partner firms. The firms in this sample learned to accept such changes as part of the nature of joint venturing and to recognize the need for continuing conversations with their partner firms.

3. The importance of partner rapport increased over time.

   Many of the JVs that these four firms maintained were over 10 years old. In fact, some were over 20 years old. Then firms experienced industry changes, market maturation, and their own growth and development. Initially it did not seem that partner firms were closely investigated: they were chosen because they were known by the parent firms. Now however these partner firms are chosen for good business reasons. With time, the firms in the study have learned how to assess markets, partners, and potential contributions of partner firms.

There is the knowledge that JV management is difficult and time consuming and as a JV matures, it is harder to control (Prahalad & Doz, 1981). Therefore it is very important to have a good partner and to maintain a good relationship with that partner. Social relations with your partner remain important because they help to build trust into the relationship.

4. Management attitudes have changed over time from viewing JVs as a „choice" to a „necessary evil."

A widely help belief among researchers and practitioners is that if one wants to do business on a golbal scale, it is necessary to JV (Hout, Porter, & Rudden, 1982). The firms in this sample have learned that it is not easy to maintain a relationship over time and that it takes more time than a wholly owned subsidiary. Joint venturing is still uncomfortable: it is particularly difficult for the American firms to loosen their grip on management controls (Lyles & Reger, 1987).

5. The complexity, uncertainty, and ambiguity of JVs is still uncomfortable for the firms, but more accurate knowledge of the future probability of certain events has come with experience.

With the growth of their experience base, the firms have begun to identify certain events that may occur during a JV's life. For example, these firms have learned that partners may acquire their partners' skills, that partner firms may be merger targets and may change hands, and that technology can be a valuable asset in joint venturing. With this increased knowledge, these JV experienced firms are better able to anticipate major issues and how to handle them.

6. The development of higher-level learning spread to all levels of the organization.

The organizational learning was incorporated into the respondents' statements and was evident in the belief systems, the norms, and the value espoused. Joint venturing was an accepted norm of doing business. All four firms sought to increase their global competitiveness by introducing and marketing their products, technologies, and name recognitions abroad. Joint venturing was one acceptable method for doing this.

Good partner rapport was an accepted value. It is extremely important because each firm has to have the reputation of being a good partner. The world is getting smaller, and the partner firms within an industry generally know each other. A firm has to have the reputation of being competent but also compassionate and trusted. Fairness in negotiations and recognition of their partners' own competence became essential norms for the managers dealing with JVs. These were learned attributes of the JV experienced firms.

Strategic Implications

This paper has addressed the learning that has occurred in JV sophisticated firms. We have pointed out some of the learning patterns that emerged and the nature of the higher-level learning patterns. The firms have built upon their experiences and maintained flexibility in their approaches to JVs. This has resulted in multiple experiences, successes, experimentations, and failures that has led to the richness of their own corporate histories and schemata. It creates a depth to the organization that transcends highly decentralized organization structures. It reaffirms that the experiences, beliefs, and norms are transmitted through the people and management of the firms (Martin, 1982).

The JV experience of these firms may be viewed as a „window of opportunity" for increasing their global competitiveness. It creates a competitive advantage for them by establishing their presence worldwide, by giving them information about operating in various countries and about environmental events, and by the development of a skill base that has prior knowledge of the likelihood of certain events. This increases their strategic capabilities and provides them a competitive advantage (Jemison, 1986; Lenz, 1980). It provides them power and influence.

The firms recognize that the quality of their partner relationships may be just as important as the JV mission since they may affect the firm's corporate global strategy (Thorelli, 1986). This provides them a sense of cautiousness and patience. It provides them a motivation to develop their reputations as trustworthy bedfellows, which allows them to influence others. It provides them a strategic advantage over firms with less experience.

The strength of this study lies in the in-depth nature of the investigation of each firm. However, it is only the first step in analyzing the importance of learning as a strategic capability. Future investigations need to address whether the learning patterns are useful to other firms and whether the learning process can be further analyzed.

References

Berg, S. V., Duncan, J., & Friedman, P. 1982. *Joint venture strategies and corporation innovations.* Cambridge, Mass.: Oelgeschlager, Gunn & Hain.

Chakravarthy, B. S. 1982. Adaptation: A promising metaphor for strategic management. *Academy of Management Review,* 7: 735-744.

Chandler, A. 1962. *Strategy and structure.* Cambridge, Mass.: M.I.T. Press.

Cyert, R. M., & March, J. G. 1963. *A behavioral theory of the firm.* Englewood Cliffs: Prentice-Hall.

Dunbar, R. L. 1981. Designs for organizational control. In P.C. Nystrom & W.H. Starbuck (Eds.), *Handbook of organizational design,* Vol. 2. Oxford: Oxford University Press.

Duncan, R. B. 1974. Modifications in decision structure in adapting to the environment: Some implications for organizational learning. *Decision Sciences,* 705-725.

Fiol, C. M., & Lyles, M. A. 1985. Organizational learning. *Academy of Management Review,* 10, 4: 803-813.

Franko, L. G. 1971. *Joint venture survival in multinational corporations.* New York: Praeger.

Galbraith, J. R. 1973. *Designing complex organizations.* Reading, Mass.: Addison-Wesley.

Glaser, B., & Strauss, A. 1967. *Discovery of grounded theory: Strategies for qualitative research.* Chicago: Aldine.

Harrigan, K. R. 1985. *Strategies for joint ventures.* Lexington, Mass.: Lexington.

Hedberg, B. 1981. How organizations learn and unlearn? In P. C. Nystrom & W. H. Starbuck (Eds.), *Handbook of organizational design:* 8-27. London: Oxford University Press.

Hladik, K. J. 1985. *International joint ventures: An economic analysis of U.S.-foreign business partnerships.* Lexigton, Mass.: Lexington.

Hout, T., Porter, M. E., & Rudden, E. 1982. How global companies win out. *Harvard Business Review,* 60: 98-108.

Jemison, D. B. 1986. *Strategic capability transfer in acquisition integration.* Stanford University Working Paper.

Killing, J. P. 1982. How to make a global joint venture work. *Harvard Business Review,* 60, 3: 120-127.

Lenz, R. T. 1980. Strategic capability: A concept and framework for analysis. *Academy of Management Review,* 5, 2: 225-234.

Lawrence, P. R., & Dyer, D. 1983. *Renewing American industry.* New York: Free Press.

Lyles, M. A. 1986. *Parental desire for control of joint ventures: A case study of an international joint venture.* College of Commerce, University of Illinois, BEBR Working Paper #1273.

Lyles, M. A., & Mitroff, I. I. 1980. Organizational problem formulation: An empirical study. *Administrative Science Quarterly*, 25: 102-119.

Lyles, M. A., & Reger, R. K. 1987. *Upward influence in joint ventures.* Universtiy of Illinois-Champaign Working Paper.

Martin, J. 1982. Stories and scripts in organizational settings. In A. Hastorf & A. Isen (Eds.), *Cognitive social psychology*: 225-305. New York: Elsevier-North Holland.

Meyer, A. 1982. Adapting to environmental jolts. *Administrative Science Quarterly*, 27: 515-537.

Miles, R. H. 1982. *Coffin nails and corporate strategies.* Englewood Cliffs, N. J.: Prentice-Hall.

Miller, D., & Friesen, P. H. 1980. Momentum and revolution in organizational adaptation. *Academy of Management Journal*, 23, 4: 591-614.

Pennings, J. M. 1981. Strategically interdependent organizations In P.C. Nystrom & W. H. Starbuck (Eds.), *Handbook of organizational design*, Vol. 1: 433-455.

Pfeffer, J., & Nowak, P. 1976. Joint ventures and interorganizational interdependence. *Administrative Science Quarterly*, 21: 398-418.

Pfeffer, J., & Salancik, G. R. 1978. *External control of organizations: Resource dependence perspective.* New York: Harper & Row.

Prahalad, C. K., & Doz, Y. L. 1981. An approach to strategic control in MNCs. *Sloan Mangement Review*, Summer: 5-13.

Starbuck, W. H. 1983. Organizations as action generators. *American Sociological Review*, 48: 91-102.

Stopford, J. M., & Wells, L. T. 1972. *Managing the multinational enterprise.* New York: Basic.

Thorelli, H. B. 1986, Networks: Between markets and hierarchies. *Strategic Management Journal*, 7: 37-51.

Wright, R. W. 1979, Joint venture problems in Japan. *Columbia Journal of World Business*, *14*, 1: 25-31.

** Funds for this research were supplied by the University of Illinois Research Board, the Department of Business Administration and the Hewlett Fund.

[21]

© Academy of Management Review
1993, Vol. 18, No. 2, 227–268.

"MESSY" RESEARCH, METHODOLOGICAL PREDISPOSITIONS, AND THEORY DEVELOPMENT IN INTERNATIONAL JOINT VENTURES

ARVIND PARKHE
Indiana University

Dramatic advances have recently marked the study of international joint ventures (IJVs). The progress has been mixed, however. Although several theoretical dimensions have been emphasized in the literature, researchers have not addressed certain crucial questions at the heart of the IJV relationship. Consequently, individually useful IJV studies have not coalesced into a collectively coherent body of work with an underlying theoretical structure. This weakness in theory development, I argue, may stem from the convergence of "hard" methodological approaches with "soft" behavioral variables. In proposing and justifying a research program toward deeper understanding of voluntary interfirm cooperation, I offer a theoretical framework for IJVs, develop a typology of theory-development approaches, and apply this framework and typology to demonstrate how a near-term shift in foci can accelerate rigorous IJV theory development.

It is correct to argue that the field of international management is in a nascent, preparadigmatic stage of development (Adler, 1983; Black & Mendenhall, 1990), and therefore it is not surprising that such subareas as international joint ventures (IJVs) also lack a strong theoretical core or an encompassing framework that effectively integrates past research and serves as a springboard for launching future research. What is perhaps surprising, however, is the extent to which current empirical IJV research, which boasts a large number of methodologically impeccable studies, fails to address concepts that are theoretically deemed *central* to the IJV relationship. In their provocative essay on "A theory of cooperation in international business," Buckley and Casson (1988: 32) noted that the essence of voluntary interfirm cooperation lies in "coordination effected through mutual forbearance." Forbearance becomes possible only when there is reciprocal behavior (Axelrod, 1984; Oye, 1986) and mutual trust

---

This study was supported by a research grant from the Graduate School of Business, Indiana University (Bloomington). Earlier versions of this paper were presented at the 1991 Academy of International Business Meeting, Miami, and at the 1992 Academy of International Business Meeting, Brussels. My thanks to Farok Contractor, John Daniels, Marc Dollinger, George Dreher, Cherlyn Granrose, Paul Marer, Janet Near, Dennis Organ, and Charles Schwenk for their helpful comments.

(Thorelli, 1986), which in turn only come about given an absence of opportunism (Williamson, 1985). Yet the core concepts of trust, reciprocity, opportunism, and forbearance have received scant systematic attention except in theoretical treatises (Buckley & Casson, 1988; Ring & Van de Ven, 1992; Williamson, 1985), computer simulations (Axelrod, 1984), and aggregated studies (Kogut, 1989; Parkhe, In press) that conceal the intricacies and dynamism of such relationships.

I argue that acceleration of theory development in IJVs is needed and possible, and that it must be preceded by a deeper understanding and systematic incorporation of core concepts in future research. Further, I challenge whether existing theory-building approaches that emphasize deductive/theory-testing/nomothetic research are adequate or satisfactory in achieving such acceleration. As Kaplan (1964: 312) noted, "Science is governed fundamentally by the reality principle, its thought checked and controlled by the characteristics of the things it thinks about." One such controlling characteristic is the methods used to connect with, and apprehend, the empirical reality; if those methods are inappropriate, then mere theoretical diagnosis of the centrality of certain concepts cannot readily be translated into theoretically grounded, rigorous research. I demonstrate instead that a near-term shift to inductive/theory-generating/idiographic research may provide a powerful stimulus that is particularly well suited for the current stage of evolution of IJV research.

Thus, this article is in response to the "methodological anomaly" that many IJV researchers appear to be employing methods that are unlikely to yield needed advances in theory. I probe why, despite repeated pleas in favor of achieving a better balance between the above two types of studies over the past quarter century (Administrative Science Quarterly, Special Issue, 1979; Bettis, 1991; Daft, 1983; Daft & Lewin, 1990; Dubin, 1969; Eisenhardt, 1989; Glaser & Strauss, 1967; Mendenhall, Beaty, & Oddou, In press; Morgan & Smircich, 1980; Phillips, 1992; Schwenk & Dalton, 1991; Swamidass, 1991), the anomaly has persisted. Also, inasmuch as the content and process of scientific inquiry are intertwined, this anomaly has spawned concomitant weaknesses in theory development. I propose and justify a fresh epistemologic approach to theory development, using a balanced, methodologically rigorous program of research, and I suggest how this program may lead to a mid-level theory of IJVs without its current weaknesses, by "loosening the straitjacket of incremental, footnote-on-footnote approach of a premature normal science" (Bettis, 1991: 318).

This article is organized as follows. First, the state of extant IJV research is evaluated, registering the significant achievements to date, but focusing on some major issues that have been left unaddressed. Next, the gaps in theory are traced to the contemporary preference for certain theory-building approaches, possible reasons underlying this preference are explored, and these approaches are placed in the context of a larger typology of approaches to theory building. How the case study methodology can be employed to address the major gaps in IJV theory is shown through a program of multiple case studies that iteratively link data to theory in an inductive process moving toward the generation of an empirically valid theory that is subject to testing and refinement through replication logic. Finally, the discussion is extended to later phases of IJV theory development in which the emergent grounded theory from the case study method is eclectically integrated with other, complementary research methods.

CURRENT RESEARCH IN IJVs

Conceptual and Methodological Foci

The vast and growing literature on IJVs, spanning from the pioneering work of Friedmann and Kalmanoff (1961) up to the present, reveals uneven development along various lines. Although certain areas have received enormous scholarly attention, others continue to be virtually ignored. The major theoretical dimensions that have been emphasized, their interconnections, and an indicative bibliography for each dimension are modeled in Figure 1.

Thus, various researchers have noncumulatively focused on different dimensions; this heterogeneity is compounded by the diversity of research lenses employed to analyze IJVs, including transaction cost (Hennart, 1991), organization theory (Habib, 1987), resource dependence (Pfeffer & Nowak, 1976), game theory (Parkhe, In press), strategic behavior (Kogut & Singh, 1988), and networks (Walker, 1988). Even though each individual study may cast new light on some aspect of IJVs, taken together, existing studies have tended to remain fragmented in their orientations. An overarching theme is required to cohesively pull together the theoretical advances into a unified theory addressing the *nature* of the IJV relationship.

Development of IJV theory centering around the core concepts of trust, reciprocity, opportunism, and forbearance can clearly provide the needed theoretical underpinning. Furthermore, not only do these concepts tap behavioral variables at the heart of voluntary interfirm cooperation, but they can also be linked effectively with each of the dimensions identified in Figure 1, as shown in Figure 2. As Daft and Lewin (1990) suggested, significant research requires breaking out of current conceptual boxes, often by authors' reaching into an area of ambiguity to define new variables or create a new logic rather than examining relationships among traditional variables.

Conceptual research stemming from Figure 2, and subsequent empirical testing, would elevate IJVs from *substantive* theory that focuses on selected organizational problems (e.g., identifying the best IJV partners, minimizing conflict), to *formal* theory (Glaser & Strauss, 1967) that permits higher-order positive and normative implications. Such empirical research, however, may be constrained by methodological barriers, which in turn limits the potential for theory advancement. As Bettis observed,

FIGURE 1
Core Theoretical Dimensions of Extant IJV Research Streams

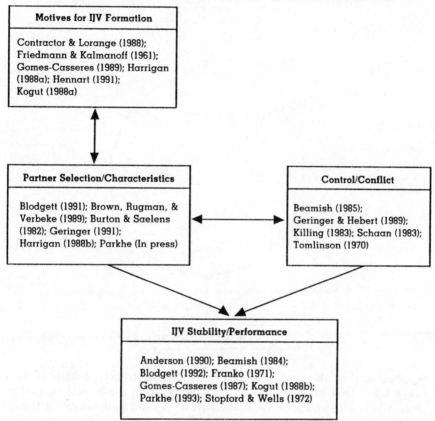

"Current norms of the field seem strongly biased toward large sample multivariate statistical studies. This leads to a large database mentality, in which large-scale mail surveys and ready made databases such as Compustat, CRSP and PIMS are often favored. . . . Qualitative studies do appear in the journals but they are the exception" (1991: 316). This view has been echoed by Hambrick (1990: 243), who noted "a clear tendency toward multivariate number crunching," and by Dubin (1982: 377), who protested the "overuse" of mail surveys and secondary data.

These "hard" data sources are unlikely to capture the "soft" core concepts outlined in Figure 2. Relatively few theorists utilize "qualitative" research (such as case studies or participant observation) that may permit deeper understanding and sharper delineation of concept domains, and fewer still resort to "joint" research (combining qualitative and quantitative approaches). For example, Mendenhall and his colleagues (In press)

FIGURE 2
Integrating Research in IJVs

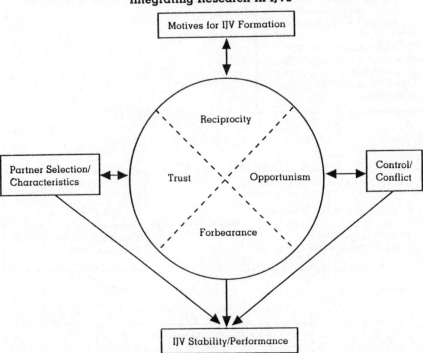

reported that of the international management articles published between 1984–1990, only 14 percent utilized qualitative approaches, and a
mere 4 percent used joint methodologies.[1] A high percentage of these
papers (82%) used research approaches characterized as "theory-thin and
method-driven" (Bedeian, 1989), even though it has been noted that in the
social sciences, as in the natural sciences in their preparadigmatic/
atheoretical stage of development, qualitative research tends to precede
the discovery of natural laws, theory development, and a field's evolution
toward maturity (Dubin, 1969; Van Fleet & Beard, 1988). As Butler, Rice,

---

[1] Parallel statistics were cited in recent papers addressing other areas of Academy of
Management as well. Schwenk and Dalton (1991) found that over 72 percent of research in
strategy relied on archival and questionnaire data. Noting that "One category may be
notable by its near absence," they concluded, "We recommend greater use of qualitative
methods" (1991: 297). Discussing operations management (OM), Swamidass (1991) con-
tended: "The scope of OM cannot be captured and explained in its entirety by purely deductive tools . . . unlike mathematics or logic, OM is embedded in the empirical universe
. . . (the lack of an empirical dimension in past OM research) is a reflection on the unbalanced research emphasis in the area, which is correctable and deserves correction by
increasing the pace and quality of descriptive, empirical investigations" (1991: 794).

and Wagstaff (1963) asserted, at a stage of development where phenomena are not well understood and the relationships between phenomena are not known, precise experiments that precede rather than succeed field studies amount to being precise about vagueness.[2] In these situations, a novel, testable, and empirically valid approach is the use of case studies because such research is

> particularly well-suited to new research areas or research areas for which existing theory seems inadequate. This type of work is highly complementary to incremental theory building from normal science research. The former is useful in early stages of research on a topic or when a fresh perspective is needed, while the latter is useful in later stages of knowledge. (Eisenhardt, 1989: 548–549)

In sum, current conceptual and methodological foci inhibit systematic study of crucial aspects of IJVs, resulting in serious theoretical lacunae. Before discussing these in the next section, however, I stress two important points. First, lack of rigor is not the problem with the extant literature. It includes many studies addressing diverse aspects of IJVs in theoretically imaginative and methodologically sound ways. The problem is that these diverse aspects have remained inchoate, as if they were unconnected, rather than being tightly interwoven aspects of the common phenomenon of IJVs. Put another way, it is not that existing research is flawed, but rather that some of the pivotal questions have not yet been asked. Thus, absent a "connective tissue" that organizes them around a coherent framework (such as Figure 2), current studies' intrinsic value has not been fully tapped.

Second, several excellent IJV case studies do exist, which have eschewed the typical focus on "hard" methods. Researchers who have examined particular industries such as aluminum (Stuckey, 1983), commercial aircraft (Mowery, 1987), and telecommunications (Kogut, 1988) and problem areas of special interests (e.g., Lyles, 1988; Stopford & Wells, 1972) have contributed valuable insights on the IJV phenomenon. But again, because they were lacking a shared set of research questions (Larsson, 1992) organized around an analytical framework, cross-case comparisons that may aid systematic IJV theory development have not been feasible, leaving these studies open to the familiar criticism of lack of generalizability.

Significant Gaps in IJV Theory

The casual remark, "It's a cold day today," may bring a flood of underlying theoretical notions and interrelationships to a meteorologist's

---

[2] In contrast, as shown later in the paper, research in the "advanced" sciences is often vague about preciseness. There is frequent reference, for example, to "order of magnitude" (Kaplan, 1964: 204).

mind, including the origination of a jet stream near the north pole, latitude and longitude of the observer, isotherms and isobars that indicate
temperature and pressure gradients, the earth's tilt away from the sun,
and so on. Likewise, the observation that "managers at IJV partner firms
A and B trust each other in their dealings," though rather dimly understood today (just as complex weather systems were not too long ago),
ought to represent the tip of the theoretical iceberg in a business scholar's
mind. Researchers must develop theoretical explanations, falsifiable hypotheses, and empirical tests that tap the psychological, sociological,
and strategic elements of "trust" and other central phenomena in voluntary interfirm cooperation. More broadly, three major areas await deeper
theoretical insights, none of which is easily accessible through research
approaches in vogue today: choice of organizational structure, alliance
structure design, and dynamic evolution of the cooperative relationship.

Choice of organizational structure. The rapid growth of IJVs (Hergert
& Morris, 1988) suggests that IJVs may be perceived by managers to meet
their competitive needs in a superior fashion relative to competing modes
of organizational structure, which include market transactions, internal
development, and merger/acquisition. The outcome is known (more frequently IJVs are being chosen), yet the process remains shielded from
scientific investigation: How and why? Few studies have examined in
depth the critical management decision-making process that weighs the
expected costs and benefits associated with the choice of IJVs, including
their fit into an overall global strategy.

> *Research Questions 1–2: How are the alternative orga-
> nizational structures evaluated (weighting system for
> comparing pros and cons of competing structures),
> and why is the IJV mode of organization chosen (per-
> ceived ability of the IJV to uniquely satisfy important
> strategic needs of the firm)?*

Alliance structure design. IJVs are voluntary cooperative relationships in which participating firms are exposed to the risk of opportunism.
This problem suggests a need for (a) careful screening and selection of
partners as well as (b) negotiating a partnership structure that provides
incentives to forbear and discourages opportunistic tendencies (Parkhe,
1993), both ex post (contractural safeguards in the formal partnership
agreement, inflicting penalties in the event of defection) and ex ante (e.g.,
mutual hostages, reciprocal agreements, and other nonrecoverable investments in the IJV).

> *Research Questions 3–5: How do companies assess (a)
> likely partners' motivation and ability to live up to
> their commitments (and how significant are reputa-
> tion effects in this assessment)? (b) potential areas for
> opportunism due to overlapping product or geo-
> graphic market interests? and (c) the "appropriate" IJV*

structure to provide ex ante and ex post incentives that
promote robust cooperation?

Dynamic evolution. The final major area in need of research concerns
longitudinal study of changes in the nature of the relationship (Parkhe,
1991; Thorelli, 1986), and hence of the partnership structure (Buckley &
Casson, 1988). As managers of partner firms gradually gain working
knowledge of, and trust in, each other, the partnership structure may
change as the relationship takes on more hierarchical (and less market)
characteristics, with diminished emphasis on formal ex ante and ex post
measures to deter opportunism, and a corresponding reduction in coordination efforts and compliance costs. Such dynamic changes have received perhaps the least amount of systematic attention in existing literature, a critical omission in the development of a more complete theory of
IJVs.

> Research Questions 6–7: (a) How does a growing collab-
> orative history (number and duration of working part-
> nerships) modify the fear of opportunism, level of
> trust, and therefore the structuring of the IJV? (b) What
> deliberate steps do companies take to install mecha-
> nisms for recognition, verification, and signaling de-
> signed to increase behavior transparency and thus ac-
> celerate the modification outlined in (a)?

Clearly, this is but a representative sample of the important and
provocative areas as yet unaddressed in IJV research, but it may include
what Blalock (1984) refers to as a "core set of questions and a reasonably
small number of important variables to examine," as shown in Figure 2.
These questions are inextricably interlinked. Choosing a partner (Qs.
3–5), for example, may strongly have an impact on evaluation of alternative organizational structures (Qs. 1–2), including whether to choose
the IJV mode of organization at all, depending upon the availability of
"attractive" partners. In turn, the choice of a partner (Qs. 3–5) will also
determine the structuring and dynamic evolution of the relationship (Qs.
6–7), depending upon a prospective partner's reputation and the subsequent matching of expectations with actual behaviors to form impressions of *future* ability and willingness to keep promises.

Thus, the important dimensions that have already been investigated
(Figure 1) cannot prudently be viewed as separable phenomena, but need
to be reconceptualized in an integrative framework (Figure 2) that (a)
recognizes and incorporates the valuable insights of previous IJV studies;
(b) rejects a treatment of the dimensions of Figure 1 as isolated areas of
study, as in the parable of the blind men and the elephant, each man
"seeing" only a distinct part of an elephant; but rather (c) fuses these
partial, related dimensions into a theoretical whole. Although this recon-
ceptualization may have theoretical merit, it reveals a methodological
problem: namely, that answering the above research questions is ham-

pered by the impotence of the approaches currently emphasized in IJV research to deal with the "messiness" that is an integral, inescapable part of such relationships, and therefore of each question posed above. To put this problem into perspective, it is necessary for researchers to view these approaches against the backdrop of a broader typology of approaches to theory development.

BARRIERS TO SYSTEMATIC THEORY DEVELOPMENT

Theory-Development Approaches: Scientific Foundations and a Typology

At the outset, I define select terms from the philosophy of science that recur throughout this article. *Ontology* refers to fundamental assumptions being made about the primitive elements of reality (specifying what exists); *epistemology* is the study of the nature and grounds of knowledge about phenomena (how a person comes to know what he or she knows); and *methodology* is the nature of ways of studying those phenomena (Mitroff & Mason, 1982; Morgan & Smircich, 1980). A typology comprising the three primary, interrelated dimensions of the theory-development process is shown in Figure 3. Each dimension will be discussed in turn.

Inductive/deductive. A person's understanding can be enhanced through the epistemologic paths of critical thought, observation, or experiment. Each path involves distinct human reasoning processes. Churchman (1971) developed these paths in terms of five "inquiring systems" (ISs): Leibnizian, Lockean, Kantian, Hegelian, and Singerian. Given the preliminary, fragmented state of knowledge of IJVs, the last three ISs are inappropriate for IJV research because they require the resolution of *multiple* realities and frameworks, whereas little theory building has occurred that advances even a *single*, widely accepted view of the nature of the IJV relationship.

FIGURE 3
Approaches to Theory-Development Research

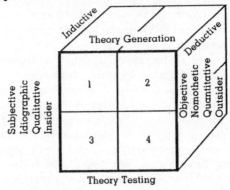

Theory Testing

For example, in Kantian and Hegelian ISs, multiple models and contrasting definitions are forced into contact with each other in order to resolve differing views of reality (Churchman, 1971), such as the devil's advocate method. Similarly, in a never-ending process, the Singerian IS calls for deeper, more refined probings if there is too much agreement about any phenomenon, and broader, more general probings if there is too little agreement (Mitroff & Mason, 1982). Whether too little or too much agreement, an implicit assumption in each IS is that competing models and definitions have been developed, so the only remaining problem is for researchers to work out differences among them. This assumption cannot be said to hold in IJV research, given theorists' lack of progress in defining and setting boundaries around core concepts, and in light of the near-total silence of IJV scholars on the crucial, context-setting research questions posed previously.

Therefore, I will focus on the Leibnizian and Lockean ISs, which reflect deductive and inductive approaches, respectively. The former bases the formulation of a problem on analytical (logical-rational) origins. Thus, axiomatic theory generation is followed by empirical data collection. However, the most basic problem of the Leibnizian IS is inventing an initial theory that is reasonably "fully formed," because, otherwise, empirical researchers will exclude essential aspects of the phenomenon under study (Mitroff & Mason, 1982), such as the core concepts suggested in Figure 2. The deductive approach underlies much of the current management research; a rendering of this dominance is shown in Figure 4.

The inductive approach, or Lockean IS, attempts to infer general patterns of order or structure from particular sets of empirical data (Robinson, 1951). In contrast to Leibnizian IS, Lockean IS does not assume an a priori axiomatic structure prior to knowledge of the phenomenon through

FIGURE 4
A Representation of the Dominance of a Theory
Testing-Deductive-Objective-Nomothetic-Quantitative-Outsider
Approach in Management Research

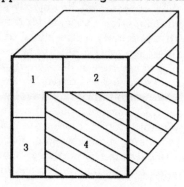

direct experience. That is, whatever order a person finds emerges from the data and is not due to imposition of a conceptual or logical pattern on the data (Mitroff & Mason, 1982). The fundamental problem of the Lockean IS is that it is impossible both to define and measure all the variables for any phenomenon and to select the significant causal relationships from among the infinite number of possible relationships. Thus, some judgment and intuition become necessary, and hence the process no longer remains purely Lockean.

In reality, of course, there is no competition, but rather an essential continuity and inseparability between inductive and deductive approaches to theory development. Bourgeois (1979) correctly pointed to the *complementarity* between induction and deduction, insisting that the process must continuously weave back and forth between them. "Bacon's inductive method was superseded by the inductive-deductive method—generally attributed to Charles Darwin—which combines Aristotelian deduction with Baconian induction. . . . This approach is the essence of modern scientific method" (Sax, 1968: 31).

Subjective-idiographic-qualitative-insider/objective-nomothetic-quantitative-outsider. Another important dimension in approaches to theory-development research was offered by Morey and Luthans (1984). The significance of these authors' contribution lies in their insight to *cluster* terms often merged or used interchangeably into dichotomous groups, each with a common core. These groups are, as in the dimension of inductive/deductive, not mutually exclusive but mutually reinforcing.

The first of these terms, *subjective/objective*, derives primarily from the work of Burrell and Morgan (1979), who asked: Ontologically, is the "reality" to be investigated external to the individual—imposing itself on individual consciousness from without—or the product of individual consciousness? Their question is neither trivial nor rhetorical because its answer suggests the apposite epistemological stance and, thus, the nature of what constitutes necessary and sufficient knowledge, to study the reality.

For example, in voluntary interfirm cooperation, when can we say that opportunistic behavior occurred? An objectivist view gives rise to an epistemology of positivism, with a concern for a form of knowledge that specifies a concrete structure and precise "facts" about social phenomena (Skinner, 1953). This idea suggests a need to map out the legal structure of the IJV relationship as specified in the formal, written contract and to measure actual versus promised behaviors by the partners. But in any such relationship, forbearance implies abiding by the letter *and spirit* of the formal agreement (i.e., forgoing potential opportunities for mutual exploitation). To access this crucial, hidden slice of reality, a subjectivist perspective is required. Using a phenomenologically oriented epistemology, subjectivists emphasize the importance of understanding the processes through which human beings make concrete their relationship to the world (Morgan & Smircich, 1980). It is evident, then, that in a phenomenon as subtle and complex as IJVs, neither objective nor subjective perspective alone can adequately inform theory.

The same can be said of the other dichotomous terms. Luthans and Davis (1982) described a nomothetic perspective as one that is group centered and uses standardized, controlled environmental contexts and quantitative methods to establish general laws. They describe an idiographic perspective as one that is individual centered and uses naturalistic environmental contexts and qualitative methods to recognize the particular and unique experience of the subject. Miller and Friesen (1982) argued that even though qualitative studies are often rich and exciting and can reveal deep insights into the complex and dynamic interplay among relevant forces, quantitative studies permit more objective, replicable, and reliable findings. Finally, an insider's perspective of science takes the view of the organizational participant in research, whereas the outsider's perspective takes the nonparticipant "scientific" researcher's view (Morey & Luthans, 1984).

As indicated previously, the terms in each dichotomous group share a common core. In making "[a] case for qualitative research," Morgan and Smircich (1980) have advanced a powerful argument that at once integrates the previous discussion and illustrates the folly of overstressing one core at the other's expense in theory development:

> The case for qualitative research in social science begins as one departs from the objectivist extreme of our subjective-objective continuum. The quantitative methods used in the social sciences, which draw principally on the methods of the natural sciences, are appropriate for capturing a view of the social world as a concrete structure. In manipulating "data" through sophisticated quantitative approaches, such as multivariate statistical analysis, social scientists are in effect attempting to freeze the social world into structured immobility and to reduce the role of human beings to elements subject to the influence of a more or less deterministic set of forces. . . . The large-scale empirical surveys that dominate much social research stand as examples of the principal types of method operating on assumptions characteristic of the objectivist extreme of our continuum. Once one relaxes the ontological assumption that the world is a concrete structure, and admits that human beings, far from merely responding to the social world, may actively contribute to its creation, the dominant methods become increasingly unsatisfactory, and indeed, inappropriate. . . . The requirement for effective research in these situations is clear: scientists can no longer remain as external observers, measuring what they see; they must move to investigate from within the subject of study and employ research techniques appropriate to that task. (Morgan & Smircich, 1980: 497–498)

Theory generation/theory testing. Though it is widely acknowledged that the accumulation of scientific knowledge involves a continual cycling between theory and data, most empirical studies lead from theory to data (Eisenhardt, 1989). As Dubin (1969) noted, most books on research methods and statistical technology contain approximately the following statement: " 'If you want to test an hypothesis, then . . .' There follows extensive elaboration of many ways for making the empirical tests. If, in innocence, you ask, 'But where do I get the hypothesis to test?' you may search fruitlessly for adequate explanation" (1969: 1). The importance of rigorously testing existing theory cannot be minimized. Yet there is an equally important role for the reverse direction, that of discovering theory from systematically obtained and analyzed data, for theory *development* is an iterative combination of theory *generation* and theory *testing*; indeed, Bacharach (1989) called the distinction between them a "false dichotomy."

Drawing upon the above typology, I now address the basic question that goes to the heart of the unbalanced (Figure 4), nonadditive nature of research in IJVs today: Why is there a chasm between theoretical recognition and empirical study of crucial IJV variables (Figure 2)? The answer may be two-fold: (a) "messiness" of social science research and (b) contemporary methodological predispositions.

Real-World Complexity and Fuzziness of Social Reality

The formidable complexity of studying unobservable individual processes in organizational behavior, such as learning, social perception, motivation, and attribution, is exacerbated in IJVs by intrafirm group decision making, subtle interfirm phenomena such as trust, reciprocity, opportunism, and forbearance, and often sharp differences in the relevant actors' cultural, national, and organizational settings (Parkhe, 1991). Many researchers deal with this complexity by following Ohm's Law (path of least resistance), that is, by simply ignoring it. However, this solution to the problem, acceptable in the well-established paradigm in economics (cf. Bettis, 1991), is hardly suitable for management scholars, inasmuch as these complexities are among the primary phenomena demanding concerted attention. As Teece and Winter (1984: 118) pointed out, the discipline of economics is shaped by very different concerns from those of management, including "unquestioning faith in the rational behavior paradigm, . . . and a delight in the construction of 'parables of mechanism' that provide a sharply defined view of an imaginary world in which the logic of a particular economic mechanism stands out with particular clarity."

In the so-called real world, uncontrolled variables abound, predictor and criterion measures interact, alternative hypotheses cannot be ruled out, and standard statistical procedures cannot be applied without massive violation of assumptions (Boehm, 1982). Serious complications can arise from "irrational, fluid, fickle" human behavior, from disentanglement of substantive findings and measurement artifacts, and from unwieldy and noncomparable analyses of managerial decision making driven by multiple goals and enacted under diverse, unique, and perpetually changing conditions. Thus, Marshall and Rossman (1989: 21) observed, "Quite unlike its pristine and logical presentation in journal articles, real research is often confusing, messy, intensely frustrating, and fundamentally nonlinear."

Intense though this frustration may be, it is imperative that theorists step back and put IJV research in its preparadigmatic, early evolutionary-stage context relative to many other sciences and recall that today's "advanced" fields once went through a similar phase of messy research, ill-defined core concepts, and unknown relationships. Today's international management theorizing roughly resembles the fledgling state of 17th-century physics and chemistry, 19th-century geology, early 20th-century quantum mechanics, and mid-20th-century psychology. A comparative/evolutionary perspective is gained when researchers consider that the particle physicists of the 1990s have in their intellectual lineage, inter alia, Newton (1642–1726) and Einstein (1879–1955), whose most seminal papers were published in 1687 and 1905, respectively. In contrast, the formal study of management is much more recent. Introductory college courses in business were first offered at Illinois and Michigan in 1901, and the first academic journal in business, the *Journal of Marketing*, began publication only in 1936.[3]

This incipiency of study undoubtedly burdens many social scientists with a sense of insurmountable, *uniquely* overwhelming complexity. But as Blalock (1984) noted, the social sciences are not alone in dealing with highly complex phenomena. Comparable difficulties exist in the physical and biological sciences, in which achievement of the status of a "science" took a long time.

One brief example from each of these fields (meteorology, the human organism) may serve to shed multidisciplinary light on confronting high complexity in scientific inquiry, may broaden social scientists' appreciation of complexity outside of the social sciences, and may illuminate how researchers must embrace, not shun, messy empirical reality. In attempting to forecast the weather, the National Meteorological Center employs a global model that calculates systems of 500,000 equations using a Cyber 205 supercomputer that operates in multiple megaflops (millions of floating-point operations per second) and processes data from a global grid of points 60 miles apart. These data on temperature, pressure, humidity, and so on, pour in hourly from every nation on the globe and from air-

---

[3] A chronology of commencement dates of leading journals in management exposes the discipline's infancy: *Administrative Science Quarterly*, 1956; *Academy of Management Journal*, 1958; *Journal of International Business Studies*, 1970; *Academy of Management Review*, 1976; *Strategic Management Journal*, 1979; *Organization Science*, 1990. These dates may be contrasted, for example, with leading journals in medicine (e.g., *New England Journal of Medicine*, 1812) and science (e.g., *Scientific American*, 1845; *Science*, 1880).

planes, satellites, and ships. Even so, accurate prediction of the weather has proved impossible beyond a short time frame (at most a few days) (Gleick, 1987). And weather prediction is probably simple compared to modeling the heart's behavior:

> A physician listening to the heartbeat hears the whooshing and pounding of fluid against fluid, fluid against solid, and solid against solid. Blood courses from chamber to chamber, squeezed by the contracting muscles behind, and then stretches the walls ahead. Fibrous valves snap shut audibly against the backflow. The muscle contractions themselves depend on a complex three-dimensional wave of electrical signals. Modeling any one piece of the heart's behavior would strain a supercomputer; modeling the whole interwoven cycle would be impossible. (Gleick, 1987: 282)

Incredible complexity, then, is an integral part of research in *any* discipline; nature does not selectively handicap social scientists vis-à-vis other scientists. To be sure, important differences set apart the social sciences from other sciences, and it would be incorrect to infer an ontological equivalence among them.[4] Kaplan argued:

> What is distinctive of behavioral science . . . is basically its subject-matter. . . . Behavioral science deals with those processes in which symbols, or at any rate meanings, play an essential part . . . the data for behavioral science are not sheer movements but actions—i.e., acts performed in a perspective which gives them meaning or purpose . . . we (must) distinguish between the meaning of the act to the actor . . . and its meaning to us as scientists, taking the action as subject-matter. (1964: 32)

On this basis, Kaplan suggested that the behavioral scientist seeks to understand behavior in just the same sense that the physicist, say, seeks

---

[4] Van Fleet and Beard (1988), drawing upon Comte's hierarchy of the sciences, suggest a hierarchy of knowledge: "The lowest level is space and number, and so it is mathematical. Add time and it becomes mechanical. Further assumptions bring in astronomy, physics, chemistry, and then geographic/geologic studies, and then mineralogy/crystallography. Add life to the hierarchy and you get biology and all its branches and associated disciplines. Then add the 'spirit of man' and the result is the humanities and social sciences" (1988: 3). The special nature of this last hierarchical level was discussed in an influential paper by Boulding (1956), who observed that social organizations, unlike clockworks, control systems, cells, plants, or animal systems, pertain to human groups or communities that have unique characteristics that emerge only in group settings. Religion, art, music, morals, value systems, the ability to produce and share symbols, awareness of time and history, and ability to process information and abstract concepts are manifestations of human interaction and emotion that are unique to organization systems. Since the ontological entities in the social sciences are so fundamentally different from those of the physical or biological sciences, we must reconsider the aptness of developing theories in the former using research approaches borrowed with little adaptation from the latter.

to understand nuclear processes. The difference is not that there are two kinds of understanding, but that the behavioral scientist has two different things to understand. Thus, the IJV researcher must first construe what conduct a particular piece of behavior represents (e.g., an act of forbearance), and second, search for the meaning of the interpreted action and its interconnections with other actions or circumstances (e.g., study of why forbearance occurred, placed in the network of related concepts in Figure 2).

Awareness of these important ontological differences, however, only reinforces a basic pattern observed by historians of science (Kuhn, 1970; Van Fleet & Beard, 1988): In any field in its early stages of development, complexity seems totally overwhelming. Thus, today's "elementary" notions of astronomy might initially have seemed fuzzy to Copernicus; "simple" gravitational principles might at first have seemed slippery to Newton; and the "basic" double-helix structure of the DNA molecule might originally have seemed obscure to Watson. Yet these powerful ideas about unknown, *invisible* phenomena were conceptualized, empirically tested against *observable* phenomena, and refined to the point where they are now an accepted part of scientific heritage, taught to school children at an early age.

Similarly in the social sciences, *verstehen* of phenomena presently considered hopelessly intractable can be significantly improved, and today's "messy" organizational notions can be made part of tomorrow's scientific heritage. But this will require researchers to abandon the debilitating myth that social science phenomena are typically so highly complex as to be intrinsically unmeasurable. As Kaplan argued, "whether we can measure something depends, not on that thing, but on how we have conceptualized it (and) on our knowledge of it" (1964: 176), adding an unequivocal "No" to the question of whether in the subject matter of behavioral science some things are intrinsically unmeasurable. Blalock (1984) suggested, further, that in answer to complexity theorists need formulations that take "rather vague assertions" about nonmeasureability, noncomparability, free will, and so on, and translate them into specific complications that can be studied systematically.

Such systematic study may transform international management scholarship from nascency into a more "advanced" stage, reflecting better conceptualization, finer-grained measurement, and deeper understanding. However, the transformation will likely be neither easy nor quick. This is not to suggest that authors must (in the Newtonian tradition) undergo a learning curve spanning several centuries before reaching maturation, particularly since our discipline can leapfrog by drawing upon the advances in many other areas (e.g., psychology, economics, ecology, sociology, game theory, and anthropology) in an eclectic, interdisciplinary manner. Rather, it is to candidly admit the relative youth and immaturity of the management discipline, impressive recent advances notwithstanding, and to point to the need for putting the conceptual horse before the quantitative methodological cart: The development of intersubjective agreement among the scientific community on core *concepts* that deal with the phenomena of central interest (Reynolds, 1971).

Arguably, in IJVs, these core concepts are trust, reciprocity, opportunism, and forbearance. If these concepts (and the bilateral interfirm interactions they represent) appear "messy," this is because at their present stage of development, they are. To some extent, they may always remain beyond researchers' grasp, but the gap between the known and the knowable[5] can be narrowed by breaking down complexity into its essential components and linking these components to related variables (Figure 2) in rigorous theory development.

In sum, social scientists face no less—but perhaps no more—of a daunting challenge than the proverbial rocket scientist who, presumably, grapples with some of nature's high complexities and best-kept secrets. Enormous difficulties also surround empirical and conceptual study of the infinitesimal amount of energy released when an electron "jumps" from a higher to a lower orbit around the nucleus; of the temperature of the sun's core; and of the deadly behavior of cancer cells and the AIDS virus. These physical and biological sciences are indeed ontologically distinct from the social sciences, as noted. Yet there is a fundamental "unity of science" that cuts across disciplines, because "all sciences, whatever their subject matter, are methodologically of one species" (Kaplan, 1964: 31). So the task ahead for management theorists lies in recognizing the challenges unique to international management and in using methods appropriate to the nature and evolutionary stage of each area of inquiry, such as IJVs. This process of theory development may be thwarted, however, by researchers' strong emphasis on certain methods.

Methodological Predispositions

As was noted, approaches to research are dominated by the southeastern portion of Figure 4. Because this domination has implications for the *fruits* of research as well (i.e., the *content* of IJV theory development), a brief backward glance is in order before charting a path for future

---

[5] There may, however, be as yet unknown limits to deterministic knowledge in the social sciences, much as there are in the ostensibly exact sciences such as physics. A good illustration is Heisenberg's principle of uncertainty (1927), which refers to the indeterminateness in the possible present knowledge of the simultaneous values of quantum theory variables. Heisenberg showed that every experiment destroys some of the knowledge of the system which was obtained by previous experiments, and it is thus impossible to know with certainty both the velocity and location of an electron simultaneously. The epistemological bases of certainty and determinism in scientific knowledge were in fact eroded earlier with Einstein's general relativity theory (1916), when Newtonian, deterministic "absolute time and absolute length were dethroned" (Bishop, 1991: A1). However, a precondition for attaining such limits of possible knowledge seems to be a deep understanding of central phenomena; for many areas of social sciences, therefore, such limits may be distant.

research that effectively breaks out of the conceptual and methodological boxes imposed on it by a normal science straitjacket (Daft & Lewin, 1990).

Many researchers' propensity to discount certain approaches and favor others betrays an intellectual mindset unwarranted by the current stage of life cycle of international management studies (Bhagat & McQuaid, 1982; Mendenhall et al., 1991; Schollhammer, 1975) and is reflected, first, in the very purpose of research undertaken. Most researchers attempt validation of existing theories rather than creation of new theory. The result, according to Lindblom (1987), is that theorists often write trivial theories because their process of theory construction is hemmed in by methodological strictures that favor validation rather than usefulness. Weick (1989) therefore suggested that theory cannot be improved until theorists improve the theorizing process, and theorists cannot improve the theorizing process until they describe it more explicitly, operate it more self-consciously, and decouple it from validation more deliberately. In order to rectify the "undue emphasis on verification of theory, not enough on discovery," Glaser and Strauss (1967: viii) argued that researchers need canons more suited to theory generation, parallel to canons derived from vigorous quantitative verification on such issues as sampling, reliability, validity, frequency distribution, construction of hypotheses, and presentation of evidence.

This emphasis on theory testing is, of course, characteristic of Kuhn's normal science, "mopping up" operations, in which theorists add a brick here, reshape a cornice there, in a wall of theory. As Kuhn (1970) himself described it:

> Under normal science conditions the research scientist is not an innovator but a solver of puzzles, and the puzzles upon which he concentrates are just those which he believes *can be both stated and solved within the existing scientific tradition* (emphasis added).

Yet a legitimate question remains: In light of the underdeveloped conceptual and theoretical base, and absent a guiding paradigm, why is the research work typical of normal science? Going beyond Daft and Lewin's (1990) valid assertions that convergent thinking has overtaken the field before it has matured and that the field has prematurely settled into a normal science mindset, I offer two possible reasons. First, being relative newcomers to the scientific establishment, there is a strong tendency on the part of some social scientists to emulate the methods of the "mature" sciences, irrespective of the propriety of such practices; this creates the "hard versus soft" cleavage (elaborated in the next section). Second, the high complexity of the phenomena under investigation has impelled many researchers to study isolated variables, as opposed to *systems* of interrelationships among clusters of variables (Mintzberg, 1977), such as those shown in Figure 2. Whereas the former may permit study through objective-nomothetic-quantitative-outsider approaches familiar in the physical or biological sciences, the latter would necessitate revisiting the ontological and epistemological bases of knowledge and understanding, and devising custom-made approaches unique to social science (e.g., direct involvement in organizations and the use of human senses to interpret organizational phenomena). This creates the "parsimony versus scope" debate.

Hard versus soft cleavage. Kuhn (1970) showed that there is nothing natural or automatic about the choice of problems and methods; these choices are heavily influenced by the contours of acceptable science at a particular time.[6] And as Kaplan (1964) cautioned, there is a real danger that some preferred set of research techniques will come to be identified with scientific method as such, for the pressures of fad and fashion are as great in science, for all its logic, as in other areas of culture. In addition to the social pressures from the scientific community, there is also at work a very human trait of individual scientists that Kaplan called "the 'law of the instrument': Give a small boy a hammer, and he will find that everything he encounters needs pounding. It comes as no particular surprise to discover that a scientist formulates problems in a way which requires for their solution just those techniques in which he himself is especially skilled" (1964: 28). As strongly argued above, focusing on a limited array of preferred techniques can curtail the feasible scope of research problems. Blalock (1984: 29) suggested that we may be studying "problems that are theoretically or practically trivial, as long as they are scientifically tractable. We examine only those variables that are easily measurable, neglecting the truly important ones. . . . Our methods dictate the problems we study rather than vice versa."

Institutionalization of the law of the instrument and the social pressures biasing researchers toward, and against, particular methodologies begins during doctoral seminars on research methods and is reinforced by universities' reward systems of promotion and tenure that encourage researchers to conduct empirical studies employing tight experimental or survey designs (Mendenhall et al., In press) and by the publication process itself. Daft and Lewin (1990) complain that reviewers for established journals seem to value articles whose theses are anchored in established theories or that use "legitimate methods, thus implicitly creating a pub-

---

[6] Indeed, Kuhn's point can be extended to the history of human thought even *before* the advent of science. The relationship between philosophy and religion began to be questioned in the 14th century. The process of alienation started with nominalism, an early and primitive attempt to question the dependence of philosophy on theology. The idea of the separation of philosophy from theology gained momentum with the development of the *scientific method*, when Francis Bacon (1561–1626), John Locke (1632–1704), and David Hume (1711–1776), among others, raised the issue of the supremacy of reason and knowledge over revealed truth. Awareness of these historical developments should be sobering to social scientists steeped in the ways of "correct" methodology, and to those who have internalized strong beliefs about "good" science, in that it lays bare the potential fragility and transience of what is considered acceptable, with shifting times.

lication barrier for research that falls outside mainstream topics or methods" (1990: 1).

This untimely emphasis on "hard" issues (e.g., precision of measurement, multivariate data analysis) is accompanied by a reluctance to tackle "softer" issues that most need advancement (e.g., delineation of conceptual domains and deepening our understanding of core concepts such as trust, reciprocity, opportunism, and forbearance). As Blalock (1984) argued, this hard versus soft cleavage has been with us for a long time, but is only intensified by the rapid introduction of sophisticated statistical tools of analysis. This situation creates an interesting paradox. Even as the neophyte social sciences toil toward ever greater precision and stringent methodological strictures, research in the advanced sciences is marked by growing appreciation for uncertainty (e.g., Heisenberg's principle of uncertainty) and tolerance for imprecision. Kaplan put it bluntly:

> I have always been impressed with the frequency with which in scientific practice, especially in the so-called 'exact sciences,' use is made of approximations, and even of determinations of no more than 'order of magnitude.' The anxiety of many behavioral scientists to be precise in their measures is often, in my opinion, an overanxiousness, possibly reflecting a lack of assurance of the scientific worth of their endeavors. (1964: 205)

Parsimony versus scope debate. The extraordinary complexity of organizations (Boulding, 1956), at multiple levels of analysis, presents researchers with tough conceptual and methodological barriers. Unfortunately, as noted previously, the response has frequently been one of ignoring away the messy concepts and the soft issues, of studying the outcomes but not the processes, and of nomothetically treating firms as black boxes. Such an orientation allows the investigator to zero in on correlations between selected variables felt to be salient for a particular problem under study, although the value added to the study is considerably diminished by the absence of a unified, coherent framework. As Daft (1983) suggested, authors typically report very thin descriptions of a large number of relationships, never touching the *why* of the correlations, dealing only with the fact that variable Y is related to variable Z, as if that constituted everything.

At issue here is the essential trade-off between the competing virtues of scope and parsimony. Bacharach (1989) noted that for adequate scope, the variables included in the theoretical system must sufficiently, although parsimoniously, tap the domain of the constructs in question, whereas the constructs must, in turn, sufficiently, although parsimoniously, tap the domain of the phenomenon in question. He further argued that scholars have sometimes sacrificed broad scope for the sharper focus that they believe enhances accuracy and parsimony. However, "this process has led to *theories which are no more than compilations of isolated variables and constructs*, making impossible a truly parsimonious theoretical system" (Bacharach, 1989: 507).

This focus on isolated variables is likely to be particularly strong in phenomena involving high complexity and soft issues, such as IJVs. Theory-development efforts in such situations, given the bias toward consistency, can produce partial theories that leave critical issues unaddressed. As Poole and Van de Ven (1989) observed, because organizational theories attempt to capture a multifaceted reality with a finite, internally consistent statement, they are essentially incomplete. As researchers perfect and test a theory, it tends to dominate their thinking, bind their judgment, and create a "trained incapacity" to appreciate aspects not mentioned in the theory. As this progression toward consistency continues, the theory becomes more and more "perfect," with less and less correspondence to the multifaceted reality it seeks to portray.

To recap the chief barriers stunting IJV theory development: Extant empirical research largely skirts around the core concepts in IJVs (Figure 2). Yet deeper understanding may be impossible until research breaks out of current conceptual boxes (Figure 1) and reaches into these critical areas of ambiguity. This shift in conceptual focus, in turn, may necessitate a near-term shift in methodological focus, away from the southeast portion of Figure 4 to the northwest portion.

Two related points emerge from the foregoing discussion. First, pushing to the limit of reductio ad absurdum, some studies seem preoccupied with using number-crunching data analytic techniques to process "hard" data collected on coarse measures of amorphous variables representing fuzzy concepts involving peripheral sections of a complex phenomenon, in order to generate hard conclusions with high precision! Quantification to a high degree of exactitude is simply sexy, even if the theoretical foundation may sometimes be made of quicksand. At our current level of development, prospects for genuine theoretical payoffs may be heightened if CPU denoted not central processing unit time on computer printouts, but core phenomenon understanding time out in the field.

Second, current studies are largely nonadditive. For reasons of expositional convenience, analytical ease, opportunistic choice of research topics, or simply the satisfaction of deep expertise within a narrow speciality, researchers often dissect the study of the empirical world into ever narrower niches (such as the boxes in Figure 1). But a certain degree of complexity inheres in the phenomenon of IJVs; studying it at less than its level of complexity would represent, as Kaplan (1964) suggested, not oversimplification, but "undercomplication." Examining the tightly interrelated IJV aspects piecemeal, without concomitant efforts to reintegrate them, reflects the erroneous belief that these phenomena are surgically separable. However, *empirical reality is a seamless whole*. In Figure 2, I attempt to organize the study of the complex reality around a coherent framework of analysis that may reduce the nonadditivity problem and synergistically combine existing studies. And because Figure 2 has at its center subtle, yet crucial, interfirm phenomena such as trust, reciprocity, opportunism, and forbearance, acceleration of theory development may require curtailment of paper-and-pencil questionnaires and secondary data, which presume that the social world can adequately be captured through objective measures because reality is a concrete structure (Morgan & Smircich, 1980), and adoption of unorthodox research approaches.

REDIRECTING THE RESEARCH FOCUS:
A NORMATIVE PROGRAM FOR THEORY DEVELOPMENT IN IJVs

I argue that the maximally efficient procedure for advancement of IJV theory in its current evolutionary stage may be one inaugurated with exploratory research,[7] followed by descriptive research, and, finally, by explanatory research. As Yin (1984) noted, exploratory research allows an investigator to examine a phenomenon and develop suggestive ideas in a flexible way. In the next stage, descriptions of patterns that were suspected in the exploratory stage are developed. Attempts to explain these empirical generalizations form the basis of the final stage (explanatory research), which is a continuous cycle of theory generation, theory testing (falsification), and theory reformulation. Thus, a recommended program of research consists of a single-case study (Phase 1), systematic replications of the initial case study (Phases 2 and 3), and finally other methodologies that complement case study research and raise the level of theory development in IJVs (Phase 4).

Initial Phases: Concept Development and Inductive Theory Generation Through the Case Study Method

Phase 1: Single-case study. In a departure from objective-nomothetic-quantitative-outsider studies, a case study would permit researchers to "get close to the action" of the formation, structuring, and stability of IJVs, for example, through open-ended interviews with top management and persons directly involved in the IJV, attendance at select executive meetings, and even quantitative data from questionnaires (a survey embedded within a case study) (see Yin, 1984). In the interviews, key actors are asked about the *facts* of the IJV, in addition to the respondents' *opinions and insights* about the events (Eisenhardt, 1989; Yin, 1984). (Mail surveys and secondary data typically sacrifice this richness and subtlety of un-

---

[7] As noted next, case studies represent a good vehicle to conduct exploratory research, because preliminary models that purport to include essential concepts and relationships in IJVs, such as Figure 2, can be subjected to in-depth investigation and modified as necessary to fit the empirical reality. However, a hierarchical view—that case studies are appropriate only for the exploratory phase, surveys for the descriptive phase, and experiments for the explanatory phase—is incorrect. Experiments with an exploratory motive are often conducted, and some of the best and most famous case studies (see Yin, 1984) have been descriptive and explanatory.

derstanding because in them there is little opportunity for clarification of questions or elaboration of answers.) Such interviews can be extremely fruitful, because interviewees can provide crucial insights, suggest sources of corroboratory evidence, and initiate access to such sources.

However, interviews can be subject to problems of bias, poor recall, and poor or inaccurate articulation (Yin, 1984). Therefore, in order to test for convergence, the interview evidence must be triangulated with multiple data sources. These include archival records and documentation. Archival corroboration involves cross-reference to databases, news clippings, and other reports in the mass media. Documentation research involves the systematic collection and examination of relevant company records and documents, including particularly the proposal, formal studies, and progress reports regarding the IJV.

The data thus obtained are epistemologically valid (Tsoukas, 1989) and lend themselves to systematic and rigorous data analytic techniques (Miles & Huberman, 1984; Yin, 1984). Yin describes three such techniques (explanation building, pattern matching, and time series analysis), which are especially well-suited for the set of Research Questions posed in the previous section.

Research Questions 1–2 (choice of organizational structure) represent explanation building. To "explain" a phenomenon is to stipulate a set of causal links about it, while ruling out rival explanations (Yin, 1984: 107–109). These explanations are not merely narratives, but rather reflect some theoretically significant propositions. The final explanation is the result of a series of iterations between an initial proposition and the findings of an initial case, accompanied by revisions in the proposition, and similar repeated comparisons of the facts in multiple cases to the proposition, with repeated revisions as necessary. For example, in the choice of organizational structure, the theorist may begin with the following set of propositions:

A. Managers are aware of, and formally compare, alternative modes of organizational structure.
B. The fundamental goal of this evaluation is to maximize the long-term competitive strength of the parent firm.
C. A formal weighting system is developed and deployed in order to thoroughly assess the advantages and disadvantages of each alternative.
D. This analysis indicates that the most favorable net outcome for the parent firm would be generated by a management decision of IJV over alternative structures.

Research Questions 3–5 (alliance structure design) represent pattern matching. The pattern-matching logic compares an empirically based pattern with a predicted one (Yin, 1984: 103–107). If the patterns coincide, a case study's internal validity is strengthened, particularly if alternative patterns of predicted values are not found. And when there are multiple outcomes of a phenomenon, the resulting pattern is labeled a "nonequivalent dependent variables design" (Yin, 1984: 103); if the results are as predicted for the overall pattern of outcomes covering each of these variables, strong causal inferences can be made about the phenomenon under study. Even stronger conclusions can be drawn if, additionally, this first pattern is different from that predicted and produced by a separate case that is expected a priori to differ from the initial case.

Certain behavioral patterns can theoretically be expected in IJVs, because they represent voluntary, self-enforcing agreements between "sovereign" parties in which courts and other exogenous mechanisms are generally not utilized because of the high costs involved in their use (Williamson, 1985), and the desire to minimize exposure to opportunistic behavior predictably sets in motion certain measures. Thus:

A. The selection of an IJV partner will prominently include an analysis of potential candidates' hidden agendas and incentives for opportunism.

     1. This analysis will be deeper the closer the IJV is to the parent firm's current and anticipated core businesses, markets, and technologies (i.e., the corporate mission).

     2. This analysis will be deeper in the absence of a positive reputation of a partner (i.e., given no historical basis for judgment, or given a negative reputation).

B. In turn, perceived high potential for opportunistic behavior will be positively related to establishment of certain steps, including

     1. Specific ex ante measures that reduce the attractiveness of cheating and thereby seek to deter defection.

     2. Ex post channels of remedy such as a "tight" legal document that specifies strong safeguards against agreement violation.

C. Conversely, a low perception of opportunistic behavior will be associated with a reduced emphasis on the above steps.

Research Questions 6–7 (dynamic evolution) represent time series analysis. A major methodological strength of case studies is that they are not limited to static assessments, but rather permit the tracing of changes over time (Yin, 1984: 109–114). The essential logic underlying a time series design is the match between a trend of data points compared to a theoretically significant trend specified a priori. In complex time series analysis, these trends may reflect multiple sets of variables, each potentially following a different predicted pattern over time. For instance, several competing trends can theoretically be expected in IJVs, each having an impact on alliance stability and performance.

A. A successful history of collaboration with a given partner may be accompanied by a diminished emphasis on defending against opportunism, particularly because such defenses are not costless. This change may cause future transactions between the two parties to be based more on trust, reciprocity, and forbearance, with less reliance on explicit measures to show good faith.

B. On the other hand, the interfirm differences (interdependencies) that IJVs are specifically created to exploit may erode over time as one partner acquires the skills and technologies it lacked at the time of alliance formation. The IJV may become destabilized as the raison d'etre of the partnership (reciprocal strengths and complementary resources) vanishes.

C. Finally, the differences in partner characteristics along various dimensions (such as societal culture, national origin, and corporate culture) that often negatively affect the longevity and effective functioning of IJVs can be progres-

Strategic Alliances

sively mitigated by the processes of organizational learning and mutual adaptation (Parkhe, 1991). This change would, ceteris paribus, tend to strengthen the partnership.

Phases 2 and 3: Literal and theoretical replication through multiple-case studies. The initial IJV case study between companies X_1 and X_2, headquartered in countries Y_1 and Y_2, and operating in a common industry Z_1, shown as $X_1Y_1Z_1/X_2Y_2Z_1$ in Figure 5, may be followed by a multiple-case design using replication logic. Specifically, Phase 2 represents "literal replication" (Yin, 1984), in which one $(X_1Y_1Z_1)$ or the other $(X_2Y_2Z_1)$ of the initial companies is examined in partnership with a third company $(X_3Y_2Z_1$ or $X_4Y_1Z_1)$ from the same country of origin and industry as the original partner. Phase 2 may also include an IJV involving different companies than X_1 or X_2, controlling for country of origin and industry $(X_5Y_1Z_1/X_6Y_2Z_1$ in Figure 5). In literal replications the theoretical propositions induced from the initial case study in our program would be expected to satisfactorily explain the available empirical evidence.

Phase 3 represents "theoretical replication" (Yin, 1984), in which other IJVs are deliberately selected such that they are theoretically expected to yield contrary results for predictable reasons. For instance, the characteristics of IJVs importantly depend upon the nationality of the partner (Parkhe, 1991, In press) and industry sector (Kobrin, 1988; Kogut & Singh, 1988) and, hence, may be expected to shift with changing countries or industries. The examination of the original IJV participants in partnership with companies from third countries $(X_1Y_1Z_1/X_7Y_3Z_1$ or $X_8Y_4Z_1/X_2Y_2Z_1)$, the selection of an IJV from a different set of countries $(Y_9Y_5Z_1/X_{10}Y_6Z_1)$, or the selection of IJVs from a different industry (not shown in Figure 5) would systematically help authors to ferret out these important differences, hastening theory development.

It must be recognized that each individual case study in the program consists of a "whole" study, or a stand-alone entity, in which convergent evidence is sought regarding the facts and conclusions for the case; each case's conclusions are then considered to be the information needing replication by other individual cases (Yin, 1984). If all the cases in Phases 2 and 3 turn out as anticipated from the propositions induced in Phase 1, the total program can be said to have provided compelling support for the theoretical framework (Figure 2), which then becomes a vehicle for generalizing to new cases. But if the cases are in some way contradictory, those initial propositions must be revised and retested with another set of cases. The potential usefulness of our program spans beyond merely the actual IJVs examined in Phases 1, 2, and 3, because the power of the case study method stems from its capacity to aid theory development beyond the immediate case at hand, not through *statistical* generalization (as in most quantitative studies), but through *analytic* generalization in which the researcher tries to generalize a particular set of results to a broader theory through induction (Robinson, 1951; Yin, 1984).

In formulating research questions outlined earlier, and tentatively

FIGURE 5
A Multimethod, Eclectic Program of IJV Theory Development[a]

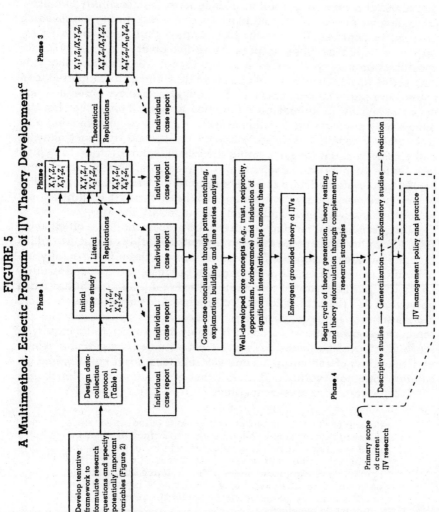

[a] X_i = IJV Company Under Study; Y_i = Headquarters Country of X_i; Z_i = Industry Sector of X_i.

specifying potentially important variables (Figure 2), I take roughly a middle position concerning the sharp disagreement in the literature on the appropriate starting point for case study research. Yin (1984) emphasized that the initial step in designing the study must consist of theory development, in which the researcher relates the study to previous theory and aims for a priori explanation. This ignores the possibility of discovering new variables and/or relationships of interest *during* the research process. In contrast, Eisenhardt (1989) argued that theory-building research is begun as close as possible to the ideal of no theory under consideration and no hypotheses to test, though she conceded that it is impossible to achieve this ideal of a clean theoretical slate (referred to in the present paper as pure Lockean IS). Both extremes are untenable and unnecessary: By its draconian adherence to prior theory, the first approach may preclude the creation of truly original, groundbreaking new concepts/relationships/theories, whereas the second approach may in many cases amount to "reinventing the wheel," and a failure to exploit and build upon previous scientific achievements. The approach presented here systematically combines extant IJV literature, core behavioral variables in voluntary cooperation, and the evidence in multiple cases, to iteratively move between data and grounded IJV theory.

Unique potential for rigorous theory advancement. In an oft-cited article, Macaulay (1963) noted the ubiquity and centrality of "soft" variables in many business relations. Systematic study of these is especially important in voluntary interfirm cooperation because, given bounded rationality, IJV partners cannot anticipate all eventualities, much less make provisions for them in a formal contract. Much importance therefore hinges on trust, reciprocity, and forbearance. In this context, case studies represent a powerful and particularly timely mode of scientific inquiry. If the reader moves northwest in Figure 4, case studies can permit a deeper understanding of soft variables and key relationships (Figure 2), and accelerate rigorous, valid, and useful theory development. Mintzberg's (1977: 94) argument is still compelling:

> Research will bear the most fruit when it is inductive, since the need is to build new theories; when it is creative, since the need is for significant conceptual leaps forward; and when it is focused in the field, where the richness of complexity is found. . . . A significant share of the research efforts should be devoted to intensive probes into single organizations. Small sample research will bring order to the array of soft variables in question.

Further, Boyacigiller and Adler (1991) have strongly recommended that scholars study foreign organizations on their own terms (idiographic research) and develop thick descriptions of other cultures and their management systems. This advice parallels Daft's message (1983: 543) urging theorists to "[l]earn about organizations firsthand: (When) trying to understand animal learning, no matter how much research money you may have, or how many assistants you may hire, always handle your own rat." The use of case studies would initiate empirically grounded theory development that is evolutionary-stage-appropriate for IJVs.

Finally, case studies uniquely satisfy Yin's (1984) three conditions for choosing a research strategy: the type of research question, the control an investigator has over actual behavioral events, and the focus on contemporary versus historical phenomena. "What," "who," and "where" questions (or their derivatives, "how many" and "how much") favor survey strategies, which are advantageous when the research purpose is to describe the prevalence or frequency of a phenomenon, and when it is too expensive or impractical to survey the entire universe. In contrast, "how" and "why" questions on a contemporary phenomenon in which the investigator has little control over events are more explanatory and likely to lead to the use of case studies. Thus, to study "who" participates in IJVs (the types of firms) and "how much," a researcher might survey firms, examine secondary data, and so on. But management scholars must urgently move beyond mere frequencies or incidence, or even correlational analyses between important yet isolated variables bearing on the IJV phenomenon, and delve deeply and holistically into fundamental questions involving causal explanation of interconnected, hitherto opaque events unfolding over the lifecycle of the IJV, such as: *Why* was the IJV mode of organization chosen over competing organizational structures? *How* was the IJV established (partner screening, partner selection, precontractual negotiations, etc.)? After establishment, *how* did the passage of time modify the relationship? To answer such questions, the theorist cannot rely solely on a survey or an examination of secondary data, but he or she must draw upon a wider and deeper array of information as provided by the case study method.

Classic studies that led to considerable theory development and empirical research at the *intra*firm level often obtained their penetrating insights from case study research. For instance, Lawrence and Lorsch (1967) conducted a multiple-case study of 10 companies in 3 industries. Likewise, Cyert and March (1963) were empiricists who observed phenomena and made inductive inferences about managerial behaviors.[8] In the rapidly growing *inter*firm cooperative relationships, case study research

---

[8] These studies should be methodologically distinguished from Chandler's (1962) pathbreaking work, which uses a *historical* method. Chandler takes as his ontological entities observational data on the behavior of the firms themselves (Mitroff & Mason, 1982). Though his focus was also on "how" and "why" questions, histories differ from case studies in the access an investigator has to contemporary behavioral events. When there is virtually no access, when dealing with the "dead" past—that is, when no relevant persons are alive to report, even retrospectively, what occurred—and when a researcher must rely on primary documents, secondary documents, and cultural and physical artifacts as the main sources of evidence, histories are the preferred strategy (Yin, 1984).

can similarly be a useful method to build on existing knowledge, to form new concepts and hypotheses, to test and refine theories, and to provide theoretical explanations and normative guidelines for IJVs.

Limitations of the case study method. The above program of research led by case studies is rooted in logic, philosophy of science, and an evolutionary view of scientific knowledge; however, the case study method is not a panacea. First, it can lead to overly complex theories, sacrificing parsimony. Eisenhardt (1989) suggested that faced with vivid, voluminous data, researchers are tempted to build theory which tries to capture everything. This should be less of a problem in executing the research program, however, because the research is guided by an initial, tentative framework (Figure 2) that attempts parsimoniously to tie core variables into an integrated theoretical system and that is subject to modification to fit the empirical reality.

Another weakness of the case study method is pragmatic and derives not from the method per se but from the institutional biases against it, as seen above. Fresh theory generation through induction is a major strength of case studies, but this requires replication. As Blalock (1984) observed, replications are rarely accomplished because practically all funding in the social sciences is short term in nature, and researchers must frequently make tenure at their universities or apply each year for new grants. Although this problem plagues other modes of inquiry as well, its impact on case study research may be especially pronounced due to the legitimate concern about external validity.

Related to the previous discussion are the nature and degree of commitment required from the researcher. Even though surveys can be costly in terms of time, money, and energy, case studies are perceived as "riskier" (Bedeian, 1989), and in international management, such studies may require preliminary study of the history, culture, and language of the people whom one is investigating (Wright, Lane, & Beamish, 1988); they also may involve logistical problems and operational difficulties arising from large geographical distances (Mendenhall et al., In press). These problems, perceived or real, militate against rapid and smooth adoption of case studies.

Finally, no single approach to theory development, including case studies, is self-sufficient and capable of producing a well-rounded theory that simultaneously maximizes the research quality criteria of construct validity, internal validity, external validity, and reliability. It was therefore argued earlier that the various approaches to theory development in our typology complement and reinforce each other. Sustaining the momentum of IJV theory development, after the initial jump-start with case study research, will require that researchers gradually employ other methods of empirical research. That is, even though case studies can act as the catalyst at this early (exploratory) stage, once the core concepts become better understood, the unique strengths of the other approaches should be exploited by the researcher's undertaking descriptive and explanatory studies that not only draw upon the emergent grounded theory from case studies, but go further to develop new theory.

Phase 4: Raising the Theoretical Level of IJV Research

Rigorous planning and execution of Phases 1–3 will end the paucity of "empirical basis for induction" (Klimoski, 1991), and the output of this process may be an emergent grounded theory in which the multifaceted complexity shrouding fundamental aspects of the IJV relationship may be unraveled. Systematically building upon these advances, it may then be possible to raise the theoretical level of IJV research by (a) increasing the generalizability threshold and (b) increasing the "efficiency of laws."

At this stage, hypotheses *deductively* derived from the emergent theory may meaningfully be combined with theory *testing*, using a combination of subjective-idiographic-qualitative-insider and objective-nomothetic-quantitative-outsider research approaches. Such research would now be meaningful because the heightened understanding of core concepts and major interrelationships among them can serve as the input for other methodologies, which may have their own unique set of advantages. Thus, in the future, researchers may utilize a sampling logic on data collected from a broader pool of respondents (e.g., through a mail survey), so that the generalizability of findings is enhanced and the resulting theory builds upon *both* replication and sampling logics, and eclectically combines the best features of both Leibnizian and Lockean ISs. (Larsson, 1992, and McClintock, Brannon, and Maynard-Moody, 1979, provide excellent discussions of combining quantitative generality across broad samples with rich, detailed qualitative data from intensive case studies.)

It is worth reiterating, however, that irrespective of the ontological nature of the subject matter or the developmental stage of a field, there is never a final output or a finished stock of theory. Ongoing theory advancement is essential, not to produce *the* ultimate grand theory, but simply to lessen the gap between the known and the knowable.[9] This process requires continuous interplay between deductive and inductive, theory testing and theory generation, and objective-nomothetic-quantitative-outsider and subjective-idiographic-qualitative-insider approaches. In other words, because these approaches complement and reinforce each other, Phase 4 *beginning* of research in the southeast part

---

[9] Much as a scientist cannot formally accept a hypothesis but merely fail to reject it (Popper, 1968), so we strive not for perfect theories, but for less imperfect theories of the infinitely complex real world. IJV theory development is thus a never-ending process. No single author or work can lay claim to having had the "last word," for that would be in the realm of metaphysics, not science. Indeed, an exciting aspect of scientific research is the discovery of the open-endedness of knowledge: The more we know, the more we appreciate how much we do not know (hence the importance of systematically outlining for one's peers "future research directions").

of Figure 3 should not imply the end of research in the northwest part, although the emphasis placed upon the former relative to the latter may grow as one advances in the research program from Phase 1 to Phase 4, and from exploratory studies to explanatory studies. Indeed, in an ongoing developmental process, there should ideally be close cooperation between researchers as they simultaneously explore the same IJVs using the two types of studies, and their data can be mixed using triangulation (Jick, 1979) to yield rich, novel insights.

Another way of raising the theoretical level of IJV research is by increasing the efficiency of laws, defined as "the range of variability in the values of one unit when they are related by a law to the values of another unit" (Dubin, 1969: 110). Where the range of unit values is broad, the law has low efficiency, and vice versa. Dubin identifies four cumulatively inclusive levels of efficiency of a law: presence/absence (lowest level of efficiency), directionality, covariation, and rate of change (highest level of efficiency). Thus, in the lowest level of efficiency are laws that state that a unit will have some values when its lawfully related unit also has some values. The highest level of efficiency is attained when it is possible lawfully to state that a direction and amount of change in value in one unit is correlated with a fixed direction and amount of change in another unit.

Thus, Level 1 in IJV research may involve specifying whether an absence of opportunism is associated with a presence of trust, and vice versa. Just as genuine peace involves more than the absence of a hot war (John F. Kennedy), and the opposite of love is not hate but indifference (Sigmund Freud), what can be said about the conceptual domains (mutual exclusivity or nonorthogonality) of the crucial variables of trust and opportunism in IJV relationships? In this context, how do reputation effects affect managers' precontractual analysis of potential IJV partners? When are reputations a good proxy for a long and successful working relationship that may shift the nature of a partnership toward more closely resembling a hierarchy, and less an arm's-length market transaction? Posing and attempting to answer such questions can deepen our understanding of "soft," ill-defined variables, more sharply delineate their conceptual domains, and progressively increase the efficiency of laws linking them as we move from Phase 1 to Phase 4 of the research program.

Finally, in Phase 4 researchers may begin to develop theoretically grounded descriptive studies to confirm/disconfirm patterns uncovered in the earlier phases. Based on these empirical generalizations from larger IJV populations, the first explanatory studies can be conducted, leading to prediction. This class of studies is characteristic of disciplines farther along in the evolutionary cycle and may permit useful normative recommendations for IJV management policy and practice.[10] Because theory

---

[10] Several scholars have recently expressed disappointment at the lack of relevance of

development is so intimately tied with empirical evidence along each step of the process, and because the inception point of the process is an initial framework that focuses directly on central variables often excluded in the past, the resulting theory should overcome major weaknesses that characterize extant IJV theory. In addition, and for the same reasons, the resulting theory is likely to satisfy the evaluative criteria of falsifiability and utility (Bacharach, 1989) and parsimony, testability, and logical coherency (Pfeffer, 1982).

Major Prejudices Against Case Studies and Methodological Antidotes

Case studies are the target of much skepticism in the scientific community. Because they comprise critical, initial phases in the proposed program, and because they represent a fundamental shift in research orientation for many researchers, it is important to frankly assess the reasons underlying these reservations. Some of the criticisms against case studies are justified, while others reflect a basic misunderstanding of the epistemologic roots of the case study method. The two concerns most frequently heard are lack of rigor and little basis for scientific generalization (Yin, 1984).

Sloppiness of logic, inadequate documentation, and investigator bias can, of course, create problems in case study research, as they can in the conduct of experiments (Rosenthal, 1966) or surveys (Dilman, 1978). And often in the past, superficial "case studies" have lacked scientific rigor, relying instead on rich story telling and anecdotes (Eisenhardt, 1991). However, strong measures can be taken to build rigor into case studies at the research design, data collection, data analysis, and composition stages, as shown in Table 1.[11] Indeed, Eisenhardt (1989) argued that one of the strengths of building theory from cases is that the constant juxtaposition of conflicting realities forces individuals to reframe perceptions into a new gestalt and tends to "unfreeze" thinking, and so the process has the potential to generate theory with *less* researcher bias than theory built from incremental studies or armchair, axiomatic deduction. Similarly, systematic steps can ensure and convey logical consis-

---

much of the research to management practice (Bettis, 1991; Daft & Lewin, 1990; Mintzberg, 1991; Van de Ven, 1989). For example, the failure rate in IJVs is estimated to be very high (Hergert & Morris, 1988; Parkhe, 1993), yet few studies have systematically explored such failures (although much anecdotal evidence exists), perhaps because of lack of an integrated theoretical framework. The research program proposed herein may represent initial steps toward bridging the gap between managerially significant problems and empirically rigorous theory development.

[11] Contrary to widespread belief, rigorous qualitative research is not an oxymoron. Canons for such research do exist (see Table 1 in this paper; Eisenhardt, 1989; Glaser & Strauss, 1967; Marshall & Rossman, 1989; Miles & Huberman, 1984; Yin, 1984). The problem, however, is that given current methodological predispositions, these canons remain largely unutilized.

tency in building a chain of triangulated evidence, as well as data files that are auditable by other researchers wishing to replicate the study.

The ultimate goal of any scientifically rigorous study is to generate data with high reliability and validity, to treat the data fairly, to produce compelling analytic conclusions, and to rule out alternative interpretations (Yin, 1984). Several authors have published case studies (e.g., Dutton & Dukerich, 1991; Eisenhardt & Bourgeois, 1988) that demonstrated meticulous attention to each stage of the research process, with results that are equal in credibility, rigor, and persuasive power to any other research method, and often theoretically more exciting. The use of multiple data sources, coupled with data analytic strategies of pattern matching, explanation building, and time series analysis in multiple cases using replication logic, can be as scientifically compelling as surveys using sophisticated multivariate techniques. In fact, Reynolds (1971) maintained that good research design and asking important research questions take precedence over tidy statistics in evaluating research quality, and "the best research design is one that does not require statistical analysis, because the results are so obvious that other scientists have high confidence in the results without considering the statistical significance" (Reynolds, 1971: 127, emphasis in original). In short, well-planned and well-executed case studies can contribute significantly to rigorous IJV theory development.

The concern about generalizability of results reflects an unfortunate confusion. Multiple-case studies are *not* analogous to multiple respondents in a survey or to multiple subjects within an experiment; rather, as outlined above, they follow a replication logic (as opposed to a sampling logic) (see Glaser & Strauss, 1967: 62–65; Yin, 1984). According to sampling logic, a number of respondents is assumed to "represent" a larger pool of respondents, so that data from a small number of persons are assumed to represent the data that might have been collected from the entire pool, and inferential statistics are used to establish the confidence intervals for which this representation is actually accurate. In contrast, an individual case is akin to a single experiment, and the analysis must follow *cross*-case rather than *within*-case design and logic. That is, each case must be carefully selected (called "theoretical sampling" in Table 1) so that it either (a) predicts similar results (Phase 2, a literal replication) or (b) produces contrary results but for predictable reasons (Phase 3, a theoretical replication). Each case serves to confirm or disconfirm the inferences drawn from the others.

CONCLUSIONS

International joint ventures are complex, mixed-motive (competitive + cooperative) relationships in which theoretically identified key variables have received meager empirical attention. The primary scope of a significant portion of extant research is on organizationally evoked what,

TABLE 1
"Scientific Rigor" and IJV Case Study Research[a]

To Maximize This Criterion of Research Quality	This Strategy is Advantageous	During This Phase of Research	Comments
Construct validity	Triangulate multiple sources of evidence to test for convergence	Data collection	Open-ended interviews with top management officials and board members, attendance at executive meetings, archival records, documentation
	Establish chain of evidence	Data collection	Explicit links among the questions asked, data collected, and conclusions drawn
	Have key informants review draft	Composition	From both partners in the IJV
Internal validity	Do within-case analysis, then cross-case pattern matching	Data analysis	Systematically match patterns obtained in initial case study (Phase 1), with literal replications (Phase 2), with theoretical replications (Phase 3)
	Do explanation building: shaping hypotheses by searching evidence for "why" behind relationships	Data analysis	Linking data to emergent theory, while ruling out alternative explanations and rival hypotheses

	Do time series analysis	Data analysis	Using simple time series, complex time series, or chronologies, array events on a time axis to determine causal events (ruling out compelling rival causal sequences), the logic being that the basic sequence of a cause and its effect cannot be temporally inverted
External validity	Theoretical (not random) sampling of IVs from specified population to constrain extraneous variation and focus on theoretically useful categories (see Figure 5)	Research design	Systematically match patterns obtained in initial case study (Phase 1), with literal replications (Phase 2), and with theoretical replications (Phase 3)
	Use replication (not sampling) logic in multiple-case studies	Research design	Analytic (not statistical) generalization through induction
	Comparison of evidence with extant literature	Data analysis	Uncover commonalities and conflicts, then push to generalize across cases
Reliability	Develop case study data base	Data collection	Formally assembled qualitative and quantitative evidentiary materials
	Use case study protocol	Data collection	Thorough and systematic documentation to enhance external reviewers' confidence

a This table developed from Yin (1984) and Eisenhardt (1989).

who, and where questions, not on theoretically grounded how and why explanations; on substantive, not formal theory; and on isolated variables, not theoretically integrated frameworks that include core concepts at the heart of the IJV relationship. However, not all areas of research in IJVs are in a preparadigmatic stage; greater progress has been made in developing theories of outcomes than of processes. Yet observable outcomes are merely the end products of invisible processes, and the two are quintessentially connected. Until theories of processes evolve substantially beyond their current stage and are effectively merged with theories of outcomes, development of an overarching IJV theory may remain stalled. Further, given the "soft" nature of these underresearched aspects of voluntary interfirm cooperation, it seems unlikely that even in the future IJVs can be satisfactorily studied using currently emphasized "hard" methods. To address this important gap, a fundamental shift is needed in the approach to research. Employing a typology of theory development approaches, this paper outlined an evolutionary-stage-appropriate program of research that strives to overcome barriers constraining theory development.

Following Kaplan (1964), Phillips (1990), and others, the major argument proposed here is that research methodology represents the *technology* of scientific knowledge advancement, and that being wedded to a specific technology can potentially undermine the core purpose of research itself. Technology consists of tools, techniques, and know-how. It is not an end in itself; rather, its raison d'etre is some deeper goal. According to Kaplan (1964: 23), this goal is to "help us *understand*." If the most basic goal of scientific research is deeper understanding through theory development, then social scientists must be more flexible with respect to their choice of technologies (methods) in the service of that goal. Merely emulating the natural sciences, which have had a vastly different and longer history, can be not only wasteful, but counterproductive: Mendenhall and his colleagues (In press), noting the dearth of published qualitative and joint studies in international management, pointed to an "alarming trend: the field's overreliance on (hard research methods) is subtly moving it *further away* from theory development."

Taking a metaperspective on the purpose and process of research (as in Figure 3) can contribute to more rapid, rigorous, and fruitful advancement of theory. The initial focus suggested in this article (northwest portion of Figure 3) represents research approaches particularly appropriate in fields striving to become "sciences," yet that are in their infancy. In more mature sciences, theory far outpaces practice. The reverse is true in growingly important areas of management, such as IJVs, where theory is struggling to catch up to practice.[12] In this context, mere armchair theo-

---

[12] For example, articles published in the *New England Journal of Medicine* may take several years to become FDA-approved medical practice, and theoretical physics papers in

rizing and testing of deductively derived hypotheses seem wholly inappropriate. Rather, it is apt, indeed essential, that scholars initially "learn about organizations firsthand" (Daft, 1983) and induce falsifiable propositions toward generating new theory.

Finally, the broad implications of messy research and methodological predispositions on theory development can perhaps be extended to areas other than IJVs. Scholars working in various subfields of management (e.g., as represented by the 20 Divisions and 1 Interest Group of the Academy of Management) may wish to consider (a) whether theory advancement is hamstrung by the bewildering complexity of the phenomena under study and (b) whether the empirical studies in their areas are unduly skewed toward the southeast portion of Figure 3. If this is found to be the case, then the central tenet of this article's argument may have implications there as well (see footnote 1). However, nowhere are these issues more salient than in IJVs. If as a consequence of this article some of the IJV empirical research is redirected or, at a minimum, a vigorous and cathartic debate is initiated, its purpose will have been well served.

REFERENCES

Adler, N. 1983. Cross-cultural management research: The ostrich and the trend. *Academy of Management Review*, 8: 226–232.

Administrative Science Quarterly. 1979. Special issue on qualitative research methods. 24: 519–712.

Anderson, E. 1990. Two firms, one frontier: On assessing joint venture performance. *Sloan Management Review*, 32 (Winter): 19–30.

Axelrod, R. 1984. *The evolution of cooperation*. New York: Basic Books.

Bacharach, S. B. 1989. Organizational theories: Some criteria for evaluation. *Academy of Management Review*, 14: 496–515.

Beamish, P. W. 1984. *Joint venture performance in developing countries*. Unpublished doctoral dissertation, University of Western Ontario, London, Ontario, Canada.

Beamish, P. W. 1985. The characteristics of joint ventures in developed and developing countries. *Columbia Journal of World Business*, 20(3): 13–19.

Bedeian, A. 1989. *Totems and taboos: Undercurrents in the management discipline*. Presidential address presented at the annual meeting of the Academy of Management.

Bettis, R. A. 1991. Strategic management and the straightjacket: An editorial essay. *Organization Science*, 2: 315–319.

Bhagat, R., & McQuaid, S. 1982. The role of subjective culture in organizations: A review and directions for future research. *Journal of Applied Psychology Monograph*, 67: 653–685.

Bishop, J. E. 1991. The scientist. *Wall Street Journal*, December 9: A1, A6.

Black, J. S., & Mendenhall, M. 1990. Cross-cultural training effectiveness. *Academy of Management Review*, 8: 226–232.

the prestigious *Physical Review Letters* may take even longer to become commercial reality. The substantial lag of IJV theory behind practice affords rich opportunities for creative scholarship.

Blalock, H. M. 1984. *Basic dilemmas in the social sciences.* Beverly Hills, CA: Sage.

Blodgett, L. L. 1991. Partner contributions as predictors of equity share in international joint ventures. *Journal of International Business Studies,* 22: 63–78.

Blodgett, L. L. 1992. Factors in the instability of international joint ventures: An event history analysis. *Strategic Management Journal,* 13: 475–481.

Boehm, V. R. 1982. Doing research in the "real world." In M. D. Hakel, M. Sorcher, M. Beer, & J. L. Moses (Eds.), *Making it happen: Designing research with implementation in mind:* 25–37. Beverly Hills, CA: Sage.

Boudling, K. E. 1956. General systems theory: The skeleton of a science. *Management Science,* 2: 197–207.

Bourgeois, L. J. 1979. Toward a method of middle-range theorizing. *Academy of Management Review,* 4: 443–447.

Boyacigiller, N. A., & Adler, N. 1991. The parochial dinosaur: Organizational science in a global context. *Academy of Management Review,* 16: 262–290.

Brown, L. T., Rugman, A. M., & Verbeke, A. 1989. Japanese joint ventures with Western multinationals: Synthesizing the economic and cultural explanations of failure. *Asia Pacific Journal of Management,* 6(2): 225–242.

Buckley, P. J., & Casson, M. 1988. A theory of cooperation in international business. In F. J. Contractor & P. Lorange (Eds.), *Cooperative strategies in international business:* 31–53. Lexington, MA: Lexington Books.

Burrell, G., & Morgan, G. 1979. *Sociological paradigms and organizational analysis.* London: Heinemann.

Burton, F. N., & Saelens, F. H. 1982. Partner choice and linkage characteristics of international joint ventures in Japan. *Management International Review,* 22(2): 20–29.

Butler, J. M., Rice, L. N., & Wagstaff, A. K. 1963. *Quantitative naturalistic research.* Englewood Cliffs, NJ: Prentice-Hall.

Chandler, A. D. 1962. *Strategy and structure.* Cambridge, MA: MIT Press.

Churchman, C. W. 1971. *The design of inquiring systems.* New York: Basic Books.

Contractor, F. J., & Lorange, P. 1988. Why should firms cooperate? In F. J. Contractor & P. Lorange (Eds.), *Cooperative strategies in international business:* 3–28. Lexington, MA: Lexington Books.

Cyert, R. M., & March, J. G. 1963. *A behavioral theory of the firm.* New York: Prentice-Hall.

Daft, R. L. 1983. Learning the craft of organizational research. *Academy of Management Review,* 8: 539–546.

Daft, R. L., & Lewin, A. Y. 1990. Can organization studies begin to break out of the normal science straitjacket? *Organization Science,* 1: 1–9.

Dilman, D. A. 1978. *Mail and telephone surveys: The total design method.* New York: John Wiley.

Dubin, R. 1969. *Theory building.* New York: Free Press.

Dubin, R. 1982. Management: Meanings, methods, and moxie. *Academy of Management Review,* 7: 372–379.

Dutton, J. E., & Dukerich, J. M. 1991. Keeping an eye on the mirror: Image and identity in organizational adaptation. *Academy of Management Journal,* 34: 517–554.

Eisenhardt, K. M. 1989. Building theories from case study research. *Academy of Management Review,* 14: 532–550.

Eisenhardt, K. M. 1991. Better stories and better constructs: The case for rigor and comparative logic. *Academy of Management Review,* 16: 620–627.

Eisenhardt, K. M., & Bourgeois, L. J. 1988. Politics of strategic decision making in high velocity environments. *Academy of Management Journal,* 31: 737–770.

Franko, L. G. 1971. *Joint venture survival in multinational corporations.* New York: Praeger.

Friedmann, W. G., & Kalmanoff, G. (Eds.). 1961. *Joint international business ventures.* New York: Columbia University Press.

Geringer, J. M., & Hebert, L. 1989. Control and performance of international joint ventures. *Journal of International Business Studies,* 20: 235–254.

Geringer, J. M. 1991. Strategic determinants of partner selection criteria in international joint ventures. *Journal of International Business Studies,* 22: 41–62.

Glaser, B., & Strauss, A. 1967. *The discovery of grounded theory: Strategies for qualitative research.* London: Wiedenfeld & Nicholson.

Gleick, J. 1987. *Chaos: Making a new science.* New York: Penguin Books.

Gomes-Casseres, B. 1987. Joint venture instability: Is it a problem? *Columbia Journal of World Business,* Summer: 97–107.

Gomes-Casseres, B. 1989. Ownership structures of foreign subsidiaries: Theory and evidence. *Journal of Economic Behavior and Organization,* 11: 1–25.

Habib, G. M. 1987. Measures of manifest conflict in international joint ventures. *Academy of Management Journal,* 30: 808–816.

Hambrick, D. C. 1990. The adolescence of strategic management, 1980–1985. In J. Frederickson (Ed.), *Perspectives on strategic management:* 230–251. Cambridge, MA: Ballinger.

Harrigan, K. R. 1988a. Joint ventures and competitive strategy. *Strategic Management Journal,* 9: 141–158.

Harrigan, K. R. 1988b. Strategic alliances and partner asymmetries. In F. J. Contractor & P. Lorange (Eds.), *Cooperative strategies in international business:* 205–226. Lexington, MA: Lexington Books.

Hennart, J. F. 1991. The transaction costs theory of joint ventures. *Management Science,* 37: 483–497.

Hergert, M., & Morris, D. 1988. Trends in international collaborative agreements. In F. J. Contractor & P. Lorange (Eds.), *Cooperative strategies in international business:* 99–109. Lexington, MA: Lexington Books.

Jick, T. D. 1979. Mixing qualitative and quantitative methods: Triangulation in action. *Administrative Science Quarterly,* 24: 602–611.

Kaplan, A. 1964. *The conduct of inquiry: Methodology for behavioral science.* San Francisco: Chandler.

Killing, J. P. 1983. *Strategies for joint venture success.* New York: Praeger.

Klimoski, R. 1991. Stay the course (and be open to possibilities). *Academy of Management Review,* 16: 7–9.

Kobrin, S. J. 1988. Trends in ownership of U.S. manufacturing subsidiaries in developing countries: An interindustry analysis. In F. J. Contractor & P. Lorange (Eds.), *Cooperative strategies in international business:* 129–142. Lexington, MA: Lexington Books.

Kogut, B. 1988a. Joint ventures: Theoretical and empirical perspectives. *Strategic Management Journal,* 9: 319–332.

Kogut, B. 1988b. A study of the life cycle of joint ventures. In F. J. Contractor & P. Lorange

(Eds.), *Cooperative strategies in international business:* 169–185. Lexington, MA: Lexington Books.

Kogut, B. 1989. The stability of joint ventures: Reciprocity and competitive rivalry. *Journal of Industrial Economics,* 38: 183–198.

Kogut, B., & Singh, H. 1988. Entering the United States by joint venture: Competitive rivalry and industry structure. In F. J. Contractor & P. Lorange (Eds.), *Cooperative strategies in international business:* 241–251. Lexington, MA: Lexington Books.

Kuhn, T. S. 1970. *The structure of scientific revolutions.* Chicago: University of Chicago Press.

Larsson, R. 1992. *Case survey methodology: Quantitative analysis across case studies.* Paper presented at the annual meeting of the Academy of Management, Las Vegas.

Lawrence, P. R., & Lorsch, J. W. 1967. *Organization and environment.* Homewood, IL: Irwin.

Lindblom, C. E. 1987. Alternatives to validity: Some thoughts suggested by Campbell's guidelines. *Knowledge: Creation, Diffusion, Utilization,* 8: 509–520.

Luthans, F., & Davis, T. R. V. 1982. An idiographic approach to organizational behavior research. *Academy of Management Review,* 7: 380–391.

Lyles, M. A. 1988. Learning among joint venture-sophisticated firms. In F. J. Contractor & P. Lorange (Eds.), *Cooperative strategies in international business:* 301–316. Lexington, MA: Lexington Books.

Macaulay, S. 1963. Non-contractual relations in business: A preliminary study. *American Sociological Review,* 55: 55–70.

Marshall, C., & Rossman, G. B. 1989. *Designing qualitative research.* Newbury Park, CA: Sage.

McClintock, C. C., Brannon, D., & Maynard-Moody, S. 1979. Applying the logic of sample surveys to qualitative case studies: The case cluster method. *Administrative Science Quarterly,* 24: 612–629.

Mendenhall, M., Beaty, D., & Oddou, G. R. In press. Where have all the theorists gone? An archival review of the international management literature. *International Journal of Management.*

Miles, M. B., & Huberman, M. A. 1984. *Qualitative data analysis.* Beverly Hills, CA: Sage.

Miller, D., & Friesen, P. H. 1982. The longitudinal analysis of organizations: A methodological perspective. *Management Science,* 28: 1013–1034.

Mintzberg, H. 1977. Policy as a field of management theory. *Academy of Management Review,* 2: 88–103.

Mintzberg, H. 1991. *Parting shots: Our real ridge.* Presidential address presented at the annual meeting of the Strategic Management Society, Toronto.

Mitroff, I. I., & Mason, R. O. 1982. Business policy and metaphysics: Some philosophical considerations. *Academy of Management Review,* 7: 361–371.

Morey, N. C., & Luthans, F. 1984. An emic perspective and ethnoscience methods for organizational research. *Academy of Management Review,* 9: 27–36.

Morgan, G., & Smircich, L. 1980. The case for qualitative research. *Academy of Management Review,* 5: 491–500.

Mowery, D. C. 1987. *Alliance politics and economics.* Cambridge, MA: Ballinger.

Oye, K. A. (Ed.). 1986. *Cooperation under anarchy.* Princeton, NJ: Princeton University Press.

Parkhe, A. 1991. Interfirm diversity, organizational learning, and longevity in global strategic alliances. *Journal of International Business Studies,* 22: 579–601.

Parkhe, A. 1993. *The structuring of strategic alliances: A game-theoretic and transaction cost examination of interfirm cooperation.* Working paper, Indiana University.

Parkhe, A. In press. Partner nationality and the structure-performance relationship in strategic alliances. *Organization Science.*

Pfeffer, J. 1982. *Organizations and organization theory.* Marshfield, MA: Pitman.

Pfeffer, J., & Nowak, P. 1976. Joint ventures and interorganizational interdependence. *Administrative Science Quarterly,* 21: 398-418.

Phillips, D. C. 1990. *Philosophy, science, and social inquiry.* Oxford, England: Pergamon Press.

Phillips, N. 1992. *Method and metaphysics in the study of management: Postpositivism and its consequences for management research.* Paper presented at the annual meeting of the Academy of Management, Las Vegas.

Poole, M. S., & Van de Ven, A. H. 1989. Using paradox to build management and organization theories. *Academy of Management Review,* 14: 562-578.

Popper, K. 1968. *Conjectures and refutations.* New York: Harper.

Reynolds, P. D. 1971. *A primer in theory construction.* Indianapolis: ITT Bobbs-Merrill.

Ring, P. S., & Van de Ven, A. H. 1992. Structuring cooperative relationships between organizations. *Strategic Management Journal,* 13: 483-498.

Robinson, W. S. 1951. The logical structure of analytic induction. *American Sociological Review,* 16: 812-818.

Rosenthal, R. 1966. *Experimenter effects in behavioral research.* New York: Appleton-Century-Crofts.

Sax, C. 1968. *Empirical foundations of educational research.* Englewood Cliffs, NJ: Prentice-Hall.

Schaan, J. L. 1983. *Parent control and joint venture success: The case of Mexico.* Unpublished doctoral dissertation, University of Western Ontario, London, Ontario, Canada.

Schollhammer, H. 1975. Current research in international and comparative management. *Management International Review,* 15(2): 29-45.

Schwenk, C. R., & Dalton, D. R. 1991. The changing shape of strategic management research. *Advances in Strategic Management,* 7: 277-300.

Skinner, B. F. 1953. *Science and human behavior.* New York: Macmillan.

Stopford, J. M., & Wells, L. T. 1972. *Managing the multinational enterprise.* New York: Basic Books.

Stuckey, J. 1983. *Vertical integration and joint ventures in the aluminum industry.* Cambridge, MA: Harvard University Press.

Swamidass, P. M. 1991. Empirical science: New frontier in operations management research. *Academy of Management Review,* 16: 793-814.

Teece, D. J., & Winter, S. G. 1984. The limits of the neoclassical theory in management education. *American Economic Review,* 74: 116-121.

Thorelli, H. B. 1986. Networks: Between markets and hierarchies. *Strategic Management Journal,* 7: 37-51.

Tomlinson, J. W. C. 1970. *The joint venture process in international business: India and Pakistan.* Cambridge, MA: MIT Press.

Tsoukas, H. 1989. The validity of idiographic research explanations. *Academy of Management Review,* 14: 551-561.

Van de Ven, A. H. 1989. Nothing is quite so practical as a good theory. *Academy of Management Review,* 14: 486–489.

Van Fleet, D. D., & Beard, J. W. 1988. *Lessons for management research from the history of science.* Paper presented at the annual meeting of the Academy of Management.

Walker, G. 1988. Network analysis for cooperative interfirm relationships. In F. J. Contractor & P. Lorange (Eds.), *Cooperative strategies in international business:* 227–240. Lexington, MA: Lexington Books.

Weick, K. E. 1989. Theory construction as disciplined imagination. *Academy of Management Review,* 14: 516–531.

Williamson, O. E. 1985. *The economic institutions of capitalism.* New York: Free Press.

Wright, L., Lane, H., & Beamish, P. 1988. International management research: Lessons from the field. *International Studies of Management and Organization,* 18: 55–71.

Yin, R. K. 1984. *Case study research: Design and methods.* Beverly Hills, CA: Sage.

Arvind Parkhe is an assistant professor in the School of Business, Indiana University (Bloomington). He received his Ph.D. in international business from Temple University. His research focuses on trust, opportunism, and reputation effects in interfirm cooperation, effective structuring of voluntary cooperative agreements, and management of interfirm diversity in global strategic alliances.

[22]

ORGANIZATION SCIENCE
Vol. 4, No. 2, May 1993
Printed in U.S.A.

PARTNER NATIONALITY AND THE STRUCTURE-PERFORMANCE RELATIONSHIP IN STRATEGIC ALLIANCES*

ARVIND PARKHE

Department of Management, School of Business 650, Indiana University,
Bloomington, Indiana 47405

The dramatic growth of global strategic alliances between firms is fundamentally reshaping the nature of international business. Indeed, interfirm *cooperation* has become a crucial component of the pursuit of global *competitive* advantage. Yet such alliances are enormously complex to manage successfully, in part because of the opportunity and incentive to cheat, and profit at the partner's expense, that is an inescapable part of these relationships. Consequently, strategic alliances are frequently subject to high instability, poor performance, and premature dissolution.

Thus, an important question arises: Is it possible to promote more stable cooperation and higher alliance performance through a realignment of companies' incentives? This question is addressed empirically in the present paper using recent work in game theory, which suggests that high performance is linked to specific elements of the alliance structure. Further, this study applies insights from international business literature, suggesting that alliance partners from different countries are often characterized by sharp cultural, national, and organizational differences, to test this linkage in an international context.

The study's data strongly support the hypothesis that alliance performance is linked to alliance structure. This finding has broad implications both for managers and management scholars, in suggesting that "up front" attention to alliance structure may help arrest the high failure rates, and improve alliance stability and performance levels. However, the data also support the hypothesis that the linkage between structure and performance varies by partner nationality. This finding points to the need for: (a) systematic assessment of salient characteristics of potential international partners; (b) development of programs to effectively deal with important differences between partner firms; and (c) attention to different key alliance structure dimensions, depending upon partner nationality. Finally, this study shows game theory to provide an extremely useful perspective in understanding crucial aspects of strategic alliances, although in the analysis of cross-border strategic alliances, the perspective must be enriched by an appreciation of interfirm diversity.

(STRATEGIC ALLIANCES; INTERCOUNTRY DIFFERENCES; STRUCTURE-PERFORMANCE RELATIONSHIP; GAME THEORY; INTERFIRM COOPERATION)

Global strategic alliances (SAs) are the relatively enduring interfirm cooperative arrangements, involving cross-border flows and linkages that utilize resources and/or governance structures from autonomous organizations headquartered in two or more countries, for the joint accomplishment of individual goals linked to the corporate mission of each sponsoring firm (Parkhe 1991a). Recent years have witnessed a dramatic acceleration of SA formation (Anderson 1990, Harrigan 1988, Hergert and Morris 1988, Wysocki 1990), and SAs are increasingly perceived as strategic weapons, even for competing within a firm's *core* businesses, markets, and technologies (Harrigan 1987). Indeed, SAs are becoming an essential feature of companies' overall organizational structure, and competitive advantage increasingly depends not only on a company's internal capabilities, but also on the types of its alliances and the scope of its relationships with other companies.

---

*Accepted by Richard L. Daft; received April 1991. This paper has been with the author for two revisions.

1047-7039/93/0402/0301/$01.25
Copyright © 1993, The Institute of Management Sciences

Paradoxically, however, the increasing frequency and strategic significance of SAs is accompanied by problems of instability and poor performance, with estimates of mortality rates ranging up to 70% (*Business Week* 1986, Geringer and Hebert 1989, Harrigan 1985, Porter and Fuller 1986).[1] Clearly, such problems are not costless. SAs typically involve commitment of substantial resources on both sides, in cash and/or in kind. And failure can result in a loss of competitive position far beyond merely the opportunity cost of the resources deployed in the SA itself; synergistic gains and expected positive spillover effects for the parent firm may not be realized.

Writers from multiple research traditions have examined the problem of enhancing the stability of such voluntary, self-enforcing cooperative agreements. For example, previous studies in the theory of the firm (Buckley and Casson 1988), international military/security agreements and political/trade relations (Schelling 1963), institutional microeconomics (Williamson 1985), and social psychology (Deutsch 1973) are unanimous in their agreement on the need to *structure* alliances to promote robust cooperation, by providing ex ante incentives.[2] However, these authors stop short of recommending just how such incentives might be provided. Recent advances in the theory of cooperation and game theory (Axelrod 1984, Oye 1986) may provide this missing piece, since they explicitly address partnership structures that improve alliance stability and performance levels. The present study sought to empirically test whether alliance structure was in fact linked to alliance performance.

Powerful though it may be in capturing the incentives and motivations that characterize different classes of relationships, game theory nevertheless rests on several assumptions whose ability to travel cross-culturally, cross-nationally, and cross-organizationally has yet to be conclusively established. In light of prior research suggesting significant differences in the characteristics of international alliances from different countries (Beamish 1985, Geringer and Hebert 1991, Harrigan 1985), the present study stratified the total sample into subgroups by partner nationality and retested the structure-performance relationship. Disaggregation of the data into U.S.-Japanese, U.S.-European, and U.S.-U.S. alliances permitted a test of the applicability of game theoretic formulations in diverse settings. A potential divergence of the results by partner nationality would raise serious doubts about the universal applicability of familiar behavioral and environmental assumptions, and in turn suggest a redirection of future research on interfirm cooperation along important new paths.

The rest of this paper is organized as follows. After reviewing the theoretical grounding and developing the hypotheses in the next section, we discuss the research methods employed to collect data. The following section presents the empirical results. Next, we critically assess the role of partner nationality in the structure/per-

---

[1] Of course, factors such as hidden agendas and conceptually flawed logic of the SA may account for a portion of the high mortality rates and low performance levels. Moreover, dissolution of the SA does not necessarily constitute failure, just as survival and longevity do not necessarily signal success. When SAs are used as "stepping stones," or transitional modes of organizational structure (Gomes-Casseres 1989) in response to current challenges as firms grope to find more permanent structures, their termination may be planned, and may be viewed by the parents as a success, not a failure. Conversely, longevity may be associated not with high performance, but with high exit barriers. This discussion notwithstanding, in a significant number of cases premature, unintended dissolution is sought to be avoided by each parent company (Harrigan 1985; Lewis 1990), and this subset of SAs is the focus of the present paper.

[2] "Structure" is often used to describe the hierarchical chart of the relationship, or the equity division of the alliance. In interorganizational relations (IOR) literature, structure may refer to the comparative or relational properties between organizations. The former include the dimensions of homogeneity, domain consensus, stability, resource distribution and overlap in membership, the latter include formalization, intensity, reciprocity, and standardization (Hall and Clark 1975, Mulford 1984, Whetten 1981). As discussed in the next section, however, in this paper structure refers to three specific attributes of the alliance: pattern of payoffs, shadow of the future, and the number of players.

formance relationship, discuss the theoretical implications flowing from this study, and conclude with some observations regarding provocative possibilities for multidisciplinary research in the increasingly important organizational phenomenon of cross-border strategic alliances.

Theoretical Development

In his celebrated book on *The Economic Institutions of Capitalism*, Williamson (1985) observes that "The benefits of cooperation notwithstanding, the achievement of cooperation (in bilateral relations) is widely thought to be frustrated by the relentless logic of the prisoners' dilemma... I submit that the feasibility of crafting superior ex ante incentive structures warrants more attention" (p. 204). Other scholars have also recently drawn attention to the isomorphism of SAs with the prisoners' dilemma game, in which cooperation is desirable but not automatic, and in which individually rational actions produce a collectively suboptimal outcome. For example, Kogut (1989) emphasizes the high instability of cooperative ventures because of the incentive to cheat, and Buckley and Casson (1988) refer to the "inalienable de facto right of all the parties involved in a venture to pursue their own interests at the expense of others" (p. 34). It is fruitful to briefly examine the structure of the prisoners' dilemma game.

In this game, two players are suspected of a major crime (such as murder). They are imprisoned and held incommunicado, so each must decide whether to cooperate or to defect, without knowing what the other will do. The authorities possess evidence to secure conviction on only a minor charge (such as illegal possession of weapons). If neither prisoner squeals, both will draw a light sentence on the minor charge (payoff of MC, for Mutual Cooperation). If one prisoner squeals and the other stonewalls, the squealer will go free (UD for Unilateral Defection) and the "sucker" will draw a very heavy sentence (UC for Unilateral Cooperation). If both squeal, both will draw a moderate sentence (MD for Mutual Defection).

Each prisoner's preference ordering is: UD > MC > MD > UC. Each prisoner will be better off squealing than stonewalling, no matter what his partner chooses to do, because UD > MC (the temptation of the squealer payoff) and MD > UC (the fear of the sucker payoff). But if both defect, both do worse than if both had cooperated (MC > MD). Hence the dilemma.

Prisoners' dilemma belongs to a broader class of relationships called nonzero-sum games, in which cooperation is necessary to the realization of mutual benefits. In nonzero-sum games, preplay communication can play an integral role as it can provide a way for the players to make joint binding agreements, unlike in zero-sum (or strictly competitive) games, where such agreements would be useless because one side gains what the other loses, and it is impossible for the players to achieve mutual benefit. Thus, SAs are nonzero-sum games, enhanced by the cooperation-inducing feature of communication, in which both parties to the arrangement anticipate benefits (due to an "expanding pie").

The troublesome phrase here is "joint binding agreements." If two autonomous firms are dealing with each other, and if exogenous enforcement mechanisms such as courts are typically assumed away because of their high costs (Williamson 1985), who is to enforce the so-called joint binding agreements? There exists, on one hand, an incentive to defect from the agreement and gain at the expense of the partner, as noted above. On the other hand, there are the gains to be made by remaining in the cooperative agreement. This uncertainty by each partner regarding the other's next move introduces inherent instability into the cooperative relationship.

However, firms need not necessarily accept circumstances as given, but rather can reshape the alliance structure through deliberate strategies to create the preconditions for robust cooperation. Specifically, Oye (1986) and Axelrod and Keohane (1986) identify three structural dimensions that serve both as proximate explanations of cooperation, and as targets of higher-order strategies to promote cooperation: (1) pattern of payoffs, (2) "shadow of the future," and (3) the number of players. Firms can reduce behavioral uncertainty, and enhance the robustness of cooperation, by appreciating the role each dimension plays in the partnership, and willfully altering the dimensions as necessary. The theoretical basis of each structural dimension is outlined next.[3]

Pattern of Payoffs

Payoffs affect the prospects for the emergence and maintenance of cooperation because, first, cooperation cannot emerge unless there are perceived gains from mutual cooperation for both firms (MC > 0). Moreover, certain patterns of payoffs produce more stable relationships than others. For instance, a very large difference in the gains to be made by unilateral defection (UD), versus the payoff from mutual cooperation (MC), will prove to be destabilizing and negatively affect performance. Likewise, if the payoff from mutual defection (MD) is sufficiently high relative to the payoff from mutual cooperation (MC), then the arrangement would be jeopardized because whether or not Firm B defects, Firm A can still count on a sizeable gain. And finally, the likelihood of cooperation will decrease as the gains from unilateral defection (UD) increase relative to the gains from unilateral cooperation (UC).

Thus, three residuals reflect the pattern of payoffs and can be expected to be related to performance: (UD-MC), which captures the joint product lost to unilateral defection; (MC-MD), which captures the loss to complete breakup of the SA; and (UD-UC), which captures the cost of unrequited cooperation.[4] As outlined above, we anticipate a negative relationship between performance and the first and third residuals, and a positive relationship with the second one.

Strategies to alter the payoff structure seek to enhance the robustness of cooperation and diminish the attractiveness of defection, by reducing the gains from exploitation, increasing the costs of defection, and increasing the gains from cooperation. Ex ante strategies include the placement of hostages (Williamson (1983), reciprocal agreements, and nonrecoverable investments in the alliance (Teece 1986). Ex post strategies include contractual safeguards built into the formal partnership agreement (Practicing Law Institute 1986).

The Shadow of the Future

The prospect of continuing interaction, signaled by expectations of a (1) durable and (2) strategically desirable relationship, affects the likelihood of cooperation by encouraging strategies of reciprocity (Axelrod 1984). Thus, the future casts a shadow back upon the present, affecting current behavior patterns. Cooperation is promoted

---

[3]*Ceteris paribus*, an increase in the number of players (N) has been posited to adversely affect the durability and performance of an alliance for three reasons (Cartwright and Zander 1968). First, as N increases, identification and realization of common interests becomes harder as transaction and information costs rise. Second, as N (and the probable heterogeneity of firms) increases, meshing each partner's calculations of expected utility from cooperative behavior becomes more difficult. And third, as N increases, recognition problems increase (creating the possibility of free-riding), and control problems increase as the feasibility of sanctioning unilateral defection decreases, with greater difficulties in implementing strategies of reciprocity. However, the following discussion focuses primarily on the structural dimensions of pattern of payoffs and shadow of the future because, as elaborated later in the paper, N is a constant (N = 2) for our purposes, since this paper delimits its scope to two-firm partnerships. Readers interested in the theory underlying this dimension are referred to the work of Shubik (1975) and Oye (1986).

[4]I would like to thank an anonymous reviewer for pointing out these intuitive characterizations of the residuals.

by the establishment of a direct connection between an actor's present actions and anticipated future benefits.

A long shadow of the future (and, in turn, reciprocal behavior and robust cooperation) is associated with the iterative character of the situation, effective recognition and control capabilities, i.e., the ability to distinguish between cooperation and defection by others and to respond in kind, and a farsighted outlook. As Schelling (1963) observes, iterativeness can be increased by slicing up an activity into increments instead of attempting one big jump. Such decomposition over time reduces the temptation to defect, and renders cooperation more tractable. Tied to iterativeness are the notions of frequency of interaction and regularity of stakes (Axelrod 1984, Smith and Aldrich 1991, Axelrod and Keohane 1986). As partner interactions become more frequent, shorter time spans elapse between alliance outcomes assessments. With this increasing regularity of stakes, each firm's next move looms larger than it otherwise would, deterring defection and enlarging the shadow of the future (see Heide and Miner 1990, pp. 8–9, and Axelrod 1984, pp. 129, 180).

Cooperation can be further reinforced by improving behavior transparency. Poor behavior transparency limits actors' ability to recognize cooperation and defection by others, separates beliefs from reality, and serves to sever the critical link between current actions and future consequences. Establishment of structured mechanisms that provide real-time information and accurate feedback regarding each other's actions, including effective recognition, verification, and signaling systems between the partners, minimize misperceptions and enhance behavior transparency.

The three game-theoretic structural dimensions enumerated above are not perfectly orthogonal, but rather are significantly interrelated. For example, the number of participating firms strongly affects the payoff distribution in an alliance, and payoffs are tied to the shadow of the future. Thus, the institution of hostages (Williamson 1983, 1985) serves both to alter the payoff structure (by increasing the costs of unilateral defection [Axelrod 1984]), and lengthen the shadow of the future (by signaling good faith intentions and long time horizons [Schelling 1963]).

To summarize, it is evident from the foregoing discussion that alliance structure—defined in terms of the three structural dimensions—and alliance performance can be expected to be related. Some structures are likely to be associated with high incentive and opportunity to cheat, high behavioral uncertainty, and poor alliance stability, longevity, and performance levels (and vice versa), leading to the hypothesis:

H1. *Game-theoretic structure and performance of strategic alliances will be significantly correlated.*

H1 is clearly significant, in that it suggests higher-order strategies in the form of ex ante modification of structure as a way of improving performance. However, it is useful to push beyond the somewhat partial and oversimplified view provided by game theory. We attempt to do so in two ways: (1) By linking the discussion to some of the existing dominant explanations of interfirm cooperation, and (2) By assessing the assumptions on which the prisoner's dilemma formulation rests.

Broadening the Theoretical Perspective

With the proliferation of SAs, a growing body of literature is addressing the motives and costs of interfirm cooperation. Porter and Fuller (1986), for instance, implicitly link the time horizon (a component of the shadow of the future) of an alliance to the motives behind its formation:

> Coalitions involving access to knowledge or ability are the most likely to dissolve as the party gaining access acquires its own internal skills through the coalition. Coalitions designed to gain the

benefits of scale or learning in performing an activity have a more enduring purpose. If they
dissolve, they will tend to dissolve into merger or into an arm's-length transaction. The stability of
risk-reducing coalitions depends on the sources of risk they seek to control. Coalitions hedging
against the risk of a single exogenous event will tend to dissolve, while coalitions involving an
ongoing risk (e.g., exploration risk for oil) will be more durable (p. 329).

Likewise, Anderson and Weitz (1989) propose a model in which "perceived
continuity of relationship" is a dependent variable, determined in part by trust,
reputation for fair play (i.e., an absence of perceived opportunism), and communication between the parties. A confluence of the latter variables promotes long-term
relationships, which in turn facilitates the attainment of the alliance motives of
flexibility, scale economies, efficiency, and low overhead (Anderson and Weitz 1989,
p. 310). And according to Kono (1984), vertical SAs often represent "quasi-integration" driven by the goals of reduced uncertainty, stabilized production and lower
costs, and quicker adaptation to market, technological, and environmental shifts as
changes in consumer markets are passed rapidly upstream, and technical changes in
production flow downstream quickly as well.

Not only is the shadow of the future related to the alliance motives discussed in
these and other studies (cf. Beamish and Banks 1987, Contractor and Lorange 1988,
Nielsen 1988, Anderson and Narus 1990, Oliver 1990), but alliance motives are also
directly tied to the payoff structure dimension through, for example, anticipated
economies of scale, access to markets or technologies, and so on. Payoffs are further
shaped by alliance costs. Porter and Fuller (1986) partition the costs of alliancing into
three categories: (1) coordination costs, (2) erosion of competitive position, and
(3) creation of an adverse bargaining position. The second and third categories are
echoed by Bresser (1988), who emphasizes the uncontrolled disclosure of strategic
information as competitive intentions are disclosed through the information links
resulting from collective strategies. Finally, payoffs also tend to be impacted by other
dysfunctional outcomes: reduced strategic flexibility; increased effect of external
disturbances; lower organizational adaptability; and the attraction of new entrants
(Bresser and Harl 1986, p. 408).

While the linkage of the basic framework of the present paper with extant SA
literature attempted here is necessarily indicative and not exhaustive, it does suggest
that many of the core issues in this topic can usefully be viewed through the research
lens of game theory to gain powerful new insights about the structure-performance
relationship. The applicability of game theory to international SAs is constrained,
however, by several simplifying assumptions, to which we turn next.

Examining the Assumptions

The prisoner's dilemma game, and, in turn, the proposed structure-performance
relationship (H1), rests on certain fundamental behavioral and environmental assumptions. The behavioral assumptions include "strong self-interest orientation," i.e.,
opportunism (Williamson 1985, p. 47); "strategic rationality" (Snidal 1986), i.e.,
(a) expected utility maximization and (b) complete knowledge of players in very
complex situations (Luce and Raiffa 1957); and that each player recognize and
remember the interaction. The environmental assumptions include (1) the absence of
a mechanism available to enforce threats or commitments, and (2) uncertainty
regarding the other player's move (Axelrod 1984, p. 11). Further assumptions are that
the meaning of "cooperate" and "defect" is unambiguous, that detecting the actions
of all players is straightforward (i.e., high behavior transparency), and that the unitary
nature of the decision makers (prisoners) obviates problems of factional, organizational, or bureaucratic dysfunctions.

Each of these assumptions becomes suspect, however, when examined in light of sharp differences in the actors' *cultural, national, and organizational backgrounds*. For example, a dominant social science paradigm is self-interest seeking with guile (Williamson 1985), which impacts alliance structure as each partner predictably attempts to reduce exposure to the risk of defection by the other. However, management and economics scholars have increasingly questioned the "assumption that managers have an underlying propensity to behave opportunistically" (Barney 1990, p. 384; Bromiley and Cummings 1991; Hill 1990; Mansfield 1990). Barney (1990) maintains instead that "There is plenty of room in organizational economics for trust, although a great deal more research in this area is needed" (p. 385).

This propensity for trust is likely to vary significantly among SA partners of different nationalities. As Thorelli (1986) observes, especially in Oriental cultures, trust is a vital supplement to contractual arrangements, and it may even take their place. In pre- and extra-contractual contexts the establishment of trust frequently takes more time and patience than Western executives spontaneously would like to invest. Similarly, Sullivan and Peterson (1982) note that whereas for Japanese managers cultural values make trust salient, and organizational variables such as position power, interpersonal relations, and decision control modify the trust-building perceptions and behaviors in predictable ways, American managers tend to rely on formal contracts and binding arbitration to resolve areas of conflict. The point is that if "transaction costs are the economic equivalent of friction in physical systems" (Williamson 1985, p. 19), as originally argued by Coase (1937), then we may conceptualize trust as the behavioral lubricant that can improve a system's (an alliance's) operating efficiency, and the role that trust is accorded in the formation, structuring, and maintenance of alliances by each firm may be highly culture-specific.

The Western tendency for being "too pessimistic about the responsiveness of the other side" is also reflected in the results of Axelrod's (1984) famous computer tournament on the prisoner's dilemma. Axelrod concluded that many participating game theorists from economics, political science, mathematics, sociology, and psychology made the "systematic error of being too competitive for their own good." Even Williamson (1985, p. 392) concedes that alliances "are more costly to forge in a low-trust than in a high-trust society." More broadly, Williamson (1985, p. 23) recognizes the need to locate his transaction-cost economizing analysis in the larger context of which the costs are a part, since:

1. The social context in which transactions are embedded—the customs, mores, habits, and so on—have a bearing, and therefore need to be taken into account, when moving from one culture to another; and

2. The argument relies in a general, background way on the efficacy of competition to perform a sort between more and less efficient modes and to shift resources in favor of the former.

Clearly, significant variation may exist along *each* of these two factors characterizing the larger context of each partner of an international alliance. The industry structure and institutions, and government laws and regulations, surrounding a company in its home country (the company's "national context"), vary greatly across countries, differentially impacting companies' ability to enter and operate SAs. For example, national attitudes about simultaneous competition and cooperation are vastly different in Japan (where companies have a long history of cooperating in some areas while competing in others), versus in the U.S. (where strict antitrust regulations reflect the federal government's suspicion of cooperation between companies competing in the same markets). Such differences in home country environments spawn companies with different experience levels in successfully structuring and managing interfirm cooperation.

Further, in some countries the cultural embeddedness of economic transactions (Granovetter 1985) and of group behavior (Cox, Lobel, and McLeod 1991) may result in an emphasis on competition and efficiency as yardsticks of performance measurement (Homans 1958; Polanyi 1957), while in other countries the preferred evaluative criteria may be stability and social justice (Grossman 1975), as reflected in the practices of lifetime employment at the individual level and long-term, "relational" contracting at the organizational level. Diversity in societal cultures and national contexts may also generate disparate perceptions about criteria for utility maximization, such as the strikingly different temporal orientations of U.S. versus Japanese firms. The former, pressed by investors and analysts, may tend to focus on quarterly earnings reports, while the latter focus on establishing their brand names and international marketing channels, a *sine qua non* of higher-order advantage leading to greater world market shares over a period of several years. Such interpersonal comparisons of utility add a "penumbra of indeterminateness" (Harsanyi 1977, p. 277) to the basic prisoner's dilemma formulation, so that the highly useful deductive framework of game theory may become less apposite in certain situations, e.g., cross-border alliances.

This important point can be reinforced in the context of the environmental assumptions of lack of enforcement mechanisms and uncertainty regarding the other player's actions. The presence of strong norms may provide the necessary mechanism for making enforceable threats or commitments in some countries (Terpstra and David 1990, John 1984). And these strong norms may lessen uncertainty about another party's probability of cooperation than in countries where such norms are absent. Examining marketing channels, for instance, John (1984) concludes that "social contract" is important in maintaining efficient exchange in long-term relationships that are vulnerable to opportunism. Appropriate role behavior and execution of agreements is ensured not by the open market (large numbers, competitive pressures, etc.), but rather by: (1) the force of administrative control and (2) the web of norms, attitudes and perceptions that constitute the social contract.

SA partners of different national heritages may vary widely not only along societal- and national-level dimensions as discussed above, but also along organizational-level dimensions that are crucial in the SA interaction (Parkhe 1991a). These firm-specific attributes include corporate culture, strategic direction, and management practices. For instance, distinct differences can exist on the need for power and control, fundamentally shaping each partner's approach toward the SA. Americans may believe that power, not parity, should govern collaborative ventures, while the Europeans and Japanese may consider partners as equals, subscribe to management by consensus, and rely on lengthy discussion to secure stronger commitment to shared enterprises (Perlmutter and Heenan 1986). Likewise, according to Ohmae (1989), the need for control is deeply rooted in the tradition of Western capitalism. He asserts that this tradition has long taught managers the dangerously incorrect arithmetic that equates 51% with 100%, and 49% with 0%.

Finally, Hamel, Doz, and Prahalad (1989) report sharply different tendencies (by partner nationality) to use SAs to enhance one's own internal skills, while guarding against transferring competitive advantages to alliance partners (Bresser 1988). In the U.S.-Japanese SAs studied by Hamel et al., for example, the U.S. company merely wanted to share investment risk, whereas the Japanese company, in addition to sharing risk, made great efforts to absorb their partner's skills as well. And when both partners are equally intent on internalizing the other's skills, distrust and conflict arises. This is why SAs between Korean and Japanese companies have been few and tempestuous. Neither side want to "open the kimono."

In sum, international SA partners may be characterized by major differences along multiple levels of analysis. Culturally-, nationally-, and organizationally-inculcated norms of managers weaned in different countries may differentially impact their propensity and capacity to take a long-term perspective and to deliberately reshape the alliance structure to promote cooperation. Consequently, the customary assumptions underlying game theoretic and economic frameworks that are erected in a unicultural environment, with homogeneous actors, may *not* be universally applicable to all firms, suggesting the following hypothesis:

H2. *The structure-performance relationship of strategic alliances* (H1) *will be moderated by partner nationality*.

The next section describes the first empirical study designed to test our two hypotheses in a realistic (i.e., nonlaboratory) business context.

Methods

Sample Selection

Under investigation in this study is the structure/performance relationship in mixed-motive (competitive + cooperative) interfirm partnerships. Our ideal choice of a sample would be a sample from the total population of such alliances. In practice, however, it was not feasible to draw a random sample from such a broad population. Rather, some degree of external validity was sacrificed and a small sample was chosen judgmentally with the hope that the focal (performance) variables could be examined in relation to structural characteristics while other factors were held relatively constant (Cook and Campbell 1979).

Five selection criteria were employed: (1) time period; (2) industrial scope; (3) firm nationality; (4) number of participants; and (5) nature of participants. The first criterion attempts to capture the recent rapid growth of SAs, and major trends of current and future relevance, by selecting SAs formed between 1983–1988. The second criterion recognizes that a limited number of industry groups are the most prolific in SA activity (Hladik 1985, Porter and Fuller 1986, Hergert and Morris 1988), and targets those groups: chemicals and allied products (SIC 28); machinery, except electric (SIC 35); electrical and electronic equipment (SIC 36); and transport equipment (SIC 37). The third criterion deletes SAs without at least one U.S. partner, primarily because of constraints on access, time, and funding. The fourth criterion includes SAs with $N = 2$ only, since a vast majority (81%) of SAs are between two firms (Hergert and Morris 1988). The fifth criterion restricts the study to interfirm, for-profit SAs, even though there is important (and increasing) cooperation between business-universities, business-government, and government-universities. Taken together, these five criteria generate a domain of inquiry that is relevant and significant, and that permits the issues of alliance structure/performance relationships to be addressed without consequential confounding effects (Parkhe 1989).

Data Collection

Data collection proceeded in three phases. In Phase I, an original database of 342 firms was constructed. This database satisfies the selection criteria and meets the needs of this research particularly well. Phase II ran parallel to Phase I, and consisted of designing a data collection instrument (questionnaire) which could effectively gather data on the relevant variables. In Phase III, the results of the first two phases were pooled with personal interviews and survey literature to conduct a nationwide mail survey of senior executives.

Phase I. The primary source for original database construction was Funk and Scott's (F & S) *Index of Corporate Change* (1983–1988). Depth was added to the database by cross-checking and supplementing relevant facts on alliance activity, by

310   ARVIND PARKHE

reference to the original citations in the *Index*. Numerous citations of probable future SA activity were excluded from the database, since these proposed SAs frequently fizzle out before getting off the ground. Application of the above selection criteria generated a gross sample of 396 firms.

These firms were checked in the *Standard & Poor's Register of Corporations, Directors and Executives* to obtain the name of a specific executive, his/her title, complete address, and phone number. The executive VP was selected, unless another person more clearly matched the needs of this survey (e.g., VP-joint ventures). Where neither officer could be found, a higher level executive was targeted. This process resulted in a sample size of 349 firms, to whom "executive pre-identification" phone calls were made in order to verify the accuracy of available information, and to request assistance in this research project. Though expensive and time-consuming, this step was most useful and is highly recommended. Massive compilations of business data sources involve considerable lead time, rendering those sources somewhat obsolete by publication time in a fast-changing business world. The effectiveness of our database was sharply increased by making many changes reflecting recent events as uncovered through these phone calls. (In addition, the receptivity to the questionnaire may also be expected to increase as a result of these calls.) Deleting the seven companies that had ceased to exist, a net sample size of 342 firms was obtained.

Phase II. The questionnaire performs the actual interrogation function in a mail survey, and therefore warrants considerable attention. The design and administration of the questionnaire in this study heavily used the "total design method" of Dilman (1978), who uses social exchange theory to develop various ways to encourage response. Most of these suggestions were implemented, including the use of professional typesetting and printing services. Details on the instrument construction steps of item generation, questionnaire pretesting, and purification of measures are described in the Measures section.

Phase III. Effective mail survey administration seeks to maximize the response rate through various techniques (Kanuk and Berenson 1975, Dilman 1978, Harvey 1988). A variation of the recommended techniques was used in this research, with the following sequential steps: (1) Executive preidentification phone calls before the first wave of mail. (2) First wave. (3) Reminder/thank you postcards to all executives. (4) Second wave of mail to nonrespondents. (5) Follow-up phone calls to all second-wave recipients.

Respondents

Of the 342 senior executives receiving questionnaires, 152 (45%) responded, and 111 (33%) of the responses were usable. One-way ANOVA in terms of firm size, product categories, and geographic markets served showed no significant differences between respondents and nonrespondents, indicating an absence of any systematic nonresponse bias in the findings. Approximately 60% of the usable responses came from persons most directly responsible for the SA, usually a functional VP; 21% came from executive VPs, and 19% came from the Chairman and/or President.

Significant cross-sector and cross-border alliance activity was present in the sample, confirming current trends (cf. Wysocki 1990). For example, the primary products of the respondent and partner firms, respectively, were as follows: chemicals and allied products, 42.3%, 33.3%; machinery except electric, 19.8%. 8.1%; electrical and electronic equipment, 23.4%, 14.4%; and transport equipment, 14.5%, 13.5%. Similarly, while the respondent firms were all U.S. firms because of sample selection criteria, the nationalities of the partner firms varied widely, as shown in Table 1. This finding is consistent with prior research (Hergert and Morris 1988).

TABLE 1
Nationality of Partner Firm

Nationality	No. of cases
U.S.A.	33
CANADA	2
MEXICO	1
JAPAN	28
SAUDI ARABIA	1
TURKEY	2
"EUROPE"	1
FRANCE	8
WEST GERMANY	8
ITALY	3
U.K.	3
SWEDEN	4
NETHERLANDS	4
SWITZERLAND	3
AUSTRIA	1
AUSTRALIA	1
PEOPLE'S REPUBLIC OF CHINA	2
**	6
TOTAL	111

** Did not indicate.

Measures of the Dependent and Independent Variables

Exploratory research typically uses several techniques to generate measurement items: literature searches, experience surveys and focus groups involving relevant actors (in our case, experienced executives who could offer ideas and insights into SAs), and critical incidents (Churchill 1979, Nunnally 1978). Wording and question construction for this study began with the literatures cited earlier, with a special focus on generating a pool of items that tap the core theoretical constructs of structure and performance. Business school faculty and doctoral students were used as expert judges to assess the face validity of the selected items, most of which were developed specifically for this study, given the paucity of prior empirical work in this area. (However, some published items were also adopted.) After several iterations of item editing and refinement, a team of three researchers undertook rigorous content analysis to determine the overlap of the remaining items with the conceptual domain of the constructs. With the resulting instrument, pretest interviews were conducted with SA-experienced executives in Philadelphia and Baltimore, to identify any problems with question wording and questionnaire layout. These interviews ranged from 70 to 130 minutes, and yielded many useful suggestions that strengthened the content and concurrent validities of the instrument.

Operationalizing Performance. To cover the breadth of this construct, performance is conceptualized to be a composite variable consisting of three components: (a) Σ(importance × fulfillment of strategic needs), or PERF1; (b) net spillover effects, or SPILLNET; and (c) overall performance assessment, or OVRALPER. PERF1 is included because when very important strategic needs are being fulfilled very well, the SA may be said to be performing well. Strategic needs are adapted from Contractor and Lorange (1988), who provide a 16-item inventory of the strategic contributions of SAs. Sample items included "risk reduction through product portfolio diversification," "lower average cost from larger volume," and "utilization of partner's special skills in R & D." Importance is rated by the respondents on a 3-point Likert scale ranging from "not important" to "very important," and Fulfillment is rated on a 5-point scale ranging from "very poorly" to "very well." A factor analysis of these items yields one factor with an eigenvalue greater than one (eigenvalue = 5.77), attesting to the internal reliability of the items, so the items were summed to form an index (Cronbach α = 0.94).

The single-item measure of SPILLNET read as follows: "Many SAs result in 'spillover' effects for their parent firms. For example, positive spillover effects may occur when knowhow that is gained from SA activities can be applied profitably to non-SA operations as well. Negative spillover effects may occur from competition between the SA and other parent firm operations, such as when geographical markets overlap. In the present SA, the net spillover effects for your firm are: 5-point scale, "strongly negative" to "strongly positive" (test-retest reliability = 0.79)."

OVRALPER was measured on a 5-point scale ("very poorly" to "very well") with the statement "In your overall assessment, how has the SA performed as compared to your expectations?" (test-retest reliability = 0.92).

There is much disagreement among business scholars on a valid measure of performance, and the disagreement is likely to persist for some time. However, the multidimensional operationalization proposed here seeks to overcome some of the drawbacks of prior measures of performance that relied heavily, for example, on survival and duration of the SA (cf. Harrigan 1988). Our performance operationalization achieves the combination of financial, operational, and effectiveness measures recommended by Venkatraman and Ramanujam (1986).

Operationalizing Structure. Recalling that sample selection criteria specify N = 2, the number of firms as a dimension of alliance structure becomes controlled for in this study. We therefore focus on the other two dimensions, the shadow of the future and the payoff structure.

Following Axelrod (1984), Axelrod and Keohane (1986), and Oye (1986), we note that the specific factors that make the shadow of the future an effective promoter of cooperation are: behavior transparency (TRANS), frequency of interaction (FRQINT), and long time horizons (HORIZON).

TRANS (α = 0.81) refers to the speed and reliability with which alliance partners learn about each other's actions (or "moves"). Speed (TIMELAG) was measured on a scale specifying four ranges ("over 1 month" to "within 1 day"), and reverse scored. As Axelrod (1984, p. 185) maintains, "The speed of response depends upon the time required to detect a given choice by the other player. The shorter this time is, the more stable cooperation can be." Reliability was measured by asking about the source (INFOSOR) and accuracy (INFOACCU) of information regarding the partner's behavior, with a choice of sources typically used (own firm's employees, SA itself, partner firm) and a 4-point range of accuracy ("never" to "always"), similar to John (1984). Formalized arrangements that shape the need to monitor the partner's ongoing actions, including "bureaucratic, formal controls" (Smith and Aldrich 1991), often constitute an important part of the SA contract (see Practicing Law Institute 1986). Such arrangements are proxied here in the "SA itself" category. The following model of the foregoing variables was assumed to represent behavior transparency:

$$\text{TRANS} = \text{INFOSOR} \times \text{INFOACCU} \times \text{TIMELAG}.$$

The postulation of a multiplicative (rather than additive) model is atheoretical; it is supported, however, by Habib's (1987) observation that in certain situations adding scores is much less well grounded conceptually than is multiplying them. For example, summing the responses may result in overlooking some revealing and interesting off-diagonal cases, such as respondents high on speed and low on reliability, or those low on speed and high on reliability.

FRQINT ($\alpha = 0.87$), the frequency of interaction, was measured as the product of two items: (a) "How many times do senior executives from your firm and the partner firm typically meet per year?" and (b) "At lower levels (for example, R & D at one firm, Manufacturing at another), how frequently does communication take place (by any means)?" (4-point scale, "never" to "frequently"). Business press has well documented the importance of top management commitment and involvement for the success of SAs, but less well recognized is the reality that regular communication at lower (operational) levels is equally critical, and this is where SAs can flourish or be destroyed. The two components are therefore weighted equally.

HORIZON ($\alpha = 0.64$) attempts to measure the expected durability of the SA, since this theoretically increases the likelihood of cooperation by encouraging reciprocal behavior in the present (Axelrod and Keohane 1986). Likewise, Kogut (1989) argues that embedded, long-term economic relations between partners (reflecting a long shadow of the future) generate reciprocation and enhance the stability of alliances. HORIZON is the product of two items, intended duration and perceived likelihood. (a) Intended duration: "Some SAs are envisioned to last an indefinite period of time, while others are created explicitly with short-term goals in mind. At the time it was launched, what was the intended duration of this SA?" (3-point scale, "short term" (1–3 years) to "long term" (over 5 years)); (b) Perceived likelihood: "In your estimation, what is the likelihood that the SA will actually last for the intended duration?" (3-point scale, "low" to "high").

The payoff structure (test-retest reliability = 0.91) was completed by the respondents using a four-cell matrix in which one cell (mutual cooperation) served as the anchor: MC = \$1.00. That is, the respondents estimated their own payoffs under different behavioral combinations (unilateral defection, mutual defection, and unilateral cooperation), using the instructions as reproduced in the Appendix. Our approach of estimating payoffs in relation to an anchor is validated by at least three considerations:

1. The magnitude of payoffs for various firms may vary greatly, depending on the scale of the SA and the level of commitment of each partner. However, our central concern is with the *interrelationships* among the payoffs.

2. The likelihood of response can be expected to be greatly heightened by not asking the executive to reveal the absolute amounts of payoffs in each scenario, but only the *relative* amounts.

3. Interval scale preference orderings of payoffs can sufficiently capture the motivations and incentives of firms in alliances.

It must be clearly recognized that there are dangers inherent in relying on the subjective assessment of respondents (cf. Schwenk 1985), and since data were collected from a single source (individual executive) at one time, the possibility of common method variance exists. Researchers have widely acknowledged the problem of using self-report measures from key informants (Houston and Sudman 1975, Phillips 1981); however, at times reliance on key informants may be the only realistic, feasible way to get the information desired (Huber and Power 1985). Along the lines of Provan and Skinner (1989), therefore, we argue that the impact of common method variance may not have been so great as to invalidate the results. Since survey participants were senior executives closely involved in structuring and running the alliance, it is not unreasonable to expect that the respondent was among the most knowledgeable people concerning the SA. Moreover, questionnaire construction involved active input from several executives during pretest interviews so as to minimize ambiguity or bias, and to prepare the wording and format for accurate understanding of the underlying behavioral constructs. Finally, although objective data (e.g., detailed audit of confidential files) from multiple sources (e.g., both parents and the alliance general manager) would have been desirable, collection of such data would have been exceptionally difficult and costly, if not impossible, especially for a large, international sample such as ours.

Data Analysis

Canonical correlation analysis (CCA) is a useful procedure when analyzing several dependent variables and independent variables simultaneously, because it can uncover complex relationships that reflect the structure between *sets* of dependent and independent variables (Andrews et al. 1981). CCA is particularly appropriate when the dependent variables are themselves correlated; in our study, PERF1, SPILLNET, and OVRALPER can certainly be expected to be intercorrelated.

CCA seeks two linear combinations, one for the independent set of variables and one for the dependent set of variables, such that their product-moment correlation is maximal. The "standard" output of CCA is canonical loadings (analogous to factor analysis) and canonical weights (analogous to beta weights in multiple regression analysis). With these statistics it is possible to test the strength and directionality of the association. Canonical weights indicate the predictive qualities of the variables, and canonical loadings are necessary for the interpretation of the relationship (Barker and Barker 1984, Hair et al. 1979).

Why not perform separate multiple regression analyses (e.g., repeated ANOVA or ANCOVA), one for each of the dependent variables? As Dillon and Goldstein (1984) caution, this approach is not recommended. Separate regression analyses would not provide as strict a test of differences in means across the dependent variables as CCA, and would defeat the purpose of having multiple performance measures, since the information provided by the interrelationships among the dependent variables would not be taken into account. The other possibility, of collapsing the performance measures into a single index, would create needless loss of information and diminish some of the advantages of having this multidimensional operationalization.

Checks for instability caused by sample-specific coefficients, and for CCA's two major data assumptions—multivariate normal distribution of variables and homogeneity of covariance matrices across groups—yielded generally satisfactory results. However, certain departures from strict assumptions were found in the data, such as the presence of heteroscedasticity. Though these departures are not serious in most instances (Ito 1970; Olson 1976), they nevertheless suggest a need for (a) caution in interpretation and analysis (cf. Dillon and Goldstein 1984, pp. 354–359), and (b) replication with data from another sample.

Data analysis must control for rival explanations of performance that might confound the structure-performance relationship under study. In other words, our interest is in the effects of alliance structure on performance, above and beyond the effects of exogenous variables (or covariates) at the firm, industry, and national levels. Three important covariates were identified: firm sizes; primary product categories of alliance partners; and top geographic markets served by the partners. For example, alliance performance may be spuriously higher in large firms; be lower in industries that are suffering; or be a function of specific country market conditions. Collection of demographic data on these three variables, coupled with use of the MANCOVA option of the MANOVA package in SPSS-X (SPSS 1988, p. 617), permitted the effects of the covariates to be parcelled out in the canonical correlation analyses performed.

Finally, there is disagreement in the literature on the appropriate statistic to report overall association between the dependent and independent variables in CCA. Olson (1976) recommends the use of Pillai's V, whereas Stevens (1979) suggests the use of Hotelling's T^2, Wilks' Λ, and Roy's greatest common root (GCR). Due to the

TABLE 2
Descriptive Statistics and Pearson Product-Moment Correlations[a]

Variables	Means	s.d.	Correlations					
			1	2	3	4	5	6
1. Σ(Importance × fulfillment of strategic needs)	0.37	0.12						
2. Net spillover effects	3.52	0.77	0.59***					
3. Overall performance assessment	3.31	1.10	0.67***	0.44***				
4. Behavior transparency	0.30	0.19	0.23**	0.07	0.19*			
5. Frequency of interaction	0.92	0.13	0.27**	0.02	0.22**	0.39***		
6. Length of time horizon	9.30	3.77	0.32***	0.16	0.31***	0.17	0.23*	
7. Payoff from unilateral defection	1.73	0.73	-0.07	-0.11	-0.10	-0.28**	-0.01	-0.09
8. Payoff from mutual defection	0.41	0.58	0.15	0.13	0.16	0.18*	0.02	0.11
9. Payoff from unilateral cooperation	-1.28	1.39	0.10	0.06	0.14	0.03	0.14	0.19*

[a] $N = 111$.
* $p < 0.05$.
** $p < 0.01$.
*** $p < 0.001$.

ARVIND PARKHE

TABLE 3
Multivariate Test Statistics for Combined Canonical Variates

Test	Statistic	Approx. F (DF)	Significance of F	Critical Value
Pillai's V	0.659	2.96(18,189)	0.001	
Hotelling's T^2	1.003	3.37(18,179)	0.001	
Wilk's Λ	0.441	3.14(18,173)	0.001	
Roy's GCR	0.417			0.275^a

^{a}Critical value ($p < 0.01$) derived from Kres (1983, p. 97).

TABLE 4
Eigenvalues and Canonical Correlations of Three Extracted Canonical Variates

Variate Number	Eigenvalue	Percent	Cumulative Percent	Canonical Correlation	Squared Correlation
1	0.714	71.315	71.315	0.635	0.403
2	0.179	17.907	89.222	0.359	0.129
3	0.108	10.778	100.000	0.311	0.097

unresolved controversy, we shall report values for all four statistics and significance levels for Pillai's V, Hotelling's T^2, and Wilks' Λ.

Results

Descriptive statistics are shown in Table 2. Not unexpectedly, the three measures of performance are highly intercorrelated. Indeed, any interpretation of contribution to performance by the structural variables from this zero-order correlation matrix would be hazardous due to the multicollinearity present in the data.

Table 3 shows the overall multivariate test statistics for the combined "canonical variates," which are statistical artifacts generated by CCA to secure maximal correlation between the variate and independent variables on one hand, and variate and dependent variables on the other hand. Pillai's V, Hotelling's T^2, and Wilks' Λ are all significant at $p < 0.001$. Roy's greatest common root (0.417) also exceeds the critical value (0.275), confirming these tests ($p < 0.01$). Further, the eigenvalues and canonical correlations of the canonical variates, shown in Table 4, indicate that summing the squared correlations column results in 0.629, i.e., 62.9% of the total variance in performance is captured by these three variates. Thus, H1 appears to be strongly supported by the data, establishing empirically the linkage between game-theoretic structure and performance for the total sample.

As argued above, however, this aggregation may conceal important differences. Testing H1 separately by partner nationality results in Table 5, which shows the emergence of distinct patterns for the different subgroups. The significance of F value associated with Pillai's, Hotelling's, and Wilks' statistics (which was 0.001 in Table 3 for the total sample) indicates excellent support for a structure-performance relationship when considering U.S. partners only, as well as for non-U.S. partners taken as a group. But for SAs with partners from Europe, the statistics are weaker, with only Hotelling's T^2 significant at the $p < 0.10$ level. SAs with Japanese partners find the least support for a relationship between SA structure and performance. We conclude therefore that H2 is supported, confirming the moderating role of partner nationality.

As indicated earlier, canonical loadings are analogous to factor loadings in factor analysis. To probe deeper into the nonuniformity of results, it is useful to compare

TABLE 5
Comparison of Structure-Performance Relationship by Partner Nationality[a]

Test	U.S. Partner $N = 33$	Non-U.S. Partner $N = 78$	European Partner $N = 35$	Japanese Partner $N = 28$
Pillai's V	0.017	0.031	0.186	0.262
Hotelling's T^2	0.009	0.022	0.069	0.339
Wilks' Λ	0.007	0.036	0.118	0.284

[a]Significance of F values reported.

TABLE 6
Canonical Loadings on Variate #1 by Partner Nationality[a]

Variable	U.S. Partner	non-U.S. Partner	European Partner	Japanese Partner
PERF1		0.512	0.431	−0.724
SPILLNET	1.211	0.477		−0.799
OVRALPER	0.531		0.620	
HORIZON		0.414		−0.706
FRQINT	0.848		0.811	−0.366
TRANS	0.428	0.368	0.400	
UD-MC	−0.493	−0.349	−0.868	
MC-MD	0.307			
UD-UC			−0.309	0.519

[a]Only loadings > 0.300 are reported.

the canonical loadings for each subgroup, as shown in Table 6. This comparison is made only with respect to canonical variate #1, since this variate is dominant in capturing the variance in the performance variables (as shown in Table 4, variates #2 and #3 are statistically much less significant). Table 6 provides the basis for comparisons among structure-performance relationships of SAs originating in different countries.

Discussion

In this paper we asked whether performance and game-theoretic structure of strategic alliances are significantly related (H1) and, if so, whether this relationship is moderated by partner nationality (H2). The robust results of H1 for the full sample vindicate recent advances in the theory of cooperation (Axelrod 1984) and game theory (Oye 1986), while the mixed results of different subgroups by partner nationality lend support to H2. Though the sample size in each subgroup is small, and hence the results should be regarded as tentative, the empirical erosion of the explanatory power of game theory in dissimilar settings raises important questions and provides fresh opportunities to deepen our understanding of SAs. We begin with Table 6 and then discuss broader implications for theory and research.

In Table 6, the HORIZON measure is significant for non-U.S. partners as a whole, and strongly significant for Japanese partners, but statistically insignificant for U.S. and European partners. Conversely, frequency of interaction (FRQINT) and behavior transparency (TRANS) loaded heavily for SAs with European partners, even more heavily for SAs with U.S. partners, but were much less significant for SAs with Japanese partners. These findings corroborate the work of Thorelli (1986) and Sullivan and Peterson (1982), who argued that Western (U.S.-U.S. and U.S.-European)

SAs may place much greater emphasis on overt behaviors (e.g., frequent interactions) and explicit understandings (e.g., formal contracts) than the informal understandings and trust that characterize SAs involving Japanese firms.

Indeed, these findings may be representative of the deep impact of societal and corporate cultures on SA management. The interactions found in international SAs bring together people who may have different patterns of behaving and believing, and different cognitive blueprints for interpreting the world (Kluckhohn and Kroeberg 1952). One example can be found in the partners' approaches to conflict resolution. In some cultures, conflict is viewed as a healthy, natural, and inevitable part of relationships and organizations. In fact, programmed or structured conflict (e.g., the devil's advocate and dialectical inquiry methods) has been suggested as a way to enhance the effectiveness of strategic decision-making (Cosier and Dalton 1990) in the West. But in other cultures (e.g., Japan, South Korea, the Middle East), vigorous conflict and open confrontation are deemed distasteful. Embarrassment and loss of face to either party is sought to be avoided at all costs by talking indirectly and ambiguously about areas of difference until common ground can be found, by the use of mediators, and other techniques. Such fundamental differences in partners' approaches may also be found in problem solving, goal setting, temporal orientations, trust levels, and other crucial areas of SA interactions that may in turn create differences in the structuring and ongoing management of SAs; a corollary of this is to focus managerial attention on the most salient structural dimensions (e.g., frequency of interaction) for each SA, depending upon partner nationality.

Where payoff structure loadings are significant (> 0.300), Table 6 shows them to follow theoretically expected patterns: Performance is negatively associated with (UD-MC) and (UD-UC), and positively associated with (MC-MD). Interestingly, U.S.-European alliances loaded most heavily on the joint product lost to unilateral defection measure of payoffs (UD-MC), and the cost of unrequited cooperation (UD-UC) correlated most negatively with performance for U.S.-Japanese SAs.

While the implications of the former finding are unclear, the latter finding is significant in that it reflects widely-held perceptions regarding the costs of unintended transfer through the alliance (Bresser 1988) that allegedly differ widely by partner nationality (Reich and Mankin 1986). Hamel et al. (1989) explain the relative openness of Western technicians in SAs with Japanese firms on the basis of cultural and professional reasons. "Japanese engineers and scientists are more loyal to their company than to their profession. They are less steeped in the open given-and-take of university research since they receive much of their training from employers. They consider themselves team members more than individual scientific contributors" (p. 138). According to this view, the SA becomes a race to learn, with the company that learns fastest dominating the relationship and eventually discarding the partner (unilaterally defecting from the agreement). As a result, companies from certain countries have acquired a reputation for entering into SAs as Trojan Horses, with the concomitant impact on alliance structuring and performance.

Each category of nationality exhibited differences in the importance of the three dimensions of performance. SAs with U.S. partners loaded significantly on SPILLNET and OVRALPER; with European partners, on PERF1 and OVRALPER; and with Japanese partners, on PERF1 and SPILLNET. While it is risky to draw sweeping conclusions given our small subgroup sizes, these findings may nonetheless indicate that the success of SAs is judged more heavily on the attainment of strategic objectives and positive synergies for SAs with Japanese partners. Combined with a dominant role of HORIZON in the alliance structure, this suggests a special role of U.S.-Japanese SAs in the strategic profile of their parent firms; namely, while overall performance assessment (OVRALPER) per se was not found to be significant, performance evaluation rests on long time horizons, with direct (PERF1) and indirect

TABLE 7
Linking Interfirm Diversity and Alliance Structure in International Partnerships

Conceptual Level	Phenomeno-logical Level	Dimension of Diversity (A_i)	Sources of Tension	Alliance Structure Components (B_j)		
				Pattern of Payoffs	Shadow of the Future	Number of Players
Meta	Supranational	Societal culture	Differences in perception and interpretation of phenomena, analytical processes	A_1B_1	A_1B_2	A_1B_3
Macro	National	National context	Differences in home government policies, national industry structure and institutions	A_2B_1	A_2B_2	A_2B_3
Meso	Top management	Corporate culture	Differences in ideologies and values guiding companies	A_3B_1	A_3B_2	A_3B_3
Meso	Policy group	Strategic direction	Differences in strategic interests of partners from dynamic external and internal environments	A_4B_1	A_4B_2	A_4B_3
Micro	Functional	Management practices	Differences in management styles, organizational structures of parent firms	A_5B_1	A_5B_2	A_5B_3

(SPILLNET) SA contributions to the competitive strength of the parent company being important factors.

The preceding conclusions and inferences regarding differences in the structure-performance relationship of different nationality subgroups are not distinct and unrelated; rather they share a common core that touches international SAs. It was argued earlier that international SA partners may be characterized by major differences in culturally-, nationally-, and organizationally-developed norms; this, in fact, was the theoretical basis of H2. Table 7 pulls together the important dimensions of interfirm diversity, A_i, into a unified typology (Parkhe 1991a); further, it systematically links each diversity dimension with the components of alliance structure, B_j. The interactive elements, A_iB_j, provide a rich avenue for future research that explicitly focuses on the impact of interfirm diversity on alliance structure, although it must be recognized that both diversity dimensions and the structural components are often interrelated, and therefore cannot be treated as mutually exclusive.

Indeed, a promising research project that would raise the theoretical level of SAs involves the disentanglement (through path analysis, covariance structure modeling, or other techniques) of the directions of causality and feedback loops among the variables involved. H1 in the present study established only correlation, not causality. For example, a long shadow of the future could result in high performance; or high performance could result in a lengthening shadow of the future. Disentangling the relationships would unlock important aspects of mixed-motive relationships, although such studies would obviously be considerably more complex than the present one.

An interim step may be to identify and categorize how each B_j (e.g., alliance payoffs) is differentially affected by various A_i's. Alternatively, one might examine

320   ARVIND PARKHE

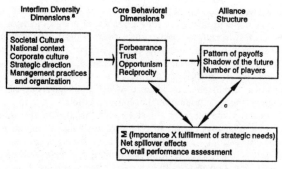

Interfirm Diversity Dimensions [a]	Core Behavioral Dimensions [b]	Alliance Structure

FIGURE 1. Revised Agenda for Future Research on Interfirm Cooperation.

how differences in a given A_i (e.g., societal culture) affect various B_j's.[5] Such studies would add to our knowledge of important factors influencing SAs, and also pave the way for more sophisticated theory-building in which A_i's, B_j's, and C_k's (the performance measures) can be integrated.

Finally, an expanded research agenda must also consider the behavioral chain that interlinks core variables at the heart of cooperation: forbearance, reciprocity, trust, and opportunism (Parkhe 1991b). Buckley and Casson (1988) pointed out that the essence of voluntary interfirm cooperation lies in "coordination effected through mutual forbearance." Forbearance becomes possible only when there is reciprocal behavior (Axelrod 1984) and mutual trust (Thorelli 1986), which in turn only come about given an absence of opportunism (Williamson 1985). Building on the above discussion, two timely research questions are posed: (1) How are these critical variables of forbearance, reciprocity, trust, and opportunism influenced by each of the dimensions of interfirm diversity? (2) In turn, how do these variables manifest themselves in alliances through differential interfirm approaches to the structural variables of pattern of payoffs, shadow of the future, and number of players? Posing these important questions significantly extends the research agenda beyond the empirical study reported in this paper, as shown in Figure 1.

Conclusions

The data from this study simultaneously validate and challenge game theory. The compelling support found for H1 suggests that the deductive power of game theory can potentially contribute extremely useful insights into enhancing the stability, longevity, and performance levels of SAs. Yet the support also found for H2 illustrates that game theory, as any other single perspective, cannot alone capture the rich complexity of real-world SAs.

There arises therefore a need to revisit game theory's major assumptions and to acknowledge that assumptions are a function of time and place. The validity of

[5]As suggested by Table 6, however, *particular* elements of the structural dimensions may be more salient for given nationality combinations. Specific and interesting hypotheses can be developed from Table 6, providing the basis for replication and corroboration of the present study's results with another sample of domestic and international SAs.

assumptions in a given place may shift over time, and at a given time assumptions may not be equally valid in all places. For example, although much of the theory-building in the organizational sciences springs from a pure-competition, zero-sum paradigm, the worldview in many countries is shaped by the realization that "nature is not always red in the fang and claw," and that competition and cooperation can coexist. These and other dimensions of interfirm diversity (Table 7) can strongly influence companies' approaches to alliance structuring; as such, context-specific applicability of game theory's assumptions becomes a crucial concern.

Exploiting powerful game-theoretic concepts and insights on the incentives and motivations present in various classes of relationships, while laying bare embedded assumptions and integrating the analysis with contextually significant aspects of interfirm cooperation, can lead to exciting possibilities for theory advancement. The present paper took one step in this direction, by offering Figure 1 as an expanded research agenda. It may be adduced, for instance, that this paper not only tested the suitability of game theory as a theoretical underpinning of the study of SAs (an underpinning that survived the empirical test), but also that it extended the literature by introducing additional theoretical considerations (the cultural, national, and organizational elements). That is, if H1 represents an innovation *within* the literature on strategic alliances, then H2 *extends* that literature and is therefore, arguably, more significant. So the next phase of research must address the following question: If the ethnocentrically derived game-theoretic and economic formulations do not apply to certain alliance partners, what higher-level rules of the game *do* govern the behaviors of highly heterogeneous international firms from diverse nationalities?

As Camerer (1985) argued, game theory may be one of the most important and underutilized sources for developing deductive theorizing in organizational research. A broadened, multidisciplinary application of game theory can prove to be extremely useful toward generating needed progress, both positively (advancing understanding) and normatively (improving prescription), in the increasingly important phenomenon of global strategic alliances.

Acknowledgements

This study was supported by a University Fellowship from Temple University and a research grant from Indiana University (Bloomington). I thank Professors Rajan Chandran, Farok J. Contractor, Richard L. Daft, John D. Daniels, Jose de la Torre, Donald Lessard, Janet P. Near, Sankaran P. Raghunathan, Charles R. Schwenk, and the anonymous reviewers of *Organization Science* for their developmental help and important contributions at various stages of this paper.

Appendix

Please provide a quantitative assessment of the impact of four different behavior patterns as pictured below. In this question, "cooperative behavior" means full cooperation in the letter and spirit of the agreement, and "opportunistic behavior" means one firm acting to maximize its gains, even if this involves heavy losses for the partner and a breakup of the SA. If your firm's payoff from Scenario II is assumed to be $1.00, what would be the relative payoff in Scenarios I, III, and IV?

Note. Even if you are not sure of the answers, please give us your best estimates.

Your firm-Firm A
Partner firm-Firm B

Scenario I	Scenario II
A opportunistic, B cooperative Payoff to Firm A would be _____	A and B both cooperative Payoff to Firm A = $1.00
Scenario III	Scenario IV
A and B both opportunistic Payoff to Firm A would be _____	A cooperative, B opportunistic Payoff to Firm A would be _____

References

Anderson, Erin (1990), "Two Firms, One Frontier: On Assessing Joint Venture Performance," *Sloan Management Review* (Winter), 19–30.

———— and Barton Weitz (1989), "Determinants of Continuity in Conventional Industrial Channel Dyads," *Marketing Science*, 8, 4, 310–323.

Anderson, James C. and James A. Narus (1990), "A Model of Distributor Firm and Manufacturer Firm Working Partnerships," *Journal of Marketing*, 54, 42–58.

Andrews, F. M., L. Klem, T. N. Davidson, P. M. O'Malley and W. L. Rodgers (1981), *A Guide for Selecting Statistical Techniques for Analyzing Social Science Data*, Ann Arbor, MI: Institute for Social Research.

Axelrod, Robert (1984), *The Evolution of Cooperation*, New York: Basic Books.

———— and Robert O. Keohane (1986), "Achieving Cooperation under Anarchy: Strategies and Institutions," in *Cooperation under Anarchy*, K. A. Oye (Ed.), Princeton, NJ: Princeton University Press.

Barker, H. R. and B. M. Barker (1984), *Multivariate Analysis of Variance (MANOVA)* University, AL: University of Alabama Press.

Barney, Jay B. (1990), "The Debate Between Traditional Management Theory and Organizational Economics: Substantive Differences or Intergroup Conflict?," *Academy of Management Review*, 15, 382–393.

Beamish, Paul W. (1985), "The Characteristics of Joint Ventures in Developed and Developing Countries," *Columbia Journal of World Business*, 20, 3, 13–19.

———— and John C. Banks (1987), "Equity Joint Ventures and the Theory of the Multinational Enterprise," *Journal of International Business Studies*, 1–16.

Bresser, Rudi K. (1988), "Matching Collective and Competitive Strategies," *Strategic Management Journal*, 9, 375–385.

———— and Johannes E. Harl (1986), "Collective Strategy: Vice or Virtue?," *Academy of Management Review*, 11, 408–427.

Bromiley, Philip and Larry L. Cummings (1991), "Transactions Costs in Organizations with Trust," Working Paper, University of Minnesota.

Buckley, Peter J. and Mark Casson (1988), "A Theory of Cooperation in International Business," in *Cooperative Strategies in International Business*, F. Contractor and B. Lorange (Eds.), Lexington, MA: Lexington Books.

Business Week (1986), "Odd Couples" (July 21), 100–106.

Camerer, Colin (1985), "Redirecting Research in Business Policy and Strategy," *Strategic Management Journal*, 6, 1–15.

Cartwright, C. and A. Zander (1968), *Group Dynamics: Research and Theory*, New York: Harper & Row.

Churchill, G. (1979), "A Paradigm for Developing Better Measures of Marketing Constructs," *Journal of Marketing Research*, 16, 64–73.

Coase, Ronald (1937), "The Nature of the Firm," *Economica*, 4, 386–405.

Contractor, F. J. and P. Lorange (1988), "Why Should Firms Cooperate?," in *Cooperative Strategies in International Business*, F. J. Contractor and P. Lorange (Eds.), Lexington, MA: Lexington Books.

Cook, T. D. and D. T. Campbell (1979), *Quasi-Experimentation: Design and Analysis Issues for Field Settings*, Chicago: Rand McNally.

Cosier, Richard A. and Dan R. Dalton (1990), "Positive Effects of Conflict: A Field Assessment," *International Journal of Conflict Management* (January), 81–92.

Cox, Taylor, Sharon A. Lobel and Poppy L. McLeod (1991), "Effects of Ethnic Group Cultural Differences on Cooperative and Competitive Behavior on a Group Task," *Academy of Management Journal*.

Deutsch, Morton (1973), *The Resolution of Conflict*, New Haven, CT: Yale University Press.

Dillon, W. R. and M. Goldstein (1984), *Multivariate Analysis*, New York: John Wiley & Sons.

Dilman, Don A. (1978), *Mail and Telephone Surveys: The Total Design Method*, New York: John Wiley & Sons.

Geringer, J. Michael and L. Hebert (1989), "Control and Performance of International Joint Ventures," *Journal of International Business Studies*, 20, 235–254.

———— and ———— (1991), "Measuring Performance of International Joint Ventures," *Journal of International Business Studies*, 22, 249–263.

Gomes-Casseres, Benjamin (1989), "Joint Venture in the Face of Global Competition," *Sloan Management Review* (Spring), 17–26.

Granovetter, Mark (1985), "Economic Action and Social Structure: The Problem of Embeddedness," *American Journal of Sociology*, 91, 481–510.

Grossman, Gregory (1975), *Economic Systems*, Englewood Cliffs, NJ: Prentice-Hall.

Habib, Ghazi M. (1987), "Measures of Manifest Conflict in International Joint Ventures," *Academy of Management Journal*, 30, 808–816.

Hair, J. F., R. E. Anderson, R. L. Tatham and B. J. Grablowsky (1979), *Multivariate Data Analysis*, Tulsa, OK: The Petroleum Publishing Co.

Hall, Richard H. and John P. Clark (1975), "Problems in the Study of Interorganizational Relationships," in *Interorganization Theory*, A. R. Negandhi (Ed.), Kent, OH: Kent State University.

Hamel, Gary, Yves L. Doz and C. K. Prahalad (1989), "Collaborate with Your Competitors—And Win," *Harvard Business Review* (January & February), 133–139.

Harrigan, Kathryn R. (1985), *Strategies for Joint Ventures*, Lexington, MA: Lexington Books.

_____ (1987), "Strategic Alliances. Their New Role in Global Competition," *Columbia Journal of World Business* (Summer), 67–69.

_____ (1988), "Joint Ventures and Competitive Strategy," *Strategic Management Journal*, 9, 141–158.

Harsanyi, John C. (1977), *Rational Behavior and Bargaining Equilibrium in Games and Social Situations*, Cambridge: Cambridge University Press.

Harvey, L. (1988), "Factors Affecting Response Rates to Mailed Questionnaires," *Journal of the Market Research Society*, 29, 341–353.

Heide, Jan B. and Anne S. Miner (1990), "The Shadow of the Future: The Effects of the Anticipated Interaction and Frequency of Delivery on Buyer-Seller Cooperation," working paper, University of Wisconsin, Madison.

Hergert, Michael and Deigan Morris (1988), "Trends in International Collaborative Agreements," in *Cooperative Strategies in International Business*, F. Contractor and P. Lorange (Eds.), Lexington, MA: Lexington Books.

Hill, Charles W. L. (1990), "Cooperation, Opportunism, and the Invisible Hand: Implications for Transaction Cost Theory," *Academy of Management Review*, 15, 500–513.

Hladik, Karen J. (1985), *International Joint Ventures*, Lexington, MA: Lexington Books.

Homans, George C. (1958), "Social Behavior as Exchange," *American Journal of Sociology*, 52, 597–606.

Houston, M. J. and S. Sudman (1975), "A Methodological Assessment of the Use of Key Informants," *Social Science Research*, 4, 151–164.

Huber, G. P. and D. J. Power (1985), "Retrospective Reports of Strategic Level Managers: Guidelines for Increasing Their Accuracy," *Strategic Management Journal*, 6, 171–180.

Ito, K. (1970), "On the Effect of Heteroscedasticity and Nonnormality Upon Some Multivariate Test Procedures," in *Multivariate Analysis*, P. R. Krishnaiah (Ed.), New York: Academic Press.

John, George (1984), "An Empirical Investigation of Some Antecedents of Opportunism in a Marketing Channel," *Journal of Marketing Research*, 21, 278–289.

Kanuk, L. and C. Berenson (1975), "Mail Surveys and Response Rates," *Journal of Marketing Research*, 12, 440–453.

Kluckhohn, C. and A. L. Kroeberg (1952), *Culture: A Critical Review of Concepts and Definitions*, New York: Vintage Books.

Kogut, Bruce (1989), "The Stability of Joint Ventures: Reciprocity and Competitive Rivalry," *Journal of Industrial Economics*, 38, 183–198.

Kono, T. (1984), *Strategy and Structure of Japanese Enterprises*, London: The Macmillan Press.

Kres, Heinz (1983), *Statistical Tables for Multivariate Analysis*, New York: Springer-Verlag New York, Inc.

Lewis, Jordan D. (1990), *Partnerships for Profit: Structuring and Managing Strategic Alliances*, New York: Free Press.

Luce, R. Duncan and Howard Raiffa (1957), *Games and Decisions*, New York: John Wiley & Sons.

Mansfield, J. (1990), *Beyond Self-Interest*, Chicago: University of Chicago Press.

Mulford, Charles L. (1984), *Interorganizational Relations*, New York: Human Sciences Press.

Nielsen, Richard P. (1988), "Cooperative Strategy," *Strategic Management Journal*, 9, 475–492.

Nunnally, J. (1978), *Psychometric Theory*, New York: McGraw-Hill.

Ohmae, Kenichi (1989), "The Global Logic of Strategic Alliances," *Harvard Business Review* (March-April), 143–154.

Oliver, Christine (1990), "Determinants of Interorganizational Relationships: Integration and Future Directions," *Academy of Management Review*, 15, 241–265.

Olson, C. L. (1976), "On Choosing a Test Statistic in Multivariate Analysis," *Psychological Bulletin*, 83, 579–586.

Oye, Kenneth A. (Ed.) (1986), *Cooperation under Anarchy*, Princeton, NJ: Princeton University Press.

Parkhe, Arvind (1989), "Interfirm Strategic Alliances: Empirical Test of a Game-Theoretic Model," unpublished Ph.D. dissertation, Temple University.

_____ (1991a), "Interfirm Diversity, Organizational Learning, and Longevity in Global Strategic Alliances," *Journal of International Business Studies*, 22, 579–601.

Parkhe, Arvind (1991b), "The Case Study Method in International Joint Ventures Research: A Critical Assessment and an Application," paper presented at the Academy of International Business Meeting, Miami, October 17–20.

Perlmutter, H. V. and D. A. Heenan (1986), "Cooperate to Compete Globally," *Harvard Business Review*, (March-April), 136–152.

Phillips, L. W. (1981), "Assessing Measurement Error in Key Informant Reports," *Journal of Marketing Research*, 28, 395–415.

Polanyi, Karl (1957), *Trade and Market in the Early Empires*, Glencoe, IL: Free Press.

Porter, Michael E. and Mark B. Fuller (1986), "Coalitions and Global Strategy," in M. E. Porter (Ed.), *Competition in Global Industries*, Boston: Harvard Business School Press.

Practicing Law Institute (1986), *Corporate Partnering: Advantages for Emerging and Established Companies*. New York: Practicing Law Institute.

Provan, Keith G. and Steven J. Skinner (1989), "Interorganizational Dependence and Control Predictors of Opportunism in Dealer-Supplier Relations," *Academy of Management Journal*, 32, 202–212.

Rapoport, Anatol (1988), "Editorial Comments," *Journal of Conflict Resolution*, 32, 2, 399–401.

Reich, Robert B. and E. D. Mankin (1986), "Joint Ventures with Japan Give Away Our Future," *Harvard Business Review* (March-April), 78–86.

Schelling, Thomas C. (1963), *The Strategy of Conflict*, Cambridge, MA: Harvard University Press.

Schwenk, Charles (1985), "The Use of Participant Recollection in the Modeling of Organizational Decision Processes," *Academy of Management Review*, 10, 496–503.

Shubik, Martin (1975), *Games for Society, Business and War: Towards a Theory of Gaming*, New York: Elsivier.

Smith, Anne and Howard E. Aldrich (1991), "The Role of Trust in the Transaction Cost Economics Framework," paper presented at the Academy of Management Meeting, Miami.

Snidal, Duncan (1986), "The Game Theory of International Politics," in K. A. Oye (Ed.), *Cooperation under Anarchy*, Princeton, NJ: Princeton University Press, 25–57.

SPSS Inc. (1988), *SPSS-X User's Guide*, Chicago: SPSS Inc.

Stevens, J. P. (1979), "Comments on Olson: Choosing a Test Statistic in Multivariate Analysis," *Psychological Bulletin*, 86, 355–360.

Sullivan, J. and R. B. Peterson (1982), "Factors Associated with Trust in Japanese-American Joint Ventures," *Management International Review*, 22, 30–40.

Teece, David (1986), "Profiting from Technological Innovation," *Research Policy*, 15, 285–305.

Terpstra, Vern and Kenneth David (1990), *The Cultural Environment of International Business*, Cincinnati: Southwestern Publishing Co.

Thorelli, Hans (1986), "Networks: Between Markets and Hierarchies," *Strategic Management Journal*, 7, 37–51.

Venkatraman, N. and V. Ramanujam (1986), "Measurement of Business Performance in Strategy Research: A Comparison of Approaches," *Academy of Management Review*, 11, 801–814.

Whetten, David A. (1981), "Interorganizational Relations: A Review of the Field," *Journal of Higher Education*, 52, 1–28.

Williamson, Oliver E. (1983), "Credible Commitments: Using Hostages to Support Exchange," *American Economic Review*, 73, 519–540.

———— (1985), *The Economic Institutions of Capitalism*, New York: Free Press.

Wysocki, Bernard (1990), "Cross-Border Alliances Become Favorite Way to Crack New Markets," *Wall-Street Journal* (March 26), A1, A12.

[23]

How to control a joint venture even as a minority partner

Jean-Louis Schaan

> We do not enter joint ventures unless there is no other way of taking advantage of a business opportunity. We like to have full control over our operations. We always have majority ownership.
>
> Vice President, large Electronics firm

> Joint ventures? Why? Our policy is that if an investment is worth making to get 50% of the profits, it is worth making to get 100%. In addition we find that sharing in the control of the venture is too messy and not worth the hassle.
>
> President, Consumer Products firm

The two quotes above reflect a widely shared concern about joint ventures, namely the exercise of control by the parents. However, as understandable as this concern is, it fails to take account of means available to control joint ventures despite the difficulties of shared control, indeed even from the perspective of a minority shareholder. If sufficient care is taken to focus objectives and expectations that are critical to the partners' respective criteria of joint venture performance, control measures can be installed that facilitate each partner's achievement of success. And this is possible without skewing matters in the interest of one parent at the expense of another.

In some situations joint ventures are the only possible form of organisation available. But those who reject joint ventures also reject these possibilities. This is what the author seeks to avoid. These organisations need a lot of attention from their parents. Many underestimate this and pay a price. The high failure rate among joint ventures certainly confirms that managers are founded in their scepticism about this type of organisational form. Independent studies show that 70 per cent of joint ventures fail to meet their

Author's note: I would like to acknowledge the editorial and technical consultation provided by William B. Bindman, C.M.C., who brought many years of relevant managerial experience to bear. I also thank J. Peter Killing for his insightful comments and the School of Business Administration, University of Western Ontario, for funding the study that led to this paper.

parents' expectations or are disbanded (*Business Week*, 21 July 1986). My prediction is that the proportion of joint venture failures will remain high because of inherent difficulties in this area of activity.

Joint ventures have all the control problems wholly-owned subsidiaries have plus those that stem from joint ownership. This article, while not excluding the former, places emphasis on the latter. Joint ownership is both the source of opportunities and difficulties peculiar to joint ventures. On the one hand it provides access to the skills and resources of two or more parents instead of just one, therefore significantly enhancing their potential to succeed. On the other hand, if the partners' objectives and philosophies are not in harmony, there may be harmful conflict.

Joint ventures occur because two or more parties see a mutual benefit in co-operating not otherwise available. The benefits come as a result of the need that each has for the other. Significantly, since both (all) partners are essential to success, it follows that even the minority shareholders are in a position to exert much influence upon the operations and upon the control of the enterprise. In effect, in joint ventures, minority shareholders can exert a degree of control quite disproportionate to their shareholdings.

The paper is based on the experience of 23 joint ventures operating mainly in North America, Mexico and Europe. The author has interviewed 48 senior executives at both the joint venture and the parent company levels. At the time of the interviews, 13 per cent of the joint ventures had been terminated, 35 per cent were unsuccessful in the eyes of at least one parent, and only 52 per cent were successful. From a comparison of the successful and unsuccessful cases, specific recommendations to enhance the likelihood of successful control are proposed.

The Joint Venture Management Dilemma

In order to ensure the success of a joint venture, managers seek to strike a subtle balance between the desire and need to control the venture on the one hand, and the need to maintain harmonious relations with the partner(s) on the other hand. The inability to manage such balance is a major reason for failure germane and peculiar to joint ventures.

Joint ventures can be deemed successful in spite of poor financial performance, and conversely, they can be considered unsuccessful in spite of good financial performance. A parent may tend to attach relatively little importance to the joint venture's financial performance if it obtains profits through transfer prices for components, fees for management or other services, royalties for the transfer of technology or when it buys and distributes the joint venture's production. On the other hand, profitable joint ventures may be terminated because the chemistry between parents dissolves or because one parent's interests or priorities have changed. Hence the need to consider the terms of the joint venture management dilemma.

Ineffective parental control. Although managers are concerned about control, they are not always prepared to spend the time and effort required to exercising it, with very harmful results. An executive from a major US chemical company explained that not paying enough attention to its Spanish joint venture eventually led to its collapse. The same scenario applied to the problems encountered by Warner Amex Cable Communications Inc., a joint venture where AmEx ended up selling its stake to partner Warner (*Business Week*, 21 July 1986).

A combination of causes conspire to defeat the effectiveness of joint venture control as exercised by parent companies. The most significant of these are as follows:

First, managers often have no clear understanding of what they expect from the joint venture and therefore do not focus their control needs properly. In 60 per cent of the joint ventures studied there was no attempt by managers in the parent companies to stipulate expectations or mutually acceptable objectives. Not surprisingly, these managers had problems deciding how to measure success or what to control.

In the absence of a comprehensive statement of control needs, developed at the outset, parent company executives tend to dabble at control. Initially, they involve themselves in those matters which interest them and not in others, even though these may be deserving of attention. These managers go through a period of trial and error learning how to control the joint venture which can be costly in terms of bringing balanced control coverage to all critical needs.

Second, parent company managers frequently provide too little time for the joint venture. Their priorities may lie elsewhere or they may simply underestimate the venture's requirements of their time. As a result, they tend to respond to problems *ad hoc*, to firefight without proper analysis and understanding, with obvious consequences. This is commonplace among heavily burdened parent company executives (in one case, a VP International had 17 operations reporting directly to him).

Third, there is often a failure to adapt control practices as circumstances change. Business conditions are never static. As circumstances change, so should priorities in both parent companies and the joint venture. If the latter does not adapt, it may decrease in relative importance to one or another parent company. As the joint venture adapts, so should the focus of its control system.

The significance of proper control should not be underestimated. Among companies the author has studied and from which the article is derived, failing ventures have been turned around by rectifying inadequate control systems so that parent company executives could more easily attend to critical operational issues. Moreover, thoughtfully organised control systems make a difference because who controls what makes a difference. There is evidence that where one parent is dominant in managing the joint venture, the results are better than when parents share the control task equally (J. P. Killing, HBR May-June 1982, p. 121).

Failure to develop a good working relationship. Divorces can happen as a result of incompatibility in personalities. This is less of a problem in growing and profitable joint ventures because managers from the parent companies will typically meet in a positive atmosphere where the most important item on the agenda could be 'how much dividend should we pay this year?' This is not much of a challenge to the strength of the relationship between partners.

A better test of relationships occurs when the joint venture encounters and overcomes rough times. Often, however, the parents have not established working relationships based on trust. When joint venture difficulties arise, this triggers a power struggle between the parents which will compound the problems. In such circumstances, parents expend energy in fighting each other instead of solving problems.

Mechanisms for Control

As suggested earlier, the effective control of joint ventures relies importantly upon an articulation at the outset of the objectives and expectations of the partners to the venture. Presuming that such articulation is adequate, covering the joint venture's economic performance, the parents' respective contributions to the venture, and any important goals which motivated the creation of the venture, then a number of mechanisms can be used to enable all interested parties to monitor developments and shape decisions affecting the joint venture.

Board Meetings
This seems too elementary to deserve mention. Yet this device too often escapes proper attention and use. The frequency of meetings and the minimal required agenda coverage are subjects that may not be agreed upon by the partners in the first instance. If not, there will be a tendency to

overlook this most important opportunity to keep significant matters under appropriate review. As well, this discipline provides for keeping all partners adequately informed, especially on those subjects where executive authority has been delegated to one of the partners but the others have an interest and a right to hear what is happening. Especially at the outset, poor communications may impair confidence and well planned board meetings provide effective protection.

In the absence of safeguards built into the joint venture contract to protect the interests of the minority shareholder, majority ownership ultimately confers control over issues covered by the board of directors. It is a useful device to avoid deadlocks. It provides for a final judge to resolve situations where the parents cannot reach a compromise through negotiations and therefore enables the joint venture to continue operating without potentially harmful consequences.

However, a majority parent cannot consistently overrule, or refuse to compromise with its partner without building significant ill-will and risking the long-term survival of the relationship. Further, minority parents can prevent their majority partner from implementing unilaterally decisions that they do not agree with by negotiating the inclusion, in the joint venture contract, of a veto right over decisions important to their interests. Among the decisions that minority partners want to be able to veto are: dividend policy, exports, approval of major projects, financing of expansion, transfer pricing, choice of suppliers, divestments, selection of key executives, etc.

Finally, control at the board level is not simply a matter of votes. Control also results from the ability to influence other board members on important issues. This is, to a large extent a matter of competence and negotiating skill. As a result, minority partners have an opportunity to influence the management of the joint venture if they are careful to appoint as their board representatives people with a strong grasp over the joint venture's operational strategic circumstances, good bargaining skills and empathy for the partner's culture.

Provision of Parent Company Services
Joint ventures are often subjected to special contractual constraints stipulating such matters as which partners bear responsibility for which decisions, the transfer of technology, sales to and from the venture, the provision of staff services and the like. Indeed, the development of such agreements constitutes an articulation of goals and expectations as mentioned earlier. It follows that the preparation of such agreements should be

Vol. 14 No. 1 Autumn 1988/9

extended, as an important control mechanism, to the definition of reporting responsibilities associated with appropriate clauses in the agreement.

In order to increase the likelihood that specific tasks in the joint venture be performed in conformity with their expectations, parent companies offer staff services and training, sometimes at no cost to the joint venture. Such services can be provided irrespective of ownership positions. As a result, increased control can accrue to parent companies in three ways: (i) increased predictability of behaviour in the joint venture because its managers will more likely do things using the guidelines and methodologies they have been taught; (ii) increased loyalty from the joint venture employees who identify more with the parent and have assimilated the parent's ethos; and (iii) greater awareness and sensitivity on the part of the parent to conditions within the joint venture because of enhanced dialogue with the venture employees.

Key Personnel Appointments

Control requires knowledge of events and circumstances. Such knowledge is most readily available to the venture's parents if key personnel running the operation, or critical functions such as marketing or R&D, are supplied by those parents, or are otherwise in a position to monitor the venture at close quarters. Thus, the appointment of key personnel is a control mechanism for parents especially if they are in a minority position or geographically remote. This, however, can raise loyalty questions and needs careful handling. A policy of open communications to all parents is recommended.

Organisational and Structural Context

Managers in parent companies can exercise control by shaping the context in which decisions are made through formal and informal means. The following mechanisms provide majority and minority partners alike with opportunities for increasing their sphere of influence:

- *Capital budgeting and resource allocation.* Managers can influence the kinds of projects that a joint venture is going to undertake by participating in the formulation of the Capital Appropriation Requests which set the criteria and conditions for approval. Providing feedback on those requests can prove an effective device to educate the joint venture managers about a parent's expectations and priorities.
- *Policies and procedures.* As in any other business, the behaviour of executives in a joint venture is influenced by the design of business plans and reporting requirements as devised by the owners. When these matters

are clearly set out and the parents' demand for prompt and accurate reporting is made manifest, a response from the management of the venture is likely to follow.

Informal Mechanisms

Finally, a proper regimen of control should not rely exclusively upon formal mechanisms such as board meetings, written reports and briefing sessions. It is important that the recipients of reports or formal exchanges be in a position of sufficient knowledge of operations and of sufficient acquaintance with joint venture personnel that they can intelligently interpret and evaluate the information and signals being received. This can be facilitated by visits to the joint venture and some social contact with its people. Properly handled, there need be no suggestion of 'intrusiveness'. The president of a large chemical corporation found that a major challenge to him when his firm was a minority partner was to obtain sufficient information to avoid asking 'dumb' questions and being perceived as interfering.

Integrating the Parent Organisations

To be effective, the foregoing control mechanisms need integration to the parent organisations. This means that parents must assign responsibility for the joint venture reporting and control mechanisms to one executive and that this party is given adequate time and resources to perform the job properly. If the control mechanisms are well conceived, if the organisation for control is appropriate both in the parental and joint venture locations, and there is reasonable flexibility in the exercise of control, the chances of success are significantly enhanced.

This 'reasonable flexibility' in the exercise of control has one feature worthy of mention. It is the gradual relaxation of control after operations are established. At the outset of operations, all parties should be relatively close to events from day to day. However, as experience is gained, as relationships become established and as the general financial health of the venture discloses itself, a degree of relaxation can occur with safety. An important effect of the relaxation of control is to signal confidence by the parents in each other and in the joint venture management. This is stimulating all around.

Naturally, such an approach should not be overdone. The author knows of cases where the parental involvement was inadequate, being limited to occasional board meetings. Then, the venture got into severe trouble and the arm's length relationship had to stop, to be followed by close intervention. The attempt to intervene will be resisted, and much trouble results if one

Vol. 14 No. 1 Autumn 1988 / 11

partner has demonstrated its inability to manage the joint venture successfully on its own.

The trick is to clarify the expectations of all parties, put good people in
place, get out of the way and let them operate but keep a handle on what
they are doing at all times.

Measures to Enhance the Likelihood of Successful Control

In the light of the foregoing potential problems inherent to the management
of any joint venture, a series of measures are recommended to enhance the
likelihood of successful control, even in a minority situation. These cover:

- Policies governing parental intervention
- Being diplomatic
- Governance of the manager
- Formal evaluations
- Arrangements for resolving disagreements.

Each of these is discussed next.

Policies Governing Parental Intervention

The intervention of the parent companies in a joint venture's affairs is a
particularly sensitive area because of the risk that one parent may perceive
that the other is trying to take undue advantage of the joint venture. There is
a clear distinction between useful contribution, which has positive results,
and interference.

A strategy consciously followed by some firms is to select joint venture
partners with no expertise in the joint venture's business with the
expectation that such partners will play a passive role in the joint venture
management. This is risky. When the passive partner starts questioning the
managing partner's judgements or decisions because it does not understand
the rationale behind them, or even worse, when it decides that it can make
those decisions better, managing the joint venture can quickly degenerate.

In joint ventures where the parents contribute complementary skills or
resources, it is sensible to allow each parent to control the area it is best
qualified in. A joint venture in the hotel industry was turned around after
two years of poor performance when the board of directors agreed to
formally allocate marketing decisions to the foreign partner which already
was in the joint venture's line of business, and financial and political
decisions to the local partner – one of the country's largest banks. Both
parents had control but over different areas. Two parents can share in the

mangement of a joint venture when they control different sets of activities or decisions that are important to the achievement of their own expectations, and both perform well.

A parent company should control areas in which it has a distinctive expertise and stay away from areas in which it does not contribute skills necessary to the joint venture. In some cases this allocation of responsibility is decided during the planning phase mentioned earlier. However, in most cases it is done *de facto*, as the parents discover over time where they can contribute best to the joint venture, and as they gain the confidence of their partner.

Being Diplomatic

Because a joint venture involves at least two partners with different personalities and expectations, one partner is rarely able to impose its wishes upon the others continuously. As a result, it must exercise influence subtly and indirectly, finding ways of shaping people's behaviours and decisions through inducement, persuasion and negotiations, rather than through command.

The following example (a Mexican petrochemical joint venture) illustrates the subtleties involved:

> Managers in a US company in a joint venture with a Mexican partner felt a strong conviction that the venture's basic strategy should be altered and, indeed, kept under continual control. This company faced the problem of how to do this given the Mexicans' resistance to interference from the US parent, both at the Mexican partner level and at the joint venture management level.
>
> The US partner resolved the foregoing dilemma by participation in the venture's planning and control processes. In this involvement, the American participation led to the development of plans and reports by venture managers not previously in use. In turn, this led to discussions and decisions beneficial to all parties and along the lines originally believed necessary by the Americans, and all this in good blood (in fact a divestiture occurred of a division hitherto a favourite of the joint venture general manager).

In this example, the foreign parent successfully influenced strategic decisions by using control mechanisms and being diplomatic. The process was incremental in nature; it involved selling the idea of the strategy papers, building the local parent's awareness of problem areas, creating commitment, building a coalition and negotiating with the joint venture general manager.

Joint ventures are less flexible than wholly-owned subsidiaries. Indeed, parent companies have to be prepared to make tradeoffs and compromises. It is imperative that managers take into consideration their partner's expectations, attitudes, norms and beliefs. Adequate focus should be placed on those issues upon selecting an appropriate partner. Failure to assess the degree of compatibility with such matters as the partner's interests, expectations, integrity, financial strength and competitive situation, leads to bad marriages.

Pursuing the marriage analogy, for a joint venture to succeed in the long term, mutual trust and respect are essential. Once destroyed trust is very hard to rebuild. A key rule in joint ventures is avoid surprises. Control is easiest and most effective if a good working relationship prevails. This does not happen by chance. Managers need to work at it and learn how to co-operate.

Managers in some parent organisations make it a priority to develop a working relationship with their partner. When going to attend the board meeting of a foreign joint venture, a senior Vice President at a major Aluminium company spends 50 per cent of his time with the partner's representatives discussing business matters, and 50 per cent visiting an archeological site, a museum or exhibit, or going fishing.

Governance of the Manager

Who will run the joint venture? In addition to general management skills, the managers of joint ventures need particular skills at interfacing with two parents, often of different nationalities or of different corporate cultures, at facilitating communications and conflict resolution, and at finding their way through the parent organisations to tap the skills, resources or support they need to get their job done. This is not child's play.

In particular, junior managers often lack the requisite skills. As some firms have found, using a joint venture as a training ground for junior managers can prove costly if appropriate safeguards are not provided. Besides his inexperience, a junior general manager can run into difficulties if, due to his immaturity, he does not carry enough weight with the executives to whom he reports in the parent companies and therefore lacks the authority required to get things done.

The joint venture general manager needs adequate support from both parents. They, in turn, need particular performance from their manager. At the outset, the three parties should get the 'drill' straight.

A common belief is that the ability to appoint a 'loyal' joint venture general manager is a sure way for a parent to secure control of the joint venture. As most joint venture general managers will testify, this is not always the case. The ability to appoint the joint venture general manager increases the chances that the parents' interests will be observed, but it is no guarantee that the joint venture general manager will always accommodate that parent's preferences.

In the words of a joint venture general manager: 'I cannot give preference to one partner, otherwise the other rebels'. Life for the joint venture general manager can be made impossible by the partner who feels discriminated against. In addition, in most joint ventures where one parent assigns the joint venture general manager, the other parent has a veto power and can force the resignation of the joint venture general manager.

It may be strategically important for the success of the joint venture that the parents do not interfere with its management unduly, or that one parent interfere more than another. In such circumstances, parents should appoint someone with status and credibility, who is respected by all. A senior executive from a large US Telecommunications firm was chosen as the first general manager of a joint venture with a large European firm operating in the same industry in order to prevent a struggle over joint venture control from emerging between two powerful parents. Further, his credibility enabled him to make decisions quickly and to gain the support he needed from both parents.

In general, the joint venture general manager's scope of freedom can be constrained indirectly through the resource allocation process (levels of capital expenditures allowed, capital appropriation request approval process . . .), and directly through face-to-face meetings. Control can also be exercised through determining the general manager's bonus and promotions. Some parents are at pains to reinforce the joint venture general manager's allegiance by keeping him on the parent's payroll, not the joint venture's, by tying his bonus to the parent's results, not just the joint venture's, by controlling his future promotions, or by requiring him to submit project proposals to his parent before they are presented to the partner or to the joint venture's board. The practice of obtaining one parent's approval before presenting project proposals was referred to as the 'no-objection' system by an executive in one organisation and the 'filter' system by a president in another. More normally, control is exercised through the feedback on specific decisions or reports, and through persuasion.

Formal Evaluations

A formal evaluation is a management audit or operational review. The extent of these can vary with circumstances but, for purposes of joint

Vol. 14 No. 1 Autumn 1988 / 15

ventures, might be a review to determine the degree to which parents' expectations are being met, the nature and extent of important problems inhibiting performance, and the adequacy of control measures in use. Such evaluations should be conducted by independent outside parties, or such parties in collaboration with parental and joint venture personnel.

The author has not found widespread use of formal evaluations. Two exceptions occurred in the case of two joint ventures which had been operating unsuccessfully for some years, and in which the parents were out of touch.

It would seem useful, especially at the early stages of a joint venture, to make use of formal evaluations. This could greatly accelerate new-found partners' acquaintance-building and more rapidly detect operational areas in need of attention at a time when the operation is relatively untested and vulnerable to difficulties. The evaluations could also bring a focus upon parental goals or expectations in need of amendment.

Resolution of Disagreements

No matter how much planning goes into setting up a joint venture, differences can arise. Typical sources of conflict in joint ventures include: dividends, joint venture's exports, financing of expansion (debt or equity), transfer pricing, choice of suppliers, growth vs profitability, investment and divestment decisions, role of each partner in the management of the joint venture or criteria of good management. It may be relatively easy to plan for the resolution of a conflict over how much dividend to pay in a given year. It is more difficult to define a mutually acceptable standard of managerial or operational performance.

To avoid stalling the joint venture's operations, parents should agree that one or the other partner should have final authority over well defined areas in the event of disagreement. Such a convention should be used in extreme situations only so as not to jeopardize the relationship between the partners. Both partners should be prepared to lose on some issues and be flexible.

Differences between parents may be such that the only solutions are to dissolve the joint venture or to let one partner out by bringing a new investor or by selling to the other partner. When buyouts are considered, one very effective clause is to stipulate that once a partner offers to buy out another, should the other refuse the offer, he is required to buy out the offering partner at the same price. As a result, the likelihood of unreasonable offers is greatly diminished.

Conclusion

Clearly, the successful management of joint ventures is a challenge to the resolve and ingenuity of all parties involved. The fact of shared ownership complicates management and control significantly as compared with more conventional forms of ownership, and confers no special advantages not enjoyed by the latter.

The growth and internationalisation of business tends to increase the incidence of joint ventures, thus increasing the incidence of complex cultural and logistical problems which influence success. At the outset of this article, I stated that minority partners in joint ventures can exert control disproportionate to their share in the ownership of the business. It should now be clear to the reader that this is so provided the minority partner contributes an equal or greater share of the intellectual effort to design the management and control practices of the venture, plus an equal or greater participation in the exercise of that control. This is as relevant to the situation of companies expanding abroad as minority investors as it is to that of local minority investors in operations financed from abroad.

However, there is positively no suggestion that the interests of minority shareholders should be served at the expense of those of other shareholders. Quite the contrary, in joint ventures the interests of one partner are best served when those of everyone else are also. The point is that where the market opportunities can best be exploited via the joint venture form of organisation, a particular kind of management and control is essential to success. If this is done, all partners will be gratified. Both minority and majority partners will secure an outcome not otherwise attainable.

[24]

ROLE CONFLICT AND ROLE AMBIGUITY
OF CHIEF EXECUTIVE OFFICERS
IN INTERNATIONAL JOINT VENTURES

Oded Shenkar*
Tel Aviv University and University of Hawaii-Manoa

Yoram Zeira**
Tel Aviv University

Abstract. This study examines the organizational and personal correlates of role conflict and role ambiguity of chief executive officers heading international joint ventures. Role conflict was found to be lower when the number of parent firms was higher and when the CEO had spent more years with the organization. Role ambiguity was found to be lower when the CEO had more years of education, when the Power Distance and Masculinity/Femininity gap between parents were lower, and when the Individualism/ Collectivism and Uncertainty Avoidance gaps were higher. The implications of these findings for role theory and international management are discussed.

Despite the growing body of knowledge on role conflict and role ambiguity in different types of uninational organizations, little is known of the processes leading to such situations in multinational enterprises. It has been frequently suggested that the existing body of knowledge is unsuitable for international operations [Adler 1983; Robock and Simmonds 1983]; hence, the examination of role conflict and role ambiguity theories in a multinational context can be fruitful for at least two reasons: First, it may serve to extend the scope and relevance of role theory beyond the uninational corporation. Second, such examination is likely to increase the theoretical depth of international

---

*Oded Shenkar is with the Faculty of Management, Tel Aviv University, Ramat Aviv, Tel Aviv 69978, Israel; and the College of Business at the University of Hawaii-Manoa, Honolulu, Hawaii 96822. His main research interests are in comparative and international management. His edited book, *Management in China*, was published by M.E. Sharpe in 1991. Requests for reprints may be addressed to him at either address.

**Yoram Zeira is a member of the Faculty of Management at Tel Aviv University. His main research interest is in international human resource management, a field in which he has widely published and consulted.

The authors acknowledge the assistance of Edna Shamir-Dar in the collection of data, and helpful comments and suggestions made by Reginald Worthley and anonymous reviewers.

Received: November 1990; Revised: May & July 1991; Accepted: August 1991.

management studies, and therefore our knowledge of an increasingly popular form of organizations. A case in point are international joint ventures (IJVs), which have recently become the fastest growing, most popular type of international direct investment [Janger 1980; OECD 1981; Walmsley 1982; Greene 1984; Hladik 1985; Harrigan 1986].

This article focuses on role conflict and role ambiguity of Chief Executive Officers (CEOs) in IJVs. Since different scholars define IJVs in different ways, and since there is no unanimity in these definitions, we decided to define an IJV, for the purpose of our research, as "a separate legal organizational entity representing the partial holdings of two or more parent firms, in which the headquarters of at least one parent firm is located outside the country of operation of the joint venture. This entity is subject to the joint control of its parent firms, each of which is economically and legally independent of the other" [Shenkar and Zeira 1987]. As in other types of international operations, IJVs bring together individuals who differ in national origin, cultural values and social norms, with the attendant political, economic and legal system differences. In the IJV's context, these differences take, however, a unique form. In many cases, incongruence of national interests is what produced the IJV in the first place, obliging parent firms to accept joint ownership despite their preference for complete control in the form of wholly owned subsidiaries [Bivens and Lovell 1966]. The resulting suspicion towards the objectives of the other parent firm(s) [Young and Bradford 1977] adds to the tension between the parties.

Furthermore, whereas in wholly owned subsidiaries of multinational corporations (MNCs) there is only one parent firm and usually only two major employee groups (parent country nationals and host country nationals), IJVs have at least two parents and may have a great variety of employee groups. Each of the parent companies has its unique goals, structure, and operation mode. By definition, at least two of the parent firms are anchored in different national and cultural environments. In addition, each employee group (parent country or host country expatriates, parent country or host country transferees, host country nationals, or third country nationals) has its own characteristics which derive from its nationality, recruiting entity, place of work, position in the IJV hierarchy, legal rights and promotion possibilities [Shenkar and Zeira 1990].

In the midst of this complex system stands the CEO, who is responsible for the daily operation of the IJV. This person faces the simultaneous demands of the different policy makers in each parent company and of the various employee groups in the enterprise, as well as the internal and external stakeholders in the host country and other countries in which the IJV conducts business; and must translate their different, ambiguous or conflicting expectations into workable strategies. As role theory predicts, such office holders are likely to face considerable role conflicts and role ambiguities [Rizzo, House and Lirtzman 1970; Katz and Kahn 1978].

This paper examines the role conflict and role ambiguity faced by CEOs of IJVs. It sets to identify organizational and personal factors that influence the role conflict and role ambiguity of these executives, and to propose implications for role theory on that basis. To the best of our knowledge, this study represents the first attempt to examine role theory in the context of IJVs and possibly in a multinational context in general. The study may also be unique in its choice of the CEO as the focal person in the role analysis; most studies on role conflict and ambiguity examine rank-and-file employees or middle managers [Fisher and Gitelson 1983; Jackson and Schuler 1985].

ROLE CONFLICT AND ROLE AMBIGUITY IN THE CONTEXT OF INTERNATIONAL JOINT VENTURES

Katz and Kahn [1978, p. 197] state that "the process of organizational role-taking is simplest when a role consists of only one activity, is located in a single subsystem of the organization, and relates to a role-set all of whose members are in the same organizational subsystem." None of these conditions is met in the case of IJVs. Role conflict can be defined as a situation in which the priorities of one system conflict with the priorities of the other systems. The CEOs of IJVs, with their inherent system multiplicity, are prone to such conflicts. As Schaan and Beamish [1988, p. 279] note, the task of general managers in IJVs is more complicated than that of their counterparts in wholly owned subsidiaries because "with essentially two bosses and two sets of expectations, they must simultaneously accommodate the interests of two partners" (and sometimes more).

The CEOs of IJVs are also likely to experience role ambiguity because they lack sufficient information regarding the specific expectations of the different policy-makers in each parent firm [Schaan and Beamish 1988], the different expectations of the different employee groups in the ventures, as well as the different expectations of the host country organizations with which they must interact.

Role theory distinguishes between four principal types of role conflict: Intrasender conflict, i.e., incompatible demands made by a single member of the role set; interrole conflict, i.e., incompatible pressures stemming from membership in multiple groups; intersender conflict, i.e., opposing pressures from different role senders; and person role conflict, i.e., a conflict between the focal person's values and the prescribed role behavior. Our assumption is that the unique structure of IJVs as multipartite, multicultural organizations would give rise to intersender conflict in particular, because of conflicting sent expectations of their parent firms.

Role theory does not emphasize as much different types of role ambiguity. However, it has been proposed that role ambiguity is generated by either of several conditions: A lack of required information, a lack of communication of existing information, or the receipt of contradictory messages from different role senders [Kahn, Wolfe, Quinn, Snoek and Rosenthal 1964].

Research findings reveal that the consequences of role conflict and role ambiguity may be numerous, among them: stress, hostility, dissatisfaction, low productivity, difficulties in decisionmaking, and distortion of reality [Cohen 1959; Kahn et al. 1964; Katz and Kahn 1978; Merton 1957; Rizzo et al. 1970; Seeman 1953]. While such effects are likely to adversely influence the effectiveness of any organization, they are especially threatening to the operation of multipartite, multicultural organizations like IJVs, and may be a contributive factor to the high rate of failure of IJVs [Franko 1971; Holton 1981; Sullivan and Peterson 1982; Vaupel and Curhan 1969]. Following Katz and Kahn [1978], we assume that the level of role conflict and role ambiguity of the CEOs of IJVs will vary according to organizational and personal variables (see also Rogers and Molnar [1976]; Van Sell, Brief and Schuler [1981]).

Organizational Factors

The organizational factors suggested here follow the major elements in role theory: The number of role senders (#1), the diversity of role senders (#2, #3 & #7), the frequency of sent roles (#4), and the consistency of sent roles (#5 & #6).

The Number of Parent Firms. Role theory suggests that the higher the number of role senders, the higher the potential for intersender role conflict. Since each additional parent represents another source of a set of sent roles (from marketing, finance, production, R&D, personnel, quality control or other divisions in the parent firms), our first hypothesis is that:

Hypothesis #1A: The larger the number of parent firms, the higher the role conflict of the CEO.

A greater number of parent firms is also likely to increase the probability of receiving messages from the different role senders perceived by the focal person to be obscure, vague or indefinite. Thus, the second hypothesis suggests that

Hypothesis #1B: The larger the number of parent firms, the higher the role ambiguity of the CEO.

Ownership. Different ownership structures were found to be problematic for the management of IJVs, particularly in ventures with both state-owned and privately-owned parents. State-owned parents in such IJVs were frequently suspected by the private parent of introducing political considerations into the venture's management [Bivens and Lovell 1966; Daniels, Krug and Nigh 1986]. IJVs involving a state-owned parent(s) were described as having complex decisionmaking processes and severe internal conflicts. U.S. managers judged IJVs with a state-owned parent firm as the least preferable mode of foreign direct investment [Raveed and Renforth 1983]. In role theory terms, parents with diverse ownership structures are likely to submit to the IJV's CEO incompatible requests that are inherent in the beliefs, procedures and policies embedded in each parent's ownership structure. The hypothesis is therefore that

> Hypothesis #2A: The role conflict of CEOs of IJVs whose parents have similar ownership structure will be lower than for CEOs of IJVs whose parents have different ownership structures.

Diverse ownership is also hypothesized to be correlated with higher role ambiguity for the venture's CEO, since it may cause parent firms to refrain from sending information, to block communication of existing information or to send equivocal messages in order to conceal their latent intentions. Thus, the hypothesis is that

> Hypothesis #2B: The role ambiguity of CEOs of IJVs whose parents have similar ownership structure will be lower than that of CEOs of IJVs whose parents have different ownership structures.

Size. Studies on IJVs identified particular difficulties when parents differed significantly in their size [Roberts 1980; Walmsley 1982; Young and Bradford 1977]. In role theory terms, differences in size imply diverse norms and modes of operation and hence diverse expectations on the part of the role senders. For instance, large companies tend to be more formal in their operations (e.g., Blau [1970]; Glueck [1977]; Harari, Crawford and Rohde [1983]) and expect the IJV to operate in a similar manner; while smaller parents expect a more informal, "common sense" approach. This brings us to the next hypothesis, namely,

> Hypothesis #3A: The greater the difference in parents' size, the higher the role conflict of the venture's CEO.

The literature survey does not indicate that differences in size are likely to increase role ambiguity. This difference is not likely to affect the transfer of necessary information to the CEOs of the IJVs or the ability of the parent firms to send clear-cut messages. Our hypothesis, therefore, is that

> Hypothesis #3B: Differences in parents' size will produce, if any, only a minor effect on the role ambiguity of the venture's CEO.

Parents' Dominance. When parents are equally involved in the daily management of the IJV, decisionmaking in the venture becomes complex and cumbersome [Bivens and Lovell 1966; Harrigan 1984; Janger 1980; Killing 1980]. This may explain why Killing [1980] found that 86% of the ventures he studied were of the "dominant parent" rather than the "shared management" type (in the former type, one parent is responsible for daily operations; in the latter type, the parents share those responsibilities). In role theory terms, the CEOs of "dominant parent" ventures are less likely to receive a set of sent roles simultaneously from more than one source. The hypothesis is therefore, that

> Hypothesis #4A: The role conflict of the CEOs who manage IJVs of the "dominant parent" type will be lower than that of CEOs in "shared management" IJVs.

Having a dominant parent should reduce the likelihood of receiving mis-leading messages with several meanings, since most important messages would be coming from a single source. Also, because dominant parent ventures are based on trust among parents [Killing 1980], there is a lesser likelihood that the parents involved will withhold relevant information from the CEOs and make it impossible for them to make decisions. Thus, the hypothesis is that

> Hypothesis #4B: The role ambiguity of the CEOs who manage IJVs of the "dominant parent" type will be lower than that of CEOs in "shared management" IJVs.

Parents' Objectives. The literature mentions various objectives accounting for the entrance of parent companies into IJV agreements, among them: (1) reducing antitrust objection [Young and Bradford 1977]; (2) spreading the risks involved in starting new ventures [Berkman and Vernon 1979]; (3) entering new or unfamiliar markets; (4) getting vital raw materials; (5) gaining technical and scientific know-how; (6) mobilizing financial resources; (7) employing qualified, experienced staff; (8) achieving cooperation with competitors [Boyle 1968; Pfeffer and Nowak 1976]; (9) making use of laws and regulations devised to encourage investment in developing countries [Dobkin et al. 1986]; and (10) overcoming nationalistic feelings towards foreign ownership [Bivens and Lovell 1966; Friedman and Beguin 1971], feelings which are frequently translated into legal barriers prohibiting full foreign ownership [Janger 1980].

Inconsistency in the objectives of the host and foreign parents (and those of other stakeholders) is quite common in IJVs [Simiar 1983]. Sawyer [1980] suggests three types of problems surrounding parent objectives: (1) the existence of latent objectives, (2) unexpected consequences resulting from the set objectives, and (3) a conflict of objectives. Lack of agreement among parent firms about the desired objectives usually results in conflict-ing directives to the ventures' CEOs and was found to be a major factor in the failures of IJVs [Peterson and Shimada 1978]. In role theory terms, conflicting objectives are likely to give rise to incompatible requests from the parents directed at the venture's CEO. Thus, we hypothesize that

> Hypothesis #5A: The more similar the parents' objectives, the lesser the role conflict of the CEO.

To avoid conflict, parent firms may want to conceal the fact that they have contradictory goals. Hence, they will tend to avoid clear-cut messages in order to avoid open conflicts with their partners. Thus, we suggest that

> Hypothesis #5B: The more similar the parents' objectives, the lesser the role ambiguity of the CEOs in IJVs.

Contract Specificity. The literature on IJVs highlights the positive role of a detailed contract and documents of incorporation in reducing the level of conflict among the parents and the IJV (e.g., Dymsza [1979]; Killing [1982];

Kobayashi [1967]; Dobkin et al. [1986]). It is emphasized that the contract should specify the (a) responsibility domains of each parent, (b) mode of dispute settlement between parents, (c) selection methods of senior office holders, and (d) the objectives of the parents and of the IJV. Detailed contracts were found to be very effective means of preventing conflicts, confusion and misunderstandings, especially when new and non-routine problems had to be resolved[1] [Young and Bradford 1977; Dobkin et al. 1986]. In role theory terms, a detailed contract decreases the probability of receiving incompatible requests from parents because many of the potentially conflicting demands have already been settled during contract negotiations. We therefore hypothesize that

Hypothesis #6A: The more detailed the contract and documents of incorporation, the lesser the role conflict of the CEO.

A detailed contract implies that information which is required by the CEOs in making decisions is readily available to them. When the contract specifies domains of responsibility for each parent, messages are likely to come from one parent at a time, with each parent required to transmit clear-cut information pertaining to its exclusive domain. The probability of receiving obscure messages thus decreases, and hence we hypothesize that

Hypothesis #6B: The more detailed the contract and documents of incorporation, the lesser the role ambiguity of the CEO.

Cultural Distance. The "cultural distance" variable, namely the differences between the national cultures of the parent companies, has a particular importance in the present study, since it distinguishes IJVs from domestic joint ventures. Following Hofstede [1980], we used four dimensions of culture: Collectivism/Individualism (namely, the degree to which collective or individual values and interests are emphasized in a society); Uncertainty Avoidance (namely, the extent to which unstructured or unpredictable events are tolerated); Power Distance (namely, the degree to which an unequal distribution of power is acceptable); and Masculinity/Femininity (namely, the extent of differentiation of male and female roles). We assumed that a considerable cultural distance is likely to increase role conflict because it implies a greater likelihood of receiving contrasting expectations which are embedded in each parent's national culture. Thus,

Hypothesis #7A: The larger the cultural distance between parents, the higher the role conflict of the CEO.

Cultural distance implies that the environments from which role senders' messages are sent are more diverse, and messages are therefore more likely to contradict or be misunderstood by the recipients, giving them several possibilities of actions or making them perplexed. Thus, we hypothesize that

Hypothesis #7B: The larger the cultural distance between parents, the higher the role ambiguity of the CEO.

62   JOURNAL OF INTERNATIONAL BUSINESS STUDIES, FIRST QUARTER 1992

Personal Factors

Length of Service. The findings on the relationship between length of service and role conflict in uninational organizations are inconsistent. Walker, Churchill and Ford [1985] found that the longer the service in an organization, the lower the level of role conflict; whereas Kelly, Gable and Hise [1981] found longer service to be associated with higher role conflict. Other studies failed to find any significant results [Dubinsky and Mattson 1979; Brief, Aldag, Van Sell and Melone 1979; Oliver and Brief 1977]; Two meta-analyses [Fisher and Gitelson 1983; Jackson and Schuler 1985] also found no relationship between length of service and role conflict. We assume that because of the unique structure of IJVs, executives who are more experienced in running such an operation have probably learned how to reduce the conflicting demands of the different role senders, for instance by making each sender aware of the other senders' demands [Katz and Kahn 1978]. Hence our hypothesis was that

> Hypothesis #8A: The longer the service of the CEOs in the IJVs, the lesser their role conflict.

Fisher and Gitelson [1983], Jackson and Schuler [1985] and Walker et al. [1985] found a weak negative relationship between length of service and role ambiguity. In the context of IJVs, one can expect CEOs who have served longer in their position to experience lesser role ambiguity because they have learned how to "extract" the required information from each role sender. Thus,

> Hypothesis #8B: The longer the service of the CEOs, the lesser their role ambiguity.

Education. A positive correlation between role conflict and level of education was found for production personnel and managers [Getzels and Guba 1954] as well as for retail managers [Kelly, Gable and Hise 1981], salesmen [Dubinsky and Mattson 1979], and nurses [Vredenburgh and Trinkaus 1983]. Brief et al. [1979] found a positive correlation between level of education and role conflict. Two meta-analyses [Fisher and Gitelson 1983; Jackson and Schuler 1985] also found positive, albeit low correlations between education and role conflict. These studies were conducted in uninational organizations.

The findings of Kelly et al.'s [1981] were explained in terms of the respondents' feelings of being overqualified for their current positions. In the present study, however, the respondents were occupying the most senior and responsible position in their organization. Hence we do not expect them to feel overqualified, but rather to have learned to use their knowledge in a sophisticated way to respond to conflicting messages; and assume that

> Hypothesis #9A: The higher the CEOs' level of education, the lower their role conflict.

Brief et al. [1979], Fisher and Gitelson [1983] and Jackson and Schuler [1985] found weak positive relationship between level of education and role ambiguity. In the case of IJVs, education may be inversely related to role ambiguity because it may make the CEOs more aware of the complexity of internal and external role senders' environments and hence of their inability to send clear-cut expectations. Hence, our hypothesis is that

> Hypothesis #9B: The higher the CEOs' level of education, the lower their role ambiguity.

Autonomy. Several studies in uninational organizations found job autonomy to reduce levels of role conflict and role ambiguity [Kahn et al. 1964; Brief and Aldag 1976; Oliver and Brief 1977; Rizzo, House and Lirtzman 1970; Schuler, Aldag and Brief 1977; Vredenburgh and Trinkaus 1983; Jackson and Schuler 1985]. The explanations for these findings were that job autonomy lowers the number and frequency of sent roles. In the case of the CEOs in our study, autonomy reflects the discretion granted to them by the parent organizations. It also reflects their feeling of independence and hence their ability to ignore conflicting messages and act according to their own expectations. Thus, we hypothesize that

> Hypothesis #10A: The higher the CEOs' autonomy, the lower their role conflict.

Higher autonomy tends to reduce role ambiguity because it allows for a better role definition by the focal person [Kahn et al. 1964; Jackson and Schuler 1985]. This should also hold for IJVs, because autonomy implies a lesser need for receiving information from internal and external role senders, and the ability to interpret incoming messages, even obscure ones, in a way which fits the needs or goals of the focal person. Hence the hypothesis is that

> Hypothesis #10B: The higher the CEOs' autonomy, the lower their role ambiguity.

METHOD

Sampling

This article is based on a study that took part in Israel between 1985 and 1987. Using a wide variety of sources, a population of forty-four IJVs has been identified though in-depth consultations with such organizations as the Israeli Investment Authority, Government Ministries, foreign embassies, Dun and Bradstreet, as well as a thorough examination of the Official Company Registry. All forty-four fit our definition of IJVs. All other types of strategic alliances were excluded. The ventures operate in a wide array of industries: Finance and insurance (five IJVs), electronics and electric products (fourteen), chemicals (eight), heavy industry (seven), consumer products (four) and services (six). Twenty-six IJVs were established prior to 1969, ten were established between 1970 and 1979, and eight were established after 1980. As for size—eighteen of the ventures had less than 100 employees, twenty-one had between 100 and 1000 employees, and only five employed more than 1000 workers each. The average size of the parent firms was 8,640 full-time employees. The foreign parent firms were located in Europe and North and South America.

All forty-four IJVs have been contacted. In-depth interviews were then conducted with twenty-two CEOs randomly selected from the population. On the basis of these interviews and on a vast comprehensive survey of the literature on management in IJVs (see Shenkar and Zeira [1987]), detailed questionnaires were formulated and pretested among MBA students employed in international settings. The final questionnaires were mailed to the CEOs of the IJVs (all of them were males). After two follow-ups, all forty-four responded, for a very rare response rate of 100%. Thus, the present findings are not based on a particular sample but rather on the entire population of IJVs in Israel at that time (1987). In the last stage, after receiving the filled-out questionnaire, most CEOs were interviewed regarding the questionnaire findings.

Instruments

The role conflict and role ambiguity questionnaire was based on the fourteen-item instrument developed by Rizzo et al. [1970] which has been frequently used [Schuler, Aldag and Brief 1977; Jackson and Schuler 1985].[2] The questionnaire has been translated into Hebrew and back into English with excellent results. A factor analysis of the fourteen-items yielded the same role conflict and role ambiguity factors as in the original Rizzo et.al. instrument. Reliability (Cronbach *alpha*) was 0.889 for role conflict (0.816 in the Rizzo et al. study) and 0.647 for role ambiguity (0.780 in the Rizzo et al. study).

Independent variables were measured as follows:

1. The Number of Parent Firms: the numbers of firms/individuals with at least 10% of the venture's equity.
   *From here on, for the twelve IJVs with more than two parents, data were collected for the two parents with the largest stake in the venture. However, in some questions (e.g., Parent Dominance) respondents were asked to compare the host and the foreign parents, respectively, as a group.
2. Ownership: private, public (more than 50% of voting shares traded in the stock market) or state owned;
3. Size: the number of permanent, full-time employees in each parent organization;[3]
4. Parent Dominance: self-reported by the CEO for each parent separately on a 5-point Likert-type scale.
5. Parents Objectives' Gap: calculated as the importance of each objective for one parent vs. its importance to the other parent.

The importance of each objective was assessed by the IJVs'
CEOs on a 5-point Likert-type scale.

6. Contract Specificity: calculated as the sum of self-reported
   specifications (we randomly examined documents to assure accuracy) on a 5-point scale ranging from "very high degree of
   specification" to "not specified" on each of the following four
   items: (a) areas of responsibility of each of the parents concerning the IJV, (b) methods of solving disagreements between the
   parents and the IJV's management, (c) rules for appointing
   personnel in the IJV, and (d) the goals of the parents and the
   IJV. Cronbach *alpha* for these items was .692.

7. Cultural Distance: calculated as sum of the score differences
   between each pair of parents on Hofstede's [1980] four cultural
   dimensions.

8. Length of Service: self-reported by the CEO;

9. Level of Education: self-reported by CEOs; and

10. Autonomy: self-reported by the CEO on a 5-point Likert-type
    scale.

Data Analysis

The nature of the dependent variables analyzed in this paper calls for some
care in the statistical analysis. These variables are created by summing over
responses to a series of statements. Each dependent variable is the sum of
responses from the statements, thus the dependent variables are non negative
and are limited on both the high and low end. These facts rule out the use
of standard multiple regression techniques that require normally distributed
errors and homoscedastic distributions. In general, least squares methods
lead to potentially seriously biased estimates. In our analysis we use a Tobit
model [Tobin 1958] with both upper and lower limits, using the method of
estimation of maximum likelihood. Two excellent surveys of limited dependent variables are Amimiya [1985] and Maddala [1984], and we refer the
reader to these sources for more details on these models. The results presented
in Tables 1 and 2 include the standard regression coefficients, standard
errors, "*t*-ratios" and significance levels. These ratios are not true *t*-values,
but are variables that are asymptotically normal.

FINDINGS

Table 1 and Table 2 list the Tobit findings pertaining to the relationship
between the organizational characteristics of the IJVs and the personal
characteristics of the CEOs on one hand, and the level of role conflict and
ambiguity of the CEOs on the other hand.

Two hypotheses have been confirmed at the .05 level: Role conflict was
found to be significantly lower for CEOs with more years in service; while

TABLE 1
Estimate of a Two-Limit Tobit Model
with Role Conflict as Dependent Variable

Variables	Coefficient	Standard Error	T-Ratio	Significance Level
CEO's Length of Service	-.1	.042	-2.385	.017
CEO's Education	-.035	.09	-.384	4.701
Size Differential	.483	.402	1.202	.229
CEO's Autonomy	-.006	.255	-.025	.98
Number of Parents	-.93	.432	-2.152	.031
Objectives Gap	.152	.35	.422	.673
Ownership Differential	-.337	.413	.815	.415

Constant	2.86385
Sigma	1.11476
Log-Likelihood	-62.467

role ambiguity was significantly lower for CEOs with more years of education. Other hypotheses have not been statistically confirmed but followed the hypothesized direction: Role conflict was positively correlated with differences in ownership, with size differential, and with an objectives gap; and inversely correlated with autonomy and education. Also as predicted, role ambiguity was inversely correlated with autonomy.

One hypothesis has been rejected at the .05 level: Role conflict was inversely correlated with the numbers of parent firms (that is, the higher the number of parents, the lesser the role conflict). One hypothesis has been rejected at a lower confidence level: Role ambiguity was negatively correlated with the number of parent firms. These surprising findings—and their implications—are further referred to in the Discussion section.

A number of hypotheses could neither be confirmed nor rejected: Role conflict was not found to be related to the Cultural Distance between parents, to parent dominance, and to the level of contract specificity. Role ambiguity was not found to be related to parent dominance, and to the level of contract specificity. Role ambiguity was not found related to parent dominance, type of contract and Cultural Distance.

While Cultural Distance (as an aggregate of the four culture dimensions) had no significant relationship with role ambiguity, a very different result appeared when we examined the four dimensions of Cultural Distance separately: All relations came out significant at the .05 level. Two dimensions— Power Distance and Masculinity/Femininity, were positively correlated with role ambiguity, while the other two—Individualism/Collectivism and Uncertainty Avoidance, were negatively correlated with role ambiguity. The averaging of the four dimensions in the Cultural Distance variable therefore canceled each other's significant impact. Implications of these findings are proposed in the Discussion Section.

TABLE 2
Estimate of a Two-Limit Tobit Model
with Role Ambiguity as Dependent Variable

Variables	Coefficient	Standard Error	T-Ratio	Significance Level
CEO's Length of Service	.259	.137	1.889	.059
CEO's Education	-1.152	.283	-.407	.000
Power Distance Differential	-.316	.093	3.396	.000
Uncertainty Avoidance Diff.	-.268	.126	-2.119	.034
Individualism/Collectivism Diff.	-.251	.103	-2.445	.014
Masculinity/ Femininity Diff.	.31	.103	3	.003
Size Differential	-2.14	1.292	-1.662	.097
CEO's Autonomy	-1.143	.846	-1.351	.177
Number of Parents	-1.593	1.405	-1.134	.257
Objectives Gap	1.375	1.285	1.07	.285
Ownership Differential	-.783	1.294	-.605	.545

Constant   -.943303
Sigma   3.29386
Log-Likelihood   -100.2

DISCUSSION

The limited support obtained for the role theory-derived hypotheses challenges the universality of role theory and hence should be discussed in some detail. A number of explanations can be offered for the findings: First, it is possible that the dynamics of role conflict and role ambiguity in international operations are substantially different than those pertaining to domestic operations because of the multiplicity of environmental systems. If this were the case, role conflict and role ambiguity dynamics in wholly owned foreign subsidiaries would be similar to those in IJVs rather than to those typical to uninational firms.

Second, it is possible that the dynamics of role conflict and role ambiguity in IJVs are substantially different from those of single ownership firms because of the multiplicity of substantial equity-sharing stakeholders. If this were the case, then the dynamics of role conflict and role ambiguity in domestic joint ventures should be similar to those in IJVs rather than to those of single ownership or to those of companies in which ownership is divided among multiple small shareholders.

A third possibility is that the dynamics of role conflict and ambiguity in IJVs are unique because of the combination (interaction effect) between multiple environments and multiple ownership. This would mean that the dynamics revealed here would not be replicated in either wholly owned subsidiaries or domestic joint ventures.

A fourth possibility is that the dynamics revealed in this study are unique to Israeli managers; while role theory was developed on the basis of US managers. Zand [1978], who studied management in Israel, observed a number of special circumstances. He noted the prevalence of very high external uncertainty at the political, military and economic level, as well as internal uncertainty stemming from such factors as misallocation of scarce materials by government authorities. As a result, Zand noted, "creative improvisation" has become possibly the most important function of a senior executive and an institutionalized norm. Since all CEOs in the present study are Israeli nationals, it is legitimate to ask whether the findings will hold with another nationality, characterized by different traits and operating in another environment. On the other hand, studies on work attitudes found Israelis to be somewhat similar to managers from Anglo-Saxon countries, such as the United States and Australia [Ronen and Shenkar 1985].

Fifth, it is possible that the "non findings" reflect the very senior level of the executives under study, which stand in contrast to the middle or first line supervisory management included in most role conflict and ambiguity studies [Jackson and Schuler 1985]. Due to their boundary-spanning role with the environment, senior executives may be faced with a very different set of role senders than their subordinates who have to answer mostly to their superiors within the organization. Answers to this possibility, as well as to the previous ones, can only be determined by future research. Some suggestions for further research appear later in the paper.

The generalizability of role theory to CEOs of IJVs is also challenged by the statistically significant findings. In particular, the lower level of role conflict (and, at a lower confidence level, role ambiguity) associated with running an IJV which has a larger number of parents, challenges a basic assumption in role theory—that the more role senders there are, the higher the role conflict. The explanation of this phenomenon given by interviewees (in the last stage of the research project) seems logical, at least in retrospect: The more parents there are, the more free the CEO is to maneuver among them and lead the IJV in pursuing its own objectives rather than follow the directives of a particular parent. In contrast, when there are two parents only, they are more likely to struggle for dominance over the IJV, send conflicting messages, and limit the ability of the CEO to reach decisions which fit his own expectations.

This finding suggests that role theory be "fine-tuned" to include not only the number of prominent role senders but also the discretion of the focal person in heeding the sent messages. The CEOs of multiple parent IJVs stated that broad discretion is an inherent part of their job and hence, it is easy for them to successfully apply such conflict reduction techniques as making role senders aware of contradictory demands or simply ignore conflicting messages and use their own judgement in making strategic decisions.

The somewhat weaker relationship between role conflict and autonomy suggests, however, that the issue is not merely that of CEO's discretion but also involves information processing considerations [Galbraith 1977]. According to Galbraith's model, organizations facing information overloads can do either of two things: Reduce the need for information processing through environmental management, creation of self-contained tasks, and creation of slack; or, increase capacity for information processing by investing in vertical information systems or by creating lateral relations. The CEO of the venture with multiple parents seems to be in a position to reduce his/her need for information processing by buffering organizational tasks and, possibly, by creating an "information slack," thus reducing the likelihood of contradictory messages.

The lack of relationship (−.106) between role conflict and role ambiguity in this study, which stands in sharp contrast to most previous domestic studies, also seems to suggest a unique dynamics of role processes in international settings. We propose that this lack of relationship is the result of a unique source of role ambiguity, which has very little to do with role conflict. (The currently acknowledged sources of role ambiguity [Kahn et al. 1964]—lack of necessary information, failure to communicate existing information, and in particular the receipt of contradictory messages—partially overlap with the sources of intersender role conflict and the incompatible requests it involves). Rather, international operations are characterized by *frequent failures to "decode," understand, and properly interpret communicated information.* The interviews conducted during the last stage of the research suggested that this indeed is the case and that such decoding failures are the crucial source of role ambiguity for the CEOs of IJVs. The CEOs emphasized that a major problem which they often face is *understanding* a sent role issued by a foreign parent or other prominent foreign role senders; although in some instances, they could not determine whether the messages were intentionally or unintentionally obscure. This finding is in line with that of Schaan and Beamish [1988], who reported that in 70% of the IJVs they studied, general managers acknowledged difficulties in understanding parents' expectations, and that in 10% of the ventures, such obscurity was intentional.

The lack of relationship between role conflict and ambiguity in the present study is also related to the differential explanatory power of the Cultural Distance variable for these two constructs. As earlier reported, while the aggregate of cultural dimensions had no significant relationship to either role conflict or role ambiguity, *all* four dimensions were each correlated significantly with role ambiguity. The two cultural variables which were positively correlated with role ambiguity were Power Distance (the degree to which steep stratification is legitimated) and Masculinity/Femininity (differentiation of male and female roles), while Collectivism/Individualism (emphasis of individual or collective values) and Uncertainty Avoidance (tolerance for unpredictable events) were inversely correlated with role ambiguity.

These results can be explained in the following way: When parents differ in Uncertainty Avoidance, namely in their tolerance of the unexpected, there is no adverse impact on the communication of information. On the contrary, the foreign parents communicate more so as to reduce uncertainty in decisionmaking.

Similarly, if parents differ on Collectivism/Individualism, communication is enhanced because the parents want to make sure that clear information will reach the actual decisionmakers. On the other hand, differences in Power Distance result in disagreement on who should communicate what, leaving the CEO "in the dark" and bringing about more role ambiguity. The same is true for the Masculinity/Femininity differential which implies potential disagreement regarding such goals as achievement and decisiveness and therefore inability of the CEO to properly interpret sent messages.

Another possible explanation is that certain cultural values, although not locally held, are more esteemed and therefore present less of a problem. For instance, although Israel is a more collectivist society than the U.S., there is a general trend towards further individualism, and as a result there is greater tolerance towards it.

Implications for IJV Managers

The findings of the present study suggest a number of implications for managers working in or with IJVs. On a strategic level, the findings lend support to the formation of IJVs with multiple parents. In addition to the advantages implicit in the strategic management literature, e.g., greater risk sharing [Boyle 1968] and a broader pool of complementary assets [Kogut 1988], multiple-parent IJVs also seem to offer a more conflict-free and hence a more productive CEO. On the other hand, such IJVs appear to exercise more freedom of operation, which is not necessarily in line with the desire of the parent firms. Thus, if IJVs represent a midpoint between markets and hierarchies [Kogut 1988], then multiple-parent IJVs may be more closely situated to the market pole from the point of view of the investing parents. It is also interesting to note that a belief in the superiority of multiple-parent arrangements was communicated in other national contexts as well. For example, an American CEO of a China-based IJV attributed the success of his venture to the inclusion of two Chinese parents, one controlling the central power contingencies while the other serving as a bridge to local authorities, all the while leaving substantial autonomy to the CEO [Shenkar 1990].

Another lesson with both strategic and managerial implications has to do with the "Cultural Distance" among parent firms and between them and the IJVs. The present findings suggest that such a distance should be taken into account in both partner selection and on-going management processes. This is supported by empirical evidence showing, for instance, that most China-based IJVs involve Hong Kong parents (there are of course other reasons, e.g., logistics, supporting this pattern). We do not recommend, however, that parent firms avoid formation of IJVs in "culturally distant" countries or involving "culturally distant parents." Our findings suggest that certain cultural differences my be regarded as complementary rather than conflicting assets (see also Schaan and Beamish [1988]). In other words, it may be easier to manage an IJV where one parent is, say, aggressive and the other is not, than to manage one with two aggressive parents which struggle to outdo each other (this is in turn related to Killing's [1980] dominant parent argument). One of our interviewees later pointed out that "the cultural distance between two parent firms allowed him more freedom to operate on his own." Another noted that he used the cultural distance to his advantage by gaining concessions from his workers on the pretext that "he had to comply with the demands of the foreign parent who did not understand the local conditions."

The present findings also suggest that CEOs who are more experienced suffer less from both role conflict and role ambiguity and hence may be better performers. The finding, which should have important implications for recruitment, selection and employment tenure of CEOs in IJVs, were explained in terms of "learning to work in the multi-constituency environment of IJVs," to quote one of the participants. Another explanation for the inverse relation between length of service to role conflict and ambiguity has to do with the normally declining influence of parent firms during the venture's life. One CEO commented: "In the past, the foreign parent was very much involved because of the need to transfer technology to the IJV. Nowadays there is a much lesser need for that." Thus, learning processes in IJVs [Kogut 1988] should be addressed both in terms of the human agents and organizational life cycle.

Role theory offers various techniques to avoid or reduce conflict and ambiguity, techniques which may be very useful to CEOs of IJVs and which may be used in their training or preparation for IJV assignments. Among the techniques are *cognitive solutions*, i.e., solutions where the focal person reduces the conflict through *ordering, separating* or *buffering* identities [Ashforth and Mael 1989]. For instance, the CEO may identify himself with the parent who represents the most salient social identity for him, e.g., the host parent. *Non-Cognitive* solutions may include *withdrawal* (e.g., resignation; compromise, namely, deciding on an "average" between conflicting demands [Getzels and Guba 1954] or performing the "subtle balancing act" that Schaan and Beamish [1988, p. 284] describe); *shifting*, e.g., switching from one parent to another on the basis of visibility [Merton 1957; Rogers and Molnar 1976]; or *initiation*, that is, calling the role senders' attention to the conflict and seeking changes in demands [Kahn et al. 1964]. Rogers and Molnar [1976] also found that interaction among directors on an agency's board reduced role ambiguity, a finding which may have important implications for IJVs, where the board fulfills a crucial buffering function.

Suggestions for Further Research

It is strongly recommended that role theory be expanded to take account not only of personal and organizational-level variables, but also of national-level variables. While the present study examined only culture, other national-level

72 JOURNAL OF INTERNATIONAL BUSINESS STUDIES, FIRST QUARTER 1992

variables involving economic, social and political systems should be considered as having a potential impact on role conflict and role ambiguity. Indeed, a number of interviewees suggested that foreign parents explained a low level of involvement in the venture's affairs in that they "don't understand the local economy and its ground rules" and would therefore avoid issuing explicit directives on such matters as personnel and domestic marketing. Another interviewee noted that "for a partnership to succeed, there must be a mutual interest binding the two *nations* together." Both statements suggest a need for a more sophisticated treatment of national environments.

It is also suggested that the role conflict and role ambiguity of CEOs in IJVs be compared to those of CEOs in wholly owned subsidiaries of MNCs, and to those of such CEOs in other national settings. It is also highly desirable to study role behavior of CEOs in uninational organizations in general and domestic JVs in particular. These comparative studies will clarify whether our findings relate only to CEOs in IJVs or are more general, and relate to CEOs in both uninational and multinational settings.

Finally, the present study has been confined to the CEOs of IJVs and did not include other major players in the IJV system which could also be faced with role conflict and ambiguity. Two such groups are the transferees sent by the host parents to work in the IJVs and the expatriates sent by the foreign parents to work in the venture. In both cases, individuals could face a significant role conflict stemming from their dual membership in both the IJV and the parent organization. Thus, it is proposed that in the future, role conflict and ambiguity will be studied for the various actors in the system, including members of the board of directors and various employee groups.

NOTES

1. The one exception to that rule is probably Japan, where detailed, written contracts are not culturally sanctioned, and where contracts are frequently considered subject to change should circumstances so require [Peterson and Shimada, 1978; Wright and Russel 1975; Kobayashi 1967].

2. Five items specifically relevant to IJVs were added: (1) The local market situation is such that it forces me, the CEO of the IJV, to act in a way which does not fit the preferred action of the foreign parent(s); (2) I encounter problems when doing my job as CEO of the IJV because the parents do not clearly specify their interests; (3) I find it difficult to show the same degree of loyalty to each of the parents at the same time; (4) decisionmaking processes at the IJV take too long because I have to get approval from the parents concerning every decision; and (5) expectations of the host parent(s) force me to manage the IJV in a way which is contradictory to the foreign parent(s) expectations. Four of these items were intended to measure role conflict, while one item (#2) was intended to measure role ambiguity. One item from the original Rizzo et al. questionnaire, "explanations of what has to be done are clear," has been dropped from the role ambiguity inventory because it has reduced reliability estimates.

3. The calculation of size as the number of permanent, full-time employees in each enterprise is based on suggestions in Altman, Valenzi and Hodgetts [1985]; Evers, Bohlen and Warren [1983]; Harari, Crawford and Rohde [1976]. The number of employees has been preferred over other measures, such as the number of clients or geographical distribution [Lioukas and Xerokostas 1982], and despite problems related to its validity (e.g., Gupta [1980]; Price [1972]), because: (a) this is the most popular operational definition in the literature [Kimberly 1976] and (b) it permits to operationalize the variable in a population of diverse industries (e.g., insurance and manufacturing).

REFERENCES

Adler, Nancy J. 1983. Cross-cultural management research: The ostrich and the trend. *Academy of Management Review*, 2(3): 226-32.

Altman, Steven, E. Valenzi & R.M. Hodgetts. 1985. *Organizational behavior*. New York: Academic Press.

Amimiya, Takeshi. 1985. *Advanced econometrics*. Cambridge, Mass.: Harvard University Press.

Ashforth, Blake E. & Fred Mael. 1980. Social identity theory and the organization. *Academy of Management Review*, 14 (1), 20-39.

Bivens, Karen Kraus & Enid Baird Lovell. 1966. *Joint ventures with foreign partners, international survey of business opinion and experience*. New York: National Industrial Conference Board.

Blau, Peter M. 1970. A formal theory of differentiation in organizations. *American Sociological Review*, April 1970: 201-18.

Boyle, Stanley Eugene. 1968. An estimate of the number and size distribution of domestic joint ventures. *Economics Review*, 1:81-82.

Brief, Arthur P. & Ramon J. Aldag. 1976. Correlates of role indices. *Journal of Applied Psychology*, 61(4): 468-72.

_____, Mary Van Sell & Nancy Melone. 1979. Anticipatory satisfaction and role stress among registered nurses. *Journal of Health and Social Behavior*, 20(2): 161-66.

Cohen, R. Arthur. 1959. Situational structure, self esteem and threat-oriented reactions to power. In Dorwin Cartwright, editor, *Studies in social power*. Institute for Social Research, University of Michigan.

Daniels, John D., Jeffrey Krug & Douglas Nigh. 1986. Joint ventures in China: Motivation and management of political risks. *California Management Review*, 27(4): 46-58.

Dobkin, James A., Jeffrey A. Burt, Mark J. Spooner & Kenneth J. Krupsky. 1986. *International joint ventures*. Washington, D.C.: Federal Publications.

Dubinsky, Alan J. & Bruce E. Mattson. 1979. Consequences of role conflict and ambiguity experienced by retail sales people. *Journal of Retailing*, 55(4): 70-86.

Dymsza, William Alexander. 1979. *Multinational business strategy*. New York: McGraw-Hill.

Evers, Frederick T., Joe M. Bohlen & Richard D. Warren. 1976. The relationship of selected size and structure indicators in economic organizations. *Administrative Science Quarterly*, 21(2): 326-42.

Fisher, Cynthia D. & Richard Gitelson. 1983. A meta analysis of the correlates of role conflict and ambiguity. *Journal of Applied Psychology*, 68(2): 320-33.

Franko, Lawrence G. 1971. Joint venture divorce in the multinational company. *Columbia Journal of World Business*, 6(3): 13-22.

Friedmann, Wolfgang Gaston & Jean-Pierre Beguin. 1971. *Joint international business ventures in developing countries*. New York: Columbia University Press.

Galbraith, Jay R. 1977. *Organization design*. Reading, Mass.: Addison-Wesley.

Getzels, Jacob Warren & Egan G. Guba. 1954. Role conflict and effectiveness: An empirical study. *American Sociological Review*, 19(2): 164-75.

Glueck, William F. 1977. *Management*. Illinois: The Dryden Press.

Greene, James. 1984. The new trading stratagems. *Across the Board*, 21(3): 29-35.

Gupta, Nina. 1980. Some alternative definitions of size. *Academy of Management Journal*, 23(4): 759-66.

Harari, Oren, Kenneth S. Crawford & John Grant Rohde. 1976. Organization size and member attitudes: An empirical study. *Industrial Relations*, 22(1): 94-104.

Harrigan, Kathryn Rudie. 1984. Multinational corporate strategy: Editors introduction. *The Columbia Journal of World Business*, 19: 2-6.

_____. 1986. *Managing for joint venture success*. Lexington, Mass.: Lexington Books.

Hladik, Karen J. 1985. *International joint ventures: An economic analysis of U.S.-foreign business partnerships*. Lexington, Mass.: Heath.

Hofstede, Geert. 1980. *Culture's consequences: International differences in work related values.* Beverly Hills: Sage Publications.

Holton, R.H. 1981. Making international joint ventures work. In Lars Otterbeck, editor, *The management of headquarters subsidiary relations in multinational corporations.* Great Britain: Biddles Limited.

Jackson, Susan E. & Randall S. Schuler. 1985. A meta analysis and conceptual critique of research on role ambiguity and role conflict in work settings. *Organizational Behavior and Human Decision Processes*, 36:16-78.

Janger, A.K. 1980. *Organization of international joint ventures.* New York: The Conference Board.

Kahn, Robert Louis, Donald M. Wolf, Robert R. Quinn, Diedrick J. Snoek & Robert A. Rosenthal. 1964. *Organizational stress: Studies in role conflict and ambiguity.* New York: John Wiley.

Katz, Daniel & Robert Louis Kahn. 1978. *The social psychology of organizations* (second edition). New York: John Wiley.

Kelly, J. Patrick, Myron Gable & Richard T. Hise. 1981. Satisfaction in chain store manager roles. *Journal of Retailing*, 57(1): 27-42.

Killing, J. Peter. 1980. Technology acquisition: License agreement or joint ventures. *Columbia Journal of World Business*, 15: 38-46.

_____. 1982. How to make a global joint venture work. *Harvard Business Review*, 60(3): 120-27.

Kimberly, John R. 1976. Organizational size and structuralist perspective: A review, critique and proposal. *Administrative Science Quarterly*, 21(4): 571-97.

Kogut, Bruce. 1988. Joint ventures: Theoretical and empirical perspectives. *Strategic Management Journal*, 9: 319-32.

Kobayashi, Noritake. 1967. Some organizational problems. In Robert J. Ballon, editor, *Joint ventures and Japan*, 99-118. Tokyo: Sophia University.

Lioukas, Spyros R. & Demitris A. Xerokostas. 1982. Size and administrative intensity in organizational divisions. *Management Science*, 28(8): 854-68.

Maddala, Gangadharrao Soundaryarao. 1977. *Econometrics.* New York: McGraw-Hill.

Merton, Robert King. 1957. *Social theory and social structure.* New York: Free Press.

OECD. 1981. *International investment and multinational enterprises.* Paris.

Oliver, Richard L. & Arthur P. Brief. 1977. Determinants and consequences of role conflict and ambiguity among retail sales managers. *Journal of Retailing*, 53(4): 47-58.

Peterson, Richard B. & Justin Y. Shimada. 1978. Sources of management problems in Japanese-American joint ventures. *Academy of Management Review*, 3(4): 796-804.

Pfeffer, Jeffrey & Phillip Nowak. 1976. Joint ventures and inter-organizational interdependence. *Administrative Science Quarterly*, 21: 398-418.

Price, James L. 1972. *Handbook of organizational measurement.* Boston: D.C. Heath and Company.

Raveed, S.R. & William Renforth. 1983. State enterprise-multinational corporation joint ventures: How well do they meet both partners' needs? *Management International Review*, 23: 47-57.

Rizzo, John R., Robert J. House & Sidney T. Lirtzman. 1970. Role conflict and ambiguity in complex organizations. *Administrative Science Quarterly*, 15: 150-63.

Roberts, Edward B. 1980. New ventures for corporate growth. *Harvard Business Review*, 58: 134-42.

Robock, Stefan Hyman & Kenneth Simmonds. 1983. *International business and multinational enterprises.* Homewood, Ill.: Richard Irwin.

Rogers, David L. & Joseph Molnar. 1976. Organizational antecedants of role conflict and ambiguity in top level administrators. *Administrative Science Quarterly*, 21: 598-610.

Ronen, Simcha & Oded Shenkar. 1985. Clustering countries on attitudinal dimensions: A review and synthesis. *Academy of Management Review*, 10(3): 50-57.

Sawyer, G.C. 1980. The hazards of goal in conflict in strategic planning. *Managerial Planning*, 28: 11-13.

Schaan, Jean-Louis & Paul W. Beamish. 1988. Joint venture general managers in LDCs. In Farok J. Contractor and Peter Lorange, editors, *Cooperative strategies in international business*, 279-99. Boston: Lexington Books.

Schuler, S. Randall, Ramon J. Aldag & Arthur P. Brief. 1977. Role conflict and ambiguity: A scale analysis. *Organizational Behavior and Human Performance*, 20: 111-28.

Seeman, Melvin. 1953. Role conflict and ambivalence in leadership. *American Sociological Review*, 18: 373-80.

Shenkar, Oded & Yoram Zeira. 1987. Human resources management in international joint ventures: Directions for Research. *Academy of Management Review*, 12: 546-57.

_____. 1990. International joint ventures: A tough test for HR. *Personnel*, 66(1): 26-31.

Shenkar, Oded. 1990. International joint ventures' problems in China: Risks and remedies. *Long Range Planning*, 23(3): 82-90.

Simiar, Farhad. 1983. Major causes of joint venture failures in the Middle East: The case of Iran. *Management International Review*, 23(1): 58-68.

Sullivan, Jeremiah & Richard B. Peterson. 1982. Factors associated with trust in Japanese—American joint ventures. *Management International Review*, 22(2): 30-40.

Tobin, James. 1958. Estimation of relationships for limited dependent variables. *Econometrica*, January: 24-36.

Van Sell, Mary, Arthur P. Brief & Randall S. Schuler. 1981. Role conflict and role ambiguity: Integration of the literature and directions for future research. *Human Relations*, 34(1): 43-71.

Vaupel, James W. & Joan P. Curhan. 1969. *The making of multinational enterprise*. Boston: Harvard University Press.

Vredenburgh, D.J. & R.J. Trinkaus. 1983. An analysis of role stress among hospital nurses. *Journal of Vocational Behavior*, 23: 82-95.

Walker, Orville C., Jr., Gilbert A. Churchill, Jr. & Neil M. Ford. 1985. Organizational determinants of the industrial salesman's role conflict and ambiguity. *Journal of Marketing*, 39(1): 32-39.

Walmsley, John. *1982 Handbook of international joint ventures*. London: Graham and Trotman.

Wright, Richard W. & Collin S. Russel. 1975. Joint ventures in developing countries: Realities and responses. *Columbia Journal of World Business*, 10(2): 74-80.

Young, Richard G. & Standish Bradford, Jr. 1977. *Joint ventures planning and action*. New York: Arthur D. Little Inc.

Zand, Dale. 1978. Management in Israel. *Business Horizons*, 36-45.

[25]

A MANAGERIAL DECISION MODEL OF INTERNATIONAL COOPERATIVE VENTURE FORMATION

Stephen B. Tallman*
University of Utah

Oded Shenkar**
Tel-Aviv University and University of Hawaii at Manoa

Abstract. This paper develops a model of international cooperative venture formation that is centered on the decisionmaking process of MNE executives. Central issues for managerial decisions are developed from the organizational studies literature. A framework delineating the sequence and criteria used in the decision to form international cooperative ventures is developed from these defined issues and from existing models. Propositions pertaining to the venture formation decision process are outlined.

People (i.e., individuals) have goals; collectivities of people do not.

(Cyert and March 1963)

INTRODUCTION

International cooperative ventures are a rapidly proliferating variety of foreign direct investment [Beamish 1988; Contractor and Lorange 1988].[1] As with most foreign direct investment models, cooperative venture formation is typically explained in terms of the market imperfections concepts of industrial organization economics models [Stopford and Wells 1972; Harrigan 1984; Beamish 1985] or the transaction cost economics approach of internalization models [Beamish and Banks 1987; Hennart 1988; Buckley and Casson 1988]. These economics-based models have had success in providing rationales for the existence of joint operations. However, such models do not provide a

---

*Stephen B. Tallman (Ph.D., UCLA) is an Associate Professor of Management at the David Eccles School of Business of the University of Utah, Salt Lake City, Utah 84112. His primary research interests are business strategy, global strategic management, and international business alliances.

**Oded Shenkar (Ph.D., Columbia University) is with the Faculty of Management at Tel-Aviv University, Tel-Aviv 69978, Israel; and the College of Business Administration, University of Hawaii at Manoa, Honolulu, Hawaii 96822. His research interests are in international and comparative management.

The authors would like to thank Dr. Nakiye Boyacigiller for her encouragement on this project and the editor of *JIBS* and three anonymous reviewers for their insightful comments which undoubtedly improved this article. Naturally, the ideas and opinions expressed remain our responsibility.

Received: July 1992; Revised: January, May & September 1993; Accepted: September 1993.

sufficient explanation of the original decision by multinational enterprise (MNE) managers to establish an international cooperative venture (ICV), nor do they adequately address the contractual joint ventures that comprise a majority of ICVs [Contractor and Lorange 1988]. While the number of studies of equity joint ventures is growing rapidly, only a small number of studies address contractual ventures; most authors take an economic perspective that focuses on ownership issues and treat all non-equity ventures as simple market transactions.

Economic models also do not explain the myriad of interpersonal and organizational factors affecting the formation and stability of ICVs [Sherman 1992]. To follow on a popular analogy of viewing ICVs as marriages, the decision to form an ICV, as well as the selection of cooperative strategies, organizational forms and partners, is not strictly economic, but also a social, psychological and emotional phenomenon. Thus, what is nominally a legally contracted economic partnership is in fact a relationship involving many considerations, only a few of which are economic in nature. It is no coincidence that ICVs are frequently described using such terms as "trust," "shared visions," and "understanding." Notice, for instance, how Dow executives recount their venture with personal care:

> We eventually had a contract with many details on paper, but our alliance was really formed by the shared vision and understandings we developed before then . . . . Our informal understanding was a central feature of the alliance. Building the management commitment and people commitment is what it's all about. Dow would not have proceeded without this.

> *(quoted in* Lewis 1990, p. 104)

Jemison and Sitkin [1986] suggest that full comprehension of acquisitions requires knowledge of strategic and organizational fits and a process perspective on acquisition strategies. In a similar manner, this article develops a model of ICV formation that focuses on the managerial processes leading to the ICV formation decision. It provides a framework of reference within which a variety of theories—economic, organizational, sociological and psychological—are applied to ICV formation. As such, the article takes a phenomenological perspective, appealing to theory to aid in understanding an event that is often observed but inadequately explained. It goes beyond the economic imperatives of most current models to address strategic and organizational factors in cooperative venture formation. The purpose of the article is to suggest that the observer of ICV initiations can focus on the phenomenon and use different theoretical constructs to provide perspective and further an inductive process of model development. More knowledge of the managerial activity may accrue to this approach than to the deductive process of selecting a single theory and using ICV formation as a test of that theory. This approach is in keeping with the comments of Parkhe [1993], who recommends that international joint venture research should still be in the "test of realism" phase, not having matured to the level of positivist theory testing.

The article begins with a brief description of current economics-based models of the ICV. This is followed by the identification of several key considerations derived from the strategic management, organizational theory, and decisionmaking literatures which are relevant to the ICV decision. A managerial decision framework is presented to explain how managers choose to use ICVs in international markets as well as why and when they are likely to select equity joint ventures (EJV) versus contractual joint ventures (CJV). Researchable propositions follow the sequence of the decisionmaking process.

Current Models of International Cooperative Ventures

Oligopoly Models. Early studies of ICVs focused on MNE-local shared equity joint ventures and were conducted within the industrial organization or oligopoly power model of competition [e.g., Franko 1971; Stopford and Wells 1972]. These studies generally view the EJV as the result of bargaining between an MNE and the local government. Motivated by strategic attempts to deter competitive market entry and improve oligopoly profit potential, MNEs establish EJVs in less developed countries in order to extend their home country market power into a new location at lower cost and with less interference than a wholly owned subsidiary (WOS) would generate [Harrigan 1984; Kogut 1988]. In the oligopoly model, EJV formation is the result of industry structure, competition based on market share, and exogenous forces such as government policy. When those exogenous forces make sole ownership impossible (for instance, when host government regulations require a local equity position), or strategic maneuvering requires cooperation rather than confrontation on unfavorable terms, EJVs are accepted as second best, temporary solutions, to be used until the venture can be converted to a WOS, or a host market presence is no longer necessary. The local party typically offers a short-term solution to market-specific difficulties in the host nation and the EJV serves to control potential competition in the host market [Beamish 1985]. More recently, the oligopoly model has come to see ICVs involving multinationals as a way of extending collusive control of an industry internationally in order to reduce competition and increase profitability.

Internalization Models. In keeping with the general literature of multinationals, most recent work on ICVs has worked in the internalization paradigm [Buckley and Casson 1976]. Internalization models focus on imperfect markets for intermediate goods, particularly knowledge skills, rather than oligopoly power in final goods markets [Kogut 1988]. These models emphasize minimizing the sum of transaction and governance costs to explain the structural forms of foreign direct investment [Teece 1986; Buckley 1988]. Hladik [1985], for instance, has shown that while early ICVs established by U.S. MNEs fit the oligopoly model, more recent ventures tend to be independent of the MNE's home country market power.

As in the oligopoly model, the internalization approach focuses on EJVs while treating non-equity cooperative ventures as purely market transactions.

EJVs are treated as quasi-hierarchical modified forms of contractual governance structures, with partial equity positions taken to minimize the opportunistic behavior embedded in competitive market activity at a lower resource cost than whole ownership. Thus, Buckley and Casson [1988] suggest that EJVs provide a compromise contractual arrangement that reduces the impact of mistrust when the costs of co-ownership are lower than whole ownership. In other words, the residual profits of EJVs are held mutually hostage to desired behavior by the partners, hence reducing transaction costs [Kogut 1988; Hennart 1988]. In keeping with the internalization concept, Beamish and Banks [1987] state that only by reducing the expected costs of transactions—due to opportunism, bounded rationality, uncertainty, and small numbers conditions—can EJVs be justified on other than political grounds. The transaction cost school does address ICVs between MNEs as well as MNE-local ventures, but continues to focus on equity forms of cooperation as a means of ensuring trustworthiness under conditions where complete hierarchical merger is not desirable. As derivatives of structural economics, transaction cost models treat EJVs as situated at a midpoint between market and hierarchy, hybrids with intermediate degrees of the same transactional characteristics attributable to markets and hierarchies [Williamson 1991].

Most importantly, the transaction costs approach does not go beyond oligopoly models in highlighting the *process* leading to ICV formation. Borys and Jemison, in their model of hybrid organizations, state that "transaction cost analysis offers a rigorous post hoc discussion of the criteria for (venture) boundary definition; yet, it has little to say about how to identify important factors ex ante or about organizational dysfunctions associated with (organizational issues)" [1989, p. 240]. Yet, as Sherman notes, "the difficulty (with ICVs) lies not only in the management of the business but also in fuzzy areas, such as the personal relationships of managers form divergent corporate cultures. When conflicts erupt, they are typically much harder to resolve than in conventional companies . . ." [Sherman 1992, p. 78]. Parkhe [1991] draws a distinction between "Type I" resource diversity that generates alliances in a search for synergy and "Type II" organization cultural diversity that tends to disrupt alliances.

Horaguchi and Toyne [1990] argue that transaction cost minimization cannot explain the creation of a new market, and as a whole it assumes a reactive rather than a proactive approach on the part of the investing firm. Indeed, even the less deterministic economic theories, such as evolutionary economics [Nelson and Winter 1982], fail to provide a realistic account of managerial behavior, e.g., the preference for "satisficing" solutions [Simon 1945]. Donaldson [1990] and Hirsch, Friedman, and Koza [1990] note that economic models essentially allow for merely one type of individual activity—that of opportunistic agents seeking their net advantage, while failing to acknowledge other bases for managerial action.

As the following pages suggest, a proactive approach towards the study of the ICV decision can be derived from organization theory concepts, providing an essential value-added input to the current economic models. By expanding the conceptual basis for the study of ICVs, it becomes possible to address their unique formation process beyond simple economic hybridization [Larson 1992].

UNDERSTANDING THE DYNAMICS OF ICV FORMATION: TOWARDS A MANAGERIAL DECISIONMAKING MODEL

The ICV decision is a multistep, complex process. This process is guided by a variety of non-economic issues, and by a quasi-rational assessment of economic costs and benefits that also are filtered through behavorial processes of perception and interpretation. The decision process is not limited to dealings with other firms. Rather, it also involves *intra*-organizational decision-making dynamics negotiated among the coalitions of the firm [Simon 1945; Cyert and March 1963]. It is a process that pits one organization unit against the other in an intense bargaining game [Allison 1971]. The process also involves isomorphic development of organizational forms unrelated to transactional efficiency [Meyer and Rowan 1978]. These and other considerations stemming from organization theory and strategic management are described below.

Organizational Issues in the ICV Formation Decision

An organizational analysis assuming managerial choice requires the fulfillment of a number of rules or conditions, going appreciably beyond the economic issues of market power or transaction costs, in the ICV formation process.

Managerial Discretion. ICVs are the result of managerial decision processes, influenced by expectations of economic performance as well as by the dynamics of internal and external organizational demands. While economic expectations are certainly part of the decision to undertake an ICV, the actual economic costs and benefits of the venture are typically recognized only after the ICV is in active operation. Transaction costs are incurred as soon as an exchange is begun, but the bulk of the costs and all of the benefits occur during operation, and can only be estimated during ICV formation. Deterministic models imply that companies making decisions regarding the formation of ICVs operate as unitary, single-minded, rational actors [Allison 1971]. The managerial decision approach proposed here asserts that economic and noneconomic factors are assessed and given priorities in the parent firms by human actors with limited information processing capabilities and a tendency toward "satisficing" decisions [Simon 1945; Cyert and March 1963]. These actors have variable degrees of access to relevant information by virtue of their divisional, functional and interpersonal affiliations, as well as variable perceptions regarding the accrued benefits and costs to themselves and to their firm should an IJV be formed. The role of individual discretion is particularly important given the centrality of "champions" in the ICV formation process. Since many ICVs are the result of aggressive promotion by champions (whose motives will be explored later), individual judgement tends to weigh more than it would in other decision circumstances.

The Limits of Environmental Determinism. One organization theory model explicitly addressing interfirm cooperation is resource dependence [Pfeffer and Salancik 1978], which attributes organizational processes to the dependencies of organizations on their environments for vital resources. It has been applied to the study of domestic JVs, showing their formation to be related to reducing potential uncertainties among interdependent firms [Pfeffer and Nowak 1976; Berg, Duncan and Friedman 1982]. While its economic counterpart— transaction costs—treats organizational responses as economically efficient, the resource dependence approach suggests that strategic purposes lie behind such adjustments.

However, while allowing for meaningful organizational discretion in enacting the environment and negotiating the organization's position in it, the resource dependence perspective still treats these negotiations as purely rational responses to exogenous dependencies [Romanelli and Tushman 1986]. The same is true for Borys and Jemison's [1989] model of hybrid organizations, which combines Williamson's [1975] model of transaction costs and resource dependence effectively with other theories of the organization but retains the deterministic outlook of its parent models. Although not applied to firms in an international setting, the hybrid model's inherently deterministic outlook would suggest that while the MNE may consider various investment forms, the formation of an ICV is still ultimately determined by a strict accounting of costs, dependencies, or other contextual factors.

From a strategic management perspective, the multinational firm (or any firm, for that matter) develops strategies that do not merely represent anti-competitive maneuverings, but are rather intended to protect and exploit competitive advantages based on the unique resources or competencies of the firm. Tallman [1992] suggests that entry strategies and structures are the result of managers attempting to reduce uncertainty and improve performance in host markets. Constrained by the idiosyncratic resources of the firm and its worldwide strategy, these managers are also subject to a variety of subjective concerns related to their inherent bounded rationality. In such circumstances, the economic rationality of cost minimization and profit maximization plays a role in providing feedback to an ongoing decision process, but is difficult to estimate in the initial entry process.

The ICV Decision as an Internal Bargaining Game. Simon [1945] and Cyert and March [1963] show that managerial limitations result in coalition building and a negotiated internal organizational environment. Organizational issues, both inside and outside the firm, become political power concerns when managers are active participants in strategic and organizational processes, with the negotiated aspect of internal decisions also reflecting the difficulty of finding an optimal outcome in an uncertain environment. The balance of risk and return represented by an ICV may thus be the result of a political process in the parent firm [Bower and Doz 1979]. As Aharoni [1966] notes, a firm's commitment to the establishment of an ICV as well as to its continued existence has much to do with the initial and ongoing status of ICV proponents in the parent firm and with the internal political power of their coalition. For instance, Lewis [1990, p. 3] notes that senior executives at both General Electric and SNECMA "had to use their authority to overcome internal resistance" to the proposed CFM International EJV, by executives who, in the case of SNECMA, questioned GE's lack of market experience, and, in the case of GE, feared the creation of a new competitor. In SNECMA's case, its president had to "retire or fire" individuals who opposed the alliance [Lewis 1990, p. 185]. When such extreme steps are not taken, the choice of an ICV, and the particular ICV form, may provide a compromise solution between conservative supporters of a limited market commitment and aggressive supporters of a WOS.

The ICV Decision as a Reflection of Corporate Culture and Structure. From the MNE's point of view, corporate culture can be used as a means for 'behavioral control' [Schneider 1988]. In other words, a strong corporate culture can serve to lower the cost of transactions as the subsidiary becomes more similar to the parent firm [Casson 1990]. Some corporate cultures may be more amenable to IJV formation than others. For example, Corning Glass Works' preference for IJVs has been explained in terms of its "unpretentious— almost humble corporate culture." Corning's management offers that looking for partners with similar culture is the secret of their IJV's success [Goldenberg 1988].

Litwak and Hylton [1962] discuss the relative similarity in organizational structures as a predictor of the types of organizational linkages that are likely to emerge between given organizations. Differences in organizational structure, they point out, can be as much a basis for conflict as incompatible objectives. Lane and Beamish [1990] make the same point with explicit reference to ICVs. Companies with global structures may have different decision procedures on ICVs than companies with an international division. In the former case, a decision may be based more on technical and product criteria; in the latter case, on country-specific information.

ICV Decisions as Institutionalized Responses. Institutional models [Meyer and Rowan 1978; DiMaggio and Powell 1983] also address organizational issues under uncertainty. These models suggest that isomorphism, or the use of institutionalized standard responses, is an expected outcome of uncertainty. Managers respond to environmental pressures by following standard organizational procedures, whether explicit or implicit, to reduce their perceived uncertainty. To draw on Cyert and March's [1963] "attention flows" concept, as well as Aharoni's [1966] findings on the foreign investment decision process, it is possible that the sequence of decisionmaking will also become institutionalized, e.g., acceptable equity positions will be determined prior to partner selection. Thus, decisions become a matter of organizational inertia, artifacts of a previous context [Romanelli and Tushman 1986].

ICVs as Solutions to Partial Interdependencies in an External Bargaining Relationship. MacMillan [1979] describes negotiated interorganizational relationships as an expected consequence of interdependencies under uncertainty. These interorganizational relations are effectively portrayed by Litwak and Rothman ([1970; see also Litwak and Hylton [1962]), who identify six variables affecting the formality of organizational linkages: the interdependence among organizations, the extent to which organizations are aware of that interdependence, the number of organizations or linkages involved in a relationship, the uniformity of transacted events, the resources devoted to maintaining interorganizational linkages, and the structure of the organizations involved in a relationship. The model emphasizes that, at any given time, organizational members are aware of only some of the organization's interdependencies and act only on those of which they are aware, precluding purely "rational" response. Therefore, choices are the products of a managerial decision, rather than being driven by invisible forces of technology, transaction economics, or resource dependence.

ICVs can be seen as solutions to states of "partial interdependence" [Litwak and Hylton 1962; Litwak and Rothman 1970], that is, instances where organizational decisionmakers conclude that *some* of the firm's objectives will be better served by cooperative arrangements than by other options, which range from "go-it-alone" to a full-fledged merger. Parameters for such decisions include the *perceived* value of the potential partner's resources for one's firm, the substitutability of those resources, their vitality and scarcity [Pfeffer and Salancik 1978], and (from an economic perspective), the *relative* cost of the transaction vis-à-vis that of alternative options [Buckley and Casson 1988].

In MacMillan's [1979] model, ICVs make sense in symbiotic relationships (vertical relations), when the two parent MNEs have only partial interests in common. In such a case, organizational capital can be acquired, and performance can be better assessed than in a market relationship [Balakrishnan and Koza 1993]. In commensal, or horizontal, relationships, ICVs are established to reduce competitive interaction [Pfeffer and Nowak 1976] or other dependencies (e.g., Harrigan [1988]; Kogut and Singh [1988]).

National Cultural Differences. Differences in the national cultures of the partners in an ICV are widely seen as affecting managers in making the formation decision, but the actuality is less well defined. Brown, Rugman and Verbeke [1989] propose that ambient culture can be regarded as a country-specific advantage. In an attempt to incorporate culture into the economic explanations of IJV formation, they present a matrix of cultural and economic 'compatibility' to explain IJV failure. Woodcock and Geringer [1991] suggest that cultural 'divergence' is likely to increase the probability of contractual inefficiency by one or more of the principals as it becomes more difficult to monitor agent's behavior, making some ownership necessary. Anderson and Gatignon [1986] acknowledge that the transaction cost based entry mode literature presents conflicting views regarding the impact of sociocultural distance. One view is that when the distance is high, firms that want to impose their mode of operation in the host country will acquire transaction-specific assets and therefore are better off seeking control of the affiliate. The other view is that when the cultural distance increases, firms adjust to local methods while relinquishing control. Anderson and Gatignon explain that both views are compatible with the transaction costs approach, and that the choice of either alternative depends on "the gains from doing business in unconventional foreign ways for a given culture" [1986, p. 18]. However, the gains mentioned are unclear. For example, how would one measure the gain (loss) from imposing U.S. organizational practices in Japan?

The "cultural distance" approach represents an oversimplistic perception of culture as a unitary coherent construct while in reality culture is a multi-dimensional variable. For instance, Shenkar and Zeira [1992] find that while cultural distances on power distance and masculinity (see Hofstede [1984]) increase the role ambiguity of CEOs of EJVs, individualism and uncertainty avoidance distances actually *reduce* such ambiguity. When cultural differences are properly constructed, the universality of existing models of ICVs can be challenged. Similarly, Dore [1986] suggests that transaction cost theory is not universally applicable but that in Japan, for example, norms of reciprocity alter the risks of opportunism.

ICVs as Product of Bargaining among Key Stakeholders. ICVs are formed following intense bargaining among prospective partners as well as other stakeholders in the environment of the foreign, and especially host, country. As Ghoshal and Bartlett [1990] point out, such stakeholders as customers, suppliers, and regulators are part of an external network with whom various organizational units interact. By virtue of the dependencies they create, such entities affect the parameters within which IJV formation decisions are made without necessarily participating directly in the bargaining process. It is important to realize that the impact of stakeholders on the IJV decision is more complex than the bargaining school assumes (e.g., Gomes-Casseres [1990]). Not only do such stakeholders include non-government entities, but their impact is also influenced by a multitude of factors. Lorange and Roos [1990] define "stakeholder strength" in terms of whether the IJV would have been pursued in a different form without its support, identifying significant differences in how Swedish and Norwegian firms reacted to such differences. Koh and Venkatraman [1991] examine the role of shareholders as significant stakeholders, showing that IJV formation tends to increase market value.

A Decision Tree Analysis of ICV Formation

A number of key considerations relevant to the ICV formation decision have been discussed. In this section, a decision tree framework is proposed to illustrate what we perceive to be a realistic, albeit stylized, portrayal of the ICV formation decisionmaking process incorporating these issues (see Figure 1). The framework focuses on the initial market entry decision, whether into a national market or a global product market. While the same basic decision process would be expected in subsequent restructurings, the complete organizing cycle would involve various feedback mechanisms and interactive decisions that would complicate the essential message delivered here. Therefore, the model focuses on how economic, organizational, and behavioral considerations influence managers to choose cooperation and then to select one general cooperative form—shared equity or contractual—over the other *at initial entry*. The extent to which the decision process described here is actually followed in all its detail will obviously vary. Large firms with ICV experience, such as Dow Chemical, follow "each branch, to the smallest leaf, to see where it leads" (*cited in* Lewis 1990, p. 129). In other firms, the process may be less robust and more intuitive, but the model is still generally applicable.

The model presented here focuses on the decisionmaking process leading to the establishment of various types of ICVs. We do not discuss performance, survival and stability of such ventures, except to acknowledge that the perceived prospects for success—whether based on past experience or not— are likely to influence formation. In addition to portraying what we believe is a realistic sequence of the decision process leading to ICV formation, we seek to predict when an ICV is likely to be used and in what form. In making such predictions, we incorporate economic variables derived from existing theories, as well as behavioral, organizational and strategic variables emanating from the considerations described earlier.

As can be seen in Figure 1, the decision to use an ICV is structured as a multistage process. In any particular case, the actual decision process may well have both simultaneous and sequential aspects, but a stepwise approach improves clarity and will be followed. In the first stage, a variety of considerations lead to a choice among pure market transaction, cooperative, and single-owner hierarchical control structures in a particular market. For instance, Ford "generally compares alliance opportunities with internal possibilities," while Corning decides "whether it can be in the business on its own . . . or whether it can do better with a partner" [Lewis 1990, p. 288, 28]. If cooperation is chosen, for reasons outlined below, decisionmakers are faced with a second basic decision, whether to use contractual or shared equity forms of cooperation. If an extended contractual relationship is selected, then one or more of a variety of contracts can be used. If a shared EJV is selected, the partners must then negotiate their relative degrees of control over managerial decisions [Gatignon and Anderson 1988; Yan and Gray 1992].

FIGURE 1
The ICV Decision Tree

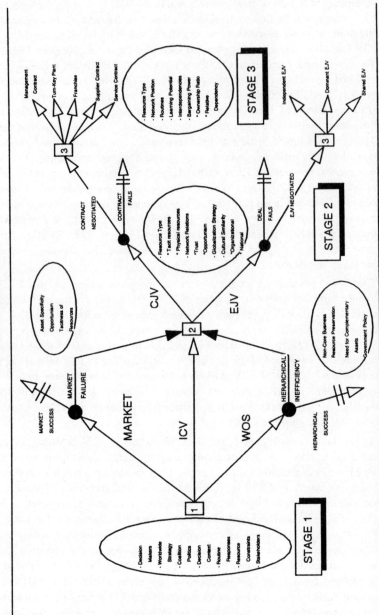

Note: The selection of actual partners will be made between Stage 1 and Stage 2, in order to choose ICV type based on known resources.

During the process of structural decisionmaking, firms also scan the environment for potential partners. Such scanning can be broad, encompassing all major players in a particular market, as with Corning, or keyed initially towards a targeted partner, as in the ICV between Apple Computer and Northern Telecom [Lewis 1990]. As earlier suggested, previous cycles are important. For example, firms with partners already in place may seek to upgrade their level of involvement without scanning a full range of potential partners, choosing a satisficing rather than an optimizing solution. The scanning process itself may be routinized also. For example, Corning "often uses third parties to learn how a potential ally conducts itself as a partner" [Lewis 1990, p. 221]. Our model addresses two key decision steps in the selection of venture structure, ICV vs. market vs. WOS; and contractual JV vs. shared EJV [Contractor and Lorange 1988], without dwelling on partner-specific adjustments. Recognize, however, that the specific capabilities of targetted or committed partners will interact with more abstract considerations in actual venture structure decisions.

Stage 1: To Cooperate or Not to Cooperate?

The initial decision for a new international market entry permits a choice among pure market transactions (exports or one-time licensing), ICVs, and WOSs. A specific objective here is to highlight the contention that a cooperative form may be the preferred, "first-best" solution of MNE managers contemplating entrance into a new market. The issues addressed in the previous section influence this decision, as follows.

The Decisionmakers. Assuming that managers are subject to bounded rationality and are affected by their own past experiences and learned responses, we expect managers in the respective partner firms to input their personal value systems, stereotypes, and interests into this decision process. Thus, managers with personal interests or relationships in a particular country or in a particular foreign firm are likely to be influenced in their choice of location and entry form. In making the decision, managers will also be influenced by their anticipated reward in regard to venture formation and failure, as well as the value they attach to that reward. Fornell, Lorange and Roos [1990] emphasize the importance of internal push by champions or sponsoring managers to the formation of cooperative ventures. Beamish [1988] notes that the reward systems in MNEs encourage executives to "show results" for their trips by returning with signed contracts, not for opting out of a risky ICV, while Lane and Beamish [1990] describe how an MBO process pushed an executive to support the formation of an ICV. While agency theory recognizes individual reward as a key consideration, we clearly go beyond that in assuming that executives may opt for foreign direct investment in countries in which they have inherent interest (and where the value of their country-specific expertise will be enhanced). In the case of Beijing Jeep, the key American Motors executive had a personal interest in China that led him to champion the joint venture [Mann 1990].

Proposition 1: The greater the economic uncertainty of a potential international transaction, the more likely an ICV will be used in a target market where key managers have a personal interest.

Worldwide Strategy. From a resource-based strategy perspective, firms pursue market entry only if their particular competencies are perceived to yield competitive advantage in a given market. However, application of firm-specific resources typically involves the use of complementary assets such as distribution networks, production facilities, laborers, and market knowledge, which represent a major variable for MNEs considering an ICV. Even an experienced firm may find that its location-sensitive assets are inappropriate to a new country or region [Tallman 1992]. Unless the firm wishes to risk failure during an adjustment period, use of a local partner to provide location-specific complementary assets is to be expected. Thus, even as WOSs become legal in markets such as China or Russia, most foreign investors continue to seek local partners. However, because competitive advantage accrues to the core competencies that the MNE brings to the new market, the managers of the multinational also seek to control the ICV in such a way as to fit their overall strategic position. Global firms which must closely control the interactions of their subsidiaries to exploit global resource bases are most likely to find partners to be strategic encumbrances.

Proposition 2: ICVs with local partners are more likely to be formed by MNEs with multidomestic strategies and independent subsidiaries than by global multinationals with interdependent subsidiaries.

Coalition Politics. When the internal negotiations surrounding the MNE entry decision are intense, an ICV may be used as a hedge against failure. A cooperative venture requires commitment of fewer resources, hence a lower opportunity cost, and implies a limited commitment to the project. MNEs also attempt to capitalize their contribution of intangible assets to ICVs, particularly in areas seen as high risk, such as China. The low commitment of the firm also implies a need to continually reaffirm the value of the venture. Thus, Tod Clare, vice president for international operations and the "champion" of Beijing Jeep at American Motors, said, "the importance of the opportunity must be demonstrated again and again, since many people at a company have not traveled outside the United States" [Goldenberg 1988, p. 34].

Proposition 3: The choice of an ICV is more likely than whole ownership when top management of the MNE is divided on issues of internationalization or of entry into particular markets.

Organizational Decision Context. The choice of structural form for an investment will be influenced by the organizational "identities" of the partners which provide internal contexts for decisionmaking. Thus, the corporate culture of some firms seems to entail a perception of the corporation as a loose network with an increased willingness to undertake boundary obscuring activities such as alliances. For instance, Corning defines itself as a network of organizations, and an executive suggests that only an organizational commitment to long-term relationships can justify the huge investment in time and energy needed to make cooperative ventures work [Sherman 1992]. Less mechanistic, more decentralized structures are more amenable to ICV formation. Thus the more decentralized structure of General Electric in the 1980s is acknowledged to be vital to the formation of its venture with Huntsman Chemical; the same is true for Ford's domestic venture with Excel [Lewis 1990].

> *Proposition 4*:   ICVs are more likely to be formed among loosely coupled, decentralized MNEs.

Routine Responses. Companies tend to find routine ways to do things such as choosing an entry form [Nelson and Winter 1982]. Franko suggests that cooperative organizational forms are related to "corporate tolerance for joint ventures" [1971, p. 204] (see also Bivens and Lovell [1966]). Beamish [1988] notes that in many companies, attitudes towards IJVs have become institutionalized [Meyer and Rowan 1978] or, in the words of Nelson and Winter [1982], their use has become an organizational routine, whether explicit or not. Writes Lewis [1990, p. xii]:

> Successful companies that shared their experiences ... have had few guidelines for strategic alliances .... That they have not translated their mastery into formal guidelines is probably because, having learned by doing, they absorbed key lessons implicitly.

An example of routine responses is British Aerospace's recent announcement that "all its future aircraft development programs would involve joint venture arrangements with international partners" [Fullick 1991, p. A7B]. When this is the case, the decision is no longer whether or not to establish an ICV, and the ICV is no longer measured against other entry mode options. Rather, the decision is limited to partner selection, specific ICV form, ownership stake and location.

> *Proposition 5*:   Firms with ICVs in place will tend to use ICVs in new markets more often, and firms in industries with a large proportion of ICVs will use cooperative forms of investment more than firms in general.

Perceived Resource Constraints. We have already suggested that certain conditions within an MNE may make its managers more receptive to the use of cooperative forms. However, since cooperation requires a partner, we must also address external considerations. Partial interdependencies, of which parents are explicitly aware, represent a recognition on the part of a parent firm that it has limited but critical interests in the other's competencies, suggesting not only the use of ICVs, but also the choice of specific partners. Awareness of the interdependencies appears to be a key factor. Hladik [1988] suggests that the recognition of resource dependencies influences the decision to conduct R&D operations in EJVs. While transaction cost economics also predicts the formation of ICVs when only some organizational assets are of interest, the full costs of a transaction are known only after the fact. Gomes-Casseres [1989] finds that U.S. MNEs are less likely to establish IJVs in their core business than in domains in which they have had less experience, and therefore have greater dependence on the partner.

> *Proposition 6*: MNEs in the same industry will form ICVs in markets perceived to be secondary as a way to reduce competitive interactions when the parents compete in primary markets.

Participating Stakeholders. Although forming an ICV involves bargaining between the principals to the deal, other stakeholders in the venture will have an impact on the process and the outcome. For instance, the government of the People's Republic of China allows the formation of WOS, but frequently creates incentives for a foreign firm to form an ICV (such as permitting it to sell in the domestic market), thus altering the relative value of an ICV without changing the transaction costs (a similar condition is argued in Kogut [1988]). Thus, when an external stakeholder has considerable power, the outcomes of the bargaining may be bounded from the start.

> *Proposition 7*: MNEs are more likely to use ICVs in centrally planned or hybrid economies when the government indicates a preference for cooperation, even if a WOS is permitted.

The seven propositions outlined above are intended to indicate specific conditions under which an MNE is likely to prefer an ICV form in international markets as its first choice. Figure 1, while illustrating the ICV decision-making process in the proposed model, also delineates boundaries of the ICV decision from the oligopoly and internalization perspectives in which it is seen as a second-best alternative. Internalization economics suggest an ICV when opportunism and asset specificity cause market failure, but resource constraints or governance costs make a WOS seem excessive. The market power approach suggests an EJV as the second-best choice, selected when exogenous factors, such as government policy, rule out the preferred WOS or when financial and managerial resources must be conserved. Internalization models suggest that non-core businesses or needs for complementary assets will push firms toward EJVs rather than full hierarchical relationships with subsidiaries. These positions are argued at great length in the literature [Kogut 1988; Madhok 1991], and will not be pursued here. However, note that even if cooperation is seen as the result of market or hierarchical failure, noneconomic pressures still affect the selection of an ICV form in Stage 2.

Stage 2: Contract or Equity?

Once a cooperative venture is proposed, managers must choose between shared equity forms (EJVs) and extended contractual relationships of various types. This is a key distinction, in that a contractual relationship is specified as to duration and purpose, while an EJV is more likely to be open-ended in both senses. This generality holds, although contractual relationships can be, and often are, renewed indefinitely and some shared equity ventures have a set duration (which may be extended by mutual agreement). While a given contract will specify payment terms, and an EJV is proclaimed to be an efficient hostage to mutual residual payments, the two forms are often mixed such that the reality of economic relations is hardly clear. Perhaps the only absolute distinction between the two forms of ICV is that an EJV involves creation of a new organizational entity with shared ownership and separate management while contractual joint ventures (CJVs) provide defined relationships without a separate organizational life.

Resource Considerations. By the time the choice between an EJV and a CJV is made, the potential partner, or a short list of prospects, should have been identified. The resources on which the venture is dependent are then identified in terms of their "tacitness," or organizational embeddedness. As Kogut [1988] suggests, tacit resources do not cause market failure, but do make knowledge transmission difficult unless organizational forms are shared. Organizational learning models [Fiol and Lyles 1985] suggest that tacit resources will greatly encourage a formal merging of organizational strategies, structures, and cultures in an equity venture in order to transmit both the skills and their milieu.

An ICV formed to improve market access to a foreign country is likely to be an MNE-local firm EJV in which the MNE provides the product and the local firm provides local expertise that is primarily tacit knowledge [Kogut 1988]. Such a venture is formed with the understanding that it will have a short life, unless mandated by the local government, as rapid learning on the part of both partners will make the ICV redundant by eliminating per-ceived dependencies [Beamish 1985].

An ICV formed to share complementary technical knowledge is likely to take place between two MNEs with equivalent levels of sophistication, both seeking equal access to the other's new technology, and may well take the form of cross-licensing, as technical knowledge is usually codifiable [Osborn and Baughn 1990]. Stuckey [1983] finds that both vertically and horizontally integrated aluminum firms established EJVs because of a perception that managerial and technical know-how was not easily transmitted (see also Beamish and Banks [1987]), while Osborn and Baughn [1990] find that the formation of EJVs was more likely when organizationally embedded knowledge was involved than in cases of transferable technology, despite the focus of transaction cost theorists on the opportunism risks to explicitly identifiable high technology. This suggests that EJVs are selected when the perceived dependencies are focused on the organization rather than the technology.

Proposition 8:   EJVs are more likely to be formed than CJVs when the partners are sharing organizational skills rather than specific technologies.

Trust Formation. Trust between partners has been frequently highlighted as the essence of successful ICVs (e.g., Sherman [1992]). Most discussions of cooperative ventures as network organizations, as opposed to simple hybrids, revolve around social control processes involving "reciprocity norms, personal relationships, reputation, and trust" [Larson 1992, p. 76]. For instance, Jarillo [1988] describes clan mechanisms of control based on trust developed over an extended reciprocal relationship. Dwyer, Schurr and Oh [1987] show that, from a social exchange perspective [Emerson 1976], trust makes working out all contingencies in formal contract form unnecessary. While network models do not require a priori faith in a partner, the trust developed over a period of time is seen as a viable alternative in time-extensive contractual relationships to the need for mutual hostages in the face of possible opportunism characteristic of an EJV. Anderson and Weitz state that "Stability of relationships [in a distribution channel] can be maintained without creating special relationships . . . by cultivating trust" [1989, p. 322]. Thus, unless the parents are comfortable with a situation of "shared opportunism" [Lewis 1990, p. 121], contractual relations will be preferred due to personal trust or higher tolerance for ambiguity.

Proposition 9:   Extended relationships between partners resulting from perceived fair dealing will generate trust and result in greater use of long-term CJVs.

International Strategy and Structure. The strategies and structures of the venture partners will be significant to the choice of cooperative form. Specifically, firms that operate with multidomestic strategies and are structured with essentially independent national subsidiaries are more likely to employ EJVs if they take a partner. The independence of the subsidiary permits both parents to focus on local market performance and makes alignment of ownership interests likely. The likelihood of a long-term relationship and the consequent need for flexibility make an equity venture attractive as well. On the other hand, a globally oriented MNE desiring a subsidiary that will be part of a worldwide integrated network may be more satisfied with a contractual alliance. If the MNE is concerned with overall network performance while the local partner is interested in returns on a single venture, the inherent incompatibility of interests makes long-term shared ownership problematic. However, with an explicit role in the network, with agreed objectives and payments, partners may be able to work together for different purposes.

Proposition 10:   CJVs are more likely to be selected by MNEs with global strategies and structures, while EJVs are more likely to be selected by MNEs with a multi-domestic strategy.

Organizational Cultures. The limited and defined interactions of a contractual relationship may reduce the strains of constantly evolving shared ownership. Therefore, firms with very different organizational cultures may prefer contractual relationships. While complementarities in hard skills and assets are widely considered to be at the root of most joint ventures [Contractor and Lorange 1988], dissimilarities in culture or style may create strains and speed failure when two firms are meshed in an EJV [Parkhe 1991]. Organizational culture is a multidimensional construct, similar to national culture, according to Sackmann [1992]. Different aspects of firm culture may be more or less central, more or less difficult to transmit, and more or less critical to operations. In a two-stage process, great differences in organizational operating style or culture may make meshing the organizations in an EJV difficult and failure-prone. However, the strictly defined terms of a contractual relationship may make such organizational factors less intrusive on the joint activities.

> *Proposition 11*:   Firms with similar organizational cultural aspects are
>   more likely to choose EJVs over CJVs and vice versa.

National Cultural Similarities. While organizational culture has a direct impact on the operation of MNEs, differences in national culture between prospective partners raise the uncertainty of decisionmakers. Kogut and Singh [1988] find that cultural distance increases the likelihood of joint venturing over whole ownership. Erramilli [1991] shows that cultural distance and experience interact to effect ownership in a nonlinear function. As suggested above, however, aggregate measures of cultural differences are unlikely to be accurate, so specific constructs must be developed. Shane [1993], for instance, proposes that people in collectivist societies tend to be less opportunistic and therefore managers in such societies will see lower costs in any given transaction.

> *Proposition 12*:   EJVs are more likely to be used than CJVs when
>   the parent firms are from more individualistic national
>   cultures than if the parents are from collectivist
>   cultures.

We also suggest that an EJV is more likely when the dominant parent comes from a high power distance environment while the other comes from a low power distance environment or when the dominant parent has low uncertainty avoidance while the less dominant parent has high uncertainty avoidance and hence is willing to perform operational, "programmed" tasks.

> *Proposition 13*:   Complementarity of power needs or uncertainty
>   avoidance in parent firms' national cultures should
>   favor the use of EJVs over CJVs.

Stage 3: Specifying the Terms of the Relationship

The decision about ICV type eventually will proceed to a specific definition of the relationships between the partners and with the venture organization in which the type of contractual venture is decided or, in an equity deal, in which the control relationships between the partners are settled. Full discussion of the details of this decision stage are beyond the scope of this paper. However, compatible models for this decision are available. Contractor and Lorange [1988] discuss the possible contractual cooperative forms and the costs and benefits of these over whole ownership from strategic and economic perspectives. Yan and Gray [1992] and Blodgett [1991] describe bargaining models in which overall and specific control responsibilities are negotiated between partners. Interestingly, ownership is formally modelled as only one input to the bargaining, although a significant one. Bargaining over equal, majority, or independent status for an equity venture is based largely on a set of concerns similar to those described above. For example, it may become formal or informal company policy not to accept a minority stake in an EJV, or not to accept a state-owned partner, regardless of what "rational" economic analysis would suggest. Alternatively, the organizational embeddedness of resources critical to a contractual venture may well determine the type of contract to be executed. The managerial issues which we use to depict the Stage 1 and 2 decisions would appear to be equally relevant to the final negotiation of control and responsibility between partners.

SUMMARY

The decision to form an ICV appears to be a managerial and organizational process, in which economic factors play a vital, if nonexclusive and indirect, role. Some of these factors come into play subsequent to the failure of another mode of control and as feedback to managers evaluating a cooperative venture once it has already been in operation. Obviously, performance expectations are an important component in the ICV decision process, although, as other authors have suggested, economic measures of performance are not always an important consideration [Kogut and Singh 1988; Hladik 1988]. Even when superior economic performance is the purpose of the ICV, economic success can be measured only after competition develops. Managers make decisions based on incomplete, perceptual visions of economic and noneconomic relationships. Environmental (usually economic) factors probably do drive out highly ineffective structural forms of ICV, even though the equilibrium conditions favored in economic models are never attained in real systems. Hence, managers should anticipate the high levels of failure associated with ICVs [Beamish 1985], given their complex cost structures and complicated reasons for initiation.

The complex, intuitive framework that we have proposed reflects many of the same concerns about current economics-based research into ICVs that are expressed by Parkhe [1993]. Parkhe suggests that positivist, single-theory-oriented conceptual and empirical models will not illuminate critical concerns about international joint ventures. His key research questions revolve around the choice of organizational structure, the design of alliance structures, and the evolution of collaborative ventures. He specifically questions the realism of strict assumptions of opportunistic behavior. Parkhe proceeds to a discourse on methods of scientific inquiry. We have focused on detailed examination of and specific explanations for managerial behavior rather than typologies of investigation. However, it does seem that our phenomenological, realism-oriented approach provides certain specific suggestions about answers to Parkhe's questions that he does not find in traditional modelling.

Many issues of venture formation and activity have not been treated fully in the present paper. Future studies should focus more on the variety of ICVs (e.g., Osborn and Baughn [1990]), and examine contractual relationships in common with equity forms of cooperation. Most importantly, the full range of motivations for embarking on a cooperative venture must be considered across functional and regional lines, with a special emphasis on hitherto neglected cognitive processes. Studies may be initially limited to certain venture types or to MNE-local firm ventures and then generalized across other ICV options. We have, perhaps, reached the point in the study of ICVs at which simplifying models must make way for models with mixed motives, multiple alternatives, and imprecise outcomes.

NOTE

1. International cooperative ventures are broadly defined here as any formal, cooperative activities between separately constituted, legally autonomous, business organizations across national boundaries. This definition of ICVs is considerably more limited than that of "strategic alliances" (e.g., Contractor and Lorange [1988]) in that it does not include activities that are either limited to specific product technology (e.g., licensing, joint R&D) or impinge on the legal autonomy of the participating parties (e.g., cross share-holding).

REFERENCES

Aharoni, Yair. 1966. *The foreign investment decision process.* Boston, MA: Harvard University Press.

Allison, Graham T. 1971. *Essence of decision: Explaining the Cuban missile crisis.* Boston: Little, Brown.

Anderson, Erin & Hubert Gatignon. 1986. Modes of foreign entry: A transaction cost analysis and propositions. *Journal of International Business Studies,* Fall: 1-26.

Anderson, Erin & B. Weitz. 1989. Determinants of continuity in conventional industrial channel dyads. *Marketing Science,* 8: 310-23.

Balakrishnan, Srinivasan Balak & Mitchell P. Koza. 1993. Information asymmetry, adverse selection, and joint ventures: Theory and evidence. *Journal of Economic Behavior and Organization,* 20: 99-117.

Beamish, Paul W. 1985. The characteristics of joint ventures in developed and developing countries. *Columbia Journal of World Business,* Fall: 13-19.

_____. 1988. *Multinational joint ventures in developing countries.* London: Routledge.

_____ & John C. Banks. 1987. Equity joint ventures and the theory of the multinational enterprise. *Journal of International Business Studies,* 19: 1-16.

Berg, Sanford V., Jerome Duncan & Philip Friedman. 1982. *Joint venture strategies and corporate innovation.* Cambridge, MA: Oelgeschlager, Gunn & Hain, Publishers.

Bivens, Karen K. & Enid B. Lovell. 1966. *Joint ventures with foreign partners, international survey of business opinion and experience.* New York: National Industrial Conference Board.

Blodgett, Linda L. 1991. Toward a resource-based theory of bargaining power in international joint ventures. *Journal of Global Marketing*, 5(1-2): 63-78.

Borys, Bryan & David B. Jemison. 1989. Hybrid arrangements as strategic alliances: Theoretical issues in organizational combinations. *Academy of Management Review*, 14: 234-49.

Bower, Joseph L. & Yves Doz. 1979. Strategy formulation: A social and political process. In D. Schendel & C.W. Hofer, editors, *Strategic management*, 152-66. Boston: Little, Brown.

Brown, Lee T., Alan M. Rugman & Alain Verbeke. 1989. Japanese joint ventures with western multinationals: Synthesizing the economic and cultural explanations of failure. *Asia Pacific Journal of Management*, 6(2): 225-42.

Buckley, Peter J. 1988. The limits of explanation: Testing the internalization theory of the multinational enterprise. *Journal of International Business Studies*, 19(2): 181-94.

_____ & Mark Casson. 1976. *The future of the multinational enterprise*. London: Macmillan.

_____. 1988. A theory of cooperation in international business. In Farok Contractor & Peter Lorange, editors, *Cooperative strategies in international business*, 31-54. Lexington, MA: Lexington Books.

Casson, Mark. 1990. Entrepreneurship and business culture. Paper presented at the Academy of International Business Meetings.

Contractor, Farok J. & Peter Lorange. 1988. Why should firms cooperate? The strategy and economics basis for cooperative ventures. In Farok Contractor & Peter Lorange, editors, *Cooperative strategies in international business*, 3-30. Lexington, MA: Lexington Books.

Cyert, Richard M. & James G. March. 1963. *A behavioral theory of the firm*. Englewood Cliffs, NJ: Prentice-Hall.

DiMaggio, Paul J. & Walter W. Powell. 1983. The iron cage revisited: Institutional isomorphism and collective rationality in organizational fields. *American Sociological Review*, 48(2): 147-60.

Donaldson, Lex. 1990. The ethereal hand: Organizational economics and management theory. *Academy of Management Review*, 15(3): 369-81.

Dore, Ronald P. 1986. *Structural adjustments in Japan, 1970-1982*. Geneva, Switzerland: International Labor Office.

Dwyer, F. Robert, Paul H. Schurr & Sejo Oh. 1987. Developing buyer-seller relationships. *Journal of Marketing*, 51(2): 11-27.

Emerson, Robert M. 1976. Social exchange theory. *Annual Review of Sociology*, Vol. 2. Annual Reviews, Inc.

Erramilli, M. Krishna. 1991. The experience factor in foreign market entry behavior of service firms. *Journal of International Business Studies*, 22(3): 479-501.

Fiol, C. Marlene & Marjorie A. Lyles. 1985. Organizational learning. *Academy of Management Review*, 10(4): 803-13.

Fornell, Claes, Peter Lorange & J. Roos. 1990. The cooperative venture formation process: A latent variable structural modeling approach. *Management Science*, 36(10): 1246-55.

Franko, Lawrence G. 1971. *Joint venture survival in multinational corporations*. New York: Praeger Publishers, Inc.

Fullick, N. 1991. British aerospace, Japanese, discuss jet joint venture. *Wall Street Journal*, December 2: A7B.

Gatignon, Hubert & Erin Anderson. 1988. The multinational corporation's degree of control over foreign subsidiaries: An empirical test of a transaction cost explanation. *Journal of Law, Economics, and Organization*, 4(2): 305-36.

Ghoshal, Sumantra & Christopher Bartlett. 1990. The multinational corporation as an interorganizational network. *Academy of Management Review*, 15(4): 603-26.

Goldenberg, Susan. 1988. *Hands across the ocean: Managing joint ventures*. Boston: Harvard Business School Press.

Gomes-Casseres, Benjamin. 1989. Joint ventures in the face of global competition. *Sloan Management Review*, Spring: 17-25.

_____. 1990. Firm ownership preferences and host government restitutions: An integrated approach. *Journal of International Business Studies*, 21: 1-22.

Harrigan, Kathryn R. 1984. Joint ventures and global strategies. *Columbia Journal of World Business,* Summer: 7-13.

_____. 1988. Strategic alliances and partner asymmetries. In Farok Contractor & Peter Lorange, editors, *Cooperative strategies in international business,* 205-26. Lexington, MA: Lexington Books.

Hennart, Jean-François. 1988. A transaction costs theory of equity joint ventures. *Strategic Management Journal,* 9: 361-74.

Hirsch, Paul M., Ray Friedman & Mitchell P. Koza. 1990. Collaboration or paradigm shift?: Caveat emptor and the risk of romance with economic models for strategy and policy research. *Organization Science,* 1(1): 87-97.

Hladik, Karen J. 1985. *International joint ventures.* Lexington, MA: Lexington Books.

_____. 1988. R&D and international joint ventures. In Farok Contractor & Peter Lorange, editors, *Cooperative strategies in international business,* 187-204. Lexington, MA: Lexington Books.

Hofstede, Geert. 1984. *Culture's consequences.* Beverly Hills: Sage Publications.

Horaguchi, Haruo & Brian Toyne. 1990. Setting the record straight: Hymer, internalization theory and transaction cost economics. *Journal of International Business Studies,* 21(3): 487-94.

Jarillo, Jose-Carlos. 1988. On strategic networks. *Strategic Management Journal,* 9: 31-41.

Jemison, David B. & Sim B. Sitkin. 1986. Corporate acquisitions: A process perspective. *Academy of Management Review,* 11(1): 145-63.

Killing, J. Peter. 1983. *Strategies for joint venture success.* New York: Praeger Press.

Kogut, Bruce. 1988. Joint ventures: Theoretical and empirical perspectives. *Strategic Management Journal,* 9: 319-32.

_____ & Harbin Singh. 1988. Entering the United States by joint venture: Competitive rivalry and industry structure. In Farok Contractor & Peter Lorange, editors, *Cooperative strategies in international business,* 241-51. Lexington, MA: Lexington Books.

Koh, Jeongsuk & N. Venkatraman. 1991. Joint venture formations and stock market reactions: An assessment in the information technology sector. *Academy of Management Journal,* 34(4): 869-92.

Lane, Henry W. & Paul W. Beamish. 1991. Cross-cultural cooperative behavior in joint ventures in LDCs. *Management International Review,* 31 (Special Issue): 87-102.

Larson, Andrea. 1992. Network dyads in entrepreneurial settings: A study of the governance of exchange relationships. *Administrative Science Quarterly,* 37: 76-104.

Lewis, Jordan D. 1990. *Partnerships for profit: Structuring and managing strategic alliances.* New York: The Free Press.

Litwak, Eugene & Lydia F. Hylton. 1962. Interorganizational analysis: An hypothesis on co-ordinating agencies. *Administrative Science Quarterly,* 6: 395-420.

Litwak, Eugene & Jack Rothman. 1970. Towards the theory and practice of coordination between formal organizations. In William R. Rosengren & Mark Lefton, editors, *Organizations and clients: Essays in the sociology of service,* 137-86. Columbus, OH: Merrill.

Lorange, Peter & Johan Roos. 1990. Formation of cooperative ventures: Competence mix of the management teams. *Management International Review,* 30: 9-86.

MacMillan, Ian C. 1979. Commentary [on Bower & Doz]. In D. Schendel & C.W. Hofer, editors, *Strategic management,* 166-72. Boston: Brown, Little.

Madhok, Anoop. 1991. Joint venture formation: A review and comparison of the internalization and competitive strategy perspectives. Paper presented at the Academy of International Business Conference.

Mann, Jim. 1990. *Beijing jeep.* New York: Touchstone.

Meyer, John W. & Brian Rowan. 1978. The structure of educational organizations. In J.W. Meyer & Associates, editors, *Environments and organizations,* 78-109. San Francisco: Jossey-Bass.

Nelson, Richard R. & Sidney G. Winter. 1982. *An evolutionary theory of economic change.* Cambridge, MA: Belknap Press of Harvard University Press.

Osborn, Richard N. & C. Christopher Baughn. 1990. Forms of interorganizational governance for multinational alliances. *Academy of Management Journal,* 33(3): 503-19.

Parkhe, Arvind. 1993. "Messy" research, methodological predispositions, and theory development in international joint ventures. *Academy of Management Review*, 18(2): 227-68.

_____. 1991. Interfirm diversity, organizational learning, and longevity in global strategic alliances. *Journal of International Business Studies*, 22(4): 579-602.

Pfeffer, Jeffrey & Phillip Nowak. 1976. Joint ventures and interorganizational interdependence. *Administrative Science Quarterly*, 21: 398-418.

Pfeffer, Jeffrey & Gerald R. Salancik. 1978. *The external control of organizations: A resource dependence perspective*. New York: Harper & Row.

Romanelli, Elaine & Michael L. Tushman. 1986. Inertia, environments, and strategic choice: A quasi-experimental design for comparative-longitudinal research. *Management Science*, 32(5): 608-21.

Sackmann, Sonja A. 1992. Culture and subcultures: An analysis of organizational knowledge. *Administrative Science Quarterly*, 37: 140-61.

Schneider, Susan C. 1988. National vs. corporate culture, implications for human resource management. *Human Resource Management*, 27(2): 231-45.

Shane, Scott. 1993. The effect of cultural differences and the perception of transaction costs on national differences in the preference for international joint ventures. *Asia-Pacific Journal of Management*, 10(1): 57-69.

Shenkar, Oded & Yoram Zeira. 1992. Role conflict and role ambiguity of chief executive officers in international joint ventures. *Journal of International Business Studies*, 23(1): 55-76.

Sherman, S. 1992. Are strategic alliances working? *Fortune*, September 21: 77-78.

Simon, Herbert. 1945. *Administrative behavior*. New York: The Free Press.

Stopford, John M. & Lewis T. Wells. 1972. *Managing the multinational enterprise*. New York: Basic Books, Inc.

Stuckey, John A. 1983. *Vertical integration and joint ventures in the aluminum industry*. Cambridge, MA: Harvard University Press.

Tallman, Stephen. 1992. A strategic management perspective on the host country structures of MNEs. *Journal of Management*, 18(3): 455-71.

Teece, David. 1986. Transactions cost economics and the multinational enterprise. *Journal of Economic Behavior and Organization*, 7: 21-45.

Williamson, Oliver E. 1975. *Markets and hierarchies*. New York: Free Press.

_____. 1991. Comparative economic organization: The analysis of discrete structural alternatives. *Administrative Science Quarterly*, 36: 269-96.

Woodcock, C. Patrick & J. Michael Geringer. 1991. An exploratory study of agency costs related to the control structure of multi-partner, international joint ventures. *Academy of Management Proceedings*, 115-19.

Yan, Aimin & Barbara Gray. 1992. A bargaining power approach to management control in international joint ventures: A multi-case study of U.S.-Chinese manufacturing joint ventures. Paper presented to the Academy of Management.

[26]

OWNERSHIP-BASED ENTRY MODE STRATEGIES AND INTERNATIONAL PERFORMANCE

C. Patrick Woodcock,* Paul W. Beamish,** and Shige Makino***
Western Business School, University of Western Ontario

Abstract. This study examines the relationship between ownership entry modes and performance. The ownership entry modes examined are the wholly owned modes of acquisition and new venture entry, and the non-wholly owned mode of joint venture entry. A theoretical relationship is developed for international entry modes that is based on the contingency characteristics of resource requirements and organizational control factors. This model suggests that different entry modes have different performance outcomes based upon their resource and organizational control demands. The theoretical model, although developed using the eclectic theoretical approach, is based largely on concepts and relationships previously delineated in contingency theory. Our hypotheses suggest that new ventures should outperform joint ventures, and joint ventures should outperform acquisitions. An empirical test using a sample of 321 Japanese firms entering the North American market provides supporting evidence.

The importance of entry mode selection to a firm's competitive advantage in a new international market has been studied widely, yet the majority of these studies have not examined mode performance. Many of the normative studies that examine entry mode performance contend that ownership-based modes such as acquisitions, joint ventures and new ventures perform poorly. Examples of this are Porter's [1987] study which found evidence of poorly performing acquisitions; various joint venture studies that concluded that joint ventures are intrinsically inefficient because of the inherently complex management relationships [Janger 1980; Killing 1983]; and new venture

---

*C. Patrick Woodcock is a doctoral student at the Western Business School, University of Western Ontario. His research has focused on international joint venture and wholly owned entry mode strategies.

**Paul W. Beamish is an Associate Professor at the Western Business School, University of Western Ontario.

***S. Makino is a doctoral student at the Western Business School, University of Western Ontario. His research has focused on international joint ventures and other strategic alliances.

We would like to thank *JIBS* Associate Editor Harry Lane, David Sharp, and the three referees for their comments.

Received: June 1993; Revised: October 1993 & January 1994; Accepted: February 1994.

254   JOURNAL OF INTERNATIONAL BUSINESS STUDIES, SECOND QUARTER 1994

research which described the new venture mode as risky, having highly variable performance outcomes [Burgleman 1983, 1985; Drucker 1974; Hill and Jones 1989]. Despite this evidence, few researchers have explicitly measured and compared the performance of the various international entry modes, and fewer still have attempted to develop a parsimonious theoretical argument for performance differences.

The object of this study is to discern which international ownership-based entry mode in general outperforms others, given that the firms have selected the entry modes based on specific contingent positions. The study develops a generalized theoretical argument applicable to both domestic and international environments, and then tests the arguments with an international sample. This study examines three ownership-based entry modes: acquisition, new venture, and joint venture.[1] The theoretical model is tested using data on Japanese ownership-based entries into the North American market.

REVIEW OF ENTRY MODE LITERATURE

The preponderance of research on international entry modes has examined the contingent relationship between firm characteristics, environment, and selected entry mode. Stopford and Wells [1972] developed one of the first international entry mode models when they argued that entry mode selection was contingent upon the firm's international experience and product diversification. Johanson and Vahlne's [1977] case-based research along with empirical studies by Dubin [1975] and Davidson [1980] provide further support for this contingent, incremental entry mode relationship. The latter studies also found that cultural and other national differences between the host and home countries appear to influence entry mode decisions.

More recently, a variety of studies have considered country, industry, and firm-specific factors and their contingent influence on wholly owned entry mode decisions. Caves and Mehra [1986] found that entry mode selection was influenced by a variety of industry and firm-specific factors, including firm size, advertising intensity, research intensity, industry growth, and industry concentration. A subsequent study by Zejan [1990] confirmed many of Caves and Mehra's results.

Other studies have compared the joint venture and wholly owned entry modes. Gatignon and Anderson [1987] found that locational factors, the degree of multinationality, and research and advertising intensity influence the selection decision between joint ventures or wholly owned entry modes. Kogut and Singh [1988] found that industry, firm, and country-specific factors influence the selection decision between the three ownership-based entry modes: joint venture, acquisition, and new venture. More recently, Kim and Hwang [1992], and Agarwal and Ramaswami [1992] examined a wide variety of entry modes. They found that locational, ownership and internalization advantages contingently influenced all of the various entry modes. In conclusion, there is considerable theoretical and empirical support for the contingency entry mode argument.

This study accepts the notion of contingency theory, which suggests that the selected entry mode must conform to the particular industry, firm, and country factors faced by the entering firm. However, supplemental theoretical reasoning complementary to contingency theory may more fully explain performance differences between entry modes. The objective of this study is to extend this line of theoretical reasoning to explain what affect contingency factors have on the performance of the different international ownership-based entry modes. Therefore, this study examines whether certain contingent mode characteristics produce performance differences between the three international ownership-based entry modes.

Empirical research comparing international ownership-based entry mode performance has been sparse, owing to the difficulty associated with collecting valid and reliable data for a firm's international joint venture and/or subsidiary performance. Subsidiary performance data are difficult to obtain because they are usually confidential. Furthermore, when performance values are obtained they are often hard to interpret because management accounting practices differ between firms and countries, and internal subsidiary performance measures do not have to conform to legal or accounting standards.

Domestic-based research on acquisition performance has been widely studied. In general, two approaches have been used: ex ante financial event studies, and ex post studies. The numerous ex ante studies, in general, suggest that acquisitions provide mixed returns to acquirers and positive returns to sellers [Caves 1989; Jensen and Ruback 1983]. The limitation of many of these studies is that they do not consider the long-term gains or losses to acquiring firms, but rather focus on the short-term stock market reaction to the acquisition event. Some of the long-term factors that have not been fully considered in this approach are organizational integration, synergy and redundancy issues, all of which become more apparent over time [Caves 1989].

Ex post financial studies examine the longer term returns available to the acquiring firm, and these studies generally conclude that negative returns accrue to acquiring firms [Caves 1989]. Behaviorally based ex post acquisition research typically has examined the ability of firms to integrate after acquisition. A variety of these studies have both qualitatively and normatively suggested that strategic implementation and organizational cultural differences make it very difficult for organizations to merge efficiently and effectively. For example, Nahavandi and Maleksadeh [1988] developed a model suggesting that the fit between two firms' strategies and cultures will influence their joint ability to synergistically develop resources and strategies after the acquisition. Chatterjee et al. [1992] and Datta [1991] empirically found that post-acquisitional performance was negatively influenced by the two firms top managers' divergent views of organizational culture.

Noncomparative studies of domestic joint ventures, in general, conclude that joint venture performance is contingent upon industry and firm-specific factors. One of the most thorough studies on this topic is Harrigan's [1985] study, in which she found that industry-specific and strategic factors contingently influence the success of joint ventures.

Comparative entry mode research explicitly measuring performance is sparse. Simmonds [1990] compared the two ownership-controlled entry modes, acquisition and new venture, in a domestic setting. He found some evidence that the new venture mode outperformed the acquisition mode while controlling for product diversification. A more ambitious study by Li and Guisinger [1991] looked at performance differences between all three ownership-based entry modes. They defined performance as the failure rates of the individual entry modes in the U.S. market. The study hypothesized that new ventures would have the lowest failure rate, acquisitions the highest, and joint ventures a median rate. This empirical study found the relationship between new ventures and acquisitions to be in the hypothesized direction and significant. However, the relationship of joint venture to these other two modes was in the predicted direction, but not significant.

This study first attempts to develop a more complete theoretical logic for the performance differences between the three international ownership-based entry modes relative to the prior two studies. Second, we empirically test the performance differences using financial performance measures rather than proxies, while at the same time controlling for locational factors. This study uses a more refined methodology and a larger sample size than previous work.

In conclusion, few studies have considered the performance variance between entry modes, and the two studies that have looked at this issue provide abbreviated theoretical arguments. In particular, these studies have not fully acknowledged the evidence of contingency theory and the impact of this theory on the entry mode versus performance relationship.

THEORY DEVELOPMENT

This study develops a theoretical model for entry mode performance differences given the fact that most entry modes are selected on a contingency basis. We use the eclectic theory approach to develop causal arguments to explain entry mode performance differences, and to explain why poorer performing modes are contingently selected by firms. Many of the arguments originate from previous contingency entry mode research, although many have been conceptually and theoretically abstracted to ensure methodological parsimony.

The theoretical development of the eclectic model used in this study focuses on industry and firm-specific factors as delineated in ownership and internalization advantages (see Figure 1). Locational advantages are controlled for both in the theoretical development and the empirical testing of the model.

The ownership advantage explains a firm's resource commitment, and the internalization advantage explains a firm's organizational control difficulties. Historically, resource commitment and organizational control, or at least close proxies of these concepts, have been studied extensively by contingent entry mode researchers. Resource-based concepts or proxies that have been empirically supported in entry mode contingency studies include country experience, competitive position, and firm size [Caves and Mehra 1986; Kim and Hwang 1992; Kogut and Singh 1988]. Organizational control concepts or proxies that have been empirically supported include ownership control, organizational culture, and managerial transfers [Agarwal and Ramaswami 1992; Amit, Livnat and Zarowin 1989; Caves and Mehra 1986; Kim and Hwang 1992; Kogut and Singh 1988; Li and Guisinger 1991; Wilson 1980; Yip 1982]. Variables that relate to both concepts and which have been supported in contingency entry mode research include product diversification and multinational experience [Caves and Mehra 1986]. Thus, resource commitment and organizational control have been shown to support the contingency factor and entry mode relationship.

Two general theoretical arguments are made in this study through the resource commitment and organizational control theoretical approaches. The first is that firms should contingently select entry modes, and the second, that contingent factors as well as the inherent characteristics of the entry mode produce differing performance levels. Clearly, these two arguments are consequential and interdependent because otherwise firms would always select the best performing entry mode irrespective of contingency theory. Therefore, to produce a realistic theory both arguments must be made simultaneously.

Entry Modes and Resource Requirements

Entry Mode Selection Based on Resource Requirements. Many researchers have suggested that different entry modes require different resource commitments. Among the first to outline a relationship between resource commitments and international business growth were Daniels [1970] and Vernon [1983]. Anderson and Gatignon [1986] developed a transaction cost model that considered the trade-off between the costs of mode control and the costs of mode resource commitment. Hill, Hwang and Kim [1990] elaborated on this idea of resource commitment when they differentiated between licensing, joint ventures and wholly owned entry modes. They defined resources as "dedicated assets that cannot be re-deployed to alternative uses without cost" (p. 118). Resources in this context could be either tangible resources such as plant and capital, or intangible resources such as market or operational know-how. The argument that a firm's entry mode is contingent upon the required resources is further developed in this study to include the relationship between entry mode and performance.

258   JOURNAL OF INTERNATIONAL BUSINESS STUDIES, SECOND QUARTER 1994

FIGURE 1
Eclectic Theory Model

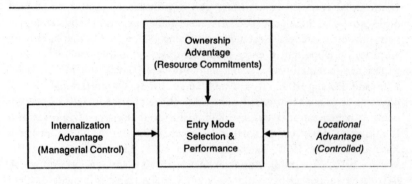

Resource commitment has been used widely to contingently differentiate between joint ventures and wholly owned entry modes. Many studies have used the degree of ownership control as a proxy for resource commitment. The greater the degree of ownership in the entry mode, the larger the resource commitment. For example, in a joint venture, a firm's resource commitment is minimized relative to a wholly owned entry mode because of the shared resource commitment between firms [Anderson and Gatignon 1986]. A firm not having the resources, and wishing to share the risks associated with having such resources is, thus, compelled to enter the market through a joint venture. Other entry mode studies have empirically corroborated the above resource-dependent relationship using nonownership proxy measures for resource commitment. Erramilli [1991] and Erramilli and Rao [1990] used market knowledge to explain why firms use specific entry modes, and Davidson [1982] found that firms having lower market knowledge tended to reduce the strategic risk by entering these markets through licensing agreements or joint ventures rather than wholly owned modes. Therefore, resource-based contingency theory has been used extensively to differentiate between joint venture and wholly owned entry mode selection.

The resource commitment concept can also be used to differentiate between the wholly owned entry modes. Firms that use the acquisition entry mode are procuring a new set of resources, while firms using the new venture mode are relying on their historic and previously developed set of resources. This concept suggests that firms having suitable resources will use the new venture mode, while firms not having suitable resources will use the acquisition mode and trade financial resources for the required resources. The necessary and appropriate resources may range from tangible resources such as product characteristics to intangible resources such as market experience. Empirical evidence of a relationship between resource commitment and wholly owned entry mode selection has been found by Caves and Mehra [1986], who observed that multinational experience was related to wholly owned entry mode selection.

The above theoretical arguments and evidence provide a model for the contingent selection of new venture entries relative to the two other modes. To contingently differentiate between the acquisition and joint venture modes, however, one has to consider the nature and type of resource requirements. Two types of resource requirements are used to make this differentiation; the first is the perceived inimitability or transferability of the resources, and the second is the core nature of the resources in the parent firm.

The important difference between the acquisition and joint venture modes is that firms in a joint venture share and provide access to some of their internal resources, while in the acquisition mode no such access is provided. A firm will use the joint venture mode to rectify a resource deficiency only if it is willing to risk providing access to such resources, and can find a willing and suitable partner(s) having appropriate resources to share or provide access [Hill, Hwang and Kim 1990]. The critical factor in the joint venture is finding partners that are predisposed to providing such access to resources. This predisposition must be based on inter-firm trust, and a perception that access and sharing of resources will not negatively impact the firm strategically [Daniels and Magill 1991]. A firm will tend to favor an acquisition entry mode if it cannot find a suitable partner predisposed to providing access or sharing the required resources, or if it is not itself predisposed to providing access to internal resources.

A firm's predisposition to providing another firm with access to its resources will depend upon its perception of the risk of exposing its critical resources. The risk of such resource access is perceived by management to be lower when the exposed resources are non-core, or if the resources are difficult to imitate or transfer to the partnering firm. A firm unnecessarily exposing critical resources to either imitation or transfer may provide its partnering firm with a competitive advantage in the future. Therefore, the perceived nature and type of resources being exposed is important to the entry mode selection process.

A variety of researchers have suggested that core resources or competencies are vital to long-term competitive advantage [Collis 1991; Hamel and Prahalad 1990; Prahalad and Bettis 1986; Stalk, Evans and Shulman 1992]. Collis [1991, p. 52] defines core competencies as "the irreversible assets along which the firm is uniquely advantaged." These are the type of resources that a firm would tend to be unwilling to share or expose unnecessarily to a potential competitor. The critical element is the perceived risk of either exposing or sharing the resources, and the resulting loss of future competitive advantage, given the benefits of the joint venture mode. If firms want to protect these vital core resources and the perceived risks of having them transferred to the second firm are high, then they should procure the needed resources through an acquisition.

A variety of studies have provided evidence that these core resource contingencies influence entry mode selection. In particular, the inimitability of the core resources has been examined. Singh and Kogut [1989] examined the contingent relationship between acquisition and joint venture selection and found that joint ventures were favored in research-intensive firms and industries. This relationship, they concluded, suggests that firms having research and development core competencies are less susceptible to losing them in joint ventures because of their inimitable nature. Their argument was similar to that put forward by Teece [1982] who suggested that research and development resources are tacit in nature, and therefore, more difficult to transfer and imitate. Other researchers have shown that the long-term viability of a joint venture and a firm's competitive position are threatened by sharing or exposing core resources [Hamel 1991; Inkpen 1992]. Therefore, differentiating between core and non-core as well as the inimitability and transferability of resources by managers is critical to the selection of an entry mode.

Another stream of research has looked at the effects of risking core resources on the selection of joint venture and wholly owned modes. Agarwal and Ramaswami [1992] empirically examined whether contractual risk influenced the choice of entry mode. They found that the higher the risk the more ownership control desired. Kim and Hwang [1992] investigated the effects of the value of firm-specific knowledge and the tacit nature of firm knowledge on a firm's entry mode selection. They found that the value of firm-specific knowledge was not significantly related to entry mode selection, but the tacit nature of the knowledge was significantly associated with the selection of wholly owned entry modes. These studies provide considerable evidence of a relationship between the exposure of core competencies in various entry modes and the selection of these modes.

In conclusion, resource requirements influence the contingent selection of entry modes. These contingent decisions are illustrated in Table 1.

Performance Implications of Resource Requirements. The contingency relationships delineated above not only influence the selection of the entry modes, but also their profitability. In particular, firms already having the appropriate resources incur minimal resource-based costs during market entry. However, firms not having the required resources must procure them using a joint venture or acquisition. Such a transaction will have an associated cost.

A firm using an acquisition entry mode will have several costs associated with procuring the necessary resources for market entry particularly in the inefficient market situation which an acquisition (a single and unique transaction) represents. First, the firm incurs the cost of searching for an appropriate acquisition target. Second, the acquiring firm has a cost associated with the risk of paying too much for the target firm, and therefore, the resources being procured. The cost of this risk is associated with the asymmetric information problem confronting the acquiring firm due to the firm's inferior

TABLE 1
Resource Requirement Contingency Decision Matrix

Entry Mode	New Resources Are Deemed Necessary for Entry Mode	Concern over Exposure to, or Sharing of, Core Resources
New Venture	No	Not Applicable
Joint Venture	Yes	No
Acquisition	Yes	Yes

knowledge of the resources being purchased. The firm to be acquired, on the other hand, has an information advantage because of its superior knowledge about its industry, its internal resources, and the market for these resources. This puts the acquiring firm at a disadvantage for evaluating the value of the resources being purchased. The seller may ask a price in excess of the value of the business and resources, or the acquirer may overbid for them.

An additional problem makes the economic transaction even more risky for the acquiring company. This problem is related to the singular nature of the transaction, which allows the sellers to cheat an acquirer, and provides the acquirer with little or no recourse to exact retribution from the sellers. Such a situation puts the seller at an advantage relative to the acquirer. Therefore, acquisitional risk or premium costs are associated with information asymmetry combined with the singular nature of the acquisition transaction process. Risk or premium costs can be lowered by increasing initial search costs, but this again is an added cost that is associated with an inefficient market.

Teece [1982] makes a similar argument for a firm that selects the acquisition mode compared to the new venture mode by suggesting that the new venture firm has excess or slack resources that can be expended on the creation of a new venture. Utilizing these slack resources more fully improves the overall effectiveness and efficiency of the firm. Furthermore, Teece's thesis is applicable to the whole firm while the theoretical argument in this paper is focused only on the entry mode itself. Other researchers have made similar information asymmetry arguments specific to the acquisition entry mode [Yip 1982].

New joint ventures, on the other hand, have minimal risks associated with resource overpayment because of the symmetrical and ongoing nature of the transaction process. The risk of paying too much for these resources is limited because all partners face the same potential information asymmetry problem. Therefore, neither partner has a clear ability to induce the other partner to overpay or overcommit without incurring the same problem themselves. This situation leads to a situation where neither party wants to induce the other to retaliate. For instance, the other firm(s) can retaliate if one firm attempts to cheat because of the ongoing relationship or multiple transactions present in a joint venture. In such an economic transactional dilemma (called a prisoner's dilemma), all parties can hold the other parties in line with the threat of reciprocal retaliatory action in future transactions.

262   JOURNAL OF INTERNATIONAL BUSINESS STUDIES, SECOND QUARTER 1994

In addition to the above retaliatory or negative motivational game, a positive motivational economic game is also present. Given that firms in a joint venture are benefiting from either sharing resources or remuneration, all parties will be reticent to cheat for fear they will lose these benefits. Therefore, all parties attempt to actively support the joint venture and do not cheat. This positive economic game dilemma (called a stag hunt) produces a non-cheating environment based on the accruing benefits to all parties. These two economic dilemmas or games tend to discourage cheating in joint ventures.

The only situation where cheating becomes advantageous is when an asymmetric retaliatory position exists between two partnering firms. In this situation, one firm can cheat and the other cannot retaliate in an equal and reciprocal manner. It is assumed, however, that joint venture partners have appropriately selected their partners to avoid such a position. This argument highlights the one resource-based cost that joint ventures incur. This cost is the search and examination cost related to selecting a partner with the required resources, as well as a partner with a symmetrical retaliatory position so that cheating is minimized. It should be noted that a symmetrical retaliatory position not only includes considerations such as strategic position, but also organizational culture, and managerial values and attitudes.

On the basis of the above assessment, the total cost of procuring necessary resources in a joint venture is more than that in a new venture because of search costs, but less than that in an acquisition, as shown in Table 2.

Entry Mode and Management Control Requirements. Organizational control costs are also dependent upon the entry mode selected. In this study, organizational control is defined as the efficient and effective management of the relationship between the parent and entry entity that enables the parent to best meet their overall goals and objectives.

Organizational control has frequently been associated with different entry modes. Previous research has suggested that entry modes having different ownership levels are associated with specific control capabilities and capacities [Anderson and Gatignon 1986; Calvet 1984; Caves 1982; Davidson 1982; Gatignon and Anderson 1988; Root 1987]. In a joint venture, the multiple ownership arrangement has costs associated with negotiating an initial control relationship between the parents, as well as costs associated with the ongoing management of the relationship [Beamish and Banks 1987; Killing 1983]. Thus, based on management control issues, the wholly owned modes appear to be intrinsically distinct from the joint venture mode.

The costs associated with managing organizational control mechanisms are related to the type of control mechanism used and the number of control relationships required. Schaan and Beamish [1988] delineated over two dozen nonownership control mechanisms used in joint ventures. Such a large number of alternative mechanisms were deemed necessary and applicable because of the lack of direct ownership control. Killing [1983] similarly

TABLE 2
The Costs Associated with Utilizing the Entry Modes

Entry Mode	Costs of Procuring Additional Resources	Ownership and Managerial Control Costs	Total Costs
New Venture	Low	Low	Low
Joint Venture	Medium	High	Medium to High
Acquisition	High	High	High

believed that nonownership control mechanisms were slower and less efficient than the more direct mechanism of ownership control in subsidiaries. Nonownership control mechanisms are often considered more costly because ultimately the various parties have greater scope to act opportunistically or cheat, given that there is no ultimate legal control mechanism such as ownership control. Furthermore, nonownership control mechanisms require that behavioral-based values such as trust and respect be developed over a period of time before an effective control relationship results. Effort is expended in initially installing and then maintaining these control mechanisms.

The joint venture mode also has more relationships to be managed. Ensuring that control mechanisms produce maximum synergies between the various entities requires that the parents not only establish a relationship with the joint venture, but also with the other parent(s). These multiple relationships increase the probability that one of the parties will act in an opportunistic manner. All of these relationships incur organizational and management control costs.

Several researchers have found evidence of such control differences between joint ventures and wholly owned entry modes. Agarwal and Ramaswami [1992] empirically found that joint ventures were positively associated with the contractual risks associated with different degrees of ownership. In addition, Kim and Hwang's [1992] empirical study on global entry modes discovered that wholly owned modes were associated with more effective and efficient control mechanisms relative to the joint venture mode.

Acquisitions also incur supplementary control costs. In particular, the resource deficiency perceptions that constrain a firm to contingently select the acquisition mode also tend to cause management control problems. The information asymmetry created by the resource deficiency may limit the firm's ability to understand and effectively control newly acquired entities in several ways. First, organizational culture differences may exacerbate the management control problem between the two merging entities. In particular, cultural differences may limit the effectiveness of behavioral-based control mechanisms that rely upon trust, value congruence and respect. This may force the acquiring company to use a restricted set of control mechanisms which in turn may decrease the implementation efficiency of the organizational control process, and increase the risk of opportunistic action by the acquired company's work force. Organizational culture differences may also impede organizational integration, yet executives often erroneously predict that organizational integration will produce post-acquisitional synergies. The opportunity costs of not gaining these synergies immediately may be significant.

Organizational cultural problems of this sort have been reported by a variety of researchers [Adler and Graham 1989; Alstom and Gillespie 1989; Balakrishnan 1988; Caves and Mehra 1986; Conn and Connell 1991; Datta 1991; Harrison, Hitt, Hoskisson and Ireland 1991; Hopkins 1987]. Datta [1991] correlated acquisition performance with the degree of similarity between the management styles in the entities before acquisition. He found that similar management styles, a proxy measure for organizational cultural characteristics, led to better performance. The costs of controlling for an organizational cultural gap are incurred both prior to acquisition, when significant searching costs are required to differentiate appropriate from inappropriate organizational cultures, and subsequent to the acquisition, when a variety of management and organizational integration techniques must be used to merge the two cultures.

The second problem associated with acquisitions is that of maximizing synergies and minimizing redundancies in the new entity. Many researchers have investigated the potential for different types of synergies in acquisitions. However, the vast majority of these studies have found no significant relationship between synergies and post-acquisitional performance [Caves 1989]. Chatterjee [1992] found that synergies, in general, do not create value in acquisitions. The more significant value-creating strategy is management restructuring, a tactic that could be implemented by the previous management independently of the acquiring firm. Furthermore, for every synergy created in an acquisition there are several costly redundancies. An empirical study by Chatterjee [1990] found that, from a resource-based perspective, acquisitions have the potential to create more resource redundancies or duplications than synergies. Despite this evidence, most managers continue to suggest that acquisitions are made for synergistic reasons [Walter and Barney 1990]. This enigma of managers claiming synergies, which often are not present, to justify an acquisition is further evidence of the information asymmetries present in this mode. Based on these management control problems, it can be concluded that control costs are higher for acquisitions than for new ventures.

Table 2 summarizes the management control inefficiencies associated with various entry modes. New ventures are least inefficient while both acquisitions and joint ventures incur considerable management control costs.

Hypotheses Development

These resource deficiency and management control arguments produce the hierarchy of entry modes illustrated in Table 2. The new venture mode is the most efficient because it incurs the lowest ownership advantage costs.

The joint venture is the next most efficient because, although it incurs management control costs, it does not incur the high resource deficiency costs. Acquisitions, however, incur both high direct resource deficiency costs and high management control costs and therefore, are deemed the most inefficient mode.

Based on this analysis the following hypotheses are derived:

H1: New venture entry modes will on average outperform the joint venture and acquisition modes of international market entry.

H2: Joint ventures will on average outperform the acquisition mode of international market entry.

DATA AND METHODOLOGY

The database used in this study resulted from a survey of all Japanese manufacturing subsidiaries in North America (i.e., Canada and United States) whose parent companies were listed on the Tokyo, Osaka, or Nagoya stock exchanges in 1991 [Toyo Keizai 1992]. The information in the database was compiled using public information and a survey of the top Japanese manager in each foreign subsidiary during 1991 [Toyo Keizai 1992]. The effects of locational advantage were controlled for by using only Japanese entries into the North American market. Industry-specific effects were partially controlled for by using only entries that involved manufacturing firms with established manufacturing operations in North America.

The database tends to underrepresent small parent firm entries and overrepresent larger parent firms because of the public nature of the database source. This may reduce the generalizability of the study, but it helps control for organizational size influences. Although no organizational variables were used in the model, the three modes appear to include cases having comparable operational scope and scale. An analysis of variance indicates that sales volume, total employment and capitalization values were not significantly different between the three modes. This analysis also tends to confirm that radically different industries (i.e., capital-intensive versus non-capital-intensive industries) were not present in the three mode subsamples. The sample consisted of subsidiaries having average sales of $51 million, average investment of $30 million and an average of 197 employees.

The operational definition of the modes are as follows: a new venture was defined as an entry that involved only one parent, which built and operationally equipped the plant; an acquisition was defined as an entry that involved only one parent, and its plant and equipment were purchased from the previous owner; and a joint venture was defined as an entry that involves more than one parent, and its plant was built and operationally equipped by these parents. These definitions ensure that the entry modes are mutually exclusive.

The database contained information on the initial entry mode type, the initial entry mode objective, and the present ownership structure of the entity.

From this information only those modes that appeared to fit the defined operational types were used in the study. A total of 321 database entries or market entries were used in this study; 166 of these were new ventures, 79 were joint ventures and 76 were acquisitions.[2] This sample size is large for such a constrained international theoretical problem.

The measurement of performance was a survey question that asked the top Japanese manager in the subsidiary to evaluate its overall financial performance in terms of financial profitability in 1991. The scale for the performance indicator had only three choices: profitable (1), break-even (0), or a loss (−1).[3] This financial performance measurement, although limited, represents the only information Japanese firms are willing to provide given their very private nature. The use of different accounting approaches and individual assessments of performance is likely to be minimized because respondents are from the same country and from the same level in the organization. Furthermore, the analysis eliminated startup period variations when unusual one-time accounting charges are most likely to create anomalous performance variations.

Chi-squared, Spearman's Rank Correlation and Kruskal-Wallis tests were used to assess the relationship between performance and entry mode. Pearson's *chi*-squared is the most commonly used test for the relationship between categorical variables. The measure is based on the differences between actual and expected frequencies in a multi-way table [Freund and Walpole 1980]. The Kruskal-Wallis and Spearman's Rank Correlation tests are used to further test the relationship using tests that are specific to interval-based and categorical variables. The Kruskal-Wallis test is a nonparametric alternative to the one-way analysis of variance test. It is based on the generalized rank-sum test that investigates the null hypothesis and it tests whether the samples come from the same population [Freund and Walpole 1980]. Spearman's Rank Correlation is a measure of variance accounted for in the relationship and is computed from the ranks of the variables present [Freund and Walpole 1980]. These three statistical tests were employed to ensure the results were duplicable, and were not the result of an inherent mathematical bias within one statistical technique.

Analytical Approach

When investigating the relationship between performance and entry mode, one must consider the effects of entry age. The internationalization literature has consistently shown that entry into a new international market requires a learning period over which entering firms establish themselves [Cardozo, Reynolds, Miller and Phillips 1989; Forsgren 1989; Johanson and Vahlne 1977; Johanson and Wiedersheim-Paul 1975; Juul and Walters 1987; Newbould, Buckley and Thurwell 1978]. During this startup period, performance is depressed because a new entrant is trying to establish market penetration and achieve economies of scale and scope. During this period of establishment, financial performance may be poor and unstable for a variety of reasons. First, new entrants require time to adjust to new markets, new organizational processes and systems, or new competitive factors in the new market mentioned above. A lag effect would probably be most pronounced in new venture and joint venture entry modes because of their newness and initial vulnerability. Second, the average performance of an entry may be low at first because some firms have selected the wrong entry mode or market and require time to recognize their error and abandon the entry. This study attempts to control for these effects by defining and excluding the initial adjustment period. Therefore, the data were examined to see if an initial adjustment period was present.

A visual check of the data indicated that all of the entry modes had an initial startup period having low unstable performance which subsequently increased and stabilized at a higher level. Furthermore, regression analysis confirmed this relationship as illustrated in Table 3. The regression results showed a positive slope for all entry modes, indicating that performance was initially low, and as age increased, performance increased. The low R^2 values suggested that the curves may be nonlinear, and thus, may level off over time. Therefore, the influence of age must be either controlled for or eliminated. Controlling for age statistically is unworkable because it reduces the cell size to less than 5.

The technique used to eliminate the effects of entry age was based upon the notion that, for each entry mode, performance would initially improve and then, after several years, it would stabilize and oscillate around this new level. Thus, a technique was needed to isolate the stable period from the growth or initial startup period. We used a nonlinear regression technique, piece-wise linear regression with a breakpoint.

Piece-wise linear regression with a breakpoint maximizes the correlation (R^2) by fitting two linear relationships appropriate to the subsamples; one prior to an x variable breakpoint and one subsequent to the breakpoint. Thus, the technique not only searches for the best slopes and intercepts for the subsamples, but it also searches for the best point on the x-axis for an appropriate breakpoint to occur between the two subsamples. Using age as the x variable we can attempt to describe the point at which the relationship between performance and entry age stabilizes. Furthermore, we can see whether the second regression line which describes the data beyond the solved-for breakpoint is horizontal, and thus stable.

Table 4 illustrates the results from the breakpoint regression analysis. These analyses used all of the statistical evidence in the data to develop the breakpoint lines, and thus, the significance of these relationships cannot be assessed. However, several interesting attributes provided strong evidence of an appropriate region from which to select a stable sample for subsequent analysis. First, the breakpoints all occurred at approximately two years. Furthermore, as one would suspect, the new venture entry required a slightly longer period to stabilize than the joint venture or acquisition modes. Second,

Strategic Alliances

268   JOURNAL OF INTERNATIONAL BUSINESS STUDIES, SECOND QUARTER 1994

TABLE 3
The Regression of Entity Age after Entry to Performance

Entry Mode	Regression Model	R^2
New Venture	Performance = 1.9 + .1 * Age	.05
Joint Venture	Performance = 1.6 + .1 * Age	.15
Acquisition	Performance = 1.6 + .1 * Age	.05

TABLE 4
Breakpoint Regression of Entity Age after Entry to Performance

Entry Mode	Regression Model #1	Break Point	Regression Model #2	R^2
New Venture	Perf.= 1.4 + 0.0 * Age	2.1 years	Perf.= 3.0 + 0.0 * Age	.80
Joint Venture	Perf.= 1.0 - 0.0 * Age	2.0 years	Perf.= 2.5 + 0.0 * Age	.84
Acquisition	Perf.= 1.0 - 0.0 * Age	1.9 years	Perf.= 2.5 - 0.0 * Age	.80

the linear relationships subsequent to the breakpoints were flat. This evidence suggests that a stable relationship between entry mode, age, and performance was established. Therefore, the subsamples used in the subsequent analysis stages were limited to entities over two years old.

RESULTS

Results are illustrated in Table 5. As shown, all tests were statistically significant; the *chi*-squared and Kruskal-Wallis tests better than the .10 level and Spearman's Rank Correlation better than the .05 level. In addition, the direction of the relationship supported the originally delineated hypotheses as shown by the means in Table 5.[4]

DISCUSSION AND CONCLUSIONS

The above analysis provides evidence that different entry modes have different performance levels. In particular, the results suggest that the new venture mode outperforms the joint venture mode and the joint venture mode outperforms the acquisition mode. These results support previous studies that have attempted to assess the relationship between performance and entry mode by Li and Guisinger [1991] and Simmonds [1990]. Therefore, there is considerable supporting evidence that international ownership-based entry modes have different performance levels.

This study did not test the theoretical arguments that cause performance variance. However, previous contingency research has provided support for many of the relationships outlined in the theory development section. This study concentrated on two arguments pertinent to the contingency-based process: resource-based and organizational control contingencies. The theoretical

TABLE 5
The Performance Difference in Entry Modes
for Entries Over Two Years of Age
(given as performance frequency per entry mode in percent)

Entry Mode	Performance Gain (%)	Performance Break Even (%)	Performance Loss (%)	Mean[1]
New Venture	44	29	27	2.17
Joint Venture	39	20	39	2.02
Acquisition	25	32	43	1.82

Chi-square: *p*=   .04
Kruskal-Wallis Test: *p*=.03
Spearman's Rank Correlation: *p*=.01
[1]Mean is based on 3 being gain, 2 being break even and 1 being loss

model argued that entry mode selection was based on a firm's resource requirements. Most of these resource-based contingency arguments have been empirically tested, with positive results, by other researchers [Erramilli and Rao 1990; Hill, Hwang and Kim 1990; Kim and Hwang 1992]. The theoretical model then suggests that contingency factors modify the transaction costs related to obtaining the appropriate resources and controlling the new organizational entity, which in turn affects mode performance. Many of these contingency relationships have also been supported in previous research [Buckley and Casson 1988; Caves and Mehra 1986; Daniels and Magill 1991; Hennart 1988, 1991].

Our evidence provides preliminary support for the theoretical model developed in this study. It must be acknowledged, however, that this study represents only an exploratory investigation of an otherwise complex causal relationship. As such, it establishes a base theoretical model and some preliminary evidence upon which subsequent work can be based. Further analysis should concentrate on developing a more generalized model that includes other contingent influences and incorporates the complexities of within-mode differences.

This study is particularly equivocal in two areas. First, it did not control for a number of firm and industry-specific contingency variables such as strategic intent, size, and organizational characteristics. These variables may provide further insight into the above relationships. In addition, industry-specific factors, such as barriers to entry and exit, may improve the explanatory capacity of the model. Some firm, industry, and country-specific variables were partially controlled for in this study, but clearly a preferred methodological approach would include controls for more of these ancillary variables. Therefore, future work must investigate the effect of these variables on this entry mode-performance relationship.

It should also be noted that many organizational and industry-specific variables may enhance our model. For instance, one firm-specific variable that explains

270   JOURNAL OF INTERNATIONAL BUSINESS STUDIES, SECOND QUARTER 1994

entry mode selection is organizational size [Caves and Mehra 1986; Hill et al. 1990]. Previous research has not related size to entry mode selection except as a measure of the number of resources available. However, size may also produce concerns related to the bounded rationality problems in an organization. This bounded rationality could influence top managers perceptions of core or inimitable resources, and thus influence the entry mode selection process.

The second limitation of this study is that it uses a data set comprised of Japanese parents entering the North American market. Locational advantages have been shown to influence entry mode [Agarwal and Ramaswami 1992], and such a locational effect may have influenced the relationships above. In particular, Japanese firms have strong organizational cultures. This location-specific effect may have an influence on the above relationship. This constrains the generalizability of the study in that culture-specific factors could influence a firm's transaction costs in certain entry modes, and a firm's perception of its core or non-inimitable resources.

In conclusion, further research incorporating a variety of other performance measures and including many other potential contingency effects is needed to broaden our understanding of the complex international entry mode selection process.

NOTES

1. The joint venture mode in this study was limited to the new venture case. Therefore, joint ventures that were established through acquisitions were not included.

2. In the joint venture sample 58% of the cases had local partners while 42% did not have local partners.

3. The sample performance variance was as follows: 38% reported profitable, 26% reported break-even, and 36% reported a loss.

4. It should be noted that an analysis using the total database including entities having an age of less than two years also provides evidence supporting the hypotheses. The chi-squared was nonsignificant at $p=.11$, Spearman's Rank Correlation was significant at $p=.05$, and the Kruskal-Wallis test was significant at $p=.02$. The directions of the results also supported the hypotheses.

REFERENCES

Adler, Nancy J. & John L. Graham. 1989. Cross-cultural integration: The international comparison fallacy? *Journal of International Business Studies*, 20(3): 515-37.

Agarwal, Sanjeev & Sridhar N. Ramaswami. 1992. Choice of foreign market entry mode: Impact of ownership, location and internalization factors. *Journal of International Business Studies*, 23(1): 1-28.

Alstom, L. J. & W. Gillespie. 1989. Resource coordination and transaction costs: A framework for analyzing the firm/market boundary. *Journal of Economic Behavior and Organization*, 11(2): 191-212.

Amit, Raphael, J. Livnat & P. Zarowin. 1989. The mode of corporate diversification: Internal ventures versus acquisitions. *Managerial and Decision Economics*, 10: 89-100.

Anderson, Erin & Hubert Gatignon. 1986. Modes of foreign entry: A transaction cost analysis and propositions. *Journal of International Business Studies*, 17(3): 1-26.

Balakrishnan, Srinivasan. 1988. The prognostics of diversifying acquisitions. *Strategic Management Journal*, 9(2): 185-96.

Beamish, Paul W. & J. C. Banks. 1987. Equity joint ventures and the theory of the multinational enterprise. *Journal of International Business Studies*, 18(2): 1-16.

Buckley, Peter J. & Mark Casson. 1988. A theory of cooperation in international business. In Farok Contractor & Peter Lorange, editors, *Cooperative strategies in international business*. Lexington, Mass.: Lexington Books.

Burgleman, Robert A. 1983. A process model of internal corporate venturing in the diversified major firm. *Administrative Science Quarterly*, 28: 223-44.

_____. 1985. Managing the new venture division: Research findings and implications for strategic management. *Strategic Management Journal*, 6: 36-54.

Calvet, A. Louis. 1984. A synthesis of foreign direct investment theories and theories of the multinational firm. *Journal of International Business Studies*, 12: 43-59.

Cardozo, Richard, P. Reynolds, B. Miller & D. Phillips. 1989. Empirical evidence on developmental trajectories of new businesses. In R. Brockhaus, N. Churchill, J. Katz, B. Kirchhoff, K. Vesper & W. Wetzel, editors, *Frontiers of entrepreneurship research*, 360-69. St. Louis: St. Louis University, Babson College.

Casson, Mark. 1992. Internalization theory and beyond. In Peter J. Buckley, editor, *New directions in international business: Research priorities for the 1990s*. Aldershot, U.K.: Edward Elgar Publishing Limited.

Caves, Richard E. 1982. *Multinational enterprise and economic analysis*. New York: Cambridge University Press.

_____. 1989. Mergers, takeovers, and economic efficiency: Foresight vs. hindsight. *International Journal of Industrial Organization*, 7: 151-74.

_____ & S. K. Mehra. 1986. Entry of foreign multinationals into U.S. manufacturing industries. In Michael E. Porter, editor, *Competition in global industries*. Boston: Harvard Press.

Chatterjee, Sanjit. 1990. Excess resources, utilization costs, and mode of entry. *Academy of Management Journal*, 33(4): 780-800.

_____. 1992. Sources of value in takeovers: Synergy or restructuring—Implications for target and bidder firms. *Strategic Management Journal*, 13(4): 267-86.

_____, M. H. Lubatkin, D. M. Schweiger & Y. Weber. 1992. Cultural differences and shareholder value in related mergers: Linking equity and human capital. *Strategic Management Journal*, 13(5): 319-34.

Collis, Stephen. 1991. A resource-based analysis of global competition: The case of the bearings industry. *Strategic Management Journal*, 12 (Special Issue, Summer): 49-68.

Conn, Robert L. & F. Connell. 1990. International mergers: Returns to U.S. and British firms. *Journal of Business Finance & Accounting*, 17(5): 689-712.

Daniels, John D. 1970. Recent foreign direct manufacturing investment in the United States. *Journal of International Business Studies*, 1(1): 125-32.

_____ & Sharon L. Magill. 1991. The utilization of international joint ventures by United States firms in high technology industries. *Journal of High Technology Management Research*, 2(1): 113-31.

Datta, Deepak K. 1991. Organizational fit and acquisition performance: Effects of post-acquisition integration. *Strategic Management Journal*, 12(4): 281-97.

Davidson, William H. 1980. The location of foreign direct investment activity: Country characteristics and experience effects. *Journal of International Business Studies*, 12: 9-22.

_____. 1982. *Global strategic management*. New York: John Wiley & Sons.

Drucker, Peter. 1974. *Management: Tasks, responsibilities, promise*. New York: Harper & Row.

Dubin, Michael. 1975. *Foreign acquisitions and the spread of the multinational firm*. Unpublished doctoral dissertation, Harvard.

Dunning, John H. 1980. Toward an eclectic theory of international production: Some empirical tests. *Journal of International Business Studies*, 11(2): 9-31.

_____. 1988. *Explaining international production*. London: Unwin Hyman.

Erramilli, M. Krishna & C. P. Rao. 1990. Choice of foreign market entry modes by service firms: Role of market knowledge. *Management International Review*, 30(2): 135-50.

Erramilli, M. Krishna. 1991. The experience factor in foreign market entry behavior of service firms. *Journal of International Business Studies*, 22(3): 479-502.

Forsgren, Mats. 1989. *Managing the internationalization process: The Swedish case.* London, U.K.: Routledge.

Freund, John E. & R. E. Walpole. 1980 (third edition). *Mathematical statistics.* Englewood Cliffs, N.J.: Prentice-Hall Inc.

Gatignon, Hubert & Erin Anderson. 1987. The multinational corporation's degree of control over foreign subsidiaries: An empirical test of a transaction cost explanation. In *Report Number 87-103,* Cambridge, Mass.: Marketing Science Institute.

_____. 1988. The multinational corporation's degree of control over foreign subsidiaries: An empirical test of a transaction cost explanation. *Journal of Law, Economics, and Organization,* 4(2): 305-36.

Haar, Jerry. 1989. A comparative analysis of the profitability performance of the largest U.S., European and Japanese multinational enterprises. *Management International Review,* 29(3): 5-18.

Hamel, Gary. 1991. Competition for competencies and inter-partner learning within international strategic alliances. *Strategic Management Journal,* 12 (Special Issue, Summer): 83-103.

_____ & K. C. Prahalad. 1990. The core competence of the corporation. *Harvard Business Review,* (May-June): 79-93.

Harrigan, Katheryn R. 1985. *Strategies for joint ventures.* Lexington, Mass.: Lexington Books.

_____. 1988. Joint ventures and competitive strategies. *Strategic Management Journal,* 9: 141-58.

Harrison, J. S., Michael A. Hitt, R. E. Hoskisson & Duane R. Ireland. 1991. Synergies and post-acquisition performance: Differences versus similarities in resource allocations. *Journal of Management,* 17(1): 173-90.

Hennart, Jean-François. 1988. A transaction costs theory of equity joint ventures. *Journal of International Business Studies,* 9: 361-74.

_____. 1991. The transaction costs theory of joint ventures: An empirical study of Japanese subsidiaries in the United States. *Management Science,* 37(4): 483-97.

Hill, Charles W., Peter Hwang & Wi Chan Kim. 1990. An eclectic theory of the choice of international entry mode. *Strategic Management Journal,* 11: 117-28.

Hill, Charles W. & G. R. Jones. 1989. *Strategic management: An integrated approach.* Boston: Houghton Mifflin Co.

Hopkins, H. Donald. 1987. Acquisition strategy and the market position of acquiring firms. *Strategic Management Journal,* 8: 535-47.

Inkpen, Andrew C. 1992. *Learning and collaboration: An examination of North American-Japanese joint ventures.* Unpublished doctoral dissertation, The University of Western Ontario.

Janger, Allen R. 1980. *Organization of international joint ventures.* New York: Conference Board.

Jensen, Michael C. & Richard S. Ruback. 1983. The market for corporate control: The scientific evidence. *Journal of Financial Economics,* 11: 5-50.

Johanson, Jan & Jan-Erik Vahlne. 1977. The internationalization process of the firm—A model of knowledge development and increasing foreign market commitments. *Journal of International Business Studies,* 8(1): 23-32.

Johanson, Jan & Finn Wiedersheim-Paul. 1975. The internationalization of the firm: Four Swedish cases. *Journal of Management Studies,* (October): 303-22.

Juul, Monika & P. G. P. Walters. 1987. The internationalization of Norwegian firms—A study of the U.K. experience. *Management International Review,* 27(1): 58-66.

Killing, J. Peter. 1983. *Strategies for joint venture success.* New York: Praeger.

Kim, W. Chan & Peter Hwang. 1992. Global strategy and multinationals' entry mode choice. *Journal of International Business Studies,* 23(1): 29-54.

Kogut, Bruce & Harbir Singh. 1988. The effect of national culture on the choice of entry mode. *Journal of International Business Studies,* (Fall): 411-32.

Li, Jiatao & Stephen Guisinger. 1991. Comparative business failures of foreign-controlled firms in the United States. *Journal of International Business Studies,* 22(2): 209-24.

Nahavandi, Afsaneh & Ali Maleksadeh. 1988. Acculturation in mergers and acquisitions. *Academy of Management Review,* 13(1): 79-90.

Newbould, Gerald D., Peter J. Buckley & J. C. Thurwell. 1978. *Going international—The experiences of smaller companies overseas.* New York: John Wiley & Sons.

Porter, Michael E. 1987. From competitive advantage to corporate strategy. *Harvard Business Review,* 65(3): 43-59.

Prahalad, C. K. & Richard A. Bettis. 1986. The dominant logic: A new linkage between diversity and performance. *Strategic Management Journal,* 7(6): 485-501.

Root, Franklin R. 1987. *Entry strategies for international markets.* Lexington, Mass.: D.C. Heath.

Schaan, Jean-Louis & Paul W. Beamish. 1988 Joint venture general managers in developing countries. In Farok Contractor & Peter Lorange, editors, *Cooperative strategies in international business.* Lexington, Mass.: Lexington Books, D.C. Heath & Co.

Simmonds, Paul G. 1990. The combined diversification breadth and mode dimensions and the performance of large diversified firms. *Strategic Management Journal,* 11: 399-410.

Singh, Harbir & Bruce Kogut. 1989. Industry and competitive effects on the choice of entry mode. In *Academy of Management Best Paper Proceedings:* 116-20.

Stalk, George, P. Evans & L. E. Shulman. 1992. Competing on capabilities: The new rules of corporate strategy. *Harvard Business Review,* 70(2): 57-69.

Stopford, John M. & Louis T. Wells. 1972. *Managing the multinational enterprise.* New York: Basic Books.

Teece, David J. 1982. Towards an economic theory of the multiproduct firm. *Journal of Economic Behavior and Organization,* 3: 39-63.

Toyo Keizai. 1992. *Japanese overseas investments 1992* (in Japanese). Tokyo: Toyo Keizai, Inc.

Venkatraman, N. & Vasudevar Ramanujam. 1986. Measurement of business performance in strategy research: A comparison of approaches. *Academy of Management Review,* 11: 801-14.

Vernon, Raymond. 1983. Organization and institutional responses to international risk. In Richard Herring, editor, *Managing international risk.* New York: Cambridge University Press.

Walter, Gordon A. & J. B. Barney. 1990. Management objectives in mergers and acquisitions. *Strategic Management Journal,* 11(1): 79-86.

Wilson, Brent D. 1980. The propensity of multinational companies to expand through acquisitions. *Journal of International Business Studies,* 12(Spring/Summer): 59-65.

Yip, George S. 1982. Diversification entry: Internal development versus acquisition. *Strategic Management Journal,* 3: 331-45.

Zejan, Mario C. 1990. New ventures or acquisitions: The choice of Swedish multinational enterprises. *Journal of Industrial Economics,* 38(3): 349-55.

[27]

° *Academy of Management Journal*
1994, Vol. 37, No. 6, 1478–1517.

BARGAINING POWER, MANAGEMENT CONTROL, AND PERFORMANCE IN UNITED STATES–CHINA JOINT VENTURES: A COMPARATIVE CASE STUDY

AIMIN YAN
Boston University
BARBARA GRAY
Pennsylvania State University

This article reports a comparative case study of four joint ventures between partners from the United States and the People's Republic of China. The bargaining power of potential partners affects the structure of management control in a joint venture, which affects venture performance. Several informal control mechanisms interacting with formal control structure and influencing performance are identified. We also investigated the joint ventures' evolution over time. An integrative model of management control in joint ventures is presented.

International joint ventures are a rapidly growing organizational form that has received increasing interest from researchers in a variety of academic disciplines. Despite this attention, academic understanding of joint ventures is still limited in scope and in depth. Previous studies have reported high failure and instability rates among joint ventures (Franko, 1971; Harrigan, 1986; Kogut, 1989; Levine & Byrne, 1986), and the factors predictive of successful venture performance remain unclear (Geringer & Hebert, 1991; Parkhe, 1993a). In addition, the empirical studies that have been done to test existing conceptual models have either produced contradictory results or been difficult to compare because of differences in how variables were measured.

This study adopts an interpartner negotiations perspective on joint venture formation. We envisioned joint ventures as mixed motive games between partners who cooperate and compete simultaneously (Lax & Sebenius, 1986; Hamel, Doz, & Prahalad, 1989). According to the negotiations perspective, the relative bargaining power of each joint venture partner shapes the pattern of management control that a venture adopts. In addition, parent control is hypothesized to be a critical factor that determines performance. Although previous researchers have empirically investigated the first rela-

---

We would like to thank Martin Kilduff, James Thomas, and two anonymous reviewers for this journal for their insightful comments on the earlier versions of this article.

tionship (Blodgett, 1991; Fagre & Wells, 1982; Killing, 1983; Lecraw, 1984), the studies are difficult to compare because they have measured both variables differently. Research findings on the relationship between control and performance offer conflicting results (see Geringer and Hebert [1989] for a review). Lecraw (1984) noted that the relationship between parent control and performance generates continuing controversy in the international joint venture literature.

Additional problems with prior research also warrant further study. For example, (1) conflicting results have been obtained for joint ventures in developing and developed countries (Beamish, 1984, 1985, 1988); (2) longitudinal studies are underrepresented in research to date and, as a result, little is known about how joint ventures evolve over time; (3) most joint venture research on developing countries adopts the perspective of the multinational partner and excludes the views of the developing country partner; and (4) only two studies have examined the relationships between bargaining power and control and control and performance simultaneously (Killing, 1983; Lecraw, 1984).

In this research, we utilized a comparative case study approach to reexamine the relationships among bargaining power, control, and performance. We sought to overcome the limitations mentioned above in several ways. First, we looked at the relationships among all three variables in the same study. By adopting in-depth, comparative case studies, we tried to sort out the confusion and inconsistencies with respect to these relationships in the existing literature. By providing detailed explanations that survey methods miss, case studies offer the prospect of new insights into the connections among these variables (Eisenhardt, 1989; Glaser & Strauss, 1967; Yin, 1989). Second, we sought to improve on existing models by accounting for the dynamic aspects of joint ventures, a topic largely ignored in research to date (Parkhe, 1993a). By tracing the evolution of joint ventures, we identified changes in the ventures over time. In this respect, comparative case studies are useful because they are particularly appropriate for studying organizational changes (Van de Ven & Poole, 1990). Third, our data reflect the interpretations of both parents. Fourth, research on international joint ventures that has examined bargaining power, control, and performance has primarily focused on ventures created among developed country partners. In our study, we aimed at a deeper understanding of joint ventures in a developing country, the People's Republic of China, thus enriching the literature with the Chinese experience.

Recent research has focused on the rapid proliferation of international joint ventures in transformational economies (those in transition from central control to a market orientation) such as that of the People's Republic of China (Beamish, 1993; Child, 1991; Daniels, Krug, & Nigh, 1985; Davidson, 1987; Pearson, 1991; Pomfret, 1991). Virtually no research on the relationships among bargaining power, control, and performance in joint ventures in China has been reported. What research exists either focuses on the macro environments in China for direct foreign investment (e.g., Campbell, 1988;

Ho, 1990; Mathur & Chen, 1987; Shan, 1991; Tung, 1982) or is descriptive
(e.g., Campbell, 1988; Eiteman, 1990; Hendryx, 1986; Mann, 1989; O'Reilly,
1988; Schnepp, Von Glinow, & Bhambri, 1990). In-depth empirical research
on the management and organizational issues in international joint ventures
in China has been limited, though more studies have been done very recently (e.g., Beamish, 1993; Child, 1991; Lo, 1989; Newman, 1992; Pearson,
1991; Teagarden & Von Glinow, 1990). The applicability of research findings
generated in the West to the Chinese setting remains an open question
(Child, 1991).

The economic reforms in China have stimulated a wealth of joint ventures in the past decade. More than 20,000 international partnerships with a
total investment of more than $26 billion were signed in the 1980s (U.S.–
China Business Council, 1990). This rapid growth of Chinese joint ventures
presents an interesting and challenging opportunity to study international
alliances in a new institutional context (Child, 1991).

In the next section, we introduce the preliminary conceptual framework
derived from the existing literature. Following Yin (1989), who argued that
case studies should start with theoretical propositions,[1] this research began
with a theoretical framework linking bargaining power, management control, and performance. We then used analytic induction (Cressey, 1953; Glaser & Strauss, 1967; Robinson, 1951; Znaniecki, 1934) to analyze four U.S.–
Chinese joint ventures.

THEORETICAL BACKGROUND

As noted earlier, we adopted a negotiations perspective to explain the
distribution of control between the partners in a joint venture. The negotiations perspective suggests that the relative bargaining power of partners is
a critical variable in determining patterns of control in joint ventures
(Blodgett, 1991; Harrigan & Newman, 1990; Lecraw, 1984). Below, we develop the meaning of these constructs and provide support for the relationships among them.

Bargaining Power

Bargaining power refers to a bargainer's ability to favorably change the
"bargaining set" (Lax & Sebenius, 1986), to win accommodations from the
other party (Dwyer & Walker, 1981; Tung, 1988), and to influence the outcome of a negotiation (Schelling, 1956). Researchers investigating bargaining

_____

[1] Yin's (1989) position that case studies should start with a priori theoretical propositions
obviously contrasts with Eisenhardt's (1989) argument that case studies should start with a
clean theoretical slate so that researchers are less likely to be bound by preconceived theoretical
notions. However, a clean theoretical slate is virtually impossible to achieve (Parkhe, 1993a),
given the accumulative nature of scientific inquiry (Kuhn, 1970), the education researchers
have received from studying prior theories, and the potentially infinite number of variables
affecting a phenomenon under study.

and those investigating resource dependence have each identified a source of bargaining power.

Advocates of bargaining theory have proposed that the stakes of the bargainers in a negotiation and the availability of alternatives influence their bargaining power (Bacharach & Lawler, 1984). A stake is a bargainer's level of dependence on a negotiating relationship and on its outcomes. Stakes are negatively related to bargaining power. Alternatives available to negotiators specify the extent to which they can choose different arrangements for achieving the same goals sought in the negotiation. Thus, availability of alternatives is positively related to bargaining power. The bargaining partner who has more alternatives is more powerful because it can threaten to walk away from the current bargaining and exercise its best alternative to a negotiated agreement (Fisher & Ury, 1981). Since stakes and the availability of alternatives are associated with the context in which a negotiation occurs, we refer to them as sources of context-based bargaining power.

In another vein, resource dependence theory (Pfeffer & Salancick, 1978) suggests that the possession or control of critical resources constitutes power in interorganizational relations. If a firm contributes more critical resources to an interorganizational arrangement than its partner, it will be more powerful than the partner in the partnership between them. Put simply, the relative bargaining power of potential joint venture partners is determined by who brings what and how much to the venture (Harrigan, 1986). A partner gains bargaining power if the joint venture depends heavily on resources it contributes that are "costly or impossible for other partners to replace" (Root, 1988: 76) and critical to the venture's success (Harrigan & Newman, 1990).

Management Control

Management control refers to the process by which an organization influences its subunits and members to behave in ways that lead to the attainment of organizational objectives (Arrow, 1974; Flamholtz, Das, & Tsui, 1985; Ouchi, 1977). Conceptualization of control in joint ventures is more problematic, however, because two or more parents may influence a venture's activities. In this study, we focused on the structure of management control exercised by the sponsoring organizations in influencing a joint venture's strategic decisions and regulating its important activities.

Geringer and Hebert (1989) characterized parent control in international joint ventures as composed of three parts: the scope, extent, and mechanisms of control. The scope of control specifies the areas of the joint venture's operation in which control is exercised. The extent of control is the degree to which the parents exercise control. The mechanisms of control refer to the means by which control is exercised. Previous studies have each focused on a different dimension of control: Killing (1983) and Lecraw (1984) on extent, Geringer (1986) on scope, and Schaan (1983, 1988) on scope and mechanisms. Thus, their results are virtually noncomparable. Our multidimensional approach to management control enhanced comprehensiveness and comparability with other studies.

Relationships Between Bargaining Power and Management Control

Prior research has attempted to articulate the relationship between the bargaining power of the partners in a joint venture and the level of control they exercise. Lecraw (1984) found that three aspects of bargaining power—the technical leadership, advertising intensity, and export capability of the multinational partner—significantly contributed to control. In a study of 35 international joint ventures between developed countries, Killing (1983) reported that the partners' respective contributions shaped the control structure of the joint ventures. For example, if one partner contributed technology while the other had expertise in marketing, shared control was the most feasible arrangement. Other studies (Blodgett, 1991; Fagre & Wells, 1982) have also reported a positive relationship between bargaining power and control, but in these studies, control was measured by ownership split between the partners.

Performance

Configuration of performance has been a controversial topic in the organizational literature (see Goodman and Pennings [1980] or Lewin and Minton [1986] for a review). The controversy derives from the facts that performance can be evaluated in several ways and that few indicators of performance have been widely accepted. Performance evaluation becomes even more problematic in joint ventures because each party in the partnership is likely to adopt idiosyncratic criteria. The literature on joint venture performance reveals three areas in which major inconsistencies occur: (1) whose perspective (that of one parent, two parents, or the joint venture's management) is used for performance measurement, (2) variation in performance measures, which may range from subjective judgments to financial indicators, and (3) variation in the appropriateness of different performance measures as a venture matures (see Yan and Gray [1994] for a review). These inconsistencies make cross-study comparisons and generalizations about joint venture performance particularly problematic.

Following Schaan (1983, 1988) and our earlier research (Yan & Gray, 1994), we adopted a multidimensional approach to joint venture performance and incorporated the perspectives of multiple players. Specifically, we used each partner's assessment of the extent to which it had achieved its strategic objectives as a measure of performance.

Relationship Between Management Control and Performance

Studies of the relationship between parent control and performance have produced ambiguous results (Geringer & Hebert, 1989). In a study of international joint ventures between developed country partners, Killing (1983) found that ventures with one dominant parent outperformed those with shared management and that the relationship between control and performance was U-shaped. Drawing from a sample of international joint ventures in a developing country, Beamish (1984, 1985) reported that dominant control by foreign firms was negatively related to performance. But when local partners dominated ventures, no such relationship was found. Beamish therefore suggested that the type of economy in which a joint venture operates may moderate the control-performance relationship. However, Lecraw's (1984) study showed that the status of the economic development of a joint venture's host country may not be as critical as Beamish suggested. Using a sample of joint ventures in five developing Asian countries, Lecraw found a positive, roughly linear association between control and performance, a finding consistent with Killing's (1983) findings. Other researchers have noted that the control-performance relationship is indirect and thus subject to contingent factors (see Geringer and Hebert [1989] for a review). We argue that additional research is needed to sort out the conditions under which the relationship between control and performance is positive and that the type of economy in which a joint venture operates still deserves to be considered an important contingency.

Structural Reconfiguration in International Joint Ventures

Researchers have characterized joint ventures as transitional forms of organization (Davidson, 1982; Harrigan, 1986; Porter, 1990; Vernon, 1977). Though not all international joint ventures are necessarily transitional or unstable, they are far more dynamic than single, stand-alone organizations (Franko, 1971). Structural changes and reconfigurations in joint ventures are likely to occur over time for several reasons. First, international partnerships may be an expedient way for multinational corporations to enter foreign markets when conditions prohibit whole foreign ownership (Davidson, 1982; Fayerweather, 1982). Whenever such constraints are removed, joint ventures tend to become wholly owned affiliates (Contractor, 1990). Second, a joint venture can be phased out because its importance to one or both parents' overall strategies depreciates (Bartlett & Ghoshal, 1986; Harrigan & Newman, 1990). A third predictable transition in joint ventures occurs when there is an "obsolescing bargain" (Vernon, 1977: 151)—when substantial learning by one partner over time devalues the expertise or knowledge contributed by the other, thereby breaking down the initial bargaining relationship between them (Hamel, 1991). The obsolescing bargain also occurs when the partners gain bargaining power over time as a result of environmental changes (Harrigan & Newman, 1990). Dymsza (1988) noted that in joint ventures between developed and developing country partners, the former's contribution is likely to become less important over time; thus, it should turn major managerial responsibilities over to the developing country partner. Similarly, we noted in previous research (Gray & Yan, 1992), as did Hamilton and Singh (1991), that joint ventures need to reconfigure over time in response to changes in the partners' relative bargaining power to ensure stability and overall performance.

However, the dynamic aspect of joint ventures has been understudied and has received "the least amount of systematic attention in the existing literature," representing "a critical omission in the development of a more complete theory of international joint ventures" (Parkhe, 1993a: 234). Previous studies on changes in joint ventures have focused on different dimensions and had varying perspectives. In particular, empirical findings on the dynamic characteristics of international partnerships have been very sketchy. With the case study reported here, we attempt to provide inductively generated accounts of how joint ventures evolve over time, what factors trigger their structural reconfigurations, and how parents deal with changes in their joint ventures.

Summary

The above review suggests that although many studies of bargaining power, management control, and performance exist, they suffer from inconsistent conceptualizations and noncomparable empirical results. In Figure 1, we offer a model that synthesizes past research on bargaining power, management control, and performance in international joint ventures. Although the main thesis of the model may apply to all joint ventures, the nature and strength of the relationships depicted may vary from international to domestic joint ventures and from ventures in developed countries to those in developing countries. This research investigated the model by focusing on international joint ventures in a developing country. Following Yin (1989), we used our theoretical model as a benchmark, comparing our data against the model using analytic induction.

METHODS

Case Selection

Researchers have called for rigorous case studies of international joint ventures (Parkhe, 1993a; Parkhe & Shin, 1991). In this study, we conducted case analyses of four joint ventures between partners from the United States and the People's Republic of China. Table 1 summarizes the major characteristics of these partnerships. The companies and individuals are disguised to ensure confidentiality. (Detailed descriptions of each joint venture are available upon request.)

FIGURE 1
A Theoretical Model of Bargaining Power, Management Control, and Performance

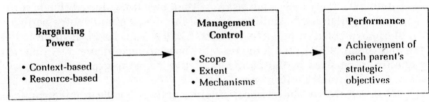

We considered several factors in selecting the cases. First, we limited our study to manufacturing ventures to minimize extraneous variation (Eisenhardt, 1989) that might be derived from differences between the service and manufacturing sectors (Chowdhury, 1988). Second, the ventures

TABLE 1
A Summary of the Major Characteristics of the Joint Ventures

Characteristic	OfficeAid	IndusCon	DailyProduct	BioTech
Product	Electronic office equipment	Industrial process control	Personal hygiene products	Pharmaceuticals
Length of negotiation in years	4	3	2	3
Formation	1987	1982	1981	1982
Total investment in millions of dollars	30	10	2.85	10
U.S.–China equity shares	51/49	49/51	50/50	50/50
Duration in years	30	20	20	15
Product market	Mainly local; small percentage for export	Local, import substitution	50% for export	Mainly local; small percentage for export
Parents' objectives				
United States	Profit Market share Low-cost sourcing	Business growth Market penetration Profit	Learn how to do business in China Establish credibility Profit Business expansion	Market Profit
People's Republic of China	Technology and management Export for foreign exchange	Import substitution Manufacturing technology Upgrade suppliers' technology	Profit Export for foreign exchange Technology Growth	Technology Gain management expertise Business expansion

were widely representative of U.S.–China joint ventures operating in various industrial sectors. Manufacturing ventures represent 69 percent of U.S.–China joint ventures (U.S.–China Business Council, 1990), and the four ventures included in this study represented the three industrial sectors in which about 50 percent of all U.S.–China manufacturing joint ventures were found. A third factor considered for case selection was that the joint ventures had to be in operation for a period of time so that data on their performance were available. A final and practical factor was access to informants. By design, we needed at least two parties from each partnership to agree to participate. The joint ventures eventually included in this study are among the first for which all parties involved agreed to interviews.

Data Collection

We collected data for this study from both interviews and archives. We conducted in-depth interviews with executives of both the U.S. and Chinese partners and the managers of the joint ventures following a predesigned interview protocol. Most of our informants (see Table 2) had personally participated in the initial negotiations for a venture or been involved in the venture's management in its early stages. Each interview lasted an average of three hours; some informants were interviewed more than once. Interviews were tape-recorded unless informants objected. To assure the accuracy of the interview data, we conducted member checks (Lincoln & Guba, 1985) in which the original informants verified our tape transcripts or interview notes. All the interviews were conducted during the eight months between May 1991 and January 1992. In addition to interviews, approximately 20 pages of archival data were collected for each partnership, including the highlights of the joint venture contracts, the joint venture's and the parents' organizational charts, corporate brochures and annual reports, published case descriptions, and newspaper and magazine reports about the partnership.

Data Coding

Data from different sources were coded using typical content analysis procedures (Diesing, 1972; Lincoln & Guba, 1985; Strauss, 1987; Taylor & Bogdan, 1984). First, we coded all data into a number of categories according to the proposed theoretical model (Yin, 1989). These categories are (1) negotiation context factors, (2) strategic objectives of the partners for participating in the venture, (3) initial contributions of each partner to the joint venture, (4) the venture's management structure when it was formed, (5) changes that occurred during the joint venture's operation in each of the above areas, and (6) the extent to which each partner achieved its strategic objectives. Table 3 provides examples of data coding.

Second, we created subcategories using classifications adopted in previous research when they were appropriate; for example, partner contributions in product design, special equipment, and production know-how were grouped into "technology." Third, within each subcategory, if data collected from different sources were inconsistent, we reconciled differences either

TABLE 2
Sources of the Interview Data[a]

Joint Venture	Interviewees
OfficeAid	Manager for business strategy of the U.S. parent, member of the joint venture's board of directors, former head negotiator of the U.S. team, and the first general manager of the joint venture
	Chairman of the board and general manager of the Chinese parent firm
	Deputy general manager of the joint venture, member of the joint venture's board of directors, and former executive general manager and head negotiator of the Chinese partner
	Two department managers of the joint venture: a marketing manager who was on the Chinese negotiation team and a quality control manager
IndusCon	Directing manager for international joint ventures of the U.S. parent, member of the joint venture's board of directors, and former deputy general manager of the joint venture
	Deputy general manager of the joint venture, member of the joint venture's board of directors, former member of the Chinese negotiation team
	Manager of marketing of the joint venture
DailyProduct	Regional general manager for the China operation of the U.S. parent, vice chairman of the joint venture's board of directors, one of the two members of the former U.S. negotiation team, former second general manager of the joint venture
BioTech	Director of finance for the Asia-Pacific region of the U.S. parent, and active participant in the joint venture negotiations
	Vice president of the joint venture, former member of the Chinese negotiation team
	Director for general administration of the joint venture

[a] Each paragraph represents one individual.

with additional sources of data or through verification by the original informants. For example, interview data on viable alternatives available to IndusCon's Chinese partner during the negotiation did not converge. We adopted the information provided by one of the informants because we found support for this source in archival data contained in a published report by a third, independent source. Overall, as Table 4 shows, triangulation across different data sources revealed a high level of consistency.

Data coding was conducted by both of us. First, we jointly developed the coding scheme and used it to analyze one case. Then, we divided the labor in coding the other three cases, with one of us coding the data while the other acted as an auditor (Lincoln & Guba, 1985). Auditing consisted of verifying both the process (the steps followed by the coder) and the product of data coding (the maps and tables derived from the interview data).

Case Analysis Method

The method adopted in analyzing the cases is analytic induction (Glaser & Strauss, 1967; Robinson, 1951; Znaniecki, 1934). In contrast to enumera-

TABLE 3
Examples of Data Coding

Coding Category	Example
Negotiation context	The Chinese were negotiating with a Japanese company the same time [while] negotiating with us.
Strategic objectives	Our goals? We went to China to earn money, no question about that. We went there also to develop a significant market share in China, and to develop a low-cost sourcing base.
Initial contributions	Most technology, about 80 percent, was imported from our American partner, but we contributed some equipment. Some of our equipment is still in use now.
Management structure	Management of the firm will be two-tiered. The board of directors will have 10 members with equal representation for each side. . . . The chairman of the board will be from the PRC, and [the U.S. parent] will name the vice chairman. The second tier of management, which will handle the day-to-day activities of the joint venture, also will be headed by the board chairman and vice chairman. The vice chairman, [the U.S. parent's] man, concurrently will hold the post of president of the joint venture.
Achievement of objectives	[The U.S. firm] now is one company who knows how to do business in China. I think this objective has been definitely achieved . . . . We have established our credibility with the local people. . . . Profitability? We are very profitable today. Profit margin is 49 percent.
Changes and dynamics	In 1987, [the U.S. partner] shifted the production of this product to the joint venture, which significantly increased the joint venture's export and generated additional foreign exchange for us.
	It takes much longer than we expected to transfer management to the Chinese. . . . Though they have been pushing hard to cut the number of U.S. expatriates, . . . I would be reluctant to take any expatriates out in the first ten years of the joint venture.
	Our first two objectives have been achieved. Low-cost sourcing [the third goal] has not. . . . So, from an emphasis standpoint, probably the three objectives are now getting equal emphasis.

tive induction, which relies on statistical methods to generate simple, aggregate, and stable mental rules, analytic induction is a method of extending or refining existing theories by constantly comparing them with crucial instances or typical cases (Glaser & Strauss, 1967; Lindesmith, 1947; Znaniecki, 1934). "The exceptional instance is the growing point of science. . . . Cumulative growth and progressive development of theory is obtained by formulating a generalization in such a way that negative cases

TABLE 4
Triangulation of Data[a,b]

Variables	Negotiation Context Factors	Strategic Objectives	Resource Contributions	Management Structure	Changes and Dynamics	Achievement of Objectives
Timing of assessment	Largely retrospective	Current and retrospective	Retrospective and current	Current and retrospective	Current and retrospective	Current
OfficeAid						
Data sources	Interviews with 1, 2, 3, and 4	Interviews with 1, 2, 3, and 4 and archival	Interviews with 1, 2, 3, and 4 and archival	Interviews with 1, 2, 3, and 4 and archival	Interviews with 1, 2, 3, and 4	Interviews with 1, 2, 3, and 4
Cross-source agreement	Modestly high	High	Modestly high	High	High	Modestly high
IndusCon						
Data sources	Interviews with 1, 3, and 4 and archival	Interviews with 1, 3, and 4 and archival	Interviews with 1, 3, and 4 and archival	Interviews with 1, 3, and 4 and archival	Interviews with 1, 3, and 4	Interviews with 1, 3, and 4 and archival
Cross-source agreement	Modestly high	High	High	High	High	High
DailyProduct						
Data sources	Interviews with 1 and 3	Interviews with 1 and 3 and archival	Interviews with 1 and 3 and archival	Interviews with 1 and 3 and archival	Interviews with 1 and 3	Interviews with 1 and 3 and archival
Cross-source agreement	High	High	High	High	High	High
BioTech						
Data sources	Interviews with 1, 2, and 4 and archival	Interviews with 1, 2, and 4 and archival	Interviews with 1, 2, and 4 and archival	Interviews with 1, 2, and 4 and archival	Interviews with 1, 2, and 4	Interviews with 1, 2, and 4
Cross-source agreement	High	High	Modestly high	High	High	High

[a] Informants are coded as follows: 1 = U.S. parent representative, 2 = Chinese parent representative, 3 = American venture representative, 4 = Chinese venture representative.

[b] High = All sources of data are in agreement: modestly high = at least two sources in agreement, others are not. Where no agreement is indicated, data were from single individual who was both a regional general manager of the U.S. parent and a general manager of the joint venture.

force us either to reject the generalization or to revise it" (Lindesmith, 1947: 12). Analytic induction involves the following steps:

> First, a rough definition of the phenomenon to be explained is formulated. Second, an hypothetical explanation of that phenomenon is formulated. Third, one case is studied . . . with the object of determining whether the hypothesis fits the facts in that case. Fourth, if the hypothesis does not fit the facts, either the hypothesis is reformulated or the phenomenon to be explained is re-defined, so that the case is excluded. . . . Fifth, practical certainty may be attained after a small number of cases has been examined. . . . Sixth, this procedure . . . is continued until a universal relationship is established, each negative case calling for a redefinition or a reformulation. Seventh, for purposes of proof, cases outside the area circumscribed by the definition are examined to determine whether or not the final hypothesis applies to them (Cressey, 1953: 16).

Following this procedure, we started with one case study and compared the findings with the theoretical model shown in Figure 1. Then, we modified the model in view of the findings in the first case. This comparative process was repeated for each successive case. Parkhe (1993a) argued that the comparative case method is particularly appropriate for the study of joint ventures, given the need for rigorous theory development on the topic.

RESULTS

Although the logic of analytic induction was strictly followed—the cases were analyzed one by one in an incremental manner—because of space limitations, we report only the final revision of the model. However, research findings on the relationships among the variables and the dynamic aspects of joint ventures are presented case by case.

Bargaining Power

Across the four cases, we identified two context-based and seven resource-based components of bargaining power (see Table 5). For each case, we list only components that both partners acknowledged.

Context-based. Evidence supporting the importance of the two components of context-based bargaining power, stakes and availability of alternatives, was present in all four cases. The measure of stakes was the perceived strategic importance of the joint venture to the overall business of a parent. For example, BioTech was critically important to its U.S. parent because the latter regarded China as one of its worldwide strategic markets. For the U.S. parent in DailyProduct, on the other hand, because the joint venture was nothing more than an experiment to test the Chinese market, the stakes were only marginally important.

Context-based bargaining power can also be derived from having alter-

TABLE 5
Relative Bargaining Power of Partners

Components of Bargaining Power	OfficeAid U.S.	OfficeAid China	IndusCon U.S.	IndusCon China	DailyProduct U.S.	DailyProduct China	BioTech U.S.	BioTech China
Context-based								
Alternatives available	Higher	Moderately higher	Moderately lower	Moderately lower	Equal		Equal	
Strategic importance	Moderately higher		Moderately lower	Moderately lower	Moderately higher	Moderately higher	Equal	
Resource-based								
Technology	Higher	Moderately higher	Higher		Moderately higher	Moderately higher	Moderately higher	Moderately higher
Management expertise	Moderately higher		Equal				Equal	
Global service support	Higher							
Local knowledge	Moderately lower		Lower		Moderately lower	Moderately lower	Moderately lower	Moderately lower
Product distribution	Moderately lower		Moderately lower		Higher		Lower	
Material procurement	Moderately higher		Moderately higher		Equal		Equal	
Equity	Approximately equal		Approximately equal		Equal		Equal	
Overall bargaining power	Higher		Approximately equal		Higher		Approximately equal	

natives, such as other potential partners with whom to negotiate or other channels through which to accomplish the same mission the joint venture is to achieve. For example, the potential Chinese partner in IndusCon was simultaneously engaged in negotiations with a Japanese firm and the U.S. partner. This situation enabled the Chinese to choose between two mutually competitive foreign firms, thereby increasing their bargaining power in negotiating with the U.S. company. In DailyProduct, because the Chinese government had "assigned" the local partner to the U.S. parent, the latter had no alternatives. In another example, additional bargaining power accrued to the U.S. parent of OfficeAid because it had existing business channels in China that could serve as alternative outlets. The U.S. firm's regional division in Hong Kong had previously exported to China, and doing so remained a viable alternative to forming the joint venture.

Resource-based. The components of resource-based bargaining power signify the resources and capabilities committed by the partners to a joint venture. These resource contributions are either explicitly specified in the joint venture agreements (contracts, memorandums, and licenses) or verbally recognized by both partners during negotiations. We saw a consistent, complementary pattern across all four cases with regard to the types of resource committed by the partners. Predictably, the foreign firms contributed more heavily than their local partners in the areas of technology (product design, manufacturing know-how, and special equipment) and global support (technical, marketing, and maintenance services), and the Chinese firms contributed more in the areas of knowledge about and skills for dealing with the local government and other institutional infrastructures. IndusCon's U.S. parent's comments were illustrative: "We have the technology and certain know-how. The Chinese partner knows how to make things happen in China. You put the two together right, it works." In other areas, although both partners made contributions, apparent complementarity also existed. The U.S. partners tended to provide imported materials, channels for exporting the joint ventures' products, and expertise in production management, and the Chinese partners contributed in areas of local sourcing, domestic distribution, and personnel management. In equity investment, both partners injected roughly the same amounts of capital in all four joint ventures.

Although both partners possessed bargaining power during the initial negotiations, the patterns of the relative bargaining power between the partners varied from one partnership to another. Since data with which to assess the relative significance of each component to bargaining power were not available, we assessed the relative bargaining power between the partners in each joint venture by assuming that all components contributed equally. In two of the four joint ventures (IndusCon and BioTech), bargaining power was balanced, or approximately equally shared between the partners. On the other hand, a significant imbalance in the partners' bargaining power existed in the other two ventures (OfficeAid and DailyProduct), with much more bargaining power accruing to the U.S. partner. The bottom of Table 5 summarizes the overall patterns of relative bargaining power in the ventures studied.

Management Control

Our data analysis revealed several unambiguous indicators of management control, which is congruent with the notion that control is multidimensional (Geringer & Hebert, 1989). Like Schaan (1983, 1988), we found that nominations of members of a venture's board of directors and general manager were important control mechanisms. Both interview and archival data supported the importance of the role played by the boards of directors in making strategic decisions for the joint ventures and solving critical problems regarding the partnerships in general. The following quotes provide some evidence:

> We [the board] approve the annual budgets submitted by DailyProduct's management and decide everything important for its operation. When anything unexpected happens in China, I have to be there to talk to the Chinese chairman (vice chairman of DailyProduct).

> The board of directors is empowered to discuss and take actions on all fundamental issues concerning the venture, namely, expansion projects, production and business programs, the budget, distribution of profits, plans concerning manpower and pay scales, the termination of business, the appointment or hiring of the president, the vice-president(s), the chief engineer, the treasurer and the auditors as well as their functions and powers and their remuneration, etc. (law of the People's Republic of China on joint ventures using Chinese and foreign investment).

The board of directors of each joint venture in this study met at least twice a year to set annual goals, review performance, and approve operational plans for the venture.

Our data also suggest that substantial power is associated with the position of general manager in joint ventures. In each of the four ventures in this study, the general manager had always been a board member and served as the executive officer of the joint venture. The general manager made important operating decisions for the venture and represented each parent in negotiations with the other partner on issues that arose unexpectedly. However, the difference in the decision power attached to the general manager and deputy general manager of a venture, each of whom is nominated by a different parent, varied significantly across our cases. In two joint ventures, OfficeAid and DailyProduct, the general manager exercised more control than the deputy general manager, but in the other two, the positions were roughly equal in terms of control. For example, the former general manager of OfficeAid, who was from the U.S. parent, stated:

> Eighty percent of the time he [the Chinese deputy general manager] would say "yes" when I made a decision . . . because I was the general manager, he was the deputy. If we didn't agree on anything, I made the decision.

This pattern was confirmed by a Chinese manager at OfficeAid, who observed that "in the offices where there is an American manager, he will be in control though we have a deputy manager there." However, the IndusCon and BioTech data suggest different patterns, as the following quotes reveal:

> The Chinese general manager and I were equals, co-managers. Mutual consulting between us continued throughout my term. This relationship was passed on to me from by predecessor. And it's true even today (IndusCon's former deputy general manager, from the U.S. parent).

> In organization design, our president [of the joint venture] should report to the Chinese chairman. However, in managing the joint venture, they are equally involved in making important decisions (representative of the U.S. parent of BioTech).

Joint venture parents also exercise control through the structure of a joint venture. We found that when the management system, decision process, and corporate policies of a joint venture were similar in structure to those of one parent, that parent exercised a higher level of control than its partner. In fact, the ability of a partner to replicate its way of managing in the joint venture reflected its level of control over the partnership, as the following quotes suggest:

> Three weeks after we hired the senior staff, we started training them in our corporate principles. . . . We wanted to go through a process which is part of our management process, our management styles. . . . I created a culture at the joint venture (OfficeAid's first general manager, from the U.S. parent).

> We structure the joint venture in China exactly the same way as we structure our organizations in other countries. In comparing with the Chinese state-run enterprises, we don't have the [Communist] party event and the union plays a very small role (vice chairman of DailyProduct, from the U.S. parent).

Our data also provide information about the overall control by each parent perceived by our interviewees. This indicator reflects both the scope and the extent of control (Geringer & Hebert, 1989). Although relying on subjective judgments, the measure of perceived overall control may capture some aspects of control that other, more objective measures could not capture. The following comments suggest that this indicator of control is important:

> [The U.S. company] always considers the joint venture as one of their own children and uses their own "standard model" to format it. They try to control it in great detail (OfficeAid's Chinese deputy general manager).

> In making important decisions for BioTech, both sides make compromises. "Compromise" is the most appropriate word here (representative of BioTech's U.S. parent).

Table 6 summarizes the degrees of control the partners exercised in each case on the above four dimensions. Overall, an imbalance in control favoring the U.S. parent occurred in OfficeAid and DailyProduct. In contrast, control in IndusCon and BioTech was approximately balanced between the parents.

Venture Performance

There were considerable differences in the strategic objectives of the partners (see Table 7). The Chinese partners focused on upgrading technology and management and earning foreign exchange through export, and the U.S. partners aimed at penetrating the local market and earning a profit in China. These divergent, though potentially complementary, objectives implied that significant bias would occur if performance were assessed from only one partner's perspective or by simply using available standard financial indicators. Moreover, we found that the joint venture managements did not provide performance assessments independent of those of the parents because all the joint ventures operated under close parent control. A joint venture's managers did not represent the partnership itself; rather, each acted as the representative of the parent firm of his or her own nation. Therefore, it was inappropriate in this study to count the joint venture managers' assessments of performance as independent of their parents', as previous researchers have suggested doing (Anderson, 1990; Killing, 1983).

The performance measure we used was the extent to which a venture's partners had achieved their strategic objectives in initiating the joint venture. If an objective represented a long-term goal of a partner, we measured the extent to which satisfactory progress had been made. Using this measure fits well with the ways that partners actually evaluated performance. The following comments by a U.S. firm are representative:

> The only appropriate criterion for performance evaluation is whether or not the partners and their stakeholders are happy with the joint venture's operation. The happiness for us is measured by its profitability and market share—the two most important goals we had. . . . Our stakeholders are happy with what we have done in China.

Table 7 presents information about performance assessment for the joint ventures.

Relationship Between Bargaining Power and Management Control

The theoretical framework in Figure 1 shows a positive relationship between the relative bargaining power of a venture partner and the management control it exercises. Data from all four of our cases support this relationship. The relative bargaining power of the partners in two joint ventures (OfficeAid and DailyProduct) was uneven: the U.S. parent had higher bargaining power than the local parent. Accordingly, in these two joint ventures, the U.S. partner exercised a higher level of management control than its Chinese partner for all indicators except representation on the board,

TABLE 6
Management Control of Partners

Components of Management Control	OfficeAid		IndusCon		DailyProduct		BioTech	
	U.S.	China	U.S.	China	U.S.	China	U.S.	China
Percent of board membership	Equal		Slightly lower		Equal		Equal	
Nomination of key personnel	Higher		Approximately equal		Higher		Slightly lower	
Similarity of management systems to parents'	Higher		Approximately equal		Higher		Approximately equal	
Perceived level of overall control	Higher		Approximately equal		Higher		Approximately equal	
Overall pattern of management control	Higher		Approximately equal		Higher		Approximately equal	

TABLE 7
Achievement of Strategic Objectives by Partners

Strategic Objectives	Degree of Achievement			
	OfficeAid	IndusCon	DailyProduct	BioTech
United States				
Profit	Yes	Yes	Yes	Yes
Market share	Yes	Yes		Yes
Growth		Yes	Partially	
Local sourcing	No			
Learning			Yes	
Credibility with Chinese government			Yes	
Overall	Largely achieved	All achieved	Largely achieved	All achieved
China				
Technology	Partially	Mostly	Yes	Yes
Export	No		Yes	
Growth			Partially	Partially
Management				Yes
Import substitution		Yes		
Up-stream technology		Yes		
Profit			Yes	
Overall	Largely not achieved	Mostly achieved	Largely achieved	Largely achieved

which was equal. For these two ventures, unevenly distributed bargaining power was associated with imbalanced management control. The partner who gained more bargaining power during the negotiations exercised more management control in the venture. In the other two joint ventures, IndusCon and BioTech, each partner possessed roughly even bargaining power and exercised equal management control over the venture. Overall, the pattern of partners' relative bargaining power is consistent with, and positively related to, the pattern in which management control is shared between the partners (see Table 8).

Relationship Between Management Control and Performance

In the theoretical model, we predict a direct, positive relationship between management control and performance. The bottom two rows in Table 8 depict the general patterns of management control and performance for each joint venture. Our findings suggest that the relationship between management control and performance was not as straightforward as was predicted. To better understand how the cases deviate from the prediction, we focus on each case in the "stepwise" manner Cressey (1953) suggested.

OfficeAid. As discussed above, OfficeAid's U.S. parent exhibited more control than the Chinese parent. With regard to performance, the U.S. parent had achieved its two most important objectives, profit and market share, though its objective of building a low-cost sourcing base in China had not yet

TABLE 8
Overall Patterns of Bargaining Power, Management Control, and Performance

Variables	OfficeAid		IndusCon		DailyProduct		BioTech	
	U.S.	China	U.S.	China	U.S.	China	U.S.	China
Relative bargaining power	Higher		Approximately equal		Higher		Approximately equal	
Management control	Higher		Approximately equal		Higher		Approximately equal	
Venture performance	High	Low	Very high	Very high	High	High	Very high	High

been achieved (see Table 7). In contrast, the Chinese partner had only partially achieved one of its two equally important objectives, updating technology. Because the joint venture exported at a loss, the second Chinese objective, generating foreign exchange through export, had not been achieved. The significant imbalance at OfficeAid in achieving its parents' strategic expectations hindered the overall performance of the venture, which was the lowest among the four joint ventures.

The OfficeAid data seem to support the positive relationship between control and performance reported by previous studies (Killing, 1983; Lecraw, 1984). In other words, the partner who exercises a higher level of management control achieves a higher level of performance from its own point of view.

IndusCon. In IndusCon, the strategic objectives of both partners were realized (Table 7). The U.S. partner had achieved its objectives of profitability and business expansion. IndusCon had been very profitable since its second year of operation. Because both partners reinvested all profit the joint venture earned in the first five years, the venture grew rapidly. Regarding market penetration, a representative of the U.S. parent made the following assessment:

> Probably a couple of companies are bigger than we are in terms of volume per year. I think, the market sees us as a quality company. . . . We are definitely the leader in quality. We are high enough up there in volume. I think, on overall basis, if you ask the most potential customers in China who they consider as the quality leader company, they would probably say "IndusCon."

Nonetheless, the U.S. parent perceived IndusCon as still having room to grow because its market share was still below 10 percent and the Chinese market was far from saturated.

The Chinese partner had also achieved its three objectives. First, by manufacturing locally, the joint venture enabled the Chinese partner to reduce its imports of industrial control equipment, its principal objective. In the past ten years of operation, IndusCon had produced a variety of control systems installed in many key Chinese industries. Second, regarding the objective of updating technology, the Chinese were satisfied to the extent that IndusCon had become an important source of high-technology products in China. Third, IndusCon's efforts to upgrade the technical capacity of the local suppliers had increased localization of material sourcing, creating a ripple effect throughout the Chinese economy. As a result, the Chinese government had twice selected IndusCon as one of the "best-run China–foreign joint ventures" in China in recent years. The Chinese partner was satisfied with the progress of technology transfer to date, though the U.S. partner still held the key technology. Overall, IndusCon stood as the best performer among the four ventures in this study because it had achieved the objectives of both of its parents.

In IndusCon, the partners exercised equal management control, and both had achieved their strategic objectives. This finding contradicts previous studies' prediction of inferior performance in joint ventures with shared management (Killing, 1983) but is consistent with Beamish's (1984, 1985, 1993) findings that shared or split control is superior for international joint ventures in developing countries. The inconsistencies between the OfficeAid and IndusCon data suggest that the previously proposed relationship between control and performance (as being proportional for each parent) underspecified the relationship. The inconsistencies can be reconciled, however, if we raise the level of analysis from the individual-parent level to the between-parents level. In OfficeAid, a relatively unbalanced level of management control (control was unequally shared) between the parents was associated with unbalanced levels of performance (high for the U.S. parent but low for the Chinese parent). Similarly, in IndusCon, the balanced management control of the partners resulted in balanced levels of performance (both high in this case). To sum, then, balance or imbalance in partners' management control is associated with a similar pattern of performance assessed in terms of the achievement of both partners' strategic objectives.

DailyProduct. Three of the four strategic objectives of the U.S. partner, namely, learning how to do business in China, establishing credibility with the Chinese government, and earning a profit in operating the joint venture, had been completely achieved. The U.S. partner indicated that the joint venture achieved a 49 percent profit margin. With regard to the U.S. partner's fourth objective, expanding the Chinese market for personal hygiene products, some progress had been made—the venture's production had exceeded the planned capacity by 50 percent. However, their hope for market expansion had been achieved to only a limited extent.

The Chinese partner had achieved its three most important objectives: earning a profit, exporting for foreign exchange, and updating the manufacturing technology at the joint venture. The Chinese objective of growth had been achieved only to the extent that the volume of the existing products had been increased beyond the original expectation. However, since the U.S. partner had some reservations about transferring other products to the joint venture, the Chinese partner had not yet fulfilled the objective of expanding to its partner's other businesses. Nevertheless, DailyProduct had been successful in meeting most of its parents' expectations. Its overall performance was much higher than OfficeAid's, though slightly lower than IndusCon's.

The relationship between control and performance at DailyProduct somewhat differed from what we found in the two ventures previously described. Management control was unequally shared between the parents, but performance had been balanced, with both partners achieving their most important strategic objectives. In other words, at DailyProduct unbalanced control was associated with balanced and moderately high performance. This pattern forced us to reconsider the proposed direct relationship between balanced (unbalanced) control and high (low) performance.

Further examination suggested several factors that might have accounted for the relationship between control and performance revealed by DailyProduct. First, unlike the previous two ventures, in which the partners had radically different strategic goals, the DailyProduct partners had some common objectives, such as profitability in hard currency. Thus, the achievement of one parent's objectives meant the achievement of the other parent's. Also, because the partners shared a common destiny, conflict over how to operate the business was less likely to occur. Common goals may serve as an informal control mechanism that renders the pattern of formal management control less critical than it is when partners' objectives radically diverge.

A second factor that might have accounted for the control-performance relationship in DailyProduct is that the most important objectives of the Chinese (the low-control partner) were incorporated into the partnership's operating plans, which were part of the joint venture contract. Both parties agreed that within the first 18 months after start-up, the joint venture should (1) achieve an annual capacity of 50 million units for product one and 4 million units for product two, (2) make a profit, (3) achieve surplus in foreign exchange, and (4) export 30 percent for product one and 70 percent for product two. These specific contractual stipulations probably served as an alternative means of control for the weaker partner to ensure that its goals were reached.

A third and probably most important factor was the high level of trust that developed between the partners in DailyProduct after the first 18 months of operation, when the joint venture's plan had been realized. After that, "Trust was no longer a problem. They trust us and leave the business to us," the U.S. partner's informant observed. Therefore, mutual trust may be an important contingent or moderating factor in the control-performance relationship when the management control of partners is unequal.

BioTech. The U.S. parent of BioTech had achieved both of its strategic objectives, market share and profit. BioTech had been very profitable and acquired the highest market share of all international pharmaceutical joint ventures in China. The Chinese partner had achieved its first and second objectives: to update manufacturing technology and to learn advanced Western management techniques for running a high-technology pharmaceutical enterprise. The Chinese were satisfied with the venture's business growth because it had continuously added new pharmaceutical products. However, this objective has been achieved to only a limited extent because the Chinese expectation of extending the business to the U.S. partner's other products (e.g., nutrition products) had not yet been met. Overall, like DailyProduct, BioTech demonstrated strong performance in achieving most of its parents' objectives.

The BioTech data provided confirmatory evidence for the relationship between management control and performance revealed in the previous cases: equal management control was associated with balanced and relatively high performance for both partners. In fact, BioTech's control-performance relationships were very similar to IndusCon's.

1502   *Academy of Management Journal*   December

Dynamic Aspects of International Joint Ventures

The findings reported above are based on static analyses, but because joint venture arrangements do not necessarily remain static, we also secured information about how the joint ventures had changed since their formation to the date of the study. We sought to identify sources of change that had prompted shifts in partners' bargaining power and driven structural reconfigurations. The feedback arrows in Figure 2 indicate such changes. In the following subsections, we analyze the dynamic development of each joint venture and summarize the cross-case effects.

OfficeAid. Since the joint venture's inception, its Chinese personnel had acquired some management expertise, operational techniques, and production know-how associated with the existing products. At the same time, the Chinese engineers had become involved in the R&D process, thus making a technological contribution to the joint venture. These changes had a positive effect on the Chinese partner's bargaining power.

Changes also occurred in the U.S. partner's bargaining power. First, the U.S. partner had gradually become experienced in operating in the Chinese system. The former American general manager indicated that he made friends with several important officials in the local municipal government, including the mayor. Second, the U.S. partner continuously provided new product designs for the venture, therefore firmly maintaining its position as a principal contributor in technology. Third, since the ten-year technology transfer agreement was subject to renegotiation, the U.S. partner began using the renewal as leverage to gain additional bargaining power. All these factors had increased the bargaining power of the U.S. partner and offset the gains in the Chinese partner's bargaining power.

In addition, the growth of the partnership itself and changes in the local environment had altered the bargaining power of the partners. For example, the increase in local content and establishment of separate distribution channels enabled the joint venture to become less dependent on its U.S. parent for imported materials and on its Chinese parent for marketing skills, thus reducing the bargaining power of each parent. Additionally, because of the legalization of swap markets for obtaining foreign exchange in the mid-1980s,[2] export became less necessary, and the U.S. partner's international distribution channels were less valuable to the joint venture than they had been.

No significant changes in the initial pattern of control in OfficeAid occurred. Despite a reduction in the number of U.S. expatriate managers from seven to five in the four years preceding our study, the remaining five

---

[2] In the mid-1980s, the Chinese government legalized swap markets for foreign exchange in some major Chinese cities, allowing companies to trade foreign currencies among themselves. Typically, however, a company pays a premium when it converts the Chinese currency (yuan) to a foreign currency—the conversion is made at a rate higher than the official exchange rate set by the Bank of China.

FIGURE 2
An Integrative Model of International Joint Ventures

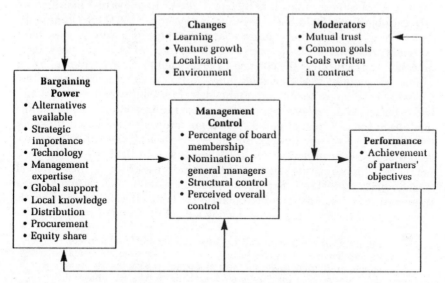

expatriates had the same scope of management responsibilities as their predecessors.

However, an undercurrent of struggle for control between the partners persisted in OfficeAid. The Chinese kept urging reductions in the number of U.S. expatriates and allocations of greater management responsibility to the Chinese staff. For example, the Chinese partner expected the next general manager of the joint venture to be Chinese. On the other hand, the U.S. partner continuously tried to enhance its control. In 1988, the U.S. partner proposed adding a nonvoting U.S. observer to the board, but the Chinese countered with a similar request to keep the balance. Subsequently, the U.S. partner proposed the following restructuring:

> We have been hoping to go to a board of nine members instead of eight by adding a ninth from us. We were rejected, expectedly rejected. We may be able to throw in some sweeteners to make it more acceptable.

And with regard to potential shifts of management responsibilities to the locals, our informant from the U.S. partner said

> We are absolutely convinced if we let them manage the operations tomorrow, things will fail six months from now.... I would be reluctant to take any expatriates out in the first ten years of the venture.

Several changes in the partners' strategic objectives were reported. First, because swap markets became available for foreign exchange and the joint venture had been running a loss in export, the Chinese partner modified its original objectives. On a board meeting in December 1991, the Chinese directors proposed that the venture abandon export as a way to earn hard currency. Also, the Chinese partner added profit to its list of objectives, presumably as a result of the changes in government policies, which allowed Chinese companies to keep a substantial portion of their operational gains. Since the U.S. parent's most important goals (profitability and market share) had been reached, low-cost sourcing increased in importance. As the informant from the U.S. parent noted, "From an emphasis standpoint, probably the three objectives are now getting equal emphasis." Overall, OfficeAid's record of unbalanced performance had induced mistrust between the partners. The Chinese partner attributed the loss in export to the low internal transfer price set by the U.S. partner and perceived the U.S. partner's heavy intervention in the joint venture's operation as taking the child away from its Chinese parent. The U.S. partner acknowledged the issue of mistrust,

> I don't think we have, in all honesty, the level of trust between the parties that we should have. . . . There always has been such a level of distrust, always a level of suspicion, specifically from the Chinese, that the foreigners are trying to take advantage of them.

IndusCon. The Chinese partner in IndusCon, like its counterpart in OfficeAid, had gained some bargaining power by learning about management techniques and gaining technological know-how over the past 10 years. However, since technology in this industry is rapidly outdated and key production know-how was still kept at the U.S. partner's headquarters, the U.S. partner retained significant bargaining power because the joint venture still heavily depended on it for up-to-date technology and new product designs. In 1987, the U.S. partner gained additional bargaining power by shifting production of a product marketed worldwide to China. This move significantly increased the joint venture's volume of product for export and generated additional foreign exchange for the local partner.

Procurement and marketing changes prompted additional shifts in bargaining power. By the end of the study, IndusCon had its own procurement staff in the United States and no longer depended on its U.S. parent for imported parts. Second, with the increase in local content, the joint venture had become more dependent on the Chinese sourcing channels, which increased the Chinese partner's bargaining power. Third, the Chinese partner's bargaining power diminished significantly when one of its wholly owned companies was acquired by the joint venture. This company was the exclusive distributor for the joint venture's products in the Chinese market.

The pattern of parents' management control of IndusCon had not significantly shifted because changes in bargaining power occurred simultaneously to both parents and were relatively equal. More important, the superior performance of IndusCon enhanced the level of trust between the partners and confirmed that its control structure worked well and that no changes were necessary. Because both parents' strategic objectives were long-term, no changes in objectives were in evidence in IndusCon.

DailyProduct. As in the previous cases, at DailyProduct the local partner had gained power by acquiring technical know-how and management techniques. However, the U.S. partner's bargaining power had increased more significantly overall. Its contribution in management expertise, though initially not valued by the Chinese partner, was now acknowledged as a critical asset. Additionally, because the U.S. firm had achieved its strategic objectives (learning how to operate in China and building credibility with the Chinese), the partnership's strategic importance to it had decreased significantly. These two changes, coupled with the more open foreign investment policy in effect in China since 1984, enabled the U.S. partner to launch negotiations for a majority joint venture in another Chinese city. Finally, high performance levels satisfied the Chinese partner's most important objective and thereby strengthened the U.S. parent's dominance. As the venture's American vice chairman observed,

> Over time, decision-making process has changed. In the beginning we had to argue on some issues, but now, they would just let us make decisions though it is still a 50:50 joint venture.... They absolutely trust us. They know that we can make money for them.

BioTech. The Chinese partner in BioTech gained bargaining power by gaining Western management techniques and technical know-how and through increased local content in the joint venture's products. However, the bargaining power of the U.S. partner increased substantially through its contribution in marketing expertise. When BioTech was formed, all its products were purchased and distributed by the local partner. As China was transforming its economic system from reliance on central planning to a market orientation, the original distribution networks collapsed in 1986 when the U.S. partner was informed that its former Chinese partner had been dismantled and that the local government would no longer buy any products from the joint venture. Since the local partner was not familiar with selling in a free market, the U.S. partner's contributions in building a distribution network and in training the venture's marketing staff increased its relative bargaining power.

These changes in the partners' bargaining power produced only a slight adjustment in control, the nomination of one more expatriate manager responsible for marketing. As in IndusCon, a key factor that might have stabilized the pattern of control in BioTech was its superior performance.

In short, several factors appear to prompt shifts in partners' bargaining power and trigger structural reconfigurations in joint ventures over time. They are summarized below.

Partners' learning. Previous researchers have noted that joint venture partners learn from each other. Vernon (1977) coined the term obsolescing bargain to capture the impact of learning on bargaining power. More recently, Hamel (1991) argued that the effective learner in an international joint venture will raise the "price" for its continued participation in the partnership. We observed this learning effect in all our cases for both partners. However, our data suggest that the Chinese partners did not significantly gain bargaining power through learning. They probably did not gain because the U.S. partners were cautious in transferring their technologies to their joint ventures and kept the key technological secrets firmly in their own hands or because these technologies were low in transparency, raising high barriers to learning (Hamel, 1991).

Growth of a joint venture's own capacity. Over time, international joint ventures accumulate their own bases of knowledge and skills, becoming less dependent on their parents (Prahalad & Doz, 1981). However, if this accumulation is accomplished in an unbalanced manner, by acquiring knowledge or skills only from one parent, this parent's contribution will eventually be devalued. As a result, changes in the existing pattern of bargaining power between the parents will occur. OfficeAid exemplified this type of change when it adopted the Chinese parent's distribution channels and developed the network for its own use.

Localization. Our data suggest that material procurement channels for a joint venture constitute a source of bargaining power for the partner who provides those channels. Since both partners have inherent, though different, motivations for increasing local content—the local partner wants to cultivate domestic suppliers, the foreigner wants to reduce cost, and both want to save foreign exchange—this change can diminish the bargaining power of the partner, typically the foreign partner, on whom the joint venture depends for imported materials. Bargaining power changes resulting from localization were observed in all our case studies.

Environmental changes. Changes in a venture's local environment, particularly in government policies, can trigger structural reconfigurations in joint ventures. Relaxation of the prohibitions on direct foreign investment enabled IndusCon to acquire the sales and service company formerly owned by its Chinese parent. Similarly, this policy change afforded DailyProduct's U.S. parent the opportunity to form a new majority joint venture and thus reduced the strategic importance of DailyProduct to that parent. More strikingly, the collapse of the state distribution network caused by the macro system transformation induced the U.S. partner in BioTech to contribute its marketing expertise, thereby increasing its bargaining power. These findings support the theoretical prediction that environmental changes can shift the original bargaining agreement between partners (Harrigan & Newman, 1990; Sharfman, Gray, & Yan, 1991), thereby reconfiguring a venture's structure.

Performance. The ongoing performance of joint ventures has an important feedback effect on the partners' relative bargaining power and the existing structure of control. Killing (1983) noted that joint venture parents enhance or loosen control over ventures as a response to their performance, but our data suggest that performance also shapes the relative levels of bargaining power and the pattern of the sharing of management control between the parents. Superior performance creates an additional bargaining chip for the partner currently in control (the situation in DailyProduct) or reinforces the extant control pattern (in the other three ventures). In addition, performance may also have a feedback effect on moderating variables, especially the trust between partners. Superior performance enhances interpartner trust over time, as was shown in all the joint ventures except OfficeAid, and mediocre or poor performance, like the significantly unbalanced performance of OfficeAid, will cause distrust between the partners, which can in turn depress a ventures' long-term performance (Killing, 1983).

Toward an Integrative Model of Bargaining Power, Control, and Performance

Figure 2, an integrative model, summarizes our findings regarding bargaining power, management control, performance, and the dynamic aspects of international joint ventures. The consistent evidence generated across all the case studies suggests a direct, positive relationship between bargaining power and management control. Though our data are not sufficient to allow a test of the relative importance of each component of bargaining power in shaping joint venture structure, they suggest that the overall pattern of the partners' relative degrees of bargaining power is highly related to how they share control. In addition, the pattern of management control in joint ventures is directly related to venture performance. When the partners' control is even, each partner's performance, as assessed from its own perspective, is equal. When control is unevenly shared by partners, the prediction of performance is less straightforward. The data suggest that three alternative control mechanisms moderate the relationship between formal management control and performance: the level of trust between the partners, the commonality of their strategic objectives, and the level of institutionalization of those objectives—whether or not they are contractual. When these moderating variables are present, management control is less predictive of performance. In addition, the relative bargaining power of two partners changes over time as a result of their learning, the growth of a joint venture's own capacity, localization of the joint venture's operation, and environmental changes. The ongoing performance of the partnership exerts an important feedback effect on the partners' bargaining power, the pattern of management control, and the quality of the cooperative relationship between the partners. The following propositions summarize the relationships discussed above and depicted in Figure 2:

> Proposition 1: The bargaining power of a potential joint venture partner will be positively related to the extent of its management control over the joint venture's operation.

> Proposition 2: The structure of the sharing of management control between joint venture parents will be related to the pattern of venture performance.

1508   *Academy of Management Journal*   December

Proposition 3: Relational characteristics of joint venture partners, including trust, commonality of strategic objectives, and institutionalization of goals, will moderate the relationship between parent control and performance.

Proposition 4: Changes in partners' bargaining power prompted by a joint venture's environment, their strategies, and the venture's maturity will trigger reconfigurations of the venture's management control structure, which will in turn cause changes in performance.

Proposition 5: Changes in the performance of a joint venture will alter the balance of the partners' bargaining power, the current structure of control, and the trust relationship between the partners.

DISCUSSION AND CONCLUSIONS

Ownership and Management Control

Our findings lead us to question the validity of previous studies' use of ownership as a proxy for management control in joint ventures (Blodgett, 1991; Fagre & Wells, 1982; Stopford & Wells, 1972). By and large, all four joint ventures in this study were equally owned.[3] However, although two of them showed balanced management control, the other two demonstrated an unbalanced, one-parent-dominant pattern of control. Within each joint venture, we found that the ownership split was consistent with only one dimension of control, board membership. With respect to other dimensions, no consistent relationship was observed.

The results of our study also challenge the assumptions prevailing in the literature that all potential joint venture partners prefer 100 percent ownership and that the equity split between the partners is an outcome of negotiation representating the relative power of participating interests (Blodgett, 1991; Fagre & Wells, 1982). Our data tell a different story. In all four joint ventures studied, ownership structure was voluntarily decided between the partners at the outset of the negotiations. As our interviewee at OfficeAid's U.S. parent noted, "We could go wholly owned but I am against it. I don't see we have a brilliant future in China with a wholly owned foreign enterprise. You go there as a foreign company and you really have nothing to work with." Moreover, potential partners see agreement on an ownership split as

---

[3] Most international joint ventures formed in the early 1980s in China adopted relatively equal ownership structures or foreign minority ownership, though this pattern has been changing in recent years as a result of the more open attitude of the Chinese government toward foreign investment in China. However, Chinese joint venture laws dated July 1, 1979, and April 7, 1990, specify only a lower limit (25%) of the level of foreign ownership in joint ventures. In fact, foreign majority partnerships and even wholly owned foreign subsidiaries were possible prior to 1985 (Pearson, 1991), though only a few such ventures were actually formed.

a threshold to cross before the serious start of negotiations. As one of our interviewees noted, "You either accept it, at least in principle, to start the negotiation; or you reject it. Then, negotiations will never happen." This evidence is consistent with previous reports that the ownership pattern in international joint ventures in China reflected both partners' needs and did not pose a major issue in joint venture negotiations (Davidson, 1987; Pearson, 1991).

Overall, our findings provide additional evidence that equity structure is not equivalent to management control. Rather, as a type of resource committed by the partners, equity investment constitutes a source of bargaining power that in turn contributes to management control. Once the equity structure is agreed on, it delineates the relative positions of the partners and sets a tone for the successive negotiations on control.

Each Partner Versus the Partnership

This research provides consistent evidence across the four cases that the way bargaining power is shared between partners varies with patterns of management control. It is important to note, however, that this positive relationship exists only at the interpartner level, when the patterns of bargaining power and control are examined from both partners' perspectives and the relationship between the partners is the unit of analysis. This finding helps explain the conflicting results regarding the relationship between bargaining power and control in previous studies examining this relationship from only one partner's perspective (Beamish, 1984; Lecraw, 1984). Our data suggest that control in joint ventures is not unilaterally chosen by one or the other partner, but is a result of bargaining. Our approach also helps reconcile the inconsistencies suggested by previous studies in the relationship between control and performance (Geringer & Hebert, 1989). A positive control-performance relationship does not hold at each partner's level in our results. We suggest that the prevailing assumption that the higher the level of control by a partner, the higher the level of performance from this partner's point of view is incomplete at best. Instead, the positive relationship between control and performance exists only at the interpartner level when the patterns of control between the partners and performance from both partners' point of view are examined.

Furthermore, our findings are consistent with those of previous researchers who have argued that the control-performance relationship is not always positive and direct (Geringer & Hebert, 1989). However, the indirect effects identified in this study (interpartner trust, the commonality of goals, and institutionalization of goals) are different from those previously identified, which include the multinational parent's strategy (Franko, 1971), strategy-structure fit (Geringer & Hebert, 1989; Janger, 1980), and fit between the areas of control and control mechanisms (Schaan, 1983, 1988). The variation between our results and those of previous research again reflects the different unit of analysis adopted in this study, the interpartner relationship instead of the multinational partner. Since previous studies have typically not even queried host country partners, their arguments may be distorted or, at best, incomplete. One recent study, however, has provided evidence that cultural differences between partners affects how they define trust and its importance in structuring performance assessment (Parkhe, 1993b).

Shared Versus Dominant Control

With respect to findings on the impact of different control types (Gray & Yan, 1992; Killing, 1983), this study also differs from previous work. According to Killing, shared control is the most problematic type of control and often leads to inferior performance. Our data suggest the opposite: the joint ventures with equally shared control, IndusCon and BioTech, demonstrated superior performance. This inconsistency may reflect differences between the two sets of joint ventures studied; Killing looked at ventures between two developed countries, but we examined ventures with a partner from a developing country. In developing country joint ventures, the management control exercised by the foreign and the local partners may be more differentiated and complementary, and thus less likely to prompt struggles and conflicts between the partners than in ventures between developed country partners. In this respect, our findings are consistent with those of Beamish (1988, 1993), who recommended a shared management structure for international partnerships in less developed countries. However, our case data do not consistently support the negative relationship between foreign parent dominant control and performance that Beamish (1984) found. Rather, our findings suggest that such a relationship holds only when alternative means of control (reflected by the moderating variables) are absent. When a high level of mutual trust exists between partners, or they share objectives, or those goals are highly institutionalized, joint ventures in which the foreign parent is dominant can still satisfy both partners' needs. This finding supports Beamish's (1988) and Koenig and van Wijk's (1991) arguments that interpartner trust is critical to venture success and Thorelli's (1986) observations that trust may supplant contractual arrangements in Asian cultures (cf. Parkhe, 1993b). The moderating variables revealed in this research suggest that the use of both formal and informal means of control is necessary to predict joint venture performance. These conclusions are suggestive at best given our methodology, but they do offer insights that clarify the inconsistencies emerging from previous research on the control-performance relationship.

The Imprinting Effect

These in-depth case studies also enabled us to explore the dynamic aspects of international joint ventures. We identified several factors that prompted changes in the bargaining power of partners. However, we did not observe structural reconfigurations in these four joint ventures. Significant shifts in the partners' levels of management control did not occur. This structural stability seems to suggest the imprinting effect organization theorists (Scott, 1987) have noted. Since each organization requires a particular

combination of economic, technical, and social resources during its formation stage, the building of such resource bases may set the organization on a
course from which it is difficult to deviate (Stinchcombe, 1965). Scott (1987)
argued that once an organization is established, it tends to retain the basic
characteristics present at its founding for a long time. Although our data
revealed no shifts in management control patterns, we observed changes in
the components comprising the bargaining power of both partners in each
joint venture. However, in none of the cases did the relative bargaining
power of the parents shift significantly. In each venture, the foreign partner's
resource contributions increased over time, but it did not experience a com-
mensurate increase in control, probably because its bargaining power diminished over time (Dymsza, 1988), particularly when the local partner was
learning-oriented (Hamel, 1991). This diminishing effect may be also attributable to sunk costs, or the fixed, highly specific investment the foreign
partner makes in a joint venture (Smith & Wells, 1975; Williamson, 1983).
Therefore, the U.S. partners' increased resource contributions to the partnerships simply replenished their naturally depleted power or offset increases in the Chinese partners' bargaining power resulting from their learning. Thus, an overall balance of bargaining power and control was preserved.

Conclusions

The findings of this comparative case study provide confirmative evidence that the relative levels of joint venture partners' bargaining power has
a significant impact on the pattern of parent control in the venture's management. By adopting a negotiations perspective focusing on the partners'
interdependence, we were able to unpack some of the complexities of joint
venture formation, management, and performance and to clarify the reasons
for some of the conflicting or incomplete results of previous studies, which
have focused on the multinational partner's perspective only. By identifying
factors that induce changes in the partners' bargaining power, our analyses
also provide insight into the dynamic development of international joint
ventures.

Are theories initiated in the West applicable in China? Our findings
suggest the answer is yes. The key relationships in the theoretical model
(Figure 1), which was primarily based on the works of Western researchers,
received significant support from our Chinese data. In addition, our findings
on the relationships among the key variables, the variables moderating the
relationship between parent control and performance, and the dynamic evolution of international joint ventures enrich the current literature and provide new clues for future research on joint ventures in other countries,
particularly on partnerships formed between developed and developing
country sponsors.

Some special characteristics of Chinese joint ventures are noteworthy.
First, significant differences existed in the strategic objectives of the foreign
and the local partners. Multinational firms form joint ventures in China
primarily to penetrate the local market and to pursue financial goals. To

them, market share and profitability are important measures of venture performance. In contrast, for Chinese partners the overwhelming goal for cooperating with the West is to learn the more advanced Western technology. These strongly contrasting objectives, though they may be complementary, give both partners strong incentives to exercise control over a venture's operation because both will perceive control as the most critical means of fulfilling their strategic intentions. Second, in the interest of learning, the Chinese expect from the outset that management will be shifted from the foreigners to themselves over time. As a result, in order to maintain control, the foreign partner will have to make continuing commitments of resources to maintain the original balance of bargaining power. Therefore, in Chinese joint ventures management control is a long-term issue, about which continuing renegotiations between the partners should be expected.

Limitations. Several limitations of the study should be acknowledged. First, the empirical research reported here was based on data from U.S.–Chinese joint ventures. Characteristics idiosyncratic to Chinese joint ventures, such as government influence and the seemingly strong complementarity of partner objectives, might have affected the research results. Therefore, generalization of our findings to other joint ventures should be made with caution. The resultant model of this study needs further testing on a larger number of Chinese joint ventures and on joint ventures in other countries. Second, Chinese joint ventures necessarily have short histories, which limits our analysis of the dynamic evolution of these international alliances. Additional research using longitudinal data is needed to clarify how joint venture structural reconfigurations prompt changes in venture performance over time. A third limitation is associated with the homogeneity of the firms studied, most of which were relatively strong performers. Although the firms studied may be representative, because Chinese joint ventures have in general been more successful than their counterparts in other countries (Beamish, 1993), our performance variable may not have had enough variance to ensure that we captured all potential factors affecting venture performance. Fourth, the analyses conducted in this study were partially based on retrospective data, which might have introduced an additional source of bias as a result of faulty memory or retrospective sense-making on the part of our informants. This problem is not critical, however, because in most cases and for most variables multiple sources of data were available and data triangulation among these sources revealed a high level of consistency. A final limitation may be related to sampling. This study is restricted to manufacturing joint ventures. Future work on Chinese joint ventures needs to investigate the applicability of the model to international partnerships in service industries.

Future research directions. Finally, we offer several suggestions for future research that will extend this study and overcome several of its limitations. (1) Regarding international joint ventures in countries like China, in which the local government plays a role, greater specification of the functions performed by the government and the local company is needed. Additional research should investigate whether the achievement of the individual Chinese partner's objectives supersedes those of the Chinese government in newly formed joint ventures. (2) This study suggests that formal and informal control mechanisms interact and jointly affect venture performance. Future research should pay more attention to the informal aspects of control, particularly, the interpartner trust relationship, partners' long-term commitment, and joint development of partner competence, and their impact on performance. (3) Valuable insights into the dynamic relationship between bargaining power and management control can be gained from studies that trace formation processes in detail over time. Doing so may further clarify the causal relationships between the two phenomena and the relative importance of the contextual power and resource-based power of partners. It would also shed light on the intriguing question of whether characteristics of joint venture formation imprinted at birth ultimately determine the success and failure rates of international partnerships. (4) The model derived from this research needs to be tested by using larger samples and joint ventures created by partners from different countries. In order to capture the dynamic characteristics of joint ventures, investigations using longitudinal, repeated-measures designs are needed.

REFERENCES

Anderson, E. 1990. Two firms, one frontier: On assessing joint venture performance. *Sloan Management Review*, 31(2): 19–30.

Arrow, K. J. 1974. *The limits of organization.* New York: W.W. Norton.

Bacharach, S. B., & Lawler, J. L. 1984. *Bargaining: Power, tactics, and outcomes.* San Francisco: Jossey-Bass.

Bartlett, C. A., & Ghoshal, S. 1986. Tap your subsidiaries for global reach. *Harvard Business Review*, 64(6): 87–94.

Beamish, P. W. 1984. *Joint venture performance in developing countries.* Unpublished doctoral dissertation, University of Western Ontario, London, Ontario.

Beamish, P. W. 1985. The characteristics of joint ventures in developed and developing countries. *Columbia Journal of World Business*, 20(3): 13–19.

Beamish, P. W. 1988. *Multinational joint ventures in developing countries.* New York: Routledge.

Beamish, P. W. 1993. Characteristics of joint ventures in the People's Republic of China. *Journal of International Marketing*, 1(1): 29–48.

Blodgett, L. L. 1991. Partner contributions as predictors of equity share in international joint ventures. *Journal of International Business Studies*, 22: 63–78.

Campbell, N. 1988. *A strategic guide to equity joint ventures in China.* New York: Pergamon.

Child, J. 1991. *Managerial adaptation in reforming economies: The case of joint ventures.* Paper presented at the annual meeting of the Academy of Management, Miami Beach.

Chowdhury, M. A. J. 1988. *International joint ventures: Some interfirm-organization specific determinants of success and failure—A factor analytic exploration.* Unpublished doctoral dissertation, Temple University, Philadelphia.

Contractor, F. J. 1990. Ownership patterns of U.S. joint ventures abroad and the liberalization of foreign government regulations in the 1980s: Evidence from the benchmark surveys. *Journal of International Business Studies,* 21: 55–73.

Cressey, D. R. 1953. *Other people's money.* Glencoe, IL: Free Press.

Daniels, J. D., Krug, J., & Nigh, D. 1985. U.S. joint ventures in China: Motivation and management of political risk. *California Management Review,* 27(4): 46–58.

Davidson, W. H. 1982. *Global strategic management.* New York: Wiley.

Davidson, W. H. 1987. Creating and managing joint ventures in China. *California Management Review,* 29(4): 77–94.

Diesing, P. 1972. *Patterns of discovery in the social sciences.* London: Routledge & Kegan Paul.

Dwyer, F. R., & Walker, C. C. 1981. Bargaining in an asymmetrical power structure. *Journal of Marketing,* 45(1): 104–115.

Dymsza, W. A. 1988. Successes and failures of joint ventures in developing countries: Lessons from experience. In F. J. Contractor & P. Lorange (Eds.), *Cooperative strategies in international business:* 403–424. Lexington, MA: Lexington Books.

Eisenhardt, K. M. 1989. Building theories from case study research. *Academy of Management Review,* 14: 532–550.

Eiteman, D. K. 1990. American executives' perceptions of negotiating joint ventures with the People's Republic of China: Lessons learned. *Columbia Journal of World Business,* 25(4): 59–67.

Fagre, N., & Wells, L. T., Jr. 1982. Bargaining power of multinationals and host governments. *Journal of International Business Studies,* 13(2): 9–23.

Fayerweather, J. 1982. *International business strategy and administration.* Cambridge, MA: Ballinger.

Fisher, R., & Ury, W. 1981. *Getting to YES: Negotiating agreement without giving in.* New York: Penguin Books.

Flamholtz, E. G., Das, T. K., & Tsui, A. S. 1985. Toward an integrative framework of organizational control. *Accounting, Organizations and Society,* 10: 35–50.

Franko, L. G. 1971. *Joint venture survival in multinational corporations.* New York: Praeger.

Geringer, J. M. 1986. *Criteria for selecting partners for joint ventures in industrialized market economies.* Unpublished doctoral dissertation, University of Washington, Seattle.

Geringer, J. M., & Hebert, L. 1989. Control and performance of international joint ventures. *Journal of International Business Studies,* 20: 235–254.

Geringer, J. M., & Hebert, L. 1991. Measuring performance of international joint ventures. *Journal of International Business Studies,* 22: 249–263.

Glaser, B., & Strauss, A. 1967. *The discovery of grounded theory.* Chicago: Aldine.

Goodman, P., & Pennings, J. 1980. Critical issues in assessing organizational effectiveness. In E. Lawler, D. Nadler, & C. Cammann (Eds.). *Organizational assessment:* 185–215. New York: Wiley-Interscience.

Gray, B., & Yan, A. 1992. A negotiations model of joint venture formation, structure and performance: Implications for global management. In S. B. Prasad (Ed.), *Advances in international comparative management,* vol. 7: 41–75. Greenwich, CT: JAI Press.

Hamel, G. 1991. Competition for competence and inter-partner learning within international strategic alliances. *Strategic Management Journal,* 12: 83–103.

Hamel, G., Doz, Y., & Prahalad, C. K. 1989. Collaborate with your competitors and win. *Harvard Business Review,* 67(1): 133–139.

Hamilton, W. F., & Singh, H. 1991. Strategic alliances in technological innovation: Cooperation in biotechnology. *Journal of High Technology Management Research,* 2: 211–221.

Harrigan, K. R. 1986. *Managing for joint venture success.* Lexington, MA: Lexington Books.

Harrigan, K. R., & Newman, W. H. 1990. Bases of interorganization cooperation: Propensity, power, persistence. *Journal of Management Studies,* 27: 417–434.

Hendryx, S. R. 1986. Implementation of a technology transfer joint venture in the People's Republic of China: A management perspective. *Columbia Journal of World Business,* 21(1): 57–66.

Ho, A. K. 1990. *Joint ventures in the People's Republic of China.* New York: Praeger.

Janger, A. R. 1980. *Organization of international joint venture.* New York: Conference Board.

Killing, J. P. 1983. *Strategies for joint venture success.* New York: Praeger.

Koenig, C., & van Wijk, G. 1991. Interfirm alliances: The role of trust. In R. A. Thietart & J. Thepob (Eds.), *Microeconomic contribution to strategic management:* Chapter 9, 1–16. North-Holland Elsevier: Advanced Series in Management.

Kogut, B. 1989. The stability of joint ventures: Reciprocity and competitive rivalry. *Journal of Industrial Economics,* 2: 183–198.

Kuhn, T. S. 1970. *The structure of scientific revolutions* (2nd ed.). Chicago: University of Chicago Press.

Lax, D. A., & Sebenius, J. K. 1986. *The manager as negotiator.* New York: Free Press.

Lecraw, D. J. 1984. Bargaining power, ownership, and profitability of transnational corporations in developing countries. *Journal of International Business Studies,* 15(1): 27–43.

Levine, J. B., & Byrne, J. A. 1986. Corporate odd couples. *Business Week,* July 21: 100–106.

Lewin, A., & Minton, J. 1986. Determining organizational effectiveness: Another look and an agenda for research. *Management Science,* 32: 514–538.

Lincoln, Y., & Guba, E. 1985. *Naturalistic inquiry.* Beverly Hills, CA: Sage.

Lindesmith, A. R. 1947. *Opiate addiction.* Bloomington, IN: Principia Press.

Lo, T. W. 1989. *New developments in China trade: Industrial cooperation with the West.* Unpublished doctoral dissertation, City University, London.

Mann, J. 1989. *Beijing Jeep.* New York: Simon & Schuster.

Mathur, I., & Chen, J. S. 1987. *Strategies for joint ventures in the People's Republic of China.* New York: Praeger.

Newman, W. H. 1992. Focused joint ventures in transforming economies. *Academy of Management Executive,* 6(1): 67–75.

O'Reilly, A. J. 1988. Establishing successful joint ventures in developing nations: A CEO's perspective. *Columbia Journal of World Business,* 23(1): 65–71.

Ouchi, W. G. 1977. The relationship between organizational structure and organizational control. *Administrative Science Quarterly,* 20: 559–569.

Parkhe, A. 1993a. "Messy" research, methodological predispositions, and theory development in international joint ventures. *Academy of Management Review,* 18: 227–268.

Parkhe, A. 1993b. Partner nationality and the structure-performance relationship in strategic alliances. *Organization Science,* 4: 301–314.

Parkhe, A., & Shin, R. 1991. *The case study method in international joint ventures research: A critical assessment and a program of application.* Paper presented at the Academy of International Business meetings, Miami, Florida.

Pearson, M. M. 1991. *Joint ventures in the People's Republic of China: The control of foreign direct investment under socialism.* Princeton, NJ: Princeton University Press.

Pfeffer, J., & Salancick, G. R. 1978. *The external control of organizations.* New York: Harper & Row.

Pomfret, R. 1991. *Investing in China: Ten years of the open door policy.* Ames: Iowa State University Press.

Porter, M. E. 1990. *The competitive advantage of nations.* New York: Free Press.

Prahalad, C. K., & Doz, Y. L. 1981. An approach to strategic control in MNC's. *Sloan Management Review,* 22(4): 5–13.

Robinson, W. S. 1951. The logical structure of analytic induction. *American Sociological Review,* 16: 812–818.

Root, F. R. 1988. Some taxonomies of international cooperative arrangements. In F. J. Contractor & P. Lorange (Eds.), *Cooperative strategies in international business:* 69–80. Lexington, MA: Lexington Books.

Schaan, J. L. 1983. *Parent control and joint venture success: The case of Mexico.* Unpublished doctoral dissertation, University of Western Ontario, London, Ontario.

Schaan, J. L. 1988. How to control a joint venture even as a minority partner. *Journal of General Management,* 14(1): 4–16.

Schnepp, O., Von Glinow, M. A., & Bhambri, A. 1990. *United States–China technology transfer.* Englewood Cliffs, NJ: Prentice-Hall.

Schelling, T. 1956. An essay on bargaining. *American Economic Review,* 46: 281–306.

Scott, W. R. 1987. *Organizations: Rational, natural, and open systems.* Englewood Cliffs, NJ: Prentice-Hall.

Shan, W. 1991. Environmental risks and joint venture sharing arrangements. *Journal of International Business Studies,* 22: 555–578.

Sharfman, M., Gray, B., & Yan, A. 1991. The context of interorganizational collaboration in the garment industry: An institutional perspective. *Journal of Applied Behavioral Science,* 27: 181–208.

Smith, D. N., & Wells, L. T., Jr. 1975. *Negotiating third world mineral agreements.* Cambridge, MA: Ballinger.

Stinchcombe, A. L. 1965. Social structure and organizations. In J. G. March (Ed.), *Handbook of organizations:* 142–193. Chicago: Rand McNally.

Stopford, J. M., & Wells, L. T. Jr. 1972. *Managing the multinational enterprise.* New York: McGraw-Hill.

Strauss, A. 1987. *Qualitative analysis for social scientists.* New York: Cambridge University Press.

Taylor, S. J., & Bogdan, R. 1984. *Introduction to qualitative research methods* (2d ed.). New York: Willey.

Teagarden, M. B., & Von Glinow, M. A. 1990. Sino-foreign strategic alliance types and related operating characteristics. *International Studies of Management and Organization,* 20(1–2): 99–108.

Thorelli, H. 1986. Networks: Between markets and hierarchies. *Strategic Management Journal,* 7: 37–51.

Tung, R. L. 1982. *U.S.–China trade negotiations.* New York: Pergamon Press.

Tung, R. L. 1988. Toward a conceptual paradigm of international business negotiations. *Advances in International Comparative Management,* 3: 203–219.

U.S.–China Business Council. 1990. *Special report on U.S. investment in China.* Washington, DC: China Business Forum.

Van de Ven, A. H., & Poole, M. S. 1990. Methods to develop a grounded theory of innovation processes in the Minnesota Innovation Research Program. *Organization Science,* 1: 313–335.

Vernon, R. 1977. *Storm over multinationals.* Cambridge, MA: Harvard University Press.

Williamson, O. E. 1983. Credible commitments: Using hostages to support exchange. *American Economic Review,* 73: 519–540.

Yan, A., & Gray, B. 1994. Reconceptualizing the determinants and measurement of joint venture performance. In L. R. Gomez-Mejia & M. W. Lawless (Eds.), *Strategic alliances in high technology,* vol. 5: Forthcoming. Greenwich, CT: JAI Press.

Yin, R. K. 1989. *Case study research: Design and methods* (rev. ed.). Newbury Park, CA: Sage.

Znaniecki, F. 1934. *The method of sociology.* New York: Farrar & Rinehart.

Aimin Yan is an assistant professor in the Department of Organizational Behavior, School of Management, Boston University. He received his Ph.D. degree from the Pennsylvania State University. His current research focuses on negotiations, structuring, and effective management of interorganizational arrangements and business partnerships. He is also interested in performance assessment and development and changes in international joint ventures.

Barbara Gray is a professor of organizational behavior and director of the Center for Research in Conflict and Negotiation at Pennsylvania State University. She received her Ph.D. degree from Case Western Reserve University. Her research interests include dispute resolution and negotiations, particularly environmental disputes, international joint ventures, collaborative partnerships, and organizational change.

Name Index